Capitalist Development and Democracy

Dietrich Rueschemeyer is Professor of Sociology and Director of the Center for the Comparative Study of Development at Brown University. He is the author of *Power and the Division of Labour* and co-editor (with Peter Evans and Theda Skocpol) of *Bringing the State Back In.*

Evelyne Huber Stephens is Professor of Political Science and Sociology, a member of the Research Faculty at the Center for Urban Affairs and Policy Research, and Director of the Latin American and Caribbean Studies Program at Northwestern University. She is the author of *The Politics of Workers' Participation: the Peruvian Approach in Comparative Perspective*, and other writings on Latin America and the Caribbean.

John D. Stephens is Professor of Political Science and Sociology and on the Research Faculty at the Center for Urban Affairs and Policy Research at Northwestern University. He is the author of *The Transition from Capitalism to Socialism* and co-author (with Evelyne Huber Stephens) of *Democratic Socialism in Jamaica*, and related articles on reformist socialism.

Capitalist Development and Democracy

Dietrich Rueschemeyer,

Evelyne Huber Stephens,

and John D. Stephens

University of Chicago Press
Chicago

The University of Chicago Press, Chicago 60637
Polity Press in association with Basil Blackwell
© 1992 by Dietrich Rueschemeyer, Evelyne Huber Stephens,
and John D. Stephens
All rights reserved. Published 1992

14 13 12 11   6 7 8 9

ISBN 0-226-73142-1 (cloth)
ISBN 0-226-73144-8 (paper)

Library of Congress Cataloging-in-Publication Data

Rueschemeyer Dietrich.
Capitalist development and democracy / Dietrich Rueschemeyer,
Evelyne Huber Stephens, and John D. Stephens.
p. cm.
Includes bibliographical references (p.) and index.
1. Democracy—Case studies.   2. Capitalism—Case Studies.
3. Economic development—Case studies.   I. Stephens, Evelyne Huber.
II. Stephens, John D., Ph.D.   III. Title.
JC423.R78 1992
321.8′0724—dc20

Contents

Preface

The social origins of this book lie in seven years of close collegial and social interaction between 1978 and 1985 when the three co-authors all resided in Rhode Island. The precipitating event for this volume was a presentation to a seminar at the Center for the Comparative Study of Development at Brown University in 1984 by Dietrich Rueschemeyer. He argued the thesis that forms the core hypothesis of this book: the finding of cross-national quantitative studies that economic development and democracy are positively related was essentially correct, but not for the reasons given in those studies. Rather, industrialization transformed society in a fashion that empowered subordinate classes and made it difficult to politically exclude them. Seeing a close link to his own work on the political development of modern Europe, John Stephens proposed at the close of the seminar that they and Evelyne Huber Stephens co-author a comparative historical study that would explore the thesis further. All three of us had wrestled with the question of the social origins of democracy and dictatorship in earlier research and in courses we had taught year in and year out and had concluded that the existing theory and research in this area, though rich, was deficient in one way or another.

Since the early 1970s, Dietrich Rueschemeyer had taught a seminar on the impact of development on constitutional form, contrasting the growing body of quantitative cross-national research with the quite different tradition of comparative historical work. This seminar grew out of earlier courses on development and his work with graduate students such as Robert Hill and Ken Bollen who did their own research on development and democracy. A first formulation of a systematic synthesis of the two traditions – one that yielded quite optimistic predictions for democracy in Latin America – was his contribution to a Festschrift for Peter Heintz, written in the late 1970s.

In her research and teaching on Latin American politics, Evelyne Huber Stephens was insistently and persistently confronted with the weakness of democracy and the prevalence of harsh forms of authoritarianism in the region. Influenced by the dependency perspective and O'Donnell's accurate observation that it was precisely in the Latin American countries at more advanced stages of industrialization where the harshest authoritarian regimes emerged in the 1960s and 1970s, she found the arguments which linked the rise of democracy to a set of historically specific circumstances in early industrializing countries rather convincing. Dissatisfied with the political implications of this view, she was intrigued by Rueschemeyer's thesis, though initially somewhat skeptical. She clearly wanted to pursue the question, and a large-scale systematic comparative analysis was the most promising way to develop a better theoretical understanding of the relationship between development and democracy and of the differences between early and late developers.

At Brown, John Stephens taught a course on the breakdown of democratic regimes, which had its origin in a graduate seminar with Juan Linz on the same topic some ten years before. In the course, he assigned both Barrington Moore's structural historical account of the origins of dictatorship and the Linz–Stepan volumes, which present more process-oriented accounts of the events leading to the demise of democracy. Each year he taught the course he was pushed to further historical study in an attempt to reconcile the two accounts.

Ironically, soon after we decided to write this book, Evelyne Huber Stephens and John Stephens departed from Rhode Island, and the entire volume was written while the authors were half a continent and sometimes continents apart. This led to many conference phone calls, to air travel, and to such unlikely meeting places as Madrid and Lenzerheide, Switzerland. In these intense discussions, we scrutinized every passage and talked through points of disagreement until we reached consensus and produced what we feel is a thoroughly co-authored volume despite the fact that most chapters were the primary reponsibility of one or two of the co-authors. Rueschemeyer was the primary author of chapters 1, 2, and 3, John Stephens of chapter 4, Evelyne Huber Stephens of chapter 5, and Evelyne Huber Stephens and John Stephens of chapter 6. We jointly drafted the concluding chapter.

We would like to thank especially the following people for comments on earlier drafts of various chapters: Ronald Aminzade, Jesse Biddle, Valerie Bunce, Daniel Chomsky, James Cronin, Johan DeDeken, Leo Despres, Gøsta Esping-Andersen, Roger Friedland, Manuel Antonio Garretón, Daniel Garst, Jack Goldstone, Jeff Goodwin, Peter Hall, Peter Katzenstein, Prema Kurien, Antonia Maioni, Jane Mansbridge, Pierre Martin, Philip McMichael, Guillermo O'Donnell, Benjamin Page, Charles Ragin, Frank Safford, Michael Shalev, Arthur Stinchcombe, and Samuel Valenzuela. Michael Mann was kind enough to read and comment on the entire draft of the manuscript. Our debt to Peter Evans is particularly great as he read and commented in detail on successive drafts of the manuscript. Chapters 2 and 3 were drafted while Dietrich Rueschemeyer was a fellow of the Institute of Advanced Study Berlin in 1987–8. He acknowledges with deep gratitude the Institute's hospitality and the stimulating company of its fellows. Much of the research for Chapters 4 and 5 was completed while Evelyne Huber Stephens and John Stephens were faculty fellows at the Kellogg Institute, University of Notre Dame, and they would like to thank the Institute for its support.

An adapted version of chapter 2 is being published in Charles Ragin, ed. , *Issues and Alternatives in Comparative Methodology*, a special issue of the *International Journal of Comparative Sociology* ((32 (1/2)), © 1991 by E. J. Brill). Parts of chapter 4 were published in the *American Journal of Sociology* ((94 (5), © 1989 by the University of Chicago) and parts of chapter 5 in *Politics and Society* ((17 (3)), © by Butterworth Publishers). We thank the publishers for permission to reprint them here.

We dedicate this book to three political thinkers and activists who influenced our own political development in very personal ways. In his own way, each of these men has defended and fought for formal democracy as a value in and of itself. But they all understood that democracy does not stop at the factory gate or the office door and that deepening democracy and making it more real requires far-reaching reductions in economic and social inequality.

For Ed Broadbent,
the late Walter Dirks,
and the late Michael Harrington

Fighters for democracy – formal and substantive

1

Introduction: the Problem of Capitalist Development and Democracy

This book examines the relation between capitalism and democracy or, more precisely, between the transformations of society that came with capitalist economic development and the long-term chances of democratic forms of rule. We will review past research, offer a new theoretical framework that can account for the apparent contradictions of earlier findings, and put the framework to the test in three sets of broad historical comparisons – of the advanced capitalist countries, of Latin America, and of Central America and the Caribbean islands.

That capitalism and democracy go hand in hand is a widely held belief. Indeed it is a commonplace of western political discourse. Editorials and political pronouncements insist regularly that capitalist development – economic development driven by capital interests in competition with each other – will also bring about political freedom and democratic participation in government. In fact, democracy and capitalism are often seen as virtually identical.

The East–West confrontation gave this proposition a special quality of proud assertiveness. And the downfall of the state socialist regimes of eastern Europe is celebrated by many as the final proof. Ironically, a quite similar proposition was central to the views of Lenin, though he gave it a very different slant. "Bourgeois democracy" was for him the constitutional form that perfectly fits the capitalist economic order. But in this view capitalism and democracy go hand in hand because democracy, while proclaiming the rule of the many, in fact protects the interests of capital owners. Whatever their differences in the conception and valuation of democracy, both these views share an important claim: the unrestrained operation of the market for capital and labor constitutes the material base of democracy. Democracy is the characteristic political form of capitalism.

The classics of nineteenth-century political theory also tended toward the view that the transformations wrought by capitalist development would bring democracy. But their reactions to this prospect were very different from what one might expect knowing the thought of their twentieth-century heirs. Alexis de Tocqueville and John Stuart Mill were apprehensive about full-fledged democracy, and they were not alone in this. Their fear of "false democracy" (Mill) and of the "tyranny of the majority" (de Tocqueville) expressed the anticipations of many Liberals and bourgeois conservatives of the time. By contrast, at the left of the political spectrum Marx opted for full democracy and saw in universal suffrage a major step in the transition from capitalism to socialism. His "dictatorship of the proletariat" was not so very different from de Tocqueville's "tyranny of the majority," except that for Marx this was a vision of hope while for de Tocqueville it was one of disaster.

These reactions give us a first sense that the questions surrounding the relationship between capitalism and democracy may be more complex than current orthodoxies allow. Actually, the twentieth century has made this even more clear than it was already in the nineteenth. Our century offers many examples of capitalist political economies that prospered without democracy; many were in fact ruled by harshly authoritarian political regimes. South Korea and Taiwan after World War II come to mind as well as, in recent decades, such Latin American countries as Brazil and Chile. And even Nazi Germany and the various Fascist regimes in Europe between the two Word Wars do not exhaust the list. On the other hand, virtually all full-fledged democracies we know are associated with capitalist political economies, and virtually all are creatures of the twentieth century. If this is the century of repressive regimes vastly more burdensome than any known in history, it is also the century of democracy.

Even a cursory review of history suggests some generalizations that point to an association between capitalist development and democracy but do not settle the question. An agrarian society before or in the incipient stages of penetration by commercial market relations and industrialization is unlikely to gain or sustain a democratic form of government. Democracy by any definition is extremely rare in agrarian societies – both in the agrarian societies that constitute the bulk of recorded history and in today's less developed countries that still rely largely on agriculture for their subsistence. The ancient Greek democracies, of which Athens was the most famous, were at best rare exceptions in the pre-capitalist history of Europe.[1] Whether or not we accept them (as well as a few other cases) as true exceptions, the typical forms of rule in agrarian societies are and have been autocracy and oligarchy.

To this one must add immediately that government in the agrarian societies of history was almost invariably inefficient and weak when compared to the power and capacity of modern states. The most tyrannical regimes of history did not have the capacity to shape and transform society that we take for granted even in today's democracies. It is this increase in the capacities of states that accounts for the fact that ours is also the century of totalitarian and very repressive authoritarian rule.

The relationship between capitalist development and democracy has not only been the object of political argument and broad speculation in political philosophy. For several decades now, it has been subjected to careful and systematic empirical research in sociology, political science, and history. It is this research that constitutes the foundation on which our own work builds.

Empirical research on democracy has in fact been a major concern of social science in the post-World War II era. After World War II, when Nazi Germany was defeated, when Stalinist rule had conquered eastern Europe, and when virtually all former colonies became independent "new states," social scientists devoted very considerable energies to identifying the conditions that make democracy possible and likely. The rise of authoritarian regimes in relatively advanced countries of South America stimulated a new wave of research (see e.g. O'Donnell 1973 and Collier 1979). More recently, the return of democracy to such countries as Spain, Portugal and Greece as well as advances of democratization in Latin America gave this research another impetus (see e.g. O'Donnell, Schmitter and Whitehead 1986).

The results of these decades of research are in many ways impressive. We can with confidence go beyond quite a few commonplace views that still inform much of the public discussion on democracy and its chances. But neither are the results of these nearly two generations of research conclusive. In particular, the impact of capitalist development on the chances of democracy is still controversial.

Two distinctive traditions of research have come to quite different and as yet unreconciled results. They employed radically different research strategies and methods, so different that scholars in either camp often barely took notice of the work of the other side. Quantitative cross-national comparisons of many countries have found consistently a positive correlation between development and democracy. They thus come to relatively optimistic conclusions about the chances of democracy, not only in the advanced capitalist nations but also in the developing countries of today. By contrast, comparative historical studies that emphasize qualitative examination of complex sequences tend to trace the rise of democracy to a favorable historical constellation of conditions in early capitalism. Their conclusions are therefore far more pessimistic about today's developing countries.

The contradictory results of the two research traditions represent a difficult problem precisely because they derive from different modes of research. Given contrasting methodologies, by which criteria is one to evaluate the inconsistent findings? Our own work takes off from this impasse. It builds on the research of both traditions and seeks to reconcile their methodological and substantive contradictions.

In chapter 2, after describing and evaluating the two research traditions, we develop a methodological approach which, when combined with the theoretical ideas developed in chapter 3, promises to transcend the impasse. In the following three chapters, we put these ideas to the test in fresh analyses of the complex evidence. Based on an integrated theoretical and methodological framework, we present our own comparative historical investigations of a large number of cases. These will, we submit, resolve the controversy about the relationship between development and democracy. And since this controversy has been at the center of empirical democracy research, our study will do more than merely resolve an esoteric scholarly debate; it will throw new light on the major conditions favoring and inhibiting democracy.

We are convinced that the main finding of the cross-national statistical work – a positive, though not perfect, correlation between capitalist development and democracy – must stand as an accepted result. There is no way of explaining this robust finding, replicated in many studies of different design, as the spurious effect of flawed methods. Any theory of democracy must come to terms with it. At the same time, such a correlation, no matter how often replicated, does not carry its own explanation. It does not identify the causal sequences accounting for the persistent relation, not to mention the reasons why many cases are at odds with it. Nor can it account for how the same end can be reached by different historical routes. The repeated statistical finding has a peculiar "black box" character that can be overcome only by theoretically well grounded empirical analysis.

Comparative historical studies, we argue, carry the best promise of shedding light into the black box. This is not only because comparative historical work has been particularly rich in theoretical argument. Far more important, historical research gives *insight into sequences* and their relations to surrounding structural conditions, and that is indispensable for developing valid causal accounts. Causal analysis is inherently sequence analysis.

At the same time, comparative historical research is able to go beyond conventional history's preoccupation with historical particularity and aim for theoretical generalization. Analytically oriented comparative history builds on a series of case analyses. It seeks to establish satisfactory explanatory accounts that do justice to each case and at the same time are theoretically coherent and consistent with each other. In the process it develops a body of theorems of proven explanatory power.

Such comparative historical case analysis must be guided from the beginning by a framework of theoretical ideas. Without that, the analysis lacks orientation in the face of an endless multitude of possibly relevant facts. The framework which we develop in chapter 3 builds on past research, it informs the accounts of individual cases and gives them theoretical unity and coherence, yet it is in turn subject to revisions suggested by the case analyses.

A framework of theoretical concepts and propositions also mitigates another problem that haunts the comparative historical study of large-scale phenomena – the fact that only a limited number of cases can be studied in the required detail. We tackle this problem directly by stretching the scope of our own investigations to the limit. We analyze a large number of cases, close to the universe in the three groups of countries selected, and we trace their development over relatively long periods of time. In fact, our comparative historical studies include more cases than quite a few cross-national statistical studies. Yet the cases are still too few in number to allow, by themselves, secure analytic conclusions. For this there are too many possibly relevant factors and too complex interrelations among them. It is here that a carefully built theoretical framework makes a critical contribution. It represents in an important sense the findings of a vast body of previous work, and it thus enlarges the reach and validity of the analysis substantially.

Our theoretical framework incorporates the major findings of the cross-national quantitative studies. However, we depart from the theoretical under-pinnings of much of the cross-national statistical work, which often adopted the then current models of modernization theory. In this structural–functional conception of social order, society, polity, and economy are seen as more or less well-functioning systems integrated primarily by shared values and cultural premises. Democracy arises due to its functional fit with the advanced industrial economy. To the extent that the development of democracy is attributed to an agent, as in Lipset's (1959) classic article, it is the middle class that is seen as the primary promoter of democracy. The upper-class, and especially the lower class, are seen as the enemies of democracy.

By contrast, we employ, like most of the comparative historical work from Max Weber to Guillermo O'Donnell, a "political economy" perspective that focuses on actors – individual as well as collective actors – whose power is grounded in control of economic and organizational resources and/or of coercive force and who vie with each other for scarce resources in the pursuit of conflicting goals. While such a perspective does recognize the role of ideas, values and non-material interests, especially when they are grounded in institutions and collective organization, it differs sharply from the functionalist and culture-centered premises of modernization theory.

How, then, do we conceive of democracy and its conditions? Our most basic premise is that democracy is above all a matter of power. Democratization represents first and foremost an increase in political equality. This idea is the ground upon which all of our work stands. The central proposition of our theoretical argument virtually follows from this: it is power relations that most importantly determine whether democracy can emerge, stabilize, and then maintain itself even in the face of adverse conditions.

There is first the balance of power among different *classes and class coalitions*. This is a factor of overwhelming importance. It is complemented by two other power configurations – the structure, strength, and autonomy of the *state apparatus* and its interrelations with civil society and the impact of *transnational power relations* on both the balance of class power and on state–society relations.

A focus on class and class coalitions may be surprising to some, while it is perhaps too easily accepted by others. We emphasize social class, first, because the concept is in our view a master key to understanding the social structuring of interests and power in society, and second, because the organization of class interests is constitutive of major collective actors. The organization of class interests is, however, a complex process in which not only the forms of collective action but the very interests actually pursued are socially and historically constructed. Thus, the subjective understanding and political posture of class actors cannot be read off the underlying class structure in any one-to-one fashion.

None the less, the political postures of given classes are not infinitely variable either. Based on our theoretical understanding and past historical and sociological research, we expected classes to exhibit definite central political tendencies in the struggle for political democracy. One central axis was defined by what benefits and losses classes could expect from extensions of political inclusion; the other was the class's ability to organize itself and engage in collective action in defense of class interests. This led us to the hypothesis, following Barrington Moore, that large landlords engaged in "labor repressive" agriculture would be the most implacable opponents of democracy. However, in contrast to Moore, as well as to Leninists and liberal social scientists, we also expected the bourgeoisie[2] to oppose suffrage extension to the working classes as such a move posed a potential treat to their interests. We expected the urban working class to be the most frequent proponent of the full extension of democratic rights because this promised to include the class in the polity where it could further pursue its interests and because the working class, unlike other lower classes, had the capacity to organize itself. It is the capacity to organize and express its interests that differentiated the working class from the small peasantry. We hypothesized that the middle classes would favor their own inclusion, but would be ambivalent about further extensions of political rights, perhaps swinging to one side or another on the basis of possible alliances. Thus, in a given historical case, one would have to examine the *structure of class coalitions* as well as the *relative power of different classes* to understand how the *balance of class power* would affect the possiblities for democracy.

Class power is in our view intimately related to the development of, the increasing organizational density of, civil society. This proposition seems at first glance similar to – but in reality is quite distinct from – claims of modernization theorists and pluralists that the growth of intermediate groups and associations tends to be supportive of democracy. Civil society, in our conception, is the totality of social institutions and associations, both formal and informal, that are not strictly production-related nor governmental or familial in character. Capitalist development furthers the growth of civil society – by increasing the level of urbanization, by bringing workers together in factories, by improving the means of communication and transportation, by raising the level of literacy. Strengthening the organization and organizational capacity of the working and middle classes serves to empower those classes and thus to change the balance of class power. A dense civil society also has an importance for democracy on its own, because it establishes a counterweight to state power.

In modern societies the state – the set of organizations involved in making and implementing binding collective decisions, if necessary by force – is invariably one major component of the overall landscape of power in society. There is no contemporary society in which the structure of domination can simply be understood by looking at the distribution of economic and social power in civil society. And the state is in varying degrees set off from and independent of other power centers. Since the state is not only an apparatus of implementation and enforcement but also the arena in which binding collective decisions are arrived at, it is of obvious importance to an understanding of the conditions of democracy. The shape of state structures and their relations to other power concentrations are therefore a second cluster of conditions shaping the chances of democracy.

A third cluster of conditions is constituted by transnational power relations. Obviously, power relations do not stop at the borders of politically organized societies. States stand in close interaction with power centers beyond their borders. In fact they often derive much of their autonomy vis-à-vis their own societies from this involvement in external relations. In addition, economic relations and economic organizations have increasingly transcended national borders. These, too, are likely to be modified by state action. Yet, however modified, the impact of powerful interests – political as well as economic – beyond a country's borders also enters the balance of power that determines the chances of democracy. In varying degree, they influence the balance of class power and they affect states and state–society relations.

One critical aspect of all three clusters of power, as well as of their interrelations, is the fact that social patterns, once forged, often persist beyond their original conditions. This negates the possibility of a "presentist" explanation of democracy, one that involves only factors observably active in the present moment of history, and it voids any mechanical account of the impact of class, state, and transnational power on constitutional form. Here is another powerful rationale for engaging in comparative *historical* analysis, which can take such persistencies into account and respond sensitively to alternative paths of causation.

Our own comparative investigations not only cover a very large number of cases in historical depth but also focus on the areas of the world most important for the history of democratization. We first turn to the advanced capitalist countries focusing on how democracy was first fully established as well as how democratic rule subsequentlty fared in the critical period between the two World Wars. We secondly study the complex processes of democratization – often only partial democratization – and of reversals of democratic rule in the countries of Latin America. Thirdly, we compare the countries of Central America with the island societies of the Caribbean. The whole set of cases examined represents the areas with the most extensive democratic experience. At the same time, there are many examples of stable non-democratic regimes as well as of breakdowns of democratic political systems that can be analyzed comparatively side by side with instances of democratization and stable democratic rule, giving ample opportunity to use the analytical comparative historical method to the fullest extent.

What is the upshot of our analyses? First, it is not an overall structural correspondence between capitalism and democracy that explains the rise and persistence of democracy. Some have conceived of such a correspondence as a simple mutual reinforcement between a free market for goods and services and a market for political outcomes. Others (as for instance Cutright 1963) have seen democracy more diffusely as a highly "differentiated" political form that fits the more differentiated social structures produced by capitalist development. Our analyses do not lend support to such overall correspondence propositions. Neither do they confirm the view of the bourgeoisie as the main agent of democracy that has been central to both classic liberal and marxist–leninist theory. Rather – we conclude – capitalist development is associated with democracy because it transforms the class structure, strengthening the working and middle classes and weakening the landed upper class. It was not the capitalist market nor capitalists as the new dominant force, but rather the contradictions of capitalism that advanced the cause of democracy.

A brief summary of our main findings should help to prepare and guide the reader through the theoretical arguments and the historical evidence presented in the following chapters. We found that social classes behaved in a quite systematic manner across our historical cases and in accordance with our expectations. The working class was the most consistently pro-democratic force. The class had a strong interest in effecting its political inclusion and it was more insulated from the hegemony of dominant classes than the rural lower classes. Exceptions to the pro-democratic posture of the working class occurred where the class was initially mobilized by a charismatic but authoritarian leader or a hegemonic party linked to the state apparatus.

The landed upper-classes which were dependent on a large supply of cheap labor were the most consistently anti-democratic force. Democratization for them posed the possibility of losing this labor supply. The bourgeoisie we found to be generally supportive of the installation of constitutional and representative government, but opposed to extending political inclusion to the lower classes. For the landed classes as well as the bourgeoisie threat perception was important both at the time of the initial installation of democratic rule and for its later consolidation. If these classes felt acutely threatened in their vital interests by popular pressures, they invariably opposed democracy and, once democratic rule was installed, attempted to undermine it.

The middle classes played an ambiguous role in the installation and consolidation of democracy. They pushed for their own inclusion but their attitude towards inclusion of the lower classes depended on the need and possibilities for an alliance with the working class. The middle classes were most in favor of full democracy where they were confronted with intransigent dominant classes and had the option of allying with a sizeable working class. However, if they started feeling threatened by popular pressures under a democratic regime, they turned to support the imposition of an authoritarian alternative.

The peasantry and rural workers also played varied roles, depending on their capacity for autonomous organization and their susceptibility to the influence of the dominant classes. Independent family farmers in small-holding countries were a pro-democratic force, whereas their posture in countries or areas dominated by large landholdings was more authoritarian. Peasants living on large estates remained by and large unmobilized and thus did not play a role in democratization. Rural wage workers on plantations did attempt to organize, and where they were not repressed, they joined other working-class organizations in pushing for political inclusion.

As anticipated, we did observe systematic variation across regions in the class structure and therefore in class alliances and the dynamics of democratization. Most importantly, the working-class was smaller and weaker and the landed class stronger in Latin America and the Caribbean, which made for a balance of class power less favorable for democratization than in the core countries. Due to the relative weakness of the working class, the middle classes played here the leading role in pushing for democratization, with the result that democracy often remained restricted.

We also found systematic variation across regions and time periods in the role of the state. Consolidation of state power was an essential prerequisite for democratization. This process was more difficult in Latin America than in the other regions we investigated, and this contributed to the long delay of even an institutionalization of contestation in many cases.

The state was stronger relative to civil society in Latin America and the Caribbean than in the core countries. This was partly related to the comparative weakness and heterogeneity of the dominant classes and partly to the history of state formation and to external support for the military in the post-World War II period. The effects of this lopsided balance of power were greater state autonomy and intervention into politics, or outright imposition of authoritarian rule by the coercive apparatus of the state.

The impact of transnational structures of power on democratization also varied across our regions, being stronger in Latin America and the Caribbean than in the core countries. Economic dependence had negative effects, though mostly in indirect ways. It shaped the class structure in ways inimical for democratization. Economic growth led by agrarian exports reinforced the position of large landholders. Industrialization with imported capital intensive technology kept the working class small and weak. Geo-political dependence relations were even more important. Geo-political interests of core countries generated direct interventions and support for the repressive apparatus of the state and thus created an unfavorable balance of power between state and civil society for democratization. The effects of British colonialism, though, deviated from this negative pattern in so far as the colonial presence prevented the dominant classes from using the state apparatus to repress the emerging organizations of subordinate classes. Instead, it allowed for the gradual emergence of a stronger civil society, capable of sustaining democracy after independence.

Political parties emerged in a crucial role as mediators in both the installation and consolidation of democracy. Strong parties were necessary to mobilize pressures from subordinate classes for democratization, but if their programs were too radical, they stiffened resistance among the dominant classes against democracy. Once democracy was installed, the party system became crucial for protecting the interests of the dominant classes and thus keeping them from pursuing authoritarian alternatives. Democracy could be consolidated only where there were two or more strong competing political parties at least one of which effectively protected dominant class interests, or where the party system allowed for direct access of the dominant classes to the state apparatus.

The main focus of our analysis allowed us to reinterpret the central, and robust, finding of the cross-national statistical studies that economic development is associated with democracy. In the course of our comparative work, we were also able to provide reinterpretations of other findings of these studies: the positive association of democracy with a legacy of British colonialism and Protestantism and the negative association of democracy with ethnic diversity. In each case, the comparative historical analysis showed that the modernization interpretation was inadequate and that the relations of class, state, and

international power were essential in understanding why these societal characteristics aided or impeded the development of democracy.

One last issue has to be taken up in this brief introduction to the problems we
intend to pursue. The concept of democracy has been given very different
meanings. Clarifying one's conception of "democracy" is not just a question of
finding an adequate and precise operational definition. Rather it involves more
complex issues of meaning. The marxist critique of "bourgeois democracy"
raises perhaps the most central issue: is the claim of democracy to constitute the
rule of the many real, or is this claim a sham that makes the de facto rule of the
few more effective and secure behind a screen of formally democratic
institutions? To anticipate our position and put it with apodictic brevity: no
actually existing democracy can claim to constitute in a realistic sense the rule
of the many; but "bourgeois" or formal democracy does make a difference for
the process of political decision-making and for the outcomes of that process.
　This position has methodological consequences. The concepts of democracy
used in our research – as well as in virtually all other empirical studies – aim to
identify the really existing democracies of our world and to distinguish them
from other forms of rule. Our operating concepts are therefore not based on the
most far-reaching ideals of democratic thought – of a government thoroughly
and equally responsive to the preferences of all its citizens (Dahl 1971) or of a
polity in which human beings fulfill themselves through equal and active
participation in collective self-rule (Macpherson 1973). Rather, they orient
themselves to the more modest forms of popular participation in government
through representative parliaments that appear as realistic possibilities in the
complex societies of today. Our definitions of democracy focus on the state's
responsibility to parliament (possibly complemented by direct election of the
head of the executive), on regular free and fair elections, on the freedom of
expression and association, and on the extent of the suffrage. Robert Dahl,
whose careful conceptualizations probably had the greatest influence on
empirical democracy research, reserved the term "polyarchy" for this more
modest and inevitably somewhat formal version of democracy (Dahl 1956,
1971).
　Why do we care about formal democracy if it considerably falls short of the
actual rule of the many? This question assumes particular saliency in the light of
two of our findings, namely that democracy was a result of the contradictions of
capitalist development and that it could be consolidated only if the interests of
the capitalist classes were not directly threatened by it. The full answer to this
question will become clear as we proceed with our analysis. But it is possible to
anticipate our conclusion briefly already here. We care about formal democracy
because it tends to be more than merely formal. It tends to be real to some
extent. Giving the many a real voice in the formal collective decision-making of
a country is the most promising basis for further progress in the distribution of
power and other forms of substantive equality. The same factors which support
the installation and consolidation of formal democracy, namely growth in the
strength of civil society in general and of the lower classes in particular, also
support progress towards greater equality in political participation and towards

greater social and economic equality. Ultimately, we see in democracy – even in its modest and largely formal contemporary realizations – the beginning of the self-transformation of capitalism.

The structure of this volume is simple and follows the line of reasoning just sketched. Chapter 2 offers a review of existing research, describing and evaluating the two traditions of research on development and democracy. It concludes with reflections on the methodological problems of reconciling contradictory results of research employing very different methods. Chapter 3 develops our theoretical framework for the study of development and democracy focusing on the three power clusters of class, state, and transnational relations. Chapter 4 presents the comparative analyses of advanced capitalist countries. Chapter 5 deals with democratization in Latin America, and chapter 6 compares the Caribbean islands and the countries of Central America. The concluding chapter 7 reviews the theoretical positions developed at the outset in the light of these comparative historical investigations. It ends by exploring the implications of our findings for the future of democracy.

2

Capitalist Development and Democracy: The Controversy

In the comparative study of macro-social phenomena two radically different research traditions coexist with each other – cross-national statistical work and comparative historical studies. This may be – and is often – seen as just another instance of the age-old opposition between quantitative and qualitative inquiry or, more radically, between social science and humanistic scholarship.

A minority of scholars – among them Jeffery Paige (1975), John Stephens (1979c), and Charles Ragin (1987) – have insisted that the two research modes should complement and be integrated with each other rather than treated as irreconcilable opposites. In research on development and democracy, the opposition between the two modes of work has a particularly intense character. Here we encounter not just a divergence of method but sharply contradictory findings. As noted, this constitutes a difficult dilemma unless one is prepared to dismiss one mode of research out of hand as inadequate. This chapter describes and evaluates the two bodies of research and seeks to lay the basis for a way to reconcile and transcend the contradictions.

Comparative Historical and Cross-national Quantitative Research on Development and Democracy

The contradictions between these two research traditions did not often lead to actual controversy and debate. Many who worked in the more qualitative, comparative historical mode hardly became aware of the other side, because they simply could not conceive of a research strategy that claims to come to valid results by taking a few pieces of information about many countries and subjecting them to statistical, correlational analysis. In turn, the emphasis on historical particularity and the small number of cases to which the historical approach could be applied, appeared radically unsuited for an exploration of the causal conditions of democracy in the eyes of students who conceived of the quantitative analysis of a large number of cases as the only viable substitute for the experimental approach that is impossible in macro-social analysis; they therefore searched for ways of studying the conditions of democracy through statistical inference from cross-national research covering many countries. The gulf between these methodological conceptions was – and is – so deep that the work of the other side was easily dismissed if it was noticed at all.

Ignorant dismissal was especially frequent among the historically minded students of democracy. The quantitative analysts paid more attention to the comparative historical work, though, as we will see, they often disregarded the more sophisticated theoretical ideas advanced by the other side, especially if these could not be tested with the crude measures suitable for macro-quantitative statistical analysis. This asymmetry has little substantive justification. Both sides grapple with difficult, yet fundamental methodological issues that are hard to do justice to at the same time; and each side makes different strategic decisions on which issues are to be given the most attention and which are to be treated with relative neglect.

We will first offer a selective account of both research traditions. This will introduce not only the problems at issue in the contrast between comparative historical and statistical investigations of the conditions of democracy but also a large number of ideas used in our own account. The chapter then turns to reflections on the questions raised by the divergence of the two research traditions. We will offer methodological arguments for an approach that can transcend the impasse and reconcile the contradictory findings.

Early quantitative cross-national studies

Seymour Martin Lipset published in 1959 a now classic paper linking democracy to economic development. It opened a long line of increasingly sophisticated quantitative cross-national studies. Lipset's theoretical position derived from the nineteenth-century classics of social theory, especially from Durkheim and Weber but also from Marx, combining a systemic conception of society with a revised version of social evolutionism. In many ways, his approach to the problems of development resembled that of modernization theory. At the same time, Lipset did not subscribe to the value determinism and the equilibrium assumptions that came to characterize especially later versions of modernization theory as well as his own later work. He combined a systemic view of social change with a resolute focus on divergent class interests and conflict.

Lipset begins with the observation that greater economic affluence in a country has long been thought of as a condition favorable for democracy: "The more well-to-do a nation, the greater the chances that it will sustain democracy" (Lipset 1959/1980: 31). He then proceeds to put this idea to the test by cross-national comparison.

He compares European and Latin American countries on the interrelated dimensions of wealth, industrialization, education, and urbanization and demonstrates that European stable democracies scored on average higher in all of these dimensions than European dictatorships. Examples of the indicators he uses are per capita income, telephones per 1,000 persons, percent of people employed in agriculture, percent literate, and percent living in cities of different sizes. A comparison of democracies and unstable dictatorships with stable dictatorships in Latin America comes to very similar results at a lower level of development.

In his theoretical account for these relationships, Lipset focuses on moderation and tolerance. Education, he contends, broadens one's outlook, increases tolerant attitudes, restrains people from adopting extremist doctrines, and increases their capacity for rational electoral choice. Increased wealth moderates the lower classes and thus makes them more prone to accept gradual change. Actually, it is the discrepancy in wealth rather than its overall level that is decisive, but since there is generally more inequality in poorer countries these two factors are closely related. In countries with great inequality of wealth, the poor are more likely to be a threat to the privileged and the established order. The rich in turn tend to be hostile to democracy, both because they feel threatened and because they often view it even as morally wrong to let the poor and the wretched participate in political decisions – an arrogant attitude which in turn feeds the resentment of the poor. Thus, the middle class emerges as the main pro-democratic force in Lipset's analysis, and this class gains in size with socioeconomic development. In sum, Lipset argues that industrialization leads to increases in wealth, education, communication, and equality; these developments are associated with a more moderate lower and upper class and a larger middle class, which is by nature moderate; and this in turn increases the probability of stable democratic forms of politics.

Subsequent studies employed far more refined statistical techniques. But they confirmed the positive relation between development and democracy. While they explored alternative as well as complementary hypotheses and sought to detail the causal mechanisms underlying the connection between development and democracy, they added little to a more comprehensive interpretation of this relationship.

Phillips Cutright (1963) brought correlational – and more generally multivariate – analysis to bear on these problems. He argued that averages of different social and economic indicators are far too crude a measure of development, discarding the more precise information available. Furthermore, differences in the character of the political order must not be just crudely classified because they then cannot be related with any precision to the quantitative information on social and economic conditions: "It makes little difference that in the verbal discussion of national political systems one talks about shades of democracy if, in the statistical assessment, one cannot distinguish among nations" (Cutright 1963: 254).

Cutright constructed scales of economic development, of "communications development" as well as of "political development" or, in effect, democracy, each combining several specific measures.[1] He then subjected these quantitative scores for 77 countries to a correlational analysis.

The correlation between the indices of communication development and democracy (or political development) was r = 0.81, while the correlation of democracy with economic development was 0.68, significantly lower. Cutright concluded that his main hypothesis – that political institutions are interdependent with the level of social and economic development – was confirmed.

The theoretical account Cutright offered for these findings is simple and not fully developed. More strongly than Lipset's it reflects the assumptions of modernization theory – of evolutionism and functional system integration. National societies are conceived as interdependent systems with sttrong equilibrium tendencies. Greater division of labor and structural differentiation in economy and society demand more complex and specialized political institutions, if the system as a whole is to be in equilibrium. He considers representative democracy as the form of government sufficiently complex to deal with a modern, increasingly heterogeneous social order. This identification of representative democracy with political differentiation is also the reason why the title of his paper speaks of "political development" rather than democracy.

In any less than perfect correlation, many countries will stand significantly above or below the regression line. Relative to its level of social or economic development a country may have "too much" or "too little" democracy. Commenting on this, Cutright offered on the one hand a number of ad hoc hypotheses explaining such "deviations" from a presumed equilibrium. For instance, he speculated, democracy may have flourished in the western hemisphere more than in Europe because of the absence of large-scale international conflict. And he suggested that case studies focus on deviant cases in order to gain further insights into the particular conditions favoring or hindering "political development".

On the other hand, he turned the mathematical equation representing the overall relations between social, economic and political development in all 77 countries into a "prediction equation:"

> The concept of interdependence and the statistical method of this study (lead) us to consider the existence of hypothetical equilibrium points toward which each nation is moving. It is possible for a nation to be politically overdeveloped or underdeveloped, and we suggest that either political or non-political changes will occur to put the nation into equilibrium. (Cutright 1963: 264)

This prediction presupposes an extremely tight integration of national systems. It furthermore implies the assumption that the social and economic development indicators represent the structural conditions that in the long run are decisive for the chances of democracy. However, these factors cannot explain on their own why any deviations from the predicted configuration should exist in the first place. Other conditions, such as those considered in the ad hoc hypotheses, become then by implication merely temporary obstacles to representative democratic forms of government or passing favorable circumstances.

Six years later, Cutright and Wiley (1969) published a study that responded to a number of questions raised by critics. It constituted a significant advance in quantitative comparative research on democracy. They selected 40 countries that were self-governing throughout the period from 1927 to 1966, thus excluding the effects of foreign occupation and colonial rule on the form of government. This represents a small, but significant advance toward the ideal of employing units of analysis that are independent of each other – a technical presupposition of causal inference from correlational analysis that can never be fully met for human societies, especially in the twentieth century.

With this sample of countries they studied democracy in relation to social and economic development in four successive decades, 1927–36, 1937–46, 1947–56, and 1957–66. In this way they were able not only to examine the same relationships in four different periods but also to subject the question of causal direction to a "cross-lagged" correlational test. Their conclusion: the positive association between social and economic development and democracy holds for all four decades, and the data suggest a causal priority especially for economic development.

The analysis then turned to the conditions of change in political representation over time. What accounts for stability of regime form in the face of social and economic change? And which factors are associated with declines in political representation, which occur in spite of the fact that literacy rates and energy consumption, the indicators of social and economic development, hardly show similar declines? Here a simple measure of social security provisions, based on the age and number of national social security programs, proved illuminating.

Changes in political representation were virtually confined to nations that rated low in the provision of social security and at the same time high in literacy. This led Cutright and Wiley to a revision of Cutright's earlier equilibrium theorem which predicted that countries with a political representation "too high" or "too low" in view of their level of social and economic development would decline or increase in political representation. Only nations high in literacy and low in social security provisions conformed to this expectation. Where literacy as well as social security were low, little or no change was observed. Neither did any significant political change occur in countries with high social security, whatever their levels of literacy.

The interpretation of these results given by Cutright and Wiley stayed as close as possible to the original equilibrium model: economic development entails division of labor and social differentiation to which representative democracy is the most adequate constitutional response. This functionalist argument is now complemented by a causal hypothesis concerning *social* development: increasing literacy and related aspects of social change foster a population's interest and capability in political participation and thus engender pressures for democratization.

The stabilizing effect of social security provisions, which constitutes the main new finding, is explained by two ideas, the second of which is only obliquely hinted at. First, satisfying major economic interests of the population strengthens people's allegiance to the political status quo, independent of constitutional form. Demands for democracy, in this view, derive their strength from unmet economic needs.

The second explanation can be combined with the first, but it is a sharply distinctive argument once fully developed. The capacity of a government to deliver social security programs can be taken as an indication of a strong and effective state apparatus, and – so we interpolate the argument – such state apparatuses may be strong enough to maintain the constitutional status quo: strong enough to defend itself against forces in society demanding a voice in collective decision-making, effective enough to "bribe" them into quiescence, and even powerful enough to crush them.

Retreat from comprehensive theoretical interpretations

Subsequent studies changed and refined the indicators for democracy[2] as well as the measures of social and economic development; they analyzed different samples of countries, and examined constitutional change over time. More important, however, was a subtle but significant shift in the relation of these studies to issues of theory. Typically, they explored propositions derived from alternative theoretical views of the relation between development and democracy, considering now in addition to modernization theory also the more conflict-oriented ideas of world-system and dependency theories. At the same time, they tended to refrain from such broader theoretical interpretations as offered by Lipset and Cutright and focused more and more on specific testable hypotheses.

Ken Bollen's work, arguably the most careful of this type, brought further methodological refinements together with confirmation of the basic empirical generalizations. Bollen also responds to a wider range of theoretical arguments. His paper on "Political Democracy and the Timing of Development" (Bollen 1979) takes off from the skepticism about any clear-cut relationship between socioeconomic development and democracy that we will encounter when we turn to the comparative–historical studies. To anticipate, this view sees favorable conditions for democracy rooted in the particular historical constellation of early capitalism and it maintains that such favorable conditions are not going to be repeated.

Bollen formulated this as the hypothesis that "the earlier a country begins to develop, the higher its level of democracy," noting that one could well argue the opposite by virtue of a diffusion of the democratic ideal over time which would exert more pressures for democracy in late developing countries. Using two different measures for the "beginning" of development, he found no significant association between the timing of development and political democracy. The interpretation of this negative finding is carefully left open. It could, for instance, be the result of the opposite – and mutually canceling – effects of different factors associated with the timing of development.

His analysis demonstrates again a rather robust association between economic development and democracy. This is especially significant because he examines a very large sample of 99 countries and because he employs a different set of indicators for political democracy. The association between political democracy and economic development was fundamentally unaffected by this different operationalization.

Bollen's study also throws light on the role of cultural factors and on the impact of state strength on democracy. He found political democracy to be positively associated with the proportion of Protestants in a country and negatively with the fraction of domestic economic production used for government expenditures. In subsequent publications, Bollen explored the interrelations between political democracy and income inequality as well as between democracy and the degree of a country's dependence on other countries in transnational economic relations. To these issues we now turn.

The relation between income inequality and democracy had been a central issue for Lipset (1959/1980) as well as for some of the classic authors on whose work he built his own argument. If these arguments lead us to expect chances for democracy to be more favorable under conditions of reduced inequality, the reverse direction of causation is equally plausible: wherever democracy is more than a mere formal sham, it should over time contribute to a reduction of inequality. Either or both of these relationships between inequality and democracy should result in fairly clear-cut negative correlations, although both are likely to involve time-lags the length of which is not easily specified. Empirical analyses have had trouble identifying clear-cut patterns.

A number of early quantitative studies came to contradictory results. Bollen and Jackman (1985b) concluded from their review of these studies as well as their own analysis that no relationship could be established once the level of development was taken into account. Muller (1988) argued that this was true only if democracy and inequality are measured at a single point in time. He found that the length of a country's experience with democracy has a significant negative impact on income inequality – independent of level of development, position in the world system, and the population's age structure. This is a gradual impact, measurably effective only after about two decades of democratic experience. Conversely, while the degree of income inequality does not seem to affect the *inauguration* of democracy, it does show a close relation to the chances of *maintaining* a democratic form of government.

The issue is far from settled. Muller's findings were challenged by Weede (1989) who introduced literacy in addition to level of development and the age structure of the population as control variables; this eliminated the central finding of Muller – the negative correlation between inequality and democratic experience. In turn, Muller (1989) replicated his earlier findings even with literacy as a control, using new measures for democratic experience and literacy.[3]

The exploration of the relation between democracy and economic dependence led to results one must judge ambiguous. Various authors had argued, on the basis of qualitative assessments and theoretical considerations, that the impact of advanced "core" countries on the political economy of dependent, "peripheral" countries would diminish the chances of democracy. "Outside the core, democracy is a rarity" (Chirot 1977: 22). Thomas and others (1979) drew from several, not altogether consistent, empirical tests the conclusion that economic dependence was indeed associated with political centralism.[4] However, Bollen (1983: 476, n.13) found no significant effect modifying the relation between democracy and level of development when he introduced such variables as penetration by multinational corporations, foreign trade concentration and US foreign aid. A complex classification distinguishing countries at the core of the capitalist world system, peripheral countries and semiperipheral countries, which was based on political as well as economic considerations – on treaty memberships, military interventions, and diplomatic relations as well as trade flows – did lead to the conclusion that democracy had, independent of a country's level of economic development, worse chances in peripheral and – to a lesser extent – in semiperipheral nations.[5] This finding suggests that geo-political international configurations may be more important than economic dependency as determinants of the chances of democracy. Shifting the focus to political international relations is also suggested by the results of Muller (1985), who found no evidence that breakdowns of democracy were the result of economic dependence, but observed a significant negative relation between aid, especially military aid, by the United States, and the stability of democracies.

Quite a few other cross-national statistical studies have also dealt with specific conditions or consequences of democracy – investigating further its relation to economic inequality and to a country's dependence on other countries in transnational economic relations or examining for instance the impact of democratic rule on economic performance. The details of these complex and often contradictory research findings need not detain us here. research findings need not detain us here.

A last quantitative study to be reviewed here departs from the cross-sectional mode of analysis of earlier work. Hannan and Carroll (1981) seek to identify social and economic correlates of *transitions* from one formal political structure to another. This "event–history method" partially confirms, partially modifies and complements the findings of cross-sectional research. Hannan and Carroll found that in the 90 countries studied for the period from 1950 to 1975, only a few of the variables examined had significant effects on the transitions from one of four political forms to another. High levels of economic production were negatively, ethnic diversity positively associated with overall rates of change in political form. The most stable political structures were multi-party systems: of the 39 countries with multi-party political structures in 1950, 28 had such a system still (or again) in 1975. In line with what one would expect from cross-sectional analyses, Hannan and Carroll's event–history analysis showed that richer countries are less likely to move from multi-party politics to political centralism, but the same holds for transitions away from centralized political forms: "Stated loosely, successful countries retain their political strategies." (Hannan and Carroll 1981: 30–1). Ethnic diversity was not only found to destabilize formal political structures in general, but had a particularly negative effect on democracy: it was especially associated with transitions *out of* multi-party systems and with changes *into* one-party regimes.

The whole gamut of quantitative cross-national research was dismissed by many and attacked as inadequate by a few. Its empirical conclusions as well as its – generally sparse – theoretical grounding, primarily in modernization theory, were sharply contradicted by investigations that focused on the histories of a few countries and analyzed them in the light of more complex theoretical arguments. These studies were critical of the a-historical quasi-evolutionary generalizations that informed modernization theories. Their own common ground in theoretical conception has been characterized by a focus on long-term effects of past conflicts and historical structures, by a search for the critical collective actors in historical change, and by an emphasis on the changing world historical environment of national histories. We offer a sketch of some of these comparative historical works before turning to an evaluation of both strands of research.

Early comparative historical investigations

Karl de Schweinitz (1964) formulated a theoretical position that sharply contradicts the notion that today's advanced capitalist countries represent the future state toward which less developed countries will travel on roads roughly similar to the paths taken by the "early developers". Democracy as known in the West was in his view the privilege of the original capitalist countries. Here economic development was slow. Its decentralized character encouraged liberal political conceptions and ideals. The working class was not yet mobilized. There was no demonstration effect from neighboring more advanced countries that would have stimulated individual and collective consumption demands. Thus, it was far easier than in today's developing nations to impose the disciplines of consumption, of work, and of public order that are necessary for economic development.

Later developing countries need a stronger state also for a number of other reasons – among them a very different international economic environment, which is likely to trap the less advanced countries in unfavorable positions in the transnational division of labor, and new technological options that can be exploited only with larger lumps of investment than private savings can sustain. The pressures toward greater centralization go beyond economic considerations and necessities. States in late developing countries also have more reason to intervene repressively because their rapidly changing societies are more mobilized. At the same time, they have more effective means – military and police technology, modern systems of communication and transportation, as well as better forms of organization – to impose the three disciplines of consumption, work, and public order. If that imposition succeeds, democracy is not very likely since democratization now depends largely on the values and intentions of the ruling groups. If it does not succeed, neither development nor democracy have good prospects. De Schweinitz concludes (1964: 10–11): "The development of democracy in the nineteenth century was a function of an unusual configuration of historical circumstances which cannot be repeated. The Euro-American route to democracy is closed. Other means must now be devised for building new democratic states." The remainder of the book makes clear that he sees the possibilities of developing democratic political structures as limited indeed.

Two generations earlier, in 1906, Max Weber voiced an opinion on the chances of bourgeois democracy in Russia that is similarly skeptical and roughly akin in its reasoning. While his passionate sympathies lay with the struggle of the liberal democrats in Russia, his analysis of the impact of capitalism on the

Russian economy and especially on the Russian agrarian structure led him to a rather negative prognosis.

True, the bureaucracy of the autocratic regime of the Tsar would hardly survive the tensions and conflicts of capitalist transformation: "As far as the negative side of the problem is concerned, the view of the 'developmental theorists' will be right. The Russian autocracy of the past has ... by any human estimate no choice but to dig its own grave" (Weber 1906: 350). But that does not mean that it will be replaced by a democratic regime. The project of democratization would have to rely primarily on the power of Western ideas, while it faces overwhelming structural obstacles. These obstacles are in Weber's view firstly grounded in the conditions of the Russian political economy, particularly in its agrarian problems. But the progress of democratization is also not favored by the character of advanced capitalism itself, which begins to penetrate the Russian economy. Capitalism in the twentieth century represents in Weber's judgement an increasingly hostile environment for freedom and democracy: "It is completely ridiculous to attribute to today's advanced capitalism an elective affinity with 'democracy' not to mention 'freedom' (in *any* meaning of the word)." Successful democratization in Russia now has to overcome obstacles that derive from the political and economic problems of late and uneven capitalist development as well as from the changed character of capitalism anywhere. Its only hopes are in Weber's view the *ideals* of bourgeois liberal reform – a slender reed to lean on.[6]

An even more skeptical view of the relation between capitalism and democracy that applies to early capitalism as well can be inferred from his analysis of the role of law and bureaucracy in the rise of capitalism. Here Weber (1922/1968) argues for a functional correspondence or "elective affinity" between early, competitive capitalism and the predictability of formally rational law and bureaucratic administration. Formal rationality and thus predictability are compromised by substantive demands of justice. Democracy, however, is in Weber's view precisely the institutional arrangement through which such substantive demands are invading and transforming the pure formalism of law. In critical ways, then, democracy and even early capitalism were at odds with each other.

More recent comparative historical work

Guillermo O'Donnell (1979b) sought to explain authoritarian developments in South America during the 1960s and 1970s that seemed at odds with the optimism implied in modernization theory. Argentina, Brazil, Uruguay, and other countries turned away from democratic constitutional forms at fairly high levels of development and, he argued, for reasons precisely related to their comparatively advanced stage of development. O'Donnell's analysis was based on a political economy framework, roughly comparable to that of Max Weber and de Schweinitz. He gave particular attention to the economic and political dependence of a late developing country on the developed core of the capitalist world economy and to the responses of the state and of class-based politics to the problems engendered by this dependency.

Import substitution industrialization (ISI) had expanded the urban middle and working classes and brought to power populist coalitions which deliberately activated popular forces, particularly through labor organization, and included them in the political process. Economic growth underwrote the costs of social welfare policies. However, the progress of "easy," or "horizontal," i.e. consumer goods import substitution behind high tariff walls depended on growing imports of capital goods, paid for by exports of primary goods. This development strategy ran into trouble when the foreign exchange reserves accumulated during World War II were exhausted and both prices and demand for Latin America's primary exports declined in the 1950s. The severe balance of payments problems caused domestic inflation. Attempts to impose stabilization policies hurt the popular sectors, divided the populist coalitions, and created political crises.

The growth of ISI had also enlarged the number and range of technocratic roles in the public and private sectors. Prominent on the minds of these technocrats was the "deepening" of industrialization, i.e. the creation of a capital goods industry. However, successful pursuit of this strategy entailed reduction of popular consumption in order to generate higher domestic investment levels (as taxation of the wealthier sectors was not even considered as a realistic alternative), and attraction of foreign capital. The crucial obstacles in this path were militant labor movements and populist politicians. This constellation led to the formation of a coup coalition among civilian and military technocrats and the big bourgeoisie. They discarded democracy as incompatible with further economic development and installed bureaucratic–authoritarian regimes. These regimes insulated economic policy makers from popular pressures and deactivated unions and left-wing political parties, by force if necessary. Thus, it was exactly in the more advanced of the Latin American countries that particularly harsh authoritarian rule was imposed in the 1960s and 1970s.

O'Donnell asserted on the basis of these findings an "elective affinity" between advanced capitalist development in dependent political economies and bureaucratic authoritarian rule. Though the wider and longer-term significance of such developments is treated with caution, his perspective is radically different from the optimism of much of modernization theory: "It is impossible to say, without systematic comparative research, but it is a disquieting possibility that such authoritarianisms might be a more likely outcome than political democracy as other countries achieve or approach high modernization (O'Donnell 1979b: 90).

O'Donnell places great emphasis on a country's dependent position in the international economic system. Dependency theory – as well as its close cousin, world system theory (see Wallerstein 1974 and 1976) – generally tends to see economic dependence as creating pressures toward authoritarian rule (see, e.g. Chirot 1977; Thomas 1984).

Seven years before O'Donnell's book, Barrington Moore, Jr. , had published *The Social Origins of Dictatorship and Democracy* (1966). This was without doubt the most important comparative historical research on development and political form, and it achieved paradigmatic influence in the field. Through historical case studies of six countries – England, France, the United States, Japan, India, and China – and extensive research on two more, Germany and Russia, Moore identifies three distinct paths to political modernity, each characterized by specific conditions: the path to parliamentary democracy, the path to fascist dictatorship, and the path to communist dictatorship. These three routes, he argues, are not alternatives that are in principle open to any society. Rather, they are tied to specific conditions characteristic of successive phases of world history. Thus he sees the conditions favorable for democracy – like Weber and de Schweinitz – bound up with the historical constellation of early capitalism: "the route that ended up in capitalist democracy ... was itself a part of history that almost certainly will not be repeated" (Moore 1966: 5).

A strong concern with historical particularity and process leads Moore to a principle that informs all of his interpretations and explanations: past conflicts and institutional structures have long-term effects and are of critical importance for later developments. Any attempt to explain current change without attention to these continuing effects of past history – any "presentist" analysis – is doomed to fail.[7]

Moore's specific analyses proceed in the by now familiar political economy framework: economic change, state structures and state actions, and social classes are the central categories. Basically marxist in orientation, the study focuses on peasants and lords, though the bourgeoisie is given a critical role as well. Moore's emphasis on the role of the rural classes derives, of course, from the principle of long-term effects of past history. It is noteworthy, however, and it will occupy us later, that the working class is virtually absent from the picture he gives of the rise of democracy.

In his conceptions of rural class conflict, the distinction between labor-repressive and market-dominated modes of labor control plays a crucial role. This has found striking support in a study of agrarian social movements in contemporary developing countries by Jeffery Paige (1975). Paige found that the most radical agrarian movements emerged when a landlord class relied on coercive labor policies while facing a cultivating class that derived its income primarily from wages rather than directly from the land and that was able to organize for collective action.

Moore asks of his cases a number of central questions, and it is these questions that constitute the core of his theoretical framework. The analysis focuses (1) on the strength of the state in relation to the power of landlords and bourgeoisie, (2) on the incidence of repressive agriculture for which the landlords need the help of the state, (3) on the relative strength of the rural and the urban dominant classes, (4) on the alliances of domination among the crown and the dominant classes, alliances shaped by the relative strength and the interests of these partners in power, and (5) on the chances of the peasantry to come to collective action depending on the presence or absence of solidary village and work structures.

The conditions for the route to communist revolution can now be listed in skeletal fashion: a highly centralized state, a weak bourgeoisie, a land owning class that relies on political means of labor repression, and a peasantry with good chances of collective action that are due to solidary village communities and weak ties to the – often absent – landlords. This picture bears a striking similarity to the sketch of the factors Weber considered relevant in the early stages of the Russian revolution. The communist take over occurred in Russia only after the system of domination broke down in the revolution at the end of World War I, which was fueled by peasant discontent.

Moore's view of the conditions for the reactionary revolution from above that ends in fascist dictatorship can be put in similarly apodictic form as follows: a coalition led by a strong state and powerful landowning classes includes a bourgeoisie that is not without some strength but depends on the support of the state through trade protectionism, favorable labor legislation and other measures that in different combinations characterize top-down, state-sponsored industrialization. Agricultural labor remains significantly controlled by repressive means rather than primarily through the market. Owing to village and work structures that do not favor solidarity, the peasant revolutionary potential is low. The internal tensions and contradictions of industrialization under reactionary sponsorship lead to experiments with democracy that do not, however, yield results acceptable to the dominant classes. Fascist repression is the final outcome. The similarity of this path to the developments in Argentina and Brazil in the 1960s and 1970s did not escape the notice of O'Donnell. In fact, he explores the broader theoretical implications of his own analysis precisely by linking it to Moore's work and by extending Moore's ideas beyond the cases of Japan and Germany (O'Donnell 1979b: 88–90).

The emergence of parliamentary democracy represents the oldest route to modernity. The picture Moore offers here is more complex than in the case of the other two routes. Conflict and a fairly even balance of power between the lords and the crown are a first condition. A strong bourgeoisie, at odds in its interests with the rural dominant class and even able to entice landlords into commercial pursuits, is of critical importance: "No bourgeoisie, no democracy" (Moore 1966: 418). Moore also notes that in all three cases of democratic development studied there was a revolutionary, violent break with the past, unsettling the established domination of landlords and crown. Other conditions that emerged as significant in the rise of communist revolution and fascist dictatorship show, however, no clear-cut pattern in the histories representing the democratic route: while labor repressive agriculture was present in France and the United States, English agriculture relied rather exclusively on the market. The capacity of rural labor for collective action – the revolutionary potential of the peasantry – was high in France but low in England and the United States.

On the case of India, Moore takes a similar position as de Schweinitz: there are complex conditions that allow the institutional legacy of post-colonial democracy to survive. But due to the limited compatibility of freedom and efficiency under current conditions, Indian leaders have to face cruel choices between effective democracy and effective development. The argument reveals a conviction that informs Moore's analysis of all routes into the modern world: "The tragic fact of the matter is that the poor bear the heaviest costs of modernization under both socialist and capitalist auspices." Therefore, modernization is not possible without "either masked coercion on a massive scale, as in the capitalist model including even Japan, or more direct coercion approaching the socialist model" (Moore 1966: 410).

In her incisive review of *Social Origins*, Skocpol (1973) takes Moore to task on a number of points, among them his neglect of the variably autonomous role of states and his lack of an intersocietal perspective.[8] She argues that a strong state with a capacity for repression – something absent in England for example, due to the reliance on the navy for military power – is an essential element of the authoritarian class coalition. Her argument for the importance of the intersocietal perspective is, in part, a plea for integrating Moore's domestic class analysis with the central ideas of dependency theory and Wallersteinian world-system theory. But at the same time, it is an argument for the importance of interstate relations in analyzing domestic politics and the variably autonomous role of the state. Conceptualizing states as standing at the intersection of domestic and international power relations proved to be exceptionally fruitful in her own comparative study of social revolutions (Skocpol 1979).

Moore's analysis is open to quite important other criticisms. One was briefly noted earlier and will occupy us later at some length: the role of the working class in democratization is rather radically neglected. This is in part a consequence of Moore's focus on long historical gestation periods. In addition, it follows from his definition of democracy which focuses on public contestation of political issues rather than on inclusive participation in the political process. The democratic struggles of the working class then appear only to extend an otherwise already largely established pattern. We will argue for a very different view.

Another important critique takes off from the apparently innocuous fact that the time periods taken into account for the different countries vary considerably in length. While the cases of democratization are pursued over very long time periods, the discussion of Japan and Germany breaks off with the establishment of Fascism. This can be defended only by arguing that post-war democratization in these two countries was exclusively a result of foreign imposition, which in turn is – like all questions of international context in Moore's analysis – excluded from the explanatory framework.

If this exclusive focus on domestic developments is modified and if the time periods considered are adjusted in theoretically meaningful ways, it is possible to argue that the reactionary path to political modernity has some potential for leading – by tortuous detours – to democratic political forms. This argument goes far beyond the cases of Japan and Germany. France came at various points in the nineteenth century quite close to the reactionary path model, yet it rightly figures as one of the main cases of democratization.[9] Spain, Portugal, and Greece as well as Argentina and Brazil may well be seen as instances of a similar development toward democracy in the twentieth century (Rueschemeyer 1980).

Yet, these as well as other critiques notwithstanding, Moore's book represents a towering achievement. It helped transform the social sciences by reestablishing the comparative historical mode of research as the most appropriate way of analyzing macro-social structures and developments.

Two modes of research – contradictory results

Our review of quantitative cross-national and comparative historical studies on the relation between capitalist development and democracy has shown us results that rather consistently contradict each other. We are faced with a serious dilemma because the two research traditions are separated by two things at once: by opposite findings and by different methods.

The first research tradition covers many countries, takes for each country only a minimum of standardized, aggregate, but not always reliable information into account, and translates that information – on occasion not with great delicacy – into numerical expressions in order to subject it to complex mathematical operations. It sees the quantitative analysis of a large number of cases as the only viable substitute for the experimental approach that is impossible in macro-social analysis.

The other tradition studies only a few countries at a time, and while the complexity of such analyses far exceeds the possibility of testing the explanatory propositions with so small a number of cases, these works are attentive to many factors suggested as relevant by common sense and theoretical argument, they treat historical particularity with care, they give weight to the historical genesis of social and political structures and developments, and they betray an attractive awareness of long-term historical developments in different parts of the world.

Taken together, the two research traditions highlight fundamental methodological issues that are hard to do justice to at the same time. Faced with difficult dilemmas, each makes different strategic decisions on what to give priority.

The quantitative cross-national research, which we respect for its breadth of coverage, the objectivization of analysis, and the quantitative testing of specific hypotheses, has come to a number of consistent results. The outstanding finding is that there exists a stable positive relationship between socioeconomic development and democracy.

The comparative historical tradition of research, which we respect for its analyses of historical process and for the sophistication of theoretical argument, is by contrast extremely skeptical of the chances of democracy in contemporary developing countries. These authors do not only deny that there exists a consistent and theoretically plausible relationship between democracy and development, capitalist or otherwise, but they also see the odds of democracy especially in developing countries as extremely unfavorable. They find the main reasons for this world historical change since the first rise of capitalism in the different and more powerful role of states (including the expansion and transformation of the military forces) in both less developed and advanced industrial countries, in the different balance of power between dominant and subordinate classes and different patterns of class alliance in less developed countries, and in the different transnational environment in which late-coming nations have to advance their projects of development.

How can this dilemma – created by contradictory results of different research methods – be resolved? Before that question is approached, one point should be made clear. This is not a conflict between divergent quasi-philosophical, "meta-theoretical" positions, as was argued for different theories of the state by Alford and Friedland (1985). In that case the conflicting analyses would simply talk past each other. The contradictory results at issue here can in our view be confronted with each other much more directly; they are in principle open to resolution on the basis of empirical evidence. This, too, is the way in which they have been treated in the past – by Max Weber no less than by the quantitative methodologists of today. We will first turn to some methodological arguments and reflections, giving emphasis to those that challenge the widely accepted monopoly of the quantitative cross-national methodology, and then seek to arrive at a judgement about the best foundations of a strategy of resolving the contradictions.

Methodological Reflections

Critique and countercritique

A convenient starting point for examining the contradictions between the two research traditions is O'Donnell's critique of cross-national statistical research, one of the rare responses from a comparative historical scholar to the other side. O'Donnell argues, first, that causal inferences from quantitative cross-national evidence imply the assumption that the causal conditions which affect the chances of democracy today are the same as those which shaped democratic developments during the early rise of capitalism, an assumption that may well be wrong. This, of course, invokes the fundamental claim made by all the comparative historical analysts we reviewed – that democratic developments were rooted in a historical constellation not likely to be repeated. However, quantitative research results make it difficult to sustain the lines of argument that have been advanced so far. Bollen (1979), as we have seen, found no consistent relationship between the timing of development and democracy or, more precisely, none that overrides the association between democracy and level of development. Furthermore, the statistical association between democracy and level of development holds even if the most advanced industrial countries are excluded from the analysis (see e.g. Cutright 1963: 258; Marsh 1979: 238). That means it cannot be "explained away" by a strong association between democracy and the highest levels of development achieved by the early modernizers. [10]

Next O'Donnell charges that if "deviations" from the central tendency identified by multivariate analysis are dismissed as due to idiosyncratic obstacles, "the basic paradigm is rendered immune to empirical falsification" (O'Donnell 1979b: 5). This objection seems rooted in the comprehensive interest in each case characteristic of comparative historical research; rather than dismissal, the deviant case deserves special attention. The objection is plausible in the context of comparative historical analysis. It is not convincing as a critique of the statistical approach, which focuses on a number of variables while randomizing the effects of others. True, in the early work of Cutright

(1963) we encountered interpretive arguments, wedded to the neo-evolutionism and the equilibrium assumptions of modernization theory, that fit O'Donnell's charge rather exactly. However, Cutright himself adduced the evidence for very important modifications of the assumed equilibrium tendency (see Cutright and Wiley 1969). And later studies no longer viewed the statistical associations as confirming complex macro-trends, but used them rather to test specific hypotheses.

O'Donnell also charges the quantitative studies with what he calls the "universalistic fallacy" – the assumption that since in a set of all or most contemporary countries "some positive correlation between socio-economic development and political democracy can be found, it may be concluded that this relationship holds for all the units (say, regions) included in that set" (O'Donnell 1979: 6). This raises the same question about uniform conditions of democracy across different regions as we just considered for different periods of time. The argument is central to O'Donnell's view of South America, where it seemed at the time that "political authoritarianism – not political democracy – is the more likely concomitant of the highest levels of modernization" (O'Donnell 1979: 8). Though nothing is wrong with this idea of regionally variant conditions in logic or theoretical principle, it is contradicted by the evidence of quantitative studies that varied in regional inclusiveness but not in the dominant result of a positive association between level of development and democracy. Given our present knowledge, it may be more reasonable to warn regionally specialized scholarship – such as Latin American studies – against the "particularist fallacy" of disregarding the results of more comprehensive analyses than to press the dangers of a universalist fallacy against the claims of quantitative cross-national research.

O'Donnell makes a quite valid point when he argues that variations within a country are not taken into account when cross-national analyses are based on average per capita figures for domestic production, educational attainment etc. It is quite true, for instance, that the growing wealth of some segments of the population affects national averages quite strongly even though nothing may have changed in the economic condition of the vast majority; in fact, such a development renders the groups that do not participate in the higher standard of living even less – rather than more – capable of making their interests count in political decisions.

However, one may see such inattentiveness to intra-country variation as a discrepancy between the indicators used and the theoretically relevant variables – an error in measurement. And it is well known that measurement error, unless it systematically favors the hypothesis under review, has the counter-intuitive effect of deflating correlations. This also applies to the – often quite debatable – indicators of social and economic development and political democracy. Bad measures make it harder, not easier, to confirm a hypothesis.

Another argument of O'Donnell constitutes, however, a powerful critique with far-reaching consequences: it is highly problematic to draw *diachronic* conclusions – about changes over time and thus about causation – from *cross-sectional* analyses. The same idea – that genetic, causal questions require historical information about processes rather than cross-sectional data on a given point (or short period) of time – was the starting point of a seminal paper by Dankwart Rustow (1970) that developed a simple process model of democratization whose phases moved from prolonged and inconclusive struggle through elite compromise to habituation. The systematic exploration of causal conditions through comparative analysis of historical sequences is a cornerstone of our own approach.

It is true that several quantitative cross-national studies did take the historical dimension into account, however minimally and crudely (Cutright and Wiley 1969; Bollen 1979; Hannan and Carroll 1981). The findings of these studies are suggestive for further analyses that search for genetic, processual explanations. Nevertheless, there is little doubt that causal explanations cannot be tested directly with cross-sectional studies and that it is diachronic propositions and studies of historical sequence that are needed for settling the issues of a causal interpretation of cross-sectional findings.

Where, then, do these rather complex arguments leave what we may take as established conclusions of the quantitative cross-national studies? One massive result of these studies still stands: there is a stable positive association between social and economic development and political democracy. This cannot be explained away by problems of operationalization. A whole array of different measures of development and democracy were used in the studies under review, and this did not substantially affect the results.

This result cannot be invalidated either by arguing that it may not apply to certain regions of the world. Nor can it be explained by diffusion from a single center of democratic creativity, though some associations of democracy with former British colonial status as well as the proportion of Protestants were found by Bollen (1979). It also cannot be explained by a particularly close correlation between development and democracy at the highest levels of development, because samples consisting only of less developed countries exhibited substantially the same patterns. Finally, the close concatenation of level of development and democracy cannot be accounted for by a special association between early modernization and democracy since the explicit inclusion of measures of the timing of development did not significantly affect the relationship between level of development and democracy.

Yet as the tale of storks and babies often told by statisticians suggests, any correlation – however reliably replicated – depends for its meaning on the context supplied by theory and accepted knowledge. The relation between statistical finding and theoretical account is decidedly asymmetrical. The theoretical explanations we encounter in the cross-national studies do not gain any particular credibility from the sturdiness of the findings for which they give an account. They are, to put it most starkly, pure conjecture. This is so by logical necessity, though it also finds support in well-founded reservations about the theoretical models most often used. In sum, the quantitative findings are compatible with a wide range of explanatory accounts.

The causal forces that stand behind the relationship between development and democracy remain, in effect, in a black box.[11] The explanations offered in the early quantitative research adopted the then prevailing assumptions of modernization theory. But nobody can maintain that this in any way followed from the statistical results. The correlations between development and democracy constitute *an empirical generalization* – not more and not less. In regard to the theoretical account of the conditions of democracy, this empirical generalization plays a role that is critically important and at the same time strictly limited: It has a veto power over certain explanations – those that are at odds with it; but it does not determine the choice between various theoretical accounts that are compatible with it.

If we must consider the association between development and democracy a fundamental given in any theoretical argument about the conditions of democracy, the quantitative cross-national research has yielded also a number of results that have less definite and often quite ambiguous implications. We can best treat them as important suggestions for further analysis, because the relationships emerged only in one or a few studies and were contradicted by others or because it is not clear what exactly is measured by the empirical indicators used. Among the more important suggestive findings are the following:

the possible negative impact of state strength on the chances of democracy,
the association between stability of political form and the provision of social
  security,
the negative relation between central control of the economy and democracy,
the negative effects of ethnic and linguistic fragmentation on democracy.
the possible role of cultural tradition and diffusion (British influence, percent
  Protestant),
the supportive relation of literacy and literacy gains to democracy,
the possible impact of economic and especially geo-political dependency,
and the long-term mutually supporting relation between democracy and
  lowered economic inequality.

There are no similarly explicit and refined critiques of the comparative historical approach as O'Donnell mounts against the cross-national quantitative work. That does not mean that comparative historical research is generally held to stand above such criticism. To the contrary, the very self-understanding of many quantitative social scientists is built on a dismissal of qualitative evidence as merely anecdotal – interesting for illustration and perhaps inspiration, but worthless when it comes to establishing results. The critical claims about comparative historical research implied by this view are easily listed. Comparative historical research, while theoretically often very complex, covers too few cases to come to any definitive results about these theoretical arguments. The choice of cases is often arbitrary, and there is no protection against a case selection that favors the author's line of theoretical argument. In fact, theories are rarely tested in any meaningful sense, because they are typically developed from facts known in advance. Finally, the lack of methodological self-consciousness in much comparative historical research is taken as the symptom not only of a profound unconcern but also of fatal substantive flaws.

We will take up some of the specifics of this critique in our discussion below. Here it is sufficient to make only a few fundamental points. The first, already made earlier, is excellently developed in Ragin's recent examination of comparative methods, both quantitative and qualitative (Ragin 1987): both comparative historical case studies and variable-oriented quantitative research must answer to the same fundamental standards, and both meet them – imperfectly – in different ways and with different strengths. The second is that the near-consensus of the comparative historical studies on the extremely limited chances of democracy after a favorable phase in the course of world history is at odds with the most robust finding of cross-national quantitative research. That consensus opinion must be dismissed, and the contrary result of the quantitative studies must be considered an established empirical generalization with which all accounts of democratization have to come to terms. This does not, however, follow from inherent flaws of comparative historical research; rather, it is our considered judgement after comparing the two traditions of research. Our third and final claim is that in principle comparative historical research is equally able to come to similarly pivotal results.

The comparative advantage of historical analyses

How are we going to develop an empirical theory about development and democracy that is credible in the light of general sociological knowledge, capable of accounting for the central relationship between development and democracy established by the cross-national quantitative research, and promising for further research into the conditions of democracy and for the interpretation of ambiguous and opaque findings? It is our conviction that we must turn to the richer theoretical reasoning of the comparative historical tradition if we want to lay the groundwork for an adequate theory of the conditions of democracy. We take this position in spite of the fact that so many of the qualitative historical works came to conclusions about the relation of democracy to development in today's world that are at odds with the quantitative empirical evidence. That their conclusions went far beyond the evidence actually examined in these studies may or may not be taken as an indictment; it does point to the problem inherent in theory-oriented comparative history just mentioned: the number of cases is too small for the number of variables considered. The contrast between intellectual complexity and the limited number of cases is indeed a basic dilemma of the comparative historical search for explanation and theory.

There are several reasons why nevertheless the comparative historical tradition of research on democracy appears to offer the best foundation for constructing a satisfactory theoretical account of the conditions of democracy. First, it is far richer in theoretical argument and analysis than the macro-quantitative studies. This is true whether we compare it with the quantitative studies that – like Cutright's – seek to support a broad systemic interpretation or with the later research trying to test specific hypotheses. This theoretical richness is not an accident: "One of the most valuable features of the case-oriented approach ... is the fact that it engenders an extensive dialogue between the investigator's ideas and the data" (Ragin 1987: 49). Second, and more specifically, the political economy orientation of the works reviewed has proved fruitful in a number of similar areas of inquiry – for instance in comparative work on inequality, on socioeconomic development, and on state intervention in civil society.

Finally, these studies developed their explanatory ideas grappling with historical sequences; and we are convinced that it is in sequences of change that we will find the key to the black box that mediates the relation between development and democracy. Historical sequence studies are generally best attuned to the necessities of a genetic, causal explanation. This claim will appear to many social scientists at first sight counterintuitive. Further reflection will perhaps make it more plausible.

What are the specific chances of insight, which the particular blind spots of the two modes of research? Our basic position on the methodological side of the impasse between them was already stated: neither side has an obvious superiority in principle, and neither can be dismissed. Rather, each has made choices when confronted with a situation that did not allow obedience to all mandates of methodology – not even to all major mandates – at the same time. Each side had to pay for its peculiar strengths with equally characteristic weaknesses.

Further reflection may usefully begin with the theoretical implications of a single case pursued over time. All too often it is taken for granted that the theoretical utility of studying one single case is extremely limited. It can inspire hypotheses, this argument says, but so can sheer imagination. It can perhaps force a reconsideration of those propositions contradicted by this singular set of unique facts, but it cannot go beyond that. This view overlooks that a particular sequence of historical development may rule out a whole host of possible theoretical accounts, because over time it typically encompasses a number of different relevant constellations. The continuity of a particular system of rule can for instance invalidate – by its very persistence under substantially changing conditions – quite a few claims about the conditions of stable domination. Such an effect presupposes, of course, that there are reasoned expectations, that the interrogation of the historical record is theoretically informed. This impact of a single case analysis is strengthened by the fact that for one (or a few) cases it is possible to match analytic intent and empirical observations much more precisely than in an analysis covering many cases with the help of standardized indicators. Case-centered research can examine the particular context of seemingly simple facts and take into account that their analytic meaning often depends on that historic context. It is these two features of historical analysis that led E. P. Thompson to insist on the "epistemological legitimacy of historical knowledge ... as knowledge of causation" and to speak – somewhat obliquely and perhaps extravagantly – of "history as a process inscribed with its own causation" (Thompson 1978: 225, 226).

Yet if the theoretical utility of the narration and analysis of even a single case must not be dismissed, a focus on historical lines of change does carry its own problems. Studying change within the same society implicitly holds constant those structural features of the situation that do not actually change during the period of observation. It is for this reason that process-oriented historical studies – even if they transcend sheer narrative and are conducted with theoretical, explanatory intent – often emphasize the role of voluntary decision and tend to play down – by taking them as givens – structural constraints that limit some options of historical actors and encourage others.

This consideration may throw a revealing light, for instance, on the recent controversy about the relation of German big business to the rising National Socialist party. Turner's analysis (1985) is a good example of the focus on process and agency and he comes to rather innocuous results about the role of big business in the rise of Hitler, while Abraham (1986) who uses a theoretical framework centered on structural analysis comes to very different conclusions. Similar questions are raised if O'Donnell and Schmitter (1986: 19) claim that in recent transitions from authoritarian rule "what actors do and do not do seems much less tightly determined by 'macro' structural factors during the transitions we study here than during breakdowns of democratic regimes". They may indeed offer us a fascinating empirical generalization. But the fact that their conclusion to the studies of "Transitions from Authoritarian Rule" (O'Donnell, Schmitter and Whitehead 1986) emphasizes themes congenial with a voluntarist perspective – such as political divisions within the authoritarian regime, pacts of "soft-liners" in government with parts of the opposition, and the sequences and turns of liberalization that could have taken a different course – may also derive from the design of this project, which had at its center a series of country monographs covering a relatively short period of time.[12]

If we entertain serious reservations about the voluntaristic bias that seems associated with the study of single instances of historical process or with analyses covering relatively short time periods, we do not intend to counterpose the focus on the *longue durée* of the French *Annales* school to a dismissed *histoire événementielle*. Our aim is rather to construct a framework of inquiry that is in principle equally well attuned to the study of process and to the recognition of structural constraints. This does not seem a utopian goal. Within this broader framework, our own interests do center on the structural conditions of democracy rather than on a process analysis of regime transitions.

Ragin claims that comparative historical case studies are generally inhospitable to structural explanations while "wide-ranging cross-national studies, by contrast, are biased in favor of structural explanations" (Ragin 1987: 70). There is little doubt about the latter assertion. In fact, cross-national statistical research has no choice but to be structurally oriented.[13] The former, however, truly holds only for single-case historical accounts. The voluntaristic bias of case oriented research is counterbalanced by comparison. Even in single-case studies comparative awareness and especially a longer time span of investigation can – logically analogous to cross-country comparisons – make the structural conditions of different event sequences more visible.

It is, however, actual comparison of cases featuring different structural conditions that really turns things around. Even a few comparisons have a dramatic effect in disciplining explanatory accounts. Moore's (1966) classic study does not stand alone as a case-oriented comparative inquiry that illuminates the role of structural constraints. In fact, most of the comparative historical studies we have reviewed share a strong focus on structural conditions. Clearly the strategy of case selection acquires critical importance here, because the range of cases examined determines which outcomes and which potential causal conditions can be comparatively studied. Certain case selections and choices of time horizon can also favor a focus on process and agency. This is demonstrated by O'Donnell and Schmitter's (1986) work on redemocratization and Linz's (1978) work on breakdown of democracy. Linz's extended essay compares cases in which the democratic regime collapsed and focuses on the events which led up to the demise of the regime. His emphasis on process (e.g. "the constriction of the political arena") and agency (e.g. mistakes made by the supporters of the democratic regime) are direct results of the short time horizon and the case selection. Had he compared breakdown cases with those in which democracy survived and/or selected a longer time horizon, for example comparing the breakdown with later returns to democracy, structural differences would have appeared as much more important in the analysis. Precisely the same observations could be made about O'Donnell and Schmitter's essay on redemocratization.

Case selection is a more important concern in comparative historical research than in quantitative cross-national studies because the latter typically reach for the largest number of cases for which the relevant information is available. Rational case selection depends primarily on a sound theoretical framing of the issues.

Ragin (1987) sees the special strength of comparative historical research in its particular aptitude to deal with two phenomena – multiple causal paths leading to the same outcome and different results arising from the same factor or factor combination, depending on the context in which the latter operates. He sees this as a powerful advantage because he considers multiple and "conjunctural" causation as the major reasons for the peculiar complexity of social phenomena and especially of large-scale social phenomena.

Why should the comparative case strategy have a special strength in dealing with this causal complexity? Since each case is viewed both on its own terms and in comparison, alternative causal conditions for the same or similar outcomes stand out with special clarity in comparative historical work, while macro-quantitative studies tend to view their cases as a causally homogeneous population of units. This is closely related to what we observed about the relation between indicator and analytical concept. The case-oriented approach has a strong comparative advantage in taking context into account – both in assessing the character of an event – say an insurgent social movement – and in evaluating its causal impact within a historical situation. Again, it is clear that good, theoretically guided case selection is critical for making full use of these advantages.

Finally, the comparative historical method allows the exploration of sequence and this, as claimed earlier, is indispensable for causal analysis. The claim deserves more comment. While a causal condition obviously has to precede its result in time, historical depth is not so obviously required. It is logically quite conceivable that the outcomes we wish to explain result from conditions located in the most immediate past. However, macro-social research has taught us two lessons, which make it problematic to take this logical possibility for granted. We have learned that (1) sequence often matters and (2) structural conditions, once settled, often resist transformation. It may, for instance, matter a great deal for the outlook and the organization of the working-class whether universal suffrage came early or late in the process of industrialization (Katznelson and Zolberg 1986), and – once set – different patterns of class consciousness and readiness to organize may be hard to change.

Neither sequence effects nor historical persistence can be counted on a priori. We need to know much more about the conditions under which lasting patterns form, change and break down before we can use historical persistence as an *explanatory* principle; and the same goes for sequence effects. We do, however, have sufficient knowledge to treat them as *heuristic* principles. As heuristic principles they privilege certain research strategies and cast doubt on others. What we know about sequence effects and structural persistencies in large scale social change make "presentist" explanations profoundly problematic. Therefore causal exploration in macro-social analysis requires the study of fairly long time periods, it requires comparative *historical* work.

Our insistence on the importance of comparative historical sequence studies for developing and testing genetic and causal theories will not go unchallenged. There is not only the argument of "too few cases, too many variables". There are also arguments presenting cross-sectional quantitative studies as particularly suitable for causal inference. These consider the factors that in a large cross-sectional set of cases are associated with a dependent variable as those most important in the longer run (see Bollen 1979: 583; also Bollen and Jackman 1989). If the number of cases is large enough for "accidental" variations to balance each other out, this argument maintains, it is precisely a cross-sectional analysis that will best reveal the major structural determinants of variation in the dependent variable – here democracy.

It is clear that this assertion presupposes a causal homogeneity of the universe of cases as well as long-run equilibrium tendencies. It also assumes a close correspondence of diachronic and synchronic relations among variables. Without such premises, which make the sharp differentiation between short-run and long-run, "accidental" and "major" causal factors possible, the goal of "reading off" the major causal factors from cross-sectional statistical patterns is logically impossible. Even with these presuppositions, that project remains deeply problematic. If there is more than one way to account for the same results, we encounter again the black box character of these findings. Quantitative research can sometimes help to adjudicate between competing theories (which more often than not were developed and given credible standing in qualitative research), but often this hypothesis testing runs into tremendous difficulties because such research must work with crude and ambiguous indicators the context of which is necessarily excluded from the analysis.

All this is not to deny the very considerable value of quantitative research results. It is certainly true – and bears repetition – that established cross-sectional results represent limits with which any genetic, causal explanation has to be reconcilable. This must be added to the obvious and powerful argument that cross-sectional studies – the prime case of available large-scale quantitative work – reduce even if they do not fully avoid the perennial problem of macro-social research that the number of cases is small and the number of potentially relevant variables large. This remains a major difficulty of the comparative historical strategy, a difficulty put into perspective but not eliminated by the arguments just developed.

A methodological strategy outlined

We can now describe the design of our own project. We will employ a strategy that takes the results of cross-national studies seriously but gives more weight to comparative historical research. It will be informed by a theoretical framework that builds on past research and theoretical argument and focuses attention on structural constraints as well as on process and decision. We want to develop a theoretically adequate account of the causal conditions of democracy that is sensitive to the insights of comparative historical research and capable of explaining the persistent statistical relationship between development and democracy. This account is to be further tested and developed in a series of comparative investigations that seek to combine a relatively large number of cases with qualitatively adequate information on each case. The cases and comparisons are chosen so as to elucidate critical questions about the relationship between development and democracy. We are confident that this combination of theory and research strategies will render the implications of both comparative historical findings *and* cross-national quantitative results more far-reaching.

Our strategy will be the strategy of "analytic induction," a strategy that can be observed in practical use in several of the comparative historical works reviewed.[14] It breaks with the conventional view that research based on one or a few cases can at best stimulate some hypotheses, while only research on a large number of cases can test them. In this view, case studies – even careful comparative case studies – are irrelevant for the validation of theoretical ideas. They belong to the "context of discovery" rather than the "context of validation" – along with anything else that might stimulate intelligent ideas, from reading novels and philosophical treatises to the enjoyment of food, wine and bright conversation. Yet this radical separation of validation from an essentially arbitrary process of "discovery" is manifestly at odds with the ways we come to reasonably reliable knowledge in everyday life or to historical knowledge that transcends the single case at hand and can be used in historical explanation.

Analytic induction employs in a self-conscious and disciplined way the same strategies we see used in everyday life and in sophisticated historical explanation. Yet it has a more explicitly analytic orientation. It begins with thoroughly reflected analytic concerns and then seeks to move from the understanding of one or a few cases to potentially generalizable theoretical insights capable of explaining the problematic features of each case. These theoretical generalizations are then tested and retested in other detailed case analyses.

Committed to theoretical explanation and generalization, analytic induction builds its arguments from the understanding of individual histories. The complex features of successive cases – with each factor remaining embedded in its historical context and therefore more adequately interpretable – serve as empirical "road blocks" that obstruct arbitrary speculative theorizing. In the overall process of theory building, they are the logical equivalent of the standardized coefficients relating a few selected variables in large-scale quantitative research.

The speculative element, and even arbitrariness, can never be fully eliminated from such case-based theory building. But neither does the opposite strategy, quantitative cross-national research, ever really lose its black box character when it seeks to account for its findings. In our own analysis, we will include as many cases as possible in the same analytically inductive project. In addition, building as we do on the results of both research traditions, we incorporate the empirical generalizations of quantitative cross-national studies into the premises of our own project.

A critical feature of successful analytically inductive research is the initial theoretical reflection. This may take the form of an explicitly developed theoretical framework of concepts, questions, guiding ideas and hypotheses. Yet even if the theoretical foundation is not announced with special fanfare, we can usually identify it with little difficulty. Barrington Moore, for instance, clearly worked with a consistent conceptual grid centered on economic change, the state, and social classes (and especially rural social classes); he used such ideas as the long-term consequences of past conflicts and developments as orientations for all his case analyses; he asked of each case a set of theoretically grounded questions: about the relative strength of the major historical actors and about their pacts and conflicts; and he deployed certain hypotheses – for instance about the chances of revolutionary collective action of peasants – repeatedly as he then turned to the main task: the case-by-case analyses from which he arrived at the three models of political routes into the modern world.

In her justly famous critique of "Origins," Skocpol, a student and critic of Moore, made these intellectual structures visible and subjected them to a searching evaluation. In her own book on social revolutions (Skocpol 1979), she begins with a critical assessment of alternative theoretical approaches and in effect constructs a full-scale theoretical framework that insists on a structural rather than voluntarist explanation of revolutions, on the salience of international and world-historical contexts, and on the potentially autonomous role of the state. It is with this set of concepts and theoretical premises that she then enters the analysis of the French, the Russian, and the Chinese revolutions as well the non-revolutionary developments in Britain, Prussia/Germany, and Japan.

Such a theoretical foundation of analytically inductive research has not only the function of stating explicitly which questions are asked, how they are framed conceptually, and what the theoretical premises of the analysis are. By giving reasons – preferably empirically grounded reasons – for these decisions and premises, it establishes continuity with earlier scholarship. It is critical to fully appreciate this point, because here lies one reason why the credibility of analytic induction is far greater than one could possibly justify with the few cases studied. As in everyday life we can gain powerful insights from a few encounters because these are assessed against the experience of a life-time, so the theoretical framework – when informed by previous thought and research – provides the background against which the picture of the cases studied yields more telling results. To put it slightly differently, a carefully developed theoretical foundation also eases the thorny problems of any macrosocial analysis that derive from the small number of cases; for it taps the results of earlier inquiries.[15]

The theoretical framework does not represent unchangeable assumptions. It does not constitute a "metatheory" in the sense of a set of premises upon which the validity of any finding is contingent. True, any theoretical framework, whether explicitly recognized or not, structures analytic attention and thus is more open to some findings than others. But we certainly do not wish to claim for the framework developed below a privileged status by which our findings would be protected from criticism that is based on other premises. Developing our theoretical framework in self-conscious detail should in fact make it easier to identify possible blind spots in the subsequent analyses.

The theoretical framework, once developed on the basis of earlier research and argument, then informs the comparative case investigations, and it will in turn be specified and modified through these analyses. The result is, on the one hand, a set of historical cases accounted for with a coherent theory and, on the other, a set of propositions about the conditions of democracy that have been progressively modified and are consistent with the facts of the cases examined as well as with the preceding research taken into account. We will develop our own theoretical framework for the study of democracy in the next chapter before we turn to three comparative analyses – of South America and Mexico, Central America, and the Caribbean, and advanced capitalist societies – in the main body of this volume.[16]

Our case comparisons are far-flung, stretching to the limits what can be done by comparative case analysis, but they are not exhaustive. The case selection – while it inevitably derives in part from the particularity of our intellectual journeys – seeks to accomplish specific analytic purposes. The set of cases examined, focusing on advanced capitalist societies, Latin America and the Caribbean, represents the areas with the most extensive democratic experience. At the same time, there are many examples of stable non-democratic regimes as well as of breakdowns of democratic political systems that can be analyzed comparatively side by side with instances of democratization and stable democratic rule, giving ample opportunity to use both John Stuart Mill's "method of agreement" as well as his "indirect method of difference."[17] The advanced core countries and South America also offer long stretches of recorded and analyzed history in which the question of democracy was a live issue. They thus give us the chance to explore the conditions of democracy in some historical depth.

The chapter on the advanced capitalist societies takes as its central problems a comparative review of democratization processes and the question of which democracies broke down in the interwar period and which did not. In taking on the latter question, it directly confronts Moore's analysis on some of the same cases which he studied. Since European democratization has been studied most extensively, it is most directly reflected in our theoretical framework. This gives the chapter on South America a special significance for the further development of our theoretical account of democracy and development. South America is also of special interest, because political independence here came earlier than in other parts of the Third World and liberal ideas had a strong political appeal in this area during the nineteenth century, while the fate of democracy was very different from the liberal centers of Europe. This gives an opportunity to explore the relevance of factors that could not be studied in a more limited set of comparisons. The chapter on Central America and the Caribbean, finally, analyses a startling contrast between the Spanish- and the English-speaking countries; yet it comes to conclusions quite different from a simplistic explanation in terms of the difference in cultural heritage.

3

Capitalist Development and Democracy: A Theoretical Framework

This chapter develops the analytic framework for the comparative analyses in the following chapters. It roughly represents our thinking prior to the completion of these comparisons. Our theoretical premises stand in a tradition of social theory that is roughly characterized by the questions, if not the answers, of Marx and Weber. The framework is informed by the theoretical reflections that anticipated and accompanied the process of democratization in Europe since the early nineteenth century and by the comparative research on democracy in our own time. Central to any analysis of systems of rule must be the relation between the specifically political realm and the broader structure of power. Questions of power therefore underlie virtually all the problems to be discussed in the construction of the theoretical framework for our analysis.

In four areas of inquiry we will develop and justify the conceptions, questions and hypotheses that inform the subsequent comparative studies. First, we will inquire into the *meaning of "democracy"* and relate it to social and economic inequality. Second, we will inquire into *social class divisions* – into the structure of antagonistic socioeconomic interests, their articulation in parties and other organizations which turn classes into social and political actors, and the balance of power between them. Third, we will inquire how different *state structures* affect the chances of democracy. And fourth, we will inquire into *transnational power constellations* likely to effect democratization. In systematically investigating the interplay of these three clusters of power, this study exemplifies a recently emerging research program which Evans and Stephens (1988) term the "new comparative political economy." The conclusion reviews briefly how the analytical framework can account for previous findings.

Democracy and its Relation to Social Inequality

The possibility of democracy

Political democracy inevitably stands in tension with the system of social inequality. However we define democracy in detail, it means nothing if it does not entail rule or participation in rule by the many. Yet in a class-divided society, the many have less income and wealth, less education, and less honor than the few. Above all, they have – individually – less power. Democracy, then, is a rather counterintuitive state of affairs, one in which the disadvantaged many have, as citizens, a real voice in the collective decision making of politics.

From this tension between democracy and social inequality follows a first, minimal condition of democracy: democracy is possible only if there exists a fairly strong institutional separation – the technical term is differentiation – of the realm of politics from the overall system of inequality in society. Only then is it even conceivable that those who stand at the bottom of the scales of power, wealth, and cultural participation will – by themselves or through their representatives – significantly shape collective decisions that are binding for all. A feudal agrarian society, in which control over land – the primary means of production – entails ipso facto political authority over the population living on the land, is not compatible with democracy. Except in theatrical rituals like carnival, it has no institutional provisions for such an inversion of the social order in the political realm.

The differentiation of government and politics from other spheres of social life, which is – in one form or another – characteristic of all modern societies, is often taken for granted as part of a teleological design of history. Yet it was itself the outcome of historically varied power struggles; it cannot be understood if one approaches it as the political aspect of a universal evolutionary process aiming for greater efficiency (Rueschemeyer 1986).

The conflict between democracy and social inequality does not end with the differentiation of state institutions from the overall structure of power, honor, and wealth in society. Power and privilege are mutually supportive, even if the sphere of the state and the exercise of formal political power are institutionally set off from the wider system of social inequality. It would be foolish to overlook, for instance, that the distribution of land in El Salvador creates insolvable problems for democracy in that country. This leads into complex questions about "real" and merely "formal" democracy.

In the extreme, there is indeed the possibility – and it is not a theoretical possibility only – that democratic institutions are nothing more than an ineffective pretense, a sham. Democracy takes on a realistic character only if it is based on significant changes in the overall distribution of power. Where that occurs, an egalitarian critique may still point to the distance between actual decision–making and an ideal model in which collective actions are equally responsive to the preferences of all citizens – Robert Dahl's definition of full democracy in contrast to the less demanding and more realizable version he calls "polyarchy" (Dahl 1971). Yet it is extremely problematic, intellectually and politically, to denounce and dismiss such less than perfect forms as merely formal.

The really existing democracies of today diverge without exception from such ideal models.[1] First, even majority rule – commonly seen as the very embodiment of democracy – violates, in a literal sense, the principle of an equal responsiveness of state action to the preferences of all citizens. Deciding things by majority is a tool of efficient governance, a compromise between full consent and the need for decisive action. The indirect exercise of legislative power by elected representatives is a second and more obvious limitation of "full" democracy. Third, in varying but always substantial degrees, important political decisions are made in all modern societies by the administrative state apparatus and by judicial courts. These decisions are thus removed not only from democratic discussion and decision but largely even from indirect democratic control. We will later encounter other, more subtle constraints that are related to the autonomy of such organizations as parties, unions and other interest associations vis–à–vis their own members. Such limitations deriving from the structures of the state apparatus and of the political process are ultimately unavoidable in any complex society.

At least equally important is, finally, the impact of the social and economic power structure on political decision-making. More variable perhaps across countries than the constraints of representation, administration and expertise, it depends to some extent on the institutional differentiation of politics from social structure and process. But beyond that it is shaped by the balance of power in society. The impact of social and economic power on politics and state action can be counterbalanced in varying degree, but it can never be erased completely.

Yet representative democracy – embedded in the wider structures of social and economic power, animated by party and interest group politics, and joined to a complex state machinery – did give the many *some* share in political decision-making. And in most cases this added significantly to whatever power they had in society. It did not bring that broad-based active participation in public affairs that was the essence of democracy for John Stuart Mill, nor did it even approach an equal responsiveness of state action to the preferences of all citizens. Nevertheless, it often secured very real advantages for the many: to begin with a by-product, it typically brought them more secure civil liberties – a requisite of democracy better appreciated in this century than ever before. Without reducing those liberties, it has also often resulted in substantially redistributive state action, especially where democratic socialist parties gained sufficient strength (Hewitt 1977; Stephens 1979c; Hicks and Swank 1984)[2]. In addition to material gain and protection against arbitrary power, democracy has thirdly brought a change that may be called "symbolic" but that it is unrealistic to belittle: it has made possible the dignity of full adult participation in politics that was denied to those excluded on the basis of social status or property. That this denial was felt as an insult, is not left in doubt by the histories of labor, of race, and of women.

Democracy may soften, but it certainly does not eliminate the differences of power, wealth and status in class-divided societies. Even the very premises of its own functioning have been compromised by class-inequality. Central among these premises is the axiom that all actors are fully aware of their own real interests. Offe and Wiesenthal (1980) critically examine this liberal axiom of an identity of actually expressed and enlightened interests. They raise radical questions about interest articulation and social class that are worth pondering:

> To what extent do the political forms of liberal democracy provide asymmetrical chances to the members of different classes to be able to articulate enlightened interests?
>
> To what extent do they leave room for those mechanisms to become effective that are required to overcome the specific obstacles to nondistorted interest-awareness that we find in the ranks of the working class?
>
> Or, conversely, to what extent are liberal democratic forms of political conflict, which favor the accurate articulation of bourgeois interests and impede the organizational practices that facilitate the articulation of undistorted working-class interests, imposed upon the working class?
>
> If it is true that political forms are not neutral, but are rather schemes for the preferential recognition of certain class interests (as we believe the above arguments strongly suggest), then they must themselves be considered as part of, and as objects of, the class conflict which they appear to merely regulate and to channel.

We recognize these as serious problems. But we do not agree with the conclusion of Leninists – and even of Rosa Luxemburg – that democracy is essentially an imposition on the working-class that works against its well understood interests. One does not have to subscribe to all premises of liberal political philosophy to see in really existing democracies the chance for a promising pursuit of subordinate class interests. Embracing democracy as promising was also the position taken by the vast majority of labor movements in different countries and in very different historical situations.[3]

The concept of democracy

The concept of democracy that guides our research, then, can and will be quite conventional. It entails, first, regular, free and fair elections of representatives with universal and equal suffrage,[4] second, responsibility of the state apparatus to the elected parliament (possibly complemented by direct election of the head of the executive), and third, the freedoms of expression and association as well as the protection of individual rights against arbitrary state action.

The first and the second of these dimensions, universal suffrage and responsibility of the state, define in our view the essence of democracy. If participation is limited to a few (as in mid-nineteenth-century England), the regime may be liberal because issues are openly discussed or because state action is limited by solid individual rights, but it remains an oligarchic regime; one cannot speak of democracy. If the state apparatus is not made responsible (as in the Germany of Bismarck and Wilhelm II), the most inclusive system of suffrage and the best protection of civil rights are not sufficient to create a "rule of the people" in any meaningful sense.

The third dimension of civil rights – which embodies the idea of political freedom – does not in itself constitute the exercise of democratic power; it is rather, on the one hand, a necessary condition of stable democracy and, on the other, a limitation of state power without which individual and collective liberty is not secure – under democratic or other forms of domination.[5]

All three dimensions are a matter of degree. This leads into issues of the classification of different regime forms of which we will give only a sketch at this point.[6] While minor deviations from the definition may be neglected when we identify a regime as a *democracy*, regimes that rank near zero on the first two dimensions will be called *authoritarian* regimes, those very low on all three, *totalitarian* ones. *Constitutional* or *liberal oligarchies* are those that rank low on inclusion while the state apparatus is fairly responsible to parliament and political liberties are more or less secured.

We will speak of *restricted democracies* when the stipulated conditions are met to a large extent, but significant sectors of the population are excluded (for example by suffrage restrictions through literacy or similar qualifications), responsiveness of government is significantly reduced (for example through frequent military interventions or political pacts), and/or limitations of the freedoms of expression and association significantly narrow the range of articulated political positions (for example through the proscription of political parties). Clearly this is a large and complex category that requires further differentiation. At the same time, clear distinctions are often difficult to draw because restrictions in one dimension may also have effects in one or both of the other two.

The comprehensive right to participation seems to be the most obvious component of any conception of democracy. Yet we emphasize it to an extent that is not common. It is far more common to treat inclusiveness of participation as secondary to the other dimensions – to the effectiveness of control over the state (its responsibility to parliament), and the institutionalization of opposition rights (freedom of association and expression, free and fair elections). First democracy is set up, this view holds, and then it is extended to broader and broader parts of society. The process of inclusion is not denied importance, but all too often it is merely viewed as the extension of a democratic pattern that already existed before. This view is diametrically opposed to the idea introduced earlier – that democracy means nothing if not a share of political power controlled by the many. We make the extent of the suffrage, and in particular the extent to which the right to vote transcends class boundaries, central to our concept of democracy. The justification of this decision goes beyond mere questions of definition and leads toward basic theoretical orientations that inform our analytic model.

Democracy and class-inequality

The history of thought about democracy underlines the critical relation between social class and democracy (see e.g. Macpherson 1973, 1977; Held 1987). Until the nineteenth century, it was nearly without exception assumed that democracy was a one-class arrangement, that class division could not be bridged by democracy. Aristotle as well as Rousseau not only stressed that socioeconomic inequality was a condition hostile to democracy; they also took for granted that the non-propertied classes were excluded from participation, as did most theorists before the nineteenth century. Jefferson rejected such exclusion but he, too, held that a democratic society had to be a one-class society. He viewed his own America as a case in point, a society in which the emergence of other classes than the prevailing class of independent "husband-men" were transitory or marginal developments and therefore negligible.

Jeremy Bentham and James Mill differed from the earlier consensus. Even though they did not consider it politically feasible actually to extend democratic rights to the working class, they did think democracy possible in their own class-divided society. They took this position on the assumption that working people would be either deferential to their betters or would think of themselves as potential capitalists and act accordingly.

The tension between democracy and class inequality came to a head in the thought of John Stuart Mill, the son of James Mill (see Broadbent 1966, as well as Macpherson 1973, 1977). John Stuart Mill saw democracy as inevitable. Growing prosperity, spreading literacy and the ever more widely ranging means of transportation and communication were increasing people's mobility and their chances to organize. As a result, the future system of governance would be democratic. But it would not necessarily be a good system of govern-ment – because the society was class-divided. Under the impact of the Chartist unrest and also influenced by the thought of Alexis de Tocqueville, Mill feared class rule by the working masses, Tocqueville's "tyranny of the majority." To avoid such "false democracy," he proposed a number of special arrangements including a system of multiple votes for the educated and the skilled. His conception of true or rational democracy combined active participation of the many with the leadership of an intellectual elite that was not bound by class.

Even though few of the special measures he proposed were implemented, John Stuart Mill's fears did not materialize when the vote was gradually extended to the working class. This has been variously explained – in a marxist vein, with the overwhelming social and cultural power of the dominant classes or, following a lead of Dorothy Thompson (1984: 335), by arguing that the extensions of the suffrage were paralleled by extensions of administrative and judicial decision-making more favorable to class privilege. Other explanations argue that the very instruments of collective action – of parties, unions and other organizations, which became stronger during the same time period – had a demobilizing effect (Macpherson 1977: 64–9), that the socially responsible and politically judicious actions of conservative politicians like Disraeli were of crucial importance (Lipset 1980: 297–9), or that the rising standard of living that became apparent during the same years had moderating consequences (Therborn 1977).

If Mill's position of a profound incompatibility between democracy and class-inequality proved to be wrong, the history of democratization cannot be understood without reference to class. And once democracy was established, the political behavior of both upper and working classes was such that Lipset (1980: 230–300) could analyze elections as "expressions of the democratic class struggle."

It is a central thesis of our theoretical framework that democratization was both resisted and pushed forward by class interest. It was the subordinate classes that fought for democracy. By contrast, the classes that benefited from the status quo nearly without exception resisted democracy. The bourgeoisie wrested its share of political participation from royal autocracy and aristocratic oligarchy, but it rarely fought for further extensions once its own place was secured.

Neither was democracy extended because of the universalist logic of the ideas that gave it rationale and legitimation. True, when taken at face value these ideas did not tolerate exclusions on the basis of class. But the historical record shows that such contradictions between reality and legitimating ideal had a healthy and long life, camouflaged even in sophisticated writings by a silent acceptance of various forms of exclusion. On occasion the vote was extended in order to serve the competitive electoral interests of established parties and institutions. But fundamentally, democracy was achieved by those who were excluded from rule and who acquired the social power to reach for a share in the political process. However much the democratic ideas were taken up and used by these excluded strata and classes, the notion that it was their universalist character that pushed democratization forward is an idealist illusion. Only within this process of empowerment of the subordinate classes did ideas play a role, too.

In the twentieth century, the democratic ideal has triumphed around the globe. Clearly this is largely a rhetorical triumph – open to contradictory interpretations and compatible with massive repression. Yet due to this development, the institutional forms of democracy may be introduced in order to gain a modicum of regime acceptance within the country and abroad; and this development has made it more difficult to limit the suffrage openly by class, race, or gender. However, where democratic institutions rest primarily on such bases rather than on the demand and power of formerly excluded classes, they will be more vulnerable to authoritarian reversals and they are more likely to be merely formal trappings, subject to restrictions such as a dominant influence of the military, bureaucracy, or hegemonic party.

It is ironic that not only liberal historians but also the orthodox marxist accounts of the rise of democracy see the bourgeoisie as *the* protagonist of democracy. In these views, the bourgeoisie drew strength from the growing dominance of the capitalist mode of production and thus was able to eliminate progressively feudal and absolutist political forms and finally establish democratic rule. This position can be maintained only if the issue of universal suffrage is neglected or if democracy is considered inevitably "bourgeois democracy" – irrelevant or even hostile to working-class interests. That was not Marx's own view, who considered the achievement of universal suffrage the historical task of the working-class (Marx 1852/1964; Marx and Engels 1848/1976). Therborn (1977) recovered this insight of Marx about the central role of the working class in the process of democratization for the comparative historical study of democracy.[7]

The chances of democracy, then, must be seen as fundamentally shaped by the balance of class power. It is the struggle between the dominant and subordinate classes over the right to rule that – more than any other factor – puts democracy on the historical agenda and decides its prospects. Capitalist development affects the chances of democracy primarily because it transforms the class structure and changes the balance of power between classes. The core of our analytic framework is therefore a "relative class power" model of democratization.

Our view of the tension between class inequality and democracy bears some similarity to that of Marshall (1950) and, following him, Rokkan (1970), exemplified in Marshall's (1950: 29) frequently quoted remark that in modern British history "citizenship and social class have been at war." However, in the work of Marshall and Rokkan, the advance of citizenship rights at the expense of property rights appears as an almost actorless process. Much closer to our view is that of Bowles and Gintis (1986: 27–63) and Therborn (1977) who see democracy as a product of the contradictions of capitalism, and the process of democratization as primarily a product of the action of subordinate classes.

How central is social class?

Making social class a central category of our analysis of democratization is bound to encounter reservations and objections. Is it really possible to grasp the diversity of life situations, interests and aspirations with such roughly classifying concepts as working class and bourgeoisie, rural cultivators and landlords? Are other dimensions of political goals and conflicts not equally or more important than the differences in power and privilege? We will not engage in extended argument with the positions that stand behind these questions. A few element-ary points must suffice.

Social class has been an extremely powerful explanatory tool in the classic analyses of social science during the last two hundred years. In its broadest sense, class refers – if in the marxist conceptualization only indirectly – to the structured and cumulatively unequal distribution of the objects of near-universal desire: of the material necessities of life and other economic resources, of respect and honor, and of power and influence. (Power may appear an unlikely candidate for being an object of near-universal desire – until one realizes that it takes a modicum of power to even eschew direct subjection to the whim of others or to have a chance of success in any social undertaking, however small.) Given this character of class in its broadest conception, it is hard to imagine any social science analysis in which it does not occupy a central place – in whatever disguise.

The marxian concept of class does not focus on distribution. It searches for collective actors that make a decisive difference in history. Though closely related to the structure of inequality, they are defined by their relation to the organization of production – that aspect of social formations Marx considered decisive for long-term historical change. Again, it is hard to fault this strategy of Marx in its fundamentals. Any study of social change gains much if it can identify collective actors of historical significance. And these are usefully considered in relation to the major factors otherwise seen as decisive for the persistence and change of social structures. To maintain – and if necessary retrieve – this idea of classes as potential historical actors seems to us of great importance, because social class in this sense is a concept that allows us to link structural change and political developments.

Class inequality does not exhaust the forms of social and economic inequality. Are other forms of inequality, especially those based on race and ethnicity and on gender, not equally important? Exploring the impact of these divisions and antagonisms offers a chance to define our conception more sharply and contrast it to others.

Gender relations may well be of critical importance for future developments in democracy, but they were far less important in the known histories of democratization. Vastly less blood was shed in the struggles for women's political inclusion, and their inclusion did not give rise to regime changes designed to re-exclude them. Some of the reasons for this seem clear. Power relations between social classes typically began to change well before changes in relative gender power. And the transformation of class relations are far more intimately linked to state interventions in society. This expresses itself also in the fact that when women were finally enfranchised – in a few countries before World War I, in many in the wake of that war, in some (for instance Switzerland and Liechtenstein) not until recently – their voting participation did not significantly change the political spectrum in any country. It is these considerations that led us to choose for our historical investigations universal male voting rights, rather than truly universal suffrage, as a critical threshold that allows us to speak of democracy.[8]

Racial and ethnic divisions become particularly important where they are linked to class and/or where racial and ethnic groups are differentially linked to the state apparatus. As sharp and often rigid distinctions of status, they can reinforce and deepen class differences as well as cut across class lines and weaken class cohesion. In the limiting case, these divisions may constitute social segments that must be treated much like classes themselves. Finally, racial and ethnic divisions may also affect the chances of democracy directly, especially where they put the unity of the country into question.

These propositions on ethnicity and race do not seem, at first sight, to differ strikingly from the views expressed in functionalist modernization theory and pluralist political analyses. We do believe, however, that the political economy approach we advance here – emphasizing the interrelationship between ethnic divisions and the class structure and the state – will prove more fruitful than the functional/pluralist alternative. The functionalist view basically sees ethnic divisions as contributing to the breakdown of democracy because they undermine social integration and societal consensus. While we do not dismiss this, we argue that even deep ethnic divisions are not likely to be fatal for democracy if they are not strongly related to class alignments, as the cases of Switzerland and Belgium illustrate. The pluralists have handled this with the hypothesis that if various social cleavages crosscut one another, this is more favorable to national integration than if they align with one another. The emphasis in this approach is on how strongly the individual identifies with various collectivities; if cleavages reinforce one another, the identification with the group may overpower national identity and endanger compromise and national integration. For our analysis the strength of group identification is also important, since it affects the propensity of groups to organize and therefore affects the balance of power between various groups. However, the functionalist approach peripheralizes what is at the center of our analytic frame: that is, the distribution of limited resources in a society and the competition of ethnic/class segments for power in the economy and polity in order to influence or control that distribution.

These differences in the treatment of ethnicity are mirrored in the analysis of the organizational density of society as a condition of democracy. If we see capitalist development and democracy primarily related through changes in the class structure, modernization theorists and pluralists typically build on an alternate conception that became prominent in diagnoses of the origins of totalitarianism (see, most recently, Huntington 1984: 202–3). It is grounded in de Tocqueville's analyses of democracy in America and post-revolutionary France and in the consensus-oriented sociology of Emile Durkheim and his ideas on the role of secondary groups. In this view, democracy is facilitated primarily by social mobilization and by the development of relatively autonomous groups that are arising in an ever more differentiated social structure. What is typically missed in these theories (or feared and criticized as destabilizing) is the shift in the power of conflicting class interests that is the correlate of social mobilization and pluralization – precisely the aspect of socioeconomic development we deem most important. Yet while we view the balance of class power as the factor of pre-eminent importance in the process of democratization, we do consider the density of autonomous organizations as relevant on three counts: as a way in which the empowerment of subordinate classes is realized, as a shield protecting these classes against the hegemonic influence of dominant classes, and – aside from the balance of class power – as a mode of balancing the power of state and civil society.

The Tocquevillean ideas are closely paralleled in the marxist literature by Gramsci's contention that rule through consensus is made possible by the development of a "dense civil society". A denser and stronger civil society is a by-product of capitalist development. Civil society, in this conception, is the totality of social institutions and associations, both formal and informal, that are not strictly production-related nor governmental or familial in character.[9] The concept includes, then, everything from the informal card playing group to the parent–teacher association, from the local pub to the trade union, from church groups to political parties. A dense civil society – one rich in such institutions, associations, and social interactions – should facilitate the development of democracy, first and foremost, because it creates favorable conditions for the classes previously excluded from the political arena to organize for collective action and to overcome the perennial "free rider" problem obstructing effective political organization on a large scale (Olson 1965).

In this view, the emphasis on social mobilization and pluralization of society is quite compatible with the relative class power model of democratization. Here it is not primarily the density of civil society per se, but the empowerment of previously excluded classes aided by this density that improves the chances of democratization. In fact, Gramsci emphasizes in addition that in the absence of a working-class movement, civil society can act as a conduit for the ideological hegemony of the dominant classes.[10]

From this we derive propositions that simply add specificity to the "relative class power model" of democratization: it is the growth of a counter-hegemony of subordinate classes and especially the working class – developed and sustained by the organization and growth of trade unions, working-class parties and similar groups – that is critical for the promotion of democracy. Even without a relatively strong labor movement, a dense civil society facilitates the political inclusion of the middle classes, especially of small independent farmers and the urban petty bourgeoisie, and in some cases this may be the decisive democratic breakthrough. The autonomy of these organizations is decisively important. Only quite autonomous organizations protect the subordinate classes from the ideological hegemony of the dominant classes – a necessary condition for a strong democratic impulse. This condition is of special importance for organizations of peasants and the urban middle class because they are often more easily co-opted by established elites than the working class.

Finally a dense civil society does also have an importance for democracy on its own, because it establishes a counterweight to state power, a condition favorable for democracy in conjunction with the balance of social and economic power. The impact of state structures and of their interrelations with the structure of power in society on the chances of democratization constitutes the second major component of our analytic framework, which will be discussed below.

A last contrast between our political economy approach and the theoretical strategies of functionalism concerns the role of culture and in particular of religion. Ideologies, value traditions, and religious orientations play a central role in most versions of structural functionalism and modernization theory. Such an approach seems validated for the particular issues of development and democracy by some cross-national statistical findings; Bollen (1979) reported, for instance, that the proportion of a country's population that is Protestant is positively associated with the incidence of democracy, giving credence to the hypothesis that a "Protestant-based culture" aids the diffusion of democracy and legitimizes democratic values.

As will become clear as we develop our framework further, we prefer to link values, ideologies, and religious orientations to structural and organizational realities. In particular, they must be seen in relation to the historical articulation of class interests. Much of what appears as culture in structural functional analysis can be more precisely identified as the values and views characteristic of different classes as they were historically formed through autonomous organization as well as hegemonic influence of one class on another.

The historical articulation of class interests does not exhaust all aspects of "culture." But for other cultural phenomena, too, we opt for a strategy of focusing on symbols, ideals and views of reality that are *organizationally and institutionally grounded*. We choose this strategy for two reasons. First, as we conceive of democracy as a matter of power, we focus on those ideas we consider most socially powerful, that is – we believe – those embedded in organizations and institutions. Second, our option has also methodological reasons; it is much more difficult to identify, and to assess the strength of, cultural phenomena that are not in such ways socially grounded.

Thus, cultural traditions that are embodied in state structures can be of great importance and will be considered in the comparative historical investigations. This includes most crucially the relationship of organized religion to the state. Finally, religious affiliation can be in its own right an important factor in collectivity formation. Group formations on the basis of religion will be treated in much the same way as ethnic groups: they can reinforce or weaken class cohesion; they may contribute to or weaken the cohesion of society; above all they, too, operate in the context of a struggle for control over limited resources.

Class Structures, Classes, and Class Organizations

Before we can enquire more specifically into the role of different social classes in the process of democratization, we must enter into a discussion of the concept of class. Without a careful and differentiated conceptualization, the idea of class can indeed be a rather blunt tool, one that can do more damage than it helps the analysis.

The analytic discourse about social class has become extremely complex – in large part because it is animated as well as divided by intertwined intellectual and ideological interests. Therefore, though a number of remarkably convergent developments ease our task significantly, a condensed treatment as we necessarily will present here is not without hazard. We will nevertheless simply stress a number of ideas that seem specially important, without engaging in extended explanation, justification, and critique of alternative positions. In particular we are concerned to come to a realistic conception of classes as historical actors that are grounded in the structures of antagonistic socioeconomic interests and their change.

Conceptualizations

At the most abstract level, we can begin with the definition of social class by Elster, who seeks to "make sense of Marx." It is couched:

in terms of endowments and behaviours. The endowments include tangible property, intangible skills and more subtle cultural traits. The behaviours include working vs. not working, selling vs. buying labour power, lending vs. borrowing capital, renting vs. hiring land, giving vs. receiving commands in the management of corporate property. These enumerations are intended as exhaustive. *A class is a group of people who by virtue of what they possess are compelled to engage in the same activities if they want to make the best use of their endowments.* (Elster 1985: 330–1. Italics added.)

This definition does not spell out – though it clearly implies – that classes are shaped in their fundamental characteristics by the structure of capitalist economic production and its development. For realistic historical analysis, that entails a conclusion often overlooked: different courses of economic development will lead to different class structures, some fundamental similarities of capitalist development in any historical situation notwithstanding. The United States and France never had, for instance, as large a working class as England or Germany did.[11] And dependent development today seems to sharply limit the expansion of the working class in almost all Third World countries.

As the last point already adumbrates, such differences in economic development do not simply arise out of technological and economic conditions internal to a society but are also shaped by the transnational division of labor as well as by state structures and the political constellations mediating state and society. We encounter here another instance of the interrelations between the different components of our analytic frame of reference. These will not become fully apparent until the end of this exposition.

Elster's definition also does not tell us whether and under which conditions classes have distinct boundaries or, by contrast, form a continuum and merge imperceptibly into each other. This question is of great interest because such distinctness seems to be a necessary condition for the emergence of collective action on the basis of class. For Marx this was not problematic because he predicted a polarization of classes in the course of capitalist development. But this prediction proved wrong. Following Weber (1922/1968) and Giddens (1973) we can locate distinct classes by introducing two factors – the range of social mobility and the spread of social interaction and communication. For Weber a *social* class is characterized by easy and typical mobility – within and between generations – among similar class positions. A social class is set off from others by greater difficulty of mobility. To this *mobility closure* we add as a secondary criterion *interaction closure* – a strong tendency for meaningful interaction to be confined within class boundaries (see Stephens 1979a).

With these analytic tools we can make the distinctions necessary for a meaningful class analysis of advanced as well as less developed capitalist societies.[12] We can distinguish the owners of capital who employ labor on a sizeable scale – the bourgeoisie proper – from the urban petty bourgeoisie. We can identify the lower non-manual employees – such as clerical workers and sales clerks without much of a supervisory role – as a class distinct from middle-level managers and professional experts outside the chain of command. Similarly, these tools allow us to analyze with some specificity the coalescence of skilled craftsmen and unskilled workers into a more or less unified working class or – under different historical conditions – their continued separation. We can examine whether landlords and industrial capitalists are separate classes or merge into a single class. And we can study differentiation or class unity in the peasantry.

Up to this point, the conceptualization takes class as an objective given. Class is a social category determined, in the extreme, by the observer and analyst. It is a category for analyzing the structure of conflicting interests. This objective conception of class must be complemented by an analysis of the subjective mentality, ideas, and dispositions found among members of a class and, equally important, by an analysis of the conditions of collective organization and action on the basis of class position. Neither class consciousness nor class organization and collective action follow with any simple necessity from class position. Nor do collective organization and action have a one-to-one relationship to the ideas and attitudes found among the class members. This means: not all classes are collective actors in history; nor do they become eventually such actors with any generalized necessity. It also means that the interests pursued by organizations acting on behalf of a class are not with any necessity "the" interests of that class.[13]

We distinguish, then, three levels of class analysis: (1) the class structure grounded in the organization of production and modified by patterns of mobility and interaction, (2) the ideas and attitudes of the members of a class, and (3) the determination and pursuit of collective goals through organized action on behalf of a class. These are interrelated, but one cannot derive typical ideas and outlooks or the existence and the goals of collective organization from the structural class position in any teleological fashion.

Class interests and collective action

Classes may indeed have *objective* interests, but in historical reality class interests are inevitably subject to *social construction*. The following comments focus on the working-class. They apply – appropriately modified – to all other classes as well. The interests actually pursued by landowners and peasants, industrial entrepreneurs and urban middle classes are historically articulated and cannot be deduced from their objective class situation.

Even those who are quite aware that one cannot take the organized expression of class interests for granted often assume that what these interests are is not really problematic. The deservedly famous (as well as deservedly criticized) analysis of collective action by Mancur Olson (1965) provides an example that this fallacy is not confined to Marxists blinded by hope. Olson treats the "public goods" that require collective action as obvious or, if not obvious, as objectively given. He assumes that unions function, if they come into being at all, as wage cartels rather than aiming for other goals – for a different authority structure at work, for example, for broad political class interests, or for national political goals virtually unrelated to class interests.

Yet it can easily be shown that the goals of different movements claiming to act on behalf of the same class differ considerably from each other. Communist, social democratic, liberal, Catholic, and even outright conservative organizations have competed with each other for the allegiance of the working class, and all have claimed to represent the best interests of labor. It is possible to argue about the validity of such claims, and one can probably reach agreement that some claims – for instance that of the Tories to act on behalf of the working class – do not stand up to any reasonable examination. Within narrower limits, however, such evaluations turn on ideas of what is historically possible and what is ultimately desirable. Class interests are an "essentially contested concept" (Lukes 1967, 1974). One can still reason about them, but not prove or disprove them in a more stringent sense.

Offe and Wiesenthal (1980) have argued convincingly that the interests of the working class are in a peculiar way undetermined (and thus subject to what we have called the social construction of class interests). They contrast working class and bourgeoisie and show that, while the interests of capital fall fundamentally into a single dimension, the interests of labor inevitably involve a whole array of partly contradictory goals because labor is never simply a commodity and the whole human being cannot be eliminated from the factor of production that is labor.[14] The resolution of these contradictions among potential goals or class interests is inevitably uncertain and conflictual. This is compounded by the fact that the subordinate classes face particular problems of collective organization. They cannot hope to overcome the problem of "free riding" – the individualist calculus that leads to withdrawal from the common effort – by the utilitarian means of individual incentive and threat alone:

> No union can function for a day in the absence of some rudimentary notions held by the members that being a member is of value in itself, that the individual organization costs must not be calculated in a utilitarian manner but have to be accepted as necessary sacrifices, and that each member is legitimately required to practice solidarity and discipline, and other norms of a nonutilitarian kind. (Offe and Wiesenthal 1980:79)

From these considerations they come a to conclusion that seems but is not in reality paradoxical: that a subordinate class's "*interests can only be met to the extent that they are partly redefined*" (ibid.). This redefinition is likely to be a process of tension and conflict.

One of the major factors shaping the social construction of class interests is the process of organization itself. Organization is the main means of empowering the many. At the same time, organization is inherently ambiguous in its consequences. Only through organization can the disadvantaged many develop conceptions of structural change to fundamentally alter their situation. As Mann (1973) puts it: "Socialism is learned." Neither socialism nor any other ideological orientation arises spontaneously out of the conditions of working-class life.

Any stable form of collective action creates an organizational core whose members tend to acquire a certain independence from the rank and file. Robert

Michels (1908/1949) called this the "Iron Law of Oligarchy." In its weak version just formulated, this tendency is inherent in any form of organized collective action. It follows from the variety of individual ideas and goals and from the advantages specialization can bring to collective organization as to so many other pursuits. Robert Michels and many later followers understood his law in a more rigid fashion than is justified – as an "iron law" virtually without exception. The autonomy of the organizational representatives vis-à-vis their constituents is in fact quite variable and depends on different conditions, some of which are by now quite well understood (see e.g. Lipset, Trow and Coleman 1956).

The variable autonomy of the leadership of an organization from the rank and file must be seen together with the necessity of co-operating with other power centers. The consequences of such co-operation – of worker represen-tatives with owners and managers, of union leaders with middle-class party leaders, or of the leaders of the most varied organizations with a domineering state – are again quite variable. They are contingent on a variety of factors, and they range from co-optation through direct bribes to acceptance of outside help in making the organization more effective and to common bonds of status, ethnicity or religion that link an organization's elite to other power holders. Social and cultural bonds between organizational elites shape the formation of an organization's goals without any conscious intent on the part of the other side to seek a strategic advantage in the pursuit of interests. It is even reasonable to include here also the case of negotiators from opposed interest organizations who agree on a compromise because it is expected to yield advantage for both sides – whatever the judgement of an outside observer about who got the better bargain. It is quite clear that in such bargaining relations the ability to act independently of consultation with the rank and file and to deliver their acquiescence later is an invaluable asset.

The relations of an organizational elite to other power holders and to their own rank and file – elite co-operation and oligarchy – are of critical importance for our understanding of the social construction of class interests as they are actually pursued. From a grass roots point of view, it seems reasonable to speak of an *inherent ambiguity of organized collective action*. We use the word ambiguity advisedly, so as to underline the variability of the component mechanisms. Thus, there is a great difference in the responsiveness to their members' preferences between an industrial union, say, in Sweden and its counterpart in Argentina under Peron. Any interest organization, even one turned around by an outside power center to become a means of controlling its members, must serve some interests of the rank and file in order to remain effective. At the same time, it is hard to think of a large organization representing subordinate class interests that does not have any trace of both oligarchy and cooptation.

Insisting that class interests are socially constructed and that the forms of collective organization critically affect this social construction of interests does not imply that the "real" interests are found at the grass roots, ready to be expressed in pure or distorted form by different organizations. Unions, mutual aid societies, and political parties can be, and often are, decisive in articulating class interests that otherwise would remain inchoate or completely dormant.

Even organizations without a clear-cut class program can play this role of interest articulation and political mobilization. In turn, radical parties may find it extremely difficult to create a broad following for goals that transcend the current situation. The immediate interests of the potential rank and file and their articulation in unions and other organizations may well be resistant to appeals of radical transformation. The tensions between socialist programs and a "trade union consciousness" focused on concrete gains in working conditions and income represent a well-known illustration.

The indeterminacies and ambiguities of collective action are of course not the only source of different outcomes in the social construction of class interests. The mentalities, outlooks, and ideological inclinations of the members of a class are not irrelevant for the character of class organizations and for their course of action, even though they are not simply reflected in – and are in fact partly shaped by – collective organization and action. The ideas and inclinations of class members are also influenced by a variety of other factors. They are related to their place in a particular class structure and to their chances of mobility within that structure, but they are also shaped by geographic patterns, cultural traditions, and, last not least, by the structure of politics and by state action.

The structure of the economy and its development have strong direct effects on the organizational formations of a class. For instance, whether craft unionism prevails in a working class or is replaced by more inclusive industrial unionism, depends in part on the timing and speed of industrialization and on its location in the international division of labor, since these conditions affect the relative role of small workshops and mass industrial production (Ingham 1974). Similarly, centralization of capitalist enterprises encourages centralization of labor organization; and union centralization is related to labor movement hegemony and leftism because it leads to a concentration of resources in the labor movement and forces the leadership to take a more class-wide view (Stephens 1979a: 399; see also 1979c).

We have touched briefly on the ethnic and racial composition of a class earlier. The most obvious effects are on the intermediate level of class-wide attitudes and behaviors. Here these communal identifications and divisions may reinforce class boundaries or – as is more often the case, and especially so in subordinate classes – lead to divided loyalties, weaken class identification and possibly establish communal links to opposite class segments of the same color or ethnicity. As factors that powerfully shape both mobility and interaction, race and ethnicity may in fact redraw the boundaries of social classes as we have defined the concept. In the United States, ethnic divisions of the working-class coincided to a large extent with differences in skill. Massive immigration of less skilled labor both made it harder to organize the unskilled and fostered hostile reactions on the part of native-born skilled workers. It thus strengthened craft unionism and inhibited a transition from craft to industrial unions similar to developments in continental Europe (Bridges 1986; Zolberg 1986: 442–3; Erickson 1957).

The economic, social, and political situation in which an organization – a party, a union, a pressure group association, or a whole cluster of organizations – finds itself will also affect the goals of class organizations if only by determining what makes sense under the circumstances. Here the organization and actions of opponents as well as the availability of allies are critically important.

These situational determinants must not be seen in too narrow a national frame. External influences – for instance through international affiliation of unions and parties – were and are still important in the formation of class organizations. The Second International is a great example of such diffusion. Variants of the marxist Erfurt Program of the German Social Democrats were adopted by a large number of other member parties. Furthermore, the way a situation and its future development is assessed will be shaped by historical precedent and diffusion across national boundaries. Theories – like Keynesianism for instance – have a different impact once they are tested as policy. Large events – like the French and the Russian revolutions – redefine for long periods and for many countries what is considered as great promise or an unacceptable danger. And even complex cumulative developments – like the incorporation of the working class into the politics of advanced industrial societies by class compromise and democratization – affect the perception of democracy as a realistic possibility in other countries.

Finally, the course of organized collective class action is often constrained by past choices and decisions. In fact, the initial organization of class interests typically has effects that outlast the historical constellation of its origins. Here lies a major cause for the different political orientations adopted by working-class organizations and parties in different countries and different historical periods. Of particular importance for the working class have been decisions about the relative role of economic and political action and thus about affiliations with political parties and about relations to the apparatus of the state.

In the short run, the actions and organizational structures of the past come close to determining the immediate future, while in the longer run other factors come more to the fore. There are, of course, critical turning points of long-term significance, such as the decisions about war and peace in socialist parties before World War I that tipped the balance of class and national identifications, fractured the carefully developed internationalism of labor organizations, and contributed to the split of the labor movement into a social democratic and a communist party.

Class constellations and democratization

The baseline for our analysis of the relation between class and democracy is quite simple: those who have only to gain from democracy will be its most reliable promoters and defenders, those who have the most to lose will resist it and will be most tempted to roll it back when the occasion presents itself. Elementary historical knowledge supports this proposition as a basic principle. It is a telling fact that revolutions from below, marxist–leninist or otherwise, are always carried out against authoritarian systems, not democracies,[15] and seizures of power in democracies virtually always occur from the right, not the left.

The basic proposition has implications that are less obvious. In particular, it denies the bourgeoisie that decisive role in the struggle for democracy which both marxist and liberal historians have attributed to it. The owners of the capital for the new forms of production that undermined feudalism did wrest – though in varying degrees – a significant share of control over political decisions from the aristocracy and the crown; and often this took the form of liberal oligarchy. But at least for every case in which the bourgeoisie included the working-class in the political system (sometimes with apparent willingness, in most cases only in response to actual or anticipated pressure), there is at least one other in which the bourgeoisie participated in rollbacks of democracy in order to defend economic interests against those classes that used to be called *les classes dangereuses.* Support for Pinochet's regime in Chile is only one in a long line of examples. Even disregarding such later reversals, it is only if we make no distinction between democracy and liberal forms of rule, however restricted by class, that we can assign to the bourgeoisie the role of the main historic promoter of democracy.

It is true that large landowners – especially those who still enjoy their privileges as remnants of a feudal social order immune to democracy – have a historical record of an even more systematic opposition to democracy. As we will see, this negative role of the landlord class is not confined to brief periods of transitions; in many cases it affected the constellations of class antagonism and alliance for long periods after landownership had lost its preeminent economic role. Barrington Moore has taught us the important lesson that an analysis of democratization can ignore agrarian class relations only at substantial intellectual peril.

We retain, then, in our theoretical framework Moore's emphasis on agrarian class relations and on landlord–bourgeoisie–state coalitions; but we combine this emphasis with an equally strong focus on the role of the subordinate classes in the new capitalist order. The role of different classes in the struggle about the form of government must be analyzed historically in terms of their conflicting interests, the transformation of economy and social order by capitalist development, and the changing opportunities for class coalitions and compromises.

Capitalist development is associated with the rise of democracy primarily because of two structural effects: it strengthens the working class as well as other subordinate classes, and it weakens large landowners. The first of these must be further specified: capitalist development enlarges the urban working class at the expense of agricultural laborers and small farmers; it thus shifts members of the subordinate classes from an environment extremely unfavorable for collective action to one much more favorable, from geographical isolation and immobility to high concentrations of people with similar class interests and far-flung communications.

Another major outcome of the capitalist transformation of the class structure – and in a sense the first, its premier outcome – is, of course, the rising power of the owners and managers of capital, of the bourgeoisie. Where bourgeois power came to constitute a counterbalance to the power of the nobility, the result was liberal oligarchy, possibly open to extensions toward the subordinate classes, more often closed to such an opening for long periods of time. In many cases, however, an oligarchic alliance with large landowners and the state – an alliance that guaranteed the institutional framework for continued capitalist accumulation without institutionalizing contestation – was a significant historical alternative to liberal oligarchy.

It is especially the working class that has often played a decisively pro-democratic role. Labor's role was concealed to the superficial eye precisely because in many countries workers were long excluded from the political process and thus from visible participation in democratic politics. This role becomes clear, however, if one looks at the struggles that led to an extension of political participation beyond the social circles surrounding the dominant classes. The particular politics of working-class organizations took different forms and often expressed reservations about participation in a political process biased against subordinate class interests. That rhetoric, however, which can for instance easily be found in the debates in the German Social Democratic Party before World War I, must not be allowed to obscure the basically democratic thrust of working-class interests; there was hardly a more reliably pro-democratic force in Germany than the SPD. And the SPD was not a marginal case but was typical of other national working-class parties (Therborn 1977; Zolberg 1986).

In the relative class power model of democratization that stands at the center of our analytic framework, it is a crucial hypothesis that the relative size and the density of organization of the working class – of employed manual labor outside of agriculture – are of critical importance for the advance of democracy. At the same time, the conditions under which the social construction of working-class interests takes a non-democratic form – as it did in Leninism and in Peronism – also deserve close attention.

The working class was – contrary to socialist expectations – far too weak to achieve by itself democratic rights for the subordinate classes.[16] If this was true of the countries of early capitalist development, it is an even more significant consideration in the analysis of the late developing countries of the Third World. In late developing countries the relative size of the urban working class is typically smaller because of uneven, "enclave" development, because of changes in the overall transnational structure of production, and because of the related stronger growth of the tertiary sector. That means that alliances across class boundaries become critically important for the advance of democracy.

The potential allies of the working class do not, however, emerge independently of the class structure. They can hardly be understood as groupings in a class-neutral political structure that happen to present themselves as allies of labor because of the accidental play of politics or by reason of democratic principle. It is primarily other previously excluded classes that constitute such potential allies. Historically, it was the urban and the rural petty bourgeoisie – merchants, craftsmen, farmers and other self-employed groups with at most a few employees – who were the most significant allies of the working class in Europe. In Latin America, the employed middle classes were more important. To play this role, however, it was necessary that they had considerable autonomy from dominant interests. This was of special importance for small farmers where large landowners constituted a politically significant force.

The specific patterns of alliance and conflict in class relations are contingent on the variable construction of class interests. A radicalization of working class struggle may, for instance, not only divide the working-class; it may also significantly reduce the chances of building a broad pro-democratic coalition between different segments of the middle classes and the working class. In turn, the degree of intransigence of elites may open or close alliance options for other classes.

The urban and rural middle classes also can take the lead in the struggle for democracy, with an often still small working class in a secondary role. Even professionals and entrepreneurs may play a significant role, provided that they see their interests sufficiently protected and anticipate gains from a more inclusive democratization. Yet the particular pro-democratic character of working-class interests shows itself not only in labor's role in the original process of democratization; we would also expect it to express itself in the defense of democratic institutions when these come under attack, as they did in Europe in the 1930s or in Latin America in the 1960s and 1970s.

Landlords stand at the opposite pole from the working class in their constitutional interests. A first cause of this lies in the fact that landlords were the dominant class of agrarian feudalism, which in all its varieties was incompatible with democratic rule. This typically had lasting effects on the political orientations of the landlord class well beyond the transformation of the economic system.

These historical causes are paralleled and reinforced by the current political and economic interests of large landlords. Any class that is dominant both economically and politically will not be eager to dilute its political power by democratization. More important than this near-universal tendency of the powerful to preserve their position, is – for a certain kind of agriculture – a specific interest linking the economic and political interests of landlords: Large landowners will be the more anti-democratic the more they rely for the control of their labor force on state-backed coercion rather than on the working of the market. This anti-democratic consequence of "labor repressive agriculture" was a central point of Moore's (1966) comparative historical analysis, and it received confirmation in the quantitative cross-national study of Paige (1975) that examined similar assumptions. Finally, peasants with small or no land holdings often represent a greater threat to the interests of large landowners than workers to the interests of employers, because they demand land far more frequently than workers insist on control of the means of industrial production.

A large and politically significant landlord class, especially one that relies on labor repressive agriculture, inhibits democratization in several ways. It often shapes the character of the state apparatus so as to make democratization more difficult; to this we will turn in the next section. It may be able to "co-opt" the emerging bourgeoisie or parts of it and establish an anti-democratic coalition composed of elements of both the old and the new dominant classes. It is likely to have a strong hegemonic influence on dependent peasants and often also on the rural middle classes. And it can, of course, wield its own considerable economic and social power in more direct ways.

The bourgeoisie is a much less consistently and radically anti-democratic force – similar to large landowners who are not historical descendants of a feudal aristocracy and who do not rely on repressive means of labor control. Reflection on the modal class interests of the bourgeoisie reveals its liberal potential but also indicates its limitations as an agent of democratization beyond liberalism.

The primary economic interest of the bourgeoisie as a class lies in the development and guarantee of the institutional infrastructure of capitalist development – in the institutions of property and contract, in the predictability of judicial decisions, in the functioning of markets for capital, goods and services, and labor, and in the protection against unwelcome state intervention. At the same time, the common class interest stands against the collective organization of labor and other subordinate classes – the premier mode of empowerment of the many. Furthermore, different fractions of the bourgeoisie have always had interests that involved directly favorable state action beyond the formal guarantees of property and market functioning – such as protection of monopolies, tax-financed subsidies, or tariff barriers against foreign competition.

The first set of bourgeois class interests demand a state that concentrates on formally universalistic institutions and largely limits itself to that. This state conception is liberal in its self-limitation and in its regard for individual liberties. It cannot be too democratic, however, because it cannot be responsive to interests that are at odds with the formalism of liberal law and of state bureaucracy and with the impersonal functioning of the market. The major contrary force here are the subordinate classes insisting on democratic participation and demanding that their interests be protected against injuries from the market, enforced by formalist law and a minimalist state. This clash of interests has repeatedly led to capitalist political interventions obstructing democratization or – in a later phase – suspending existing democratic institutions. The last set of bourgeois interests, finally, the interest in state action directly aiding particular forms of capital accumulation, creates a similar, though typically less strong dependence on supportive state action as we observed as a consequence of labor repressive agriculture for the landowning class.

Historical reality is, of course, far more complex than these observations on the modal interests of different classes suggest. It is more varied across countries and historical constellations. The factors that account for this complexity will therefore have to have a central place in the comparative historical analysis. The major factors relevant here are, in our view: first, the social construction of class interests in the process of collective organization; second, the persistence of organizational forms, alliances, and ideological orientations beyond the causal conditions of their original formation; and third, the perceptions of immediate and anticipations of future opportunities and threats, which are shaped by historical experience both within and beyond the borders of one country.

How these factors modify the historical articulation of class interests and result in quite contrasting constellations of alliance and conflict can be indicated here only by a few illustrative arguments. The classic (though not typical) historical sequence – represented by the English process of democratization – is the slow expansion of democratic rights from aristocracy to gentry and bourgeoisie, to petty bourgeoisie and upper working-class, to all male adults, and then to the whole adult population. This sequence may have favored the maintenance and the continuous development of liberal political institutions, but it favored at the same time the pursuit of dominant class interests and it undercut as well as shaped the articulation of subordinate class interests. We think here both of the coercive defeat of the Chartist demands for universal male suffrage and of the subsequent phased extensions of the vote, which put the Conservatives and the Liberals in competition for the new electorate but also gave them a chance to put their imprint on the organized expression of working-class interests for some time to come.

One may well consider this historical development as a deformation of working-class interests. It certainly protected dominant interests from radical threats. But the role of bourgeois-led parties can also be seen as critically positive for the mobilization of subordinate classes and the articulation of their interests. Which of these – on their face contradictory – views one adopts, depends presumably on counterfactual assumptions about the particular case. Measured against the desolate subordination, small size, and disorganization that characterize the working class in quite a few Third World countries, even bourgeois-led parties may help articulate working-class interests and advance their chances of organization far more than a class-based collective action ever could. By contrast, their impact may be judged as demobilizing on the strength of a very different evaluation of working-class organizational potential in a particular historical situation.

The English sequence of democratization is instructive in quite another way. Often taken as the paradigmatic path of political development, it actually is a precedent that was followed by more deviant than conforming cases. This is no accident. The pace of capitalist development, its timing relative to that of other countries (which affects the horizons of historical experience), and the rise of organized expression of different class interests are not chained to each other in invariant relations.

In fact, both historical learning and the changing impact of one political economy on the other make these relations systematically different from each other across time. The German bourgeoisie took a far less open and liberal political position than its English counterpart. This cannot be understood without attention to the facts that Germany was a latecomer to capitalist development (if an early latecomer), that its pace of industrialization was faster, and that the bourgeoisie already felt threatened by the emergent working-class when it was still engaged in fighting for its own right to political participation. In other countries, for instance in Latin America, we expect to find constellations of class interests and their articulations that are again very different from both England and European latecomers.

Perceptions of threat, especially those guiding the organizations acting on behalf of dominant class interests, are critically important for the chances of democratization. In many cases, the dominant interests are strong enough to foil advances in democratization if they perceive radical threats to their interests. These perceptions are not simply reflections of objective conditions but represent symbolic constructs that are subject to hegemonic and counter-hegemonic contention. Once established, they often remain a potent force for long periods of time. An obvious contemporary illustration is the fear of communism in many Third World countries that are in the midst of struggles about democratization.

State Structures and Democracy

The relative class power model of democratization has to be modified by "bringing the state back in" (Evans et al. 1985). If the struggle for democracy is a struggle about power, we cannot confine our attention to the structure of power in civil society and the economy. Any modern state is on its own a significant part of the overall landscape of power. The state apparatus is furthermore of special relevance because it is always a major actor in that field in which democratic rule must prove itself as effective and real – the power to shape authoritative decisions, binding for all.[17]

State autonomy and democracy

When we initially discussed the very possibility of democracy, we encountered a first condition without which democracy cannot exist – a fairly strong institutional differentiation of the political realm of formal collective decision making from the overall system of inequality in a society. Without it, a significant role of the many in governance is inconceivable. Such institutional differentiation – in some measure characteristic of all modern societies – gives government and politics a certain autonomy from social power and privilege, but it certainly does not make structured inequality irrelevant.

The relations between the structure of social and economic power and the state have been the subject of protracted debate, especially among marxist scholars. At the center of these discussions was the issue of the "autonomy of the state".[18] We take the position that this autonomy is variably determined by historical conditions that do not stand in a one-to-one relationship to capitalist development. The rise of the modern state cannot be explained adequately by the needs of emergent capitalism; it had its own roots and determinants, even if its relations to the capitalist transformation of economy and society quickly attained central importance for both sides – for the new state apparatuses as well as the new economic forms and elites (Weber 1922/1968; Tilly 1975).

Furthermore, modern states cannot be understood merely in relation to their own societies. Each must be seen as part of a system of states. The relations among states have their own dynamics of challenge and response, ascendancy and defeat (which give the discipline of international relations its remarkably self-contained character). Involvement in this field of interstate relations is one of the bases of the state's partial independence from the internal constellations of socioeconomic interest and power (Hintze 1975). This means that states must be seen in both contexts at once – as "potentially autonomous organizations located at the interface of class structures and international situations" (Skocpol 1979: 33).

The modern state, then, has in our view a *potential* autonomy that is far greater than most varieties of marxist conceptions of the state allow, conceptions that for instance see the state as an instrument in the hands of the dominant classes or assign it a "relative" autonomy that does exist vis–à-vis even the dominant classes but is limited to maintaining the capitalist system in good working order. However, if the modern state has indeed a very considerable potential autonomy, the actual autonomy of concrete states varies widely, depending on a constellation of factors as yet rather incompletely understood.

While this variable autonomy of the state can hardly be stressed enough, another proposition is equally important: the state is almost inevitably part of any pact of domination that in effect determines the substance of the major collective decisions. The system of domination in all modern societies includes the state; and the articulation of state power with the power structure of the society is decisive for the overall system of domination.

The colonial state represents a special case because it typically had greater autonomy from the indigenous society than virtually any other state. This is of great importance for the "new nations" of the Third World, since state structures and their articulations with civil society often persist once firmly set. True, decolonization often constituted a radical break, and one certainly cannot count on simple continuities – the "colonial inheritance" – in state–society relations in new nations. But the transformations of decolonization and their impact on state autonomy take a different form depending on the level of economic development, the density of civil society, and the relative strength of different social classes.

How is state autonomy related to democracy? One may be tempted to give the apparently obvious answer: They stand in opposition to each other. The more autonomous the state apparatus and its managers from the forces of society, the less the chances of democracy, or if democratic forms exist, the more likely that they are merely formal, a pretense.

This is a seriously incomplete view, because it treats "the forces of society" without any differentiation. Some distinctions focusing on class will make this clear. In most marxist discussions, the autonomy of the state means first and foremost autonomy from the dominant class, in capitalism from the bourgeoisie. We do not accept this as the exclusive meaning of autonomy. The concept of state autonomy must retain a more comprehensive meaning to be put to full use, but autonomy from dominant interests is clearly one facet of critical importance. Some autonomy of the state from the dominant classes, from the bourgeoisie and especially – where it still exists – from the landlord class, is a necessary condition for democracy to be possible and meaningful. If the state is simply a tool of the dominant classes, democracy is either impossible or a mere form. Such autonomy of the state is in fact but one aspect of the differentiation between political collective decision making and the wider structures of inequality.

This consideration suggests that pre-democratic pacts of domination, especially those involving – in addition to state and bourgeoisie – a landlord class that relies on labor repressive agriculture, probably have to break up before democratization has a serious chance. That hypothesis is in accord with Moore's analysis, and it is reminiscent of a condition of social revolutions which voluntaristic theories of revolution have always neglected – that revolutionary situations can hardly occur unless the system of domination is seriously damaged, that they cannot be understood just as the result of pressures from below, however desperate (Skocpol 1979).

The autonomy of the state from the dominant classes can, obviously, never be complete. Where the landowning aristocracy has close relations to the state apparatus, as is typical of landlords relying on coercive means of labor control, the interests of landowners have often been firmly imprinted on governmental organization and its corps of civil servants. Once institutionalized, this orientation and the associated anti-democratic proclivities can well persist even after the economic power of landlords has waned.

Such patterns of recruitment for top positions and the peculiar esprit de corps of higher civil servants and military officers are critical for linking the state apparatus to – or insulating it from – the interests and orientations of different classes. At the same time, recruitment patterns and esprit de corps are decisive for the degree and the character of the state apparatus's corporate identitity and its ability to act coherently.

In the context of capitalism, the state relies for its own revenue on the health of the economy. That entails a special dependence on the interests of capital owners and managers. It is above all their reactions and anticipations that represent the "business climate," which is so often decisive for the success of state policies. And it is their investment decisions that determine future economic growth, stagnation, or recession and with that the level of employment and the development of tax revenue. This is the basic dependence constraining state autonomy in capitalist societies.

These constraints do leave space for significant state action. The state apparatus may have accumulated enough power on its own to act with some autonomy even against dominant interests. Equally important, the power constellations in economy and society may have shifted so as to make state action less dependent on dominant, and more responsive to subordinate class interests. Thus, if and to the extent that working-class organizations and socialist parties acquired sufficient strength, as they did especially in the small democracies of western Europe, state–society relations were transformed and the interests of the subordinate classes were better served by the state (Stephens 1979c).

The intuitive plausibility of an inverse relation between state autonomy and democracy makes more sense if we use a broader conception of state autonomy. A state apparatus that enjoys considerable autonomy vis-à-vis the mass of the population – the petty bourgeoisie, small farmers as well as the working-class – is unlikely to be a factor favorable for democratization. The more resourceful and powerful the state apparatus, the less likely that the subordinate classes of the population are strong enough to impose democratic rule on the system of domination.[19]

Taken together with the previous point, these considerations suggest that while state autonomy vis-à-vis the dominant classes is a necessary condition of effective democracy, the same state strength that contributes to this outcome may enable the state to overpower the pro-democratic forces in the rest of the society. Processes of democratization, then, must steer between the Scylla of a dependence of the state on the dominant classes that is incompatible with democracy and the Charybdis of a state machinery too strong to be democratically tamed.

State and civil society

Is the autonomy of the state vis-à-vis the population as a whole not limited, in any political order, by the need of the system of rule to be legitimate in the eyes of its citizens? And does this need not by its very nature hand a sort of quasi-democratic control over the state to the mass of the population? Though the position expressed in these questions is rarely argued explicitly, it is quite commonly taken for granted. Yet it is fundamentally mistaken. It turns the values of democracy into empirical assumptions about the functioning of all systems of domination. The reality of history shows a quite different pattern:

> a system of domination may – as often occurs in practice – be so completely protected on the one hand by the obvious community of interest between the chief and his administrative staff . . . as opposed to the subjects, on the other hand by the helplessness of the latter, that it can afford to drop even the pretense of a claim to legitimacy. (Weber 1922/1968: 214)

Legitimation as well as other, weaker forms of consent are important only where people already have significant social power. Only if the subordinate classes have acquired significant power does it make any difference whether a state is legitimate in their eyes or not.

The many acquire power primarily through organization. As we have seen, capitalist development has two consequences that are relevant here. It makes generally for a denser civil society, and that eases the problems of organization for collective action. And it shifts agricultural workers and small farmers into the urban labor force, where they have far better chances of collective organization.

High organizational density in society – among all classes but especially among the subordinate classes – is an important counterweight to the power of the state apparatus. A dense civil society widens the passage between the Scylla of a state so dominated by landlords and bourgeoisie that democracy becomes impossible or meaningless and the Charybdis of an authoritarian leviathan strong enough to overwhelm all democratic forces in society.

At the same time, the state has many ways of shaping the development of civil society. It can ease or obstruct the organization of different class interests; it can empower or marginalize existing organizations; it may succeed in co-optation and, in the extreme, use whole organizational networks as conduits of hegemonic influence. The complex interdependence of state and civil society creates a wide variety of possible relations between the state and different social classes and, consequently, of conditions conducive or hostile to democracy.

The ways in which organized religion is related to the state is of great importance for our inquiry. Whether there is religious division, whether a church is closely allied with the state and/or dominant classes, whether a strongly organized church stands apart from and possibly in opposition to the state apparatus, whether religious movements and sects have developed an autonomous and dense organizational network – these questions are critical in analyzing the overall relations of state and civil society. Again, we will emphasize the impact these differences have on the chances of dominant classes to gain and maintain cultural hegemony as well as on the chances of subordinate classes to retain some autonomy. As indicated earlier, we will seek to relate earlier scholarly work that took its cues from different theoretical orientations to the class analytic framework we develop here. Especially relevant is the comparative historical work of Lipset and Rokkan (in particular Lipset and Rokkan 1967; Rokkan 1970) which examined the lasting imprints of state formation, church-state relations, and class on political alignments.

The monopoly of violence

The modern state claims a monopoly on the use of coercion and violence. It denies these means of power to any other actor in society. Even where this policy does not succeed fully, it leads to a massive concentration of the coercive tools of power in the hands of the state. At the same time, the monopoly of the use of coercion is the basis of authoritative decision making binding for all. It is, in fact, yet another aspect of that differentiation of collective political decision-making from the wider structures of inequality we have touched on repeatedly. Where the consolidation of this authority of the state is seriously in question, where it is challenged by armed conflict and where its reach is uncertain, democratic forms of rule are impossible.

The particular role played by the means of coercion in a given state structure and in its relation to the wider society can be decisive for the chances of democratization (Stepan 1988). If the organizations of coercion and violence – the police and the military – are strong within the overall state apparatus, the situation is quite unfavorable for democracy. Even in advanced capitalist, democratic societies, a large and powerful military establishment reduces the sphere of decisions subject to democratic decision-making. Not only is the ethos of the armed forces – an ethos of command and obedience, of order and loyalty – typically at odds with democratic values, but their organizational interests and often their class position as well also predispose them against rule of the people. In the Third World, a strong military is one of the major obstacles to successful democratization. And the export of weaponry and other military technology – stimulated by East-West tensions and often supported with military aid – is one of the major ways in which western democracies undercut democratization in the Third World.

"Tocquevillean" effects of state structures

State structures and state policies have effects other than those intended by policy makers; the patterns of state organization and state action may have an impact on society that is often not noticed by the actors themselves and even more rarely intended. These "Tocquevillean" structural effects[20] profoundly influence all forms of collective action in society. They have complex and contradictory relations to democratization particularly as they affect the articulation of state and civil society and influence the formation of classes and their interrelations.

A counterintuitive example of the restructuring of state–society relations is found in European absolutism. The autocratic rule of absolutism is hardly, on its face, a phenomenon favorable to democracy. Yet it is arguable that the bureaucratic universalism of the modern state had egalitarian consequences. The equality of the subjects of absolutism in continental Europe can be analyzed as one of the foundations of democratic citizenship. By the same token, absolute rule advanced the differentiation of state and society.

State structures and the unanticipated consequences of state action are also closely interrelated with developments in the class structure. This applies with special force to landowners and the bourgeoisie because their role in the system of domination links them closely to the state. Not only are state structures imprinted with the interests and views of dominant classes, but these classes in turn are shaped in their organization and outlook by their relations with the state in the context of the wider system of domination. Yet, the same basic proposition holds also for the subordinate classes, for changes in their outlook and organization. Jürgen Kocka has, for instance, raised the possibility that the German working class was more united and broadly organized in part because of unintended consequences of state action: "Government supervision and repression did not focus on specific occupations but on journeymen and workers in general. Probably this helped them to identify as workers instead of as members of particular crafts or special skill groups" (Kocka 1985: 291). In addition, measures of control and repression were in this case complemented by social security policies that also focused on workers as such, inscribing a unitary class conception into these new institutional structures. "Tocquevillean," unintended effects shade over into intentional and consciously conceived policies. If German social policy contributed unwittingly to a unification of the working-class, many states – Germany included – carefully underline and protect in their legislation the distinction between blue collar working-class and white collar employees, however routine the work of the latter – clearly a policy of dividing the working-class.

Finally we can point to effects that democratization itself may have on the patterns of class formation. Here historical sequence matters decisively. Working classes that had to fight for democratic participation tend to be more cohesive and more politically radical than working-classes that faced less struggle or – as in the North American case – that constituted themselves structurally after the struggle for more or less inclusive democracy was won (Katznelson and Zolberg 1986).

Democracy and the Transnational Structures of Power

To the relative power of classes and the partially autonomous state we must add a third dimension of power relations: transnational power structures and their impact on the internal system of rule. Countries – their states and their political economies – do not exist in isolation from each other. The relations to other states are always a central element on the agenda of state policy. In fact, it is only as part of a *system of states* that the modern state and its development can be understood.

Equally important, no modern economy is limited to its country's borders. Increasingly, national economies have become involved in worldwide economic relations and found – or were forced into – a place in the worldwide division of labor. This integration in the transnational economy has a significant impact on the internal class structures, and international capital interests become a significant factor in internal class relations. It is quite plausible, then, to consider transnational structures of power – both political and economic international relations – as vitally important for the internal power balance of a country and thus for the chances of democracy.

The impact of the worldwide economy is not merely a matter of market forces. While the international market is much less open to economic intervention and intentional structuring than the internal economy, states as well as transnational corporations do exert a significant influence by command and agreement rather than merely through market exchange. The more powerful among them put their stamp on the world economy and relegate weaker political economies to a position of dependence.

The three broad components of our analytic framework introduced so far – relative class power, the state as a partially autonomous block of power, and the transnational power structure – are complexly intertwined with each other. We have seen that the state's involvement in transnational relations is one important basis of its very autonomy vis-à-vis the internal structure of social and economic power. Transnational relations affect the development of national economies. And the position of a country in the international division of labor is a major determinant of the relative size and power of its dominant and subordinate classes. Within often harsh constraints, states – even small states – do have some freedom of action on the international scene. They even can modify the impact of transnational economic relations on the national political economy though, to be sure, their capacity for such action varies tremendously. Finally, internal class relations and in particular the nature of the overall system of domination, which now often includes international capital as a significant actor, are in turn one major determinant of the capacity of states to act effectively in the transnational scene.

Rather than turning immediately to the effects of transnational dependence and interdependence, we begin our discussion of international power relations with the impact of the most radical disruption of transnational interdependence – the consequences of war.

War and democratization

The most dramatic manifestation of inter-state power relations certainly is war. That warfare has a close relation to democratization has often been noted. Previous arguments have prepared the explanation: any major war strengthens the hand of the state vis-à-vis its partners in the existing system of domination, and this may loosen the coherence of that coalition. More important, modern mass-mobilization warfare involves the willing participation of the many, both in the field and at home. It has therefore typically led states to make major concessions to the subordinate classes. Working-class organizations often had to be included in the ruling coalition, and the pressure to extend the vote to women and excluded racial groups mounted. Even though such social mobilization for war can also be achieved under authoritarian auspices and even though after the conclusion of a war we frequently see attempts to contain and reverse such gains (as was the case after both World Wars in the United States), modern mass warfare tends to give a powerful momentum to already existing pro-democratic pressures. A now nearly forgotten US Senator, Barkley of Kentucky, gave eloquent expression to this in 1946 in a debate on civil rights:

> I voted, Mr. President, to extend the arm of the Federal Government into every home and into every city and into every town in the United States and take from the homes and communities every able-bodied man available for military service without regard to race, color, creed, religion, ancestry, or origin. . . . I do not see how I, having voted to subject men to compulsory service in behalf of our institutions in wartime, can refuse to vote for the same kind of democracy in peace when the war has been won. (Quoted in Leuchtenburg 1986: 592)

If the economic exertions of a major war are overwhelming and especially if the war is then lost, the earlier ruling coalition may not merely be transformed in its internal balance, it may *break up* – creating profound political instability and the potential for rapid advances toward democracy. This is often over-looked when subsequent constitutional change is simply attributed to imposi-tion by the victorious powers – the commonsense view of democratization in Japan and Germany after World War II.[21] We do, of course, not deny that foreign imposition – in colonies as well as in defeated countries – may have some effect and even constitute a lasting imprint. But the outcome is inevitably shaped, especially in the longer run, by the internal structure of power, by the relations of power among the classes, and by the articulation of state structure with the patterns of economic and social power in society.

The power vacuum created by such a break-up of the system of domination need not, of course, be an opening for democracy. The outcome may well be a different form of authoritarian rule, as it was in Russia after 1917. If the power vacuum is primarily filled by an expansion of the role of the state, non-democratic outcomes are virtually inevitable. This depends partly on the international environment, but the critical question here reverts again to relative cla s power. If the subordinated classes have – or can develop – organizations strong enough to control the state apparatus, they can take advantage of the weakening of the dominant classes, and advances toward democracy become more likely. An important further question is whether the antagonisms between different potentially pro-democratic groups are seen as bridgeable or, alternatively, whether earlier divisions and cleavages are so deep as to preclude coalition building as well as even antagonistic co-operation.

There are other reasons why war has by no means unambiguously positive consequences for democracy. One of its major effects may be a strengthening of the military apparatus, which under most conditions is a development hostile to democracy. A heightening of nationalism, another likely correlate of war, often eases the hegemonic influence of dominant over subordinate classes.

The impact of economic and geo-political dependence

The less developed countries find themselves typically in positions in the international division of labor that severely affect their internal development. If this combines with an unfavorable position in the geo-political interstate relations, one can speak of sovereignty only in a very reduced and formal sense. We have seen in the previous chapter that many analysts have viewed such a condition of dependency as radically inhibiting democratization. Yet we have also seen that the empirical cross-national evidence does not support these radical claims. It is at best ambiguous.

Recent developments in dependency theory, which focus on the consequences of dependence for economic development, have led to a paradigmatic shift away from radical claims that were both rigid and unhistorical. The new views no longer see dependency as a unitary phenomenon which has homogeneous consequences – the obstruction of development and the creation of underdevelopment – across a wide range of historical situations, but adopt a more complex conception. In this conception dependence remains central but can take different forms, can interact with significant technological developments, can be counterbalanced by state action, and can lead to a variety of outcomes (Cardoso and Faletto 1979; Evans 1979; Evans and Stephens 1988). This new conception of dependency appears also best suited for the comparative study of its impact on the chances of democracy.

A dependent niche in the worldwide division of labor does not leave the class structure untouched, because it affects the internal economic development.

Therborn (1977: 31–2) offers a succinct description of the modal consequences. Though it probably paints too homogeneous a picture, it gives a powerful indication of the kinds of changes a comparative historical analysis will have to consider:

> First, dependent capitalist development has severely restricted the internal differentiation of the capitalist class, making it instead largely dependent on one external centre . . . . Secondly, the lopsided, externally dependent growth of petty and generalized commodity production has rendered the economic base extremely fragile and vulnerable to international crises, thus leaving the indigenous bourgeoisies little room for manoeuvre vis-à-vis the exploited classes . . . . The frequent intertwining of capitalist with feudal, slave or other pre-capitalist modes of exploitation, as well as the combination of enclave capitalism with subsistence farming, has impeded the development of impersonal rule of capital . . . and a free labour market, thereby seriously limiting the growth both of the labour movement . . . and of an agrarian small and petty bourgeoisie.

In this view, dependent capitalist development, then, weakens the two effects of development on the class structure we identified earlier as most favoring democratization: an expansion and strengthening of the working-class and a reduction of the large landowning class in size as well as political power. It also tends to conserve labor repressive agriculture and to weaken the autonomy of subordinate classes such as the peasantry and petty bourgeoisie from the landlords' anti-democratic hegemonic influence. More generally, dependent development has been shown to increase consistently the degree of socioeconomic inequality (Chase-Dunn 1975; Rubinson 1976; Bornschier and Chase-Dunn 1985), and that can – though it does not regularly – inhibit democratization.

Whatever the consequences of dependent development for the relative size and strength of different classes, dependency often but not always creates strong bonds of common interest between the dominant classes in core countries and their counterparts in the dependent country. The state in the dependent political economy may then become the third part, and an important instrument, of a "triple alliance" (Evans 1979) that stands in a fairly strong position against the interests of subordinate classes.

There are quite a few reasons to expect that dependent states have strong incentives to buttress as much as possible their autonomy, among them the unfavorable position of their political economies in the worldwide division of labor and the chance to modify this insertion into transnational economic relations to the country's advantage by state action. At the same time, the strengthening of civil society that may counterbalance such state strength in internal state–society relations is likely to be retarded by structural effects of dependence – for instance by the divisive effects of greater income inequality and uneven development. This would be another reason to expect negative effects of dependence on democracy.

We must remember, however, that neither Muller (1985) nor Bollen (1983) found in their quantitative cross-national studies any overall relationship between democracy and such measures of economic dependence as the presence of transnational corporations and the concentration of foreign trade on one or a few partners. Bollen did find a negative correlation between democracy and dependence – independent of level of development – only when he used a measure for dependence that included, in addition to trade flows, a number of political variables such as treaty memberships and military interventions.

This suggests that the effects of economic dependency as such are far less clear-cut than the impact of radically unequal interstate relations. On that interpretation of Bollen's results it would be problematic to assume a generalized negative effect on democracy via the impact of dependent development on the class structure. This does not imply that an unfavorable development of the class structure becomes irrelevant nor that there are no powerful anti-democratic alliances of international capital and the local dominant classes. Rather, these effects may be less than uniform consequences of economic dependency, and they may possibly be counteracted by other factors. Furthermore, where economic dependency is joined with geo-political dependence, Bollen's results would support a fairly generalized negative conception of the effects of dependency on democracy. Such a combination of economic and political factors is likely wherever a dependent state plays a strong role in its political economy (as in the triple alliance analyzed by Evans 1979) and a core state takes a strong geo-political interest.

It seems plausible, however, both on theoretical grounds and on a rough comparative purview, to see the impact of unequal geo-political relations on the chances of democratization also as contingent on specific situational factors. East–West tensions and the fear of communism have given especially American interventions an anti-democratic cast that it may be imprudent to generalize beyond a particular world-historical constellation (Muller 1985). Even within this overall constellation, geo-politically motivated pressures and interventions differed strikingly across regions. Thus, since the early twentieth century, the role of the United States has been overwhelmingly negative in its Central American "backyard:" with rare exceptions, US interventions supported anti-democratic forces against the threat of radical social transformation. But pressures of the northern European democracies (and in part also of the United States) supported very different, democratizing developments in Spain, Portugal, and Greece (Whitehead 1986b). This may be related to the different social base of European democracies; but it is conceivable that the future American role in East Asia might resemble these latter cases more than the part played by the United States in Central America.

On these grounds we will adopt an "agnostic" position on any generalizable overall relationship between democracy and political/economic dependence in transnational relations. This does not mean, however, that the position of a country in the transnational division of labor and inter-state relations is irrelevant for its chances of democratization. It does mean that these chances are dependent on power relations among groups and institutions whose interests stand to benefit or suffer by democratization. Transnational power relations are an integral part of these constellations that interact with the other forces and developments. It is because of the variability of these interactions that simple generalizations based on transnational power configurations alone are bound to fail.

Transnational cultural flows

Dependency and world system theory have recently attempted to include also the cultural sphere (e.g. Meyer 1980). Cultural premises and ideals are certainly relevant to the process of democratization. However, the critical question concerns the extent to which they are effectively grounded in social forces and institutional structures. To include cultural traditions and innovations as a major component of our analytic framework presupposes that they have a strong enough effect on the relevant constellations of power to make a clear-cut difference for the chances of democracy.

Democratic aspirations certainly were ideals that traveled across international borders. Such transnational cultural flows had, however, little effect if the structural conditions were not favorable. For instance, the diffusion of democratic ideals to Latin America in the nineteenth century did not significantly advance democratization at that time.

As noted earlier, democracy is today an internationally accepted ideal, however variably "democracy" may be interpreted. This acceptance is based largely on the experience with Fascism and its defeat as well as on the rejection of Stalinism. Though one may be skeptical about the real meaning of that rhetorical triumph, this worldwide near-consensus is not without effect. In the second half of the twentieth century it has become difficult for dictators to promise a "Thousand Year Reich"; more often than not they rather choose to legitimate their regime as "preparing the country for democracy". Similarly, when democracy is introduced it is much harder than in the nineteenth century to privilege certain classes of voters or to institute formal limitation of the suffrage and exclude whole segments of the population. But other types of restrictions remain exceedingly common.

Clearly this worldwide cultural hegemony of democratic ideals is tied to a specific historical constellation. Its effects become more significant when it is backed by powerful transnational pressures. These may develop on a small scale from the training of professionals abroad. On a larger scale, pressure from significant foreign partners can have a powerful effect. But, as we just saw, it is hardly assured that such pressure will be forthcoming even from the most established democratic political systems, and where it does exist it cannot be expected to compensate for missing internal conditions.

On its face more appealing is the idea that specific transfers of ideas and *institutions* from a cultural "cradle of democracy" have a positive effect on the chances of democracy even in societies with a radically different social structure. One could point to England and its former colonies and cite the preponderance of democracies among the latter as support for the hypothesis. Cross-national research confirmed commonsense notions of the relation between colonial status in the British empire and later democratization (Bollen 1979; Bollen and Jackman 1985a). As argued earlier, however, it is possible to give such quantitative associations very different interpretations. Broad correlations do not explain causality – they do not explain for instance why democracy broke down in the former British possessions in Africa.

That these examples all involve pro-democratic transnational flows does of course not deny the existence of other currents that affect the chances of democracy negatively. The spread of Fascist ideas between the World Wars and the impact of the Cold War ideology after 1945 are two powerful instances.

While we remain open to the possibility of direct cultural effects, especially if they have institutional grounding, we maintain that it is the interaction of different clusters of power and interests that are decisive for the prospects of democracy.

Comparative Research on Democracy in a New Framework

The analytic framework outlined deals with the structural conditions favoring and inhibiting democratization. It does not focus on the political constellations and sequences involved in particular transitions toward or away from democracy. It conceives of democracy as a political form that must be seen first and foremost as a matter of power. In the institutionally differentiated sphere of formal political decision making it gives the many an effective share of power even though they do not rank high in the scales of wealth, honor, and social power as individuals.

We maintain that this is a realistic conception even when applied to the actually existing representative democracies, defined by free and fair elections with a suffrage inclusive of all classes, responsibility of the state apparatus to the elected parliament, and civil rights protecting freedom of expression and association. At the same time, it must be recognized that formal democratic institutions can coexist with very different degrees of real political power of the many.

Both the development of democratic institutions and the effective role of the many in collective decision-making depend on power constellations. We have distinguished three clusters of which we consider the first of paramount importance: the balance of class power, the power and autonomy of the state apparatus and its articulation with civil society, and the transnational structures of power. All three interact with each other in complex ways.

In all three clusters, we insist on the historical, sequential character of the required analysis. This is of critical importance, first, because many structures and constellations persist and are influential beyond the historical configuration of their origin. Previous state structures and regime forms shape later political developments; the original shape of class organization and the related social and political constructions of class interests are powerful determinants of later forms of class-based collective action; critical events – such as brutal repression, a successful coup, or civil war – shape the perceptions of opportunity and threat for long periods of time. A related, second, reason lies in the fact that institutionalization of most significant patterns takes time – often generational turnover. Actually, elapsed time is not the critical factor. What is essential is the experience of successful responses to challenge.

Both points significantly apply to democracy itself. Especially the civil rights of free expression and association but also the rules of the political game, which channel conflict and give procedural protection to powerful interests, require a prolonged process of habituation and institutionalization to become robust and fully effective. At the same time, once effectively grounded these institutions of mutual toleration protect the chances of oppositional forces to (re)gain political power, and they enhance the opportunities for organizing the subordinate classes. This underlies the fact that democracy itself has tendencies to persist: democracy begets democracy, at least under propitious conditions. If democracy itself is one of the phenomena that tend to persist beyond the conditions of their origin, an important methodological rule follows: one must be prepared to distinguish the causal conditions of the first installation of democracy from those that maintain it after consolidation and even from those that determine the chances of redemocratization after an intervening authoritarian regime. This rule does of course not deny that other, constant causes – such as the balance of class power – remain critically important throughout.

Finally there is a third reason – again closely related to the first two – to insist on a genetic, historical analysis. To put it simply: sequence matters. Among the many examples that spring to mind are the relative timing of state building and class formation, different sequences of industrialization and the first democratic initiatives, and worldwide historical developments that give a different character to internal changes in a set of countries which are similar except for their different world historical context.

Taken together, these reasons for insisting on historical sequential analysis entail another conclusion: except at a very high level of abstraction, we cannot expect similar forms of rule to be the result of a single set of causes, identical across a wide range of countries and historical configurations. Rather, once the analysis goes beyond the salience of the three clusters of power constellation we identified – the balance of class power, the power and autonomy of the state, and the transnational configuration of power – we must expect to find patterns of multiple causation and, historically speaking, different paths leading to democracy.

How does our framework, developed in the same political economy approach that guided most comparative historical research, account for the major finding of the cross-national statistical research – the robust correlation between socioeconomic development and democracy? The major explanation is found in the changing balance of class power. Socioeconomic development enlarges the size of the working class and it increases the organizational power of subordinate classes generally. At the same time, it erodes the size and the power of the most anti-democratic force – the large landowning classes, especially those that rely on coercive state power for the control of their labor force.

There are other relevant correlates of socioeconomic development. The state tends to gain in resources and acquires greater importance for the economy.

Where the power of the bourgeoisie counterbalances the power of large landlords, the state also has a chance to become more autonomous from dominant interests. At the same time, the growing organizational density of civil society not only constitutes an underpinning for the political organization of subordinate classes, but it also represents a counterweight to an overwhelming power of the state apparatus.

The major difference between our framework and those comparative historical studies that came to results at odds with the positive relationship between development and democracy lies in our emphasis on the empowerment of the subordinate classes, especially the working class. This is closely related to another contrast. Barrington Moore and others focused primarily on the public contestation of political issues and the institutions of mutual toleration as the major features of democracy and tended to give second place only to inclusive political participation, which for us is pivotal.

The persistent association of development and democracy in today's Third World countries may be seen as raising critical questions about our emphasis on the empowerment of the subordinate classes. If indeed the size and role of the urban working class is typically smaller, how is this continuing effect of development on democratization to be explained? While we do not think that this objection invalidates the balance of class power approach, there is little question that democratization in the early developing countries of Europe was quite different in its specifics than similar developments in the Third World of today. The particular role of the working class, and the patterns of opposition and potential alliance varied even among the European countries, and these differences become greater when the analysis includes the less developed countries of the twentieth century. Yet while the working class is typically smaller in today's Third World countries, the urban population with its better chances to communicate and organize very often is not; in fact, the urban subordinate classes in peripheral countries today may well be larger than their counterparts in the countries that developed earlier.

The relations between the different clusters of conditions may, as we just noted, change over time and vary across countries. In addition to different class constellations and different articulations of state and society, it is possible that transnational influences in the second half of this century play a greater role in favoring democracy. If this were a major substitute for a diminished role of the working class, however, we would expect to find also that democratic institutions more often are merely formal and would not represent a corresponding real role of the many in political decision-making. While such cases may in cross-national statistics appear as full-fledged democracies, a closer contextual analysis could well reveal significant restrictions of democratic rule, especially in the responsiveness of state action to elected parliaments.

It is important to remember that the correlation between development and democracy is far from perfect. This is clearly at odds with a simple functionalist teleology as we encountered in the early theoretical arguments of Cutright (1963). It is easily accounted for in our theoretical framework. First, if the struggle for democracy is indeed a struggle for power, it is contingent on the complex conditions of subordinate class organization, on the chances of forging alliances, on the reactions of dominant interests to the threats and opportunities of democratization, on the role of the state, and on transnational structures of power.

Furthermore, the chances of consolidating and institutionalizing democracy do not seem as closely related to development effects as the changing balance of class power and the resultant efforts to put democracy on the political agenda. In his sequential model of transitions to democracy, Rustow (1970) begins with an important background condition: a national unity which provides a taken-for-granted sense of mutual social and institutional attachment; this does not entail a comprehensive value consensus but rather constitutes a shared collective identity and a minimal sense of solidarity that encompasses all potential political actors. It is the social counterpart to the consolidation of state authority discussed earlier. Ethnic, linguistic, and religious fragmentation are among the main obstacles of such cohesion. These do not yield – at least not in the short and medium run – to the most obvious correlates of economic development, to more dense and far-flung communication and mobility along lines dictated by economic considerations. To the contrary, economic development may generate the resources with which these old and fragmented social identities can be maintained and refurbished (Geertz 1963; Rueschemeyer 1969).

Finally, the installation of democracy requires complex class compromises that become embodied in new institutional arrangements. These have to meet unknown tests in the future for democracy to become consolidated. Quite clearly the skills and the luck of the institutional architects do not have any direct relation to socioeconomic development.

Given the realities of differential class power, democracy is a fragile phenomenon. Democratic institutions can at their best offer subordinate classes a real voice in collective decision-making, while protecting the dominant classes against perceived threats to their vital interests. This is a delicate balance with many chances for failure.

4

Advanced Capitalist Countries

Introduction

We open our comparative historical study with an analysis of the transition to democracy in the set of countries which first made that transition, the advanced capitalist countries of the contemporary world. The cases analyzed include the universe of Western European cases which experienced some period of democracy before World War II, as well as the four British settler colonies of North America and Australasia. The analysis of the European cases focuses on the period 1870–1939. We begin our analysis in 1870 for two reasons. First, only one of these countries, Switzerland, was a democracy by our definition at that point in time. Second, the economic crisis beginning in the 1870s set off a chain of political events, particularly with regard to the tariff issue, which consolidated or reorganized class, sectoral, and party coalitions. In most countries, these coalitions affected the transition to democracy and, in some cases, its breakdown decades later in the interwar period. This depression, the European-wide industrial spurt of the subsequent decades to World War I, the war itself, and then the Great Depression form pegs around which the historical experience of almost all of the western European countries can be organized. By contrast, due primarily to geographic isolation, these events had much less if any impact on the democratic transitions in the four British settler colonies.

Twelve of the sixteen countries discussed here experienced no major reversal of democratic forms after the transition to full democracy. Four countries – Austria, Germany, Italy, and Spain – did experience such reversals and we single them out for special attention. These cases, particularly the German one, are deviations from the general rule that advanced core capitalist countries are democratic, and thus an analysis of their development promises to tell us something about the long-term structural features that condition such an historical trajectory. Though three of these modern authoritarian regimes were short lived, they were only broken by war and it is arguable that they would have lasted much longer had they avoided war.

Contending views of the experience of advanced capitalist democracies

Therborn's (1977) study of the transition to democracy in the advanced capitalist world emphasizes the role of the working-class, as represented by working-class parties and unions, and the role of geopolitics, especially foreign wars. Both of these factors appear in our theory. Lipset's more general statements on the relationship between development and democracy, on the other hand, would lead one to hypothesize that the European industrial spurt of 1870–1914 was associated with democracy because it enlarged the middle class. The long-term movement toward democracy in the English settler colonies might be linked to economic development in the same way.

Because they seek to make broad generalizations from a universe of cases, these studies do not explain deviations from the central tendency, such as highly developed countries that were nevertheless authoritarian. Drawing on Moore (1966), the theory developed in the last chapter provides an explanation which focuses on the role of large landlords and the state in the ruling coalition during industrialization. We depart from Moore's own analysis in that we consider a wider range of comparable cases. He limits himself to the analysis of a few large countries excluding two large western European countries, Italy and Spain, though he indicates that his analysis of modern capitalist authoritarianism fits these cases with some modification. As to the small countries, he argues that the "decisive causes of their politics lie outside their own boundaries" (Moore 1966: xiii). By contrast, Rokkan (1970) and Katzenstein (1985) contend that not only is this an exaggeration but also that the small western European countries have special characteristics which make them an essential point of comparison in the study of the political dynamics of all of the countries in the region. More specifically, both see the weakness or absence of the landed upper class as a distinctive feature of these countries.

To facilitate the analysis in this chapter, it is useful to explore Moore's argument in a little more detail. As Skocpol points out in her discussion of Moore, there are multiple paths to democracy, but a single path to modern capitalist authoritarianism. Thus, it is simplest to outline the path to authoritarianism and hypothesize that once a country passes an initial stage of industrialization and has avoided peasant revolution, it will develop in a democratic direction if it lacks any of the essential characteristics leading to authoritarianism. The critical condition for the development of modern capitalist authoritarianism is the development of a coalition of large landholders, the crown (the monarch, bureaucracy and military, i. e. , the state) and a politically dependent bourgeoisie of medium strength. Elaborating on Moore, we can identify the following factors which lead to the development of this coalition:

1   The landed upper classes must be strong or, more precisely, they must remain the politically dominant force into the modern era (i.e. late nineteenth century) and must retain a significant amount of that power in a "democratic interlude".

2 The maintenance of peasant agriculture under landlords oriented to the market but employing political rather than market control of labor – labor repressive agriculture – into the modern era is a second essential feature of the path to modern capitalist authoritarianism. The method of labor control leads the landlords to seek an alliance with those in control of the means of coercion, the state, and it accounts for the strong antidemocratic impulse of the aristocracy (Moore 1966: 435).

3 The country has to have experienced sufficient industrialization that the bourgeoisie is a politically significant actor, but it cannot be more politically powerful than the landed classes. Skocpol (1973) points to the difficulty involved in measuring the strength of "bourgeois impulses," but formulating it as we have done here, this is less problematic.

4 The bourgeoisie is kept in a politically dependent position as industrialization is aided, and to some extent directed, by the state through protection, state credits to industrialists, state development of infrastructure, promotion of modern skills, and even state development of enterprises later handed over to private entrepreneurs. Militarism and thus armaments production seals the bourgeoisie into the state–landlord dominated coalition and its reactionary and imperialistic politics.

5 There must be no revolutionary break from the past. Thus, peasant revolutionary potential must be low (for the reasons pointed to in chapter 2) or else the whole process, in particular the power of the landlords, would have been broken at an earlier point in history.

6 A state with a sufficient capacity to repress peasant (and worker) protest is an essential element of the authoritarian class coalition.[1] Autonomy of the state from subordinate classes and alignment of state forces with the dominant class or classes contributes to the authoritarian outcome. Such an alignment of the state is encouraged by social integration of top state personnel with the upper classes, especially the landed upper class, and a strong corporate identity, which is a result of high generational continuity among other factors. In the case of the military, both strength (repressive capacity) and corporate identity are encouraged by participation in foreign wars and aspirations to great power status.

It should be noted here that while the coalition of the state, labor repressive landlords, and a dependent bourgeoisie seems to be an essential feature of the authoritarian path, the six factors listed above may simply contribute to the outcome, that is, may make it more probable, without being completely essential. In developing this list of factors, we have focused on the elements which come closest to being necessary conditions; other contributing conditions could have been added. For instance, Moore (p. 417) initially argues that the persistence of royal absolutism into modern times is a feature of the nondemocratic path, but he later indicates that it is only a contributing feature, recognizing that Italy was a constitutional monarchy. One might add that Spain was also and, on the other hand, Sweden and Denmark, like Germany, were ruled by limited absolutist governments in which the king could appoint his cabinet without reference to the composition of parliament. Nevertheless, it is probably accurate to say that the persistence of royal absolutism in Germany and Austria did contribute to the authoritarian outcome in those countries.

Another explanation for why some countries' development culminated in authoritarianism in the interwar period is provided in recent work by Kurth (1979). Developing the line of thought of O'Donnell on bureaucratic authoritarianism in Latin America and Gerschenkron (1962) on European industrialization,[2] he argues that the timing of industrialization and the movement through various industrial phases (from light consumer goods to capital goods to consumer durables) relative to other countries influenced the political development of Europe over the last century and a half. Industrialization in early industrializers, such as Britain, France, and Belgium, was propelled by the light consumer goods industries, especially textiles. The relatively small amount of capital required for the development of these industries facilitated industrialization without dependence on the state. As a later industrializer, German industrialization was dependent on the state, first in the form of protection, and later aid in mobilizing capital in the capital goods phase, which tied the German bourgeoisie to the state and strengthened the authoritarian Junker–crown alliance. A similar situation prevailed in Austria. The entry into the capital goods phase, in which the development of the steel industry played a key role, further reinforced this pattern. The capital required (which was relatively high in this case) was mobilized from the profitable and internationally competitive light consumer goods industry in the early industrializers whereas this was not possible in the later industrializers which turned to the state for this task.

Kurth argues that it is in the saturation phase of the steel industry where the link between the timing and phasing of industrialization and the development of modern (i.e. twentieth-century) authoritarianism is most clear. Initially, the vast majority of steel output was absorbed by railroad construction. Once the domestic market for rails was exhausted, steel producers turned to other countries and overseas colonies and to armaments. Germany, with few colonies and with overseas markets pre-empted by the British, had to rely more heavily on the latter. The loss of colonies as a result of World War I exacerbated the situation and, not surprisingly, the steel industrialists favored rearmament and rejection of the Versailles Treaty and were strong supporters of the reactionary German National People's Party (DNVP) and authoritarian "solutions" throughout the Weimar Republic.

As for the "late-late" industrializers of Latin Europe, Kurth suggests that there was a link between the trasformismo/el turno politics of the late nineteenth and early twentieth century and the industrial phase at the time. The uncompetitiveness of both industry and agriculture was reflected in protection of both sectors and in a merging of interests of land and industry which was in turn reflected in the political arrangements of trasformismo/el turno. Both involved, among other things, an accommodation of interests of segments of the economic elite through bargaining and clientelistic ties. Thus, Kurth's argument suggests a different economic basis for the development of the land-owner–bourgeois coalition in Latin Europe than in Central Europe.

Though Kurth's work may be seen as complementary to Barrington Moore's argument rather than an alternative to it, there is one critical difference:

Moore's view suggests that the source of the anti-democratic posture of the bourgeoisie in the authoritarian cases is its dependence on the aristocratic dominated state, whereas Kurth suggests that there was a basis for this posture in the economic situation of the class or segments of it. Thus, political (and ideological-cultural) subordination of the bourgeoisie to the agrarian elite is not a necessary feature of his argument.[3]

To briefly foreshadow our conclusions, we will underline the role of the organized working class in the final push for democracy, but will demonstrate that, not only did the working class need allies in other classes in this final push, other social classes were, in many cases, more important in earlier extensions of suffrage and/or struggles for parliamentary government. One can account for the variation in such class coalitions in the push for democracy and the causes of the interwar breakdowns by examining the dominant class–state coalitions of the late nineteenth century. The existence of a large landed class created a set of alliance possibilities for other classes which impeded the development of democracy in the first place and, once democracy was established, facilitated its eclipse by authoritarian forces. The course of domestic events took place in the context of, and was heavily influenced by, transnational structures of power, which had its most dramatic impact in the form of wars and depressions.

The Transition to Democracy in Europe: The Democratic Cases

In 1870, only one country in Europe was democratic by the criteria laid out above. By 1920, the overwhelming majority were. Two decades later democratic rule had been eclipsed in a number of these countries. Let us now look more closely at the processes which brought democracy to these countries and at the factors which separated the democratic survivors from the cases of breakdown in the interwar period. Moore's analysis focuses heavily on the type of agricultural arrangements and labor force control adopted by the landed aristocracy. Had Moore included the smaller European countries, his focus would certainly have begun with the existence of (or absence thereof) a politically powerful landlord class. This, in turn, is largely a product of the pattern of concentration of landholding itself: in all of the small countries, there were too few large estates to support the development of a politically significant class of landholders. This one factor prevents the development of the class coalition which is fatal for democracy. And in fact, the correlation between strength of large landlords and the survival or breakdown of democracy in the interwar period as shown in table 4.1 indicates that this one factor provides a powerful explanation for the survival or demise of democracy.[4] It should be noted that large landholding may not be "dominant" in a statistical sense. In Germany, the west and south, a majority of the country in land area, was dominated by small farming, as was the north of Italy outside of the Po Valley. Spain and Austria–Hungary also contained regions in which small holding was

TABLE 4.1   Agrarian elite strength and political outcomes in Europe

	Strength of agrarian elite in late nineteenth century	
	Weak	Strong
Democracy survives in interwar period	Sweden Denmark Norway Switzerland Belgium Netherlands France	Britain
Authoritarian regime established		Austria–Hungary Spain Italy Germany

dominant. The critical factor here is that in all of these countries there were a sufficient number of large estates to give rise to the formation of a politically powerful landed elite. In all of the small countries, on the other hand, small to moderate holding was the overwhelmingly dominant form of land tenure in the entire country and no large agrarian elite existed.

A few points on the strength of the agrarian elites indicated in table 4.1 are in order before we proceed. Historically, the French agrarian elite was also very powerful, but the revolution broke its power. By the late nineteenth century, the French countryside was dominated by small peasants and the landed upper-classes no longer constituted the powerful political actor they had been a century earlier. Thus, the revolutionary break from the past which Moore hypothesizes as a necessary feature for democratic development was essential in the French case. However, as Katzenstein (1985) points out, most of the small states in Europe did not experience a revolutionary break and none the less developed in a democratic direction. Again, Moore's analysis is flawed by the exclusion of the small states. The virtually perfect correlation between country size and landlord strength is no accident. As Tilly (1975: 40–4) points out, military success was one factor which distinguished the successful state consolidation from the unsuccessful attempts and success in war was greatly facilitated by "strong coalitions between the central power and major segments of the landed elite." The small states only avoided being gobbled up by reason of geography (Scandinavia), the operation of the interstate system from the Treaty of Westphalia onwards (especially Belgium and Netherlands),[5] or both (Switzerland).

Britain stands out as a deviant case in terms of landholding, and resort to Moore's emphasis on the type of commercialized agriculture as an explanatory factor is necessary to bring this case into line. And indeed it is also accurate to classify the three authoritarian cases not discussed by Moore (Italy, Spain, and Austria–Hungary) as cases of dominance of "labor repressive" agriculture. That is, in these three countries, historically agriculture was labor intensive and landlords relied on non-market "political" mechanisms to assure themselves of an adequate supply of cheap labor. In contrast, British landlords turned to sheep raising, and, from the enclosure movement on, could rely on market mechanisms to supply the necessary labor (e.g. see Brenner 1976, 1977). Still, while the correlation presented here is suggestive of the causes of breakdown, we must examine the individual cases to uncover what social forces actually brought in democracy and what forces and dynamics appear to explain the relationship between landed class strength and breakdown.

By the eve of World War I, a handful of countries had become democratic: Switzerland (1848) was the trailblazer follwed by France (1877) and Norway (1898). In 1915, Denmark joined this group.[6] These are all nations of smallholders, urban petty bourgeoisie, and with a significant though not nearly dominant industrial sector (and therefore significant working and capitalist classes) at the time of democratization.

The first breakthrough to democracy came in Switzerland. The most clearly identifiable date for the achievement of full democracy is the adoption of the constitution of 1848. This constitution instituted representative government and male suffrage at the federal level.[7] However, in Switzerland, power was very decentralized, cantonal level development was very important, and the constitution of 1848 essentially ratified what had already become a reality in many cantons. The political structures of the so-called Restauration, imposed under the influence of the Congress of Vienna, already came under attack in the 1820s. By 1831, eleven cantons had adopted liberal constitutions (Gitermann 1941: 447). The defeat of the conservative Catholic cantons in the Sonderbund war of 1847 eliminated the last powerful pockets of resistance.

The roots of Swiss democracy reach relatively far back and are grounded in Swiss social structure. From the origin of the Swiss confederation in 1291, Swiss history is punctuated with successful intervention of family farmers in political developments. As we will see repeatedly in this chapter, such autonomous and successful intervention on the part of small farmers only occurs in countries without a powerful landed upper class and it is certainly this characteristic of the social structure of the Swiss countryside that was responsible for early political influence of farmers. Swiss cities were primarily trading centers, and exchange and artisanal production were organized in strong exclusive guilds controlled by the elites in each profession. The city economies were, thus, "feudalistic" if one can use that word for a country without significant serfdom and manor production. Under the political arrangements of 1815, the cities were privileged vis-à-vis the countryside. The politically dominant groups under this system were the guild masters and merchants in most cantons, together with patrician families in some cantons, notably Bern.

Switzerland was an early industrializer and industry, primarily textiles and watches up to the period in question, developed without state aid. Because they depended on water power, most factories did not grow up in the cities but rather were located in the countryside. In this same period agriculture also underwent significant improvements in productivity (Andrey 1983: 191–9). These economic developments generated a wide array of groups with an interest in the promotion of commerce and thus in the abolition of restrictions on inter-cantonal trade and of guild restrictions which in turn required a more centralized national state. These groups joined together in what Gruner (1977: 73–89) calls the "Freisinnige Grossfamilie," i.e. the extended family of Liberals. Originally they included the entire array of the social structure, from industrial entrepreneurs, professionals, intellectuals, and artisans to farmers and workers. Given that the beneficiaries of the traditional restrictions also held political power, the Liberal program called for extension of suffrage and representative and open government (Gitermann 1941: 441).

The Liberals did not become a real national party until 1858, and particularly in this initial period of development, the Liberal program was carried forth by a multitude of associations in the increasingly dense Swiss civil society. As Gruner (1977: 81) points out, these included "public interest and church-related, literary and professional associations, such as students', artisans' and workers' associations, and last but not least organizations devoted to the promotion of social life (gesellige Organisationen), such as rifle clubs, choral societies, and athletic clubs". The Liberal movement came to span not just all social strata but also all denominations, languages, and regions. What glued it together was the commitment to a national democratic state, an integrated national market, and anti-clericalism.

It was the anti-clerical component of the program which galvanized the conservative opposition. It should be underlined that this conservative opposition did not oppose democracy; on the contrary, they sought to extend it and mobilize their followers against the Liberals. Initially, conservative opposition came from Protestant as well as Catholic quarters. For instance, in the "Züri-Putsch" of 1839 deeply religious Protestant farmers overthrew the liberal government, demanding for instance guarantees for religious instruction in schools and the introduction of direct elections and of the popular referendum (Gitermann 1941: 458–460). However, the move of conservative Catholics to clericalization in the cantons where they were dominant, namely in central Switzerland, Freiburg and Wallis, led to their isolation and defeat in the Sonderbund war. This defeat then led to the establishment of the new democratic national state and the consolidation of liberal hegemony.

After the initial victories of the liberal democratic movement the clerical issue came to overshadow all the others; in particular, democracy in the sense of political inclusion was not controversial. The divisive political issue, bound up with the clerical question, was the degree of cantonal autonomy vis-à-vis the central government. It is worth emphasizing how limited the opposition to political democracy per se was; only the narrow stratum of beneficiaries of the Restauration system, the guild masters and local patricians, were real opponents. As we shall see, Switzerland is unusual in that the industrial bourgeoisie joined other groups in support of not only economic liberalism but also full democracy. There appear to be three primary reasons for this posture. First, as in other countries, the bourgeoisie shared an interest with other groups in the liberal movement in sweeping away the restrictions on economic activity. Second, since industry was largely located in rural areas, the bourgeoisie belonged to those politically disadvantaged by the dominant position of the towns under the Restauration political arrangements. Finally, the Swiss bourgeoisie in this period faced not only no socialist labor movement, which would not develop for decades, but no industrial labor organization whatsoever. Moreover, there was no world historical precedent of threat to bourgeois interests from organized industrial labor, as this was before the development of Chartism. As we emphasized, the liberal extended family in this period was a multi-class movement, ranging from the bourgeoisie to artisans and workers. In the four decades after the adoption of the 1848 constitution this movement underwent significant internal strain and finally broke apart into separate parties along class lines. Already in the 1850s the faction dominated by railroad and banking interests came under attack from the left wing of the liberal movement for abusing the system of representative democracy, and this stimulated the movement for an expansion of direct democracy (Gitermann 1941: 509–17). The Swiss case clearly demonstrates the importance of small-holding patterns for autonomous political action of small farmers. Regardless of their religious affiliation and their alignment on the clerical issue, the farmers in this period, sometimes through armed struggle, acted as a democratic force.

We take up the story of the transition to democracy in France where Moore ends it, with the French Revolution. Moore (1966: 106, 109) argues that the outcome of the French Revolution was decisive for the development of democracy in France because it destroyed the seigneurial system and the political power of the landed aristocracy. He then correctly notes that the Restoration returned political power to this class, but since it did not move to share it with the upper bourgeoisie, its period in power was necessarily limited. The Revolution of 1830 then finished the work of the Great Revolution and the "old aristocracy disappeared from the political arena as a coherent and effective political group" (Moore 1966: 106).

In its broad outlines, Moore's analysis is correct, but it exaggerates the demise of the political power of the nobility in this period. Since the political role of large landlords is of some importance for the analysis of the development of democracy throughout this book, it is worth examining in a little more detail what impact the French Revolution did have on the subsequent development of democracy in that country. First, it should be noted that, due to developments before the Revolution, peasant property was widespread, if insecure, before that event. The redistribution of noble land effected by the Revolution was not great; emigré nobles were expropriated and thus the total amount of French land owned by the nobility dropped from one-quarter to one-fifth (Magraw 1983: 24–5). One must add to this the church lands expropriated in 1790 and sold to the highest bidder. Naturally most of this land went to the wealthy bourgeoisie and not to peasants, but there is no question that many peasants did benefit from the land reform. More important for the peasantry was the guaranteeing of property rights and thus the securing of peasant property and the abolition of seigneurial rights. As late as the 1870s, Republican politicians used the threat that seigneurial rights would be reimposed as a potent political weapon to woo the peasantry (Elwitt 1975: 76). The abolition of seigneurial rights also meant that landlords who wanted to make a living from the land would have to turn to commercial market agriculture. As transportation improved throughout the century, especially with the advent of railroads, this was even more emphatically so.

Following de Tocqueville, Skocpol (1979: esp. 202–5) emphasizes that the Revolution and the Napoleonic reforms further centralized the state apparatus. For the development of democracy, this precluded the development of intermediate forms of restricted democracy in which full democracy prevailed in one part of the country but not in another as in the United States from the Jacksonian period to the 1960s (see pp. 122–32 below). The centralization of the French state meant that social transformation initiated in the cities often outstripped what would be sustained by the countryside and thus was subject to subsequent roll-back resulting in a pattern of democratic breakthrough and reaction. Such a pattern could already be seen in the Revolution itself. A second result of the centralized state which was more unambiguously negative for the development of democracy was that the central government's control over the prefects meant that it could, and well into the Third Republic did, use its power to staff the state apparatus with its own supporters and then to use them to mobilize voters, particularly state employees, to support the government in elections and to harrass the opposition.

Finally, the Revolution dislodged the aristocracy from its privileged position in the army and bureaucracy. In this case, in contrast to the property settlement, the Restoration temporarily rolled back this achievement of the revolution. However, this reversal was short lived.

The Restoration regime attempted to base its rule very narrowly on the nobility and this virtually insured its downfall. This is exemplified by the 1830 suffrage law which would have eliminated all but the richest landowners from the electorate. It was this law that sparked the three days of street fighting in Paris that resulted in the downfall of the Bourbon monarchy and the Restoration regime. The upper bourgeoisie, particularly those sectors based in Paris and in finance, and not the artisans that did the street fighting, was the primary beneficiary of the Orleanist July Monarchy that was subsequently installed. The suffrage law enacted, though considerably broader than the Restoration franchise, ensured that this would be so. It enfranchised males paying 200 francs or more in direct taxes and thus gave 1 in 170 inhabitants the right to vote, which was considerably more restrictive than Britain after the reform of 1832 (Magraw 1983: 48–9, 68). The main contribution of the July Monarchy to the subsequent development of democracy was the complete reversal of the Bourbons' attempt to restore the aristocracy to its pre-Revolutionary position in the army and bureaucracy.

The class alignments in subsequent events follow a general pattern. The core of the urban working class was discontented artisans whose conditions of work were undergoing a progressive transformation due to the character of French industrialization. Combining and transforming elements of their Old Regime corporatism, Revolutionary ideas about citizenship and political change, and various currents of French socialism, by 1848, this dominant faction of the working-class came to articulate an ideology of republican socialism which combined demands for democratic government with those for social and economic reform (Sewell 1986; Aminzade 1981). On the opposite side of the spectrum was the Legitimist aristocracy who favored a restoration of the Bourbon monarchy. The elite segment opposed to the Legitimists was the Orleanists, which combined some landlords, upper bourgeoisie of Paris, the financial sector, and increasingly the railroads. Both of these groups opposed suffrage extension and social reform but differed on clerical issues, which was in part an economic issue since many Orleanists had been the beneficiaries of the sale of church lands. The provincial bourgeoisie, professionals, and the petty bourgeoisie stood in between, favoring the extension of suffrage but fearing the prospect of extending democratic revolution to social revolution that might endanger property rights. The political posture of the peasantry defies easy generalization because it varied according to pre-Revolutionary traditions, varying experiences with the Revolution, variations in production relations across regions, and variations in the degree of modernization across regions. Perhaps the widest points of agreement among various factions of the peasantry were the desire to protect the property settlement of the Revolution and to advance the immediate economic interests of rural small producers. For the modal (and politically pivotal) peasant, the political form in which this was done was secondary. The social and political factions which managed to mobilize the peasantry proved to be the arbiter of the events of 1847–52 and 1868–77, the two critical periods for the development of French democracy.

On the heels of bad harvests, which had increased discontent in the countryside, various political factions, based primarily in the the middle classes, began a campaign for broadening of suffrage in 1847. The government's cancellation of a political banquet supporting this campaign in Paris in February set off a chain of events which led to a working-class revolt and culminated in the declaration of a republic by a provisional government. The provisional government called for elections with universal male suffrage to be held in April. In part because of the provisional government's land tax which fell on the backs of the peasants but primarily because of the lack of any political organization, local notables dominated the electoral process and the elections produced an overwhelming conservative victory. The subsequent changes in government composition led to the reversal of earlier social legislation and ultimately sparked the revolt of the Parisian working class in June.

The defeat of the working-class rebellion and the victory of Louis Napoleon in the presidential election of December seemed to confirm that not only did the French not favor the "democratic and social republic" favored by the working-class activists, but they also did not even favor a democratic republic at all. However, in the wake of the repression of the working-class revolt, leaders of the radical republicans and socialists regrouped and fashioned a democratic platform whose additional social content could appeal to both workers and peasants, as it guaranteed private property, called for free compulsory secular education and the right to work, and focused on big capital as the enemy.

Under the leadership of professionals, teachers, and segments of the petty bourgeoisie, this "democratic socialist" alliance organized a successful campaign which gained the support of the urban petty bourgeoisie, professionals, artisans, as well as the peasantry in regions that later elections proved to be consistent areas of peasant support for the left (Price 1972: 201–4, 228–45). Though the 35 percent of the vote reached in the May 1849 election fell far short of victory, it gratified the left and deeply alarmed the right. The left's subsequent victory in 21 of 30 by-elections led directly to a law in 1850 which reduced the electorate by 30 per cent and to rightist support for or acquiescence to the coup of Louis Napoleon of December 1851.

After the prosperity of the 1850s gave way to the more difficult times of the 1860s and after the Emperor suffered a series of diplomatic setbacks, the regime liberalized in order to shore up domestic support. With this new space for political organization, the opposition managed to poll 40 percent in the elections of 1869. Bonaparte's final diplomatic setback, blundering into the war with Prussia and the defeat of the army under his generalship at Sedan, led directly to the proclaiming of the Third Republic. Again the attempt of the urban working-class to give the republic a social content was met with repression and the first elections resulted in a victory for the right. Arguably only the inability of the Orleanists and Legitimists to arrive at a political compromise prevented a restoration of the monarchy, though in a constitutionally restricted form, at this point. The Republicans used the democratic opening to vigorously organize and overwhelmed all other groups in the 1876 elections. In the following year, the President of the Republic, General McMahon, having refused to appoint Gambetta, the leading Republican, as Prime Minister, now used a pretext to dissolve parliament and call new elections. The Republicans emerged victorious despite the President's use of the full range of his powers over the bureaucracy to secure their defeat. Thus, 1877 marks the definite establishment of cabinet responsibility to a parliament elected by universal male suffrage.[8]

Why did the Republicans succeed in establishing democracy in 1877 and not in 1849? They were, of course, a minority at the earlier date but subsequent elections, had they been held, might have changed that. The key is the nature of the class coalition they were able to put together. Leadership of the republican and democratic movement from the late July Monarchy to the Third Republic had progressively shifted from the alliance of politically active artisans and the urban middle classes to an alliance of the politically active urban middle classes and the provincial bourgeoisie. Accompanying this shift was a shift away from the demand for a "democratic and social republic" to a democratic republic without the accompanying social legislation and with a stronger emphasis on the right to private property (Elwitt 1975; Aminzade forthcoming). True, the attack on big capital, finance and the railroads was retained, but the only thing left for urban workers was the promise of compulsory secular primary education. Since the working class really had no place else to go, this not only broadened the coalition, it also facilitated an accommodation with the upper bourgeoisie and landed upper class.

A second feature that distinguishes 1849 from 1877 is the improvements in the means of transportation and communication even in this short period of time. A prime task of the Republicans was to penetrate the countryside in this largely peasant society and counter the influence of traditional local notables on the consciousness and voting behavior of the peasantry. Of course, the Republicans of 1877 could build on the successes of 1849, but when one compares accounts of the 1849 campaign (e. g. Price 1972) with those of 1877 (e. g. Elwitt 1975), one cannot help but be impressed by how much this process of penetration into previously backward regions was facilitated by extension of rails, roads, newspapers, and so on.

In the two Scandinavian countries, the working class organized in unions and political parties played some role in the drive for democracy. In the case of Norway, the working class contributed to the final push for universal suffrage (embodied in various laws passed between 1898 and 1913), though earlier suffrage extensions were largely the work of the peasantry, with the help of sections of the urban middle class (Rokkan 1966; Derry 1973). In Denmark, an alliance of the working class, small and medium farmer, and urban middle class segments as represented by the Social Democratic–Venstre coalition pressed through the 1901 introduction of parliamentary government. The driving force behind the 1915 introduction of universal suffrage were the Social Democrats and the Radikale Venstre, representing the working class, small farmers, and segments of the middle class (Miller 1968; Dybahl 1969; Christiansen 1988). It is important to note here that in Denmark and Norway (as well as Sweden), the medium farmers were ambivalent about the final suffrage extensions which resulted in the inclusion of large minorities of working-class voters not previously included, and it was among segments of the urban middle classes and the small farmers and tenants that labor found its ally. So to argue that the effect of landholding patterns on political outcomes was caused simply by the authoritarian posture of large landlords and democratic posture of small holders is inaccurate. At the same time, it is important to note that the Scandinavian peasantry was divided and even the medium and larger farmers, though not supportive of the final push to universal suffrage, generally contributed to the process of democratization by supporting earlier suffrage extensions.

In the rest of Europe, but particularly among the antagonists in World War I, the social dislocations caused by the war contributed to the breakthrough of democracy. The war and its outcome changed the balance of power in society, strengthening the working class and weakening the upper classes. The ruling class was discredited, particularly in the defeated countries. Labor support was necessary, at home for the production effort, on the front for the first mass mobilization, mass conscription war of this scale and duration. And, finally, the war economy and mass conscription strengthened the hand of labor in the economy, enabling it to extract concessions for the coming period of peace.[9] One indicator of the change in class power was the swell in labor organization from an average prewar level of 9 percent of the labor force to a post war peak of 30 percent in the antagonists, which experienced the transition to democracy in this period (1918 or 1919). Organization more than doubled in the two nonparticipants (Sweden and the Netherlands) which experienced the same transition at this time (Stephens 1979c: 115). In all these countries the working class played a key, usually the key, role in the transition to democracy. But, as Therborn (1977) notes, the working-class was not strong enough alone. It needed allies or unusual conjunctures of events to effect the introduction of democracy. As an indicator of this it could be pointed out that in no case did the working-class parties receive electoral majorities even after the introduction of universal suffrage.

In Britain, Sweden, Belgium, and the Netherlands, it can be argued that the war only accelerated the introduction of democracy. In each country, the prodemocratic coalition at the party level and the underlying alignment of social forces had formed or was in the process of formation. In most cases, the coalition had been responsible for previous suffrage extension, such as the 1907 reform in Sweden or the 1893 reform in Belgium.

In Sweden (as well as in Belgium and the Netherlands), the agrarian elites were too weak to be a significant political force.[10] The Swedish case merits special attention because, of all of the small European countries, Sweden shared the most characteristics with the countries (particularly Germany) which developed in an authoritarian direction. From its period as a great power, Sweden had a heritage of absolutist government. It developed a highly status-conscious nobility which dominated the officers' corps and the upper ranks of the bureaucracy. In the nineteenth and early twentieth century, this class and the royal family looked to Prussia and then imperial Germany for its models in social organization and culture. Indeed, this was still true after World War I, as the king was known to be sympathetic to Nazi Germany.

Sweden was also a late industrializer and the industrial structure was characterized by a high degree of concentration, and thus, as Ingham (1974) argues, a highly solidaristic and aggressive employers association. And, like its German counterpart, Swedish business carried out an extremely militant and organized fight against unionization up to World War I. Like Germany, and unlike Britain, Sweden also had a strong labor movement which was committed to socialism, the existence of which was certainly perceived as a threat by the bourgeoisie, thus stiffening its resistance to political incorporation of the working-class. By World War I, virtually the entire Swedish bourgeoisie had shifted into the Conservative Party, the most anti-democratic of the Swedish parties. Indeed, in the spring of 1914, after a bitter conflict over constitutional government, the king appointed a royal cabinet that contained many of the leading figures of Swedish industry (Söderpalm 1969: 24). Finally, as in the four authoritarian cases, the last decades of the last century witnessed the introduction of tariffs on agricultural and industrial imports, thus bringing the political interests of industrialists and the agricultural sector closer together.

However, Sweden was critically different from Germany in that it did not have a powerful landed upper class. As early as the fifteenth century, the independent peasantry owned half of the land in the country and, as both Tilton (1974) and Castles (1973) point out, the crown often played this class off against the nobility in order to reduce the latter's power. It was with such an alliance that Charles XI effected the Great Reduction in the seventeenth century, which halved the land holdings of the nobility. By the nineteenth century the Swedish nobility was a "bureaucratic aristocracy" dominated by noble government officials and military officers (Rustow 1955: 16). The converse side of this was that the independent peasantry enjoyed political rights in the old regime unparalleled in the absolutist regimes on the continent. Indeed, the parliamentary structure prior to the introduction of the bourgeois reform of 1866 provided for a peasant estate in addition to that of the nobility, clergy, and burgers.[11]

The independent peasantry played an important role in the introduction of democracy in Sweden. In Sweden, as in Norway and Denmark, it was split on the question of universal suffrage. It was the Liberals, who were based in the urban middle classes, dissenting religions and in small farmers in the north and west, who joined the Social Democrats in the push for suffrage extension. Several decades of political pressure (through strikes, demonstrations, parliamentary obstruction) by the Social Democrats and the trade unions in co-operation with segments of the Liberals resulted in the introduction of male suffrage, but not parliamentary government, in 1907.

Thus, though the Swedish bourgeoisie and the Conservatives were politically and culturally similar to their counterparts in Germany, the Swedish bourgeoisie did not have the option of allying with an agrarian upper class with an electoral base in the countryside. It was relatively isolated and resistance to democratic reform was a less realistic option. The Conservatives did stall further reform until the fall of 1918 when the German defeat in the war stimulated their capitulation. Then, as a consequence of their political isolation, they agreed to a compromise in which they consented to the introduction of universal suffrage and parliamentary cabinet government and received only preservation of the monarchy in return.

As Stråth (1988) argues, the changing class alliances in the process of democratization and the development of Swedish civil society and the transformation of its internal character in the course of the nineteenth and early twentieth century were closely interrelated processes. The 1809 constitutional reforms which introduced some protection of civil rights opened up a sphere for the development of civil society, which grew with the formation of various private associations, such as study circles and lending libraries, and the expansion of book, journal, and newspaper publishing. These groups and print media propagated liberal ideas (abolition of the estate parliament and suffrage based on property holding; free trade, press and religion) and this contributed to a movement for political reform supported by non-noble ironworks owners, wholesalers, non-noble landed proprietors, and prosperous farmers. The reform of 1866 represented the fulfillment of the program of these early nineteenth-century bourgeois Liberals. After the reform, they gradually allied with their old conservative opponents, who were based in the aristocracy, bureaucracy, and Lutheran state church clergy, to form the basis for a new conservatism.

The accelerating industrialism of the late nineteenth century led to the transformation of civil society due to the development of the "popular movements" (folkrörelser), the temperance movement, the free churches, and the labor movement (which, at this point in time, included the co-operatives as well as the trade unions and social democratic party). These movements were based in the working class and the middle classes, both rural and urban. Stråth (1988: 33) estimates that one-third of the population were members of the popular movements. They developed a whole array of associated organizations including vigorous programs of adult education. Elementary school teachers were deeply involved in the movements. The penetration of these movements into the middle classes prevented the development of a Bildungsbürgertum along German lines which would have brought the middle classes under the ideological hegemony of the upper classes. On the contrary, while the different popular movements varied in ideological orientation, they shared a puritanical bent and a commitment to egalitarianism; thus, the middle and working classes shared elements of a counter-hegemonic ideology which was democratic and anti-elitist in content. It was precisely the social forces organized by these movements which were the bases of the Social Democratic–Liberal political coalition which brought through democracy.

At some points, Stråth suggests that the contrasting development of civil society in nineteenth-century Germany and Sweden was rooted in the differing class structures without, however, developing the point. The difference was in the middle-class elements of the popular movements. Citing the examples of Scandinavia and the North and West of the United States, Rokkan has observed that strong temperance movements only develop in Protestant small-holding societies[12] and are presumably another manifestation of the tendency to rural self-organization in these societies. Dissenting protestant sects also find fertile grounds in such societies. Though the case of England shows that Protestant sects can develop elsewhere, certainly their strength in Scandinavia as compared to Germany is in part due to the rural social structure. The Lutheran and Anglican churches were important conduits of ruling-class hegemony, and escaping their hold either into the Protestant sects or into the secularism of the labor movement represented an important step in preparing the ground for the development of a democratic counter-hegemony.

Tilton (1974: 568) contends that insufficient repressive capacity in general, and the absence of a standing professional army in particular, also played a role in the calculations of the conservatives at the point of their final capitulation. Interestingly, the weakness of the repressive apparatus, in turn, can, in part, be attributed to the influence of the landowning peasantry in the late nineteenth and early twentieth century, as they used their influence in the lower house to resist appropriations for defence and called for a reorganization of defence, since the defence system was sustained largely by taxes and other obligations which fell on their backs (Rustow 1955: 26–8; Verney 1957: 100–3). The farmers' resistance to defence expenditure eventually effected a transformation to a conscript army. It is important to note that it is was primarily the questionable loyalty of the troops rather than the sheer size of the coercive forces that was the conservatives' primary concern. The Minister of War and the Minister of the Marine characterized the sentiments in the army and navy as "very revolutionary," which made a great impression at the time, immediately after the revolutions in Russia and Germany (Tilton 1974: 567–8).

In Belgium, the Workers' Party, after decades of struggle including six general strikes, found support in the social Christian wing of the Catholic party, which was based among working-class Catholics (Fitzmaurice 1983; Lorwin 1966; Therborn 1977: 12, 25). In the Netherlands, similar divisions in the religious parties and the Liberals produced alliance possibilities for the Social Democrats (Daalder 1966: 203–11). Analyzing the Dutch case in the light of the Moore thesis, Tumin (1978) makes a point which we have emphasized in the Scandinavian cases: the absence of a strong landed nobility allowed the Netherlands to develop in a democratic direction without experiencing a revolutionary break from the past. It is worth underlining that the accounts of the transition in both of the low countries make it clear that the growing importance of the working class in society created the pressures that moved these non-socialist parties toward a more democratic posture. In part, this pressure was transmitted by workers and artisans already mobilized by self-help societies and trade unions who joined these parties and, in part, the pressure was a result of the efforts of these parties to compete with the Social Democrats for the loyalties of unmobilized workers.

The British case is so singular in so many ways, both in terms of the antecedents of democracy and the process of democratization, that it is virtually impossible to decide which factor(s) was (were) the most important on the basis of comparative analysis. Various analysts have argued that it was the absence of labor repressive agriculture (Moore), the absence of a bureaucratic state and standing army (Skocpol), or the independence of the bourgeoisie due to the country's status as an early industrializer (Kurth), which separates Britain from Germany and the other authoritarian cases. To these, one might add one based on our interpretation of the relationship between development and democracy combined with Moore's arguments on the role of landlords and the elimination of the "peasant question" in Britain. Relative to the level of industrialization, and thus the configuration of the class structure, democracy came late to Britain. By the time of the first suffrage extensions to the working class in the late 1860s, less than one-fifth of the labor force was engaged in agriculture and over two-fifths were in mining, manufacturing, and construction (Mitchell 1978: 51–64). Almost no European countries reached such a labor force profile, and corresponding class structure, until after World War I or, in some cases, after World War II. Thus, when one compares Britain to other large landholding cases (the authoritarian cases) at this same period in time, one must keep in mind that the latter were much more agricultural and thus the landlords carried much more economic power and thus, potentially, political power, and the working class was a much less important potential force in the country.

The establishment view of suffrage extension in the British case argues that the "peculiarities of English history" (however specified) meant that segments of the British upper classes had settled into a pattern of peaceful political competition by the mid-nineteenth century and this competition extended to competition for working-class votes which resulted in the suffrage extensions of

1867 and 1884. Our comparative analysis of the transition to democracy suggests that in Britain this process in itself, if it were true, would be a peculiarity. In no other case did middle-class-based (and largely upper-class-led) parties unilaterally extend effective suffrage to substantial sections of the working class (except where suffrage was irrelevant for the actual governing of the country due to the lack of parliamentary government as in Germany, or due to electoral corruption as in Spain and Italy). At best, some sections of the middle classes (and in France, some segments of the bourgeoisie) allied with the working-class parties for such suffrage extensions. All cases where the working class was politically included without substantial pressure from the politically organized working class itself (Switzerland and to a lesser extent Norway) were essentially agrarian democracies in which democracy was established before the working class had become a significant political actor.

On deeper examination the establishment view appears to be flawed. As Johnson (1976) argues in his critique of Moore's view of the British route, these reforms were in large part a response to working-class pressure beginning at least as early as the Chartist movement, whose main demand was universal suffrage, and extending throughout the nineteenth century. After forcefully suppressing the immediate threat represented by Chartism, the established parties, under the pressure of electoral competition, later responded to the working-class challenge with attempts to co-opt segments of the working class by politically incorporating them. Moreover, Harrison (1965) contends that, in the case of the 1867 reform the immediate agitation by the working-class political organizations, most notably the Reform League, beginning in 1864 and culminating in the Hyde Park demonstration of May 6, 1867, had a significant effect on the 1867 reform.[13] The British case bears some resemblance to the French case, as the transition to democracy was in part a delayed response to earlier working-class agitation which predated the formation of late nineteenth-century social democratic parties.

None the less it is a peculiarity that the final political initiation of the reforms came from upper-class led parties without a strong working-class base. Part of the explanation of this lies in the late development of the Labour Party itself.[14] The Liberals and the Tories were only willing to extend the right to vote to workers because they hoped to benefit from the votes of the newly enfranchised workers. Had a substantial Labour Party already commanded the loyalty of workers, the threat perceived by the elites certainly would have made the established parties more reluctant to make such a move.[15] This is most assuredly the case with the 1867 reform as Disraeli's primary reason to support reform was the expectation that the new voters, including the workers, would support the Tory Party and thus break the Whig–Liberal monopoly on power. By the time of the 1884 reform, working-class voters had lined up behind the Liberals; thus Gladstone could feel confident that his party would benefit from a further extension of suffrage (Wright 1970: 63, 92). If this argument is correct, it also suggests that the absence of a significant socialist working-class party in France in the late 1860s and 1870s may have contributed to the willingness of significant sections of the bourgeoisie to support parliamentary government based on universal male suffrage. The support of the Swiss industrial bourgeoisie for democracy, which occurred under conditions of little working-class organization, further reinforces this generalization.

And finally the reform of 1918, which established male suffrage and eliminated all but minor provisions for multiple voting, was the culmination of the Labour–Liberal co-operation that led to the rise of the Labour Party. No one would deny the important role of the working class in this reform. Rather, it is contended that the reform was of minor significance compared to the 1867 and 1884 reforms. Blewett's (1965) careful study demonstrates that this is a mistake. Though 88 percent of the adult male population would have qualified to vote in 1911 were it not for complications and limitations in the registration procedures which were biased against the working class, less than two-thirds were on the voting rolls. The importance of these restrictions can be seen from the fact that this figure rose to 95 percent after the 1918 reforms (Matthew et al. 1976: 731). Moreover, in 1911, half a million of the eight million voters were plural voters and needless to say not many of them were working-class. The final proof of the importance of the 1918 reform is Matthew, McKibbon, and Key's (1976) analysis which demonstrates that the reform was critical in allowing Labour to displace the Liberals as the second party in an essentially two-party system.

This survey leaves us with our breakdown countries as cases where the war may have influenced more than the timing of the introduction of democracy. But before moving on to them, let us take stock of what can be learned from the development of democracy in Europe as we have outlined it. One obvious lesson, stressed by Therborn (1977), is the important role played by the working-class, that is, by its organizational representatives, the trade unions and the socialist parties. For the Swiss, French, and British cases, one can add to that the role of artisan agitation and early craft unions and, in Britain, Chartism. Workers also played a role in the confessional parties in the Netherlands and Belgium in pressing those parties toward a more democratic posture. The rapid development of industrial capitalism in the latter half of the last century stimulated working-class organization which first gradually, and then with the war and its outcome, decisively changed the balance of class power in all these countries; indeed, it changed the balance of class power in the entire core of the world capitalist system. The change in the underlying class structure as indicated by labor force figures is significant enough: between 1870 and 1910, the non-agricultural workforce grew in these countries by one-third to one-half to an average of 61 percent .[16] The change at the level of class formation and class organization was even more significant: in no country in 1870 were the socialists a significant mass-based party and the trade unions organized a miniscule proportion of the labor force; by the eve of World War I, the parties affiliated with the Second International garnered an average of 26 percent of the vote (despite suffrage restrictions in a number of countries) and the trade unions organized an average of 11 percent of the non-agricultural labor force. In the immediate post war elections, the socialists' electoral share increased to an average of 32 percent , while trade union organization grew spectacularly, increasing two and half fold. The organized working class was also the most consistently prodemocratic force in the period under consideration: at the onset of World War I, European labor movements, all members of the Second International, had converged on an ideology which placed the achievement of universal suffrage and parliamentary government at the center of their immediate program (Zolberg 1986).

This interpretation supports our theory and turns Lipset (1960) and all the cross national studies which followed on their head; the working class, not the middle class, was the driving force behind democracy. It also contradicts Moore, most marxist analysts, and many liberal social scientists (e. g. Dahrendorf 1967) who argue that the primary source of democratic impulses was the bourgeoisie. However, Therborn's (1977) focus on the last reforms in the process of democratization leads to an exaggeration of the role of the working class. First, in the two agrarian democracy cases (Switzerland and Norway), the role of the working class was secondary even in the final push to democracy. Second, in other cases, not only did the working class need allies in the final push: in earlier democratic reforms, multi-class alliances were responsible for the success of the reform (France, Britain, Denmark, Sweden, and Belgium).

However, as will become apparent in our analysis of the authoritarian cases, none of these other social classes were as consistently pro-democratic, both across countries and through time, as the working class.[17] Both the urban middle class and/or segments of the peasantry provided the mass base for authoritarianism in the breakdown cases. The bourgeoisie whose role in the introduction of democracy has been emphasized in so many accounts, from marxist to liberal, played a positive role in only three cases, Switzerland, Britain, and France. Moreover, in Britain and France, it was only segments of the class that co-operated in the push for democracy, and then only after earlier histories of popular agitation for democracy and bourgeois resistance to it. In all of the others, the bourgeoisie was one of the centers of resistance to working-class political incorporation. It did make an indirect contribution to the outcome, however. In the cases discussed so far, the bourgeoisie sought entry into the corridors of power and in all cases, except for Denmark and Sweden, it supported the drive for parliamentary government. Bourgeois political forces established parliamentary government with property, tax, or income qualifications for voting – that is democracy for the propertied – a true "bourgeois democracy" in contrast to the bourgeois democracy of leninist marxism. This system then was opened up by successive organized groups demanding entry into the system: the peasantry, the middle class, and finally the working class. There is a certain amount of truth to the extremely crude interpretation that each group worked for its own incorporation and was ambivalent about further extensions of suffrage. The positive contributions of the bourgeoisie were to push for the introduction of parliamentary government and then to capitulate to pressures for further reforms rather than risk civil war.

Transition and Breakdown: The Authoritarian Cases

As we saw, the working-class needed allies; its power alone was insufficient. Here we can turn to the characteristics of the authoritarian path outlined earlier for the social and historical conditions which foreclosed or created the possibilities for alliances. In the cases of coalitions of the landed upper classes, the state and the bourgeoisie, no alliance strong enough to overcome their opposition could be constructed. It was only the change in the balance of class power caused by the war that allowed for the democratic breakthrough. But, as Maier (1975) argues in his study of Germany, France, and Italy, this surge in the strength of labor and the political left was quickly, though not completely, rolled backed. A quick glance at union membership and voting statistics indicates that this was a general European pattern. In the cases where this surge of working-class strength was the essential ingredient in the transition to democracy, the working class and its allies (where it had any) were unable to maintain democracy when a new conjuncture presented new problems (depression, worker and/or peasant militance, etc.) and new alliance possibilities for the upper classes moved the bourgeoisie, the landlords, and state actors from passive to active opposition to the democratic regime.

This still leaves us with something of a black box in terms of the mechanism by which the existence of a relatively strong class of landlords actually influenced the political structures and events of 1870 to 1939. One might first ask what difference it makes that landlords were an element of the ruling coalition (as opposed to a simple bourgeoisie–state alliance). Moore gives a straightforward answer to this question: the landlords, who had earlier cemented an alliance with the crown/state, exercised a political and ideological hegemony over the rising bourgeoisie, in which the latter accepted the ideological leadership of the landlords, in part as a result of state support for industrialization. The authoritarian politics of the agrarian elite were transmitted to the bourgeoisie. In tracing the state's motivation, one might hypothesize that, initially, the crown/state made the alliance with the landlords because, as Tilly points out, the alliance was militarily strong. This alliance was progressively strengthened as elements of the state apparatus (the military, bureaucracy, and the judiciary) were drawn from agrarian elites directly, or the occupants of these positions were absorbed through accretion, or both. All three groups then retained these authoritarian politics in the "democratic interlude." And, to the extent that the haute bourgeoisie was drawn into the authoritarian politics of the agrarian elites, it also came to participate in the social linkages to the state apparatus strengthening the anti-democratic posture of the state.

As pointed out earlier, Kurth argues that the bourgeoisie in some countries may have had autonomous reasons for adopting anti-democratic politics, and a similar line of argument has been advanced by a number of historians critical of the dominant view of German developments (see below). The main function of a strong agrarian elite in this perspective is to create an alliance option for the bourgeoisie to pursue such anti-democratic political impulses, an option not present in the small-holding countries.

This still leaves one with a problem for the democratic period, because even a highly cohesive upper-class alliance must reach beyond its ranks to influence the political developments in the era of mass politics. Drawing on recent neo-marxist theories of the state, one can identify three basic mechanisms which translate the power of landlords and the more general antidemocratic impulses of both segments of the upper classes into influences on the events of the democratic period (and the mass politics of the period immediately before World War I). The first is conscious agency or attempts at "instrumental" use of the state, such as funding authoritarian parties and movements, using political influence to obstruct democratic procedures, as well as utilization of kinship and other social links to influence state policy in an authoritarian direction. The second mechanism is what is referred to as structural determination. As Block (1977) points out, in a capitalist society, any government must ensure that the basic conditions for capital accumulation are met. The threat of investment slowdown and capital flight is a constraint on any government. Stated in terms of our problematic, governments which do not have the confidence of capitalists (and landlords) may find that declining investment, capital flight, and so on, add economic difficulties to their other difficulties resulting in a destabilization of the regime.

The third mechanism is through the effect of ideological hegemony as elaborated in chapter 3. Following Gramsci, it was argued that the dominant classes will meet with some success in their attempts to impose their world view on significant segments of the subordinate classes. To put this into the context of this chapter, it is our argument that the political posture of the urban middle classes and the peasantry was heavily influenced by the ruling-class coalition which led the political development of the country in question. Where the authoritarian upper-class coalition was well established, it affected not only the content of the ideology propagated by the ruling classes, that is, a particularly hierarchic, rabidly anti-democratic, anti-liberal set of values, but it also affected the extent to which the ruling ideology was accepted by the urban middle classes and, especially, the peasantry.

The concept of ideological hegemony can be fruitfully combined with traditional social scientific analyses of political mobilization in Europe (e.g. see especially Lipset and Rokkan 1967; Rokkan 1970) to give a more class-analytic content to the these authors' analysis. Such a combination yields the following insights in the case of the peasantry. Lipset and Rokkan (1967: especially 44–6) point out that, in Protestant small-holding countries (or regions of countries, e. g. Swiss cantons), the peasantry themselves were the agents of their own mobilization and the political forms were agrarian parties. In Protestant large-holding countries, the mobilizing agents were the landed upper-classes: thus the political weight of the peasantry strengthened that political block. In Catholic countries (or areas of countries, e.g. southern Germany), the mobilizing agents were Catholic parties. To fully specify the ideological orientation of these Catholic parties, it is necessary to bring into our analysis both the posture of the state vis-à-vis the Catholic church in the Catholic countries and the size of the Catholic community in predominantly Protestant countries (see table 4.2). As one can see from the table, the central tendency is clear: as indicated above, the ideological posture of the parties does vary by the landholding structure and thus the role of large landholders in shaping the parties. Above all, in all countries with a significant landed elite, that class was a key force behind the party that mobilized significant sections of the peasantry. There are, of course, exceptions due to historic relations between church, landlords, and peasants in particular regions (especially within Spain and France); but the scheme presented in the table does offer a baseline that holds in most cases. A similar scheme could be presented for the urban middle class. This analysis underlines a point we made in chapter 3: the subjective interests of social classes are historic social contructions and cannot be read off of social structure in a one to one fashion. The contrast between the political postures of the German peasantry and the Scandinavian peasantry in the interwar period is a dramatic demonstration of this.

One caveat should be issued before closing: it is not our intention to attribute, directly or indirectly, all anti-democratic and reactionary impulses in peasant and middle-class politics to the ideological hegemony of the landlord–bourgeois–state coalition. This would be clearly wrong as the examples of the Lapua movement in Finland, Rexism in Belgium, and Action Française or Poujadism in France demonstrate. Moreover, mass support for Fascism or other forms of authoritarianism in the four breakdown cases cannot all be traced to that source. Rather we want to argue that the existence of a strong agrarian elite and allied bourgeoisie significantly increased the appeal of such reactionary ideologies in these other classes.

With this last mechanism in mind, the class alliance option argument can be restated: the existence of a strong class of large landholders with close ties to the state not only changed the alliance options of the bourgeoisie. Together these three groups exercised an ideological influence over segments of the middle class and the peasantry that also pushed these segments in an authoritarian direction or at least prevented them from allying with the working class in the push for democracy, thus reinforcing the viability of the authoritarian option for the bourgeoisie.

In clarifying the status of these three mechanisms, it is useful to draw on Stinchcombe's (1968) distinction between historical and constant causes. An historical cause is one which happens at a point (or in this case a period) of time in the past and then the pattern created reproduces itself without the recurrence of the original cause. So, for instance, the Kulturkampf in Germany as well as the Naval League and Agrarian League propaganda campaigns (see below) did not have to be carried on constantly for them to have an effect on the political attitudes of the peasantry and urban middle class a generation later. The instrumental and structural mechanisms are closer (though not identical) to a constant cause, which is a set of social relationships, activities, etc. that are constant from year to year and produce a constant effect. In the present analysis, we are concerned with institutional change rather than maintenance, but otherwise the argument is the same. The importance of this distinction for this analysis is that the mechanism of ideological hegemony need not have a

TABLE 4.2   Mobilizing agent of the European peasantry

		Strength of agrarian elite in late nineteenth century	
		Weak	Strong
Catholic	State allied with church	Belgium (Rightist but moderate Catholic party)	Austria (Rightist Catholic party)
	?[a]	Swiss Catholic cantons (Rightist but moderate Catholic party)	Spain (Rightist Catholic party)[b]
	Not allied with church	Northern Italy (Centrist Catholic party)	Southern Italy[b]
Protestant	Small or no Catholic minority	Scandinavia Swiss Protestant cantons (Centrist agrarian parties)	Eastern Germany Britain (Rightist Protestant parties)
	Significant Catholic minority	South and west Germany[b] Netherlands (Centrist Catholic parties and Protestant parties of the right and center)	

[a]The classification of Switzerland on this dimension is problematic since the central state clearly had no religious alignment, but the individual cantonal governments did. The Spanish case is problematic as the alliance of the crown and the state forces shifted during the nineteenth century from opposition to the church at the time of the Carlist Wars to alliance at the end of the century.

[b]These are deviant and/or problematic cases. The Protestant farmers of north-west Germany were mobilized, in part, by the Conservatives and the Agrarian League in imperial Germany and the DNVP in the Weimar Republic, all of which were dominated by the east Elbian large landlords, but particularistic and regional parties also gained support from these farmers. In southern Italy, landlords controlled the peasant vote and threw their support to the anti-clerical Liberals in the clientelistic log-rolling process characteristic of the period. In Spain, the party referred to is the CEDA, but much of the Carlist peasantry supported Basque regional parties and the southern agricultural workers and tenants supported the anarchists and socialists. The conspicuous absence of France from the table is due to the great regional variation in peasant politics due to variations in local modes of production, role of the clergy, and legacies of the revolution.

close relationship with the current economic and political strength of large landlords or the cohesion of the authoritarian coalition. Naturally, persistence of landlord power and/or the cohesion of the coalition will serve to maintain the ideological legacy of the past, but that legacy will not decline in a one-to-one relationship with the decline in landlord power or coalition cohesion.

Italy

As Lipset and Rokkan (1967) point out, the Italian state allied with the urban upper class in its drive to unify the country. This usually indicates a weak landed upper class, since European states generally chose to ally with landed interests if these were sufficiently strong. Yet Italy did contain significant large holding regions in the south and the Po Valley and the large estates in these areas were sufficiently numerous to sustain a very significant landed class. The deviation of Italy from the modal pattern is due to the fact that unification was spearheaded from the Piedmont, a small-holding region, as was most of the rest of the industrially advanced north. The south resisted incorporation into the new Italian state. But even after the incorporation of the south, it is clear that the landed upper class did not assume the political leadership of the country, thus Italy does not fit Moore's pattern of a landholder-dominated state in alliance with a dependent bourgeoisie.

Nevertheless, an alliance, or at least an accommodation, between the landed class, the bourgeoisie, and the state did develop in the period between unification and World War I. The first step in this direction was the development of trasformismo, a political barter system in which the main political and economic interests (i.e. land and industry) were accommodated through clientelistic exchanges, under first Depretis and then Giolitti (Seton-Watson 1967: 51–2, 91–7, 246–8). Second, the government attempted to encourage economic development through protection of industry, protecting agriculture as compensation. And finally, the government embarked on an armaments program which tied segments of industry to the government and a militaristic foreign policy. Lyttelton (1973: 11–12) observes:

> The political effects of the 1887 tariffs were extremely serious. The decision to create a national steel industry was defended by invoking the needs of national defence, and the new iron, steel and shipbuilding interests were heavily dependent on a lavish programme of battleship construction. The link between an uncompetitive heavy industry dependent on state contracts and the pursuit of an imperialist power policy, first forged between 1882 and 1887, was ominous for the future. The alliance between northern industrial interests and southern latifondisti brought into being by the tariff was a powerful obstacle to democratic development.

The parallels to the German tariffs of a decade earlier and subsequent developments in that country are obvious: the tariff barter brought heavy industry and agriculture into an alliance similar to the rye–iron alliance in

Germany, and the armaments program made heavy industry dependent on the state and an imperialistic policy. It is true, of course, that the landed classes never did assume a role of political leadership in Italy and thus the case differs from the coalition pattern outlined by Moore. Still, the 1887 tariffs were not an isolated instance. At the turn of the century Pelloux, the Prime Minister, made an explicit attempt to establish a heavy industry–agrarian coaltion in support of reactionary and repressive policies. Though this failed, part of the project of his successor, Giolitti, the dominant politician from the 1890s to the war, was to create links between the state and agricultural and industrial interests through protection, defense expenditure, labor peace, and economic nationalism.

In the Italian case, the working class played an important but not leading role in the introduction of democracy. Giolitti extended suffrage to all adult males in 1912 in an attempt to gain support for his government's Libyan venture.[18] Certainly one of the target groups for his co-optative efforts in this case were the Socialists and more generally the working class, because co-optation of the Socialists was a long-term project of Giolitti. However, the 1913 election was managed by Giolitti and his allies through corrupt practices and it is actually the 1919 election that marks the introduction of democracy in Italy. The mobilization of workers and peasants during the war and particularly in its wake did play an important role in this transition. This is reflected in the outcome of the 1919 election: the principal parties of these classes, the Socialists and the Catholic Populari, were the big victors, polling a slim majority of the vote together, 32 percent and 21 percent, respectively (Rokkan and Meyriat 1969: 228).

In accounting for the breakdown of Italian democracy, conscious attempts by the upper classes to influence events in an authoritarian direction were in fact very important. The post-war strike wave, factory occupations, peasant organizing, and victories by the Socialists in local council elections alarmed the bourgeoisie and the Po Valley landlords. Both groups began to fund the Fascists on a massive scale as the Fascists made violent attacks on peasant organizations, trade unions, socialist party offices and local councils controlled by the left the main focus of their activity. Increasingly, the Po Valley landholders not only provided money but actually participated in the movement whereas the bourgeoisie contributed money but not men. Moreover they used their influence to prevent any alternative to Fascist rule. As Seton-Watson (1967: 598) points out, "[b]y 1922 contributions from banks and industrial firms, particularly those of Milan, were flowing into the treasury of the Fascist party, and their representatives in Parliament were using all their influence to block an anti-fascist coalition."

Given that virtually all accounts of the development of Italian Fascism emphasize the penetration of the Po Valley as a crucial turning point in the strengthening and the transformation of the character of Fascism (e. g. see Seton-Watson 1967: 505–664; Lyttelton 1973: esp. chapter 3), it should be pointed out here that the size of landholdings in the Po Valley varied and that initially the Fascists got support from modest farmers who were dependent on wage labor as well as from large landholders. Once the Fascists had ousted the socialist and Catholic unions they were in a position to control the local labor market and dispense jobs and thus began to get support from agricultural workers, tenants, and small farmers. Nevertheless, as Cardoza's (1982; also see

Corner 1975) detailed study of the province of Bologna demonstrates, the large, commercially oriented, landlords were the most pivotal group in influencing the direction of events in the area. Their support for authoritarianism was clearly motivated by the threat to their control of labor represented by the tremendous thrust of union organization and socialist victories in municipal elections after the war.

Forces internal to the state, particularly the security forces, also contributed to the Fascist victory (Lyttelton 1973: 38–40; Tasca 1938: 97–123). Most army officers were sympathetic to the extreme nationalist organizations, and, at crucial points, such as the Fiume invasion and the March on Rome, the government was reluctant to order the army to act against the radical nationalists for fear that they would not obey. The police generally tolerated, often facilitated, and sometimes even participated in the violent attacks of the Fascists on the socialists, peasant organizations, and trade unions. Without such help from the security forces the tremendous growth of the movement in the critical winter–spring of 1920–1 would have been impossible. It is difficult to overestimate how important the posture of the coercive forces was in the Italian case: Italian Fascism was not a mass electoral movement; it came to power as a result of the use of private violence against its enemies, above all the socialists. This would have been impossible had the security forces not tolerated it.

Because the Fascists were never a mass electoral movement, upper-class ideological hegemony over other groups is less important in accounting for the outcome than in the German or Austrian cases. Moreover, the south was so underdeveloped and its civil society was so weak that no group exercised hegemony in the region; it was integrated into the country's politics through clientelistic/patronage type relations and overwhelmingly supported the more conservative factions of the Liberals who, we hasten to add, were not a pro-democratic force. In the North, the mass support for non-democratic solutions cannot be gauged by simply noting that Fascism had limited electoral support (the 1922 elections gave the Fascists only 32 of 530 seats). First, the Fascist movement was not identical to the party as it was in Germany; it had many supporters who voted for other parties. Second, the Liberals in Italy were not democrats. Farnetti (1978: 32) notes that, in part, "fascism was the outcome of the incapacity (or unwillingness) of liberalism to turn into liberal democracy based on universal suffrage and proportional representation." Thus, the Fascist vote hardly gauges the extent of anti-democratic sentiment. As to the sociological base of the support for Fascism, we have good evidence from a survey of 151,000 of the 217,000 members in October 1921 (Linz 1976: 61–62). Twelve percent of the members were landowners, 24 percent were farmworkers, 15 percent were industrial workers, and all of the rest were urban middle class. It is likely that the Fascist electorate had a similar social composition. The broader mass support for non-democratic solutions (represented by the more conservative Liberals and the Nationalists) was also drawn disproportionately from the urban middle and upper class and landowners.

To pose a counterfactual for this case, one might ask what the political situation in Italy would have looked like if there had been no large landholding class; if the countryside had been covered with small peasants. Comparative work on party support argues that these Catholic peasants would have supported the Populari, an essentially pro-democratic force, thus strengthening that party and greatly facilitating the formation of an anti-Fascist parliamentary coalition in 1921–22. Deprived of its Po Valley support, Fascism would have remained an urban, and much weaker, phenomenon.

Germany

Recent work on German history by Blackbourn and Eley (1984; also see Eley 1983) and Calleo (1978) attacks what they see as the dominant view in current historical thinking on German political development including that of Moore.[19] It is probably fair to say that few, Blackbourn, Eley, and Calleo included, would contest the assertion, common to the dominant view, that historically an alliance developed between the east Elbian landed upper class, the Junkers, and the Prussian state, and that the political leadership of unified Germany after 1870 depended on this alliance for its key political support. In the wake of the depression of 1873, the heavy industry segment of the bourgeoisie, particularly the coal and steel interests, joined the coalition, with the tariffs of 1879 and later the naval armaments program consolidating the coalition.

While the views of Blackbourn and Eley and Calleo are different on many points, they agree that the argument of the dominant view which locates the cause of German authoritarianism and imperialism in the political dominance of the Junkers and the politically dependent, indeed, "supine" posture of the bourgeoisie is flawed. Blackbourn and Eley argue that the bourgeoisie was clearly the socially and economically dominant class in Imperial Germany and that it was also politically very influential, if fragmented, and certainly did not accept the political leadership of the landed classes. Calleo (1978: 129ff) goes further with regard to the relative political roles of the Junkers and the bourgeoisie, asserting that while the Junkers had a veto power in Imperial German policy, big business was more influential in the overall formation of political and economic policy.

One key point in Blackbourn and Eley's analysis (Blackbourn and Eley 1984: 18–19; Eley 1984: 75–90) is consistent with our theory of democratic development and is strongly supported by the evidence presented here. They question the historical accuracy of the equation of the bourgeoisie with liberal politics and of liberal politics with support for democracy. They argue that not only in Germany, but also elsewhere in Europe, the Liberals not only found much of their leadership and support in other classes, they also did not enjoy the full support of the bourgeoisies. More important, the Liberals did not necessarily support the introduction of democracy, which Eley defines, following Therborn, the same way we do. It was the working class and middle strata that accomplished this task, they contend. They argue that the mistaken view that the Imperial German bourgeoisie had accepted the political leadership of the Junkers is based on the fact that the bourgeoisie did not support the introduction of political democracy and on the unwarranted assumption that it would have been in their economic interest to do so.

However, it does appear that all three authors agree that the German bourgeoisie as well as the middle classes were more anti-democratic than their counterparts elsewhere, and that that was at least part of the reason for the weakness of democratic impulses and the persistence of the authoritarian features of the Imperial German regime. At a party level, Blackbourn (1984: 284) notes that not only the National Liberals but also the left Liberals and the Catholic Zentrum opposed the introduction of equal, direct, and secret voting for the Prussian Landtag.[20] The analysis of the origins of German imperialism and authoritarianism by the authors differs somewhat. Calleo emphasizes above all the geo-political position of Germany but also its late industrialization and the accompanying high degrees of industrial concentration and its lack of a colonial empire. In an argument similar to Kurth's, he contends that this led the German bourgeoisie to support imperialism in an effort to secure foreign markets and military contracts. Here he leans heavily on the careful historical scholarship of Kehr (1973, originally published in 1930) on the Naval Laws of 1898 and 1900 who shows that the state (more specifically the Kaiser and Admiral Tirpitz) initiated the naval build-up. The program was enthusiastically supported by big business, who heavily funded the Naval League and other imperialistic associations aimed at influencing middle-class opinion. The political representatives of the Junkers, on the other hand, initially opposed the naval build-up. But he does not dismiss the role of the Junkers in sustaining German authoritarianism entirely, as he indicates that their presence tipped the balance of power in Germany toward the more reactionary, anti-labor, and protectionist heavy industry rather than the free trade oriented and more liberal light industry.

Eley (1984: 135, 147, 153–4) argues that the origins of Imperial Germany's authoritarianism lie in the combination of an aristocratic enclave in the state, the threat of a powerful socialist labor movement, and important economic and religious divisions in the bourgeoisie that prevented the presentation of a united political front. Additionally, the high degree of concentration in the German economy gave large employers a capacity for repression on the industrial front, which manifested itself in a largely successful anti-union drive, in the late Imperial period. This made compromise with labor a less necessary and attractive alternative (Eley 1984: 107). Eley (1984: 153–4) nicely sums up his view:

> ... the option of the German bourgeoisie's leading fractions for a politics of accommodation with the landowning interests after 1871 was fully compatible with the pursuit of bourgeois interests ... The bourgeoisie entered the agrarian alliance not from a lack of "political self-confidence", but as the best means of securing certain political goals. The indifference to further "parliamentarization" came less from any "pre-industrial tradition" of authoritarianism, than from a rational calculation of political interest in a situation where greater parliamentary reform necessarily worked to the advantage of the left. Likewise, it made perfect sense for German capitalists to refuse the "just" demands of the working class, once a given level of private economic power and monopoly organization bequeathed it the ability to do so.

If we accept the arguments of Calleo and Blackbourn and Eley, at least those in which they agree with one another, what damage does that do to the thesis that the position of the position of the landed upper class is a key, if not the key, to understanding the authoritarian trajectory of German development? It is worth underlining what they share with what they designate as the dominant view. They agree that German industrialization was state aided and directed, that the aristocracy held an important, if declining, position in the bureaucracy and army, and that heavy industry opted for an alliance with the landowning class in the wake of the 1873 depression. This rye–iron coalition was reaffirmed by the tariff policies of the Bülow government after the turn of the century. In 1906, even the left Liberals joined with the National Liberals and conservatives in an electoral coalition, the Bülow Bloc, in support of the government's colonial policies. What is contested is that the bourgeoisie was a "politically dependent" or even "supine" partner in the coalition. Thus, on this account, Germany would appear more similar to Italy than the traditional view has admitted, though the German aristocracy held a privileged position in the state, something not true of Italy.

Recent scholarship on German economic development further strengthens the case against attributing a subordinate posture to the German bourgeoisie as it questions the view of Gerschenkron, which is adopted by Moore, that German industrialization in this period was directed "from above" by the state. In reviewing this literature, Trebilcock (1981: 22–111, esp. 104) concludes that the phase of state directed industrialization began to decline in 1840 and by the Imperial German period, the initiative had shifted to cartelized industry and, above all, banks. While this does not question the existence of an alliance between the state, landed upper class, and heavy industry, it does question whether the bourgeois segment was a dependent partner in the alliance.

The main theoretical significance of the recent work on German political development is to question the view, as we have done, that the bourgeoisie is the "natural" carrier of democratic politics. It does not, however, undermine the contention that agrarian class relations left an important legacy which helped undermine the push for democracy in Germany. Be it Calleo's tipping the balance of power in favor of heavy industry or Eley's aristocratic presence in the state, the Junkers still figure heavily in these accounts of the origins of Imperial German authoritarianism.

Moreover, the additional explanations offered by the authors do not fare very well under comparative examination. As we saw, the late industrialization–high concentration–strong socialist labor movement argument does not hold in the Swedish case. Sweden had all of these characteristics as well as an aristocratic enclave in the state, but the Swedish bourgeoisie did not have the option of allying with a powerful landed upper class. Thus, resistance to democratic reform was a less realistic option. Likewise, the equation of Germany's imperialistic policies with the thrust toward authoritarianism is not unproblematic, because, as Calleo himself points out, other nations, notably Britain, engaged in imperialistic policies without the strong thrust to domestic authoritarianism. This is not to deny that these were contributing factors – that late development, concentration, the threat of a strong labor movement, etc. did contribute to authoritarianism in Germany. Rather, we want to argue that they cannot displace the existence of a politically significant landlord class and the landlord–state–bourgeois coalition as a critical feature of the authoritarian path.

The role of the agrarian upper classes and of the authoritarian coalition more generally in the breakdown of Weimar democracy is also a point of contention. For instance, these factors play a role but not a central one in Bracher's (1970) important work on the breakdown of the Weimar Republic. Thus, to complete our argument about the road to modern authoritarianism, it is necessary to specify how agrarian class relations and the coalition helped push Germany toward authoritarianism. Here, we will provide such a specification as well as highlight the pro-democratic role of the main working class party, the Social Democrats.

As was pointed out, on the eve of Wold War I, only the Social Democrats were supporters of parliamentary government and full suffrage reform at all levels of government. Consequently, it seems eminently plausible to argue that the transition to democracy was a direct result of the war. The defeat in World War I, the discrediting of the ruling class, and the temporary power vacuum on the right that this created changed the balance of class power in Germany. Labor organization surged to 30 percent of the labor force and the democratic parties, which now could be counted to include the Catholic Zentrum and the left liberal German Democratic Party (DDP), received 77 percent of the vote in the National Assembly elections of January 1919. Unfortunately, the right recovered quickly; these three parties only polled 42 percent in the June 1920 elections and never again reached a majority during the Weimar Republic (Rokkan and Meyriat 1969: 157–8).[21] Moreover, labor organization slid sharply backward in this same period. Without the defeat, it seems quite likely that Germany would not have become a democracy for decades, until something created a decisive shift in the balance of class forces.

In the wake of the controversy over Abraham's (1986) work and Turner's (1985) determined attempt to absolve big business from responsibility for the Nazis' rise to power, the assertion that conscious instrumentation played an important role in the German case is bound to provoke a dispute.[22] It must be said at the outset that the controversy focuses on the role of big business, and that the culpability of other elites, notably the Junkers and the closely allied top officers' corps, is not a point of contention. Indeed, Turner is eager to shift the blame to these elites, and few would contest the importance of their role in the conspiracies in the circles close to Hindenburg in the last days of the Republic, which led to the installation of Hitler as chancellor. These two groups, along with segments of heavy industry, were the backbone of elite support for and leadership in the German National People's Party (DNVP) which was always monarchist, authoritarian, and anti-democratic and increasingly closely co-operated with the Nazis after 1928.

To mediate the controversy on the role of big business, one must clearly state what the question is. First, one might ask whether big business favored and actively and consciously contributed to the installation of a National Socialist government. This is Turner's question and he argues that, to the final days of the Weimar Republic, the politically active segments of German business continued to be disturbed by the socioeconomic radicalism of the Nazis and thus did not support the installation of a government led by the Nazis, though many leading businessmen favored a DNVP-led coalition with the Nazis. Second, one might ask whether the leading segments of business subjectively favored an authoritarian outcome. A third question, finally, asks whether the actions of big business objectively contributed to the breakdown of democracy and an authoritarian outcome. We contend that the evidence presented by Turner as well as that presented by Neebe (1981) indicates that both of these latter questions must be answered in the affirmative, though we hasten to point out that only an affirmative answer to the third question is important to our overall argument. This appears to be Neebe's (1987) own evaluation of Turner's evidence.

As indicated above, most of heavy industry, primarily coal and steel, supported the DNVP throughout the Weimar Republic, an historical extension of its support for the conservatives and the rye–iron coalition of Imperial Germany. Other segments of business, export oriented industry, finance and so on, tended to support the DVP (German People's Party) or, in the case of the most liberal segments, the DDP (German Democratic Party). Under Streseman's leadership the DVP supported accommodation with the Social Democrats and a reluctant acceptance of the Versailles treaty. The former entailed acceptance of Sozialpolitik, government intervention in wage regulation, and other pro-labor measures. With the onset of the Depression and the death of Streseman, this segment of business gradually moved to the right. While it initially favored the continuation of the Grand Coalition, it increasingly came to see Sozialpolitik and other pro-labor measures to be too costly, constituting, in the view of leading businessmen, the main barrier to renewed investment and thus recovery. Business at first had high hopes for the Brüning government, but became disillusioned with it as it still relied on Social Democratic toleration and thus failed to move in a dramatically anti-labor direction. By September 1931, almost all segments of business had become very critical of Brüning's policies, though the top leadership of the important Reichsverband der Deutschen Industrie (RDI) continued to support the Chancellor to the end of his period in power (Neebe 1981: 102, 109). This drive to exclude the Social Democrats combined with the rise of the Nazi vote left business with two options: supporting a parliamentary government with Nazi support or an extra-parliamentary cabinet of the right, either of which would move the government in an authoritarian direction. Turner (1985: 272; also see Neebe 1981: 127–39) argues that the capitalists (including the RDI leadership) finally found their chancellor in Papen, whose government not only began to roll back the Weimar labor legislation and Sozialpolitik but also suspended the Prussian Landtag and drew up plans to revise the constitution in a decidedly more authoritarian direction. In all these developments, business used its money, political contacts, and media to influence events in the desired direction, and while hardly all-powerful, it is not plausible to argue that it was without significant influence.

There can be little question that, objectively, the Papen government was a groundbreaker for the Nazis. Papen himself was a key actor in the formation of the first Nazi-led government and a minister in that government. Thus, it is clear that objectively business intervention in the political process contributed to the breakdown of democracy. What did leading businessmen subjectively support? Not Nazism, Turner argues convincingly. He indicates in passages too numerous to cite (see e.g. Turner 1985: 252, 273–6) that they advocated a freeing of the cabinet from dependence on parties and a return to the "sort of mixture of freedom and authority that had prevailed in the Empire." Business support for the Papen government was not motivated only by the economic policies of the government but also by the political "reforms" on the agenda (Neebe 1981: 135–8). Thus, the evidence does indicate that business did favor a turn to more authoritarian forms of government.

The argument that the effect of upper class opposition to the sitting government and ultimately the democratic regime was mediated by structural mechanisms (lack of investor confidence, etc.) is strongest for the German case. Virtually all scholars concede that the economic situation was a very important contributor to the outcome in Germany whereas the importance of this factor has been contested (at least by its omission) in the accounts of the other breakdowns. Moreover, we know that it is plausible to argue that lack of "business confidence" in the Müller and Brüning governments did make an independent contribution to the dismal economic situation, because the attitudes of leading German capitalists toward these two governments have been so thoroughly documented.[23]

The argument that the authoritarian posture of the middle classes and the peasantry was, in part, a product of upper class ideological hegemony is important in the German case. Here one must explain why so many people were open to voting for the Nazis (37 percent in 1932) or, adding the DNVP (6 percent in July 1932), for authoritarian parties in general. To facilitate the analysis of the rise of the Nazi vote as well as a comparison of the German and Austrian cases, it is helpful to examine social and historical bases of the parties, utilizing the Lipset–Rokkan scheme (Lipset and Rokkan 1967). The DNVP was the political creature of the conservative monarchist bloc which represented an alliance of the state (or "nation-building elite", N, in Lipset and Rokkan's terminology), the state church (C, the Lutheran church in this case), and the landed upper class (L) (see table 4.3). The liberal bloc, the DVP and the DDP, represented the bourgeoisie and other elements of the urban upper and upper middle classes (U) and assumed a secular posture (S). The Catholic (R) bloc, Zentrum and the Bavarian Peoples' Party, BVP, represented the largely south and west German Catholic population. The working class primarily supported the Social Democrats and secondarily the Communists.

An examination of election results in this period indicates that the Nazis received votes from everyone who was not absorbed in the Socialist/working class or Catholic countercultures (see table 4.3). We contend that the authoritarian and militaristic ideology of the ruling groups of imperial Germany contributed to the susceptibility of every other sector of the population to the reactionary appeals of Nazism. Under the impact of the increasingly desperate economic conditions of the depression, these social groups turned from the traditional conservative authoritarianism of their old parties to the radical racist authoritarianism of the Nazis.

Our crude analysis here is confirmed by detailed empirical studies of two sorts. First, in their detailed examination of ecological data on voting patterns, Hamilton (1980) and Childers (1983), though disagreeing on many points,

TABLE 4.3   Elections in the Weimar Republic National Assembly (%)

	Jan. 1919	June 1920	May 1924	Dec. 1924	May 1928	Sept. 1930	July 1932	Nov. 1932	March 1933*
National Socialists NSDAP	–	–	7%	3%	3%	18%	37%	33%	44%
Conservatives (NCL) DNVP	10	15	20	21	14	7	6	9	8
Liberals (PSU)	23	22	15	16	14	9	2	3	2
DVP	4	14	9	11	9	5	1	2	1
DDP	19	8	6	6	5	4	1	1	1
Catholics (PR)	20	18	16	18	15	15	16	15	15
Zentrum	20	14	13	14	12	12	13	12	12
BVP	–	4	3	4	3	3	3	3	3
Labor	46	42	34	35	41	38	37	37	30
SPD	38	22	21	26	30	25	22	20	18
USPD	8	18	–	–	–	–	–	–	–
KPD	–	2	13	9	11	13	15	17	12
Other	1	3	8	7	13	14	2	3	1

*Conducted by the Nazi–Nationalist Government with significant harassment of the opposition.
NSDAP – National Socialist German Workers' Party, DNVP – German National People's Party, DVP – German People's Party, DDP – German Democratic Party, BVP – Bavarian Peoples' Party, SPD – German Social Democratic Party, USPD – German Independent Social Democratic Party, KPD – German Communist Party
Source: Rokkan and Meyriat (1969: 157–9).

concur that the Nazis failed to penetrate the socialist and Catholic countercultures. Second, Allen's (1984) fascinating and well researched community study of the Nazi seizure of power in one German town, based on newspaper reports, interviews with participants, and Nazi party documents, not only confirms the shift in voting patterns referred to above. It also provides a clear picture of how German civil society in the period was organized, with a highly cohesive working class Social Democratic subculture promoting a democratic and socialist ideology, and a somewhat less cohesive, but none the less densely organized, middle and upper class culture interpenetrated by a large number of rightist, nationalistic, and militaristic groups promoting variants of that ideological current. [24]

Our argument here admits that there is a grain of truth in the cultural interpretations of the collapse of German democracy. In its crudest journalistic form, this view contends that the Germans succumbed to authoritarianism because they were authoritarian. A slightly dressed up academic version of this is that the Weimar Republic crumbled because its culture was "illiberal." Authors such as Bracher (1970) and Lepsius (1978) present a much more sophisticated variant of the argument by breaking the German society and polity into four blocs, contending that it was in the National Liberal and Conservative Monarchist blocs in which the voters succumbed to the radical authoritarian appeals of the Nazis and in which the leaders were willing to co-operate with them. This closely follows our own argument.

The weakness of these points of view is that they either leave the strength of the authoritarian camp unexplained, as Lepsius does in his short essay, or explain it in historical terms without clearly connecting the content of ideology to the material and political interests of the economic and political leaders of the camps promoting them. Bracher (1970: 27–8) hints at a connection between the promotion of the statist–nationalist–völkisch ideology, the related Lebensraum philosophies, and the carrying out of the Kulturkampf against the culture of the Catholic southern Germans, on the one hand, and the interests of the political elite of Imperial Germany, on the other. But the mesh of this ideology with the interests and development project of the economic and political elite is nowhere made explicit and tightly tied together.

Gerschenkron (1943: esp. 53–5) does make an explicit link between Junker class interests and their, in his view, conscious and successful attempt to spread proto-Nazi ideologies among small peasants in order to maintain and increase support for the Conservative Party, the Agrarian League, and their agricultural program. Critics of this view, such as Blackbourn, Eley, and Calleo do not dispute the contention that this attempt to influence the social consciousness and political allegiance of the Protestant peasantry was successful. They contend that it had little impact on the urban middle classes. But, they, particularly Calleo, offer an alternative source and conduit for ultra-nationalistic (though not backward looking and agrarian) ideological influences on these strata. Following Kehr, it can be argued that the bourgeoisie's support for imperialism had an independent economic basis and this led the bourgeoisie actively to promote ideologies of imperialism through the Naval League and other nationalist organizations.[25] All three authors emphasize the role played by imperialism in the attempt of the Liberals to secure a mass base in response to the rise of the Social Democrats. And, while it is true that imperialism does not logically imply opposition to democracy, in Germany, in both the Imperial era and the Weimar period, they were linked: the political forces which promoted imperialism also were authoritarian. Based on the electoral and community studies cited earlier, we contend that these are specific instances of the general phenomenon of the penetration of the ideologies of the Imperial German elites (the state elites, Junkers, and the bourgeoisie) to all social groups, in varying degrees, outside the working class and Catholic blocs, thus strengthening authoritarian currents in these groups. This strongly supports our contention (see chapter 3) that the density of civil society (or strength of secondary groups, etc.) per se is not a sufficient condition for the development of democracy. In fact, as the German case shows, under certain historical conditions, the associative groups characteristic of a dense civil society can serve as organs of socialization for authoritarian ideologies.

Forces inside the state also played a role in the German case. With the strong overrepresentation of the landed aristocracy in the upper ranks of the Reichswehr, it is not surprising that the army shared the Junkers' authoritarian monarchist politics, and though they never fully supported Hitler, their neutrality was essential for the Nazis' seizure of power (Carsten 1973). In the eleventh hour, the period of presidential rule from 1930 to the seizure of power, the contribution of elements of this group went far beyond neutrality, as the circle around Hindenburg was completely dominated by the men drawn from the Junker–military–bureaucratic elite. The project of those closest to Hindenburg was to use the Nazis to install authoritarian presidential rule. This game eventually led to the Nazi entry into the government with control of the chancellorship. The German judiciary consistently treated equivalent offenses by political groups on the left and the right quite differently. The light sentence received by Hitler for the Munich putsch is a case in point here.[26] This alignment of forces inside the state is also in part a product of the coalition that consolidated the German state and the resulting imperialistic and militaristic ideologies propagated by state elites.

The counterfactual in this case is important because potential critics might correctly point out that the Protestant peasants of northern Germany were one of the first groups to whom the Nazis made a breakthrough in the post-1928 period. Thus, one might ask, why should we expect the movement to be much weaker if Germany were small-holding? Setting aside the fact that it must be agreed that it would be impossible to imagine the whole economic and political trajectory of Germany without Junkers, we can turn to Finland for an answer. Under the impact of different but equally tumultuous events (revolution, civil war, depression), sections of the peasantry did turn to the radical right Lapua movement in the 1930s, and the movement did manage to get the Communist Party suppressed (Alapuro and Allardt 1978; Alapuro 1980, 1988: esp. 209–18). But it never managed to effect the suspension of parliamentary politics. In accounting for its failure to reach this goal, Alapuro and Allardt cite several situational and structural factors. The most important of the structural factors, they contend, was the absence of a strong landed upper class.[27] As a result, the Finnish peasantry had mobilized autonomously (as in all Protestant small-holding countries) and formed its own political party decades before the rise of the Lapua movement. Thus, when the Lapua movement attempted to translate its substantial support among peasants into electoral support at the polls, it failed to make more than marginal inroads into the support of the Agrarian Union.

To summarize our analysis of Germany, the Prussian state allied with the landed upper class, and a significant segment of the bourgeoisie, heavy industry, joined this coalition in the imperial period on a platform of protective tariffs, imperialism, and political exclusion of the masses. Other segments of the bourgeoisie, though disagreeing with the economic policies of the ruling coalition, did not advocate political inclusion of the lower classes. In part through deliberate political campaigns, the dominant classes developed an ideological hegemony over significant sections of the Protestant peasantry and urban middle classes. The working class, organized by Social Democracy and the trade unions, and the Catholic minority were sufficiently insulated by their respective subcultures to resist the influence of the dominant ideology. Since even the Catholic party, though on the democratic end of the spectrum, did not join Social Democracy in the demand for full democracy, no pro-democratic coalition could be constructed before World War I. The war was decisive for the transition to democracy: it discredited the ruling class and greatly strengthened the working class. However, the support for democracy among the Protestant middle classes and peasantry and the more liberal segments of the bourgeoisie was temporary and purely tactical and, among heavy industry and the landed upper class, non-existent. Occupants of the upper ranks of the state apparatus, especially the army, sympathized with the latter groups. Thus, when the depression undermined the fragile class compromise which Weimar democracy depended on, the masses and elites outside the Catholic and working class blocs moved to the right, either taking their traditional parties with them or, in increasingly large numbers, defecting to the Nazis. Authoritarian elements in the state greatly facilitated the final transition to an authoritarian regime.

Austria

Of the other three European breakdown cases, the Austrian appears to be closest to the German. Certainly, the class–state constellations in the eighteenth and nineteenth century are quite similar. The basic state alliance was also between the crown; the army, which was very closely identified with the Habsburg Monarchy; the bureaucratic elite; and the landed nobility. The ethnic divisions within the Empire and later Austria–Hungary divided the nobility and often set the non-German nationalities, particularly the Magyar magnates, against the monarchy, but as Taylor (1976) emphasizes, when they had to choose between defending their class privileges and advancing claims for national autonomy, they virtually always chose the former. The system of labor control in the countryside can be accurately labeled "labor repressive": though Joseph II abolished true serfdom, the Robot, obligatory labor service, which remained in effect until 1848, was actually the more critical provision in limiting labor mobility (Gross 1973: 247, 255). And even in the post-Robot period, the great lords remained the predominant power in the countryside. Indeed, they gained at the expense of the minor noble landholders.

The ethnic divisions within the Habsburg Monarchy point to one contrast between Austria and Germany that does have a bearing on our argument. For obvious reasons, the conscious promotion of a nationalist legitimating ideology was out of the question for the ruling groups in the Habsburg Monarchy, particularly in German Austria, the area of main concern here.[28] Thus, while it can be plausibly asserted that the ruling groups did propagate an ideology legitimating their rule and that the content was of necessity authoritarian, one has no obvious "smoking gun" as one has in the case of the campaigns of the Agrarian League and Naval League in Germany.

At least initially, the bourgeoisie was economically dependent on the Habsburg state. The state attempted to promote industrialization through high protective tariffs; subsidies, loans and tax exemptions to businesses; armaments purchases; building of infrastructure; development of necessary skills and education in the population; and development and ownership of selected undertakings (Gross 1973: 243 ff). Austria–Hungary then followed the German pattern of a declining state role and a rising role for banks (Trebilcock 1981: 335–9; Good 1984: 251). However, due to the politics of ethnicity, this did not result in the end of the dependence of the bourgeoisie, or at least, a segment of it, on the state. In the case of the German Austrian bourgeoisie, their dependence on the state was reinforced by their (probably correct) view that the end of the Empire was inimical to their interests, despite the fact that it is arguable that the objective effect of their subordination to the imperial state was to impede the development of capitalism (Gross 1973; 250; Trebilcock 1981: 361). Gross (1973: 251) contends that the dependence of the German Austrian bourgeoisie expressed itself in the "persistent adherence to quasi-feudal social values." In a word, it accepted the ideological leadership of the monarchy and the landed nobility. The abolition of the Robot furthered the links between the landed nobility and the bourgeoisie since many of the nobles used the monetary compensation provided for the abolition to enter business on a significant scale (Gross 1973: 255–6; Taylor 1976: 73).

The transition to democracy in Austria followed a similar path to that in Germany, with the defeat in the war creating a temporary change in the balance of class power. The differences were that, on the one hand, the Socialist Party and the working class were stronger, electorally and organizationally, the Socialist movement being the very prototype of the successful application of a Gramscian strategy. On the other hand, the Socialists were the only clearly pro-democratic party, with the possible exception of the Landbund. The various parties of the German Nationalist bloc (polling together around one-fifth of the vote), which were supported by a large segment of the bourgeoisie and the Protestant middle class, participated in governments in the late 1920s which turned a blind eye to, and sometimes even co-operated with, the Fascist Heimwehr. Indeed, during German Nationalist leader Schober's chancellorship in 1929–30, his office acted as a conduit for monthly contributions of 250,000 schillings from Austrian banks to the Heimwehr (Simon 1978: 96). Moreover, by 1932 virtually all of the supporters of the German Nationalists had defected to the Nazis. The Christian Socials (polling around 40 percent) not only protected the Heimwehr while in office; the leadership of the party conspired to end democracy in 1933 and ultimately the party fused with the Heimwehr.

On the question of instrumental manipulation of the state by upper class interests, the Austrian case is again similar to the German. There is no doubt that industry did contribute to the Fascists: we have just mentioned the role of Austrian banks. Industrial interests nurtured and financially supported the Heimwehr from the outset specifically as force of coercion aimed at the Social Democrats and the trade unions (Gulick 1948: 128–30). For example, the country's largest mining and metallurgical firm, the Alpine-Montan Gesellschaft, contributed significant amounts of money to the Heimwehr (Rabinbach 1983: 55). However, perhaps more important for the fate of Austrian democracy was the support in the upper classes for non-Fascist authoritarian forces in the Catholic and German National blocs (Gulick 1948: 693, 778, 858).

The potential that the coercive forces had as an instrument for or against democracy was well realized by both the Social Democrats and the Christian Socials in Austria. In the initial years after the war the Social Democrats made efforts to reconstruct the army filling the rank and file with its own supporters, though the officers corps continued to be dominated by the old imperial officers. After the socialists left the government in 1920, the Christian Socials moved to alter the composition of the army. A similar course was followed in the case of the Vienna police who were recruited from the Christian Social villages of Lower Austria rather than from the heavily socialist capital itself (Gulick 1948: 751). The political loyalties of the coercive forces proved important. As a result of the incident on July 15, 1927, when police fired on a crowd of rioters killing 85, the government found that it could rely on the coercive forces even in the socialist stronghold of Vienna. This incident, which is considered the crucial turning point in many accounts of the breakdown of Austrian democracy, was quickly followed by a Heimwehr offensive against the Social Democrats carried out with the toleration of the Christian Socials.

The Austrian case differs from the German in that the landed upper classes themselves played little active role in the interwar events, though what contributions they did make were supportive of authoritarian forces (Gulick 1948: 7–8). Part of the reason for this is that, compared to other regions in Austria–Hungary, German Austria contained a disproportionate amount of the mountainous areas, which were predominantly small-holding. Thus, the ideological legacy of past and present dominant elites is, if anything, more important for explaining the outcome in Austria than in Germany. Based on local election results, it has been estimated that well over 50 percent of Austrians would have voted for the Christian Socials (30–5 percent) or the Nazis (over 20 percent) if a national election had been held in 1933 (Simon 1978: 110). The greater electoral strength of the authoritarian right parties in Austria compared to Germany is explained by the authoritarian (or, at the very best, ambivalent) position of the Catholic camp. This, in turn, is explained by the historical alliance of the Habsburg state and the landed oligarchs with the Catholic church. This N–R (Roman Catholic) –L alliance in the Lipset–Rokkan scheme was the historical social structural basis for the Christian Social Party. It represented a fusion of the organized Catholic institutional culture with this elite alliance, with the latter group defining the class character of the Catholic camp's political ideology. Thus, the pro-democratic camp in Austria was weaker than in Germany due to the differences in the historic alliances of the church.[29] For precisely the same set of reasons, the appeal of Nazism was considerably less in Austria than Germany and the authoritarian Catholic corporative state of the Dollfuss–Schusschnigg period much less repressive, with considerable autonomy for trade unions and other forms of non-party social organizations.

There is one weakness in the argument linking the ideology of the dominant political coalition in Austrian development to the behavior of the parties in the interwar period. The development of the Christian Social movement substantially predated its fusion with upper class interests (Boyer 1981). While it is true that the party shed much of its early radical romantic anti-capitalism and became solidly conservative with the development of the alliance, its opposition to lower-class interests and universal suffrage and its anti-semitic authoritarianism date back to its early years. Thus, if its authoritarian posture is connected to the ideology of the ruling elites, the connection is not simple or obvious.

A stronger case can be made for connecting the class–state coalitions of the nineteenth century to the outcomes of the interwar period in the Austrian case by pointing to the link between the development coalition and the weakness of, and anti-democratic posture of, Austrian liberalism. Austrian liberalism was based in the German Austrian bourgeoisie and upper middle classes and thus reflected the conservative position of those groups which was directly linked to their perception of their own self-interest in preserving the Empire and the Habsburg Monarchy as mentioned earlier. Liberalism in Austria meant anti-clericalism, rationalism, and support of property rights and little more. It lacked the democratic tendencies of English liberalism, not to speak of the strong support for democracy characteristic of Scandinavian liberalism.[30] Thus, the dependence of the bourgeoisie on the Habsburg state helps to explain the weakness of democratic currents outside of the working class in the first Austrian Republic.

The Czech case presents a nice support for a counterfactual argument on this point. For obvious reasons, the bourgeoisie in Bohemia and Moravia did not see the preservation of the Habsburg state in the same light as their German Austrian counterparts and thus developed a more aggressive and stronger liberalism. This is one factor that helps explain why democracy survived in Czechoslovakia until the German invasion, in contrast to Austria. The case of Czechoslovakia also puts into perspective the arguments that the decisive factor sealing the fate of Austrian democracy was foreign pressure from its authoritarian neighbors. While it cannot be denied that this was a significant factor, Czechoslovakia was similarly surrounded by authoritarian regimes and subject to pressures from them but did not succumb. Moreover, this argument is weakened by the fact that the trajectory toward the authoritarian seizure of power in Austria began with the events of 1927, well before the rise of Nazi influence in Germany, and the critical step toward the installation of the authoritarian regime, the suspension of parliament, occurred only a few months after Hitler was appointed Chancellor and before the Nazis had consolidated power.

Spain

There is no doubt that landholding in absolutist Spain was extremely concentrated: the nobility and the church held over two-thirds of the land in the country (Carr 1982: 39). But, as in the Italian case, the initial development of the ruling political coalition in the nineteenth century does not seem to point in the direction of the landlord–bourgeois–state alliance as responsible for the development of modern authoritarianism. The conflicts of the first decades of that century pitted the urban middle and upper classes, intellectuals and the army, supporting a program of liberal reform, against the church, nobility, and monarchy. An important part of the liberal program was an attack on corporate property rights: entailed property, seignorial rights, church-owned lands, and communal property, thus directly attacking the interests of the nobility as well as the church.

In the course of the century, however, the coalition of forces that gradually assembled around the Moderado Liberal (later dynastic Conservative) party did resemble the authoritarian coalition.[31] By the time of the first Carlist wars in the 1830s, the crown was aligned with the Moderados and increasingly most elements in the army supported this party, though the Progresista Liberals continued to enjoy some army support until late in the century. In their periods in power in the 1830s and the 1850s, the Progresistas carried through the liberal property rights reforms of the original liberal program, which resulted in a very significant redistribution of land as church properties were sold by the government and the end of entailment led many poorer nobles to sell their land. Since this land was sold on the open market rather than used as part of a land reform scheme, it was those who had the money to buy it who benefited: the affluent nobility, the upper peasantry, the local political bosses in the rural towns, and the bourgeoisie. The larger landowners, both the traditional nobles and the new landlords, also increasingly gravitated to the Moderados–Conservatives. By the time of the Restoration (after 1874), sections of the Catholic right in the form of the Catholic Union had broken with Carlism and joined the dynastic Conservatives. With the Catholic Union came the episcopate and "the more recalcitrant of the Catholic aristocracy" (Carr 1982: 355). These social supports of the Conservatives increasingly became a single social class with a common social and political outlook. Carr (1982: 284, 431–2; also see Linz 1967: 204) sketches the situation at midcentury and then at the end of the century:

> [The generals] were absorbed into the aristocracy by a continuous process of new creation [of titles]... The amalgam of speculators, industrialists, landowners, together with the prosperous lawyers and ennobled generals who were its political voice par excellence, constituted what democrats were beginning to call a ruling oligarchy – estimated at five hundred families.
>
> [The aristocracy] was conspicuous in its support of Catholic values. Since its whole history in the nineteenth-century had been one of accretion, through the incorporation of successful soldiers, hauts bourgeois, and politicians, it tended to impose these values on the upper ranges of society as it imposed its way of life.

The dynastic Conservatives' opposition within the El Turno Pacifico system was the dynastic Liberals, the heirs of the Progresistas. The Liberals were based in the provincial urban upper middle classes and, on paper, supported liberal democratic ideals. When they were in office in the last decades of the nineteenth century, they put these ideals into law, making Spain, on paper, a democracy: universal suffrage, freedom of association, freedom of the press, etc. But the reality of the situation was quite different: in the El Turno system, there was a de facto agreement that the two dynastic parties would alternate in power, and this was accomplished by fixing the electoral outcome. The parties outside the system, the Republicans and the Socialists, had no chance to gain power despite the existence of universal suffrage and the numerical significance of the classes they represented. Thus, the political situation under El Turno was very similar to that under trasformismo in Italy. The parallel does not end there. Like Italy, Spain, in 1891, introduced tariffs on both agricultural and industrial imports. Like Italy, in a conscious effort to create a national industry, it embarked on naval building programs in 1888 and again in 1908. Thus, it is probable that all these developments had the same effect as in Italy: to bring the state, the bourgeoisie, and the landed classes into closer alliance.

The Spanish situation in the closing decades of the last century shows some other interesting contrasts and similarities to the German and the Italian. In both Spain and Germany, the upper officers' corps were closely linked with the upper class(es), but in quite different ways. In Germany, many top officers were traditional aristocrats. In Spain, the officers were often of humble origin and an army career could be a way to move into the political elite (owing to the role of the military in Spanish politics) and then the economic elite, sometimes ending in ennoblement. A second contrast to Germany was that the landlord class was a mix of traditional aristocrats, ennobled haute bourgeoisie and military men, and untitled property holders. As in Italy, it cannot be said that the bourgeoisie was dependent on a landholder-dominated state.

The process of economic development in the period 1875 to 1920 and thus the increasing size of the urban lower middle and working classes put pressure on the El Turno system, as it increased the strength of the unions and Socialist and Republican parties, as well as the Anarchists. The economic boom induced by the war, in particular, greatly strengthened labor unions. Indeed, it became more and more difficult to fix elections in the urban areas and the votes of the urban electorate became known as "votos verdad." A combination of public revulsion to the excesses of El Turno and widespread indifference to the overthrow of the parliamentary system contributed to the success of the coup of Primo de Rivera in 1923, ushering in a period which the dictator himself said would be a "brief parenthesis" to clean up the corruption of El Turno (Carr 1982: 564). The institution of the Republic, and thus democracy, came as a result of the victory of the Republicans and Socialists in the larger cities in the municipal elections of 1931 and the subsequent proclamation of the Revolutionary Committee composed of Republican and Socialist conspirators. The passive role of the army was critical, it did nothing to stop the Republican conspirators.

The transition to democracy in Spain is rather like the same process in Italy, as the working class forces were the beneficiary of the introduction of democracy more than the initiator of it.[32]The principal political representative of the working-class, the Socialists (PSOE), played a secondary role in the transition to democracy as they only unified behind the Revolutionary Committee in the eleventh hour. The Socialists garnered a somewhat smaller portion of the vote than in Italy, approximately 20–5 percent (Linz 1967: 225; Linz 1978: 146–7). And even more than in Italy the immediate reaction of the upper classes (i. e. in regard to the mechanism of instrumental use of the state) to the threat represented by the political mobilization and trade union organization of the working class and landless agricultural workers was a central, if not the central, dynamic in the breakdown of the regime.[33] Not only did large estates dominate the countryside more than in the other three cases discussed here, it was also a very heavily agricultural country. Thus it is not surprising that the agrarian question was the focal point of class conflict and that the hostility of the large landholders to state intervention in local agrarian labor markets, which strengthened the hand of labor, and to the modest agrarian reforms of the first Republican government was such an important factor in the breakdown (Malefakis 1970). By the same token, given the low level of capitalist development of the country and thus the weakness of civil society, ideological hegemony of the authoritarian (upper class) forces did not play such a crucial role in the Spanish case.

There is a sense in which the Republic was a premature progressive development which was quickly rolled back because the democracy itself and the reforms it introduced exceeded the limits that the balance of class power in society would tolerate. The Republic was ushered in by developments in urban Spain and did not reflect the power balance in Spanish society as a whole. Thus, it was quite similar to a number of revolutions in nineteenth century Spain which emanated from the urban areas and resulted in the installation of a Progressive government and the promulgation of a liberal constitution or the like, and then were quickly, though not completely, rolled back. The Republic was only unusual in that its accomplishments were completely destroyed and it ushered in five decades of dictatorship. We encountered a similar pattern of changes initiated in the urban areas leading to subsequent roll-backs emanating from the countryside in France. In both cases, the existence of a centralized state prevented the co-existence of urban democracy and rural authoritarianism which we will find in the United States.

The Spanish case is exceptional in that the most crucial element of the state, the army, played not simply a passive role in the authoritarian seizure of power but rather was the instrument of seizure. Again, this was a continuation of a nineteenth-century pattern of Spanish politics rather than a new development.

Democratic Development in Britain's Settler Colonies

This group of countries, the United States, Canada, Australia, and New Zealand, differs from the European countries in that they were characterized by broad suffrage before they achieved self-government, either in independence or within the British Empire. Thus, the relationship with the colonial power and Britain's changing role in the international political and economic system are an essential part of the story of democratization. However, Britain was not in a position to dictate policy without regard to local power relations, and even when it attempted to do so, the decrees had a very different effect given the colonial social structures than they would have had in Britain itself. This can most clearly be seen in the transfer of British suffrage requirements to the North American colonies, which resulted in vastly more democratic arrangements there than in Britain. We treat the four cases in the historical sequence of their settlement because British influence on the ultimate outcome increased through time and was progressively transformed by its changing role in the international system. The United States and Australia are treated in more detail than the other two cases since they deviate from the pattern demonstrated by the European cases, that is, they are characterized by large estates engaged in labor repressive agriculture but developed in a democratic direction.

The United States

The United States does seem to pose a problem for our theory as it is clearly a case in which there was a significant class of large landholders engaged in labor repressive agriculture, yet the country apparently did become a democracy. Our qualification on the classification of the United States as a democracy contains one of the keys to our argument: the United States did not become a full democracy until late 1965 when the Voting Rights Act of 1965 allowed the federal government to ensure that blacks in the South could exercise the right to vote. However, the classification of the United States as a "restricted democracy" distorts as much as it elucidates. It may be more appropriate to classify the North, and later the West, of the country as a restricted democracy from its colonial origins to the Jacksonian period and as a full democracy thereafter.[34] The South might be more accurately described as a constitutional oligarchy or restricted democracy, depending on the time period and state in question, from its colonial origins to the late 1960s. Herein lies another key to our argument: the decentralized character of the American state, including the vesting of police power in the states and localites, is an essential element in explaining the political trajectory of the country.

In the colonial political system, the individual colonies were politically independent of one another and they were largely self-governing. The colonies' suffrage qualifications followed the prevailing British pattern, and indeed the crown enforced these qualifications in the colonies (Williamson 1960: 3–39, Dinkin 1977: 28–49). The main qualification in Britain was the "40 shilling freehold", that is, anyone owning land bringing in an annual income of 40 shillings could vote. There were also borough qualifications, usually on the basis of tax, property or trade, which allowed town inhabitants without real property to vote. In the colonies, variants of these qualifications were adopted, often substituting property value or acreage for the 40 shilling income qualification. While any deviations from the British restrictions were generally in the liberal direction, these alternative qualifications were considered to be the local equivalent of the 40 shilling freehold. In fact, the colonists generally agreed with the virtue of limiting suffrage to freeholders, and overt criticisms of property tests were extremely rare until the crisis leading to the revolution (Williamson 1960: 3, 47).

Despite the similarity of suffrage requirements in Britain and the American colonies, the colonial electorate was vastly larger in proportionate terms than the British: in the colonies, the proportion of adult white males entitled to vote varied from 50 to 80 percent, while only 15 percent of adult males could vote in Britain (Williamson 1960: 38; Dinkin 1977: 46–7, 49). By far the most important reasons for this were the much greater concentration of agricultural property ownership and the higher level of industrialization and urbanization in Britain. Thus, in the northern colonies, the suffrage was broad enough and the black proportion of the population low enough that these states would already qualify as restricted democracies. The social basis of this political regime was the same as in Norway and Switzerland in the period immediately before the breakthrough of universal suffrage, which like the US north, were not only small-holding but also experienced no or weak feudal rule and no royal absolutism. Like these countries, the diffusion of rural property ensured the development of large class of politically autonomous family farmers. In the South, the existence of a large class of black slaves and greater concentration of rural property holding resulted in a political system characterized by not only a much higher degree of political exclusion but also by a higher degree of de facto concentration of power among the politically included.

The movement from this already broad suffrage to universal white male suffrage occurred in three phases: the revolutionary era (to the adoption of the constitution), the Jeffersonian period, and the Jacksonian period. Each phase pitted roughly the same social groups against one another. The reforms of the revolutionary era began in the period before the war, as the conflict over "no taxation without representation" heated up. The very slogan implied that all those taxed should have the right to vote, and legislation moving in that direction, state by state, began in 1774. Generally, it can be said that the alignments on the issue were similar to that on the Constitution: the anti-Federalists and their precursors favored suffrage extension and the Federalists opposed it (Main 1961: 13, 19, 265). Indeed, one of the issues that divided the anti-Federalists from the Federalists in the struggle over the Constitution itself was that the Federalists favored the checks and balances incorporated in the document as a check on popular majorities and favored a greater centralization of power at the national level. The social bases of the factions divided on class lines: the Federalists were generally men of property, wealth, and prestige. If anything the alignment on suffrage was even more of a class alignment than that on the Constitution. As Main (1961: 249–81) shows, a commerce vs. subsistence farming alignment cut across the class alignment on the Constitution issue, such that all townspeople including artisans and manual laborers favored the Constitution because it was believed that the increased centralization of power would be beneficial to commerce and trade. However, these urban manual groups favored suffrage extension (Williamson 1960: 82–6). A very important group pressing for suffrage rights were the revolutionary soldiers, another instance of the pressure to politically incorporate those required to bear arms in war. By the end of the revolutionary period, many states had moved to tax qualifications for voting and Vermont even to universal white male suffrage. Most religion qualifications were also eliminated.[35] However, free blacks were qualified to vote in only five of the thirteen states (Dinkin 1982: 41–2). The proportion of white males with voting rights varied from 60 to 90 percent, with most of the states at the upper end of this range.

The adoption of the Constitution provided for a significant increase in national political authority and led directly to the development of the first modern, and national, political parties (Chambers 1967: 9). The political alignment pitted the Federalists against the Jeffersonian Republicans. At the elite level, the Federalists generally represented large banking and merchant interests while the Republicans represented planters, but in most states (except Virginia), there was also a clear tendency for the established political elites, whatever their economic base, to be Federalists (compare Ferguson 1983b: 31–5 and Goodman 1967). Thus, the Republicans stood to gain from a suffrage extension as they could expect to gain support from the politically excluded as a group and from smaller farmers due to common interests on agrarian questions (e. g. tariffs, interest rates, debtor questions). On a state by state basis, the Republicans, once in power, extended suffrage and reapportioned legislatures, thus marginalizing their Federalist opposition. The reforms of this period resulted in the adoption of universal white male suffrage in some states and tax qualifications in virtually all others, Rhode Island, North Carolina, and Virginia being notable holdouts (Williamson 1960: 138–207). Given the existence of poll taxes in many states, tax suffrage meant near universal male suffrage. Regardless of tax status, those that had served in the militia were generally granted the right to vote largely during and in the aftermath of the war of 1812.

After the deterioration of the first party system, a new set of party alignments pitting the Jacksonian Democrats against the Whigs developed, reaching full flower in 1840 (McCormick 1967). The main extensions of suffrage came early in this period during the Jackson presidency. The predominant issues were tariffs, the role of the Bank of the United States, and territorial expansion. The elite alignments in this period were complex since these issues cut across many sectors (e. g. railroads and merchants), but generally planters aligned with the Jacksonians and manufacturers with their opponents (Ferguson 1983b: 36–9) in accordance with their interests in the dominant issues of the day. This elite alignment put the Jacksonians in the position of being able to construct an agrarian alliance with small and medium farmers who held especially heavy electoral weight in the West (now Midwest) as they also favored lower tariffs, easier money, and expansion. Thus, it was also in the interest of the Jacksonian alliance to extend suffrage to the remainder of the white male electorate who were largely small farmers and tenants in the still heavily agrarian United States. The electoral outcomes of Jackson's two campaigns for the presidency reflect these elite/mass alignments: the agrarian South and the West voted overwhelmingly for Jackson, the mid-Atlantic states split, the manufacturing New England voted heavily for Jackson's opponent in 1828 and split in 1832

(McCormick 1967: 99–100). Despite the fact that universal white male suffrage became the rule for the first time in this period, the proportion of the electorate enfranchised increased marginally since so many had been included under the previous system which combined militia and tax qualifications with poll taxes.

Thus, (almost) full democracy was achieved in the North and West in this period.[36] One hastens to add that blacks were excluded from the franchise in most of these states. Only in five New England states were they allowed to vote in 1860 and these states contained only 6 percent of the black population of the North (Woodward 1974: 20). Still, given the relatively small black population in the North at this time, the political system of this section of the country and its social base can be characterized as an agrarian democracy, similar to Norway and Switzerland among the European cases. The alliance that brought this through was most similar to Switzerland as segments of the economic elite allied with the large small-farming population and sections of the much smaller urban middle and lower class. However, which segment of the economic elite was included in the alliance was quite different. In Switzerland, the early manufacturing interests promoted liberal constitutional government and suffrage extensions as part of a program to sweep away feudal barriers to capitalist development. US manufacturers faced no such barriers and, in this period, they fell on the opposite side of the political divide on the dominant issues of the day from the largest excluded group in the North, small farmers, as well as from workers. From a European point of view, what was surprising, to put it mildly, was the posture of the labor repressive landlords.[37] While an alliance between large landholders and small farmers and tenants was common in Europe, it was invariably completely dominated by the large landlords and its politics were reactionary, aimed at preserving the status quo rather than increased political inclusion. Two features of the United States allowed the southern landlords to ally with pro-suffrage forces. The first, and most important, is the racial base of American slavery which made it plausible to think that inclusion of poor whites would not be a precedent for blacks. Second was the decentralized nature of the American polity, which allowed quite different political systems (and indeed socio economic systems) to operate in different regions of the country.

The nature of the American state also supplies us with a piece in the central puzzle of American political development from the point of view of our theory: Why did the authoritarian coalition not appear in the United States given the system of agrarian class relations in the South? The character of the American state is a point that Moore neglected in his otherwise useful discussion. Though Moore poses the question in a fashion unusual for discussions of the Civil War, that is, why did the German compromise between labor repressive landlords and the bourgeoisie not materialize, he gives an answer that appears in many of the standard interpretations of the period: the breakup of the Jacksonian alliance was followed by an alignment of western farmers with northern industrialists. This alliance was based on increasing common interests with one another and different interests from the South.

The need to include the role of the state is clearest when one compares the position of the southern landlords with their counterparts in the four authoritarian cases in Europe. The southern planters never controlled the central state and thus never penetrated it the way that German, Austrian, and Spanish landed upper classes did. Thus, state actors per se did not align with landlords. Moreover, to maintain a system of labor control which relied on political mechanisms, they did not need to control the central state. All they needed was control of the local state along with assurance of no interference from outside. This is demonstrated even more dramatically by the "second serfdom" of blacks beginning in the late nineteenth century outlined below than by the ante-bellum system. However, it should be noted that the fact that control of the local state was sufficient is clearer in hindsight. The ante bellum landlords feared that they would not be free from outside interference. This fear was a primary motivation for the political struggle over the extension of slavery and ultimately for succession.

The comparison of Europe and the United States reinforces Tilly's observation that the centralized national state in Europe was built up for reasons of warfare. It was not built up because it was needed for labor control. However, once it was established, in particular, once the central state was made the repository of most coercive power, it was necessary for landlords to maintain at least very significant influence over the state to maintain the system of labor control. One can see this in somewhat different ways in the Italian and Spanish cases. In Italy immediately after World War I, the Socialists and the Populari came into control of the local states in many communities in the Po Valley, but police power remained in the hands of the central state. Thus, when the landlords turned to the use of Fascist private violence to regain control of the countryside, the Socialists and Catholics were helpless, since the central state would not enforce order. In Spain, with the left in control of the government from 1931 to 1933, the force of the national government was used to begin to dismantle the system of labor control. This led to a tremendous reaction among landlords who concentrated all of their political energies on dislodging the left from national power. Had state power been so centralized in the United States, either the southern landlords would have been forced to influence it enough to assure that police power would back up their system of labor control, or the system of labor control would have been dismantled.

Differences in bourgeois interests made an authoritarian outcome more unlikely in the United States than in Europe. This was in part due to the fact that the critical juncture in the United States, 1840 to 1860, was much earlier in relation to industrial advance than in Europe, and in part due to the position of American business and agriculture in the world economy. First, the southern landlords did not favor tariffs, so a rye–iron coalition on this basis was not possible. Second, heavy industry did not carry the weight in the American capitalist class in this period that it carried after the turn of the century. Light manufacturing and above all railroads, "America's first true 'big business'" (Ferguson 1983b: 44) were more important in this period.[38] Moreover, the railroads were by no means closely connected to steel interests as many of them preferred to import the superior British rails. Thus, the "iron" side of the "rye–iron" equation was not available at this point. Because of the historical conjuncture (that is, before the centrality of battleships and heavy artillery in warfare both of which first appeared in the Civil War), imperialism, in the form of westward expansion at the expense of Mexico, though an important political issue, was not tied to the interests of heavy industry. And finally, and most importantly, as Moore (1966: 140) points out, the northern businessmen did not face the threat of a strong and radical labor movement, such as those faced by their European counterparts at the turn of the century.

The independent farmers also differed from their counterparts in the authoritarian cases. While it can be argued that southern planters exercised a political, and perhaps an ideological, hegemony over small landholders in the South, the western farmers were much more similar in political organization and autonomy to their Scandinavian counterparts than they were to Protestant farmers in Germany or Catholic peasants in Austria. Moreover, their interests and that of southern planters were increasingly opposed: low tariffs were of less importance to western farmers because they were oriented to the domestic market and the two groups' interests were opposed on the issue of the expansion of slavery and the interconnected demand for "free soil" in the western frontier. In addition, the revolution in transportation that accompanied the building of rails and canals resulted in increasing exchange of goods between the North-East and the West, bringing the interests of these two regions closer together. Thus, the combination of the lack of traditional hegemony of the planters outside their home states with increasing divergence of interests of southern planters and western farmers led to the break-up of the Jacksonian coalition and the emergence of the Republican coalition of western farmers and eastern business.[39]

The Civil War and the end of slavery brought only a temporary period of democracy to the southern United States. As Moore points out, a land reform in the South would have been necessary to make democracy permanent in that region and the Radical Republican plan to do this failed in large part because it was too much of an attack on property rights for northern propertied interests to stomach. It might have been possible to preserve the enfranchisement of southern blacks formally guaranteed in the Fifteenth Amendment, had northern interests, even in the absence of land reform, been willing to maintain a federal presence in the South. However, the failure of the Radical Republican program was followed by the agreement after the disputed Hayes–Tilden election which allowed the Republican Hayes to take office in return for the end of occupation of the South in 1877. Then, a series of Supreme Court decisions which had begun in 1873 progressively cut federal jurisdiction and protection, culminating in the Williams vs. Mississippi case in 1898, which opened the legal door to disenfranchisement and segregation by approving of the Mississippi plan depriving blacks of the right to vote (Moore 1966: 148; Woodward 1974: 71).

The failure to implement land reform combined with the end of slavery confronted the southern landlords with the problem of how to control the rural labor force. An initial attempt before the withdrawal of federal troops to use wage labor ended in failure. As Woodward (1974: 31–66) points out, the withdrawal of federal troops from the South was not followed immediately by the disenfranchisement of blacks and blacks continued to vote in large numbers for two decades. However, in this period, a new system of labor control based on the crop liens and debt peonage was installed and the "Redeemer" governments supported the system with appropriate legislation, enforcing the crop lien system and preventing outside labor recruitment (Schwartz 1976: 7–20; also see Wiener 1978). This was accompanied by an ever increasing reliance of the southern economy on a single crop, cotton; a reliance which was reinforced by the debt peonage system as creditors forced indebted tenants to grow the cash crop even when other crops might have been more optimal from the point of view of the family economy. Though the transition to this new system proved difficult for some southern landlords, who as a consequence lost their land, this simply resulted in a circulation of elites; landholding in the South was more concentrated in 1900 than it had been in 1860 (Schwartz 1976: 84).

For a period, these Redeemer governments, which were generally led by conservative elites of Whiggish political background with noblesse oblige attitudes toward blacks, continued to rule the South, in part, by cutting deals with local black leaders. However, the conservatives' Whiggish economic policies, which championed property rights and financial, commercial, and industrial interests, were not popular and their rule rested on an odd combination of their prestige among whites for ending Reconstruction and clientelistic support from blacks. Moreover, the new tenancy and debt peonage system began to produce counter-organization among the tenant population (Schwartz 1976). This movement grew in strength with the agrarian depression of the 1880s and 1890s and then turned political in the form of the rise of Populism. The electoral success of Populism upset the fragile system of rule (Woodward 1974: 76–85). Populism, which initially was interracial in the South, united poor whites and blacks and thus represented a severe threat to the whole propertied upper class. The conservative elites then resorted to another odd combination of appealing to poor whites against the Populists on the basis of Negrophobia and of massive vote fraud in Black Belt areas in an attempt to maintain their rule. This was followed by the wholesale disenfranchisement of blacks, through the introduction of literacy requirements, property qualifications, poll taxes and the white primary. Generally, loopholes were developed to let poor and illiterate whites vote lest they rebel against the system, but it was also considered to be not undesirable to keep some of them off the voting roles as well. The system was very effective: in Louisiana, for example, 130,334 blacks were registered to vote in 1896; by 1904, only 1,342 were. This campaign of race hate was extended through a proliferation of "Jim Crow" laws which almost totally segregated blacks socially. The sequence of events clearly shows that the disenfranchisement of blacks was ultimately rooted in the incompatibility of the new repressive system of labor control and democracy.

The retreat of northern liberalism, which played an essential part in the southern reaction and began on the basis of common defense of property rights, accelerated due to the reaction of northern business to unprecedented levels of labor agitation and the turn of northern business to the support of imperialism, which, like the disenfranchisement of blacks in the South, was justified on a racial basis. The northern retreat was reinforced by the increasing reliance of northern manufacturers on cotton: consumption of cotton by domestic manufacturers increased from 800,000 bales in 1870 to 4,800,000 bales in 1910 and cotton emerged as the country's number one export accounting for one quarter of all goods shipped abroad in 1917 (McAdams 1982: 67). The northern reaction was not limited to a hands-off policy; rather, northern business engaged in its own campaign of labor repression and disenfranchisement. Employing primarily private police forces and tolerated by local and state authorities, employers responded to the strikes with a level of violence unparalleled in Europe (Montgomery 1979; Shefter 1986). They also supported efforts of the Progressive movement ostensibly to clean up electoral corruption, but whose objective effect was to exclude significant segments of the increasingly immigrant working class from the electorate through a proliferation of registration requirements and property, tax, residence, and literacy qualifications and pauper and alien disqualifications for voting.[40]

Thus, an accommodation between labor repressive landlords and the bourgeoisie did develop in this period and it was directed in large part toward the political exclusion and control of (northern) workers and (southern black) peasants. One might ask then why this did not develop into a fully authoritarian system. The most obvious answer is that, from the viewpoint of the propertied classes, there was no reason to press for greater political exclusion since the then prevailing arrangements served their interests well. The decentralized political arrangements allowed the South to politically exclude blacks totally and install a system of debt peonage which met their needs for a large supply of cheap labor. The political arrangements of the "System of '96" in the North and West were enough to effect a drastic and constant decline of electoral participation up to the New Deal and to assure the political hegemony of the party of big business in that period (Burnham 1970, 1981). The employer attacks on unions with the private use of violence were just as effective as the contemporaneous offensive on the part of German big business in keeping heavy industry in the two countries free from unions.

The lack of threat from a powerful and radical labor movement might have been another contributing factor, though the differences between Europe and the United States are not as great in this period as they were several decades later. In 1913–14, 10 percent of the US non-agricultural labor force was unionized compared to a European average of 11 percent. Politically, the differences are greater; Debs, running on the Socialist ticket in 1912, garnered 6 percent of the vote compared to the European average of 26 percent cited earlier. Thus, it is plausible to contend that a stronger left would have generated a stronger reaction in the United States, a contention that is buttressed by the post-World War I governmental persecution of the left (Weinstein 1967). Here, we enter into sheer speculation, but based on the results of the comparative analysis in this book, we doubt that the United States would have turned into a fully authoritarian regime without representative institutions and competitive elections including a substantial electorate. The urban middle class, which our comparative analyses reveal to be a pivotal group, and the family farmers of the North and West were too independent and had had too long an experience with representative institutions (over 100 years) to easily tolerate their own exclusion. The fact that the urban middle class supported the efforts of the Progressive movement which excluded many workers from the political system does not indicate that they would have tolerated their own exclusion. Indeed, the evidence to be presented in the next chapter indicates that such an attempt might well have stimulated the formation of a middle class–working class alliance aimed at the political incorporation of both groups, given the presence of a sizeable working class.

This system prevailed until the Depression and the New Deal realignment. Ultimately, the rise of organized labor and the willingness of an increasingly capital intensive segment of the capitalist class to compromise with labor changed the power balance in American society and resulted in the post-World War II incorporation of the working class (including black workers in the North) into the political and economic system, albeit on far less favorable terms than its European counterparts (see Ferguson 1983a, Stephens 1979c: 89–177). While they did not fall immediately, this change in the power balance and in political arrangements eventually led to the elimination of many of the suffrage restrictions in the North and East characteristic of the previous period.

For the completion of American democracy, the important story of the post-World War II period is the enfranchisement of blacks. Generally, this story has correctly been told as the story of the civil rights movement (e. g. see Morris 1984). The accounts of this movement focus on the actions of movement leaders, followers, their opponents, and national political leaders and thus emphasize process and agency in their analysis of the political developments. However, from a comparative perspective and in a longer time frame, it is clear that there were definite structural changes in the economy and polity, many of them duly cited in passing in these accounts (e. g. see McAdams 1982: 73–87), which allowed this movement to develop. The first of these was the decline of "King Cotton" and the mechanization of southern agriculture. As James (1988) has recently shown, even as late as 1967, there was a strong correlation between agrarian class relations and the disenfranchisement of blacks. That is, the lack of suffrage rights for blacks was still strongly related to dependence of the local (county level) economy on black tenant farmers and to the dominance of white farmer owners in the local economy. The need for tenant labor began to decline first due to declining profitability of cotton production and then to the mechanization of southern agriculture. As a result, the number of black farm operators declined from 915, 00 in 1912 to 267, 000 in 1959 (McAdams 1982: 95). This along with the accompanying process of capitalist industrialization cut the link between the economic fortunes of most white southerners and the system of labor repressive agriculture (Bloom 1981; Mandle 1978). The decline of cotton also cut the tie between northern manufacturing interests and southern landowners. Agricultural modernization in the South and industrialization in the country as a whole also created a push–pull in the labor market which led to a migration of blacks toward northern cities and toward cities within the South. By the 1960s, almost as many blacks lived outside of the old Confederacy as inside and proportionately more blacks than whites lived in cities (Woodward 1974: 192; Piven and Cloward 1971: 213–15). This increased the abilities of blacks to organize.

Second, the New Deal realignments and power shifts meant that political forces in the rest of the country became allies of southern blacks. In a precise reversal of the post-Civil War events, some northern politicians from the party that most blacks supported (now the Democrats) began to press for civil rights for blacks. The Supreme Court, whose character had been changed by the appointments of Roosevelt and Truman, in decision after decision, beginning with a 1941 decision declaring the white primary unconstitutional through the landmark Brown vs. Board school desegregation decision of 1954 and subsequent rulings supported black civil rights and asserted the right of the federal government to intervene to redress the situation, reversing exactly the post-Civil War sequence of decisions.

Third, the New Deal and the war had resulted in a centralization of the state in the United States and an extension of government functions into new areas of the economy and society associated with the expansion of the welfare state. Thus, when the federal government did decide to act in support of black rights, it could do so with greater effectiveness. For instance, the Truman administration ordered the integration of the armed forces and the end of discrimination in federal employment, with both actions being of greater significance than several decades before due to the expansion of employment in these areas.

Fourth, international power relations favored black inclusion through a number of channels. Black soldiers who had fought for democracy in World War II came back demanding the same at home. The war economy had strengthened the industrial labor confederation (CIO) and the labor shortage had brought many blacks to northern cities to fill jobs in industry. The international climate changed in ways that made the political exclusion of blacks an embarrassment for the United States. Hitler's imperialist policies and the Holocaust made it impossible to defend racist policies internationally. The advent of the Cold War resulted in further pressure from foreign policy elites for elimination of the embarrassing racist practices in the South.

Finally, in part owing to the previous changes mentioned which increased blacks' capacity for self-organization, blacks began to organize and to demand political and social rights. This first made itself felt through the organizing activity and political pressure of northern blacks. As McAdams (1982: 86) points out, the positive actions to emerge from the judiciary and the executive in the 1931 to 1954 period were frequently reactions to such activity and pressures. In the following period, the initiative shifted to southern blacks. In the final analysis, progress in the South would have been marginal had the oppressed themselves not demanded an end to the system. This can be seen from the progress of black enfranchisement and the end of legally enforced segregation which proceeded in two phases (Woodward 1974: 135). In the first phase, up to the Brown vs. Board decision of 1954, the actions of the Supreme Court and federal government dominated the situation. Primarily as a result of this, the proportion of voting age southern blacks with the right to vote increased from approximately 2 percent in 1940 to more than 20 percent in 1952. After Brown vs. Board, a southern reaction set in and progress might have stagnated were it not for the fact that southern blacks used the opportunity opened by the emergence of allies for the first time since the end of Reconstruction to organize and press for their rights. Organized black political pressure along with the post-New Deal political alignments and power shifts in society finally resulted in the passage of the Civil Rights Act of 1964 and the Voting Rights Act of 1965 which gave the federal government the responsiblity of enforcing black voting rights in the South and eventually resulted in the inclusion of southern blacks in the electorate.

To summarize our analysis of the United States, the history of democratic development can be divided into three phases: the period up to the Civil War in which the North and Midwest became democratic, from Civil War to World War II when an authoritarian system in the South co-existed with a democratic system in the rest of the country, and the period from World War II to the late 1960s in which blacks in the South were enfranchised. In the first two periods the coexistence of an authoritarian system in the South based on labor repressive agriculture with a relatively democratic system in the North was predicated on the decentralization of the state and the racial distinctiveness of the class subject to coerced labor. The democratization of the North and Midwest in the period up to the Civil War was made possible by the domination of family farmers in the countryside, the pro-democratic posture of this group, and its alliance with segments of the upper class who were willing to support the extension of suffrage in order to insure the political dominance of the party based on this alliance (the Jeffersonian Republicans and the Jacksonian Democrats). There was no movement toward a potentially authoritarian coalition of northern capitalists and southern landlords in the period immediately before the Civil War because these two groups had opposing interests on the key issues of the day and because the capitalists did not face a threat from labor. In the post-Civil War period, the northern capitalists and the southern landlords moved toward an accommodation, but this never developed into an authoritarian alliance because the political arrangements of the System of '96 protected the essential interests of both groups. Again, the threat from labor, though not absent, was lower than in Europe due, in part, to the immigrant character of the working class and its subsequent internal divisions. Moreover, the sequence of political developments was important: a move to a fully authoritarian regime was unlikely at this point because the urban middle classes and family farmers were unlikely to tolerate their own political exclusion given their relative political autonomy and long history of participation in democratic politics. Finally, the post-World War II enfranchisement of blacks in the South was made possible by the modernization of southern agriculture and industrialization in the country at large, the New Deal political realignments, the centralization of the state and expansion of its functions, changes in international power relations, and the self-organization of blacks.

Canada

The initial development of suffrage and representative government in Canada is similar to the North and West of the United States, with the exception that transition to restricted democracy with broad suffrage was delayed sixty years. This lag is easily explained by the pace of settlement and economic development. More difficult to explain is the late development of male suffrage: it was not until 1920 that Canada made the transition to full democracy. Differences in geography hold part of the answer: the Canadian Shield, an immense high plateau of pre-Cambrian granite which pushes down to the Great Lakes, prevented the development of a Canadian parallel to the Midwest and delayed the development of the prairie West (McNaught 1988: 10–11). Thus, a Canadian counterpart to the Jacksonian coalition did not develop, at least, not in the strength that it did in the United States.

As they did in the case of the thirteen American colonies, when the British granted representative assemblies to the Canadian[41] colonies, they generally applied some variant of the 40 shilling freehold and corresponding urban qualifications for voting for the legislative assemblies.[42] As in the United States, these qualifications resulted in a vastly larger proportion of adult males with suffrage rights than they did in Britain. While no precise figures on the matter exist, the changes in the vote which occurred when Nova Scotia moved from property suffrage to universal male suffrage and back to property suffrage indicate that around 70 percent of adult males were qualified to vote under the property qualification. The elected assemblies did not entail representative government as their power was limited by appointive Legislative Councils or appointed members of the assemblies and by the powers of the Governor and Colonial Office.

Significant change in this system awaited the populating of Canada and its transformation from a fur trading to an agrarian economy. This transition was achieved by the 1820s and, at this point, one sees the beginning of consistent pressure for representative government and suffrage extension. The demands for representative government came from the reform forerunners of the Liberals, though many conservatives also saw virtues in such a move. The Liberals generally made suffrage extension their cause. The social bases of the democratic movements are similar to the United States. In Ontario, the reformers around William Lyon Mackenzie and later the "Clear Grit" Liberals were based in the Protestant farming areas of the west. In Québec (which with Ontario made up over two-thirds of Canada), the radicals around Louis-Joseph Papineau and later the Parti Rouge were based among small farmers and small business. These factions, which formed the left wing of the Liberals, attacked the urban business elites, the "Family Compact" in Ontario and the "Château Clique" in Québec (McNaught 1988: 67, 84–86 117–18). Abortive rebellions by the supporters of Papineau and Mackenzie in 1837 led to the appointment of a commission under Lord Durham which recommended, and ultimately led to, the introduction of representative government. Their successors succeeded in extending the franchise in the 1850s (Garner 1969: 107–14). In Prince Edward Island, the "escheat" Liberals with a strong base in the tenant population, though unsuccessful in their land reform demands, did manage to extend the franchise to near universal male suffrage. In British Columbia, the existence of a large, and volatile, gold mining population deserves credit for the institution of a similarly broad franchise there (Garner 1969: 49, 129–30).

As was indicated by the Durham report, the British posture toward the demand for self-government had undergone a marked change since the time of the American Revolution. Britain had gone through its own process of electoral reform and, more important, with the rise of industrialism, had undergone a distinct change in economic philosophy. Departing from the mercantilism that had characterized the old empire (and before the rise of the new imperialism of the late nineteenth century), the Whigs promoted free trade, a philosophy which made sense in light of British sea hegemony and a virtual monopoly of the market for industrial goods. Colonial expenditures were seen as a liability, since free trade between nations resulted in the maximum economic benefits for all. In the mid–1860s, some members of Gladstone's cabinet, following the "Manchester theory of colonial separation" advocated the divestment of Canada even if it meant merger with the United States (McNaught 1988: 128–9). This was not lost on Canadians: conservatives, who resisted demands for self-government for fear of endangering privileged access to British markets, were shocked when Britain abolished one such privilege with the repeal of the Corn Laws in 1846.

At the time of Confederation in 1867, representative government had been achieved in Canada and the franchise, generally based on ownership, tenancy, or occupancy of property or on tax assessment, had been extended to 70 percent to 90 percent of adult males depending on the province. Subsequent changes before World War I were minimal. In 1874, the Liberal government reformed the electoral law, establishing the secret ballot among other things. Several provinces broadened suffrage by lowering the property qualification and British Columbia established universal male suffrage in 1876. The Conservative Macdonald government introduced a bill in 1885 to federalize the franchise with voting qualifications which represented a significant restriction of the franchise in some provinces (Waite 1971: 139ff). Under pressure, they were forced to lower the qualifications such that the resulting law actually extended suffrage. The Liberals returned power over voting qualifications to the provinces in 1898.

The reason for the failure of Canada to move to universal male suffrage at an earlier point as the US North and (Mid)west did was the absence of a "Midwest." As indicated in our discussion of the Jacksonian period in the United States, the US North-east, which, like the Canadian East, combined a commercial and agrarian economy, opposed Jackson whereas the purely agrarian Midwest supported him. In Canada, the Canadian Shield prevented the development of the sociological equivalent of the US "Midwest" and retarded the development of the West. As the Canadian West began to become increasingly settled by family farmers, it did support radical democratic "Jacksonian" demands. In fact, the emergence of prairie populism after 1900 led to the Canadian Council of Agriculture's Farmer's Platform which demanded democratic reforms and mildly socialistic economic reforms during World War I. This was one factor leading to the introduction of universal suffrage.

Far more important was the war itself. The Canadian war effort was tremendous: out of a population of seven and a half million, 628,000 served in the war, 425,000 of whom saw overseas duty. Moreover, the war effort was controversial; organized labor, organized agriculture, and French Canada opposed conscription (Creighton 1971: 209–10). This opposition resulted in the creation of enough loopholes that many of the young men who opposed conscription managed to avoid service. Defeats in provincial elections in Saskatchewan and Alberta convinced the Unionist (predominantly Conservative) government to take political advantage of the presumed loyalties of the armed forces and extend the right to vote to all members of the armed forces and their female relatives and to disenfranchise all post-1902 immigrants from enemy countries and conscientious objectors in 1917 (Brown and Cook 1974: 271–2). In 1920, with the Unionist–Conservative government still in power, suffrage was extended to virtually all males and females.

Australia and New Zealand

Australia is of great interest because it is one of the few cases in which the countryside was dominated by large estates and in which democracy developed at a comparatively early stage of industrialization, and, indeed, developed without the violent upheavals characteristic of the United States and Britain. Moore's analysis suggests that the low labor requirements of the extensive pastoral estates which covered the Australian countryside might provide one key to the political developments in that country. In such cases, large estates do not require repressive forms of labor control. As it turns out, it can be argued that the estates were actually "labor repressive" and one must turn to the relationship of landlords to the state for the reasons for the turn of political events.

For the first two and one half decades after the first white settlement in 1788, Australia, initially a penal colony, was a military dictatorship. The large sheep estates, which originated in land grants to officers and in purchases by immigrant capitalists, were staffed by "assigned" convict labor. As late as the 1830s, two-thirds of pastoral labor was convict labor (McMichael 1984: 154). Thus, though the labor to land ratio was very low, this was clearly labor repressive agriculture. McMichael (1984: 148–9) contends that convict labor was unfree but not slave labor as it differed from slave labor systems in that labor was controlled by the state not the landlords. The convict was not part of the landlord's capital.

When some elements of representative government were first introduced in the 1820s, the landed oligarchy, the so-called "exclusivist" landlords, came to politically dominate the new Legislative Councils. Beginning in the 1830s, a new class of pastoralist entrepreneurs, "squatters", arose. These men utilized the peripheral areas under crown ownership to run large herds of sheep, initially illegally, and then under crown license. These were hardly squatters in the American sense: the sheep runs were enormous; they averaged over 30,000 acres in New South Wales, which at this time covered the whole eastern half of the Australian continent (Hartwell 1977: 81). The short term of the lease and thus the low incentive to invest in capital improvements and the low cost of the squatting license meant that these operations were much more labor intensive than one might assume for the land to labor ratio. This, along with the use of convict labor, argues that the agricultural system was labor repressive and that both sections of the landed oligarchy had a strong incentive to oppose the extension of democratic rights. However, the squatters, in particular, had a strong motivation to demand self-government provided that suffrage was restricted enough to allow their dominance in legislative bodies, as such political arrangements would allow them to collectively gain control of land administration and individually to gain ownership of their sheep runs. It is not surprising, then, that self-government with a restricted franchise along with the continuation of convict transportation and assignment were the main political demands of both the exclusivist oligarchy and the squattocracy.

Arrayed against these two upper-class fractions was a variety of groups created by the convict system and the wool economy. Small-holders, often ex-convicts, producing wheat and other products for the domestic market favored broader democratic rights and opposed squatter attempts to monopolize crown lands. The urban centers created by the need to transport wool and service the domestic economy contained growing classes of artisans, laborers, and various middle strata which opposed squatter demands and organized to end the transportation and assignment of convicts. Initially, the urban upper and upper middle classes, merchants, businessmen, and professionals, sided with, and even led, the anti-squatter alliance (Connolly 1981).

The key factor that prevented the development of the authoritarian coalition was that the landed uppper classes did not control the state; the colonial state was still controlled by London. With all factions in the colonies demanding self-government, the Colonial Office, following the liberal climate of opinion in British politics in the 1840s, determined to do this in a way in which the squatter oligarchy would not be allowed exclusive political influence. First, in 1839, the Colonial government ended assignment of convict labor and then in 1840 terminated the transportation of convicts to New South Wales. Though transportation was continued until 1852 in Tasmania and there were occasional experiments with the use of indentured labor, this marked the end of the labor repressive system in Australia.[43] Second, as a step to local self-government in 1842, the colonial government granted New South Wales a legislative council which was one-third appointive and two-thirds elective. The franchise was restrictive; a £200 freehold or £20 annual rental were the voting qualifications. This resulted in a "squatter council" (Hartwell 1977: 67–8). However, the crown retained control over land administration and thus the squatters could not achieve their main goal: conversion to freehold.

The following decade and a half unleashed political battles in which various social groups attempted to influence the final contours of self-government, with the Colonial Office acting as a mediator. The anti-squatter alliance was strengthened by the discovery of various gold fields beginning in the 1850s. On the one hand, this created a class of "diggers" many of whom had absorbed the lessons of Chartism in Britain. Political demands from this group intensified when capital intensive mining began to replace independent gold digging. On the other hand, it strengthened the hand of the urban bourgeoisie vis-à-vis the rural upper classes. These developments helped insure the initial victory of the moderate liberal alliance and the introduction of a wide franchise, though not manhood suffrage, and responsible government. Subsequently, the leadership of the Liberals shifted to the radicals, urban middle-class politicians supported by the working and middle classes, who pressed the agenda forward advocating manhood suffrage, the secret ballot, and a democratic Legislative Council (the upper house) as well as land reform and social reform. With this left turn, the urban upper and upper middle classes defected wholesale to the conservatives (Connolly 1981). By 1860, the Liberals had succeeded in pressing through much of their agenda in all colonies except Tasmania: manhood suffrage for the Legislative Assemblies and the secret ballot had been introduced and the property qualifications for members of the legislature had been abolished (Clark 1955: 374–7). However, property holders were still allowed to vote in each district where they held property, the franchise for the Legislative Councils was restricted to property holders, and Legislative Council districts were gerrymandered to favor rural areas. Thus, the upper houses remained the domain of the landed upper class.

The resolution of the land question was also a compromise. The squatters' demand for transition to freehold was granted but they were forced to compete with family farmers and would-be family farmers who had raised the demand for "free selection" of crown lands. The transition to freehold along with the labor shortage (which was aggravated by the end of assisted immigration – part of the liberal agenda – and the gold rushes) stimulated capital investment, in particular extensive fencing. This, in turn, greatly reduced the need for labor. Together these developments transformed sheep raising into a capital intensive operation in a relatively short period of time.

While a discussion of variations in the political arrangements from colony to colony would take us too far afield here, the polar cases of South Australia and Tasmania are of special interest because they underline the contribution of agrarian class relations to the political outcomes, one of the central themes of this book. The colonization of South Australia was carried out according to Wakefieldian principles.[44] With no convicts, the domination of family farmers and wheat growing rather than sheep ranching, South Australia's social structure was more similar to that of the American Midwest than to the rest of Australia. The colonists were also drawn heavily from dissenting religions in Britain, which had fed the democratic movement there. Thus, it is not surprising that South Australia was the first colony to institute manhood suffrage, the secret ballot and no property qualification for members of the Legislative Assembly and it was the only colony in which no plural voting was permitted at this early date (Clark 1955: 374–7; McNaughton 1977: 105; Irving 1974: 132).

Because of the remnants of the convict system and the long economic depression beginning in 1856, Tasmania remained politically backward. Convicts and ex-convicts were 30–40 percent of the population and remained in "a state of near feudal dependence on their rural masters" due to the lack of land availability and inability of the towns to absorb them as a result of the depressed economic conditions (Irving 1974: 153). As a consequence of these agrarian class relations and the weakness of towns, liberalism was weak and landlord rule went unchallenged. Thus, Tasmania passed none of the liberal electoral reforms legislated by other colonies in this period and, in 1856, even passed the Masters and Servants Act which continued the arbitrary power which the magistrates had exercised in the convict period.

The political arrangements in the Australian colonies remained essentially the same from this period until the rise of the labor movement in the 1880s and 1890s. After initial success in organizing new sectors, such as sheep shearers, the movement was hit with a number of defeats in strikes in the early 1890s. These setbacks in labor market conflicts accelerated a move of labor into electoral politics which had begun earlier. The labor parties made dramatic gains in elections in all colonies in the early 1890s except Tasmania which followed suit a decade later. Labor–Liberal coalitions pushed through electoral reforms which (1) introduced manhood suffrage for the lower house where it had not already been the rule, (2) abolished property qualifications for office holding, (3) introduced payment for members of parliament, (4) eliminated plural voting for property holders, and (5) in many colonies, introduced female suffrage (Clark 1955: 374–7; de Garis 1974: 239–41). With the introduction of federation in 1901, universal suffrage was adopted at the federal level.

The colonization of New Zealand did not begin until 1840 and, thus, at its initial stages its whole development, economic, social, and political, was shaped by post-mercantilist Britain, specifically, by the liberal free trade philosophy that had penetrated the Colonial Office at this time. The colonization was carried out according to Wakefieldian principles. As in South Australia, the availability of land made it difficult to deny laborers land and, in any case, the Governor, Grey, proceeded to undermine this feature of Wakefield's scheme. The consequence was that small family farming along North American lines rather than small gentry estates worked by hired labor as Wakefield intended was the dominant pattern. True, there were a number of large sheep estates, but these employed very little labor; even the largest were populated by no more than a score of people including the owner and his family. Moreover, as of the 1880s, only 2 percent of the adult male population was involved in sheep farming (Gardner 1981: 64, 78–9). With the addition of the goldminers in the 1860s, the social structure of New Zealand was favorable to democracy.

However, the unquestionably pro-democratic forces created by these economic arrangements – small farmers, diggers, etc. – did not have to fight very hard for democracy: they were practically given it. With Earl Grey in the Colonial Office and George Grey in the Governorship, both Whigs, the initial form of government was very liberal. With little knowledge of conditions in the new colony, Earl Grey authored a constitution in 1846 which called for household suffrage, remarkable given the suffrage requirements in Britain at the time. The Governor determined that self-government should wait three or four years until colonial finances were in order and set it aside. This stimulated the colonists to demand self-government with broad suffrage (Marais 1968: 291). Governor Grey then began work on a constitution which he sent to the Colonial Office in a series of dispatches between 1848 and 1851. The Colonial Office made some minor revisions to what emerged in 1852 as the most advanced constitution in Australasia: a nominated council and an elective assembly with franchise for all males with a £30 freehold, a town tenant with £10 annual rent or a country tenant with £5 annual rent. Few males were excluded by these provisions. The powers of the assembly were wide: only the Maori policies were reserved by the Colonial Office. The first assembly then established the principle of responsible government resting on the confidence of the assembly.

Three years after their military defeat in 1864, the Maoris were granted four seats in the legislature. Manhood suffrage was not a product of class politics: it was passed in 1879 by a government of a slightly conservative character but before the emergence of all but the most rudimentary parties and certainly not ones with defined ideologies and clear-cut social bases of any sort. These emerged in 1887 when a Liberal Party supported by small farmers and the urban middle and lower classes defeated a Conservative Party supported by large landowners and businessmen. The Liberals proceeded to complete the process of democratization by eliminating plural voting with two laws in 1891 and 1893 (Dalzeil 1981: 109–10; Sinclair 1961: 167). Thus, only this very last step in the process can be seen as primarily the product of political struggle between classes. The social structure of New Zealand can be credited primarily with the maintenance of democracy rather than its introduction.

The settler colonies compared

To conclude our discussion of the British settler colonies, one can first point to a number of common features of the four cases. First, they inherited the political achievements of earlier political struggles in Britain. Thus, at a very early stage, government with representative features was implanted in the colonies and these became the primary arena for political struggle. Moreover, these British political institutions had much more democratic effects in the context of the colonial social structures than they did in Britain, a "Tocquevillian effect" of the transplanted state structures.

Second, two features of the agricultural arrangements contributed to the democratic outcome. The first of these, common to the four cases, was the wide availability of cheap land which eventually resulted in a large class of independent family farmers in all four cases. It is striking that this occurred in spite of efforts to prevent it or at least to counteract it in three of the cases. In Québec, the French attempted to transplant feudalism in the form of a seignorial system, but the obligations and payments of the habitant (tenant) and his rights were so broad that the system differed little from freehold (Garner 1969: 75). One Canadian historian has characterized the seigneur's role as "a government agent for land settlement" (Creighton 1971: 59). In Ontario, the Governor attempted to carry out the intention of the Canada Act of 1791 to recreate English social structure and avoid the leveling tendencies prevailing in the United States and France by granting huge pieces of land which were to become the bases of an aristocratic upper class (McNaught 1988: 61–6). Both of these attempts failed because land in North America was too widely available: to get people to work the land one had to sell the land as freehold or create conditions that were near to freehold. In New Zealand and South Australia, the Wakefieldian attempts to recreate the English countryside failed for the same reason. The second feature of agrarian class relations which contributed to the democratic outcome was the failure of the landed upper-classes in the United States and Australia to establish an ideological hegemony over the rural middle and lower classes in the country as a whole. This was only achieved in the case of whites in the US South. One might speculate that the reason for this was that the agrarian upper classes in these settler colonies lacked the traditional legitimacy that the European nobility with its long historic continuity held.

The third common feature of the four cases is that in no case did the agrarian upper class control the state. This was insured by the land holding patterns in Canada and New Zealand. In the United States, it was a product of the decentralized state and the southern landlords' inability to politically dominate family farmers outside the South. In Australia, it was the result of the Colonial Office's conscious attempt to limit the influence of the squatters in the process of the establishment of self-government.

Finally, one striking contrast among the four cases is how the changing role of Britain in the international system and related changes in domestic politics affected the process of democratization. In the context of mercantilism, the United States had to fight and win a war of independence to gain self-government. This war, along with the subsequent war of 1812–14 with Britain, had the unintended result of suffrage extension as soldiers successfully demanded the right to vote. By the late 1820s when Canada and Australia began to demand self-government, the industrialization of Britain had resulted in changes in the dominant thinking about representative government and international economic relations. Free trade and colonial self-sufficiency, including self-government, now had its vigorous and influential advocates. As a result, the demands for self-government were granted by the Colonial Office. Finally, the further strengthening of these liberal political forces in Britain meant that New Zealand was virtually "born free," though its social structure insured that it would stay free.

Conclusion and Discussion

Our overview of the transition to democracy confirmed Therborn's (1977) contention that the working class, represented by socialist parties and trade unions, was the single most important force in the majority of countries in the final push for universal male suffrage and responsible government, though in several of the small-holding countries, the small farmers and/or the urban middle class played the major role. This contradicts the modernization view, as advanced by Lipset (1960) which argues that economic development and democracy are connected primarily through the expansion of education, the growth of the middle class, etc. Rather, it was the growth of the working class and its capacity for self-organization that was most critical for the final breakthrough of democracy. The rapid industrialization experienced by western Europe in the five decades before World War I increased the size and, with varying time lags, the degree of organization of the working class and thus changed the balance of class power in civil society to the advantage of democratic forces.

But, by focusing only on the final step of the process, Therborn rather exaggerates the role of the politically organized working class. Not only did the working class need allies even in the final push; earlier suffrage extensions which incorporated substantial sections of the lower classes, rural and urban, were often led by other social groups, usually the urban middle class or small peasantry, with the working class playing only a supporting role. Moreover, the contribution of the working class to these reforms came in the form of artisanal agitation and delayed political responses to defeated movements (such as Chartism in Britain) as often as through the action of the Second International parties emphasized in Therborn's work. The important role of working-class segments of confessional and liberal parties is also somewhat underplayed in his analysis. And finally, where the working class had few allies (e. g. in Germany and Italy, only the Catholic parties) or none (Austria) democracy was fragile and did not survive the interwar period.

The posture of modernization theory's hero, the middle class, as well as that of the peasantry, was quite variable. In some cases, these groups' political representatives supported the introduction of democracy. In others, they were an essential element of the political coalition that led to democracy's demise. This is closely related to another deficiency in the modernization and pluralist views of democracy mentioned in chapter 3. Drawing on a line of thought that dates at least back to de Tocqueville, these theories hypothesize that economic development leads to democracy because it leads to the development of formally autonomous groups that arise in an ever more differentiated social structure. While we also argue that a denser civil society is generally favorable to democracy, in some cases it can act as a conduit for authoritarian ideas emanating from the dominant classes. The German case demonstrates this very well. This variability of the posture of the middle class, and the peasantry, across the cases also demonstrates the extent to which subjective class interests are historically socially constructed.

As expected, the landed upper class was the most consistent and intransigent opponent of democracy. In no case did it favor the introduction of full democracy, though there were significant variations in the intensity with which it opposed full democratization. The political strength of landlords varied greatly across the cases and this was one source of the different historical trajectories experienced by different countries.

The bourgeoisie, which appears as the natural carrier of democracy in the accounts of orthodox Marxists, liberal social scientists, and, to a certain extent, of Moore, hardly lived up to this role. Except in Switzerland and to a lesser degree France, it opposed the final extensions of suffrage to the working class. Its contribution was to establish parliamentary government and it did not even do this in all cases.

The bourgeoisie's resistance to the initial political incorporation of the working class and its support for working-class exclusion in some countries in the interwar period was clearly connected to working-class support for socialist parties. This factor introduces a subtle wrinkle in the argument linking the strength of the working class to introduction of democracy. Certainly a significant portion of, if still a minority of, the working class in Italy, Germany, and Spain supported the Communists, who were authoritarian in this period, or the maximalist socialists, who were ambivalent about democracy, and there is little doubt that these parties or factions of parties contributed to the breakdown of democracy. However, the example of Austrian Social Democracy, which was powerful, clearly committed to socialism, and democratic, indicates that it was not only, or even mostly, these parties' and factions' attitudes toward democracy but rather their demands for socialism, which was perceived as a threat and provoked an upper-class reaction.

This seems to suggest almost the reverse of Therborn's thesis: where the working class was well organized and committed to a moderate to radical socialist party, it hindered the development of democracy. This cannot be dismissed out of hand. We argued that one reason for the willingness of the Swiss bourgeoisie and sections of the French and English bourgeoisies to support the extension of suffrage to significant sections of the working class lay in the fact that the working class in those three countries was not organized by socialist parties at the time. It represented less of a threat to their interests. Moreover, it is true that the working-class movements in the four breakdown cases were among the stronger and more radical movements analyzed here. As is suggested by the literature on labor movement ideology, it is arguable that these movements' radicalism was in part a direct response to their exclusion.

Yet, it is worth underlining that the objective threat to upper-class interests as indicated by a combination of the strength and radicalism of the movement is not that good a predictor of where democracy would break down. The examples of Norway, where the Social Democrats were as strong as in Austria and more radical in the late 1920s, and France, where the communists were as strong as or stronger than they were in Spain, Germany, or Italy, argue against such a generalization. The relationship between working-class strength and democracy may be summarized in the following way: a diachronic analysis within each of the western European countries reveals that the growth of working-class organizational strength led to increased pressure for the introduction of democracy; a synchronic analysis across countries reveals that these pressures led to the development of stable democratic regimes where the working class found allies in other social groups. If the pro-democratic alliance was strong, the bourgeoisie was not able to act to move the country in an authoritarian direction even where it perceived a threat from the working-class movement, as it surely did in Norway and Sweden.

However, the question about the relation of the working-class threat to breakdown might be asked in a different way. After making his observation that Italian democracy broke down because liberalism was unwilling to become liberal democracy, Farnetti adds that the fact that socialism was unwilling to become social democracy also contributed to the demise of the regime. The same could be said about Spain: the radicalization of the Socialist Party did contribute to the outcome there (see Malefakis 1970: esp. 317–42). Indeed, this was the PSOE's own historical judgement and this judgement partly explains the party's extreme restraint during the process of redemocratization and in its return to power. Nevertheless, it should be pointed out that there is a false symmetry in Farnetti's statements about socialism and liberalism. By moving from liberalism to liberal democracy, the bourgeoisie moves to support a political system in which it presses for its substantive interests in competition with other classes. By contrast, by moving from socialism to social democracy, the working class must abstain from articulating demands within the democratic system which the leaders of the working-class movement see as essential to the class's substantive interest. It does not involve, at least in Europe in the first two decades of this century, a movement to support of democracy since virtually all of the Second International parties were committed to democracy in the first place. Still, it is fair to say that the analysis in this chapter indicates that the optimal configuration of working-class organization for the development of democracy would be one in which the class was well organized, both in unions and a party, but that these organizations were not radical. Indeed, it would be most optimal if they raised no substantive demands at all other than those for democracy itself, which, however is an entirely hypothetical state since workers' movements must defend at least the short-term material interests of their constituents to retain their loyalty.

The overall picture of political alignments in the transition to democracy, then, does support our contention that capitalist development strengthens civil society and both the middle and working classes, thus leading to the strengthening of democratic forces. This simple hypothesis does account for the essential elements of the process of transition in the countries which experienced an internally generated transition to democracy and in which democracy survived the interwar period. However, as the breakdown cases demonstrate, the middle classes as well as the peasantry played quite different roles in different countries. In some, such as the Scandinavian countries, they supported suffrage extension and allied with the working class. In others, such as Germany and Austria, they formed the mass base for authoritarian movements that ended democracy.

Explanation of the differences between countries with regard to the survival of democracy is where the Moore thesis proves helpful. The development of the labor repressive landlord/bourgeois/state coalition appeared to be the critical feature distinguishing the cases in which democracy broke down and in which it survived: in all four countries in which authoritarian regimes replaced democracies, a politically powerful body of large landholders survived into the twentieth century, and historically these landholders were engaged in labor repressive agriculture (see table 4.4). None of the other countries fit this description: in one of the three large-holding cases, Britain, the large landholders did not employ labor repressive techniques of labor control. In the United States, the labor repressive landlords never did establish control of the national state. They did, however, establish (and re-establish) a labor repressive agricultural system and authoritarian political system in the South that lasted

TABLE 4.4 Social and historical factors leading to authoritarianism

	Germany	Austria	Italy	Spain	Britain	France	United States	Small European Countries	Australia	Canada and New Zealand
Landed upper class politically very significant	yes	yes	yes	yes	yes	no	yes	no	yes	no
Historically engaged in labor repressive agriculture	yes	yes	yes	yes	no	no	yes	no	yes	no
Bourgeoisie strong enough to be politically very significant, but not more powerful than landed class	?	yes	more powerful than landed interests	yes	more powerful by 1900	more powerful	more powerful	more powerful	more powerful	more powerful
Bourgeoisie dependent partner in coalition	?	yes	no	no	no	no	no	no	no	no
Revolutionary break from the past	no	no	no	no	yes	yes	yes?	no	no	no

All evaluations of strength of the various forces etc. are for the late nineteenth century in Europe, immediate pre-Civil War period in the United States, late 1850s in Canada, Australia and New Zealand.

until the 1960s. In Australia, the colonial state was not controlled by the laborrepressive landlords and the colonial power instituted self-government in such a way that the landlords were not able to establish exclusive control of the state. In the rest of the countries, the countryside was dominated by small-holders by the beginning of the twentieth century.

In the detailed analysis of the four authoritarian cases, we attempted to show that historically an alliance, or at least an accommodation, did develop between the state, labor repressive landlords, and the bourgeoisie. However, in no case did the authoritarian coalition develop exactly along the lines outlined in *Social Origins*. One of the weakest points in Moore's analysis is his characterization of the bourgeoisie as the dependent partner in the coalition (See table 4.2). In Italy, the bourgeoisie, not the landholders, was the politically dominant segment of the upper classes. Recent historical scholarship on Imperial Germany questions the view that the bourgeoisie was politically dependent. Even in Spain, where the landed class was dominant in sheer economic terms, it cannot be said that the bourgeoisie accepted the political leadership of the landed classes. Only Austria seems to fit Moore's characterization, and there, the political and economic dependence of the German Austrian bourgeoisie was, in the final analysis, cemented by its position in the multi-ethnic state, and this dependence was not shared by its Bohemian and Moravian counterparts. It appears that Moore's analysis on this point suffers from the unwarranted assumption that the capitalist class has natural pro-democratic tendencies emanating from its economic interests.

Turning now to how the legacy of agrarian class relations and the authoritarian coalition more generally actually affected the events of the interwar period, we proposed the distinction between instrumental effects, that is, active intervention in the historical process by the actors in question, structural constraints on government policy, and hegemonic effects, that is, legacies (and recreations) of the ideological hegemony of the ruling coalitions, past and present, which are particularly important in explaining the behavior of the middle classes, urban and rural. In Italy and Spain, active intervention by landlords and capitalists in support of authoritarian outcomes was found to be of great importance. It cannot be overemphasized how critical the role of agrarian elites' attempts to maintain the control of rural labor was in these two cases. In Austria, the legacy of the ideological hegemony of dominant classes was decisive. In Germany, it was argued that all three factors mediated the effect of the historic developmental coalition on the interwar events.

The contrasting role played by the mechanism of ideological hegemony in the four cases, its importance in Austria and Germany as compared to Spain and Italy, is a function of the level of economic development and thus the strength of civil society. A second contrast between the four cases has been suggested by Stein Rokkan (personal conversation, 1973): it was in the two late nation builders, Italy and Germany, that the hyper-nationalism of Fascism was ideologically dominant, whereas in Spain and Austria the ideologically dominant current was clerical corporate authoritarianism. Rokkan argued that the overlapping of state consolidation and nation-building with mass mobilization created a climate favorable to the development of mass hyper-nationalism. One can add to this the experience of World War I which was also a component in the Fascist trajectory as it was directly related to the development of the right-wing paramilitary organizations that fed into Fascism. Thus, Fascism was only one form of modern capitalist authoritarianism, it is not equivalent to it.[45]

In this chapter, we have used the phrasing "historically engaged in labor repressive agriculture" when referring to the landed upper-classes of Austria, Germany, Italy, , the southern United States, and Australia. The method of labor control at the time of the transition to democracy and its subsequent demise was left open. Since we will return to the theme of the form of agrarian labor control in the next two chapters, some additional discussion of this question is in order here. One might begin by asking whether these classes were currently engaged in labor repressive agriculture and whether their mode of labor control was an important source of their opposition to democracy. Briefly, it can be said that the answer to the first question is yes in the US case but no in all four European cases and Australia. In Australia, the end of convict assignment and the development of freehold for the squatters ended the system of labor repressive agriculture and led to the rapid decline of the labor intensity of sheep ranching. As we have already pointed out, to the extent that the Moorian coalition contributed to the breakdown in Austria, it was not because of threats to the immediate interests of landlords. In Germany, landlord interests were at stake but the main issues there were policies aimed at support of prices, such as tariffs on grain, and loan subsidies for indebted landlords. Landlords and their political representative, the DNVP, certainly pressed for authoritarian solutions but not because of their need for labor control.

However, in the cases of Italy and Spain, though labor control methods cannot be described as "labor repressive," it most decidedly is true that the landlords' mode of labor control was an important source of their opposition to democracy.[46] To reconcile this assertion with our statement on the absence of labor repressive agriculture in the last paragraph, we must re-examine the concept. In both countries, rural labor was formally free in the period immediately preceding the transition to democracy. Moreover, there were no effective means of limiting labor mobility, such as the crop lien system, debt peonage, and the restraints on labor recruitment enforced in the post-bellum American South. On the other hand, organization of rural labor was difficult under prevailing political conditions and rural labor had no effective suffrage rights. The introduction of democracy changed the situation radically in ways that challenged the traditional mode of labor control. Rural labor now had rights to organize which were enforced by the state. In many localities, the parties representing the interest of rural labor (the socialists and, in Italy, also the Populari) controlled local government. The state, both the local state and, particularly in Spain, the national state, intervened on the side of rural labor, fixing wage rates, enforcing labor contracts, even limiting landlord rights to recruit labor from outside the locality, and so on. The counter-reaction of landlords was to strongly support an end to the political system that brought these problems.

What this example shows is that methods of labor control cannot be categorized into a simple dichotomy even when one's sole interest is predicting the posture of landlords toward various forms of political organization. There is a wide spectrum of political and organizational rights compatible with "market control" of labor. This holds for capitalists and workers as well as for landlords and rural labor. Indeed, in O'Donnell's (1973) argument on the transition to bureaucratic authoritarianism, the perception of capitalists that democracy and rights of organization made it impossible for them to attain wage rates compatible with future accumulation was a key reason for them to support the introduction of an authoritarian regime.

To briefly summarize the results of the analysis of the breakdown cases, it is our conclusion that the agrarian class relations and patterns of state–class alliances of the nineteenth and early twentieth centuries were necessary though not sufficient causes of the breakdown of democracy in interwar Europe. The existence of a large landed class changed the alliance options for other classes in both the late nineteenth century and in the 1920s and 1930s and as a consequence changed the political outcomes. It both opened up authoritarian options for the bourgeoisie and, to the extent that the landlord–state–bourgeois alliance affected the politics of the middle class and peasantry, it closed off options for the working class. What this amounts to is to assert that had the country in question had different landholding patterns and resultant state–class relations, democracy would have survived. As we pointed out in the discussion of Germany, this counterfactual will appear to many to be absurd, since those patterns of agrarian class relations and state–class alliances are an integral element of one's understanding of the essential features of German (Italian, Spanish, Austrian) economic and political development. In a sense, this is precisely our point.

The analysis indicated that Kurth's explanation of the paths to democracy and authoritarianism nicely supplements the explanation based on agrarian class relations. The timing and phases of industrialization reinforced tendencies created by legacies of agrarian class relations but it could not override them. On the positive side, the thesis does elucidate some features of the four authoritarian cases and highlight differences between them and the United States, Britain, and France. Late industrialization in the former four cases was associated with tariff policies and state intervention in the economy that facilitated the formation of and/or strengthening of the landlord-state-bourgeoisie coalition, and in every case this was further reinforced by an armaments policy which made heavy industry very dependent on the state and imperialistic policies. Thus, in a fashion that dovetails with the arguments of Calleo and Blackbourn and Eley, Kurth's argument supplies one with an economic explanation for the posture of the bourgeoisie in these countries, an alternative to Moore's dependence on landlords argument, which did not fare well in the present analysis.

However, Kurth's argument only holds in countries characterized by the presence of a significant landlord class, as an examination of the small European democracies reveals. Most of the small democracies were late industrializers and most industrialized with tariff protection for industry and agriculture, often introduced in reponse to the crises of 1873–96.[47] At least some of them were characterized by some of the features typical of German industrial structure, which in Eley's account forms one link between late industrialization and authoritarianism. As we saw in our analysis of Sweden, the Swedish bourgeoisie did support the essentially authoritarian Conservative Party, which is consistent with the Kurth and Eley theses. But, the Conservatives' support was limited and they had no allies in other parties, thus capitulation to the democratic forces was almost the only alternative. The political independence of the Swedish peasantry is clearly a key reason for the isolation of the Conservatives.

Kurth's argument on the importance of the saturation phase of steel production and imperialism might be saved by introducing a geo-political condition along the lines of Calleo's thesis on the German case. That is, it might be argued that imperialism was only a viable alternative for countries in a position to aspire to great power status and thus the argument simply does not apply to small countries. Without denying the importance of armaments production and imperialism in explaining the trajectory of the authoritarian cases, it can simply be pointed out again that the British and American cases show that imperialism does not imply a push toward domestic authoritarianism.

Table 4.4 classifies the countries studied in this chapter on five of the six factors listed earlier as leading to the landlord/state/bourgeois coalition. The sixth factor, features of the state, will be discussed below. One can see that most of the European small states, Canada, France, and New Zealand differ markedly from the authoritarian regimes. Much of this is traceable to landholding patterns. With overwhelming dominance of family farming, the large landholding class, where it existed at all, could not achieve political significance (point 1 in the table); labor repressive agriculture was impossible (point 2); the bourgeoisie was ipso facto stronger than the landed class (point 3); and, for the same reason, it was not the dependent partner in a coalition. In the cases of the small European democracies, New Zealand, and Canada, because there was never a strong agrarian oligarchy, a revolutionary break from the past was not necessary. In France, the revolutionary break accelerated the weakening of the role of the landed oligarchy in agriculture and thus by the late nineteenth century, it exhibited a profile similar to the small democracies. Britain differed from the authoritarian profile as the landlords were not engaged in labor repressive agriculture. However, as we noted in our discussion, it also differed in many other ways (e.g. tariff politics, early industrialization, absence of working-class socialism in a critical period, etc.) and thus the case is over-determined.

The United States and Australia come closest to Moore's characterizations. We qualify Moore's own assertion that the United States experienced a revolutionary break from the past. Certainly, the defeat of the southern landlords in the Civil War ended any possibility that they might lead a move toward the establishment of authoritarianism at the national level, but it did not stop them from re-establishing authoritarianism in the South. The nature of the state is what separates Australia and the United States from the authoritarian cases. In the United States, state power was decentralized and the labor repressive system was maintained through landlord control of the local state. In Australia, the colonial state began the dismantling of the labor repressive system and then managed the transition to colonial self-government such that the landlords were unable to control the state.

The analysis summarized in table 4.4 is intended to account for why democracy broke down in some countries but not others in the interwar period. In all cases other than France, it also helps one to understand much about the politics of democratization. It is misleading in the French case because it implies that the landed upper class was not a serious barrier to democratization in this case. While it is true that by the turn of the century this class was politically marginalized, it was still a very significant political actor in the events of 1830–77, the critical period of democratic transition in France. Even in periods of rule by parliaments elected by universal suffrage, such as the Second Republic and the initial years of the Third Republic, the landed upper class retained significant political influence through its alliance with the church and its ideological domination of the peasantry in many regions of the country. Indeed, the political power of the landed upper class is one reason why the Second Republic failed to produce a stable democracy.

Why the power of the landed upper class failed to produce a similar authoritarian outcome in the 1870s is a question of some interest. One answer is that it was too weak. It is certainly true that France in this period was an intermediate case between the small democracies of Europe and the authoritarian cases both in terms of the proportion of land controlled by large landlords and in terms of the political power of landlords. But three other features, all consequences of the French Revolution, also distinguish France from the authoritarian path as outlined earlier. First, the Revolution had ended the seigneurial system and by the 1870s agriculture was thoroughly commercialized. Second, the bourgeoisie and the traditional nobility were deeply divided politically and even the bourgeoisie itself was divided on the very question of the desirability of democratic government. Third, and perhaps most important, by the end of the Orleanist Monarchy, the aristocracy had lost its enclave in the army and the bureaucracy.

The nature of the state is the sixth factor hypothesized at the beginning of this chapter to lead to authoritarianism. It was left out of table 4.4 because the countries defy easy categorization on this variable. There is no question that forces inside the state, particularly the coercive forces, contributed to the rise of authoritarian regimes in all four cases in the interwar period. Thus, by the very outcome, for these cases, we know that the state had the capacity to act. Crucially, it had sufficient repressive capacity to install authoritarian rule. We also know that the coercive forces, and in some cases, the bureaucratic and judicial elites, were ideologically inclined to intervene. Thus, they aligned themselves with the dominant classes and exhibited autonomy from subordinate classes as hypothesized. Arguably, this alignment was in part due to social links to those classes. Finally, we know they had to have the opportunity to intervene with some possibility of success. That is, they had allies. Or, to state it more precisely in the case of the coercive forces, there had to be powerful groups in civil society calling for their intervention.

The ambiguity arises in the case of the democratic survivors. Nonintervention could be a result of "deficiencies" on any of the three factors, ideological inclination, capacity, or allies in civil society. Non-events are notoriously hard to study and a systematic analysis of cross-country variations would require primary research beyond the capacity of the present study. Nevertheless, we can venture some hypotheses on this matter.

First, did the state not intervene due to lack of repressive capacity as indicated by the size of the coercive forces? Skocpol (1973) criticizes Moore's analysis of England on this ground. Here we would express some skepticism that lack of repressive capacity per se prevented the upper-classes in any of the democratic survivors from introducing authoritarianism. The ability of the northern United States, the very opposite of a Prussian "strong state", to mobilize a massive repressive force in the Civil War against resistance (draft riots, etc.) argues that most of these states had the ability to mobilize repressive capacity were the will there. Moreover, figures on the size of the military personnel in late nineteenth-century Europe do not support the hypothesis that the authoritarian cases had significantly larger armies in proportionate terms than the democratic cases (Flora et al. 1983: 252). As of the 1870s, military personnel as a percentage of males 20–44 years of age varied from a low of 3–4 percent in Italy to 7–8 percent in Austria with no obvious social or political factor to distinguish the large establishments from the small ones. By the decade before World War I, size of the military establishment was related to great power status with the large countries ranging from 5 percent to 9 percent of males 20–44 under arms and the small countries from 1 percent to 4 percent. While this means that all of the authoritarian cases were on the high end of the spectrum, the defeat of Germany and Austria in the war resulted in the vast reduction of their armed forces. At the time of the authoritarian seizures in the 1930s the armies of these two countries were among the smallest in Europe. What mattered then were the loyalties of the coercive forces and the alliance structure in society not size of the military apparatus.

The question of allies in civil societies has, of course, already been covered thoroughly in this chapter. With regard to loyalties, the contrast between Sweden and Denmark on the one hand, and Switzerland and Norway on the other hand, suggests that a legacy of absolutism, unbroken by revolution, strengthens the reactionary posture of all state actors. The class structures of these four countries were very similar, but state resistance to the introduction of full responsible parliamentary government delayed the introduction of democracy relative to the level of industrialization in Sweden and Denmark as compared with Norway and Switzerland.[48] It can be expected that current or past status as a great power would be likely both to increase this reactionary tilt and to strengthen the army's position in the state and society. The contrast between Germany, Austria, Italy, France, Britain, Spain and Sweden on the one hand, and Norway, Switzerland, Belgium, and the Netherlands on the other would appear to support this expectation.

The importance of political loyalties can also be seen by later developments in Sweden. While, by World War I, the upper ranks of the state were still filled with officials and officers of upper-class and even aristocratic origin, the political developments of the previous decades had resulted in a conscript army, whose loyalties lay with the classes of its origins not with the officers' corps. Thus, as we noted in our discussion of Sweden, the troops could not be relied upon for domestic repression by this point in time.

To differentiate France and Britain from the breakdown cases, it can be argued that the alliance structure in civil society itself influences the political orientation of the military to intervene. Appeals for military intervention or appeals to the army to turn a blind eye to the private use of coercive power by powerful groups in society are a feature of almost every democratic breakdown discussed in this book. Moreover, to return to the theme of the authoritarian coalition, the long-term alliances of the military with other social forces and the military's roots in the social class structure affect its propensity to intervene. If the political project of these groups does not call for authoritarian solutions, it is less likely that the army will come to that political conclusion independently. Thus, the British army officers' corps differed in outlook from its German counterpart in the same way that the British Conservative Party differed from its German counterpart. As we argued above, the French aristocracy's loss of control of the officers' corps in the early nineteenth century certainly reduced its ability to affect the political developments later.

The analysis in this chapter powerfully supports our argument that transnational structures of power affect the development of democracy. The effect of geo-political pressures was most clear in the case of Austria. Foreign intervention in the Spanish Civil War became a celebrated cause though it is not clear that it changed the outcome. The threat of foreign intervention also delayed the development of democracy in Switzerland. The defeat of Napoleon III in the Franco-Prussian War at the very least sped up the process of democratization.

Far more important than selective and purposeful interventions by foreign powers is how European-wide and even world wide international economic and political developments reverberated through every country conditioning or even determining domestic political developments at critical periods. This is most apparent in the case of the British settler colonies where the colonial power influenced not only the political outcomes but the nature of that influence as Britain industrialized and her domestic politics and international economic posture changed. In Europe, it was above all the crises of the 1873–96 period, World War I, and the Great Depression which changed the course of events. These events deeply affected the politics of democratization in all European countries except Switzerland and France and even influenced most of the British settler colonies. However, the effect was different depending on the domestic alignment of forces and position in the international system (Gourevitch 1986). The economic crises of the late nineteenth century led to the class alliances on the tariff question which cemented the authoritarian coalition in the four breakdown cases. Britain's international economic position drove industry and agriculture apart. Converse alignments, competitive agriculture and protectionist business, produced similar results in the British settler colonies weakening the chances of authoritarian alliances there. Sweden did raise tariffs but a permanent coalition of domestic manufacturing interests and the agricultural sector did not result. World War I had more the uniform effect of accelerating the process of democratization in most European countries and in Canada, but where pre-war democratic coalitions were weak the turn to democracy did not survive the interwar period. The Great Depression led to the isolation of Social Democracy and the installation of Fascism in Germany and to the integration of Social Democracy and the formation of the farmer–worker alliance in Sweden. The variability of the effect of transnational structures of power and international events again underlines the complex interaction between class power, state power, class and state alliances, and transnational power that we have seen throughout this chapter.

To return to a point made in our earlier discussion of Moore, the long term development of Spain, and to some extent the American South, leads one to raise the question of whether "fascism" represented a viable system or not. Moore seems to be ambivalent on this point. On the one hand, he designates it as one of three "paths to the modern world." On the other, at several points, he indicates that these systems crashed owing to their own internal contradictions (Moore 1966: 438, 442). Our position is much less ambiguous: modern capitalist authoritarianism is an inherently unstable system as under the conditions of modern industrial social organization it is difficult in the long run to exclude working and middle classes both economically and politically.

The comparative historical analysis in this chapter confirms our contention that the correlation between economic development and democracy found in the quantitative cross-national studies is more accurately explained by our political economy approach than by modernization theory. Our discussion of hegemony and peasant mobilization in Europe and of religion and civil society in Sweden contain the seeds of a similar alternative explanation for the correlation between Protestantism and democracy found in the quantitative studies. In these studies, this correlation is also explained by concepts and relationships derived from structural-functionalism. Again it is Lipset's early essay that is the source of this explanation of the correlation. He contended that "Protestantism's emphasis on individual responsibility furthered the emergence of democratic values in these countries" (Lipset 1960: 57), an assertion which is cited by Bollen and Jackman (1985a: 31).

Our discussion of Sweden points in another direction: What was important about the dissenting religions was not the values it promoted but rather the sectarian organization. That is, they were autonomous organized communities whose development strengthened civil society. Furthermore, they were organized in opposition to the state church and the state so their existence insulated their members from ruling-class hegemony.[49] As we argued in our discussion of peasant mobilization, state churches, Lutheran and Anglican as well as Catholic, were conduits for ruling-class hegemony. The parties developed by these state church–class–state coalitions (Lipset and Rokkan 1967) were opponents of democracy. Parties with strong bases in dissenting sects were always more liberal, supporting civil liberties and suffrage expansion and in some cases full democracy. Thus, we argue that the critical distinction here is state church vs. sect, not Protestantism vs. others as indicated by the cross-national analyses.[50]

There is no question that doctrine does reinforce the political tendencies of churches and sects. Lutheranism shares with Catholicism authoritarian features: though members are encouraged to read the Bible, the church retains a monopoly on the authoritative interpretation of it. Luther also strongly emphasized obedience to political authority (Sanders 1964). However, comparative historical evidence from the European cases indicates that it was the political situation of the church that was crucial in determining the political posture of the party allied with it: where the church was not allied with the state and also was a minority, the allied political party (e. g. the German Zentrum) was a relatively democratic force and the church's subculture did insulate its followers from authoritarian ruling-class hegemony. The converse can be seen in the case of Connecticut: there the Congregationalist establishment aligned clearly with the Federalists and opposed suffrage extension. The state continued to have one of the most restricted franchises in the United States well into the nineteenth century (Goodman 1967: 80; Williamson 1960: 165–73, 265).

Some countries have been excluded from the analysis in this chapter and we close with a few comments on how their inclusion might change our analysis. Our criterion for inclusion was that the countries in question experience some period of full democracy by the end of the interwar period. An analysis of all countries in Europe (and not just western Europe) fitting this criterion would have included Czechoslovakia and Finland.[51] The inclusion of these two countries would have increased the importance of state consolidation as a variable. Alapuro's analysis of Finland and comparison with elsewhere in eastern Europe underlines the importance of the state's sudden loss of the means of coercion at the time of the Russian Revolution for the subsequent development of these countries. Thus, the state and transnational structures of power loom larger in accounting for developments in this region. At the same time, he also confirms the importance of agrarian class relations for the different outcomes in different countries.

Next it might be asked what difference inclusion of Japan and the states of the European periphery which never became full democracies or, in many cases, even restricted democracies (Portugal, Greece, and the rest of eastern Europe) might make.[52] In general, the inclusion of the European periphery would raise the importance of the level of development/strength of civil society/strength of subordinate classes as a variable for explaining differences across countries. These factors go far in explaining why these countries were never democratic in the first place. The existence of a powerful landed upper class was certainly also a barrier to the introduction of democracy in Portugal, Poland, Hungary, Latvia, and Estonia. Ethnic divisions within and between classes played a role in the events of the interwar period in a number of countries, most notably Yugoslavia. Finally, as we mentioned in the last paragraph, in eastern Europe transnational political influences and state consolidation were much more important in explaining the political trajectories of these countries in the interwar period.

Japan experienced a period of restricted democracy in the 1920s, so called "Taisho Democracy," before turning to Fascism in the 1930s. All four of the cases of modern capitalist authoritarianism examined in this chapter fit Moore's analysis in so far as all four of them did have a significant and politically influential class of large landlords into the modern era. Ironically, Japan, one case discussed extensively by Moore, does not fit this characterization (Dore

1959; Dore and Ouchi 1972; Waswo 1976). A powerful bureaucratic and military state, created in part in response to outside threats, not a powerful landed upper class, is the root of Japanese authoritarianism (Kim 1988a). This state directed industrialization "from above" and created a bourgeoisie dependent on the state for its very existence. The military retained tremendous formal governmental power even during the Taisho period and when the political agenda of the bourgeois politicians threatened the military's own project, it moved to eliminate party government. The inclusion of Japan, then, would further strengthen the autonomous role of the state and of transnational structures of power in explaining the political developments of the more advanced capitalist societies in the interwar period.

5

Latin America

The wave of (re)democratization in Latin America in the 1980s has raised the question whether this constitutes just another cycle in the rise and decline of constitutional, more or less democratic rule, or whether it constitutes a trend towards democratization consistent with the results of cross-national statistical studies. Whereas it is the case that most of the major Latin American countries rank higher on the conventional indicators of socio-economic development than they did in the 1960s (e.g. Seligson 1987a), the austerity policies necessitated by the debt crisis have exerted a highly detrimental influence on the presumed consequences of development which are traditionally invoked in the statistical studies to interpret its favorable effect on democracy. Inequality and poverty have increased in the 1980s and thus the room for tolerance and compromise has shrunk.

Much of the recent literature on redemocratization focuses on the process of transition itself, on actors and decisions (e. g. O'Donnell and Schmitter 1986; Malloy and Seligson 1987; Drake and Silva 1986), but to answer the question whether we are seeing a cycle or a trend we need to adopt a longer historical perspective and focus on power relations in society and between civil society and the state, and on the effects of economic development and of transnational structures of power on these internal power relations. In developing this analysis, we will re-emphasize a number of themes laid out in chapters 2 and 3. We begin our analysis of the conditions shaping the emergence and consolidation of democratic regimes in Latin America with a focus on the class structure and class coalitions as they emerged in the period of export expansion and were modified by the growth of import substitution industrialization (ISI).[1] The nature of large landowners and other elite sectors was crucial for the intensity of resistance against democratization, and the capability of subordinate classes to organize was crucial for the strength of pressures for an opening of the political system. The role of the middle classes was often decisive in so far as the alliances they formed determined the degree of opening and heavily influenced the consolidation of the new regimes. The attempt to understand differences in the class structure and options for class alliances directs our attention to the nature of a country's integration into the world market (foreign controlled mineral vs. nationally controlled agrarian export sectors), the labor requirements of agriculture, and the degree of subsidiary industrialization generated by the export sector.

As our theoretical framework suggests, we also include the interaction between class and state in our analysis of the effects of class structure and class alliances on regime forms. Before state power itself was consolidated, a rather lengthy process in many Latin American countries, no regime form could achieve stability. After consolidation of state power, states varied in two important dimensions, namely in the degree of relative autonomy from economically dominant classes and in the degree of involvement in the promotion of economic development and the shaping of the political articulation of emerging subordinate classes. The relative autonomy of the state tended to be higher in mineral export economies than in agricultural export economies, and it tended to grow in the period of ISI when newly emerging groups challenged oligarchic power. In the post-World War II period the relative autonomy of the state was further enhanced by the international system of states via economic and military aid. Whereas the state's growing autonomy from oligarchic interests in many cases provided an opportunity for widening political inclusion and institutionalizing contestation, the bolstering of state autonomy by external sources tended to work in the opposite direction, towards political exclusion and suppression of contestation.

As outlined in chapter 3, our analysis will also take account of transnational structures of power which affected democratic emergence and consolidation both directly and indirectly. Economic dependency shaped the class structure in ways which kept anti-democratic forces strong and pro-democratic forces weak. In agro-export economies large landowners remained economically important and politically strong. The high capital intensity of ISI kept the industrial working-class a relatively small proportion of the population and thus hampered the organizational capacity of the lower classes in general. The two World Wars, particularly the second one, temporarily strengthened pro-democratic currents but did not produce any lasting regime changes. In contrast, the Cold War significantly strengthened anti-leftist and anti-democratic forces. Though direct intervention by foreign powers in internal political affairs was much less significant in South America than in Central America and the Caribbean,[2] economic and diplomatic pressures to ensure protection of property rights often weakened reformist democratic governments. Furthermore, the emphasis on counter-insurgency training and the provision of military aid enhanced the importance and relative autonomy of the coercive arm of the state and thus reinforced the propensity of the military to restrict or abolish democratic politics.

Finally, the following analysis will draw our attention to the importance of political parties. They were crucial in institutionalizing contestation, in mobilizing pressures from below for an opening of the political system, and in mediating threat perception at the top as to the consequences of making such concessions. Essentially, democracy could only be consolidated where elite interests were effectively protected either through direct influence of elite groups on the state apparatus or through electorally strong political parties.

The relationships between these variables and democratic rule are by no means simple and unilinear. Some variables have contradictory consequences for democratization, some effects change over time, the variables interact and their relative importance changes over time. There is not a unique path to achieving democracy or preserving it. Rather, as we have argued, historical sequences are important. The emergence of class coalitions, state structures and other political institutions in an earlier phase shapes the way in which new social forces are integrated into or excluded from the political process in later phases. Accordingly, comparative analysis of historical sequences is best suited to let us explore the causal conditions for emergence and consolidation of democratic regimes.

Though the applicability of any generalizations to a particular country depends on that country's prior historical path, it is worth highlighting just a few generalizations from the very beginning. Without structural conditions which allowed the organization of effective mass pressure democracy was unlikely to emerge. Yet, at the same time the emergence and survival of democratic regimes has required first of all the development of an interest in the institutionalization of contestation on the part of elites and then the construction of effective mechanisms for protection of elite interests in the context of inclusion of non-elite sectors. The expansion of export agriculture brought generally the beginning of institutionalized contestation among elites and pressures for greater political inclusion, which however were successful only where agriculture was not so labor intensive as to make the organization of labor threatening to agrarian elites. Early growth of industrial employment further enhanced the prospects of democratization, but this could be undercut if political relations between elite and mass were articulated by the state rather than political parties. Expansion of mineral exports also led to organized mass pressure, but this pressure was likely to be institutionalized in the form of radical mass parties, which was threatening to elites and therefore created a cycle of democratic breakthroughs and authoritarian lapses. A cycle of breakthrough and collapse could also be invoked where elite and middle-class politicians turned to the military as allies in their initial quest to establish democracy.

Our analytical approach differs from that taken in the major recent interpretations of Latin American political change. Most of these other approaches tend to concentrate exclusively on structural, class analytic factors, or on political institutions, actors, and processes. O'Donnell's earlier work on the rise of bureaucratic–authoritarian regimes (1973), Cardoso and Faletto's (1979) study of dependent development in Latin America, and Bergquist's (1986) analysis of the emergence and political role of the labor movements in Argentina, Chile, Colombia, and Venezuela, all take a structural, class analytic approach. J. S. Valenzuela's (1985) and A. Valenzuela's (1989) discussions of the development of Chilean democracy concentrate on political institutions, actors, and choices. O'Donnell and Schmitter's (1986) analysis focuses mainly on political actors and their choices in the period of transition from authoritarian rule. Diamond and Linz's (1989) introduction to a large comparative collaborative study of experiences with democracy in Latin America discusses a long list of factors which range from economic and social structures to political institutions, processes, and actors, without however establishing clear priorities or systematic relationships among them. Collier's (1986) and Collier and Collier's (forthcoming) analyses of the political legacies of the initial incorporation of labor movements come closest to our own approach in that they integrate structural variables into their essentially political institutional analysis. Our approach, in contrast, integrates political institutional into an essentially structural analysis; but, like the Colliers' approach, ours takes systematic account of political conjunctures and their legacies.

Aside from the collection of essays in the Diamond, Lipset, and Linz (1989) volume, the only comprehensive attempt to explain the emergence and decline of (partly) democratic forms of rule in the Latin American countries is Therborn's (1979) study. Therborn also remains at an exclusively structural level and concludes that democracy is a conjunctural outcome resulting from the contradictions and conflicts within capitalism (1979: 96), but he does not identify clear patterns of such contradictions and conflicts. We attempt to provide here a broad gauged comparative analysis which combines an emphasis on structural variables with systematic attention to the role of political institutions and critical political phases.

We shall pursue the line of analysis suggested by our three clusters of power, looking at the development of the balance of class power, the relationship between state and civil society, and the impact of transnational structures of power. In contrast to chapter 4 where we focused on the transition to and the breakdown of full democracies, we will here take into account more restricted forms of democracy also and focus on a longer time period. If we included full democracies only, our universe would be very small indeed. A look at tables 5.1 and 5.2 shows that the South American countries by no means followed a path of linear progression from oligarchic regimes to severely restricted, then mildly restricted, and finally fully democratic ones.[3] Rather, there is a variety of paths, involving reversals and the skipping of stages.

The analysis in this chapter is quite complex and rests on many pairs and sets of comparison. To improve the clarity of presentation, we begin by laying out the argument, even though it is not an argument derived from a grand theory, but rather an argument arrived at through analytic induction. The analysis itself is not constructed as a test of theoretically derived alternative hypotheses. Rather, it is an attempt to chart the sequences of regime changes, toward and away from democratic forms, and link them to changes in the balance of class power, in the state apparatus, and in the international economy and system of states.

After presenting an analytical summary of our argument, we shall develop a more detailed comparative historical analysis of the factors leading to the establishment of the various types of regimes, the factors which support the consolidation or breakdown of democratic regimes, and finally those which promote redemocratization. The distinction between these different stages in the analysis is important because factors which support the installation of some form of democratic regime may not support its consolidation, and because the existence of a democratic regime profoundly influences future political dynamics. Comparisons with developments in Europe will serve to underline both the universal characteristics of the dynamics of democratization and its peculiarly Latin American features.

The Argument

In laying out the conditions conducive to the emergence of the different types of democratic regimes, we focus in particular on the economic power base of elites, the strength of civil society, the balance of class power, and the political articulation of civil society.[4] These factors were originally shaped by the structure of the economy and of the state, whose origins lay in part in the colonial legacies and were modified by the combination of geographical suitability and export opportunities in the nineteenth century and during the onset of industrialization. They in turn shaped the interaction between the pressures from subordinate classes (i. e. middle and working classes) needed for democratization and the level of threat perception on the part of economic elites motivating the elites to accommodate to these pressures or search for authoritarian alternatives. Once political institutions had been formed – shaped by economic structures, by the historically inherited state structures, and by the class structure – they assumed a life of their own and became important determinants of regime outcomes. Thus, the conditions leading to the emergence of different varieties of democratic regimes underwent substantial change over time.

The various sequences formed by the interaction of structural and institutional variables are sketched out in figures 5. 1 and 5. 2 below. These figures should provide a road map for the outline of the argument that follows. The argument covers a sequence of four factors that are basic antecedents to the emergence of democratic regimes: the consolidation of state power, the expansion and type of export economy, the strength of industrialization, and the agent of political articulation of subordinate classes. After a brief discussion of the class forces that give these factors their dynamic thrust, we then go on to discuss the sequences of breakdown and reconstitution that follow the initial establishment of democracy. In this second set of sequences, institutional arrangements for effective protection of elite interests play a crucial role.

Consolidation of state power

The first essential precondition for the emergence of any form of institutionalized contestation was consolidation of state power. Before state power was consolidated, there was no institutionalization of contestation and thus no movement towards democracy. This does not mean that a strong state had to be established in the sense of effective intervention in economic and social life, but simply that overt challenges to state authority had to come to an end, particularly challenges in the form of armed resistance. In other words, the state

TABLE 5.1 Classification of regimes

	Constitutional oligarchic	Authoritarian; traditional, populist, military, or corporatist	Restricted democratic	Fully democratic	Bureaucratic–authoritarian
Argentina	before 1912	1930–46 1951–55 1955–58 1962–63	1958–62 1963–66	1912–30 1946–51 1973–76 1983–90	1966–73 1976–83
Brazil	before 1930	1930–45	1945–64 1985–90		1964–85
Bolivia	before 1930	1930–52 1964–82	1982–90	1952–64	
Chile	before 1920	1924–32	1920–24 1932–70 1990	1970–73	1973–89
Colombia	before 1936	1949–58	1936–49 1958–90		

Ecuador	1916–25	before 1916 1925–48 1961–78	1948–61 1978–90		
Mexico		up to 1990			
Paraguay		up to 1990			
Peru		before 1930 1930–39 1948–56 1962–63 1968–80	1939–48 1956–62 1963–68	1980–90	
Uruguay		before 1903 1933–42	1903–19	1919–33 1942–73 1984–90	1973–84
Venezuela		before 1935 1935–45	1958–68	1945–48 1968–90	

TABLE 5.2 Types of restricted and full democracy

Contestation	Inclusion Restricted		Unrestricted	
Restricted	Argentina	1958–62; 1963–66	Brazil	1985–90
	Brazil	1945–64	Bolivia	1982–90
	Peru	1939–48; 1956–62; 1963–68	Ecuador	1978–90
	Ecuador	1948–61	Colombia	1936–49
	Chile	1920–24; 1932–58	Chile	1990
	Venezuela	1958–68		
	Uruguay	1903–19		
	Colombia	1958–90		
Unrestricted	Chile	1958–70	Argentina	1912–30; 1946–51; 1973–76; 1983–90
			Bolivia	1952–64
			Chile	1970–73
			Peru	1980–90
			Uruguay	1919–33; 1942–73; 1984–90
			Venezuela	1945–48; 1968–90

had to be able effectively to claim a monopoly on organized force. In fact, institutionalized contestation was easier to achieve if the state played only a minor or no interventionist role, because this lowered the stakes in gaining control over the state apparatus.

The difficulty of the task of consolidating state power varied with the length and intensity of the independence wars and with external warfare in the first century after independence. Exposure to warfare prior to and during the attempt to consolidate state power not only delayed the achievement of consolidation, but prolonged fighting and extensive destruction of the economy during the independence wars cast military leaders into a more prominent role in post-independence politics. Later exposure to external warfare, mostly due to the struggle over borders, further strengthened the position of military strong-men, and defeat in wars was particularly detrimental to peaceful internal competition for power. Where the achievement of consolidation of state power was delayed for a long time, the problems of institutionalization of contestation and of inclusion tended to pose themselves simultaneously because economic development had increased pressures from subordinate classes. The greater difficulties in consolidating state power in Latin America compared to Europe explain at least part of the comparative scarcity of stable institutionalized elite contestation and gradual inclusion of non-elite sectors.

Export expansion

Once state power was consolidated, a new phase in the process of democratization began, with new dynamics shaped by economic structures, particularly the expansion of the export economy, and by the legacies of the transition to independence. For progress towards democracy to be made, intra-elite conflicts due to geographical and economic diversity and due to scarcity of resources had to be moderate and thus facilitate institutionalized contestation, and pressures from subordinate classes for inclusion had to emerge. Without such pressures, no opening of the political system took place, but there was no simple linear relationship between the intensity of such pressures and progress towards democracy. If these pressures were highly threatening to elites, they tended to meet with authoritarian reactions. The degree to which they were perceived as threatening depended in turn on the agents mobilizing and articulating the pressures (radical mass parties were more threatening than clientelistic parties), on the economic vulnerability of elites (labor intensive agriculture made landowners more dependent on politically sanctioned labor control than non-labor intensive agriculture), and on the availability to elites of political institutions for control within a constitutional context (elite political parties or state corporatist institutions).

We are using labor intensity of agriculture rather than Moore's notion of labor repressive agriculture because in all systems landlords used some degree of legal coercion to ensure an adequate supply of cheap labor for their estates. Even where labor relations were based on wage labor (a characteristic of market control in Moore's terminology), politically backed restrictions, such as on labor

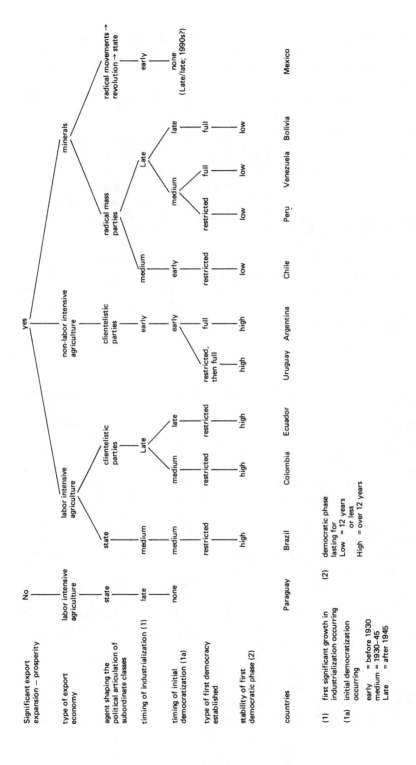

FIGURE 5.1 Paths to initial democratization after consolidation of state power

mobility or on unionization, served to keep labor cheap. The greater the supply of cheap labor needed, the more important such restrictions imposed and enforced through state power were for the landlords. Consequently, the more labor intensive agriculture was, the greater the threat perception was on the part of the landowning elite of a potential loss of control over the state apparatus in the wake of an opening of the political system.

The necessary condition for significant reduction of scarcity of resources and for the emergence of pressures for inclusion was expansion of the export economy. If no significant export expansion occurred, no movement towards democracy occurred either, and if expansion started late, movement towards democracy was delayed. The conditions most conducive to the early consolidation of state power and to institutionalization of contestation among elites were a relatively easy transition to independence, little involvement in border wars or success in such struggles, lack of great regional diversity, and early expansion of the export economy.

Export expansion was not sufficient in itself for the emergence of restricted or full democracy. Democracy depended on the sequences of social structural and political institutional developments set in motion by export expansion. The predominance of agricultural versus mineral exports, the former being under national and the latter for the most part under foreign ownership, made for crucial differences in the democratization process.[5] The nature of the export economy shaped the strength and homogeneity of the economic base of the elite and its labor requirements, the degree of subsidiary industrialization and urbanization generated by the export sector, and the strength of and alliance possibilities among subordinate classes, all of which were important for the process of democratization.

Expansion of a nationally controlled agrarian export economy produced elite prosperity and thus helped to consolidate elite contestation, but by itself did not produce any significant pressures for inclusion. If pressures for inclusion were produced by industrialization, resistance on the part of the landowning elites to any significant opening of the political system was stern where the dominant type of agriculture was labor intensive, but more moderate where agriculture had lower labor requirements. Progress towards democracy only occurred under the crucial precondition of absence of labor intensive agriculture. In fact, in no case where (1) labor intensive agriculture predominated, and (2) agriculture was the crucial export sector, was unrestricted democracy established in South America.[6] Under these conditions, the landowners feared the loss of an abundant supply of cheap labor in the wake of democratization, and they were powerful enough either to resist an opening of the political system altogether or at least to keep the rural sector excluded.

Expansion of mineral export economies produced less favorable conditions for the institutionalization of contestation, but stronger pressures for inclusion from subordinate classes. When foreign-owned mineral exports assumed the leading role, there was a greater tendency to elite heterogeneity and a greater potential for state autonomy from domestic elites. Urban commercial and financial elites, as well as owners of small and medium mines, could emerge as separate groups from agro-exporting elites, and the possibility of collecting revenue generated directly or indirectly by the mineral export sector gave the state greater potential autonomy from local elites. Conflicts of interest among elite factions, together with the centrality of the role of the state in capturing proceeds from the mineral export economy, intensified the struggle for control of the state and made constitutional elite competition for power more problematic. The early emergence of a geographically concentrated and strategically located working class with a high propensity to organization and militancy, together with the weaker hegemonic position of the landholding elite, provided the basis for the growth of radical mass parties which promoted the formation of alliances between middle and working classes. These parties articulated demands for political inclusion along with demands for radical social reform, which were initially highly threatening to elites. Thus, expansion of mineral export economies set up a sequence of political instability, with democratic breakthroughs followed by authoritarian reaction. Only later changes in the radical mass parties and/or in elite confidence in the effectiveness of the representation of their own interests through political institutions opened the possibility for the consolidation of democratic regimes.

Industrialization and agents of political articulation

Once the Latin American countries started to diversify their economies, adding industrialization to the production of raw materials, they entered a new phase in the process of democratization. Industrialization raised the potential for pressures for democratization, particularly for greater political inclusion, because it strengthened civil society by increasing the size and the interaction among middle and working classes, but its political effects were mediated by the pre-existing political institutional structures, particularly the party system and the tradition of state intervention in society. Industrialization produced or reinforced already existing pressures for inclusion, but the actual strength of these pressures and their political outcome heavily depended on the agents shaping the political articulation of civil society. The nature of these agents was rooted in the class structure and patterns of political institutionalization set before and during the expansion of the export economy.

In agricultural export economies the two principal agents shaping the political articulation of civil society were clientelistic parties and the state. In the case of clientelistic parties, threat perception on the part of economic elites was reduced by elite leadership or by participation of some elite factions if they were middle-class led. These parties typically attempted to enlist labor support to strengthen their own political base, without promoting strong labor organization. They did not always push for full democracy, which further reduced the threat posed by their activities to elites. Where the state attempted to encapsulate and control the emerging working class from the beginning, the result was a weak labor movement and a weakly articulated civil society, incapable of exerting any significant pressures for democratization.

The configuration of type of agriculture, strength of industrialization, and agent shaping the political articulation of civil society resulted in three different types of outcomes in economies where agriculture was the dominant export sector. In agrarian export economies with non-labor intensive agriculture and significant pressures resulting from early and strong industrialization, articulated by clientelistic parties, an opening to full democracy took place. In agrarian export economies with labor intensive agriculture and moderate pressures resulting from later and weaker industrialization, articulated by clientelistic parties, only an opening to restricted democracy occurred. In agrarian export economies with labor intensive agriculture and containment of pressures by strong state involvement, there was no opening at all or only a delayed opening to restricted democracy.[7]

In mineral export economies, the pre-existing radical mass parties became the primary mobilizers of the industrial working class and forcefully articulated demands for political inclusion and social change. Except in the special case of Mexico, which will be discussed at the end of the analysis of conditions for initial democratization, the state did not play a lasting role in shaping and controlling the political articulation of labor in any of the mineral export economies.[8] The radical mass parties attempted to promote labor and middle-class organization and the formation of political alliances between them in support of the struggle for full democracy. These mass parties were capable of effectively pushing for democratic openings even before industrialization had created a large urban working class and a well consolidated civil society, but they were in no case capable of consolidating the democratic regime in their first attempt. Where industrialization came late and/or remained very limited, radical mass parties did not survive in their original form; they fragmented and ceased to be an important political force, and/or abandoned their radical posture in the face of intense repression but persisted as moderate mass parties. Such changes in the mass parties then opened the possibility for the reestablishment of democracy, initially typically of a limited nature.

Class forces

If we analyze the class forces which were crucial for the move towards democracy, the middle classes emerge in a leading role, though, we hasten to add, they were frequently ambivalent concerning democracy for other subordinate classes. The parties pushing for an installation of democracy in the sense of institutionalized contestation with effective inclusion of non-elite sectors were all led by members of the middle classes and had significant middle-class bases. However, the middle classes needed allies to be successful in effecting installation of a democractic regime. In particular, in order for full democracies to be installed, a significant working-class presence was indispensable. Thus, even if we narrow our focus to full democracies, the Latin American experience does differ from the one of advanced capitalist societies we analyzed in the last chapter.

Given their leading role, the presence of identifiable middle classes was obviously a prerequisite for democratization, but the size of the middle classes per se was not a crucial determinant of the strength of pro-democratic pressures nor of the degree of inclusiveness of the democratic regime installed. Whereas in two of the countries with the largest middle classes the earliest breakthroughs to full democracy occurred, in another only restricted democracy was established. Breakthroughs to full democracy also occurred in countries with comparatively small middle classes. The role played by the middle classes in bringing about democracy depended on the type of allies available. The middle classes first and foremost sought their own inclusion and formed the alliances necessary to achieve this end.

Where sectors of elites and/or of the military served as effective allies, the middle classes were quite content with restricted democracy. Where there was a significant working-class presence, the search for allies among the working class caused the middle classes to push for full democracy. The middle classes attempted to enlist working-class support either with appeals for electoral support for clientelistic parties or through the sponsoring of working-class organizations and the formation of formal alliances with such organizations through radical mass parties. Where radical mass parties mobilized pressures for democratization, strong elite resistance resulted in preventive or reactive authoritarian responses. Where clientelistic parties appealed for support from a sizeable working class, successful democratic openings occurred.[9]

The working class generally, but not always, played a strong pro-democratic role in so far as it demanded an opening of the political system to achieve its own inclusion. Given the social construction of class interests, however, working-class organizations in some cases readily supported authoritarian regimes which accorded them material and status concessions (see e. g. Malloy 1987: 243). This was particularly likely if the leaders of such regimes were the first to mobilize and organize labor on a large scale. The most notable case is the support for Peronism in the Argentine labor movement.

Political institutions and consolidation of democracy

As the preceding discussion showed, the structure of the economy and the resulting class structure were very important in the phase of formation of political institutions, most critically political parties. Once these institutions were established, they developed a dynamic of their own and became independent determinants of regime outcomes. They played crucial roles in mobilizing pressures from subordinate classes and mediating such pressures in ways which reduced the threat level to elites. Once full or restricted democracies had been established, political institutions, particularly the party system, remained crucial for their consolidation or breakdown.

Some degree of industrialization was a necessary condition for the consolidation of democracy because it produced the organizational strength the middle and working classes needed to sustain pressures for their inclusion. In mineral export economies, radical mass parties were capable of effecting breakthroughs to full or at least restricted democracy before any significant industrialization had occurred, but not of consolidating democratic regimes. In agrarian export economies, there were no breakthroughs to full democracy without significant industrialization and only rarely breakthroughs to restricted democracy. Industrialization was not sufficient for the consolidation of even restricted democracies; the other necessary condition was the continued protection of elite interests through the party system.

The prerequisite for protection of elite interests was the existence of two or more strong competing political parties, at least one of which effectively promoted the interests of significant sectors of economic elites, and/or both (or all) of which allowed for direct access of economic elites to the policy-makers in the state apparatus. Effectiveness had two components, namely continued close articulation of the party leadership and/or policy-makers appointed by the leadership with economic elites, and capacity of the party to appeal to a large enough base to ensure its electoral strength.[10]

Breakdown and reconstitution

Where effective clientelistic parties were lacking and elite representation in the party system was perceived as inadequate from the beginning, only restricted democracies emerged, as elite appeals for military intervention to prevent unacceptable election outcomes or policies tended to be frequent from the start, and compliance with such requests reinforced military involvement in politics. Typically such regimes emerged where either popular pressures mobilized by a mass party had been strong enough to force an opening or where the military itself in alliance with sectors of the middle classes had been involved in bringing about such an opening. Repeated military intervention in turn further impeded the consolidation of political parties and the institutionalization of contestation. Where popular pressures were threatening a radicalization of policy and the incumbent government was ineffective in dealing with these pressures, military involvement behind the scenes tended to give way to direct intervention through coups and the installation of military supported civilian or military authoritarian regimes.

Full or restricted democracies, initially tolerated by elites, in the context of medium or high levels of industrialization broke down where economic elites began to perceive that their interests were inadequately protected through the party system. Economic crises tended to sharpen such elite perceptions and thus serve as catalysts for breakdowns. The only two full democracies in existence at the beginning of the 1930s, Argentina and Uruguay, fell victim to coups inspired by elite attempts to protect their economic interests from the effects of the Depression. Later breakdowns of full or restricted democracies were spurred by elite perceptions that their interests were beginning to be seriously threatened by the fractionalization of parties and the erosion of their ability to moderate social conflict in situations of economic stagnation. In a few cases, such as Chile after 1932 and Uruguay after 1942, where civil society and the party system were strong, democracies managed to survive for quite a long time.

Table 5. 3 shows the relationship between institutional protection of elite interests and stability of democratic regimes. What is important about the cases

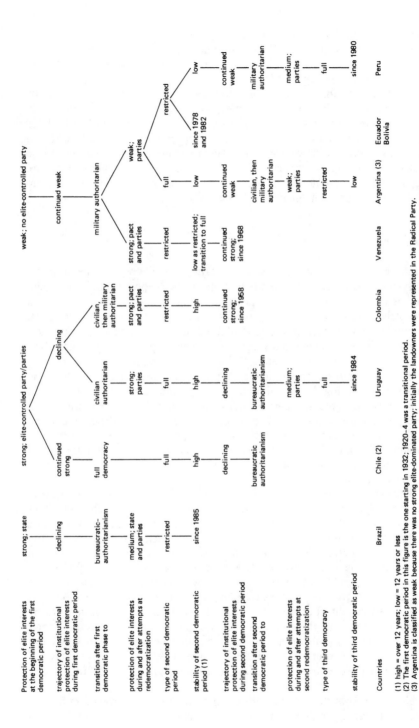

FIGURE 5.2 Political institutions and regime transformations after initial democratization

(1) high = over 12 years; low = 12 years or less
(2) The first democratic period in this figure is the one starting in 1932; 1920–4 was a transitional period.
(3) Argentina is classified as weak because there was no strong elite-dominated party; initially the landowners were represented in the Radical Party.

TABLE 5.3   Institutional protection of elite interests and democratic stability

Protection of elite interests		*Stability of democracy*[a]
	high	*low*
high	Colombia since 1958 Chile 1932–70 Uruguay 1903–19 Venezuela since 1958	
low	Brazil 1945–64 Colombia 1936–49 Uruguay 1919–33; 1942–73 Argentina 1912–30 Ecuador 1948–61	Chile 1970–3 Peru 1939–48; 1956–62; 1963–8 Argentina 1946–51; 1958–62; 1963–6; 1973–6 Bolivia 1952–64 Venezuela 1945–8

[a]low = 12 years or less
high = more than 12 years

in the deviant cell, i. e. with low protection of elite interests and high stability, is that in all of them except Ecuador effective protection of elite interests was initially provided through the state (Brazil), or strong elite-dominated parties (Colombia), or strong middle-class-dominated parties allowing for elite access to party leaders and the state bureaucracy (Uruguay), or elite representation in the strongest middle-class-dominated party (Argentina). Over the course of the democratic periods this protection declined because of party fractionalization or the erosion of corporatist institutions, and this is what led to the breakdown of the regimes. In Ecuador elite interests were initially protected by default, i. e. the lack of any strong organized pressures for significant deviations from the status quo.

Once democracies had been replaced by authoritarian regimes, pressures for a return to democracy emerged. In the majority of cases, the same forces which had originally pushed for the democracy and which had grown in strength during the democratic period pushed for a return to the same type of democracy that had been overthrown. Where they were successful in reinstalling a full democracy before the 1980s, the previous experience repeated itself; a renewed breakdown occurred. In some cases, the same or other forces supported or at least accepted a more limited form of democracy, which brought with it a higher chance for consolidation. Political engineering could make an important contribution to reinstallation and consolidation of democracies through political pacts which compensated for the lack of strong elite parties by providing for effective representation of elite interests in the political system. Such pacts, however, also entailed restrictions on democracy, at least initially. Figure 5.2 gives a schematic summary of these variables and sequences and the resulting regime forms.

The wave of redemocratization in the late 1970s and 1980s involved in some cases a regrouping of previously pro-democratic forces and in others the emergence of new such forces due to a strengthening of civil society and of subordinate classes during the period of authoritarian rule. In all cases, strains within the authoritarian regime were crucial in initiating the democratic opening, and in some cases the erosion of these regimes was much more important than civilian pressures for redemocratization. However, the revival of pre-existing political parties and/or the emergence of new parties led to important changes in the political articulation of civil society and the strength of pro-democratic forces, which offer a greater potential for consolidation of these democracies than existed before.

Having presented an overview of the general political sequences of South American development to guide the reader through what follows, we now turn to the analytically guided comparative historical analysis which led us to the identification of these sequences. Without making any claim to providing more than brief sketches of the critical junctures in individual countries, we present the historical material on which our generalizations are based. Beginning with the consolidation of state power and working forward through the diversity of historical sequences, we shall try to weave the connections between argument and cases.

Conditions for Initial Democratization

Consolidation of state power

Fulfillment of the first precondition for the emergence of a regime form with regularized contestation and more than minimal inclusion, namely consolidation of the state apparatus and the establishment of effective control over a geographically defined continuous population, was rather problematic in most of Latin America.[11] The struggles for independence and later over borders, and the foreign interventions in the nineteenth century, go a long way towards explaining the importance of caudillos and leaders of the regular military in national politics and the inability of elites to create institutionalized competition for power even among themselves. The expansion of regular and irregular armies during the wars of independence created many military leaders who, in the power vacuum left by the collapse of Spanish rule, became power contenders at the local or national level, based on control over loyal troops. The emergence of local militias in the period of struggle over the question of who should rule further contributed to the emergence of caudillos, seeking power through force of arms, not through constitutional processes.[12]

Furthermore, the economic legacy of the colonial period and continued economic dependence made national unification problematic in many cases, for great regional diversity and lack of economic integration created conflicts over the degree of political centralization (see e. g. Silva Michelena 1973), and the partial survival of elites with strong previous ties to the colonial state aggravated elite fractionalization and competition. There was great variation among the various countries in the time it took for the problems of struggles over borders and over regional autonomy, centralization of the military, and more or less assured rule enforcement to be solved. In Chile, the comparatively easy struggle for independence and the absence of strong regional diversity allowed for the earliest settlement of the question of consolidation of state power in any South American nation, namely in the 1830s (e. g. Loveman 1979: 134–49). In Venezuela, in contrast, one of the latest cases, the severe disruptions of the drawn-out independence struggle, the importance of caudillos in this struggle, and great regional diversity delayed this settlement until the turn of the century (e.g. Lombardi 1982: 157–205).

Consolidation of state power was a necessary, but not sufficient condition for the creation of relatively stable rule with institutionalized contestation by the elite alone or with wider participation. Elite prosperity based on export expansion and relative elite homogeneity were additional necessary conditions. In Peru, for instance, institutionalized elite contestation was never achieved, despite state consolidation in the period 1860–90. Only in six of the ten South American cases were there periods with institutionalized contestation among elites (see table 5.1). In contrast to western Europe, then, with the telling exceptions of Germany and Italy, the tasks of consolidating state power and establishing a stable form of elite rule were more difficult, completed later (if at all), and thus temporally closer to the next phase, that of incorporating newly emerging groups into the political system. This can certainly be considered a contributing factor to the lesser frequency of emergence and consolidation of democracy in Latin America compared to Europe. Additional important differences are to be found in the effects of dependent development on the class structure, and on the power balance within civil society and between civil society and the state.

Expansion and character of the export economy[13]

The next development necessary for the establishment of institutionalized competition for political power, a sustained period of expansion of the export economy giving rise to a prosperous class of export producers and urban merchants and financiers, also occurred at different times and to different degrees in the various cases.[14] Growth of economies with nationally controlled agrarian export production was more likely to create a prosperous and more or less homogeneous elite of large landowners with ties to urban interests than growth of foreign-controlled mineral export economies.[15] Yet, growth of agricultural export production had contradictory consequences for democratization. On the one hand, it facilitated institutionalization of contestation among elites, even where regionalism and/or different agrarian exports generated some diversity among a landholding elite with otherwise strong common interests, such as in Brazil and Colombia. On the other hand, it strengthened large landowners and thus potentially formidable opponents of democracy.

How formidable landlord opposition to democratization was, depended heavily on the labor requirements of agricultural production.

In Brazil, consolidation of state power was not a problem because of the continuity from colonial times. Export growth in coffee started in the middle of the nineteenth century, and both coffee and sugar exports increased dramatically after 1880. Accordingly, after the fall of the monarchy in 1889, the landowning oligarchy was economically secure and prosperous enough to institutionalize a system of competition for political power among its different factions, in which governors as representatives of regional oligarchies bargained over national executive power.[16] In contrast, in Colombia effective consolidation of state power and a first sustained period of export expansion, based on coffee, were delayed until the early twentieth century. Consequently, it was only after the end of the War of a Thousand Days in 1903 that the Conservative and Liberal oligarchic factions started to overcome their deep historical enmity and establish a viable system of elite contestation (Wilde 1978: 34–7).

In Ecuador, President García Moreno (1860–75) was able to consolidate state power to the extent of bringing the periods of civil war to an end (Schodt 1987: 28–33). However, tensions between the coastal agro-exporters and the highland oligarchy remained strong and obstructed the institutionalization of contestation. The cacao boom starting in the late nineteenth century then shifted power from the highland landowners, allied with the church and acting through the Conservative Party, to coastal elites and the Liberal Party as their representative. This made possible a period of constitutional Liberal oligarchic rule from 1916 to 1925, during which, however, there was little attempt to extend centralized state control over the highlands, where the landowners were left in control.

Uruguay had a rocky road to national unification, with both frequent involvement in border wars and armed confrontations between Blancos and Colorados persisting throughout the nineteenth century. However, export prosperity based on sheep and cattle set in after 1880, and this enabled the coastal-based Colorados to assert their dominance over the Blancos, led by the traditional landowners of the interior, and consolidate state power with the defeat of the Blanco rebellion in 1904 (Mendez 1977: 87–121). Given the non-labor intensive character of the agrarian export economy and the subsidiary industrialization and urbanization generated by it, a topic which will be taken up below, this defeat ushered in a form of restricted democracy, rather than simply oligarchic contestation. The contrast to Paraguay here is instructive. President Francia (1814–40) consolidated state power internally, greatly weakened the church, the Spanish landowners, and the criollo (i.e. locally born, of Spanish descent) merchants and financiers by expropriation, strengthened the military as his major support base, and pursued essentially an autarkic development (Schmelz 1981: 54). The War of the Triple Alliance devastated population, land, and state finances, and opened Paraguay's economy to the outside. Yet, there was no export boom of any kind. A quite diversified export base developed, but without bringing prosperity and strengthening export-linked groups to the extent that they would have been able to impose constitutional oligarchic rule. In Argentina, the problem of consolidation of state power was finally solved with the acceptance of the status of Buenos Aires as federal capital in 1880, though Mitre (1861–68) had already effectively unified the country. Significant export growth based on cattle, sheep, and grain began in the 1870s, consolidating the dominance of the agro-exporting groups in the littoral, who managed to institutionalize contestation among themselves (Rock 1985: 118–61).

On the anti-democratic side, growth of the nationally controlled agrarian export sector strengthened the large landowners who were rather universally opposed to full democratization. The intensity of landlord opposition to democracy depended on the character of the dominant type of export agriculture. Where that agriculture was highly labor intensive and labor relations were based on a combination of wage labor and a semi-bound labor force, as in Colombia, Brazil, and Ecuador, the landowners were implacable opponents of democratization. In Brazil, they were an important part of the forces that managed until 1985 to prevent the installation of a democratic regime with universal suffrage. In Colombia, one faction of the Liberals pushed through universal suffrage in 1936 despite strong opposition from the Conservatives and from the landowners in the Liberal Party itself, but interference in the electoral process by local landowning notables kept democracy restricted in practice. Where export agriculture was mostly ranching, with low labor requirements, and labor relations in that sector were firmly based on wage labor, as in Argentina[17] and Uruguay, the landowners were anti-democratic as well, but their opposition to democracy was less strong, which allowed for full democracy to be established in the 1910s in response to pressures from a comparatively highly urbanized and industrializing society. I shall return to the question of pressures from society below.

In the mineral export economies, in contrast, growth tended to produce less elite homogeneity. It strengthened urban commercial and financial groups who came to coexist with traditional landowners in a less close alliance than the one between urban commercial and financial interests and agrarian exporters in agrarian export economies. Thus, mineral export growth had also contradictory effects on the chances for democracy. On the one hand, it made institutionalized contestation among elites more difficult and thus tended to perpetuate military interventionism, but on the other hand it weakened the position of the large landowners as crucial opponents of democracy. The local proceeds from the export sector were primarily captured by the state apparatus, along with revenues from taxes on imports which were made possible by the mineral export expansion. Therefore, control of the state as a means for access to resources remained salient and the struggle for control of the state intense. Moreover, in mineral export economies, alliances between the middle and working classes were more likely to emerge than in nationally controlled agrarian ones, which had equally contradictory effects on democratization. On the one hand, the formation of these alliances meant that stronger pressures for democratization emerged earlier, but on the other hand these alliances tended to be radical in their demands and thus stiffened the resolve of dominant groups to keep the alliances excluded.

These alliances participated in the struggle for control of the state, and where they managed to gain such control, they were able to develop a considerable autonomy from the landowning class. Revenue from the foreign-owned export sector and from imports stimulated by it provided the resources for state expenditure. By extending the franchise to the rural sector and mobilizing rural workers, urban groups could attempt to further strengthen their base relative to that of the landowners. However, because the parties fomenting these alliances between middle and working-classes in mineral export economies, namely Acción Democrática (AD) in Venezuela, the Alianza Popular Revolucionaria Americana (Apra) in Peru, the Movimiento Nacionalista Revolucionario (MNR) in Bolivia, and the Radical, Socialist, and Communist Parties in Chile, at least initially promoted radical programs, they presented a strong threat not only to landowning but also to urban elites and united them in resistance to democracy. Thus, the typical pattern was one of breakthrough to democracy, followed by authoritarian rule and repression.[18]

In Peru and Venezuela, elite contestation was never firmly institutionalized. In Chile and Bolivia, in contrast, elite contestation took hold by the second half of the nineteenth century (Chile) or by the turn of the century (Bolivia). Chile is a special case of a mineral export economy, because it had seen a period of significant agricultural export growth and of domestically controlled silver and copper mining after 1848, before the denationalization of nitrate mining in the 1880s and the growth of the foreign copper companies after the turn of the century. Chile also had a significant domestically-owned coal mining sector, and there was a considerable overlap between landownership and holdings in other sectors. As a result, the Central Valley landlords were economically powerful and significant sectors of them were more closely connected to mining and urban interests than their counterparts in other mineral export economies.[19] Thus, institutionalized contestation became a viable option early on, and inclusion could even be widened to non-elite sectors. Early consolidation of state power, early elite prosperity, and relative elite homogeneity (before the significant growth of mining production), then, all contributed to making Chile the first country in South America to establish a political system with highly institutionalized contestation and more than minimal inclusion. However, landlord strength also explains the continued exclusion of the peasantry and the delay of the establishment of full democracy until the 1970s.[20]

Bolivia had, like Chile, an originally stronger and more cohesive dominant class than other mineral export economies, but the pattern of middle- and working-class formation and the role of the state was typical of the latter. Tin did not become important until the end of the nineteenth century; from the 1860s to the 1890s silver mining had been important. Silver was mainly under national control, and the mining bourgeoisie was closely linked to the landowning families. This led to the formation of an amalgamated elite of landed and silver interests. Before the consolidation of the industry in the 1920s, tin mining was largely controlled by foreign, particularly Chilean, financial interests. With the rise of tin, new elements achieved elite status, and the old families developed connections to urban activities and the tin companies, e. g. through family members serving as lawyers for the companies. Thus, an elite of old and new elements emerged (called La Rosca), with close links to tin and heavy involvement in politics (Malloy 1970: 38). The expansion of the export economy in the period 1870–1920 made possible the establishment of relatively stable elite contestation between 1899 and 1920. Thereafter, the economy started to stagnate, the elite's economic base was weakened, and intra-elite struggles intensified, making coups the dominant mode of transfer of political power.[21]

In Venezuela, high regional geographic and economic diversity, and the strong caudillo legacy from the independence war delayed effective unification until the turn of the century. Moreover, significant export growth, originally based on agriculture, did not occur until the early twentieth century. Thus, caudillo rule, rather than institutionalized elite competition for power, prevailed until the death of Gomez in 1935, and the military dominated politics from 1935 to 1945. The period from the 1920s on presents the clearest case of weakening of the landowning elite by a mineral export sector. The oil wealth led to an overvalued exchange rate which made agrarian exports uncompetitive and unattractive and exposed even agricultural production for the domestic market to strong competition from imports (Karl 1986: 199–200). The destruction of export agriculture and rural–urban migration left the large landowners without a strong enough economic or political base to impose their rule and effectively block pressures from a middle–working class alliance for democracy.

The Peruvian example confirms that export growth, like consolidation of state power, was not a sufficient condition for the establishment of institutionalized contestation among elites. Neither the guano boom of 1845–79 nor the export boom after 1890 was followed by such an arrangement. In part, this can be explained by the legacy of the long struggle for independence, namely the strong tradition of caudillismo. Though caudillo rule was replaced by civilian-dominated regimes after 1895 (Pike 1967: 168ff), different military factions continued to play important roles as allies sought by civilians. The reasons why civilians continued to turn to the military for political support are in turn to be sought in the elite heterogeneity produced by geographical diversity and by a strong colonial legacy, reinforced by the impact of expansion of the export economy. The guano boom did not strengthen a national class, but rather provided resources mainly through state extraction and thus raised the stakes of control over the state apparatus (Berg and Weaver 1978). In the post–1890 export boom agricultural products and domestic capital were leading, which clearly strengthened the large landowners in the coastal areas, many of whom diversified into urban activities. However, mining remained important, becoming dominant again by 1930 and coming predominantly under foreign control (Thorp and Bertram 1978: 40). Also, agricultural export production was diversified, with both highland and coastal producers participating, and significant parts of sugar production, the product accounting for the largest proportion of the value of agricultural exports, came under foreign control as well. Therefore, the coastal agro-exporters did not become a hegemonic ruling-class. Coups remained the dominant mode of transfer of power and the period 1919–30 was one of dictatorial rule.

Growth of the middle and working classes and of urbanization accompanying the expansion of the export economy was also necessary for a widening of political inclusion. With the newly emerging urban groups of employees and professionals, of workers in transport, beginning manufacturing for the domestic market, and, depending on the type of export economy, mining or subsidiary industrialization to the export sector, civil society became stronger and the weight of middle and lower classes in the power balance increased. Through the formation of unions and political parties, important segments of these classes became political actors capable of exerting pressures for both civil rights and political inclusion. The extent to which mobilization and organization of subordinate classes occurred and the form their organizations took were strongly shaped by the agricultural or mineral base of the export economy and by the extent of subsidiary industrialization generated. In agrarian export economies clientelistic parties emerged; where there was no significant subsidiary industrialization, the parties were initially weaker than where such industrialization occurred. In mineral export economies, radical mass parties emerged.

As in Europe, the effectiveness of the pressures for political inclusion depended on the one hand on the strength of these new groups, i. e. their size, the density of organization, degree of unity, and alliances with other groups, and on the other hand on the strength and resolve of the elites to resist them. Where subsidiary industrialization and urbanization generated by the export sector were extensive, these pressures were strong, and where agriculture was less labor intensive, the resolve of elites to resist was lower. Where minerals were dominant, radical mass parties exerted generally strong pressures for inclusion but threatened elites and strengthened their resolve to resist.

A closer look at Argentina and Uruguay, the two early breakthroughs to full democracy, supports the above argument in so far as these countries had achieved what was for Latin America an unusually high degree of urbanization and middle- and working-class formation and organization by 1910 to 1920. This was due to their particular type of export economy, beef, hides, wool, and grain, which generated considerable subsidiary activity not only in transport, but in meat packing, tanning, and wool processing. One might accept this as a sufficient explanation for the breakthrough to democracy, but the fact that the achievement of similar levels of urbanization and industrialization in Chile and Brazil in the 1950s,[22] for instance, did not lead to full democratization forces one to consider additional factors. The Moore thesis suggests that one should again look at the role of large landowners. Like all the other South American countries, Argentina and Uruguay have landholding patterns dominated by large estates, and large landowners have constituted the most powerful social class since colonial days. However, as discussed above, the type of agriculture and the resulting labor relations dominant in Argentina and Uruguay were unique for South America, i. e. the dominant agricultural activity during the period of export expansion was not labor intensive and labor relations were predominantly based on wage labor. Thus, it was the combination of both factors resulting from the particular character of the agricultural export economy in Argentina and Uruguay, namely the pressures emanating from society, generated by early industrialization and urbanization, and the relatively moderate anti-democratic stance of the large landowners, which made the establishment of a fully democratic regime possible in the 1910s.

The pressures from below for political reform and the fact that landowners "could afford" to give in explain a good part of why they did so in the cases of

Argentina and Uruguay. However, closer historical analysis suggests some additional important explanatory factors. Divisions within the landowning class, partly along structural lines and partly along more narrowly political lines, were another factor facilitating the opening, in so far as they impaired the formation of a closed anti-democratic power bloc, and the pressures from below were directed at political inclusion rather than radical social and economic changes. In Argentina, some landowners who were not part of the Buenos Aires export oligarchy supported the Radical Party.[23] More importantly, the oligarchy was split over the question of electoral reform. A significant sector correctly perceived that an opening of the political system would constitute no fundamental threat to their interests, as its main beneficiary would be the clientelistic Radical Party which represented middle-class interests. The working class was organized in militant unions, but two factors obstructed their effective political action. Their heavily foreign extraction disenfranchised a large proportion of the working class, and the dominant influence in the unions was exercised by anarchists and anarcho-syndicalists who did not promote party building and participation in electoral politics (Spalding 1977: 23–31; Bergquist 1986: 101–16). On the contrary, continued exclusion of the middle class carried the risk of Radical attempts to mobilize the working class into an anti-oligarchic alliance and of renewals of insurrectionary attempts. In general, mobilization of support for democratization by clientelistic parties with mass bases was less threatening to elites and thus provoked less intense resistance than mobilization by ideological mass parties.

In Uruguay, the modernizing landowners of the littoral provinces were opposed to the old Blanco–Colorado rivalry and did not support the Blancos, representing the traditional landowners of the interior, in their rebellions in 1897 and 1904 against the more urban-based Colorados (Mendez 1977: 87–122; Finch 1981: 5–11). Moreover, the heavily immigrant composition of both the modernizing landowners and urban commercial, financial, and industrial groups linked to them (Mendez 1977: 16), in addition to divisions among them, prevented them from controlling the political system to the same extent as their counterparts in Argentina. This opened the way for middle-class political leaders to form alliances with sectors of the elites and pursue political reforms to strengthen their own position (Finch 1981: 9). The defeat of the 1904 rebellion by Batlle helped to institutionalize contestation and open the way for inclusion under the 1919 constitution. As in Argentina, a significant proportion of the working class remained disenfranchised because they were immigrants, and the major force pushing for democratization, the Colorados, was a clientelistic party. These two factors reduced the threat posed by democratization to elite interests.

Import substitution industrialization

Starting in the 1930s in some countries and later in others, growth of import substitution industrialization (ISI) brought with it further growth of the middle and working classes and thus the potential for a strengthened civil society and pressures for political inclusion. Compared to the core countries, the lower level of development and the pattern of dependent development made for different timing, proportion, and composition of the emergence of the middle classes relative to the working class. At comparable levels of development, the working class was weaker relative to the middle classes than in the core countries. This pattern was set by the growth of the export economy, as this caused growth of the state and urbanization before any significant industrialization (with the above mentioned exceptions of Argentina and Uruguay), and it was perpetuated during the ISI phase. Urbanization and state expansion brought forth middle classes of state employees, private white collar employees, professionals and intellectuals, artisans, shopkeepers and small entrepreneurs. Late and dependent industrialization, though, did not lead to a corresponding formation of an industrial working class and labor movement. Even when ISI was undergoing significant growth, labor absorption by industry remained limited. Within the industrial sector, the predominance of small enterprises with paternalistic labor relations hampered labor organization.[24] Many of these small enterprises were in the informal sector, that is, outside the coverage of labor laws, social security legislation, and contractual labor relations with regular money wages.[25] This had important implications both for the strength of civil society and for the political articulation of the middle and working classes. It meant that the middle classes had to play an important role in pushing for an opening of the political system, if such an opening was to occur.

ISI also enlarged the ranks of the industrial bourgeoisie oriented towards production for the domestic market. This bourgeoisie was not strong enough to play the leading role in challenging oligarchic domination, even where it emerged as a separate group from and independent of the large landowners. However, as long as the growth potential of the economy was large, ISI opened the possibility for an alliance between this bourgeoisie and the middle and working classes, and thus for the establishment of an including regime (O'Donnell 1973). Such including regimes, though, were neither necessarily democratic (e.g. Vargas, Perón in his second term), nor did their social and economic policies necessarily weaken the oligarchy and prepare the way for democratization in the longer run (e.g. Vargas, the Liberals in the 1930s in Colombia). Nevertheless, growth made for a socioeconomic positive sum game, that is, new urban groups could gain while old groups still retained many traditional privileges. Accordingly, the political struggle came to be perceived as less of an all-or-nothing affair, and more democratic forms of rule became possible where subordinate classes exerted pressures for democratization. The gradual opening of the Chilean system from the 1930s to the early 1970s certainly was facilitated by the growth of ISI not only because it strengthened the urban subordinate classes, but also because it provided the resources for state patronage which ensured a continued strong electoral base for the right-wing parties without requiring any significant increase in the taxation of private property.

Two broad patterns of ISI growth can be distinguished in Latin America. One pattern saw initial strong growth stimulated by the depression and World War II, in some cases heavily promoted by deliberate pro-industrial policies, based mainly on domestic capital. A second pattern saw a growth spurt in the

1950s and 1960s, with heavy participation of foreign capital. The pattern of initial growth in the 1930s fits Argentina, Brazil, Chile, Mexico, and Uruguay (though in Uruguay ISI did not develop very far because of the small size of the domestic market). In Brazil and Chile, political decisions to accelerate ISI were particularly important. The pattern of growth in the 1950s and 1960s fits Colombia, Peru, and Bolivia (though Bolivia remained at a clearly lower level of industrialization). Ecuador and Paraguay fit neither pattern, as they experienced little industrialization until the late 1960s. Venezuela is a special case because of the relatively constant oil-based growth since the 1920s. On the basis of our assumptions about the impact of ISI on the development of civil society, we would expect stronger and earlier pressures for an opening of the political system in the cases of initial growth in the 1930s and in Venezuela. However, the growth of middle and working classes did not automatically and uniformly translate itself into a stronger civil society and more effective political articulation. Rather, the pre-existing political institutions, particularly the parties and the tradition of state involvement in society significantly shaped civil society, and its political articulation.

Social classes, the state, political parties, and the struggle for democracy

If one analyzes the class forces behind successful and failed attempts to install democratic regimes, the middle classes emerge as the crucial forces behind the alliances effecting initial breakthroughs to restricted democracy and, in collaboration with the working class, to full democracy. It was in the middle classes that the parties or movements mobilizing and exerting pressures for democracy had their main base. Only if we take a very long view, including every step that contributed towards greater institutionalization of contestation and greater inclusion, even if those steps were not made with the intent to include significant new groups and were accompanied by a variety of mechanisms which de facto limited inclusion, can we find cases where parts of the oligarchy itself pushed for democratization. For instance, in Chile in 1874, the oligarchy-based Conservatives supported an electoral reform whose main goal was to remove control over the electoral process from the incumbent government and which included universal male literate suffrage in order to make it more difficult for the authorities to deny the right to vote to non-elite sectors whose support for the incumbents was doubtful (J. S. Valenzuela 1985).[26] In Colombia after the War of a Thousand Days, export-oriented sectors of the landed oligarchy and commercial and industrial groups generated bi-partisan support for a new system of institutionalized contestation with safeguards for minority representation, which was established with the reforms of 1910 (Bergquist 1978: 247–62). However, in no case did significant sectors of the oligarchy actively support greater political inclusion in a situation where the majority of the subordinate classes were mobilized enough to actually participate.

As in Europe, the bourgeoisie was nowhere the driving force behind democratization. A possible exception is the unsuccessful rebellions in Chile in the 1850s where the mining bourgeoisie in alliance with artisans, craftsmen, and small farmers demanded participation in the oligarchy-dominated state (Zeitlin 1984: 30–56), though it is important to point out that other sectors of the mining bourgeoisie supported the incumbents. The emerging industrial bourgeoisie was small and weak as a political force because of their dependence on the state for protection from imports and foreign competition, except for those sectors which were closely linked to agro-exporting interests and for this reason did not challenge the political order. Furthermore, the industrial bourgeoisie in many cases was of immigrant extraction and thus lacked either the franchise or important kinship connections to establish political prominence (e. g. Argentina and Uruguay; see Rock 1985: 233, and Finch 1981: 163–70). The same was true for the commercial bourgeoisie in many cases. In other cases, the commercial and financial bourgeoisie was closely linked to the landowners through multiple holdings and/or kinship links (e. g. Chile since at least the late 19th century; see Zeitlin 1984: 165–71) and thus did not develop into an independent political force. Particularly where the ISI growth spurt came after World War II and involved strong participation of foreign capital (Colombia and Peru), the bourgeoisie remained too weak even to form a Keynesian alliance with middle and working classes to effect pro-industrialization policies. The conditions under which bourgeois groups, along with sectors of the oligarchy, supported institutionalization of contestation (though not full inclusion) were either crises of hegemony resulting in political instability and possibly even internal war (e. g. Uruguay 1903; Chile 1932; Ecuador 1948), or incumbency of corrupt dictatorial, military-backed regimes (Venezuela and Colombia 1958).

Compared to Europe the urban working class played less of a leading role as a pro-democratic force. Before the 1930s, there were only few cases where the labor movement had achieved sufficient strength to have some political impact. In the three cases where it did, its presence reinforced middle-class pressures for democratization. As already discussed, the character of the export economy in Argentina and Uruguay generated early urbanization, subsidiary industrialization, and thus labor movements which were much stronger than their counterparts in the rest of Latin America. The intensity of labor mobilization and militancy on the one hand, and the moderation of the political threat by clientelistic middle-class-led parties on the other hand motivated elites in both cases to accept political reforms, and in Uruguay in addition social welfare and labor reforms sponsored by the Colorado governments. In Chile, the labor movement was not very large and mainly concentrated in the nitrate zones and major cities and ports, but it was very militant precisely because of the importance of the nitrate mining areas (Bergquist 1986). Labor militancy was important in influencing the electoral college to bring Alessandri to power in 1920, the first presidential candidate to build his campaign on appeals to middle and lower classes (Drake 1978: 47–54). He had managed to attract working-class support despite the opposition of the Socialist Workers' Party to his candidacy (Angell 1972: 35). In Brazil, early labor organization emerged in the São Paulo area, but at the national level labor organization remained insignificant in size, and from its very beginning it was reigned in by state paternalism (Schmitter 1971: 140).

In the 1920s and first half of the 1930s the labor movements in Argentina and Chile were greatly weakened by repression, unleashed by an alliance between economic elites and the middle classes or the military. In Argentina heavy repression came in the aftermath of the semana trágica in 1919, and in Chile under Ibáñez. In Uruguay labor organization stagnated during this period. In Peru and Colombia labor organization was growing, mainly due to its promotion by Apra and the Liberal Party and government, respectively. In Bolivia, Venezuela, Ecuador, and Paraguay only isolated efforts were made in this period to form labor unions, mainly among transport workers.[27] Starting in the second half of the 1930s, ISI led to an expansion of industrial and other urban employment and thus the potential for labor organization and mobilization and for pressures for political inclusion. The trajectories of the labor movements in the South American countries in the following two decades varied with the level of industrialization and with the role of the state and political parties in labor mobilization. The state and political parties became the crucial actors shaping the social construction of class interests of the swelling ranks of the urban workforce, as well as its capacity for the concrete pursuit of these interests.

The state's role in shaping the labor movement was generally stronger in Latin America than in Europe, but there was significant variation among the Latin American countries. In some cases, the working class was incorporated into state-sponsored organizations linked directly to the state apparatus. Some regimes even attempted to extend this principle of organization to other classes and construct a corporatist state. Such forms of state involvement did not emerge in Europe except under Fascist regimes. In some of these Latin American countries corporatist structures were eroded in later phases by competitive party politics, and in others such incorporation attempts failed or were not undertaken by any regime. Nevertheless, the state still played a strong role in regulating labor organization and in mediating between organized labor and employers.

The conventional explanation for the strong state role is the colonial legacy with its corporatist tradition. However, it should be kept in mind that in most countries the independence wars thoroughly destroyed state structures and therefore interrupted any direct institutional continuity. The exception here is Brazil; yet, the fact that Brazil represents only one of the three cases in Latin America where state incorporation of the labor movement had lasting effects gives reason to doubt the importance of the colonial legacy. The other cases are Paraguay, where President Francia consolidated state power and established state dominance over society right after independence, and Mexico, where labor incorporation had even stronger lasting effects than in Brazil. For Mexico, however, the argument about colonial institutional legacies is particularly weak, because not only the independence war but also the revolution destroyed old state institutions. Only under Cárdenas were corporatist political institutions forged which linked the labor movement to the state via unions and the revolutionary party. Even in Brazil the state apparatus had become quite decentralized during the Old Republic and it was Vargas who really re-created the corporatist structures.

A more convincing argument than the legacy of colonial institutions is that state expansion took place along with the expansion of the export economy. Thus, in most cases a sizeable state apparatus existed before a significant industrial working class emerged. This provided economic and political elites with the means to intervene in the development of civil society in order to prevent disruptive consequences of industrialization. One can add to this the argument that organic statism, the normative political theory underpinning the colonial order, was available to elites as a world view, legitimacy formula, and guide to institution-building when faced with crisis situations (Stepan 1978: 40–45). This raises the question why Latin American elites perceived the rise of the labor movement as generating actual or potential crisis situations. Here, one can reasonably hypothesize that historical time was important; with the European experience as an example, Latin American elites perceived the potential power of labor and thus the need to control and/or co-opt emerging labor organizations. In many cases such attempts kept the labor movement weak, even if they were not successful in incorporating it into state-controlled structures.

The working class in Latin America only weighed decisively on the democratic side where (1) an organized middle class constituted a potential for mobilizing it into an anti-oligarchic alliance, as in Argentina before 1912, Uruguay before 1919, and Chile before 1932, (2) a middle–working class alliance was actually formed, as under the Popular Front in Chile, through Acción Democrática in Venezuela and Apra in Peru, or (3) the working class was mobilized into a revolutionary movement, as in Bolivia. Yet, such alliances were not always successful in installing full democracy, and even less so in consolidating it. The fact that in the other cases (Brazil, Colombia, Ecuador, Paraguay) the working class was too weak to play a significant political role was crucial for the problems of democracy there, and even in the just discussed cases where the working class did play a significant role, its relative weakness presented a problem for the consolidation of democratic regimes.

In three cases one might argue that the working class did play the leading role in the breakthrough to full democracy, namely Argentina in 1945/6 and 1973, and Chile in 1970. However, in the case of Argentina, the international political conjuncture at the end of World War II and particularly US pressures in the form of withholding of arms shipments until free elections were held (Potash 1969: 258–9) strengthened pro-democratic tendencies among the elites, the middle classes, and the military. Moreover, Perón's mobilization of the working class through the state apparatus was crucial, and the coalition formed by Perón for the 1946 election was multi-class, including some urban industrialists (Kenworthy 1973: 43). The mobilization of this expanding class by Perón and the significant benefits extended by Perón made its majority identify its class interests with the preservation of a Peronist regime, democratic or not; an excellent example of the importance of the social construction of class interests. For the return to democracy in 1973, the growing opposition to the Onganía regime among virtually all social classes was essential. Though the working class played a highly visible role in the events in Córdoba in 1969[28], the fact that the bureaucratic authoritarian regime had alienated a majority of all classes except for the internationalized bourgeoisie (O'Donnell 1978) was crucial in motivating the military to depose Onganía and move towards a re-establishment of democratic procedures (Smith 1983: 97–8). Chile in 1970 appears to be the one case where the working class was of crucial importance. It was the Unidad Popular that made the final step to full democracy with the enfranchisement of illiterates for the 1971 municipal elections. Though only about two-fifths of industrial workers in the Greater Santiago area supported the marxist left between 1958 and 1970, and though the Unidad Popular had important bases of support among sectors of the middle classes, its main base was in the urban working class (Smith and Rodríguez 1974: 64–7). One might counter this argument by pointing out that the Christian Democrats, a party with its main base among the urban and rural middle classes and the urban poor, also supported universal suffrage. However, it should be kept in mind that the Christian Democrats in the 1960s and 1970s were competing heavily with the Unidad Popular parties for the support of both urban and rural lower classes; thus, its support for universal suffrage can be seen as a concession to these classes.

The driving force behind the initial establishment of democracy, then, was the middle class, or rather, the middle classes, namely urban professionals, state employees and employees in the private sector, artisans and craftsmen,[29] and small entrepreneurs, sometimes joined by small and medium farmers. As pointed out above, the different size and strength of classes in contrast to Europe can be explained by the fact that the expansion of the export economy caused the growth of the state and urbanization before any significant industrialization, and that the size and organizational strength of the working class remained restricted during the phase of ISI by the capital intensive character of dependent industrialization, the large number of small enterprises, and the existence of surplus labor due to a combination of population growth and rural–urban migration. In a somewhat crude generalization we could say that in Europe the working class in most cases needed the middle classes as allies to be successful in its push for democracy, whereas in Latin America it was the other way round.

However, the middle classes by no means allied with the working-class in every case, nor did they genuinely support full democracy in every case. The very position of the middle classes, in between the elites and the masses, made for considerable ambiguity in the perception of their class interests regarding the desirability of full democracy. Moreover, the great heterogeneity of the middle classes made for diversity in the perception of class interests. Thus, historical legacies and present alliance options were important determinants of middle-class action in support of full or restricted democracy. Instead of the working class, alternative important allies were the military, dissident sectors of the oligarchy, and sectors of new economic elites (Argentina before 1912, Uruguay 1903, Brazil 1930, Chile 1932). In one case, oligarchic factions actively sought middle- and working-class support (Colombia in the 1930s). In the cases where the middle classes found military or elite allies an opening of the political system could be achieved without a high degree of popular organization and mobilization, as clientelistic parties typically played prominent roles in forming these alliances and confined their demands to political inclusion, which meant that they constituted no immediate threat to vital elite interests. However, this also meant that the strength of pro-democratic forces needed to maintain the democratic regime was quite limited, if and when the economic elites started feeling threatened and turned decidedly against it. In other words, the nature of the alliance formed in the stage of breakthrough to full or restricted democracy had important implications for the stage of consolidation or breakdown of democracy, a topic to which we shall return below.

The timing of the first significant growth in industrialization and urbanization, whether as a spin-off from the export sector or from import substitution, shaped the emergence of pressures for democratization from the middle and working-classes, in so far as these two processes strengthened civil society. As mentioned before, however, the strength of these pressures and their effects depended also on the political articulation of civil society and thus were heavily influenced by the tradition of state intervention in society, the pre-existing political parties, and party and movement builders active at the time of expanding industrialization.

In mineral export economies, the type of party that had emerged during the period of export expansion was a programmatic mass party, attempting to mobilize the working-class into alliances with the middle classes, such as Apra in Peru, AD in Venezuela, and the Radical, Socialist, and Communist Parties in Chile. The MNR in Bolivia more or less fits the type of a programmatic mass party, but its unity and organizational coherence were precarious. In nationally controlled agrarian export economies, in contrast, the predominant type of party was a clientelistic one, such as the Radicals in pre-1930 Argentina, the Colorados and Blancos in Uruguay, and the Conservatives and Liberals in Colombia. In these countries, the middle classes typically did not promote working-class mobilization into an alliance but nevertheless needed lower-class support which they attempted to enlist on the basis of patronage. This is not to say, of course, that the programmatic mass parties did not also engage in clientelistic practices, particularly at the local level.[30] However, they also had a commitment to a distinctive program at the national level, and they attempted to socialize their followers into a particular world-view, something absent in the purely clientelistic parties.

Where industrialization and urbanization occurred early in connection with the export economy, and where there was no major attempt on the part of the state to encapsulate newly emerging groups in this period, i. e. in Argentina and Uruguay, full democratization took place in the second decade of the twentieth century. This was made possible because the additional condition concerning agrarian class relations in the two countries was fulfilled. Moreover, in both cases the driving forces behind democratization were middle-class-led clientelistic parties with some elite representation. Uruguay is the case with the least direct state involvement in the formation of the labor movement. Indirectly, state policy favorable towards labor in the areas of labor and social legislation did affect the growth of the labor movement, but there was no attempt whatsoever to control unions; not even compulsory registration of trade unions existed (Alexander 1965: 61). Batlle had supported the inclusion of the labor movement as a legitimate political actor in 1895 already. In his first term (1903–7) he explicitly recognized the right to strike and passed a variety of labor laws.[31] However, he made no attempt to link the labor movement to the Colorado Party. Rather, the Uruguayan labor movement was from the beginning heavily influenced by its Argentine counterpart. Thus, the dominant political tendencies until the mid-1920s were the anarchists, and then syndicalists, socialists, and communists. Both the Argentine and the Uruguayan labor movements were kept weak politically because large proportions of the working classes were first-generation immigrants and therefore did not have the vote. In Argentina, state attempts to deal with the comparatively large but weakly politically articulated labor movement were largely repressive. In both cases, middle-class support for the parties promoting contestation and inclusion was broad based, and though they appealed for and received some working-class support, they also attracted some allies from marginal or dissident sectors of the landowning elites. In addition, sectors of the military, particularly younger officers, supported the Radicals in Argentina (Rock 1975: 48), and in Uruguay the military had fought to defeat the Blanco rebellions in 1897 and 1904 (Mendez 1977: 88–94; 118–22).

After the 1910s, however, the patterns of political development in Argentina and Uruguay started to diverge. In Uruguay, civilian supremacy over the military was established and the two main political parties became virtually the exclusive channels for competition for political power, because they provided effective representation for all major interests in society.[32] Batlle's second administration (1911–15) again brought progress in labor legislation and growth in the labor movement, thus strengthening support for the Colorados and the transition to full democracy in 1919. However, during the 1920s and early 1930s the labor movement declined in membership and was badly split politically, so that it could offer little resistance to the turn to authoritarianism in 1933. After 1938, repression eased and the increase in industrialization resulted in revival and growth of the labor movement. The labor movement in turn strengthened the constituency of the traditional urban, pro-industrialization, pro-labor Batllista faction in the Colorado Party, facilitating the return of this faction to power and the return to full democracy by 1942.

In Argentina, in contrast, sectors of the military had served as an ally of the middle classes; military participation in the revolts of the Radicals intensified the threat to the oligarchy and thus the perception by one part of the oligarchy that electoral reform was needed. However, by 1930 this alliance had turned into the opposite. As opposition to the Radicals and Yrigoyen mounted because of their populist spending and his intervention in provincial and military affairs, and as middle-class support for the government declined because of the effects of the depression, the oligarchy, lacking any strong representation in the party system and feeling threatened in addition by the economic crisis, found willing allies in the military for a restoration of authoritarian oligarchic rule (Rock 1975: 243–64). The working class at that point was not really a significant force any longer. The severe repression starting with the events of the semana trágica in 1919 had left the labor movement greatly debilitated. Yet, despite frequent

repression of militant labor actions, the comparatively high degree of industrialization reached by the second half of the 1930s began to generate a civil society
with considerable strength. Perón then further strengthened it and added much
greater weight to the working class, because his incorporation strategy involved
a heavy dose of mobilization, as he had to compete with already existing unions
in order to build his own electoral base. The holding of open elections in 1946
and Perón's victory were largely attributable to well organized working-class
support and careful coalition building with other urban groups.[33] The construction of a political party with close ties to the unions added effective political
articulation to a strong civil society.

Where significant growth of industrialization and urbanization occurred in
the 1930s and during World War II, i. e. in Brazil, Chile, and Venezuela, the
transformation of the oligarchic (or dictatorial, in the case of Venezuela) state
took different forms depending on the state's capacity to incorporate and
control newly emerging groups and the capacity of the party system to provide
effective representation to old and newly mobilized groups. In Brazil, where the
state played the strongest role in incorporating labor among the South
American countries, civil society remained rather weak and its political
articulation extremely weak until the 1970s. Given Brazil's comparatively
smooth transitions to independence and then to the republic, a well consolidated (though decentralized) state apparatus was available to the oligarchic
groups in the early decades of the twentieth century to revive the tradition of
significant state intervention in society and attempt to encapsulate new groups
and prevent their acquisition of an independent organizational power base.[34]
Unionization was legalized in 1907, but in practise it was discouraged. Aside
from the urban centers of São Paulo and Rio, there was only very little and
localized labor organization. To the extent that a labor movement emerged, the
oligarchy embarked on a strategy of government sponsorship and paternalism in
workers' organizations. For instance, government authorities paid for all
expenses for the Fourth National Workers' Congress held in 1912 with
representatives from 71 associations, the high point of the early stage of labor
organization (Schmitter 1971: 140). As of 1930, middle-class activism was
rather narrowly centered in students, intellectuals, and the military, and the
coalition bringing Vargas to power included sectors of the military, dissident
sectors of landowners, and urban elite interests, in addition to the middle
classes (Skidmore 1967: 9–12). No strong national parties of any kind had
emerged during the period of export expansion; neither elite nor middle-class
interests had effective party representation at the national level. Owing to the large
size of the country and the great regional diversity, local elites had achieved
considerable autonomy, and political activity and thus party organization were
concentrated at the state level. The result of the coup of 1930 was a hybrid
between an authoritarian system and a highly restricted democracy with
continued strong military intervention, until the breakdown into full blown
authoritarianism in 1937.[35] Under the corporatist estado nôvo, then, Vargas
pursued the incorporation strategy to the ultimate, with strong emphasis on
control via the state bureaucracy (Erickson 1977). The result was a numerically
moderately strong labor movement, but with very low mobilization capacity and

no independent political articulation. Thus, despite growing industrialization in the 1930s and 1940s, civil society did not develop many autonomous organizations nor any effective political articulation through parties at the national level, and pro-democratic pressures from popular groups remained weak until way into the post–1945 period of restricted democracy. The transition in 1945 was again largely the result of a decision by the military, influenced by the post-World War II political conjuncture (Skidmore 1967: 53). Accordingly, military intervention remained a salient feature of the following period.

Colombia represents a case of "premature" breakthrough to restricted democracy, before industrialization had generated significant pressures from subordinate classes. The driving force behind the opening was the Liberal Party, which, like its counterpart the Conservatives, was essentially a clientelistic, elite-dominated party with a mass base and was firmly entrenched in the political system. In the 1930s, the Liberals attempted to strengthen their position in the system through mobilization and inclusion of the urban lower classes (Urrutia 1969: 115–21). In this attempt, the Liberal government of 1934–8 introduced universal male suffrage. Local corruption of the electoral process, however, particularly in rural areas, remained so important that the resulting system can only be considered a restricted democracy (Oquist 1980: 104–9). It was both the local and national political influence of the two elite-dominated parties that induced the Conservatives and the landowners in the Liberal Party to tolerate this opening. Partly owing to initiatives by the Liberal government, such as promotion of labor organization and the founding of the central union organization CTC, and partly owing to further growth of the Colombian economy, civil society grew in strength, and some Liberal factions, particularly Gaitán and his followers, began to articulate the political interests of new groups more forcefully. Despite the fact that labor organization was sponsored by the Liberal government, there were no corporatist institutions created to subject the labor movement to state control, nor was the labor movement brought under control of the Liberal Party; the Liberals shared control with the Communists and Socialists until 1946 when a Catholic union confederation was established in addition (Alexander 1965: 134–7). By the mid–1940s, mobilization and partisan political as well as class based hostility and violence were increasing rapidly, and after the riots in Bogotá violence became an unsolvable problem. This presented a strong perceived threat to Conservative as well as Liberal elites, but instead of being able to compromise as in earlier times in the context of a less mobilized society, party leaders intensified competition and hostility and the parties fractionalized, which led to the installation of an authoritarian regime in 1949 (Wilde 1978: 51–8). Thus, Colombia demonstrates that the "breakthrough – close down" cycle characteristic of radical mass parties could also occur in situations of clientelistic parties when mobilization levels were sufficiently high and party leaders lost control over their organizations.

In Ecuador, the absence of a mineral export sector and of any significant industrialization before the 1960s meant that there was no base for a middle-class–working-class alliance which could have mobilized pressures for inclusion, and not even for a strong alliance between the middle classes and

sectors of the economic elites which could have installed a restricted democracy. There was little state involvement in the formation of the labor
movement, and neither one of the traditional parties (Conservatives and
Liberals) attempted to mobilize workers and link them organizationally to their
party. These parties were historically weaker thán their counterparts in
Colombia; they did not have a mass base. Some ferment and opposition against
oligarchic domination emerged after the mid–1920s, when the decline of cacao
weakened the coastal agro-exporters and the commercial and financial groups
linked to them (Schodt 1987: 37–50). However, the middle and working-
classes were too weak to take advantage of this crisis of hegemony to install an
alternative regime responsive to their interests, and the military as an institution
assumed an important political role. The combination of stalemate between the
traditional sierra landowners and the coastal agro-exporting groups, with
growing involvement of the middle classes, in part in alliance with the Liberals,
a politically fractionalized military, and a weak working class led to extreme
political instability. In 1944, an uprising by a coalition including sectors of the
elites, middle classes and the military, and supported by sectors of the urban
lower classes, toppled the incumbent president who was attempting to impose
his handpicked, unpopular successor (Cueva 1982: 34–44). The populist
Velasco assumed the presidency and soon took an authoritarian path, thus
alienating all major groups in the society; he was overthrown by the military in
1947.

In the absence of the ability of any one group or coalition to impose its rule,
the Conservatives as well as the Liberals, supported by the Socialists (Neira
1973: 360), accepted the results of the 1948 election. These elections ushered
in 13 years of restricted democratic rule, as three successive presidents were
elected and able to serve their full terms. The military, though, remained
directly involved in any matters that affected the interests of its members. The
maintenance of restricted democracy in this period was greatly facilitated by the
prosperity resulting from the rapid increase in banana exports, by the fact that
none of the elected presidents was under pressure from organized popular
groups to initiate any major departures from the status quo, and by the resulting
abstinence of all major social groups from appealing to the military for direct
intervention. Some social diversification took place, as a significant quantity of
bananas was produced by medium and small farmers and the coastal prosperity
attracted large numbers of migrants (Schodt 1987: 56–7). However, the
industrial working class remained very small, the new urban and rural middle-
and lower-class groups poorly organized, and the parties very weak personalistic institutions (Blanksten 1951: 58–71), so that there was no viable political
movement defending the democratic regime when economic problems
emerged in the late 1950s, social tensions intensified, and the military
re-entered the scene as ultimate arbiter and temporary ruler.

Paraguay was similar to Ecuador in the long delay of industrialization, the
lack of a significant mineral export sector, and the weakness of the middle and
working classes and the political parties. It differed from Ecuador in the
absence of a relatively strong landowning, commercial, and financial class
linked to the export sector, competing for power with the more traditional

landowners and their ally, the church. It also differed in the strength of the state. These two factors account for the difference between the prolonged political instability in Ecuador and the ability of authoritarian rulers in Paraguay to establish durable authoritarian regimes. The preponderance of the state and its repeated ruthless application of repression, combined with some attempts at incorporation in the aftermath of the Chaco War (Lewis 1982: 27–42), left the middle and lower classes even weaker than in Ecuador. The two traditional parties had emerged in the 1870s, but up to the seizure of power by Stroessner they remained weak, personalistic, patronage-based organizations, never making a serious attempt to organize middle and lower classes. Stroessner then effected a fusion between the state, including the military, and the Colorado party, turning the party into an instrument of incorporation and control. Thus, when social diversification did accelerate under the impact of industrialization in the 1960s, Stroessner's regime was firmly entrenched and managed to dominate the newly emerging groups from the beginning through the imposition of corporatist controls and repression (Lewis 1982: 56–61). Accordingly, Paraguay did not see even one period of democracy, whether restricted or full.

Chile, Peru, Venezuela, and Bolivia, the four mineral export economies, represent cases where the working class played an important role either as an explicit ally of the middle classes, or at least in that working-class mobilization and militancy reinforced middle-class pressures for institutionalization of contestation and inclusion. Three mechanisms account for this relationship. First, the existence of mining centers facilitated early labor organization and the emergence of labor as a potentially important political actor. Second, the importance of the mineral export sector weakened the capacity of the large landholders to establish themselves as a truly hegemonic class and consequently shape the values and political behavior of the middle classes. This meant that significant sectors of the middle classes could be organized into an anti-imperialist/anti-oligarchic alliance with the working class.[36] Third, where mineral exports were prospering, their proceeds gave the state a certain autonomy from the domestic economic elites and thus provided the potential for middle-class political leaders who managed to gain control of the state to pursue a reformist course promoting middle- and working-class interests (and thus maintaining the coalition) without necessarily generating a fundamental conflict with the urban sectors of the economic elite and concomitant economic decline.

In Chile state involvement in the formation of the labor movement had effects of intermediate significance.[37] The labor code of 1924 was an attempt to capture and contain the growing working-class organizations and militancy. Moreover, Ibáñez crushed the independent labor movement, which had been greatly weakened by unemployment, and substituted government sponsored, centralized, and paternalistic unions (Drake 1978: 59). Union growth and strength were permanently hampered by the code, but the effective control gained by the state over the labor movement never became significant, and after 1932 what control there was eroded rapidly under competitive party politics.[38] The radical mass parties became the crucial agents in the organization of the labor movement, thus not only providing political articulation for civil society but actively shaping it (Angell 1972). The transition to restricted democracy in 1932 predated the formation of the middle-class–working-class Popular Front alliance, but the high level of popular unrest in the preceding years had impressed on the oligarchy the need to accept institutionalized forms of contestation, as well as inclusion of parties representing working-class interests (Drake 1978: 60–98). Having strong political parties representing their own interests, oligarchic groups could feel confident enough that they would be able to protect these interests in the context of a restricted democracy. Party-sponsored growth of the organizational strength of civil society, facilitated by the social changes resulting from ISI in the decades after 1932, effected the gradual reduction of initially severe restrictions on contestation and inclusion, most notably the electoral reforms of 1958 and 1962 and the legalization of rural unionization in 1967 (Loveman 1979: 256–316). Nevertheless, the political strength of the landowning elites enabled them to delay the break-through to full democracy until 1970.

In Venezuela, there was no comparable attempt at co-optation of the labor movement by the state, only repression, and civil society as well as its political articulation grew very rapidly in strength when repression was eased after the death of Gómez in 1935. The economic base for greater density of civil society was provided by the oil induced economic growth. Yet, the activity of political organizers and leaders, many of whom had returned from exile in 1935, was of crucial importance for strengthening civil society and its political articulation. Particularly the leaders of Acción Democrática engaged in intense organizing activity, which enabled them to ally with sectors of the military and force a breakthrough by coup to full democracy in 1945 (Martz 1966: 49–62). The landowning elite on its part had been so weakened by the oil economy that it was unable to block the installation of full democracy at that point. Three years followed in which particularly labor organization in urban and rural areas continued to increase rapidly, and in which far-reaching reforms were initiated.[39] However, AD's strength and virtually total domination of the party system, and its emphasis on the representation of the exclusive interests of sectors of the middle classes, the working class, and the rural poor, cemented an opposition coalition including all elite sectors of the society, urban and rural, large sectors of the middle classes, and the church (Levine 1978: 89–93). When its former allies among the military also turned against AD because of their lack of influence on policy formation, the strength of AD's lower-class base was insufficient to prevent the coup of 1948 (Lombardi 1982: 224–5).

The Chilean–Venezuelan contrast underlines the importance of the party system for the mediation of pressures for democratization. What was essential for elite acceptance of restricted democracy in Chile was that the elite had viable political parties capable of protecting its own interests. In Venezuela before 1958 in contrast, the elites and even sectors of the middle classes lacked political parties capable of competing effectively with Acción Democrática and thus turned against the democratic system. In general, where elite competition through political parties was firmly established when civil society grew in strength, as in Colombia, Chile, and Uruguay, new groups were integrated into these and other parties and through them into the political system, and the result was democracy with varying degrees of restriction but low military involvement. Where elite competition through political parties was not well established, the results of the growing strength of popular groups were severely restricted democratic regimes with high military involvement (Argentina 1958–62, 1963–6; Brazil 1945–64; Peru 1939–48, 1956–62, 1963–8), or a short-lived breakthrough to full democracy (Venezuela 1945–8). Under these conditions, the modal response of elites, and partly also of non-elite groups, to high levels of social and political conflict remained appeals to the military for intervention, appeals which were heeded all too frequently.

Peru and Bolivia represent further cases where alliances between middle- and working-class forces were important in promoting political democracy. They both underwent late spurts of ISI and concomitant growth of the labor movements, but in both cases pressures for an opening of the political system emerged earlier, generated by radical mass parties. In neither case had the state made more than a short futile attempt to incorporate the emerging labor movement, and in neither case did other political parties of comparable strength compete with Apra or the MNR in mobilizing popular forces.[40] In Peru, the first strong pressures emerged in 1930–2, organized by Apra, the party that had been formed by Haya de la Torre in exile. Apra had its main base in the sugar growing areas of the north where it had been able to forge a coalition between sugar workers (through Apra-supported unions) and the large sectors of the middle classes impoverished by the expansion of the large-scale, heavily foreign owned or financed, sugar plantations and the growing domination of trade in the area by the same companies (Klarén 1973). It is interesting that the initial center of Apra's working-class base was among the sugar workers rather than the miners. The miners were more influenced by Socialists and Communists who formed the CGTP in 1929 and competed with Apra in organizing the labor movement. The sugar workers shared some essential characteristics with the mining proletariat, which made them susceptible to organization and anti-imperialist appeals. They were wage workers, concentrated on large plantations, and many of these plantations were foreign owned. Sugar workers and the déclassé middle classes were not natural allies; they had little day to day contact with each other and were only brought together by the party. Apra was also active in organizing urban unions, but the level of industrialization was very low, and the depression together with political repression greatly weakened existing unions and made organizing very difficult; thus, a significant urban labor movement did not emerge until the 1940s (Sulmont 1984).

Apra's program and style were very radical, anti-oligarchic and anti-imperialist, and after the election defeat of Haya de la Torre in 1931 the party embarked on an insurrectionary strategy, leading to the uprising in Trujillo in 1932. This provoked a very intense counter reaction from the oligarchy, large sectors of the middle classes, and the military, with the result that Apra was suppressed until 1939.[41] Since Apra was the crucial force behind popular organization, its suppression effectively dampened pressures, though only temporarily. In 1939, Apra was de facto reintegrated into the political process, and in the 1940s it was able to carry on organizational activities. Before the 1945 elections, Apra was legalized, which opened a three-year period of less severely restricted democracy, with literate male suffrage. During these three years, popular organization and mobilization led by Apra reached new levels, and there was no other political party capable of effectively competing with Apra in open elections. Apra's activities again alarmed the oligarchy and the military and provoked another coup followed by suppression of the party. In 1956 a restricted democracy was re-established, with continued strong military pressures against Aprista participation in power, ultimately enforced by direct intervention (Villanueva 1975; 1977; Hilliker 1971: 58–71). In the 1960s, when civil society had grown stronger, the oligarchic–military alliance broke apart, and after the failure of a civilian regime to effect any significant reforms, the military seized power and established an authoritarian but including regime.[42]

In Bolivia, anti-oligarchic mobilization started in the late 1920s and greatly intensified after the loss of the Chaco War with Paraguay (1932–6). By that time, economic stagnation had accentuated elite infighting and eroded what contestation had been institutionalized in the early twentieth century. The economic elite remained strong enough effectively to resist a constitutional opening of the political system, but not to prevent the emergence of a revolutionary movement and a breakthrough to full democracy through force of arms. Both nationalist and revolutionary socialist groups emerged among the middle classes, particularly the younger generation, in the 1930s (Malloy 1970: 60–77). Radical forces promoted unionization; by 1940 railroad workers and artisan groups were organized already, and the miners were in the process of being organized. The MNR emerged as the strongest middle-class nationalist group and aligned with a section of the military in 1943 to stage a coup and impose a mildly reformist government. However, in 1946 this government was overthrown, and in the following years the MNR deliberately widened and strengthened its social base (Klein 1971: 38–40). By that time, the organized working class was already strongly influenced by revolutionary socialists, and therefore the alliance sought by the MNR pushed the party's program significantly to the left. In 1951 the MNR for the first time committed itself to universal suffrage, tin nationalization, and land reform (Malloy 1971: 117).

After the successful 1952 revolt, the new MNR government did decree universal suffrage, including the large illiterate portion of the population. However, the MNR–labor alliance was fraught with tension and mutual suspicion from the beginning, and these tensions grew more severe as economic problems became pressing. Industrialization was still at a low stage and consequently civil society relatively weak, but strategically located sectors were highly organized and armed and competed for power in the context of weakly institutionalized contestation. Though the MNR continued to exist, it was unable to play the role of a cohesive, programmatic party, and its organizational strength was insufficient to weather the economic problems of the mid-1950s (Malloy 1971: 112–33). The economic austerity policies pitted labor against the center–right faction of the party, which controlled the executive, and eventually led to bloody confrontations. Furthermore, there were no other cohesive parties representing interests of important social groups and capable of competing with the MNR. Thus, the military, which had been purged and greatly reduced in size after the revolution, was rebuilt with US support and increasingly drawn into politics, with the result that it replaced the MNR by coup in 1964 (Malloy 1971: 131–44).[43]

Military involvement in politics and democracy

Having identified the differences in the timing and strength of democratizing pressures, the class forces behind these pressures, the role of parties and the state, and the response of the economic elites, we now need to analyze the conditions leading to high vs. low military involvement during periods of restricted democracy. This question, of course, has to be treated in the context of the long tradition of military involvement in Latin America. As was discussed above, the independence wars and the subsequent struggles over borders led to the great importance of military force, which interacted with the problems of consolidating state power. Military leaders competed with civilians for political power, and the existence of regional caudillos made the imposition of national rule often difficult. But the problem of military involvement in politics was by no means solved with consolidation of state power and the establishment of regular armies under central command. Rather, intra-elite struggles and the weakness of civil society caused civilian groups to appeal to factions of the military for intervention on their behalf. Dissident elite sectors and the emerging middle classes in many cases appealed for military support in their efforts to gain a share of political power, and the ruling groups frequently relied on the military to squash such challenges.

A first and easy answer to the question of why the military continued to intervene during democratic periods in some cases but not in others is that "the most frequent sequel to military coups and government is more of the same" (Nordlinger 1977: 207); in other words, a tradition and/or relatively recent precedent of military intervention increases the likelihood of renewed intervention. To a certain extent, this is certainly the case; military intervention is more likely where institutional and normative underpinnings of contestation are weak to begin with, and it weakens such institutions and norms further. For instance, military involvement in the overthrow of incumbent oligarchic governments and in the establishment of democratic rule by the middle classes or middle–working-class alliances was not particularly auspicious for the consolidation of democracy. Such military participation was mostly a result of the presence of internal conflicts in the military between supporters and opponents of the incumbent oligarchic governments. However, such conflicts in most cases perpetuated themselves and often intensified. This entailed the potential that the military opponents of the new government might get the upper hand again in the internal struggle and might respond to calls for intervention on the side of the civilian anti-democratic forces. Often, the very attempts of an incumbent government to influence military promotions in order to strengthen its supporters violated norms of professionalism and thus alienated crucial sectors of the officer corps. Argentina from 1912 to 1930, particularly during the second administration of Yrigoyen 1928–30 (Potash 1969: 29–54), and

Venezuela from 1945 to 1948 (Lombardi 1982: 223–5) exemplify this pattern well.

In statistical studies a precedent of military intervention emerges as a good predictor of renewed intervention (Putnam 1967; Hibbs 1973), but the relationship is not perfect; for us, precisely the "outliers" are the interesting cases. For instance, Chile as of 1932 had an extended recent experience of military intervention, and nevertheless civilian governments came to power and ruled constitutionally for the next forty years. Similarly, civil wars and the importance of military men in the struggle for political power gave way to successful subordination of the military to civilian governments in the early twentieth century in Uruguay and Colombia, where the military subsequently stayed out of politics until the 1960s and 1950s, respectively. Venezuela and Colombia after 1958 are further cases where military intervention was replaced by sustained civilian rule. Moreover, military involvement does not need to take the form of outright intervention through a coup; other important forms of involvement are, for instance, ultimatums posed to civilian governments and backed by coup threats, or implicit acknowledgment by civilian governments of military veto power over crucial decisions. Periods where these forms of involvement were frequent have to be included in the analysis.

In his review of the literature on the military in politics Lowenthal (1986: 9) points out that studies explaining why the military has not taken an extensive and direct political role in a number of countries and periods are scarce and "generally unilluminating." However, he also makes another point which is helpful in searching for an answer to our question, namely that the most persuasive writers on military intervention in politics stress the impact and interaction of macrosocial factors with institutional structure and interests proper. The degree of conflict in the society is a powerful incentive for military involvement, and dynamics in society and in the military institution interact (e.g. O'Donnell 1976, Philip 1985, Nordlinger 1977). Stepan (1971) has demonstrated the importance of strong civilian appeals to the military for the formation of a coup coalition and the actual execution of coups in Brazil between 1945 and 1964. Such appeals were also frequent during the period of restricted democracy in Argentina and Peru. In this group of countries, we can distinguish two patterns of relationships between civil society and the military. One pattern consists of an initially weak civil society which is undergoing a process of rapid organization, with excluded groups pressuring for inclusion and in some cases trying to ally with sectors of the military, and established groups feeling threatened and appealing to the military to protect order and keep the excluded groups excluded. This is the pattern of Brazil 1945–64 and Peru 1939–48 and 1956–68. The other pattern, occurring only in Argentina, consists of a very strong but stalemated civil society, where open conflict is high and the military is firmly opposed to the inclusion of one of the major social actors. In either pattern, military intervention of the moderator type[44] contributed nothing to the institutionalization and resolution of the conflicts, notwithstanding military claims that intervention was necessary for the installation and preservation of "genuine" democracy. Ultimately all these moderator patterns ended in a military dictatorship, of either the institutional or the personalistic variety.

If we go beyond an attempt to explain high military involvement on the basis of analyses of cases where it was present to a systematic comparison of the countries and periods with restricted democracy where military involvement was low with those where it was high, we find that what clearly distinguishes them is the existence vs. absence of two or more strong political parties.[45] Where parties were strong, they could provide for the representation of all established interests in the society, as well as for the gradual integration of new groups. The possibilities for protecting their interests and mediating conflict through the parties restrained civilians from appealing to the military for intervention and thus greatly reduced the military's propensity to do so. In particular, elites had to feel secure that their interests would be protected by a party with a strong base.[46] What is important, then, is not just the existence of a strong party, but rather of two or more such parties capable of making a credible bid for participation in political power, at least one of them being committed to protecting elite interests. Apra in Peru, AD in Venezuela, and the Peronists in Argentina were all strong parties in their organizational structure and mass base. However, they had no rival parties of comparable strength, their programs and appeals were radical and oriented exclusively towards their lower-class base, and they claimed a monopoly on the representation of popular interests. As a result, they marginalized all other political actors and generated broad opposition coalitions, which in turn, lacking strong enough parties of their own to compete electorally, appealed to the military to repress the radical parties.

Whereas the weakness of parties and thus the propensity of major civilian groups to appeal to the military for intervention on their behalf explains the frequency of intervention, the type of intervention, i. e. whether it was on the side of pro- or anti-democratic forces, can be explained with the interaction between the institutional character of the military (degree of professionalization, internal unity vs. tensions between old and new guards, recruitment and socialization patterns of officers) and the political role of the middle classes.[47] The stronger the middle classes and the more pro-democratic their posture, the more likely it was that factions of the military aligned with them in their efforts to install a democratic regime (e.g. Argentina before 1912, Uruguay in 1903–4, and Venezuela in 1945). Whether these factions were able to get the upper hand depended in part on their positions in a military hierarchy governed by professional criteria and on the strength of ties to oligarchic interests among the senior officers. In contrast, the stronger the perceived threat to stability from the lower classes, the more anti-democratic the posture of the middle classes, and the stronger the calls for intervention from economic elites, the more likely it was that the military would support oligarchic efforts to assert control or, in the case of highly professionalized military institutions, that it would intervene in a moderator role or establish a military dominated regime.

Summary of initial democratization sequences

To review briefly the paths to initial democratization, we can start with the point that the length and difficulty of the process of consolidation of state power was the first determinant of progress towards institutionalization of contestation. The next determinants of progress towards institutionalization of contestation and greater inclusion were the onset and type of expansion of the export economy. In some cases, this expansion led to the emergence of new political parties, radical mass parties in mineral export economies and clientelistic parties in agrarian export economies, and in other cases the forces generated by expansion were absorbed into pre-existing political parties or were kept politically disarticulated by a tradition of strong state involvement in society. These political institutions in turn became further important determinants of political outcomes, as they profoundly shaped the effects of the last important social structural factor shaping progress towards democracy, the expansion of industrialization.

Non-labor intensive agriculture as the leading export sector, accompanied by significant subsidiary industrialization and urbanization and by the growth of clientelistic parties led to the most favorable balance between pressures from below and resistance from above and thus the first breakthroughs to full democracy. Labor intensive agriculture as the leading export sector was favorable for institutionalization of contestation, but not inclusion. Pressures from subordinate classes for inclusion remained weak, as the agrarian economy was not conducive to the organization of subordinate classes. Later, when such pressures were generated by industrialization, they met with strong elite resistance and reliance on incorporation in state-controlled institutions and/or repression. Only where strong political parties represented elite interests, or where elites developed confidence in the control capacity of corporatist institutions, an opening to restricted democracy became possible.

Where minerals were the leading export sector contestation was facilitated in one case and there only temporarily (Bolivia), where the sector was under domestic control; but the dominance of mineral exports generated strong pressures for inclusion. The articulation of these pressures by radical mass parties in turn led to strong elite resistance, and repression followed successful as well as unsuccessful attempts to install democratic regimes. This sequence could only be broken if elites became assured by experience or a political pact that the party system would effectively protect their interests.

When subordinate classes began to exert democratizing pressures, the middle classes played the leading role. The propensity and capability of the middle classes to exert strong pressures and to demand full democratization, however, were conditioned by the presence of a significant organizational potential in the working class. Where such a potential was absent, middle-class pressures for democratization remained weak (Paraguay, Ecuador) or were absorbed and co-opted by sectors of the elites (Colombia) and/or by the state (Brazil). Where the working class had a significant numerical presence but only weak connections to working-class-based parties (Argentina and Uruguay), middle-class-based clientelistic parties appealed for working-class support and pushed for full democracy but abstained from establishing close links to unions. Where the working class had a high potential for organization and left-wing groups or parties promoted unionization and attempted to forge union–party alliances (in the mineral export economies), some middle-class-led parties did the same and developed into radical mass parties, or at least entered alliances with radical working-class parties. The comparatively greater weakness of the ideological hegemony exercised by traditional economic elites in mineral export economies facilitated the emergence of strong middle-class support for such radical parties.

Based on this set of sequences we can suggest three conditions which in combination seem to have been sufficient to allow for the establishment of viable fully democratic regimes in South America before the 1980s: (1) absence or previous elimination of large landowners engaged in labor intensive agriculture as powerful economic and political actors; (2) significant strength of subordinate classes, particularly the working class, in the balance of power in civil society; (3) political articulation of civil society through two or more strong political parties.[48] The first two conditions are a result of the structure of the economy (mineral versus agrarian export sector, type of agriculture) and of the level of economic development (industrialization and urbanization). The third, and the second one in part, are a result of historical legacies or deliberate institution building acts, but the challenges they present to would-be institution builders are formidable. The first one is also subject to deliberate political action; that is, a sweeping land reform can eliminate large landowners as a powerful class, but this is an exceedingly daunting task in the South American context.[49]

Looking at the stringency of these conditions serves, if nothing else, to remind us of the hard uphill road that democratizers have had to travel in South America. The path did not get much smoother after the initial achievement of democratic rule.

Mexico

Mexico requires special treatment because the revolution set its trajectory apart from those of the South American countries with mineral export economies. It is a case whose democratic record is clearly below what one would expect on the basis of the country's level of development. Essentially, Mexico has never had any period of democratic rule. In the 1970s and 1980s pressures for democratization resulted in some political reforms which, however, have fallen short of opening the possibility of a loosening of the symbiotic relationship between the state eclipsing the autonomous political articulation of subordinate classes. The case illustrates very clearly the potential long-run anti-democratic effects of a state eclipsing the autonomous political articulation off subordinate classes. The nature of Mexican authoritarianism is very different from that of other countries which lack any democratic record, such as Paraguay, El Salvador and Guatemala, and so are its origins. The Mexican system relies much more on co-optation than repression, it does have a mass base, it grants considerable room for the expression of political dissent, and it has proved to be very flexible and capable of adapting to changing conditions.[50] Its origins lie in the legacy of the revolution which allowed political leaders over the following decades to build effective institutions for the incorporation of subordinate classes and thus prevent the independent political articulation of these classes.

From the point of view of the questions posed in this book, two aspects of Mexican political development have to be explained, namely why the dominant classes never managed to institutionalize contestation among themselves but rather helped to bring about the revolution, and why economic growth has not generated more effective pressures for democratization from subordinate classes in the post-World War II period. The answer to the first question lies in the long and difficult process of consolidation of state power and in the great heterogeneity of economic elites; the answer to the second question in the pivotal role of the state in shaping the political articulation of civil society.

The intensity and length of the war of independence left Mexican society with only two institutional bases of power, the military and the church. The war with the United States, repeated local rebellions, and the French invasion further reinforced recourse to armed force as the major means to achieve, exercise, and also to resist political power.[51] Thus, it was only under Díaz who seized power in 1876 that a monopoly of organized force could be established and state power could be centralized. Under his rule export expansion led to great prosperity, but no sector or sectors of economic elites were capable of achieving a hegemonic position and exercising political power in a constitutional way. The Mexican economy was primarily a mineral export economy, with precious metals accounting for 79 percent of total exports in 1877–78 and still 58 percent in 1900–1 (Hansen 1971: 15). Most of mining investment in this period was foreign. Agriculture also expanded considerably, with different products being important in different areas, such as ranching in the north, wheat, grain, and sugar in the center, and henequen (a plant yielding fiber) in the Yucatan. Though agricultural production was primarily under Mexican control, foreign capital controlled the marketing of some important products. Finally, manufacturing grew in iron, textiles, and other light consumer goods, with a combination of local and foreign capital.[52] The result of this diversified pattern of growth was great heterogeneity of the dominant classes, with different ties to world markets, the local market, the state, and each other, and without a clearly dominant sector or coalition.

The state, whose role in promoting economic growth through granting concessions for railroad construction, contracting loans in world financial markets, establishing protective tariffs, etc. was essential, also became a crucial mediator among different sectors of economic elites, both domestic and foreign.[53] This role, which for a long time was a source of strength and relative autonomy for the state, became a source of vulnerability once a combination of wavering favoritism, pervasive corruption, and increasing dominance of foreign capital alienated large sectors of the dominant classes and generated militant opposition among those sectors not allied with foreign capital. At the same time, Díaz's concessions to British oil interests led to pressures and hostility from US interests, and as Díaz appeared increasingly vulnerable, US government policy became equivocal, denying him firm support. The combination of growing tensions between the regime and large sectors of the dominant classes and sectors of foreign capital, the succession crisis, withdrawal of US support, and increasing rigidity and corruption in the state apparatus, including the military, produced a crisis of the state and opened the way for the outbreak of rebellions from below.[54]

Given the lack of periods of institutionalized contestation and the dictatorial nature of the Díaz regime, no mass political parties emerged before the revolution. However, the structure of the enclave economy did produce very radical tendencies among the subordinate classes. The northern revolutionary movement led by Villa showed a social composition similar to that of the radical mass parties which emerged in the South American enclave economies in the twentieth century, namely a working-class–middle-class coalition of urban and rural workers and unemployed, and educated radical middle-class and petty bourgeois elements. The other major component of the popular revolutionary movement, Zapata's army, had its base among the members of Indian communities and small and medium peasants who were fighting for land lost to modernizing haciendas. Though Villa's and Zapata's armies temporarily gained the upper hand in the fighting, these representatives of subordinate classes were unable to construct a viable coalition, rebuild a state apparatus under their control, and establish a political system geared towards protection of their constituents' interests. Instead, victory fell to the Constitutionalist armies of Carranza and Obregón which represented mainly dissident sectors of elites and the middle classes and had managed to attract support from organized labor in Mexico City. [55] The contents of the new constitution of 1917 reflected the influence of forces within the Constitutionalist camp which defended peasant and worker interests, but they remained by and large dead letters for over 15 years, as these radical forces were in the minority among the revolutionary coalition which established control over the state apparatus and gradually managed to extend effective central control over the nation.

After the revolution, the problem of consolidating state power posed itself anew. Not only was political power very decentralized, to a large extent in the hands of local political bosses, but regionally based armed challenges to the central government also re-emerged, most prominently the Cristero rebellion of 1926–9. Thus, the primary concern of the heirs of the revolution remained effective centralization of power, rather than institutionalization of contestation and widening of political inclusion. With the founding for the 1929 election of the Partido Nacional Revolucionario (PNR) in which the military was given a major voice, Calles managed to both reduce the power of local political bosses and co-opt the military into participating in the political process and abstaining from direct intervention. The successful centralization of power laid the basis for Cárdenas to build an organized popular base for the regime and implement constitutional provisions favoring the interests of subordinate classes to a significant extent. However, his very success in catering to the interests of subordinate classes and including them into strong organizations linked to the party weakened the capacity of subordinate classes to pressure for effective political and socioeconomic participation and representation in the longer run. Rather, they became increasingly marginalized during the phase of significant industrial growth after 1940. In the absence of institutionalized contestation and independent middle- and working-class political organization, there remained only extremely limited options for mounting a challenge based in sectors of subordinate classes to the elite-dominated PRI and its alliance with national and foreign capital.

After his accession to power in 1934 Cárdenas, taking advantage of a conjuncture which provided the state with considerable autonomy, embarked on a wide-reaching program of economic redistribution and social mobilization.[56] He distributed close to twice the amount of land that all his predecessors together had distributed (Meyer and Sherman 1983: 599), and he made communal ejidos (a form of land tenure where ownership is vested in the community and land can be cultivated collectively or individually) the main beneficiaries of the land reform. He also protected the rights of labor and promoted urban and rural unionization. Members of ejidos and of peasant leagues and unions were integrated into peak associations and given formal representation in the political system through the creation of peasant and labor sectors in the party. In his efforts to incorporate the working class into state-controlled institutions, Cárdenas could build on a tradition of co-optation and collaboration between the state and organized labor.[57] In order to attract support for the Constitutionalist forces, Carranza and Obregón had reopened the Casa del Obrero Mundial in Mexico City, the anarcho-syndicalist union confederation which had been closed by the Huerta government. They also offered material and financial support and promises of favorable labor legislation, and they received support from "red battalions" of armed workers. In 1918 Carranza encouraged the formation of the Confederación Regional Obrera Mexicana (CROM). Under Obregón and Calles the CROM leadership was appointed to important political positions, and unions affiliated to CROM were favored. A combination of excessive corruption of the CROM leadership and changes in government policy away from support for CROM to generally more repressive responses to labor demands and militancy led to significant defections from CROM in 1919 and to its eventual demise. By 1932, then, the labor movement was severely divided and lacked a strong tradition of autonomous organization. Cárdenas's efforts were further aided by the low degree of organization of the working class; as of 1930 only some 5 percent of workers in manufacturing, transport, and communications were union members (Spalding 1977: 115). Moreover, the National Federal Labor Law of 1931 had already given the government significant legal control over unions and labor relations.

The formal link of organized labor to the party created by Cárdenas ensured that the political articulation of the working class would be mediated by state elites. The party was reorganized in 1938, renamed the Partido Revolucionario Mexicano (PRM), and based on four pillars: labor, the peasantry, the middle classes, and the military.[58] Middle-class organizations representing groups such as government employees, teachers, private farmers, small merchants and industrialists, and professionals were organized in the Confederación Nacional de Organizaciones Populares (CNOP), which in turn formed the basis for the "popular sector" of the PRM, just as the Confederación de Trabajadores de Mexico (CTM) did for the labor sector and the Confederación Nacional de Campesinos (CNC) for the peasant sector. In theory, the interests of each of these sectors were to be safeguarded through the election of representatives to party and government offices at all levels. If practice approximated theory under Cárdenas, the two became increasingly divorced under his successors; it was the party leadership which came to appoint sectoral leaders and government officers from the top levels down. Instead of subordinate classes shaping policy via their effective representation in the party, a partnership between the party elite and the economically dominant classes came to implement an economic model which produced sustained economic growth at the cost of increasing inequality and economic dependence.[59]

By mobilizing and incorporating labor into state-sponsored organizations Cárdenas eclipsed the democratic thrust of the expansion of the urban industrial working class, just as Vargas did in Brazil and Perón did in Argentina. What differentiates Mexico from the other two cases is that the demobilizing and control functions of these organizations have remained effective, whereas they were eroded during periods of competitive politics in the other two countries. The main reason for this difference, we would suggest, is the existence of a hegemonic party in Mexico. Cárdenas could build on and managed to greatly strengthen a pre-existing elite-based party by incorporating subordinate classes into it. In contrast, both Vargas and Perón built new parties, Vargas even two of them, one of which became more or less identified with the interests of subordinate classes, as did the Peronist party. Thus, electoral politics in Brazil and Argentina led to intense interparty competition and appeals to subordinate classes based on promises of material improvements, which allowed for greater independence from the state apparatus and growing militancy particularly of urban labor.[60] In Argentina growing class polarization under Perón led to strong support among the dominant classes and large sectors of the middle classes for an authoritarian solution. Labor militancy in the period of restricted democracy after 1958 was further aggravated by the attempt to exclude the Peronist party from the political game, and this in turn reinforced support for a renewed authoritarian takeover. In Mexico, in contrast, elections were not only compatible with PRI hegemony and low labor militancy, but they served to strengthen the legitimacy of the regime internally and externally.

In sum, problems with consolidation of state power and great elite heterogeneity prevented the emergence of a constitutional oligarchic regime. Rather, tensions between sectors of the dominant classes and the state contributed to the crisis at the top which allowed for the outbreak of successful revolution from below. Renewed problems with consolidating state power were solved by the victorious sectors of the revolutionary leadership with the creation of a party which initially subordinated local to central elites and later was strengthened by the addition of mass bases. Through the incorporation of newly mobilized and rewarded peasants, workers, and members of the middle classes into the state-sponsored party, their independent political articulation and thus their capacity to counter state control and to pressure for democratic rule was eclipsed. The PRI became truly hegemonic and thus served to bolster the longevity of the corporatist mass organizations. Close collaboration between the political and the economic elites, and the high potential of party and state to co-opt ambitious politicians, combined with selective repression, have ham-

pered the emergence of counter-elites successfully pressuring for the institutionalization of contestation and effectively competing with the PRI by breaking its
hold over organized sectors of the subordinate classes or organizing those
sectors not incorporated into PRI-linked mass organizations.[61] Moreover, the
PRI has demonstrated flexibility in responding to the challenges that have
emerged with a variety of liberalizing measures which have extended the space
for contestation but stopped short of allowing for real democratization, namely
the possibility of a replacement of the PRI by an opposition.

We will take up the issue of liberalization in Mexico in the context of our
discussion of redemocratization in Latin America in the 1970s and 1980s. Let
us now turn to an analysis of the factors underlying consolidation and
breakdown of regimes after initial democratization.

Regime Transformations after Initial Democratization

Patterns of transition

The initial installation of a full or restricted democratic regime had an impact
on later political dynamics in two ways. Democracy allowed greater freedom for
organizing among the subordinate classes, particularly the working class, which
could put strains on the alliances which had achieved democratization. The
attitudes of the dominant classes vis-à-vis democracy were affected by the
concrete experience with it; where they enjoyed strong representation in the
new system, they learned to accommodate to it, but where they were clearly
marginalized from political power and threatened by the increasing organizational power of subordinate classes, they attempted to undermine the system.

In shifting the focus to the conditions accounting for regime changes after
initial democratization, one can start by analyzing the types of transformation in
the course of which political contestation and inclusion were widened (i. e.
democratizing transitions) or restricted (i. e. transitions to authoritarianism),
and by asking whether there are connections between the patterns of democratic and authoritarian transitions. Tables 5. 4 and 5. 5 give an overview of the
types of transformation in the various cases.

The first transition to full or restricted democracy was preceded by
constitutional oligarchic rule only in three of the nine countries which
experienced such periods; in the other six countries, the transition took place
directly from authoritarian rule. If we look at the longevity of first periods of
democracy, the hypothesis about the favorable effects of institutionalized elite
contestation for the installation of democracy receives rather weak support.[62] In
two of the countries where constitutional oligarchic rule immediately preceded
the new democratic regimes, these new regimes were quite long lived
(Argentina 1912– 30; Colombia 1936–49), an average of fifteen and one half
years; the third case, Chile 1920–24, was a transitional case rather than a clear
democratic opening and was very short lived. This compares to an average life
span of 12 years for first time democracies in countries where this first

TABLE 5.4   Transitions widening inclusion and contestation

Old regime	New regime			
	Restricted democracy		*Full democracy*	
Oligarchic constitutional regime	Chile 1920 Colombia 1936	(4) (13)	Argentina 1912	(18)
Traditional, populist, or military authoritarian	Uruguay 1903 Chile 1932 Argentina 1958 1963 Brazil 1945 Ecuador 1948 1978 Peru 1939 1956 1963 Colombia 1958 Venezuela 1958 Bolivia 1982	(16) (38) (4) (3) (19) (13) (12) (9) (6) (5) (32) (10) (8)	Argentina 1946 Bolivia 1952 Uruguay 1942 Venezuela 1945 Peru 1980	(5) (12) (31) (3) (10)
Restricted democracy			Chile 1970 Uruguay 1919 Venezuela 1968	(3) (14) (22)
Bureaucratic authoritarian regime	Brazil 1985 Chile 1990	(5)	Argentina 1973 1983 Uruguay 1984	(3) (7) (6)

The numbers in parentheses after the year of the transition indicate the number of years which the new regime lasted, up to 1990.

transition came from some form of authoritarian rule. If we look at all our cases, i.e. periods of democratic rule, not countries, except for the cases of redemocratization in the late 1970s and 1980s, and compare the longevity of full or restricted democracies which had no precedent of either constitutional oligarchic or democratic rule, whether immediate or in a previous phase, with those which were preceded by constitutional oligarchic and/or democratic rule, we find that the former lasted on the average nine and one half years and the latter thirteen and one half years.

Where a first democratic regime broke down and a second democratizing transformation occurred, the same type of democracy tended to be reestablished. If a fully democratic regime had been established the first time, the

TABLE 5.5   Transitions restricting inclusion and contestation

Old regime   *New regime*

	Constitutional oligarchic	Traditional or populist or military authoritarian	Bureaucratic authoritarian	Restricted Democracy
Restricted democracy		Argentina 1962 Peru 1948 1962 1968 Ecuador 1961 Chile 1924 Colombia 1949	Argentina 1966 Brazil 1964	
Full democracy		Argentina 1930 1951 Bolivia 1964 Uruguay 1933 Venezuela 1948	Uruguay 1973 Argentina 1976 Chile 1973	

country was likely to return to the same type (Argentina 1946; Uruguay 1942); if it had been a restricted democracy, the same or similar restrictions were likely to re-emerge (Chile 1932; Colombia 1958; Peru 1956; Ecuador 1978). Only in a further step was a full opening likely to occur (Chile 1970; Peru 1980), and only after a second breakdown were greater restrictions likely to be imposed (Argentina 1955). One explanation for this is an institutionalization effect in so far as previously established political rules and procedures could more easily be revitalized than new ones shaped from scratch.[63] A second and complementary explanation is that in general traditional authoritarian regimes did not drastically change the underlying constellation of contending forces; only the populist and the bureaucratic authoritarian systems did, the former by mobilizing and thus strengthening, and the latter by demobilizing and violently breaking the organizational strength of popular forces.[64] The exception here is Venezuela; after the authoritarian regime which had replaced the short lived (1945–48) experiment with full democracy, political and economic elites decided to install a restricted democracy in 1958.

Transitions to authoritarianism

What is clear if one looks at the transformations which restricted contestation and/or inclusion is that there are no cases where any form of democracy was replaced with a constitutional oligarchic regime, nor cases where one type of democracy was replaced with another, more restricted one. What this means is that once a more open political system was established, it was not possible any longer to simply restrict participation and/or restore an oligarchic system; rather, recourse to more coercive measures and the installation of some type of authoritarian system were necessary.

To understand the transitions to authoritarianism, one needs to separate out two questions, namely (1) the factors accounting for the breakdowns of democratic regimes, and (2) the factors shaping the type of regime replacing the democratic one. The first question asks whether some types of democratic regimes had congenital weaknesses which made their breakdown likely. The most clear-cut cases are restricted democracies with high military involvement; sooner or later, they all broke down into authoritarianism (Peru 1948, 1962, 1968; Ecuador 1961; Brazil 1964; Argentina 1962, 1966). Where the military was heavily involved in the politics of a restricted democracy, it was not possible to reduce or neutralize such involvement without an intervening authoritarian period during which the military discredited itself and/or endangered its own institutional cohesion and therefore decided to withdraw from politics. Full democracies before the 1980s did not fare much better; eight of the nine cases broke down, the exception being Venezuela since 1968. In three cases, though, the breakdown occurred after extended periods of democratic rule (Argentina 1930; Uruguay 1933 and 1973).

The least likely type of democratic regimes to break down into authoritarianism were restricted democracies with low military involvement. Of the six cases established prior to the late 1970s, only two were replaced by an authoritarian regime, namely Colombia in 1949 and Chile in 1924 (the latter case not really fitting the classification but rather being a transitional case of regime to begin with); three were transformed into full democracies (Chile 1970; Uruguay 1919; Venezuela 1968); and one remained a restricted democracy but relaxed some of the restrictions (Colombia 1971). The relative stability of these regimes was due to two factors; first, the nature of the coalition which had established the regimes, i. e. an alliance between the middle classes and sectors of the economic elites, in some cases appealing for popular support but not including organized lower classes as full partners; and second, the existence of firmly institutionalized party competition, i. e. the presence of two or more strong political parties at least one of which effectively protected elite interests. The working class was allowed to organize, and its organized sectors were included (or better: tolerated) in the political process, but there was no concerted effort by the state and/or a political party to promote organization and mobilize the working class into an alliance with the middle classes. Thus, civil society grew in strength gradually, without posing an acute threat to the elites which would engender repression. Chile is a partial exception; the installation of the restricted democracy in 1932 was effected by a middle class–elite alliance, but from 1938 on the middle–working-class alliance played a very important role and generated a considerable degree of mobilization. The reasons why the restricted democratic regime nevertheless managed to survive for such a long time in Chile are the confidence of the elites in their effective representation in the political system and the moderation in the actual policies of the middle–working-class alliances when in power. When this confidence was eroded in the early 1970s and policy radicalized significantly, the elites started undermining the democratic regime.

In general, where an alliance between the middle classes, sometimes represented by a relatively autonomous political class, and sectors of the economic elites was the decisive force behind the democratizing transformation, relatively stable restricted or full democracies emerged. This was the case for the democratizing transformations in Uruguay in 1903, 1919, and 1942; Chile in 1932; Colombia in 1936 and 1958; and Venezuela in 1958 and 1968. The condition for the very formation of such an alliance was, of course, that at least significant sectors of the economic elites felt that they would be able to ensure protection of their interests under the new regime either through strong parties or through the provisions of a political pact. As long as this expectation was borne out, the democratic systems survived; where the party system appeared to lose the ability to perform this function, such as in Colombia by 1948, and Uruguay by 1933 and 1973, elites effectively promoted a turn to authoritarianism. In order for full democracies to be consolidated (Uruguay after 1942 and Venezuela after 1968), a significant degree of industrialization was a further requirement.

Where the middle classes and sectors of the elites were allied with sectors of the military in the process of democratization, there was a strong potential for perpetuation of military involvement (Brazil after 1945 and Argentina after 1958), or for an easy revival thereof in response to civilian appeals (Argentina 1930). In either case, the result was an eventual military takeover and installation of an authoritarian regime. Equally unstable situations prevailed in all cases where middle and working classes formed an alliance to push for democratization, a situation typical of mineral export economies (Peru in 1939 and 1956, Bolivia in 1952, Venezuela in 1945, and Chile in 1970). In order to be successful, these alliances needed to promote high mobilization, but the price of victory was the implacable enmity of the elites and/or the military and other sectors of the middle classes. Thus, even where such alliances were able to establish full democracies, their success entailed the danger of polarization and formation of broad opposition coalitions, and thus of rapid erosion of these democracies.[65] Moreover, except for Chile, these democracies were premature in the sense that civil society and particularly the organization of lower classes were still comparatively weak. This weakness was compensated by party mobilization of strategic sectors in the installation phase, but it impaired consolidation of the democratic regimes. In the case of Peru, high military involvement prevailed during the periods of restricted democracy, as Apra's early insurrectionary strategy and its continued strong mobilization efforts and participation in coup conspiracies made a majority in the military determined to bar Apra from access to state power; both periods of restricted democracy gave way to authoritarian military regimes.

As pointed out repeatedly, the type of coalition formed in the initial transition to democracy was in part shaped by the structure of the economy and the type of party that emerged. In mineral export economies, ideological mass parties emerged and mobilized alliances between middle and working classes. The presence of these parties had somewhat contradictory consequences for the viability of democratic regimes. On the one hand, they presented a more dramatic threat to elites than clientelistic parties with a middle- and working-class base and thus generated more repressive responses (Apra from its founding until 1978; AD 1948–58), but on the other hand they mostly enjoyed strong legitimacy among and influence on their followers and thus could ensure mass compliance with political alliances or pacts concluded by party leaders in attempts to consolidate democratic regimes (Chile after 1932; Venezuela after 1958). The MNR in Bolivia is the glaring exception here. Such compliance, in turn, was favorable for the survival of restricted and fully democratic arrangements, as it reduced threat perception among elites and prevented ungovernability. Moreover, programmatic mass parties made a positive contribution to democratic consolidation in so far as their promotion of mobilization and political education strengthened the subordinate classes and increased the level of political participation among them.

In agrarian export economies, clientelistic parties emerged and promoted alliances between the middle classes and sectors of elites and/or the military, while appealing for popular support on a patronage basis. These parties initially presented only a moderate threat to elites and thus could be successful in installing restricted democratic regimes. However, clientelistic parties were highly susceptible to fragmentation. Where historical loyalties cemented party identification (Uruguay and Colombia), the parties managed to survive and maintain both their cross-class bases and the constitutional political process for longer periods of time than where the quest for state power was the only glue holding the party together (the Radicals in Argentina). However, even in the former cases party fragmentation led to situations where party leaders lost their ability to negotiate compromises, enforce compliance of their parties, and prevent a breakdown into uncontrolled violence (Colombia in the 1940s) or creeping military domination (Uruguay in the 1960s).

The experiences of Venezuela and Colombia since 1958 demonstrate that historical legacies in the form of one-party dominance or a fractionalized party system are not necessarily permanent impediments to the installation and consolidation of democratic regimes. The political pacts concluded by leaders in the two countries established the conditions for effectively competing parties and a democratic system, albeit initially with a heavy dose of elite control and severe restrictions, whose effects are still omnipresent in Colombia. In Colombia, the pact strengthened the two traditional parties and revived an older tradition of compromise and coalition-building among them, but in Venezuela AD's position was weakened and party competition deliberately strengthened through political engineering, and accommodation and compromise were created virtually from scratch.[66]

The role of large landowners as opponents of democracy tended to change after the installation of democratic regimes, under the impact of their concrete experiences with full or limited democracy. Whereas landowners engaged in non-labor intensive agriculture acquiesced to the installation of fully democratic regimes, they turned into rabid opponents of these regimes once they saw their influence dwindle and felt economically threatened (Argentina 1930, Uruguay 1933). In contrast, landowners who depended on a mixture of market and political coercion to ensure themselves a large pool of cheap labor and who had opposed a democratic opening, tended to accommodate themselves to limited democracies if they were convinced by experience that their control over votes could assure them an influential position in the political process, or that their interests were effectively protected under a political pact (Chile after 1932; Colombia after 1958).

In most cases, though not in all, the breakdown of democratic regimes occurred in situations of acute economic problems and was clearly related to these problems. This was the case in Chile 1924 and 1973, Argentina 1930, 1951, 1966, and 1976, Uruguay 1933 and 1973, Bolivia 1964, Brazil 1964, Ecuador in 1961, and Peru in 1948 and 1968. In Venezuela in 1948 and in Colombia in 1949 this was not the case. The breakdowns in the 1920s and 1930s were related to the crisis of the nitrate industry in Chile and to the Depression in Argentina and Uruguay. In the latter two cases, the agrarian exporters felt threatened by the decline in external demand and by what they perceived as inadequate policy responses of the incumbent governments.[67] The later breakdowns were related to balance of payments problems, resulting from secular stagnation of the export sector (Argentina 1951), or decline of the export sector due to increased competition from other producers and falling prices (Ecuador), or secular stagnation aggravated by the decline in exports and terms of trade after the Korean War boom (Bolivia), or by problems in the export sector combined with the exhaustion of the easy phase of ISI (Brazil, Argentina 1966 and 1976, Uruguay). In Peru in 1948 and 1968 economic problems were present but, compared to the other cases, of lesser importance than more strictly political factors in causing the breakdown. Chile in 1973 is a special case in so far as the economic crisis was crucial in the fall of the Allende government, but its emergence was less due to economic factors per se than to their interaction with the political struggle.

Whereas the type of coalition which installed a democratic regime and the type of party system in place heavily conditioned the likelihood of the regime's breakdown, and the occurrence of severe economic problems influenced its timing, the stage of ISI reached when the breakdown occurred shaped the type of authoritarian regime which would replace the democratic one. In the early stages of ISI, traditional or populist authoritarian regimes emerged, or a type of military regime with varying degrees of reformist orientation; in advanced stages bureaucratic–authoritarian regimes emerged.

Popular mobilization at the time of the installation of the traditional authoritarian or reformist military regimes was at a comparatively still low to intermediate level, but in several cases it had been growing very rapidly and thus had raised the level of threat perception among the elites and the military (Venezuela 1945–48, Peru 1945–48, 1956–68), or led to a decay of the democratizing coalition (Bolivia 1952–64), or started to degenerate into uncontrollable violence (Colombia in the 1940s), all of which paved the way for the turn to authoritarianism. Traditional authoritarian regimes were based on an alliance including agro-exporting, commercial and financial economic elites and the military (Argentina 1930, Colombia 1949, Peru 1948), and in addition sectors of the middle classes (Uruguay 1933, Venezuela 1948, Bolivia 1964); populist authoritarian regimes were based on a populist cross-class coalition, initially mostly with military backing (e. g. Perón 1951). Reformist military regimes were based primarily in the military institution and had no significant civilian allies (Peru 1968; Ecuador 1963).[68] Foreign capital in all these cases was concentrated in extractive industries, commerce, finance, transport, and utilities, and only in Argentina, Venezuela, and Bolivia the democratic regimes had seriously threatened some of these holdings. Accordingly, foreign companies and their local representatives played a less prominent role in the traditional or populist authoritarian regimes than they would in supporting the bureaucratic authoritarian regimes at advanced stages of ISI. Under the reformist military regime of Peru, relations to foreign capital were in fact highly strained.

The goals of traditional authoritarian regimes were limited to changing political decision-making structures. They mostly sought to preserve the social and economic status quo or to return to a previous state of affairs (e. g. Argentina 1930–43). Populist authoritarian regimes sought changes in the social and economic structure as well as in the political system. They promoted domestic industrialization, attempted to restrict the role of foreign capital, pursued redistributive policies, and mobilized popular forces, particularly the urban working class. Accordingly, the form of the state apparatus and the role of the state in the economy varied. Traditional authoritarian regimes could be of a civilian or military variety, but the military regimes were more personalistic or factional than rule by the military as a professional institution. In particular, there was no militarization and no significant expansion of the state apparatus. The existing repressive and administrative capacity of the state was sufficient given the relatively low levels of economic development and popular mobilization and the limited goals of the regimes. Typically, these regimes had limited autonomy only and ruled in close alliance with factions of the economic elites. Populist authoritarian regimes were dominated by civilians but initially often enjoyed military support or acquiescence. Their ambitious goals for social and economic change entailed an expansion of the state apparatus, particularly of the bureaucracy involved in regulating the economy and providing social services. The need for repressive capacity was limited as only selective repression was needed as a complement to co-optation in ensuring the stability of the regimes. The autonomy of the state from civil society as a whole, while greater than that enjoyed by oligarchic or traditional authoritarian regimes, remained more limited than that to be achieved by bureaucratic–authoritarian regimes. The support from subordinate classes increased the autonomy of the state from dominant classes and enabled the regimes to pursue pro-labor policies resisted by the latter, but property rights of domestic capitalists and traditional prerogatives of landowners remained untouched.

While the breakdown of democratic regimes has to be explained with the class-composition of political coalitions and with institutional factors, the installation of the bureaucratic–authoritarian regimes which tended to replace critically weakened democracies at advanced stages of ISI (Brazil 1964,

Argentina 1966 and 1976, Chile 1973, Uruguay 1973) was a result of the structural conditions identified by O'Donnell (1973). The situation of completion of light consumer goods industrialization, heavily dependent on imports of capital and intermediate goods, in the context of the declining export performance, generated balance of payments crises and economic stagnation.[69] Since ISI had strengthened the labor movement, efforts to implement an economic solution to the crisis which shifted the costs onto the lower classes repeatedly failed in the framework of the democratic systems and intensified open confrontation. Moreover, the strong penetration of foreign capital into the manufacturing sector had opened new alliance possibilities for authoritarian forces (O'Donnell 1973; Collier 1979).[70] Accordingly, military regimes whose installation was initially supported by the entire economic elite and large sectors of the middle classes threatened by popular mobilization came to base themselves exclusively on support from civilian technocrats, the big internationalized bourgeoisie, exporting groups, and foreign capital (O'Donnell 1978).

The bureaucratic–authoritarian regimes sought radical changes in both the political system and the social and economic structure. Their primary emphasis was on the economic exclusion and the destruction of the organizational potential of the lower classes, but the implementation of their austerity and export promotion policies hurt not only the working and lower classes, but also the middle classes and the traditional sectors of the bourgeoisie producing for the domestic market. Consequently, the resolute pursuit of their economic policies required a closing of all channels and destruction of all institutions for the articulation of group or class interests. As a result, civil society as a whole and its political articulation were significantly weakened in all these cases, at least initially, and most dramatically so in Chile, Brazil, and Uruguay.

Bureaucratic authoritarianism is a form of rule by the military as a professional institution and entails the penetration of the state apparatus by military personnel. Whereas state capacity for the administration of economic and social affairs has undergone varying changes under different bureaucratic–authoritarian regimes, repressive capacity has undergone a tremendous expansion in all of them. In some cases, exemplified by Brazil 1964–85, the state's role in the economy as regulator and entrepreneur, in collaboration with foreign and big domestic capital, expanded greatly and entailed a significant increase in state capacity for economic planning and intervention. In other cases, exemplified by post–1973 Chile, the regimes pursued a deliberate policy of state-shrinking and withdrawal from economic entrepreneurship and regulation. In all cases, the role of the repressive apparatus of the state, particularly of the secret police, became crucial. It not only came to operate totally autonomously from civil society, but even developed the potential to escape the control of the military government and the military high command. The regimes themselves enjoyed a high degree of autonomy from civil society, from the subordinate classes as well as from the domestic bourgeoisie. However, their autonomy from transnational structures of power remained limited. Initially, the political support from some advanced capitalist states and from international public and private sources of loans increased their autonomy from transnational corporations, but the accumulation of a staggering foreign debt dramatically reduced their autonomy in the longer run.

Bureaucratic authoritarianism is a specifically modern state form. O'Donnell (1973) captured this in part in his argument that the spread of technocratic roles provided the basis for the formation of a coup coalition among technocrats in the military, the state bureaucracy, and the private sector. One can add to this that advances in information and communication technology provided the means not only for economic planning and intervention, but also for surveillance and repression. Furthermore, the external anchoring of the state in the post-World War II economic and geo-political system was essential for the rise of bureaucratic authoritarianism. External support in the form of financial assistance and training for the military and police strengthened the coercive apparatus which then extended its control over the entire state machinery. Interactions with transnational corporations and international sources of finance afforded the state considerable autonomy from the domestic economically dominant classes.

Redemocratization in the 1970s and 1980s

Where the bureaucratic–authoritarian regimes were successful in generating further industrialization, civil society grew stronger again after the initial phase of repression, and pressures for liberalization and democratization re-emerged. As Stepan (1985: 333) points out, the number of industrial workers in Brazil grew by 52 percent from 1960 to 1970, and by another 38 percent from 1970 to 1974, and the concentration of new industrial activity in the Sao Paulo area facilitated the emergence of new unions. Such new unions in crucial economic sectors, along with human rights groups, church-related organizations, and grass-roots popular movements demanded a restoration of civil and political rights.

The catholic church made a particularly important contribution to the strengthening of civil society in Brazil from the late 1960s on. Through the formation of Christian base communities the degree of organization of subordinate classes was raised considerably. They came to encompass sectors of the urban and rural unemployed and poor which are otherwise difficult to organize. Moreover, the participatory practices of these base communities predisposed their members to demand opportunities for participation in the political process (Bruneau 1982: 127–145; Mainwaring 1986: 146–223).

In Peru, under a different type of military regime from the bureaucratic–authoritarian ones, mobilization of urban and rural workers and of urban squatters greatly increased and provided the basis for forceful protests against the military government's economic policies and for a return to democratic rule (E. Stephens 1983). Though divisions within the military institutions and the regimes were crucial for the initiation of liberalization in all cases (O'Donnell and Schmitter 1986: 19), and Brazil and Peru were no exceptions, democratization would arguably not have gone as far as it did in these two cases had it not been for the greater organizational weight of subordinate classes and the consequent pressures from civil society (see e.g. Stepan 1989 for Brazil).

In Argentina, the bureaucratic–authoritarian regimes failed to achieve both their economic and political goals, and there was no clear change in the strength of civil society. If anything, fragmentation of the Peronist movement weakened an important part of civil society. However, given the conditional democratic commitment of at least sections of the Peronist movement, the fractionalization of the movement may actually have facilitated the re-establishment of democracy. The transition to democracy then was less the result of growing pressures from civil society than self-destruction of the military regime (Cavarozzi 1986: 155, 168; Viola and Mainwaring 1984). Tensions between the military as an institution and the military as a government had started already in 1980 (Stepan 1985: 329–30), were aggravated by the severe economic crisis generated by the government's policies, and were completed through the disastrous launching of the Falklands war. Thus, a situation of virtual state breakdown presented the opportunity for redemocratization.

In Uruguay the years between 1974 and 1980 brought significant economic growth (at least compared to Uruguay's record over the preceding two decades), before the balance of payments crisis of the early 1980s ushered in austerity policies and a recession. Despite this growth, civil society was drastically weakened between 1973 and 1978, mainly due to heavy repression of labor and the left (Stepan 1985: 325). However, neither the economic base for the labor movement nor the organizational infrastructure of the traditional non-left parties were destroyed. Thus, despite the previous repression of activists from all parties, the opposition managed to regroup rapidly once the first opening was provided by the military's decision to hold a referendum in 1980 (Gillespie 1986: 179–87; Handelman 1986: 209–14).

Pinochet's deindustrialization policies and the attempt to destroy the party system significantly weakened civil society and its capacity for articulating demands for political change (Valenzuela and Valenzuela 1986). As Garretón points out (1986: 121), the military's policies of deindustrialization and state retrenchment in Chile have generated marginalization, segmentation, and disintegration, in stark contrast to the consolidation of new social forces as a result of industrialization and expansion of the state in Brazil. This contrast, along with Pinochet's iron control over the military and the ruthlessness of repression, go a long way in explaining the long delay in significant progress towards democratization. The transition was initiated and heavily controlled by the military which had set the course towards the critical referendum of 1988 in its efforts to institutionalize the authoritarian regime through the 1980 constitution. Once the political space was opened, however, parties were rapidly reconstructed and managed to form a broad opposition coalition to hand an electoral defeat to the dictatorship. Still, civil society remains weakened and the parties consequently without a power base strong enough to challenge the significant restrictions on the power of the democratic government imposed by the military, and thus to re-establish a genuine, unrestricted democratic regime.

In Bolivia and Ecuador, economic growth in the 1960s and 1970s did not result in a strengthening of the working-class; the percentage of the workforce in the secondary sector remained virtually stagnant between 1965 and 1980, at about one-fifth (World Bank 1986: 238–9).[71] Unlike in Peru, the policies of the military regimes did not significantly raise the level of mobilization and organization of the lower classes either; on the contrary, the Banzer regime was highly repressive towards labor and the left. And in both cases the weakness and fractionalization of political parties persisted (Malloy and Gamarra 1987, 1988; Conaghan 1987; Handelman 1981). Accordingly, despite formal steps towards redemocratization, democracy remained highly unstable, threatened by frequent coup conspiracies and resort to unconstitutional means by incumbents, and restricted by a continued crucial role of the military. In Bolivia, the heavy involvement of the military in the narcotics smuggling industry which had flourished under Banzer was an additional obstacle to democratization (Whitehead 1986a: 64–7).[72] The result was chaotic politics, at times behind a democratic façade (Malloy and Gamarra 1987). In Ecuador, the struggle among contending forces produced an impasse between executive and legislature right from the start (Handelman 1981: 66–9); this repeated itself under the second civilian government and eventually led to constitutional crisis and resort to physical force to resolve conflicts between members of Congress and the President (Conaghan 1987: 152).

On the basis of the analysis presented here, one would venture the hypothesis that chances for consolidation of democratic regimes are generally better in the 1980s than before because the achievement of higher levels of industrialization strengthened civil society and tended to relegate large landowners to secondary importance. However, there are variations among the different countries on these conditions, and these conditions are by no means sufficient for the installation and consolidation of democratic regimes. Rather, the role of competing strong political parties was shown to be crucial for the consolidation of democratic regimes. This initially made prognoses for Argentina, Peru, and Uruguay appear brighter than for Brazil, Ecuador, and Bolivia. In the former three cases, landlords dependent on large amounts of cheap labor are not (or no longer) an important group. Argentina and Peru also seemed to meet the condition of having two or more relatively cohesive parties, whereas the continued fractionalization of the Uruguayan parties appeared from the beginning as a liability for the consolidation of democracy there (Gillespie and Gonzalez 1989). However, in the cases of Argentina and Peru it was once again borne out that clientelistic parties without strong ties to civil society are subject to rapid decay, particularly if confronted as incumbents with difficult economic problems.[73] In contrast, despite the reemergence of party factionalism in Uruguay, the comprehensiveness and flexibility of the party system, including both left and right, and the links of parties to civil society, have helped consolidate democracy by dampening labor militancy and instilling confidence in the economic elites. Brazil is handicapped in two ways: not only are large landlords with high labor needs still a formidable force, as evidenced by the problems with the land reform, but the parties are weak, lacking organizational and programmatic cohesion and firm ties to civil society (Hagopian and Mainwaring 1987).[74] In Ecuador all three conditions are unfavorable: large landlords engaged in labor intensive agriculture still exist also, and civil society and political parties remain weak. In Bolivia, the land reform basically eliminated labor repressive agriculture, but the subordinate classes are weakened by political and regional splits and the parties are extremely weak (McClintock 1986; Malloy and Gamarra 1987).

Our reason for giving separate treatment to developments since the late 1970s, then, is simply the fact that these new democratic regimes are still too young to allow for solid assessments of their potential for consolidation. We are by no means subscribing to the view, so popular with sectors of the American foreign policy establishment, that the 1980s are the glorious decade of democratization. The new democratic regimes in South America were ushered in to a large part by the effects of economic crises on incumbent authoritarian regimes, rather than by significant structural changes or international pressures to emulate the western European and North American examples. These same economic crisis conditions are now undermining the incumbent democratic regimes. Still, our analysis does suggest that chances for consolidation are better than they had been ealier because some structural changes favorable for democratic rule have taken place in at least some of these societies.

Summary of regime transformation after initial democratization

Vigorous industrialization helped preserve democratic regimes, but the strength of civil society resulting from higher levels of industrialization was not a sufficient condition for stabilization of full democracies. The real key was political institutions, namely the existence of a party system affording protection to elite interests. Once democratic regimes have been established, the direct influence of structural variables seems to diminish and the consequences of past political choices take on a life of their own. This was partly, perhaps, a result of the fact that the balance of class power did not shift enough.

The most detrimental feature for prospects of stabilization was shown to be strong military involvement in politics, which in itself was the result of a tradition of civilian appeals for military intervention due to the weakness of the party system. A factor related to the character of the party system was the composition of the class coalitions behind the breakthrough to democracy. Middle-class–elite alliances as decisive forces behind the breakthrough were most conducive to stabilization of democracy. However, such alliances only emerged if at least some sectors of the elites had representation in the party system, and in most cases they established restricted democracies only. Chances for consolidation of democracy were better where there had been a previous phase of democracy. This was true for cases where democracy was re-established after an authoritarian interlude, as well as where a restricted democracy was made fully inclusive in response to pressures from below generated by industrialization.

The political character of the military was also crucial to the democratizing transitions in the late 1970s and 1980s, but in a very different way. These transitions resulted from openings produced by tensions within the military regimes, tensions which in turn stemmed from a combination of the narrow support base of the regimes, their repressive character, and the severe economic problems of the period. None the less, the same political dynamics that helped preserve democracy were important in reconstituting it. The openings created by the fragility of military authoritarianism were taken advantage of by revived remnants of pre-existing organizations and/or by others newly formed in the context of a civil society which had been strengthened by a growth in industrialization. Where significant remnants of strong parties existed, the construction of pro-democratic alliances and the reinstallation and consolidation of democratic regimes was facilitated. In contrast, where such remnants were lacking but civil society had grown considerably in strength and new parties were formed to articulate its demands, the pursuit of a co-ordinated strategy for redemocratization and consolidation proved more difficult.

Political liberalization in Mexico

The progress of political liberalization in Mexico, and the question whether it is likely to lead to actual democratization deserve some special discussion because the case is theoretically interesting. Given the degree of urbanization and industrialization reached in Mexico, one would have expected the PRI's capacity to co-opt and control popular sectors to be eroded by challenges from forces seeking to forge an autonomous political articulation of subordinate groups quite some time ago. However, the PRI has demonstrated a surprising resilience, and though Mexico has undergone some changes towards greater political contestation, it will take considerably greater institutional innovation for this process of liberalization to evolve into democratization than it did in the South American cases.

Given the central position and tremendous patronage advantages of the unions affiliated to the official labor confederation CTM and the hazards of independent union action,[75] the primary challenges to the regime initially came not from the working-class but rather from educated sectors of the urban middle classes. Even among the unions not affiliated to the CTM, most have supported the PRI; only few of them openly supported left-wing opposition parties before 1988. A first strong challenge emerged in the form of the student protest movement of 1968. The regime appeared severely threatened by these attempts of middle-class radicals to build an alliance with disaffected sectors of the working class, the peasantry, and urban marginals, as it resorted to bloody repression of the movement.[76] In the 1970s activities of guerrilla groups as well as the emergence of several parties without official recognition continued the challenge. Moreover, growing business hostility to the government's more reformist measures, such as the land reform in the mid–1970s, increased investment in health and education, and more room for non-CTM unions, led to pressures for economic liberalization and greater political representation for the opposition. Particularly the northern conservative business groups organized themselves in a new peak association and started to actively support the opposition Partido Acción Nacional (PAN) (Kaufman 1989: 111–123).

After its initial repressive response, the regime showed a more flexible position and implemented a series of political reforms between 1972 and 1977, granting more room for party activity on the right and the left and for articulation of opposition voices in Congress, but neither substantive opposition influence on policy nor full institutionalization of contestation.[77] Strong financial support for the conservative PAN in the 1970s from business sectors concerned about their dwindling influence on economic policy helped it to develop into the main opposition party. The PAN has neither an alternative program to offer nor strong connections to other organizations in civil society, but up to 1988 it served as a rallying point for anti-PRI protest votes. Various parties to the left of the PRI remained divided by ideological issues and weak because of their lack of organizational ties to civil society.

The steadily rising real wages from the 1950s through the 1970s and the availability of patronage resources had facilitated the maintenance of a firm organizational hold of the CTM and the labor sector of the PRI over the working-class and particularly its political articulation and thus prevented the emergence of a working-class–middle-class alliance exerting pressures for democratization. However, the economic crisis of the 1980s spurred an intensification of political opposition among the educated urban middle classes (Cornelius 1986: 138), stronger tendencies towards autonomy in the labor movement, and the emergence of new autonomous grass-roots organizations (Levy 1989: 466; 487). At the national level the CTM has continued to support the government's austerity program, and it has proved capable of enforcing the wage declines, but at the local level its mobilization capacity has declined significantly (Cornelius 1986).

The weakening of the CTM's position and the emergence of new grass-roots organizations have made it possible for left-wing parties to build closer links to working-class and other lower-class organizations. The potential political significance of an emerging left with bases in civil society, representing a middle-class–working-class alliance became visible in the 1988 elections. In those elections the left for the first time mounted a serious challenge to the PRI and replaced the PAN as principal opposition. This surge of opposition from the left was in large part due to the success of some dissident PRI leaders in unifying various currents of leftist, socialist, and nationalist opposition into the Frente Democrático Nacional (FDN).[78] Cuauhtémoc Cárdenas, the son of ex-president Cárdenas, became the FDN's public leader and presidential candidate. His promises of a return to redistributive policies, a reversal of divestment of state enterprises, and a suspension of payments on the foreign debt had a strong appeal to both lower- and middle-class urban constituencies whose economic situation had deteriorated markedly under de la Madrid's austerity policies.[79]

Aside from the economic crisis, the key issue in the 1988 elections was their integrity. Despite the political reforms, voter abstention had remained very high in the 1980s, and the 1985 elections were marred by serious corruption, most so in areas where the elections were hotly contested (Cornelius 1986: 132). Though overall there appeared to be fewer instances of fraud in 1988 than in earlier elections, the delay in the announcement of election results damaged their legitimacy. Furthermore, the turnout was only 49 percent of registered voters. Both the PAN and the FDN vigorously protested and refused to acknowledge the PRI's election victory. They did take their seats in the legislature, but the issue of political liberalization is clearly kept at the top of the political agenda.

The effectiveness of opposition pressures in pushing liberalization forward and transforming it into actual democratization has been hampered by several factors. The FDN split, and its successor, the Partido de la Revolución Democrática (PRD), has been kept weak by internal tensions and its inability to expand its organizational base among the subordinate classes. The PRI has wavered in its approach toward political liberalization, as intense conflicts emerged over the extent of liberalization.[80] The strongest opponents of the liberalizing measures, which have always been decided on at the level of the presidency, are regional and local political bosses and the leaders of the CTM. The official labor leaders have feared that a strengthening of left-wing political parties which advocate more militant union action might enable these parties and independent unions to make inroads into their constituencies. It has become increasingly obvious that internal reform of the PRI itself and of the affiliated mass organizations with regard to decision-making and candidate selection is one of the main requirements for progress towards implementation of the liberalizing measures and towards democratization. Serious challenges to the government and to union leaders loyal to the PRI have continued as autonomous tendencies in the labor movement keep growing stronger. However, without a strong common front of organizations articulating the interests of subordinate classes politically, it is doubtful that the PRI will feel sufficient pressure to resolve the internal struggle in favor of democratization of the party as well as the national political system.

Regime Transformations and Transnational Structures of Power

International economic influences were important for democratizing tendencies via both economic conjunctures and the structural integration of Latin American countries into the world economy.[81] The expansion of the export economy and later ISI, stimulated by the Depression and World War II, affected the class structure and thus the strength of civil society and its political articulation. Thus, to the extent that integration into world markets generated economic growth, it also affected the class structure in a way to bring forth pressures for democratization. Moreover, where this integration took the form of an enclave it tended to weaken the economic and political power bases of anti-democratic landowners. However, other effects of economic dependence, perpetuated by the particular way in which Latin America was integrated into world markets, were negative for pro-democratic forces.

First, as already discussed, dependent industrialization led to the emergence of a comparatively small industrial working class. At the same time there was a very large urban informal sector of self-employed and of people employed in very small enterprises. This made labor organization exceedingly difficult. Where a strong current of organization in the working class was absent, middle-class organizations tended to remain weaker and less prone to promoting democratization as well.

Second, since the dependent economies were highly vulnerable to external shocks, some international economic conjunctures, such as the onset of the Depression, gave rise to economic crises which fundamentally threatened the interests of economic elites along with those of all other sectors of society. This helped to erode the confidence of elites who had shared political power in a democratic context with representatives of middle-class interests in the capacity of political parties to protect their interests, and it induced them to attempt to reassert exclusive control by imposing an authoritarian system. The most clear-cut cases illustrating this are Argentina in 1930 and Uruguay in 1933. The economic problems which contributed to the erosion of fragile democracies in the 1950s and 1960s were less attributable to clearly identifiable international economic conjunctures like the Depression, but they were equally clearly related to structural features of dependent industrialization, mainly the high import intensity of the manufacturing sector.

Third, the presence of direct foreign investment in crucial sectors of the economy also tended to weigh on the side of the anti-democratic forces in a very direct way. Foreign investors not only strongly opposed reform attempts of democratic governments, such as increases in corporate taxes and elimination of privileges (not to speak of expropriation), thus undermining these governments' economic base and political support, but also encouraged anti-democratic forces to take action. The opposition from foreign investors and their support for authoritarian transitions were most visible in the 1960s and 1970s (Brazil 1964, Chile 1973), both because the penetration of foreign capital was very extensive and because these regimes most openly challenged its position. However, opposition and retaliation also occurred where foreign capital was largely confined to extractive industries and infrastructure, if its prerogatives were attacked (Venezuela 1945–8). Particularly detrimental for democracy was the fact that US companies could mobilize pressures from their home government on democratic regimes. Chile 1970–3 is the most dramatic case (US Senate 1975), but Brazil under Goulart (Skidmore 1967: 322–30) and Peru under Belaúnde (Jaquette 1971: 172) also experienced such pressures. In these cases, pressures from international economic and political forces coincided.

Influences from the international system of states, both conjunctural and structural, which favored democracy were clearly weaker than in Europe. Only if one includes the cultural diffusion of the ideal of democracy in the nineteenth and again in the twentieth century might one arrive at a different assessment. Latin American countries were not significantly involved in either of the World Wars, and thus the aftermath of the Wars had a weaker impact on pro-democratic forces. The post-World War I political conjuncture, while in some cases seeing considerable increases in labor mobilization, most prominently in Argentina and Chile, did not produce the wave of democratization it did in Europe. Pro-democratic tendencies in the aftermath of World War I remained too weak to take advantage of the international discrediting of authoritarian regimes because the internal balance of class power, unlike that in Europe, was not significantly affected by involvement in the War. Despite the beginnings of import substitution industrialization before and during World War I, neither the position of the economically dominant classes nor the size and mobilization capacity of the subordinate classes underwent significant changes. In contrast to most of Europe, the large landholders were still economically important and politically powerful, and, with the exceptions of Argentina and Uruguay, the urban middle and lower classes were too small and/or insufficiently organized to play the role of counterweights.

By the end of World War II, organized segments of the middle and working classes, in some cases supported and in others tolerated by urban industrial elites and sectors of the military, were in a stronger position to ride the wave of international pro-democratic sentiment and pressure for the discarding of authoritarian political practices, despite the continued opposition of the large landowners and traditional sectors of the military. Still, only in Argentina, Brazil, Venezuela, and Peru did the end of World War II noticeably reinforce democratic currents. In the post-World War II period, the European powers were very concerned with consolidating democracy in their own region, and EEC pressures for democratization in southern Europe were related to these concerns. Moreover, the Socialist International played an important pro-democratic role in Europe. The European concerns and consequent pro-democratic actions in international politics had only a much weaker counterpart in the United States and its sphere of influence, as perceived security interests of the United States as a global power assumed priority (Whitehead 1986b). The one case in Latin America where US pressures for democracy were applied and where they managed to tip the internal balance of power towards the democratic forces is the Dominican Republic in 1978 (Kryzanek 1979).

In contrast, anti-democratic influences from the international state system were considerably stronger in Latin America than in Europe, most prominently the Cold War and US support for and training of the Latin American military. US pressures induced many governments to outlaw communist parties and thus to allow at best for restricted democracy, even where these parties clearly played by the democratic rules of the game. Military assistance in the 1950s and 1960s reinforced the anti-communism of the Latin American military, which tended to become co-terminous with anti-leftism and anti-popular (democratic) forces. It also strengthened the military as an institution and thus its potential to act autonomously not only from the incumbent government but from civil society and political institutions in general. It increased the centrality of organized force in the state apparatus and the capacity of this branch to take control of the other parts of the state apparatus and use it to extend control over civil society. Whereas US military aid and assistance alone by no means explain the erosion of the democratic systems (which was mainly due to the underlying forces discussed above), they helped create a state apparatus unfavorable for democracy and thus the conditions for the installation of bureaucratic–authoritarian regimes in Brazil, Argentina, Chile, and Uruguay in the 1960s and 1970s.[82] Furthermore, US pressures exercised through economic means and diplomatic channels did contribute to the undermining of the legitimacy of incumbent governments and thus to the critical weakening of democratic systems in Bolivia and Brazil before 1964, Peru before 1968, and most dramatically Chile before 1973.

Conclusion

In the preceding analysis the class structure, class alliances and the balance of class power, as well as the relationship between class forces and the state emerged as important factors shaping the installation and transformation of democracy in South America and Mexico. The formation both of class alliances and of the relationship between state and civil society were heavily influenced by the integration of these countries into the world economy and by their position in the system of states. These general relationships were highly consistent with our expectations based on the analytical framework presented in chapter 3.

In addition, the analysis of the Latin American experience has drawn our attention to three elements which elaborate our original framework and the theoretical lessons drawn in chapter 4 from the experience of advanced capitalist societies. First, the middle classes played a more prominent role in the process of democratization than they had in advanced capitalist societies. Second, political parties turned out to play a crucial role in the installation and consolidation of democratic regimes. Third, the character of the state itself changed with economic development in a way that entailed potentially detrimental consequences for democracy.

We saw that parties led and supported by members of the middle classes were the decisive forces behind democratization more often than in advanced capitalist societies. This is partly a result of the fact that in this chapter we also included restricted forms of democracy whereas in the last one we concentrated on the transition to and the breakdown of full democracies. And it is partly a simple result of the weakness of the working-class. The middle classes were not inherently more democratic in Latin America than in Europe or North America. The ambivalent attitude of the middle classes towards democracy became clear in their frequent acceptance of restricted democracy as well as in their repeated support for coups overthrowing democratic regimes which appeared to be incapable of guaranteeing economic and social stability. Since the middle classes first and foremost pursued their own inclusion, the nature of available allies determined the type of democracy they attempted to install. Only under the influence of a significant working-class presence did they fight for and defend full democracy.

Political parties emerged in our analysis in a crucial role for the mobilization of pressures for inclusion from subordinate classes, and for the achievement of the delicate balance between such pressures from subordinate classes and threat perception on the part of economic elites necessary for the consolidation of democracy. The type of party which emerged, and the class alliances it was able to mobilize were originally shaped by the nature of the export economy, namely its agricultural versus mineral base. In agricultural export economies clientelistic parties emerged and in mineral export economies radical mass parties. The clientelistic parties typically included sectors of elites and the middle classes and presented a moderate threat to elites only, in contrast to the radical mass parties which mobilized middle–working-class alliances to exert strong pressures for inclusion. Accordingly, clientelistic parties were less likely to evoke strong defensive, anti-democratic reactions than radical mass parties. However, where labor intensive agriculture dominated the export sector landlords resisted democratization anyway, with the result that the opening of the political system was delayed and extended at best to restricted democracy. In agricultural export economies with non-labor intensive agriculture and the presence of a sizeable working class, clientelisitc parties were capable of installing full democracy. Strong pressures for democratization from radical mass parties set in motion sequences of instability which could only be broken if elites were reassured through concrete experience that their interests could be well protected in a democratic system. In all types of economies, the party system assumed crucial importance for consolidation or breakdown after the initial installation of democracy. Only where it afforded effective protection of elite interests through strong parties representing or at least safeguarding these interests, or through a political pact, could democracy be consolidated.

The state apparatus itself emerged in a more prominent role than in the advanced capitalist societies. Military involvement in politics was much higher in most countries. This was originally a result of drawn-out independence wars and involvement in border conflicts in the nineteenth century. It was perpetuated in the twentieth century in many cases through civilian appeals to the military for the exercise of pressures on incumbent governments or for direct intervention. Such intervention could only be stopped where political parties became the main channels for the political articulation and promotion of the interests of all major groups in the society. In some countries the state became important in shaping the political articulation of newly emerging social forces in the early stages of industrialization. A tradition of strong state involvement in shaping civil society stemming from colonial days (Brazil), the early period of independence (Paraguay), or the period of reconstruction after the revolution (Mexico) was conducive to successful attempts to encapsulate subordinate classes, particularly the emerging working class, into state sponsored organizations and thus pre-empt pressures for democratization. Even where there was no such tradition and where state attempts at incorporating new groups had no lasting success, state expansion as a result of the expansion of the export economy and prior to significant industrialization created a situation where a comparatively large state apparatus confronted a weak civil society and thus was able to retard and/or weaken the independent articulation of the emerging working-class. At advanced stages of industrialization a new form of state domination over civil society emerged, bureaucratic–authoritarian regimes. The high autonomy of the state from civil society and the state's deliberate and successful attempts to weaken civil society rested on its strong coercive capacity and on its capacity to mobilize economic resources independent of the domestic economically dominant classes. Both types of capacity had been strengthened by economic development and the state's involvement in the international economy and system of states. Economic development, technological advance, and the imperative of dealing with the most sophisticated actors in international markets provided the incentive and the means for an expansion of administrative and managerial capacity of the state apparatus. Access to external sources of capital reduced the state's dependence on the domestic bourgeoisie. And US financial assistance and training for military and police forces had greatly increased the repressive capacity of the state.

Particularly the rise of bureaucratic authoritarianism, but also the entire experience with democratization analyzed in this chapter has revealed the importance of the context of late development and a dependent position in the world system. Late industrialization with advanced imported technology has created a class structure with a comparatively small industrial working class, which has kept the balance of class power rather unfavorable for the installation and consolidation of full democracy. Raw material export led economic growth provided the basis for state expansion before significant industrialization and thus created the possibility for a power imbalance between the state and civil society, tilted in favor of the former. The importance of the external anchoring of the state coming with economic and geo-political dependence further accentuated this imbalance. The crucial role of the state as an intermediary between the national and international economy, particularly in securing access to foreign markets, capital, and technology, strengthened its autonomy from domestic economic elites. The externally supported expansion of the repressive apparatus of the state cemented the autonomy of the state from civil society as a whole. These tendencies manifested themselves most dramatically in the rise of the bureaucratic–authoritarian regimes, but they were also noticeable in other cases and did not disappear with the redemocratization of the bureaucratic–authoritarian regimes. The role of the state and its external anchoring will appear as even more crucial in the experience of Central American and Caribbean countries which will be analyzed in the next chapter.

Finally, let us come back briefly to the studies of political change in Latin America mentioned in the beginning of this chapter and reflect on the difference between the approach that has been used here and that used in those studies as well as in the interpretations of the results of cross-national quantitative studies. First of all, we have tried to bring political institutional factors into a basically class-analytic perspective. We have argued that initially the structure of a country's economy and the class structure and class alliances it generated, in conjunction with the historical legacies of the transition to independence, shaped the prospects for democracy as well as the character of the state and the newly emerging party systems. Once these institutions had come into existence, however, they assumed a weight of their own and contributed in decisive ways to regime outcomes. Second, rather than assuming that the prospects for democracy at a particular time depend on the relative weight of different "variables" at that time, our analysis has identified sequences which are always contingent on historical legacies. The paths followed by different countries forked at critical junctures, opening some options for the future and closing others. Not just the occurrence but the timing of critical events, such as the consolidation of state power, or the expansion of industrialization, were crucial. Depending on when they occurred they set in motion different sequences of elite contestation and pressures for inclusion. Cross-sectional descriptions that do not take into account the historical processes which underlie current choices simply cannot provide satisfying accounts of the rise and fall of democratic regimes.

6

Central America and The Caribbean

Introduction

We now turn to another important part of the western hemisphere, namely Central America and the Caribbean, where the strong democratic tradition of the ex-British Caribbean stands in stark contrast to the authoritarianism and repression of the Central American countries. Both sets of cases are exceptional; the level of social conflict and repression in Central America stands out among Third World countries, as does the longevity of democratic rule in the English-speaking Caribbean. We argue that this is due to the particular nature of the state and the historical evolution of its relationship to domestic economically dominant classes and the transnational structures of power.

The development and survival of political democracy in the English-speaking Caribbean make that group of countries remarkable in comparison to other countries at similar stages of socioeconomic development. As Huntington (1984: 201) points out in his assessment of the prospects for democracy in the world, it is among the upper third of "middle income countries" (as classified by the World Bank) which he terms the "zone of transition" that democracy is at all frequent and even among this group of twenty-one countries only seven are democratic. By contrast, democracy is the rule rather than the exception in the West Indies, despite the fact that only one of these countries, Trinidad and Tobago, had reached the level of development to qualify for the zone of transition by the early 1980s. The Central American countries conform to the norm of authoritarianism at their level of development, but the intensity of social strife and the strength of revolutionary challenges as well as of repression make them exceptional also.

Both sets of countries are also of special interest because they are characterized by what one could call hyperdependency. To a greater extent than South America and Mexico, they were shaped by external economic and political forces. They came closer to being pure plantation economies (Best 1967), growing and declining with the vagaries of the world market for one or two crops, and they have been more directly dominated politically by foreign powers. British colonialism in the larger Caribbean territories lasted until the 1960s, to be followed by US hegemonic domination. The ex-Spanish Central American countries had come under US domination by the turn of the century already. Essentially, this meant that no government could consolidate its rule if it was not acceptable to the United States. For the most part, diplomatic and economic pressures were sufficient to produce the results desired by the United States; if they were not, military intervention provided the necessary leverage, from the frequent occupations in the early 20th century to the invasions of Grenada in 1983 and Panama in 1989.

Since, as we argued in the last chapter, economic and political dependency had a largely negative, if complex, impact on chances for democracy in Latin America by creating a class structure unfavorable for the self-organization of subordinate classes, state expansion and autonomy from domestic social forces unfavorable for a balance between state and civil society, and economic vulnerability unfavorable for the consolidation of constitutional regimes, one would expect a rather total absence of a democratic tradition in these small, hyperdependent countries. This expectation is widely fulfilled in Central America, but hardly in the ex-British Caribbean.

The contrast between the political development of the two sets of countries highlights two analytical themes which emerged in the last chapter. First dependency is a complex economic and political structural condition some of whose aspects can have positive and others negative effects on democratic forces, and these effects may change over time. Second, structural factors shape the emergence of political institutions, but political institutions then assume a role of their own in shaping political outcomes. Foreign domination in the form of British colonialism in the Caribbean implied state autonomy from domestic elites and allowed for the emergence of unions and political parties which became the crucial driving forces for democratization and counterweights to domestic economic elites, sustaining a power balance favorable for democratic regimes after independence. In contrast, foreign domination in the form of US hegemony in Central America reinforced the position of domestic elites and supported the build-up of strong coercive apparatuses, thus helping oli-garchic–military alliances to undermine or repress middle– and working-class organization. At a later stage, US military aid and training contributed to the growing autonomy of the military and its direct exercise of political power through highly authoritarian and repressive regimes.

This chapter attempts to explain the emergence of both types of regimes through comparative historical analysis. We will employ two kinds of compari-sons in the analysis in order to account for differences in regime outcome. First, we will compare the ex-British West Indies to the ex-Spanish plantation economies in the region in order to examine what characteristics of the political economies and histories of these two groups appear to be connected with the markedly different political destinies of the two groups of countries. Second, we examine variations within these two groups, contrasting democratic Costa Rica with the rest of Central America, and the two authoritarian cases of Burnham's Guyana and Gairy's Grenada with the rest of the West Indies.[1]

As before, we focus on the balance of class power, the relationship between civil society and the state, and the impact of transnational structures of power on the emergence and consolidation of democracy. We also continue our effort to reinterpret the findings of the cross-national statistical studies employing a different theoretical framework from that used in those studies. Compared to the experience in the advanced capitalist countries and South America, the role of the state, particularly its external anchoring, will emerge as more decisive. The analysis which follows will confirm what we have argued for the South American cases and what the cross-national statistical analyses show, namely that economic dependence per se has mainly indirect and contradictory and thus statistically not significant effects on democratic rule, but that geo-political dependence has more directly noticeable and, in the US sphere of influence, predominantly negative consequences for democratic stability. However, the example of the ex-British West Indies again cautions against undifferentiated generalizations. In these countries, geo-political dependence, i. e. their status as colonies, at a critical historical juncture had long term indirect effects favorable for the emergence and consolidation of democracy. In explaining these effects, then, we also offer a new interpretation of the positive relationship found in the statistical studies between British colonial status and democracy. Finally, our analysis of the breakdown of democracy in Guyana provides an explanation of the negative statistical relationship between ethnic diversity and democracy which links ethnicity to class and state.

Some additional comments on the arguments concerning the relationship between British colonialism and democracy prevalent in the literature are in order before we develop our analysis. The quantitative studies do hardly more than mention the correlation, but several other recent studies (Diamond 1989a; Huntington 1984; Weiner 1987) make the argument that British colonialism left a legacy favorable for democracy because it provided for a period of tutelary democracy before independence.[2] The evidence offered by Weiner (1987: 20) is that "every country with a population of at least 1 million (and almost all the smaller countries as well) that has emerged from colonial rule since World War II and has had a continuous democratic experience is a former British colony." His explanation points to the enduring legacy of the establishment by the British colonial authorities of bureaucratic structures and the rule of law, and of representative institutions and periodic elections. Owing to their socialization in these institutions, local elites internalized the norms of democratic procedure and developed organizational and other political leadership skills. In our analysis of the British settler colonies, we did find that the transfer of British institutions to the colonies did contribute to the democratic outcomes in those countries.

However, Weiner's evidence and argument on the salutary effects of British colonialism is problematic as there are only six countries which fit his criteria and, as Weiner himself admits and Huntington points out as well, many more former British colonies have not sustained democratic rule. Thus, we are dealing with a weak correlation. The argument nevertheless is rescued by these authors with the introduction of length of British colonial rule. In the Caribbean and India and Sri Lanka British colonialism had deep enough roots to leave an enduring legacy, they claim, whereas the shorter period of colonial rule in Africa meant that the institutions of tutelary democracy did not take root. What this modification of the argument overlooks is the fact that, as our analysis here will show, indigenous political leaders and parties only began to play a significant role in the British Caribbean during and after World War II, as they did in Britain's African colonies. Another problem with Weiner's and other authors' arguments is that they do not provide any systematic comparison with other forms of colonialism, particularly French colonialism. We shall return to this issue in the conclusion to this chapter.

Caribbean and Central American Cases Compared

Caribbean and Central American countries share some socioeconomic characteristics which cross-national statistical studies have shown to be inimical to democracy. As pointed out above, their levels of development in 1970 were too low to be favorable for democracy. Their economies were traditionally plantation economies, with some mining and industrialization, and tourism in the Caribbean, superimposed in the post-World War II period. This means that the societies were traditionally very hierarchical and the economies highly dependent on foreign trade and foreign investment. Both areas underwent significant economic growth in the 1960s stimulated by a combination of export expansion to advanced capitalist countries and common market arrangements, the Central American Common Market (CACM) and the Caribbean Free Trade Association (CARIFTA). This growth created similar strains, namely unabated (if not increasing) inequality and high un- and underemployment in urban and rural areas, as well as growing popular mobilization. Though Costa Rica and the major Caribbean countries except for Guyana had a higher GDP per capita in the 1960s and 1970s than the Central American countries, which corresponds to their higher level of democracy, seen on a world scale these differences are not very significant, as of all our cases only Trinidad and Tobago had reached the "zone of transition" by the early 1980s. Thus, low economic development, high inequality, rapid social change, and the specially high dependence on US interests all militated against the installation and consolidation of democratic regimes in the region.[5]

Not surprisingly, then, all but two of the Spanish-speaking countries in the Caribbean basin were ruled by authoritarian regimes in the 1960s and 1970s, and the 1970s saw increasingly violent confrontations between these regimes and reformist or revolutionary forces. The exceptions were Costa Rica and, from 1978 on, the Dominican Republic. In contrast, all but two of the English-speaking Caribbean countries had democratic regimes from the time of their independence in the 1960s throughout the 1970s. Guyana and Grenada were the exceptions. The question imposes itself why democracy could flourish in some countries, whereas in others economic elites and military establishments resorted to increasingly violent repression not only of revolutionary movements but of democratic reformist forces as well.

The first obvious hypothesis that comes to mind is that British colonialism was the critical variable as it left a legacy of democratic institutions. We will indeed see that British colonialism did make an indirect contribution to the emergence of democracy. However, the cases of Guyana and Grenada (not to speak of Britain's colonies in Africa) show that this legacy did not necessarily survive, and Costa Rica and the Dominican Republic show that other paths led to democracy in the region. The question then becomes whether the democracies in Central America and the Caribbean on the one hand and the non-democracies on the other hand share any similarities which extant theories suggest are important for the development and survival of democratic systems.

An explanation inspired by Moore would suggest the following: in the Central American non-democracies, rural class relations were characterized by a combination of wage labor and legal coercion, and there was an alliance between large landowners, still the dominant faction of the economic elites, the state, and a dependent bourgeoisie. In the Caribbean democracies, in contrast, rural labor relations were squarely based on wage labor, the economic fortunes of the planter class had declined, being replaced by foreign companies, and thus the authoritarian alliance had been eclipsed. There is undoubtedly some validity in this explanation. Landlords had remained an extremely important part of the economic elites in Central America, whereas they had lost most of their economic power in the English-speaking Caribbean. Furthermore, at the beginning of the 1960s, a clearly higher percentage of the labor force was in agriculture in the Central American countries (between 49 and 67 percent) than in our Caribbean cases (between 20 and 36 percent). Even if we follow the arguments about the reconceptualization of labor repressive agriculture laid out in the last two chapters and acknowledge that agriculture was labor intensive both in Central America and the Caribbean, a greater proportion of the population was subject to landlord attempts at keeping rural labor abundant and cheap in Central America. In fact, landowners in Central America did resort to legal and extra-legal means to prevent unionization and other forms of collective action, in contrast to the Caribbean where rural labor was well organized in unions.

Nevertheless, the examples of Barbados and Honduras caution against accepting the explanation based on landlord power as sufficient. In Barbados the planter class had remained the hegemonic faction in the economic elite, having extended its holdings into urban activities, and yet rural labor was well organized. In Honduras the large landowners had never been very prosperous and had also taken second place to foreign banana companies, but with the exception of some unionization on banana plantations, rural labor remained very weakly organized. Thus, we at least need to understand the historical conditions which prevented the planters in Barbados from suppressing rural unionization like their counterparts did in Central America. To explain our central question, why Barbados was democratic and Honduras authoritarian, we need to complement the focus on the landowner–state–bourgeois alliance with a focus on the relative strength of middle- and lower-class organizations as a whole and on the nature of the state apparatus and its relations to foreign forces, and we need to analyze the historical sequences underlying the different patterns in our three clusters of power. What was crucial in Barbados was that, by the 1960s, the power of the planter class was counterbalanced by the presence of strong political parties and labor unions. In Honduras, the military ruled the country, given the absence of a strong economic elite and the very low degree of organization of the middle and working-classes at the national level. External intervention at an earlier stage and military support in the post-World War II period had greatly contributed to making the military the most important national institution.

Barbados, then, exemplifies the dominant pattern of the 1960s in the democratic Caribbean societies and Costa Rica as far as the relative strength of civil society and, within it, of the subordinate classes is concerned. Labor unions, professional associations, and political parties gave the subordinate classes leverage vis-à-vis the economic elites. Unions and parties, along with professional associations and churches, also constituted forces independent of the state and thus the locus of some degree of power as a counterweight to state power. Moreover, these societies had weak or non-existent military establishments, which meant that the likelihood of the repressive apparatus of the state being used by any one group or acting autonomously to crush civil society was low. Conversely, Honduras exemplifies the pattern of the authoritarian regimes where civil society and particularly the subordinate classes were still weak. Attempts of unions, reformist parties, students, and church groups to strengthen their organizations and exercise pressures to extract concessions from economic elites and/or to influence political decisions met with resistance, if not outright repression, from the state apparatus. The military establishments were comparatively large and strong, i. e. well equipped, trained and financed, largely with US military aid. They acted either autonomously or in alliance with economic elites to repress challenges from civil society to their collective corporate as well as their own and the economic elite's economic interests. The external support meant that the power imbalance between the coercive apparatus of the state and civil society kept growing and that the potential for autonomous political action on the part of the security forces increased along with it.

The structural and institutional underpinnings of authoritarianism and democracy in the 1960s and 1970s, then, can be clearly identified. What remains to be explored is the theoretically important question how these structures and institutions evolved in such a different manner, given the common roots of these societies in plantation economies. The antecedents of the different situations of the 1960s lie in the developments in the 1930s. The Depression brought great disruptions to the extremely export-dependent societies in the region. In response to decreasing real wages and increasing unemployment, attempts at labor organization and labor protests emerged in all societies.[4] The reactions of the economic elites to these protests and organizing attempts were universally negative, but the reaction of the state varied widely. Here, British colonialism was important, in so far as it constituted an alternative to landlord or military control of the state and thus the use of the coercive forces of the state to repress both the protests and the emerging labor unions and allied political parties. Consequently, the 1930s marked the beginning of organized political life and opened the way for the subsequent consolidation of civil society in the Caribbean, whereas in Central America they set the precedent for the primacy of the coercive apparatus of the state and for state control over and repression of civil society, exercised either by land-owner–military coalitions or by the military alone. Costa Rica, the deviant case in Central America, resembled the Caribbean in so far as the large landowners were not in firm control of the state apparatus either and consequently unions and political parties were allowed to consolidate their organizations.

Spanish-speaking countries from the 1930s to the 1960s

To explain why the economic elites and/or the military controlled the state in Central American countries and the Dominican Republic in the 1930s and used this control to squash emerging social forces, two interdependent sets of factors are crucial, namely the economic strength of the large landowners and their relationship to the state, and the extent of US economic presence and direct political intervention. To underline the theoretical point that strength of the landed class is not the only critical variable but rather that the role of the state and foreign forces has to be taken into consideration, one can distinguish two basic types of class-state constellations in Central America in the first three decades of this century (or three types, if one takes Costa Rican exceptionalism into account, which will be discussed below). In one type, exemplified by El Salvador and Guatemala, the large landowners were very prosperous, having established commercial and financial holdings as well (El Salvador), or having merged with originally merchant elites (Guatemala).[5] They formed an oligarchy in the true sense of the word, controlling the state directly or via military officers. In the other type, exemplified by Honduras, Nicaragua, and the Dominican Republic, the landowners were not as prosperous because histo-rically the territories had been sparsely populated, had suffered many military invasions and, particularly in Nicaragua, had seen fierce fights among different factions of landowners. Also, foreign capital had a strong presence, dominating the financial system, the railroads, at times even customs collections, and, in the case of Honduras, the crucial export sector bananas. Thus, the landowners as a group were not in control of the state; rather, military strongmen, sometimes in alliance with an elite faction, exercised political power. Moreover, these three countries were the object of repeated US military intervention and occupation in the first third of this century, which further impeded the establishment of civilian control over the state apparatus. US representatives controlled the crucial parts of the state, namely the fiscal apparatus and the coercive forces. The US legacy in Nicaragua and the Dominican Republic was a US trained and equipped security force which was to perform the function of keeping peace and order after the withdrawal of US troops. In both cases, these forces were used by their commanders as stepping stones to the establishment of dictatorial rule and economic fortunes for their families.

In the early 1930s, growing unemployment and falling real incomes caused popular protests and attempts at labor organization in all the Central American countries. The response was repression of varying intensity and the establishment or consolidation of dictatorial regimes. In El Salvador, the last non-military representative of the oligarchy to hold the presidency, Romero Bosque, held open elections in 1930. However, his successor, elected narrowly and with leftist support, was overthrown by a military coup in 1931 which brought General Hernandez Martinez to the presidency. Popular uprisings in the western coffee growing areas in 1932 were repressed by the army, and in retaliation as many as 30, 000 Salvadorans were killed.[6] Hernandez Martinez held on to power until 1944; his presidency marked the beginning of the military–oligarchic pact under which the military dominated in political office holding and provided the oligarchy with the conditions for continued economic and social domination. In Guatemala General Ubico seized power in 1931, launched a purge of suspected Communists and sympathizers, and suppressed unions.[7] He centralized power in the executive, at the expense of rural notables (i. e. landowners) and was able to exercise autocratic rule until 1944. He also professionalized the military and thus laid the groundwork for increasingly autonomous military action in politics, reducing direct oligarchic control.

In Honduras, where US and United Fruit Company (UFCO) approval were the chief criteria for holding the presidency, Carias was elected as the candidate of the National Party in 1932 and proceeded to rule the country in close collaboration with United Fruit until 1949. In the Dominican Republic and Nicaragua, Trujillo and Somoza, the two commanders put in charge of the US-created security forces used their military power to achieve political control, taking advantage of political unrest and the economic weakening of the large landowners.[8] Trujillo supported an armed rebellion against the incumbent elected president in 1930 and subsequently took control of the electoral machinery and had himself made president, centralizing power in his hands and using it ruthlessly to suppress any challenges, from popular forces as well as elite circles, until his assassination in 1961. US troops still guaranteed order in the first years of the Depression in Nicaragua. Before their withdrawal in 1933 they supervised elections, but Somoza started to act independently of the elected president, for example in the crucial matter of having Sandino, the leader of the guerrilla struggle against US occupation, assassinated in 1934. By 1936 Somoza had managed to establish his control over the presidency as well, thus inaugurating the dynastic rule of his family which was to last until 1979.

Under these dictators and their successors in the 1940s and 1950s, activities of unions and political parties were heavily restricted and their growth was stifled. The degree of repressiveness of the governments varied between countries and over time, but even where parties and unions were allowed to exist, they were not able to acquire any significant organizational strength and socioeconomic or political influence.[9] Organizations of subordinate classes did not develop as significant counterweights to the economic domination of the large domestic landowners and the foreign corporations, nor did civil society develop as a significant counterweight to the state. On the contrary, the imbalance between state and civil society was aggravated after World War II, as the state apparatus, particularly its coercive arm, was strengthened through US military aid. US support for and influence on the military institutions in Central America fostered professionalization; the result of this process was a greater sense of corporate identity, but not an acceptance of the doctrine of civilian supremacy. Rather, the military developed the capacity for increasingly autonomous, though not necessarily united, political action. Splits within the military assumed relevance for political intervention, resulting in coups and counter-coups, sometimes with and sometimes without direct links to civilian forces.

Guatemala underwent a different development between 1944 and 1954, but by 1960 the subjection of civil society under a military dominated state was as strong as, if not stronger than, in the other Central American countries. The main forces responsible for this outcome were the US government and the United Fruit Company, the latter by pressuring for and the former by providing military support for the overthrow of the reformist President Arbenz. The reason why two reformist presidents could come to power in the first place is twofold: General Ubico's vast public works program had the unintended side effect of increasing the size of the middle and working classes, and his attempt to professionalize the military strengthened reformist factions. In 1944, he faced intense pressures from a rebellious middle class movement led by young officers and university students. The international conjuncture was favorable to the rebellion[10] and the US was reassured by the participation of officers. After Ubico's ouster, free elections were held and won by Arevalo who proceeded to support the rights and organizations of urban labor. Even rural unions achieved a considerable presence, and under Arbenz, who was elected in 1950, they became involved in the administration of a land reform. Thus, civil society underwent a rapid development and the balance of power started to shift somewhat in favor of the middle and working classes, but the attempts at economic and political inclusion of urban and rural lower classes threatened the oligarchy and the military, as well as United Fruit. UFCO's landholdings and control over the railroads were threatened and its executives found close allies in the US government.[11] The result was an armed invasion and the overthrow of Arbenz, organized and financed by the CIA. Castillo Armas, the leader of the invasion force and new president, erased the post–1945 labor legislation, cancelled the registration of large numbers of unions and made effective unionization virtually impossible. The number of organized workers fell from some 100, 000 in 1954 to fewer than 27, 000 in 1955 (Schoultz 1983: 193).

The real exception to the pattern prevailing in Central America was Costa Rica. The crucial factors setting it apart were the relative weakness of the oligarchy and relative strength of the rural middle class which had their roots in colonial times. Costa Rica was originally poor and sparsely populated, most settlers becoming farmers rather than hacienda owners. Coffee cultivation in the 1830s started on family-sized farms, and though later a process of land concentration took place and a landowning, coffee-exporting elite with diversified holdings emerged, a prosperous middle class of farmers and merchants remained.[12] This led to an early institutionalization of middle-class participation in politics and the growth of political parties. After 1889 responsible government and contestation became institutionalized, but property, income, and literacy qualifications kept the suffrage still highly restricted. Between 1917 and 1919 the electoral tradition was interrupted by dictatorial rule, but after the return to democratic rule registration and balloting procedures were gradually improved to effectively include larger sectors of the population; literacy qualifications were abolished in 1949. Accordingly, by the time the Depression generated significant popular protests, the large landowners were no longer in full control of the state apparatus nor could they successfully appeal to the military to re-establish such control.[13] Rather, popular organization continued to grow. A few unions had already emerged in the early decades of the twentieth century. In 1929 the Communist Party was formed which became the driving force behind the establishment of unions on the banana plantations in 1931. These unions staged a bitter but partially successful strike in 1934, thus consolidating their and the Communists'[14] base in the banana areas. At the same time, unionization increased among urban workers, and the Communists formed a central union federation which became the dominant force in the labor movement.

Under the impact of labor agitation the incumbent moderately conservative government passed a minimum wage law in 1933. The National Republican Party (PRN), a moderately reformist party, grew in strength in the 1930s, partly on the basis of presenting itself as the more moderate alternative to the Communists, and it won the elections in 1936, 1940, and 1944. To counter the opposition from economic elites to his social reform program, President Calderón in 1942 entered an informal alliance with the Communists who had won 16 percent of the vote in the 1942 congressional elections (Bulmer-Thomas 1987: 102). In 1943 major social reforms were legislated, such as the eight-hour day, the right to unionize and strike, and the establishment of labor courts. Thus, by the 1940s Costa Rica had the most active union movement in Central America, which, together with the strong middle class, made for a power balance favorable to democracy. Nevertheless, the incumbent governments in the 1940s occasionally harrassed the opposition, and consequently opposition against the PRN gained ground not only among the economic elites but also among sectors of the middle classes. The rebellion against the PRN government which clung to power through clear election fraud in 1948 was led and won by José Figueres in the name of democracy,[15] and thus did not constitute a radical break with previous political institutions.

A junta led by Figueres formed an interim government with a social democratic orientation. The junta's reform designs, such as the nationalization of banks and the imposition of a wealth tax, alarmed economic elites who managed to have parties representing their interests dominate the constituent assembly. In 1949 Ulate Blanco, the real winner in the fraudulent elections of 1948, took office. Ulate was a conservative who had won as the candidate of an opposition coalition consisting of conservative parties and the social democrats, united only by the desire to defeat the PRN. Under his administration the Communist Party, which had been outlawed by the interim government, remained suppressed. This weakened the more radical tendencies in the union movement, but labor and union rights were left untouched. In 1952 Figueres formed the PLN (Partido de Liberacion Nacional), since then the dominant party in Costa Rica, alternating in power with a variety of opposition parties. Arguably the most important outcome of the civil war for the survival of democracy in the longer run was the dismantling of the army by Figueres. One should add, though, that the experience with effective articulation of the interests of economic elites by conservative parties induced these elites to accept the prohibition of a standing army by the constituent assembly. In sum, Costa Rica entered the period of rapid transformation in the 1960s and 1970s with a comparatively well consolidated labor movement, party system, and political institutions, and without a largely autonomous repressive arm of the state.

The English-speaking Caribbean from the 1930s to the 1960s

The general pattern of state–society relations at the onset of the 1930s in the British Caribbean was direct colonial (crown colony) rule over a weakly articulated civil society.[16] Before 1865, several Caribbean colonies had significant elements of local self-government, though, of course, with such an extremely limited franchise that planter interests were completely dominant. Beginning with Jamaica in 1865 most of the Caribbean colonies were turned into crown colonies. Local assemblies, usually with a mix of appointed and elected members, and with property and/or income and literacy qualifications for the franchise, continued to exist, but their powers were subject to those of the governor. The first middle- and working-class organizations emerged shortly before the turn of the century, e.g. the Trinidad Workingmen's Association in 1897, the Jamaica Union of Teachers in 1894 and the Jamaica Agricultural Society in 1895. The first attempts at forming political parties were generally made in the 1920s. In Jamaica Marcus Garvey founded the People's Political Party in 1927, in Barbados C. D. O'Neal formed the Democratic League in 1924 and also the Workingmen's Association as popular base for the League. The same early pattern of party–union alliance under middle-class leadership existed in Trinidad where the Trinidad Workingmen's Association under the leadership of Cipriani formed the Trinidad Labour Party in 1932. None of these parties, though, were able to consolidate their organization and social base; rather, they declined quite rapidly and were replaced by the parties coming out of the ferment of the 1930s. Similarly, the trade unions remained weak until the late 1930s.

Between 1934 and 1938 a wave of labor rebellions swept the Caribbean. This unrest brought to the forefront a number of charismatic or otherwise highly prominent labor and political leaders, mostly of middle-class origin, who played crucial roles in the formation of unions and allied political parties. Though security forces, reinforced by British troops, were deployed to put down mass demonstrations and riots, and a number of people were killed and many leaders were arrested, the repression did not nearly approach the levels prevalent in Central America. Rather than physically liquidating leaders and members of popular organizations and closing the political system, the colonial government left unions intact and allowed for the formation of new political parties in the aftermath of the disturbances. The parties which emerged in alliance with trade unions out of this conjuncture became for the most part the driving forces in the nationalist movement, pushing for democratic rule and increasing local autonomy. Thus, the demands for democratization and for decolonization became inextricably linked. In reaction to the disturbances of the 1930s, the British appointed a Royal Commission to investigate social and economic conditions in the Caribbean colonies. The findings and recommendations of the Moyne Commission (as it is called after its chairman Lord Moyne) were considered so sensitive by the British that they were not made public in their entirety until after World War II, but among the proposed reforms they included steps towards more significant local participation in government (Post 1981: 85–91).

In 1935 major strikes in the oil and sugar industries took place in Trinidad. Tubal Uriah Butler emerged as the major agitator and organizer of oil workers and in 1936 he founded the British Empire Workers and Citizens Home Rule Party, to become known as the Butler Party. The labor revolts also gave rise to a number of other loosely working-class-based labor/socialist parties, which articulated the demand for universal suffrage and self-government (as well as for social welfare and usually "socialism") in the subsequent period and contested the first elections held with universal suffrage in 1946 and 1950. They took most of the seats alloted to elected members, but they lacked cohesion and were ineffective both as legislative mechanisms and in furthering the drive for responsible government and independence (Ryan 1972: 72–90). It was not until the founding of the People's National Movement (PNM) in 1956 by middle-class elements, headed by the eminent historian Eric Williams, that a cohesive, programmatic party took the lead in spearheading the nationalist movement. It immediately attracted black working-class electoral support and eventually came to be supported by most of the black trade union leadership also, thus achieving the kind of middle-class/working-class fusion accomplished in Jamaica and Barbados, albeit without adopting the mild Fabian socialism of some of these other parties.

In Jamaica the first major strikes in 1935 were still quite localized, but in 1938 strikes, protest marches, and clashes with the police spread over the entire island (see e.g. Post 1978: 276ff). The Jamaica Workers and Tradesmen Union (JWTU), founded in 1935, became the base for Alexander Bustamante's organizing efforts in 1937. He traveled the entire island, using his oratorical skills and charismatic qualities to urge workers to organize. When expelled from the JWTU for trying to seize the presidency, he formed his own union, the Bustamante Industrial Trade Union (BITU) in January 1939, with some 8,000 members (Eaton 1975: 69ff). He also became a member of the newly formed People's National Party (PNP). Efforts to form a party to give political expression to middle- and working-class concerns had started in earnest in 1937, and by 1938 Norman W. Manley, Jamaica's most prominent lawyer, had been convinced to assume the leadership in founding the PNP (Post 1978: 365). In 1940, the PNP adopted a Fabian socialist position, and it appeared that a strong PNP–BITU alliance would cement the middle and working-classes into the nationalist movement. However, in 1942 Bustamante broke with the PNP and formed his own Jamaica Labour Party (JLP) in anticipation of the

1944 general elections. This break left the PNP with weak grass-roots support, and accordingly the PNP strengthened its party organization at local levels and promoted growth of the Trade Union Council (TUC). These developments laid the ground work for the domination of Jamaican politics by the two party–union blocs and for the continued clear leadership of the PNP in the drive for responsible government and independence.

In Barbados large-scale strikes, mass meetings, demonstrations and riots broke out in July 1937. During 1938 organizing work was done for the Barbados Progressive League (later to become the Barbados Labour Party, BLP), and in 1939 Grantley Adams, a lawyer and Rhodes scholar like his counterpart Norman Manley in Jamaica, became president of the League. In November 1938, Adams represented the League at the British Guiana and West Indies Labour Congress, where resolutions were passed in support of a "Government of the Federated West Indies," self-government with universal adult franchise, the nationalization of sugar industries and limits on the size of landholdings. The spirit of these resolutions shaped the League's first formal statement, namely its submission to the Moyne Commission; its basic thrust was democratic and socialist (Hoyos 1978: 210–3). The building of an organized lower-class base for the party was started with the founding of the Barbados Workers Unions in 1941, with Adams as President General. Under a still highly restricted suffrage the League gained five seats in the lower house in 1940, and by the time of the first elections with universal suffrage in 1951, its strength had grown to the extent that it won 16 of the 24 seats in the lower house (Hoyos, 1978: 223).

In trying to explain why the responses to the labor disturbances and the subsequent development of parties and unions were so different from the developments in Central America, one can again start with the argument about the balance of class power and propose that the composition and strength of the economically dominant classes on the one hand and the strength of the middle classes on the other hand favored a reformist rather than a repressive response, more like the pattern in Costa Rica. The upper classes in Trinidad and Jamaica were clearly no longer pure plantocracies of British origin. In Trinidad, there had been a long-standing division between the British planters and French and Spanish planters and merchants. Immigration from the Middle East, China, and Portugal added families who accumulated wealth through commerce, in Jamaica as well as in Trinidad. The Guyanese upper classes were similarly divided between European, Portuguese, and Indian segments. In all three colonies, the sugar estates were moving into the hands of foreign owners, generally large multinational corporations. Thus, the domestic planter class was no longer that strong and it was ethnically distinct from the rising commercial bourgeoisie. Arguably, this decreased the likelihood of the formation of an upper-class coalition led by agricultural interests dependent on a large supply of cheap labor. However, the Barbadian case argues that one should not exaggerate the importance of this factor. There, the British planters managed to maintain their hegemony not only in agriculture but also in urban commerce.[17] Moreover, the West Indian middle class was hardly a strong counterweight to the elites; only in Jamaica had its members reached a considerable degree of organization, mainly in professional associations. Finally, cries for order from the dominant classes and denunciations of "outside agitators" were not lacking.[18] That is, it is arguable that the domestic upper classes might well have resorted to more extensive use of repression had they had the capacity to do so.

In an interesting parallel to Australia, the critical feature that prevented the formation of the Moorian coalition of landlords–state–bourgeoisie in the British West Indies was that the local elites did not control the state apparatus. It was in the hands of the imperial power. This had been true even before the period of crown colony rule in the colonies, when the local upper classes did have considerable power; if the British government was not pleased with what the local legislature did it could always suspend or alter the local constitution.

This is not to argue that planter interests were not overwhelmingly dominant under crown colony rule as well as in the earlier periods of greater (upper class) self-government (e.g. see Lewis 1968; Lutchman 1974; Hoyos 1978). We do contend, however, that the imperial power was a brake on the exploitative aims of the planter class. Emancipation is the most obvious case in point; the West Indian planters were dead set against it. Just a few examples from the subsequent period contrasting crown colony rule and planter self-rule should suffice to buttress our case. Planter self rule was perhaps most complete in British Guiana prior to 1891 where the sugar planters were in the habit of "coercing the administration to their way of thinking and in their interests, by utilizing the powers which they possessed under the constitution" (Lutchman 1974: 30). In fact, it was the attempt to use these powers to quash a report by the Medical Inspector about the deplorable conditions of workers on the sugar estates which led to the British imposition of the constitution of 1891, forcing the planters to share power with the urban bourgeoisie and middle classes. The contrast between the 1930s and the Morant Bay rebellion of 1865 in Jamaica, where the white plantocracy used its control of the state for brutal repression, killing over 400 people in retaliation for fewer than two dozen victims of the original rebellion, also serves well to underscore this point.

Subsequent progress towards universal suffrage, internal self-government and independence was similarly shaped by the interaction of domestic and international forces, and a comparative analysis suggests that developments in the international system were again the more important determinants. All this raises the question, of course, why the British colonial administration responded comparatively mildly to the labor rebellions and why it was willing to make political concessions thereafter.

Here we can extend the argument that we made in the case of the British settler colonies: not only the interests of the dominant class in Britain but also the relative balance of class power within Britain was a very important factor determining the action of the British state and thus colonial policy. The industrial capital interests that were the dominant force in Britain in the last half of the last century did not require the kind of labor repression that plantation agriculture did. Then the rising strength of the labor movement, first organizationally in the trade unions, and then politically decisively changed the balance of class power in the country and resulted first in the transition to democracy (1918) and then extensive social reform (see chapter 4 and Stephens 1979c).

We have cited some examples of how the British acted as a brake on West Indian planters' interests in the nineteenth century above. The rise of Labour and the introduction of democracy made itself felt both in changing the general political climate which helped to legitimate the struggles for democracy and self-rule in the colonies and also in specific actions of the government. For instance, in part as a result of Cipriani's, the Trinidadian labor leader's, visit to the Labour Commonwealth Conference in 1930, the Labour government responded with a circular to colonial governors suggesting reform of labor legislation. Labour outcries in the wake of the 1930s labor rebellion certainly helped to create the climate that led to the Moyne Commission recommendations. In the 1940s the Fabian Colonial Bureau became a persistent critic of colonial policy, and its West Indies Committee frequently intervened with British authorities on behalf of labor movements and like-minded political parties, such as the PNP in Jamaica (e. g. Post 1981: 155, 284, 398, 516). And, of course, most important, it is widely conceded that the Labour government of 1945–51 was critical in making major steps toward democracy and decolonization in the West Indies and elsewhere (Hintzen 1989: 31; Ryan 1972: 71; Spinner 1984: 25).

One must be careful not to go too far with this argument. Racism could and did contribute to the justification of much more repressive policies toward the lower classes in the colonies than existed in Britain or in the British settler colonies. Moreover, there was a considerable discrepancy between the class power balance and public opinion in Britain and what actually happened in the colonies as the relationship between the sitting government in the imperial power and the colonial government had to be filtered through layers of colonial administration. As Lewis notes, the colonial service was the last to be professionalized; its personnel was selected by connections and patronage in the English upper-class "old boy" network. Governors were often Oxbridge men with no knowledge of the social sciences, "usually abysmally ignorant of public opinion at home, and especially of public opinion outside of the ranks of the Establishment" (Lewis 1968: 111–12). It was difficult to rule against the interests of the local planter classes in any case and, given the political orientation and class background of the governors, they had little motivation to do so. Thus it is not surprising that the wishes of the imperial government might be circumvented as, for example, they were in Trinidad in 1932 when the government responded to the Labour government circular with meaningless legislation (Ryan 1972: 37). Perhaps more important, the colonial governors were the main source of information on conditions in the colonies for the colonial office and thus the British government. Despite these qualifications, there is still no doubt that the British government did act as a restraining influence on planters' exploitation and in its response to events of the 1930s, embodied in the Moyne recommendations, was willing to go much further than the local upper classes would have ever dreamed of.

In accounting for the post-war decolonization process "international opinion" is frequently cited as an important factor (Ryan 1972: 71; Spinner 1984: 13; Hintzen 1989: 31–2 for the Caribbean; for Africa see Gann and Duignan 1967). To raise this to the status of an explanatory factor, one must account for the change in international opinion itself. Only the briefest sketch can be offered here. We would point to two interrelated factors: the changing balance of class power in the core and changing power relations in the international system. The two World Wars were critical junctures in both cases. As we discussed in chapter 4, World War I and its aftermath corresponded with and in part caused a decisive change in the balance of class power in the core as the labor movements and parties of the left emerged much more powerful in the wake of the war and as a number of countries made the transition to democracy in the period. The defeat of authoritarian Germany and Austria–Hungary, the transition to democracy in the winners and the losers, and the emergence of the Soviet Union which, though increasingly authoritarian, was strongly anti-colonial, resulted in a change in the climate of world opinion in favor of Wilsonian self-determination (at least for white people) and at least rising criticism of colonialism.

The rise of authoritarianism in Italy, Germany, Austria, Japan, and Spain was of course a gigantic setback in this process but it set the scene for a war in which the leading colonial powers fought the Fascist countries in the name of democracy in alliance with the Soviet Union. Again the end of the War led to changes in the balance of class power in the advanced capitalist countries, as the trade unions and left emerged much stronger than before. The period between the end of the war and the beginning of the Cold War, which can be conveniently dated with the statement of the Truman doctrine in March 1947, was particularly favorable for anti-colonial forces. Labour was in power in Britain as were left coalitions, including the communist parties, in France and Italy.[19] The movements in the colonial states were encouraged by the example of Gandhi's successes in India. Whereas the Cold War and resultant shift in US policy from an emphasis on self-determination and democracy to fighting communism was a setback for this broad international anti-colonial climate, this was partly offset by the growing momentum of the process of decolonization and national liberation as the new nations pressed the process forward in international fora, such as the UN. This was critical, for example, in the penultimate stages of Guyana's struggle for independence as Jagan used the UN to put pressure on Britain.

As mentioned earlier, British colonialism and the decolonization process are generally considered to have been less conflictful and specifically more likely to contribute to democratic outcomes than colonialism and decolonization under other nations (Smith 1978; Weiner 1987; Diamond 1989a, 1989b; also see the statistical research cited in chapter 2). This view is sometimes associated with a romantic perception (on the part of apologists of British imperialism) of British colonialism as having been benevolent, a view which is hard to square with that of the West Indian nationalists of the intransigence with which the British ceded their power. As Lewis (1968: 108) observes: "For the history of the West

Indian movement for self-government and representative institutions, especially after 1918, shows decisively that (1) Colonial Office policy, in practice, was to grant minuscule reforms at the last moment, discriminating between different territories, and seeking every way to delay the inevitable; and (2) progress, in any case, was the result of the struggle of the militant progressive forces in each colony, extracted from London through protest and agitation . . ." Lewis's summary of the dynamics is certainly correct, but as our analysis showed, the British did allow for the self-organization of such militant forces, and in general for the independent organization of subordinate classes, thus facilitating the emergence of a balance of power within civil society and between civil society and the state which was favorable for the maintenance of democracy.

As the quote from Lewis indicates, progress towards democracy and independence was far from automatic and unilinear; rather, it was shaped by a very complex interaction of domestic and international forces. Internal pressures had to be credible enough to elicit concessions, but not threatening enough to provoke defensive reactions and regress. In particular, pressures for radical socio-economic reforms in addition to the political ones tended to prompt negative reactions.

Jamaica was the trailblazer in the process of constitutional decolonization; the first elections for the lower house based on universal suffrage were held there in 1944. In its statements to the Moyne Commission, the PNP had insisted very strongly on such elections as a step towards self-government. It thus gave organized and forceful expression to the desires of the Jamaican middle and working-classes for political as well as socio-economic reforms. The JLP, in contrast, which won the 1944 elections owing to its strong trade union base, was essentially non-programmatic and opposed to self-government, thus slowing progress towards this goal. Nevertheless, the PNP continued to promote it, during its time as opposition in parliament and after its accession to power in 1955. In 1957 Jamaica achieved virtually full internal self-government through the introduction of cabinet government. In 1958 Jamaica joined the Federation of the West Indies, and after the referendum favoring withdrawal from the Federation in 1961 rapid progress was made towards full independence; the Independence Constitution took effect in August 1962.[20]

Progress towards greater political participation and local autonomy in Trinidad was slower. The first elections with universal suffrage were held in 1946; thereafter, internal divisions and the weakness of the parties slowed further progress. Indeed, Creech Jones, the Secretary of State for the Colonies, argued that the lack of programmatic parties in Trinidad prevented an immediate move to a fully elective legislature, which was the policy of the Labour Government for all colonies (Ryan 1972: 83–84). This was the task that the People's National Movement took on after its formation in 1956. Its vigorous campaign resulted in virtually full internal self– government in 1961; independence was granted in 1962, as in the Jamaican case after the collapse of the Federation.

Barbados was an exceptional case in that it had not been turned into a crown colony in the second half of the nineteenth century, but rather had preserved an unbroken tradition of parliamentary institutions since 1639. In reality, though, real executive power was in the hands of the governor and his appointees, and the franchise for the House of Assembly was highly restricted. Under the "Bushe Experiment" (named after the governor who introduced it) steps toward a semi-ministerial government were taken as early as 1944, in so far as the names for membership in the appointed Executive Committee were to be presented by the majority leader in the House. However, there were still property qualifications for the franchise and the Legislative Council, dominated by planter interests, was a serious hindrance. The first general elections under universal suffrage were held in 1951, and further steps towards full internal self-government were taken in 1954 and 1958. In 1961 finally, the Legislative Council was replaced by the Senate, where members appointed on the advice of the majority leader in the House had a majority. Ever since Adams's attempt to pass measures for universal adult suffrage in the House in 1940, the BLP had exerted consistent pressures for democratization. Its alliance with the Barbados Workers Union gave significant strength to the nationalist movement. In the early 1950s, however, tensions between the BLP and the BWU paralleled tensions between left and right within the party and led to the break of the alliance and a split in the party, with the left forming the Democratic Labour Party (DLP). This split did not significantly weaken the nationalist movement, though, because the DLP pushed for progress in the same direction. After the collapse of the Federation of the West Indies in 1962, plans for a new federation of eight islands (smaller ones plus Barbados) were pursued. By 1965 these plans were defunct, and efforts towards separate independence succeeded in late 1966.

The cases of Jamaica, Trinidad, and Barbados show that the British were essentially willing to move towards decolonization in the Caribbean, but that local pressures shaped the nature of actual progress. Particularly in the early stages, local pressures were crucial. Post (1981: 152–4), for instance, documents how important the considerations of domestic Jamaican pressures were in the deliberations of the Colonial Office in 1941 about political reforms there. This might lead one to argue that progress could have been much faster and could have encompassed social and economic reforms as well, if only the middle class leadership of the nationalist movements had been less timid (or less conservative in outlook) and had engaged in mass organization and mobilization more vigorously. The example of Guyana, though, suggests that a very high degree of mobilization in support of radical proposals could at least temporarily reverse progress towards democratic self-government.[21] The Cold War and the growing role of the United States in the Caribbean considerably reinforced anti-radical pressures. As a result of a variety of such pressures, for instance, the PNP in Jamaica expelled its marxist left wing in 1952.[22]

We can identify some similarities to and differences with the analysis of the emergence of democracy in South America, Europe, and the British settler colonies. First, the planters, like the large landowners engaged in labor intensive agriculture in these other regions, were strongly opposed to any concessions to the subordinate classes. Second, the bourgeoisie was not a proponent of democracy and independence either. Moskos's (1967: 42) interviews with a systematic sample of West Indian leaders in 1961–2 found that 94 percent of businessmen opposed independence. Further analysis of the Jamaican interviews showed that a majority of businessmen paid lip service to democracy as a form of government, but were more skeptical than political and intellectual elites about the competence of the average Jamaican voter and, like their counterparts on other islands but in sharp contrast to other Jamaican elites, were opposed to independence (see Stephens and Stephens 1990).

The driving force behind democratization and decolonization was an alliance of the working-class and the middle classes. The pattern encountered in some countries in South America of middle-class inclusion through an alliance with dissident segments of the elites was impossible because the West Indian upper classes were united in their opposition to democratization and independence. This cross-class coalition usually took the form of a party–trade union alliance similar to northern European social democracy, but with greater middle class support and more heavily middle class in its leadership than in Europe.[23] Most of them adopted Fabian socialist principles in their early years, but by the 1950s the more socialist (as opposed to welfarist) elements were all but abandoned. Thus, these parties constituted no immediate threat to either the domestic economic elites or foreign capital, neither one of which openly and actively opposed democratization and independence at that point. Though historical evidence and the interviews referred to above indicate strong reservations on the part of businessmen about seeing political power pass to local democratic governments, the economic elites were isolated on this issue and, most importantly, could not enlist any allies in the state apparatus to block progress in this direction. The telling exception is Guyana, where the radical nature of the program of the dominant nationalist party galvanized the domestic economic elites, foreign capital, the US government, and the British colonial authorities into an alliance which undermined the emergence of democratic self-government. In sum, then, one can say that it was both the strength of working- and middle-class organization in unions and political parties, and the moderation of these organizations that favored completion of the process of constitutional decolonization and consolidation of democratic rule.

Spanish-speaking countries from the 1960s to the present

In the 1960s and 1970s, Central America and the Caribbean underwent similar spurts of economic growth, leading to economic and social diversification. Since growth in both areas was taking place under dependent capitalism, it increased inequality and unemployment in rural and urban areas, though the severity of rural dislocation varied. The political reactions to these economic developments were widely different, however. In the Caribbean, newly emerging groups were for the most part absorbed into the party–union blocs. Except for Guyana and Grenada, democracy survived, even where economic and political conflict put it under heavy strain as in Jamaica in the 1970s. In Central America, in contrast, newly emerging groups met with repression of varying intensity. The results of this ranged from successful to stalemated revolution and military-dominated highly restricted democracy; the achievement of full democracy became ever more remote.

In the 1960s, both import substitution industrialization and export agriculture grew considerably in Central America. Spurred by the Central American Common Market, US private investment and US aid for the military and infrastructure, production and construction increased. These processes created the conditions for growing middle- and working-class organization, and they also increased rural unrest as land concentration deprived more and more families of their traditional subsistence. However, the repeated stifling of unions and political parties through internal oligarchic–military alliances or external intervention in the previous decades, together with massive US military aid, had left the societies with an extreme imbalance between the organizational power of the middle and lower classes on the one hand and the economic power of elites and the repressive power of the state apparatus on the other hand. Accordingly, channels for the peaceful expression of discontent resulting from dislocation were largely ineffective, and efforts to make them more effective and change the power imbalance by strengthening popular organization met with continued repression. As a result, revolutionary challenges of varying intensity and effectiveness emerged; early (1965) and strong but immediately thwarted in the Dominican Republic, strongest in Nicaragua and El Salvador by the late 1970s, more localized in Guatemala, and lowest in Honduras. The intensity of such challenges was shaped by a variety of factors, such as the importance of land as a scarce resource (very high in El Salvador, high in parts of Nicaragua and Guatemala, moderate in Honduras),[24] the severity of dislocations in rural areas (high in El Salvador, Nicaragua, and northern Guatemala, low in Honduras), the existence of urban–rural contacts (high in Nicaragua and El Salvador), and ethnic divisions (weak in Nicaragua, except for the Miskito Indians, and El Salvador, strong in Guatemala). The effectiveness of revolutionary movements depended further on the unity of the economic elite (high in El Salvador, low in Nicaragua), the organizational coherence or bureaucratization of the state's repressive apparatus (high in Guatemala, very low in Somoza's Nicaragua, medium to high in El Salvador),[25] and the strength of external support for the repressive apparatus (very high in El Salvador, high in Guatemala until 1977, low in Nicaragua after 1978).[26]

In Nicaragua the Somoza dynasty maintained firm control until the 1970s. The growth of agricultural production, the highest in Central America in the period 1950–77, involved significant land concentration, such that by the late 1970s the landless rural labor force in some areas was more than ten times larger than in the 1950s (LaFeber 1983: 226–7). Rural–urban migration led to the rapid growth of urban slums, which were to become important grounds for the insurrection.[27] Urban and rural popular organizations were ruthlessly repressed by the dictatorship. Church-sponsored grass-roots organizations contributed to popular mobilization, though they were not exempt from repression (Montgomery 1982). After 1973 the revolutionary movement, which had been unable to make any major impact in the 1960s, gained momentum. The greed and repressiveness of the Somozas and their close allies eventually also drove the rest of the economic elite into militant opposition. In fact, a general strike initiated by the bourgeoisie in early 1978 marked the beginning of the final stage in the struggle. By 1979, the National Guard, which had never become a highly professional and disciplined military institution, started to disintegrate under the onslaught of the insurrection. When the United States finally cut off military aid to Somoza, the last obstacle to the victory of the revolutionary movement was removed.

Developments towards democratization after the revolution were heavily shaped by external pressures. Certainly, the US-sponsored contra war was a decisive obstacle to the installation and consolidation of a fully democratic system. Even well consolidated democracies grow intolerant towards dissent in the face of external aggression. Establishing a democracy in such a context and under the legacy of a very lopsided balance of power in civil society was exceedingly difficult. On the positive side, the Sandinista government strongly promoted popular organization and thus laid the groundwork for subordinate classes to become a counterweight to the economically dominant classes. Furthermore, despite official US propaganda to the contrary, professional observers judged the 1984 elections as conforming to democratic standards (LASA 1985), and popular participation in the elections was high. On the negative side, with short periods of relaxation, press censorship severely restricted freedom of speech. Thus, from 1984 to 1990 Nicaragua was a restricted democracy, though it was far more democratic than any of the other Central American countries except for Costa Rica.

The elections in 1990 resulted in a surprise victory of the opposition and the transfer of power to the new government ushered in a formally fully democratic regime.[28] The balance of power in civil society appears moderately favorable for the consolidation of democracy, though it remains to be seen how well consolidated and therefore capable of surviving the change from state support to state hostility the Sandinista-sponsored mass organizations are. Prospects for the future will continue to be shaped by transnational structures of power. A crucial juncture will be reached with the next elections. Heavy US partisan interference on behalf of the incumbents might well damage the legitimacy of democratic institutions critically and generate militant resistance bypassing all democratic channels. One does not even have to be able to predict the winners in the ensuing struggle to assess the prospects for democracy in this case as very bleak indeed.

In El Salvador, military rule with different degrees of toleration over time of party and, to a lesser extent union, organization prevailed. The military was internally split, some factions that were less closely tied to the oligarchy harbored mildly reformist designs, but they remained consistently weaker than the conservative factions.[29] The oligarchy took an important part in the growth of traditional and new economic activities, thus adding to its economic strength. The expansion of cotton and sugar production led to further land concentration in a situation where population pressure on the land was already extremely high.[30] From 1961 to 1971 the number of landless families more than tripled (LaFeber, 1983: 243). One escape valve was migration to Honduras, where up to a quarter million Salvadorans went during the 1960s (LaFeber, 1983: 175). In 1969, however, Honduras began to expel these immigrants, and the subsequent "soccer war" closed this escape firmly, which aggravated and radicalized the internal struggle in El Salvador. Popular organization had increased; political parties, unions and Christian base communities were demanding political and social rights and economic concessions. However, the popular forces faced a very strong and highly cohesive oligarchy and a moderately professionalized and well equipped US-supported military who offered stern resistance to any reforms and answered organization and peaceful protest with increasingly brutal repression. Growing guerrilla strength was followed by stepped-up military aid under Reagan, leading to a situation where neither side is able to win.[31] The trappings of democracy, with US-supported elections beginning in 1982 and 1984, did nothing to bring the coercive forces under control of the government. Thus, the interests of the oligarchy and increasingly the economic interests of the military itself remain protected by official and inofficial repressive actions. A democratic solution is impossible without concessions of the oligarchy on land reform, as access to land is the crucial issue for the majority of the population, but the oligarchy remains intransigent. As long as the dominant faction in the military supports this position and on its part is supported by the United States, negotiations between an elected government and the guerrillas, no matter how well intentioned on both sides, remain incapable of bringing about a transition to full democracy.

In Guatemala, the legacy of US-sponsored intervention and the follow-up with massive military aid was a very strong military institution, interested primarily in its own aggrandizement and prosperity. Military officers were becoming landowners and participants in urban ventures. Even during the short periods when the political system was relatively open, the military remained the determining force behind the scenes, blocking any significant reforms. However, the Arevalo and Arbenz periods had also left a legacy of a stronger middle class and a more mobilized (though repressed) working-class in urban and rural areas.[32] In the early 1960s the first guerrilla activity emerged, as did the phenomenon of private death squads on the right. By the late 1960s the military was engaged in a large-scale brutal counterinsurgency campaign. By the late 1970s renewed revolutionary movements emerged, particularly in areas where the expansion of oil and mining production and of export agriculture dislodged peasants from their lands. Most of those affected by the land grabbing were Indians, which made alliance-building among different rural-based guerrilla groups and between them and urban forces difficult because of the ethnic diversity. Thus, the revolutionary thrust has been contained at a lower level than in El Salvador, but similarly unfavorable conditions prevail for democratization. The installation of a democratically elected president in early 1986 did not change the fundamental power imbalance between civil society and the autonomous coercive arm of the state.

Honduras was under moderately conservative military dominated rule from 1963 to 1975. Like in the other countries, the military had been greatly strengthened, and even more so than in the others had become the sole truly important national institution. The importance of the banana plantations, the relative weakness of the domestic large landowners, and the comparatively low population pressure on the land made for less immediate and intense social conflict than in the other countries. They allowed for a considerable degree of unionization on the banana plantations and for a certain degree of peasant organization. However, in the 1960s problems were growing, as large numbers of Salvadorans were looking for land. When strikes and riots broke out in 1968 the Salvadoran immigrants began being expelled, and the continuing expulsions in the aftermath of the "soccer war" in 1969 took some pressure off the domestic situation. Protests were further dampened by the return of some land by the banana companies. Though the companies maintained the very profitable marketing activity, peasants did get land and could grow bananas in co-operatives. Nevertheless, the early 1970s were a period of significant efforts at popular mobilization. The military was divided as to the appropriate response; one faction favored a Peruvian-style reformist–co-optative approach, the others more conservative repressive approaches. The latter won out and by 1975 the country swung sharply to the right (Shepherd 1986). The return to elected government in 1981 left the military in the position of holding the ultimate say; at best one could categorize the regime since then as a highly restricted democracy. In fact, the militarization of Honduras by the Reagan administration continued to strengthen the military, thus obstructing chances for movement towards full democracy even further.

The Dominican Republic underwent a condensed version of stifled popular mobilization and attempts at an electoral path to reform, a consequent revolutionary challenge, and its repression through US intervention. The last chapter in its development has been a return to democracy, supported by US pressures at a critical juncture. The assassination of Trujillo in 1961 opened the way for elections to be held in 1962; they were won by Juan Bosch and the Dominican Revolutionary Party (PRD). After only seven months in office, however, the government was overthrown by the military. In 1965 the PRD led an insurrection which was supported by younger officers. Due to this split in the military, the rebellion got close to ending in a victory for the rebel forces, but the invasion by US marines reversed the course of the fighting. Some 3,000 people were killed in the fighting and another 1,000–2,000 in its aftermath; this had a severely debilitating effect on popular organization. Under Balaguer, then (1965–78), the Dominican Republic experienced very rapid growth, yet no significant popular challenges. Several reasons can be adduced to explain this: The lesson of 1965 was not lost on would-be revolutionaries; the most exploited segments of the labor force were (and are) migrant workers from Haiti, mainly in sugar; the rural dislocations were not as severe as for example in El Salvador and Nicaragua; and there was some, albeit very restricted, room for political and union organizing activity. Balaguer's rule was highly authoritarian, maintained through fraudulent elections, and he kept a tight rein on unions, but there was no large scale repression as in Nicaragua, El Salvador, and Guatemala. The rapid economic growth caused the middle and working-classes to expand, and though the working class did not really grow in strength because of the restrictions on unionization, the PRD's mobilizing activity demonstrated the potential power of a middle-class/working-class alliance. During Balaguer's rule, the PRD shifted towards the center and became a moderate reformist party with cross-class support (Espinal 1986: 86). Thus, an electoral victory and transfer of power to the PRD did not constitute a threat to the vital interests of the economically dominant classes. The PRD's 1978 presidential candidate Guzman, himself a large landowner, further contributed to making the party acceptable both to large parts of the domestic business community and to the Carter administration. When election fraud threatened to deprive Guzman of his apparent victory in 1978, considerable pressures, including from the Carter administration, brought the military to the point of allowing Guzman to take office.[33] The serious divisions in the PRD in the 1980s and the economic crisis substantially reduced the chances for consolidation of democracy, as they left a party system composed of personalistic political machines and kept unions extremely weak. The contested reelection of Balaguer in 1990 demonstrated the fragility of the democratic institutions (Hartlyn 1990).

Costa Rica stands in stark contrast to the other Central American cases. The repressive apparatus of the state was emasculated and the economic power of the elites was to some extent counterbalanced by the organizational power of the middle and working classes. The economic growth of the 1960s provided resources for further expansion of the social welfare system and public sector employment. The economic and social inclusion of the majority of the population supported their political inclusion and thus helped to strengthen democratic institutions. The PLN and various opposition parties alternated in power for most of the post–1952 period. Elites accepted democratic rule, as they had learned to protect their interests through the party system. As pointed out above, the first president under the post-civil war constitution was a conservative. Furthermore, there never existed an electorally strong radical mass party which could have mounted a credible threat to elite interests. The dominant party before the civil war was the populist PRN, and afterwards the moderate social democratic PLN. Accordingly, not much progress was made on reforms affecting private property. In particular the landless rural population, being poorly organized, remained a severely disadvantaged group.[34] The limits on internal reform were paralleled by a cautious foreign policy, intent on preventing a confrontation with US interests. Certainly, the lesson of Guatemala was not lost on Figueres and his successors in the PLN. Accordingly, democracy and its underlying power balance were not put to a severe test. A situation where the major internal and external actors would activate their power resources in the pursuit of their interests inside and outside of the democratic system could be avoided.[35]

English-speaking countries from the 1960s to the present

The situation in the Caribbean islands after independence resembled the Costa Rican one with respect to the repressive apparatus, that is, the military was of minimal strength. The organizational base of the middle and working-classes in the party–union complexes was for the most part even stronger than in Costa Rica. Progress in national insurance systems, education, and health services similarly contributed to popular loyalty to the parties and the democratic system of government. Elites had learned before independence already to work with and through the established parties, using financial contributions and control over print media as major sources of leverage. Rapid economic growth also led to further social diversification, but the emerging forces were for the most part absorbed by existing unions and/or integrated into the political parties through patronage. In the 1960s and early 1970s some isolated spontaneous challenges with violent components, such as the riots in 1965 and 1968 in Jamaica and the mass demonstrations in 1970 in Trinidad, occurred, as did organized expressions of protest in the form of the black power movement and various marxist–leninist groups. However, none of these groups were able to attract a significant support base and challenge the hegemony of the established party–union blocs. In the 1980s, then, the economic crisis presented a significant challenge to these democracies. It not only deprived the governments of resources to fulfill popular expectations for economic and social policies to improve mass welfare, but it also weakened unions and began to undermine state capacity to maintain the rule of law, for instance, to protect their citizens from violent crime.

Barbados underwent least strains on its democratic system, as the incumbent parties remained moderately reformist or moderately conservative and the degree of popular mobilization remained relatively stable. The DLP won the 1961 elections and proceeded to push for significant social welfare reforms. The party was re-elected in 1966 and 1971, but defeated by the BLP under Tom Adams, the son of Grantley Adams, in 1976 and 1981, only to be re-elected in 1986.[36]

In Trinidad the party system was less favorable for consolidation of democracy as the PNM was clearly dominant. Still, it managed to accommodate elite interests as well as to retain the support of major unions. The PNM was essentially pro-capitalist but mildly social reformist and stayed in power until 1986. It managed to stave off the challenges from the left, arising out of the black power movement, by the liberal use of patronage made possible by the oil revenues.[37] However, the collapse of the oil price in the 1980s induced a severe economic crisis which made these patronage resources dry up and allowed for an election victory of an opposition coalition. The soon emerging splits in this coalition and the coup attempt by a group of militant Black Muslims in 1990 demonstrated both the profound divisions in the society and the failure of the party system to integrate and effectively articulate the interests of all mobilized social forces.

Jamaica's system of government and social cohesion underwent significant strains in the 1970s. The PNP's return to a democratic socialist stance under Norman Manley and his son Michael, the attempts to build a genuine mass party and movement and the resulting increase in popular mobilization, the concrete reform policies between 1972 and 1976 and the radical rhetoric of some prominent PNP leaders, together with a high non-aligned foreign policy profile profoundly threatened economic elites and aroused US hostility.[38] The economic elites retaliated with capital flight and the United States with economic and diplomatic pressures and more or less open support for the opposition. A severe balance of payments crisis in 1976 and the ensuing IMF programs between 1977 and 1980 weakened the PNP government's support drastically, though it still maintained a large minority of loyal party stalwarts. In this situation, actions of a highly opportunistic opposition leadership contributed to a climate of strife and direct confrontation. In the 1980 election campaign some 500 people were killed in political violence. The security forces clearly turned against the incumbent PNP, but an attempted coup was put down by the top command. Ultimately, the PNP was defeated at the polls and the JLP took office in a constitutional manner.

In the 1980s, democracy came under challenge again when the PNP decided to boycott the 1983 elections which had been called by Prime Minister Seaga in clear violation of an inter-party agreement on electoral reforms. The result was a one-party parliament from 1983 to 1989. What was crucial for the survival of democracy in Jamaica in the 1970s and the 1980s was the power balance in civil society on the one hand and between civil society and the repressive apparatus of the state on the other hand. Two political blocs of roughly equal strength, both with cross-class support, confronted each other. Despite a complete shift of elite support to the JLP and a certain realignment of the middle and lower classes in 1976, followed by a significant shift of popular support to the JLP by the late 1970s, the PNP still maintained a significant mobilization capacity. In the 1980s, the PNP rebuilt its organizational infrastructure and emerged strengthened from the period without parliamentary representation, winning the 1989 elections. Given its organizational base in civil society, the PNP could only have been excluded from the political system through force of arms. The security forces, however, were not nearly as large, well equipped and self conscious a corporate institution as their counterparts in Central America. Accordingly, they were neither ready allies for one of these political blocs, nor holders of a strong belief in their own superior capacity to rule, nor in very close connections with the economic elites. Indeed, it is questionable whether the security forces, i. e. the military and police, could have imposed effective repressive rule, whether on their own behalf or on behalf of civilian groups, given the limited size of the military and the limited discipline of the police, and the high degree of popular mobilization, including the wide distribution of arms among the lower classes. The question then becomes why the Jamaican governments after independence had not been building up a stronger security apparatus. A large part of the answer is that the political parties were firmly established and represented groups whose interests were in economic development and social progress. Moreover, there were no significant internal or external threats, nor a tradition of militarism in the society. Finally, and very importantly, before the Reagan initiative of 1983 to build a regional security system there was no significant external support for militarization.

Variations within the English-speaking Caribbean

Democracy did not survive the first post-independence decade in all countries in the English-speaking Caribbean. By the late 1970s, the electoral process in both Guyana and Grenada was sufficiently corrupted that it is fair to say that it was very unlikely (Grenada) or impossible (Guyana) for the opposition to win an election and displace the government. Moreover, in both countries, opposition parties, unions, and newspapers were subject to considerable harrassment.[39] Since the social origins of authoritarianism are quite different in the two cases, it is necessary to discuss them separately.

Cross-national statistical research has shown that ethnicity is negatively related to democracy. Guyana fits this generalization as virtually all observers of Guyana agree that the ethnic division between East Indians and Africans contributed to the development of authoritarianism in that country. But the existence of this ethnic cleavage was hardly a sufficient cause, as Trinidad demonstrates. Hintzen (1989: 3) certainly points to the core of the answer when he observes that the People's National Congress (PNC) "was brought to power by relying not only upon mobilization of the black and mixed masses but, perhaps more importantly, upon the fact of black domination and preeminence in the colonial and post-colonial state bureaucracy including its armed branches." However, what differentiates Guyana from Trinidad is not that Africans[40] did not dominate the state apparatus in Trinidad (they did), but that this was not a necessary feature of the PNM's rise to power. Rather the critical difference between the two countries was that the ethnic group which dominated the state was a minority or fast becoming one in Guyana whereas it was a substantial majority in Trinidad.[41] Even to say this is to simplify matters as it is the whole pattern of the articulation of the ethnic divisions in the whole political economy which lay at the root of the Guyanese developments. Moreover, one needs to add the very important role of the Cold War and the actions of the two relevant core capitalist powers without which the PNC's initial ascent to state power might not have been possible.

There are broad similarities in the class/ethnic divisions in Trinidad and Guyana. With emancipation, the African population left the sugar estates as soon as possible and the planters brought in East Indian indentured servants to work the fields. Sugar workers in both countries are still overwhelmingly East Indian.[42] Increasingly, Africans left not only the plantations but rural life altogether and the East Indian population became the dominant group in the peasantry (rice in Guyana; cocoa, cane, and market gardening in Trinidad). Owing to discrimination in employment, the upwardly mobile East Indian gravitated to the free professions and small business. Africans dominated the urban working-class occupations, mining (Guyana), oil fields (Trinidad), and the civil service, especially the police. Thus, the two racial/ethnic groups are not only occupationally, but also geographically, segregated, which helps to preserve the separate cultures and impedes social mixing. As mentioned previously, the upper-classes in both countries were drawn from various European and Middle Eastern nationalities. By the time of the post-war events examined here, the independent sugar plantocracy was a thing of the past and sugar production was dominated by multi-national corporations.

This brings up one substantial difference between the two countries: sugar was more important in the economy of Guyana and production was far more concentrated due to the demands of Guyanese geography (Lewis 1968: 259–62; Lutchman 1974: 9–10). By 1950, there was only one independent plantation out of nineteen in the country and the huge Bookers concern owned fifteen of the nineteen (Spinner 1984: 9). Bookers was involved in the import side of the economy also. The company itself claimed that it controlled the lives of 80 percent of the population. It was said that "Bookers will do everything but bury you" (Lewis 1968: 265). And, at least up to the land reform scheme of the Jagan government, the peasantry was markedly weaker in Guyana than elsewhere in the Caribbean. In sum, the Guyanese class structure was more polarized and the middle class weaker than in Trinidad.

Lewis (1968: 259–60) suggests that the root causes of the crisis of 1953 and subsequent developments lay in this socio-economic polarization and the ethnic division without, however, being very precise on the question. In the 1930s, the thrust of the nationalist movement was weaker in Guyana than in the rest of the West Indies. The middle class component was almost absent, which can be clearly linked to the configuration of the class structure (Hintzen 1989: 32). The situation on the estates was at the same time very authoritarian and very paternalistic and, we would argue, was largely responsible for muting the labor rebellion of the 1930s . The Sugar Producers Association (SPA) managed to keep control of labor, in part, through its good relations with the sugar workers' union, the Man Power Citizens Association (MPCA), which became increasingly a company union, used by the SPA to fend off challenges from Jagan's union, which, though much more popular than the MCPA among sugar workers, never managed to win bargaining rights for them.

As a result of the weakness of the nationalist movement, constitutional reform and suffrage expansion, which were introduced as a result of West Indian wide developments, outpaced organizational developments. This left a political vacuum into which the People's Progressive Party (PPP) stepped after its formation in 1950. The PPP was working-class-based and multi-ethnic. It was led by a marxist–leninist faction centered on Cheddi Jagan, but even the social democratic Burnham wing was more radical than the other labor/social democratic parties in the British West Indies at the time. The PPP had no serious competitors in the process of political mobilization and in the leadership of the nationalist movement. Thus, the PPP represented a greater threat to the economic elites in Guyana than the nationalist movement did elsewhere in the Caribbean.

Certainly the absence of an organized middle-class component of the nationalist movement helps explain why the radical PPP came to dominate the movement. A comparison with the situation in Trinidad at the time of the first elections held under universal suffrage argues that this was not the whole story as the middle class was not politically organized in that country either until the formation of the PNM (1955). In the 1946 and 1950 elections, working-class-based parties with a labor or socialist orientation took most of the seats (Ryan 1972: 76, 89–90). The difference is that these parties were not united in a single front, the legacy of the history of mobilization of the Trinidadian working class by different movements, such as Cipriani's TLP and Butler's oil field workers' union and his party. The PPP faced no competition in the working class which we would argue was in part the result of the configuration of the political economy, especially the domination of the huge sugar estates, and the consequent retardation of working-class political mobilization.

The PPP went into the 1953 elections competing against a weakly organized middle-class, business-led party and a large number of independent candidates and swept the election, taking 51 percent of the vote and 18 of 24 seats (Spinner 1984: 36). The PPP government pressed its constitutional powers to the limit to push through its radical but essentially reformist program: land reform, removal of church control of schools, trade union legislation, and other welfare state legislation.[43] The most contentious pieces of legislation were the Rice Farmers Security of Tenure Bill, which contained a controversial provision by which the government could force the sale of land in certain cases, and the Labour Relations Bill, which, simply by providing for fair election procedures for trade union representation, would virtually assure that Jagan's union would replace the MPCA as bargaining representative on the sugar estates. True, these reforms were accompanied by much rhetoric and, in the case of both these controversial bills, the PPP government suspended normal parliamentary procedure to rush the bill through; but the program was decidedly reformist in character. This did not prevent the local press and the upper class from becoming hysterical about the government's radical policies and its alleged "communist intentions". The Governor convinced Churchill and the Colonial Secretary that action was needed and the colonial office moved to suspend the constitution after the PPP had been in government for only 133 days.

There is no doubt that the constitutional suspension was motivated by a combination of the reaction of the local upper classes, in a very class-polarized society, to attacks on their privileges and the reaction of local elites and foreign political leaders, both in London and Washington, to "communist subversion." There is equally little doubt that the PPP government was not attempting to subvert the democratic arrangements (such that they were) in the colony. But, in the climate of the height of the Cold War, the Jagan faction's marxism–leninism and Jagan's contacts with eastern bloc countries were enough to alarm the Conservative government in Britain (still the main foreign actor in the West Indies) and the United States.

One must be careful in attributing too much to the events of 1953 in accounting for the eventual installation of authoritarian rule in Guyana. The record indicates that even the Colonial Office decided that the Governor overreacted as he was relieved after only two years in office and given a lesser post. PPP activities were proscribed for a period after the suspension, but the party and its organizations were not massively repressed as were unions and parties of the left in parallel events in Central America. Moreover, Jagan's wing of the PPP won elections held in 1957, was allowed to serve out its term, and won again in 1961.

The main contribution of the events of 1953 to the development of authoritarianism in Guyana was their role in the 1955 Jagan–Burnham split and the subsequent development of racial politics in the country, and here interpretation of the events is very controversial. Jagan's (1972) view is that the split was largely the work of imperialist forces and the charge is not without ground since as early as 1951, the US trade unions did work to drive a wedge between the Jagan-led union and the main body of unions, the British governor worked to form a united front of forces against Jagan, and the Colonial Office and even the British Labour Party encouraged Burnham to split with Jagan (Despres 1967: 199; Lewis 1968: 274; Spinner 1984: 31, 58, 70, 92–3). The local media and upper-classes also encouraged the split (Spinner 1984: 61).

However the split did not immediately take on a racial character and it was that development that was most fateful for democracy in Guyana. Moreover, the turn to racial mobilization can hardly be laid entirely at Burnham's door and after all, given the racial balance, he had much to lose from such a turn. The 1956 split of the black radicals from Jagan, which was a more important turning point for the development of racial mobilization, was stimulated in part by his speech to the 1956 party congress in which he opposed the Federation partly on racial grounds and called for an attempt to appeal to East Indian businessmen on an ethnic basis. The policies of the 1957–61 Jagan government dispropor-tionately benefited East Indians as they heavily favored agriculture over urban development, helped small to medium business (and thus East Indians) at the expense of large business, recruited and promoted East Indians in civil service jobs, and passed educational reforms benefiting East Indian teachers and children (Despres 1967: 232–3, 236–7, 245–50, 252; Hintzen 1989: 49–50; Spinner 1984: 74, 80–1). While almost all of these policies could be justified on ideological grounds and the PPP leadership denied intent to promote racial politics, it is hard to believe that consolidation of East Indian support was not one of the goals of the policies given the pattern of all of them taken together. At any rate their objective effect was to feed African fears and racial antagonism and force Burnham and the PNC leadership into racial mobilization also (Despres 1967: 253–5, 260–2).

Burnham and the rest of the PNC leadership are hardly blameless as not only did they respond with racial mobilization, but more important they constantly refused Jagan's appeals to form a united anti-colonial (or, later socialist) front. Though the racial divide had by then been institutionalized in the party system, it might have been possible to work out a consociational formula for coexistence of the two groups. But, by the early 1960s, Burnham smelled power and let nothing stand in his way of achieving it alone.

The PPP won the 1961 election again as in 1957 with a minority of votes due to the disunity of the opposition (43 percent of the vote and 20 of 35 seats to the PNC's 41 percent and 11 seats, with the conservative United Force taking the remaining seats). The British Conservative government faced international pressure on two sides: from the Third World countries, which were using the UN as a forum to pressure for decolonization, and, from the United States, which, in the wake of the Cuban revolution, was pressing hard for a solution which would not allow Jagan to lead Guyana into independence. With British tolerance, the United States was now intervening in Guyanese internal affairs in a major way, indirectly via the US trade union link, and, directly, through the CIA.

Owing to PPP policies and the racial orientation of the 1961 campaign, racial tensions were very high.[44] The beginning of the end of the Jagan government (and, retrospectively, Guyanese democracy) came with a general strike in February 1962, launched by government employees and supported by the PNC and the UF. A mass demonstration by the government's opponents degenerated into a riot, arson, and looting of East Indian businesses. Though these events outwardly appeared to be spontaneous, they were in fact carefully planned by Burnham. [45] The police and paramilitary units looked on and Jagan was forced to rely on the intervention of British troops to quiet the situation. Two years of disorder followed, the high point being an 80-day general strike, covertly financed by the CIA and AFL–CIO. In these strikes, the European employers generally closed their business or, in the case of the sugar estates, even locked out their workers to add momentum to the movement. In all these events, 300 lives were lost. In the end, the PPP was forced to accept the introduction of proportional representation, a solution favored by the PNC, the UF, and Washington. The capitulation was forced by the coalition of forces referred to in the introduction to this section: the domestic upper and middle classes, the black urban lower classes, the state apparatus, and metropolitan interests.

In 1964, the Guyanese people participated in the last honest election in the country's history. The PNC polled 41 percent and the UF 12 percent and these two parties formed a government which took Guyana into independence in 1966. Through judicious use of patronage, the PNC managed to get enough parliamentary crossovers to dispense with the coalition. Given the party's race–class base and the growing number of East Indians, it was probably apparent to the PNC leadership that it was unlikely that they could ever get a majority. Thus, they moved to ensure their victory in the 1968 election through massive fraud.

As Hintzen (1989: 56) succinctly states, after 1968, "the PNC was able to assure itself of absolute domination of the state through racial mobilization, control of the machinery of elections, support from a loyal state bureaucracy, and control of a highly politicized army and police." Initially, patronage was an extremely important element of the PNC's ability to assure itself of support and its ability to dispense patronage was greatly enhanced by the government's socialist policies which involved takeover of foreign businesses and most of the domestic economy. At the same time it greatly increased the size of the security forces from 2, 135 in 1964 to 12, 751 in 1977 (Danns 1982: 162). While this build-up was partly motivated by the border dispute with Venezuela and the dispute was used as justification for it, its main purpose was domestic repression. These recruits were overwhelmingly African, mainly from the urban lower classes (Danns 1982: 121, 161). When the economy began to deteriorate very badly in the mid and late 1970s and the source of patronage began to dry up, the government came increasingly to rely on coercion and shows of force to control the country. Elections became a complete farce, with boycotts of the opposition leading to minuscule turnouts, while the government claimed large turnouts and massive majorities.

In summary, the root cause of the breakdown of Guyanese democracy was a society which was highly polarized along race and class lines with the two dominant ethnic groups being highly segregated occupationally and geographically. The smaller of the two groups, the African, was dominant in the urban areas and the civil service, above all in the police, which made it difficult for the political party representing the East Indian population to rule once the Africans began to feel threatened owing to a combination of the policies of the PPP government and demographic pressures and agricultural modernization, which were forcing the East Indians to seek urban jobs in competition with the Africans. Due to the threat they perceived from the PPP's ideological posture and its policies, the largely European domestic upper-classes aligned with the African based PNC (though, ironically, they were later to be eliminated as an important social group by the PNC's nationalization policies). The marxism-leninism of the PPP also stimulated the dominant core capitalist powers to intervene on the side of the PNC. This alliance with the domestic upper-classes and the metropolitan powers was essential for first placing the PNC in power, given the minority position of its race/class base. The PNC established authoritarian rule, a move which would have been impossible without an initially strong base in the security forces, and then consolidated it by expanding the security forces and ensuring their loyalty. Thus, the way in which ethnic divisions were articulated in the state made the coercive arm of the state an instrument of political elites representing one of the ethnic groups in their quest for state power. The quest for power of these elites, who initially lacked a decisive power base of their own as their ethnic group was a minority and composed of subordinate classes, was successful because of support from external forces and domestic economic elites. Once the African leadership had consolidated its control over the state apparatus and greatly strengthened its coercive force, it expanded its autonomy from domestic economic elites as well as foreign interests.

For space reasons, we can only deal very briefly with the case of Grenada.[46] At the outset, Grenada had some superficial similarities to Guyana: the 1930s labor rebellion left the island untouched and early constitutional advance (the introduction of universal suffrage in 1951) was the result of pressure elsewhere in the West Indies.[47] The level of labor organization was, relative to elsewhere in the West Indies, very low in 1950; there was virtually no organization on the sugar estates and even the urban unions were not strong. This left a tremendous political vacuum into which Eric Gairy stepped. In the space of two years, the charismatic Gairy succeeded in organizing the vast majority of agricultural workers in the country; leading two successful strikes, one of all agricultural workers and one general strike; and winning the first election held under universal suffrage with 64 percent of the vote and six of eight seats.

The difference between Grenada and the rest of the West Indies, we would argue, lies in the ideology of persons or forces that organized the labor movement. The organizational force of the working class in each case was harnessed in the service of the movement (or persons) who first succeeded in organizing it and advancing its material demands. As indicated in our discussion in chapter 3, given the structural position of the working class in the authoritarian capitalist societies, it is not surprising that these movements most often have democratic ideologies, since political democracy will ensure the freedom of workers to organize and advance their demands and may even give the workers' movement a share of political power. However, the example of Grenada shows that workers can develop loyalties to authoritarian movements if they advance workers' material interests. Moreover, the case of Peronism in

Argentina demonstrates that one is not simply dealing with an idiosyncrasy of a micro-society here. These ideologies, socially constructed and constituted at a given historical moment, last generations beyond.

There are, however, some peculiar features of the Grenada case due, arguably, to the extremely small size, which make it dangerous to generalize too much from the case. It seems plausible to hypothesize that the size of the society, with an electorate of less than 30,000, made it possible for Gairy to hold his "movement" together through sheer charisma and highly personalized contact with and servicing of his supporters. For instance, his party, the Grenada United Labour Party (GULP), had no constituency organization whatsoever. The electoral fortunes of GULP fluctuated with Gairy's erratic behavior, as it won the elections of 1954, 1961, and 1967 and lost the elections of 1957 and 1962.

The 1967 election, which the GULP won with 55 percent of the vote, taking seven of ten seats, marked the beginning of the move toward authoritarianism. By this time, Grenada had achieved full internal self-government (independence came in 1974), which allowed Gairy to begin to greatly increase the corruption that had begun in his earlier tenures in office and buttress it with political repression. Gairy used his office blatantly for personal gain in the manner of Somoza and Trujillo, which alienated local business, who faced unfair competition from Gairy-owned concerns. On the other hand, he tilted labor legislation heavily in the direction of employers, alienating unions and workers. To maintain his rule, he turned increasingly toward repression: he organized a personal police force, the infamous Mongoose Gang, to harrass his opponents and won the 1972 and 1976 elections through fraud. And, of course, his decidedly weird behavior, such as promoting the investigation of UFOs in the UN, hardly earned him any international supporters.

By the late 1970s, the reaction to Gairy's rule had generated an impressive coalition against him: from the Chamber of Commerce, the churches, and the conservative Grenada National Party to the Civil Service Association and the urban unions and the radical New Jewel Movement. Still, the example of Guyana in the late 1970s suggests that Gairy might have survived had he maintained a solid base in the security forces. The 300-member Grenada Defence Force was ill equipped, untrained and underpaid and had at best a tenuous commitment to the Gairy government (Jacobs and Jacobs 1980: 124–5). It is not surprising, then, that in March 1979, a mere forty-six members of the New Jewel Movement were able to defeat the army in less than twelve hours with the loss of only three lives. With massive support from the people, the rest of the security forces were then quickly disabled.

Due to the small size of Grenada, we will hazard only a few generalizations, which can be corroborated with comparative evidence. First, the cases of Grenada and Argentina underline the importance of the ideology of the initial mobilizing agents of the labor movement for the fate of democracy in the country. Second, the contrast between Burnham's success in Guyana and the failure of Gairy to institute stable authoritarian rule demonstrates the importance of strong and politically loyal security forces for such attempts.

Conclusion

Summary

As our theoretical framework suggests and our analyses in the last two chapters bore out, the crucial dimensions for explaining the emergence of democracy and authoritarianism are the balance of class power, the nature of the state, and the impact of transnational structures of power. In order for democracy to be established and consolidated, a certain degree of power balance within civil society and between civil society and the state needs to prevail. Pressures from subordinate classes have to be strong enough to make demands for their inclusion credible, and threat perception on the part of elites has to be moderated to induce them to accept such inclusion. The state has to have autonomy from dominant classes, but cannot be autonomous from civil society as a whole. Transnational structures of power should not support the aggrandizement of the coercive apparatus of the state and the strengthening of the autonomy of the state from civil society, nor, of course, should they generate interventions which undermine democratically elected governments.

The Central American cases, except for Costa Rica, have not developed such constellations. The lack of consolidated mass-based unions and political parties capable of countering economic elite and military interests is attributable to the systematic stifling of such organization since the 1930s by landowner–state alliances, or by largely autonomous militaries, or by a combination of these and direct foreign intervention. An understanding of the role of US intervention is crucial for these cases. In Nicaragua, the Dominican Republic, and Honduras US direct intervention in the first third of this century laid the groundwork for rule by elites based on control over coercive institutions. In these countries and El Salvador and Guatemala as well, large military assistance programs in the 1950s and 1960s reinforced tendencies towards increasingly autonomous political action of military institutions, from subordinate classes and from civil society as a whole. In Guatemala and the Dominican Republic renewed direct US intervention eclipsed popular movements and thus a crucial ingredient for the emergence of democratic rule.[48] Large landowners dependent on cheap labor are still important segments of the elite in El Salvador and Guatemala, and they feel acutely threatened by the potential implications of political inclusion of the lower classes in the form of land and tax reforms.

Caribbean and Costa Rican exceptionalism can similarly be explained by a combination of socioeconomic structural and political factors. In Costa Rica, the original settlement pattern had led to the formation of a quite prosperous agrarian middle class of family farmers. Despite a process of land concentration and emergence of a landless rural population in the nineteenth and twentieth century, the persistence of this middle class and its urban counterpart constituted a counterweight to the large landowners, sharing in the control of the state. Thus, at the critical juncture of the 1930s, unions and political parties were allowed to grow and contribute further to a power constellation favorable for democracy. Political events in 1948 reinforced the process of consolidation of democracy in so far as the winner of the civil war proceeded to dismantle the military. Elites gradually learned to accommodate to democratic rule and to work through political parties to protect their interests. Their vital interests were never threatened by an electorally strong radical mass party. Most crucially, there were no attempts at significant land reform.

In the English-speaking Caribbean the political conditions were decisive in so far as the local planter class did not control the state apparatus when popular organizations began to emerge on a large scale. By the time of independence, parties and unions were well consolidated. Even though significant parts of the economic elites opposed independence, they had already developed ways to work through the political parties to protect their interests. In the end, even those parties which had adopted a Fabian socialist position, once in office, pursued essentially dependent capitalist development models along with some reformist social policies. Moreover, there was no large coercive apparatus that could have been enlisted by the elites to repress these organizations, nor were the parties who controlled the government willing to build up such an apparatus. Arguably, this became important for the survival of Jamaican democracy when the PNP's departure from the pattern of dependent capitalist development in the 1970s caused economic elites to perceive a very significant threat to their interests. A massive opposition propaganda campaign managed to undermine the PNP's support base and to turn the security forces against the party (Stephens and Stephens 1986: 229–49), but the PNP survived the 1980 election defeat intact and there was no attempt to suppress it.

Guyana deviates from the West Indian pattern not merely because of the fact that it is deeply divided along ethnic lines, but because to the particular articulation of this ethnic division in the political economy of the country. Moreover, the PPP was much more radical than any other of the governing parties in the British West Indies. Accordingly, the economic elites first supported the suspension of the constitution in 1953 and then the change to a system of proportional representation in 1964, designed to prevent the PPP from continuing to hold governmental power. In 1953 this meant direct support for an authoritarian solution; in 1964 it meant an indirect contribution to the breakdown of democracy, which ironically was to turn out highly undesirable for the upper classes. The geo-political concerns of core capitalist countries also played a critical role in the development of authoritarianism in Guyana, as they did in Central America. In 1953 the British authorities intervened directly, and in 1964 British and US pressures heavily reinforced pressures from domestic elites and the PNC. The lower classes were organized, but they were split along ethnic lines. In the final analysis, it was a temporary coalition of the PNC, based in the African urban lower and middle classes and in the state apparatus, with the domestic upper classes and US and British governments that put the country on the road to authoritarian rule. Like in Central America, it was the development of a large coercive apparatus that sustained the regime once it was in power. The collapse of the Gairy regime in Grenada serves to underline the importance of this factor.

Reflections

It will hardly come as a revelation to Latin Americanists and Caribbeanists that the evidence presented here obviously leads to a categorical rejection of Huntington's (1984) rather bizarre suggestion that augmenting US military power would brighten prospects for democracy in the Third World. But neither does our evidence wholeheartedly support certain variants of dependency theory which see dependency as uniformly negative for democracy because they assume that transnational corporations and core capitalist powers are invariably hostile to democratization in the third world, a posture which is motivated by their economic interests. Despite economic and political hyperdependency, democratic regimes emerged in the English-speaking Caribbean countries.

The inadequacy of the economically deterministic dependency view is clearest in the case of the decolonization of the British West Indies. Politics in the core are not monolithic. The posture of Britain towards her colonies was progressively altered, we have argued, by the changing balance of class power in Britain and the rest of the core and changes in the power balance in the international state system. The politics of the incumbents matter: there were differences between Labour and the Conservatives on colonial policy, and it is no accident that one of the very few positive acts made by the United States, the support for fair elections in the Dominican Republic, came during the Carter administration. Moreover, the United States did encourage the decolonization process, at least up to the advent of the Cold War.

None the less, the role of the United States has been overwhelmingly negative in its "backyard." What one may question about the dependency view is to what extent US actions have been determined by immediate economic interests of American corporations. There is a lot of merit to this contention for the pre-World War II period, when a number of the US interventions could be directly linked to the defense of specific US corporate interests. Moreover, defense of the Canal Zone and actions aimed at limiting the influence of European powers in the area cannot be unambiguously labeled "geo-political" rather than "economic," since part of the aim was to establish and defend US economic hegemony in the area. On the other hand, in the post-war period, one could argue that the Cold War has led to the primacy of geo-political considerations in US foreign policy making.

There can be little doubt, on the one hand, that it would be hard to link many of the post-World War II US interventions to the defense of specific US capitalists' investments and other interests in the region and, on the other hand, that the danger of "communist takeover" has virtually always been invoked to justify US intervention. With the single exception of Costa Rica, the US interventions against "communists" involved supporting anti-democratic forces. However, there are two weaknesses in the arguments that so radically delink US geo-political and economic interests. First, they focus far too much on specific US investment in a given country or region and completely neglect the general interest of US capital in keeping in power Third World governments which do not challenge US economic interests. Second, they frequently take at face value State Department claims that US "security" interests were at stake. One must at least ask the question what role "communism" played as opposed to radical social transformation. In many of the cases where the United States intervened to help end democracy, the marxist-leninist forces were almost without influence. Even where they were influential, they were not in a position to be a danger to democracy, assuming that had been on their agenda. Despite the claims of the US State Department, the academic evidence overwhelmingly demonstrates that US security interests were not threatened.

How, then, does one explain the pattern of frequent US interventions against leftist governments in the absence of an objective threat to security interests? We suggest that the answer lies in the "dominant ideology" of the United States which is overwhelmingly influenced by capitalist interests, given the weakness of US labor and the absence of a social democratic party. This is not to suggest the existence of a seamless and monolithic dominant ideology, but rather that the center of gravity of the political debate on Third World affairs in the United States as compared to, say, Sweden has something to do with the balance of class forces in society. What might be generally recognized as a Cold War conception of Third World politics, which equates even aggressive but constitutional reformism with communism, is very strong in the United States and it has had the effect of legitimizing successive interventions in the Third World as defenses of democracy and US security. Yet, the primary objective effect of these interventions taken as a totality was to make the countries in question safe for capitalism, even if no specific US capitalist interests were threatened in a given country.

This discussion brings another point to the fore which was also highlighted by our discussion of consolidation of democracy in South America: in any given set of international and domestic power relations, there are limits to democracy, as it appears to have been incompatible with radical social reform. Like in South America, all of the surviving democracies in the Caribbean and Central America abandoned any schemes of radical reform they might have had; for example, Figueres in Costa Rica, the PNP in Jamaica in the early 1950s, and the PRD in the Dominican Republic between 1965 and 1978. The few governments which attempted such transformations provoked reactions which ended democracy. Attacks on private property, such as land reform schemes, provoked vigorous reactions not only from local upper classes but also from the United States, which tended to equate such attacks with communism, as exemplified by Arbenz in Guatemala. Even in Jamaica in the 1970s, when democracy survived the reactions of the local upper-classes and the United States to the PNP's reform schemes, the anticipation of reaction from those two sources certainly limited what the PNP even tried to do. The PNP's moderation in the 1990s similarly has to be seen as a reaction to the experience of the disruptive power of these forces, in addition to the inescapable constraints of IMF programs.

Our analysis supports the contention central to our framework that the state cannot be reduced to a mere reflection of power relations in civil society (see also Evans et al. 1985). Not only can the state act autonomously of civil society, it can profoundly shape it. In South America and Mexico we saw how attempts by the state to incorporate the emerging labor movement into state-sponsored organizations undercut the political articulation of the working class, and how state attempts to regulate unionization managed to weaken the labor movements' organizational capacity. In this chapter we encountered two forms of state autonomy from and state impact on civil society; the autonomy and impact of the colonial state in the British Caribbean, and the autonomy and impact of the sovereign state sustained by external support for the coercive apparatus in Central America. The colonial state, by allowing the formation of organizations of subordinate classes, contributed to a strengthening of civil society and a shift in the balance of class power which was favorable for democratization. The dictatorial states in Central America did the opposite in that they used their coercive capacity to partially suppress the development of civil society, particularly the organization of the rural and urban lower classes.

This is not to say that the expansion of civil society which accompanies socioeconomic development can be completely suppressed. Urbanism, factory production, literacy, and education bring with them not only the informal relationships of civil society that are almost impossible to suppress, but also quasi-formal organizations in the workplace and community, which have proved highly resilient to repression. This is clearest in the most developed of the dictatorial regimes of the 1970s and 1980s, those in the Southern Cone of Latin America and in southern Europe, where counter-regime institutions like unions managed to re-establish themselves even in the most repressive regimes such as Chile. It seems very plausible to hypothesize that repression is more effective in retarding the growth of civil society at the level of development of Central America in the 1930s than at higher levels of development.

However, as the example of El Salvador demonstrates, it is possible for the state to sustain repression of the political articulation of a strengthened civil society by force for long periods of time, if external support keeps the state apparatus strong. Support from a significant part of the economic elites for such repression, as is present in El Salvador, further facilitates its maintenance, but such support is not indispensable. Strong external support over long periods of time can lead to a situation where the coercive forces develop a high degree of autonomy from economically dominant as well as from subordinate classes and impose their rule on all of civil society. The Central American countries have moved far in this direction, which can be explained by their hyperdependence on the United States. Though this might in part be considered a product of the close proximity of these countries to a great power, the examples of South Korea and Taiwan, with very strong and autonomous states whose origins lie in the periods of massive US aid dispensed in the 1950s, demonstrate that powerful geo-political influences on state–society relations can occur in the absence of geographic proximity.

Transnational structures of power, then, emerged as even more important for the political outcomes in Central America and the Caribbean than in South America. The presence of foreign political domination or foreign intervention at critical junctures left historical legacies which shaped political regime forms for decades after the withdrawal of the foreign forces. In the Caribbean the

British presence in the 1930s provided a protective umbrella for the emergence of pro-democratic forces which then survived decolonization. In Nicaragua and the Dominican Republic, US occupying forces built coercive institutions which became the bases for dictators to establish their highly personalistic regimes after the withdrawal of US troops. In Guatemala the US-sponsored overthrow of Arbenz and subsequent military aid nipped emerging democratic forces in the bud and supported the growth of an autonomous coercive apparatus which would perpetuate repression and authoritarianism.

The importance of transnational structures of power is by no means restricted to their effects in the form of historical legacies, however. In the 1980s US direct involvement in Central America and the Caribbean remained as intense as ever. Contrary to US rhetoric, this involvement was more detrimental to than supportive of democracy in the longer run in so far as it helped to weaken unions and political parties articulating the interests of the middle and lower classes, and thus crucial elements of a pro-democratic balance of forces. Support for the military in El Salvador, with its well-known links to death squads devoted to systematically killing off the leadership of popular organizations, provides the clearest illustration of these negative effects. To reiterate the general point emerging from our analysis of US hegemonic domination, confirming the statistical results, it has operated, both historically and contemporaneously, through local coercive forces and against popular movements and political organizations, and consequently it has influenced the local balance of forces in a direction unfavorable for democracy.

Among the transnational structures of power shaping civil society and thus indirectly political outcomes in Central and South America figures the Catholic church. Its presence and therefore political influence varied greatly among the different countries, but to the extent that it had a significant presence, the direction of its influence changed. Up to the 1960s, its influence was for the most part anti-democratic in that it discouraged popular political organization and legitimized the hierarchical social order and authoritarian regimes. After Vatican II and the 1968 Medellín Bishops' Conference, however, the "preferential option for the poor" led important sectors of the church to promote the organization of christian base communities among the urban and rural lower classes. Experience with self-organization and confrontation of common problems, in turn, led to greater political involvement among the lower classes, thus adding stronger political articulation to a strengthened civil society. This helped pro-democratic forces, for instance, to widen the political space opened by bureaucratic–authoritarian regimes in South America, or to challenge the traditional repressive personalistic or military regimes in Central America.

To return to the theme of alternative theoretical explanations for the findings of cross-national statistical studies introduced in chapter 2, we have argued that the relationship between socioeconomic development and democracy can be better explained in a political economy than in a functionalist theoretical framework. In the subsequent analysis, much additional evidence was mustered supporting the political economy explanation. Likewise in chapter 5, we argued that the cross-national analyses had misinterpreted the correlation between Protestantism and democracy, and we provided an alternative interpretation.

We have also presented some evidence here on two other factors which have been shown to be consistently correlated with political democracy, the British colonial experience and the absence of ethnic diversity.

As we saw, the dominant themes in the literature on the prodemocratic effects of British colonialism are the role of "indirect rule," which supposedly tutored the indigenous elites in the exercise of power and left them better prepared for independence, and the transfer of appropriate institutions for democratic rule after independence. We did see that the transfer of British representative institutions made a contribution to the emergence of democracy in the settler colonies. Whatever the merits of the argument about "indirect rule" and "tutoring" for other areas of the Third World, which we shall consider shortly, it is almost completely irrelevant for the Caribbean. Crown colony rule was direct not indirect, and to the extent that local elites were influential in the political systems (crown colony or otherwise), it was only the plantocracy (at least up to World War I). The planters could hardly be described as indigenous and moreover they played little role in politics during the process of decolonization or the first years of independence. The experience of the Caribbean indicates that the main contribution of the British to democracy was to concede reforms when local pressures were great enough to make it a choice between reform or escalation of disorder in the colony. By the interwar period, the break of the colonial administration on planter–upper-class repression was sufficient that it allowed for the growth of middle-class associations and union organization (that is, the formal organized segment of civil society), a process which was greatly accelerated by the reforms instituted as a response to the labor rebellion. One can certainly argue that there was an element of political learning in the parliamentary institutions in the post war transition to democratic self-government, but a comparative perspective suggests that the growth of civil society and the lack of a significant coercive apparatus were the greater contributions to democracy.

It is important to qualify any statement about a positive contribution of the British at the outset. The alternative presented by history to Third World peoples was not colonialism or autonomous development but rather British colonialism or some other colonialism (including the special case of Spanish colonialism, which in Latin America resulted in the early transfer of power to local elites). In the case of the West Indies, the British were responsible for extermination or marginalization of the indigenous populations, creation of a plantation system, and the enslavement of Africans and their relocation to the Caribbean plantations. To attribute a positive contribution to West Indian democracy to British colonialism is, at best, an ironic twist to the end of a sordid history. Moreover, given the role of the Fabian Bureau and the post-war Labour government in the decolonization process, it should be observed that the British who made the positive contribution were not the same British who installed the colonial regimes.

Nevertheless, it is accurate to say that British colonial rule did have a favorable impact on the development of democratic forces if compared to a situation where a landlord–military coalition controlled the state apparatus.[49] In the British Caribbean, unions, middle-class organizations, and political parties were allowed to form and consolidate their organization. Thus, when independence transferred political power to local actors, the state of development of civil society and of the party system was favorable for the consolidation of democracy. What is important to note, though, is that colonial rule in these cases simply allowed civil society and the party system to develop out of local conditions. Where local conditions were not favorable for the maintenance of democracy, such as in Guyana due to the ethnic and class/state configuration and the dominance of the radical PPP in the early nationalist movement, colonialism did not bequeath viable democratic institutions. On the contrary, the fear of radical reforms led the colonial authorities to join forces with the local upper classes and US interests to weaken the party and thus to lay the groundwork for the erosion of democracy. The fact that colonial authorities could by no means impose democratic institutions capable of being consolidated on local conditions which did not contain the power balance favorable for democracy, becomes plainly obvious in the case of Britain's African colonies (see Diamond et al. 1989a).

This point merits some further discussion because it puts the argument about the beneficial effects of British colonialism in proper perspective. There are two main weaknesses in the recent literature on colonialism and democracy, namely the lack of systematic comparison of British to other colonialisms, and the explanation of variation within British colonialism with length of colonization. British colonialism is credited with having established bureaucratic structures, the rule of law, and representative institutions, which appropriately socialized elites into democratic values. However, Gann and Duignan (1967: 320–5) make it clear that French colonialism was in many ways similar to British colonialism in so far as the creation of the rule of law and of representative institutions was concerned. Where they differed was in the participation of local elites in executive power and in the treatment of independence as a political option; the French denied any such participation to local forces and they resisted a movement towards separation and independence for a longer period of time, insisting instead on assimilation of the overseas territories into the French Republic. Smith (1978: 73) explains this difference with the fact that the British had developed a model for a process of constitutional decolonization in dealing with their white dominions, which later could be applied to India and other colonies of Third World peoples, once movements in those countries forced the British to do so.

Diamond (1989a: 8–9) supports the view that French was similar to British colonialism in fostering local participation. He attributes the relative strength of democracy in Senegal to the long tradition of political competition under French colonial rule and the existence of an elite experienced in political organizing. British would have to be grouped with French colonialism, then, as Diamond himself does at several points (1989a: 6–10), and contrasted to Belgian and Portuguese colonialism under which no representative institutions were allowed to emerge. Whereas it is true that the latter left a clearly non-democratic, if not anti-democratic, legacy, the question still remains why democracy broke down as well in most of the former French and British colonies in Africa. The explanation based on the comparatively briefer period of colonial rule than in the British West Indies is weak because the relevant period during which representative institutions for mass constituencies functioned was similar in both cases, roughly the last two decades before independence.[50] One might finally want to argue that the longer lasting French resistance to independence meant that the process of decolonization itself was more violent and thus responsible for the subsequent problems of democracy. However, the examples of Algeria and Indo China should not lead one to overlook that in many other French territories decolonization finally came peacefully and swiftly (see e.g. Gann and Duignan 1967: 339–40). Moreover, as Smith argues (1978: 90–4), the degree of conflict during the process of decolonization had much to do with the local social structure, particularly the local power position of the predominant nationalist elite.

The crucial difference between the British West Indian colonies on the one hand and the British and French African colonies on the other hand lies in their respective level of economic development and their social structure. Freedom to organize and the right to participate in politics through representative institutions opened the way for the emergence of vigorous unions and affiliated political parties in the West Indies, which made for the balance of power in civil society and between civil society and the state that we have identified as favorable for the consolidation of democracy. In contrast, the lower level of development in Africa meant that civil society in general and the working-class in particular were weaker. Accordingly, political parties were weaker as they lacked close ties to strong unions or other organizations in civil society. This weakness of civil society and its political articulation facilitated the emergence of a predatory state[51] and attempts by the state elite to dominate civil society and control its political articulation. In fact, state elites in Africa frequently made attempts to form hegemonic parties and sponsor organizations in civil society linked to those parties. Where such attempts were successful and eclipsed the independent political articulation of subordinate classes, they created a double imbalance unfavorable for democracy. Not only did they result in state domination over civil society, but they directly reinforced domination over subordinate classes because the state elites were an integral part of the dominant class (see e.g. Sklar 1979).

The functionalist view of why ethnic divisions contribute to the development of authoritarianism is that they undermine social integration and societal consensus. The Guyanese case demonstrates that this perspective is not without its merits, but it is hardly the whole story. Nor is the hypothesis that democracy is compatible with oppression of ethnic minorities by majorities (e.g. the United States and northern Ireland) but not vice versa (South Africa). The Guyanese case (and the contrast to Trinidad) argues that one must examine the entire interrelationship between ethnic divisions and the class structure and the state to understand the political consequences of the ethnic divide.

As in the last chapter, this chapter's study of the process of democratization in the West Indies underlines the importance of analyzing historical sequences in determining the political outcomes. The state passed into local control well after strong unions and political parties had been built and after a number of elections with universal suffrage had been held. Had the plantocracy had full control of the means of coercion at the time of the labor rebellions of the 1930s, repression not concession would have been the response and the West Indies might have followed the trajectory of Central America.

7

Conclusions and Reflections

In general, the three comparative historical studies demonstrated the utility of the theoretical framework for the study of the development of democracy laid out in chapter 2. Building on this theoretical framework, we arrived at explanatory accounts of processes of democratization, of the comparative incidence of democratic and non-democratic regimes, and of breakdowns and rollbacks of democracy. At the same time, our empirical analyses introduced a number of complexities and qualifications to the framework and raised questions which we were unable to answer in the context of this study.

In our concluding comments, we will briefly outline the major findings that have implications for the theoretical framework including a number of qualifications and open questions. We will also explore how our analysis might be extended in a number of directions. Our theoretical conclusions contain some clear implications for the chances of democratic stability in Latin America (including Central America). They also suggest interpretations of developments in some countries not covered in the comparative historical analyses. And finally, we address the dilemma that stabilization of formal democracy appears to require serious restrictions on substantive democracy because of the need for protection of elite interests, and we take up the question of the prospects and possibilities of advancing democracy substantively in countries where formal democratic institutions have been established.

Theoretical Assessment

Theoretical arguments supported

Our studies confirmed the importance of the three clusters of power – of class power, state power, and transnational structures of power – for the development (and demise) of democracy in the process of capitalist development. These three factors combined and interacted in varying ways and varying sequences to determine political developments. The patterns found in each of the three regions under study were quite different; but these differences were understandable in the context of the theoretical framework.

The centrality of class power to the process of democratization was repeatedly confirmed in the comparative studies, and the classes aligned themselves for the greater part in the manner laid out in chapter 3. The organized working class appeared as a key actor in the development of full democracy almost everywhere, the only exception being the few cases of agrarian democracy in some of the small-holding countries. In most cases, organized workers played an important role in the development of restricted democracy as well. The Latin American cases bear out the expectations generated by the theoretical framework precisely because the working class played a lesser role in the historical events there: the relative weakness of the working class certainly has contributed to the infrequence of full democracy in the region and to the instability of democracy where it did emerge.

How the working class affected events was highly variable. This gave weight to our conception of a *social construction of class interests*. Even in Europe, where the main effect of working-class organization came in the form of the parties of the Second International and affiliated unions, it also expressed itself through independent artisanal agitation, delayed responses to defeated movements, and pressure from the working-class wings of confessional and liberal parties. In the West Indies, working-class pressure expressed itself first in the form of the labor rebellions of the 1930s which led the colonial authorities to introduce some measure of self-government, and then in the form of unions and multi-class parties. In Latin America, unions and parties of varying ideological persuasions and with at least some base in the working class were essential parts of alliances which introduced full democracy. In all regions, however, pressure from the organized working class alone was insufficient to bring about the introduction of democracy; the working-class needed allies.

Large landlords, particularly those who depended on a large supply of cheap labor, consistently emerged as the most anti-democratic force in the comparative studies. If an economically significant class of labor-dependent landlords had control or, at least, very significant influence on the state in a given period, the state resisted demands for the expansion of democratic rights. When on-going capitalist development, often in conjunction with immediate political or economic crises, stimulated a surge in the demands of the masses for political inclusion and/or economic amelioration, the state responded – immediately or at a later point, when the crisis had subsided – with political exclusion and repression. This key element of Moore's pioneering study bore the test of repeated examination across the countries studied in the preceding chapters. Democracy could only be established if (1) landlords were an insignificant force, or (2) they were not dependent on a large supply of cheap labor, or (3) they did not control the state. The fact that labor intensive agriculture remained a crucial export activity and large landlords a significant sector of the economic elites in South and Central America well into the second half of the twentieth century explains much about the severe obstacles to democratization in these areas.

The orthodox marxist and liberal social science view of the role of the bourgeoisie as the primary agent of democracy did not stand up under scrutiny. Though clearly not as anti-democratic as landlords, capitalists and the parties they primarily supported rarely if ever pressed for the introduction of full democracy. Beyond this, the only generalization that can be made about the posture of the bourgeoisie toward democratic reforms is that it varied from case to case and from time period to time period depending on the alliance options open to them as well as on ideological legacies of the past. In most countries, the bourgeoisie supported the opening up of contestation and the introduction of parliamentary government which, in turn, often allowed civil society to develop and opened the way for inclusion of the middle classes and later the working class. However, this was not always the case. For example, the bourgeoisies of Germany, Sweden, and Denmark supported early liberal reforms, but they opposed the call for full parliamentary government when the growth of socialist organization in the working class threatened to bring a measure of political power to the socialists were parliamentary government introduced. In Latin America, the bourgeoisies often supported the termination of parliamentary government and the ending of civil liberties by military coups, despite the fact that the resulting military dictatorships frequently deprived the bourgeoisie itself of direct access to the state.

Yet, in contrast to labor-dependent landed upper classes, our comparative analyses uncovered cases in which the bourgeoisie did support a political arrangement which entailed significant extensions of suffrage to the lower classes. Nineteenth-century suffrage reforms in Switzerland, Britain, and France and the Venezuelan pact of 1958 spring to mind as examples. It is important to note that in these cases the threat posed by the working class was small owing to the absence of socialist organization in the class or to the arrangements of the political pact. In England, successive reforms came only after the suffrage demands of the Chartists had been safely subdued a generation earlier. A much more frequent contribution of the bourgeoisie to democracy has been to accommodate to it and even support it once it is established. Yet, this is hardly a universal response: all three of our comparative studies were riddled with examples of bourgeoisies supporting the termination of democratic regimes once new conditions increased their motivation to do so or presented them with allies in such a project.

The contrasting posture of the landed upper class and the working class contains the core of our argument of why capitalist development and democracy are related: capitalist development weakens the landed upper class and strengthens the working class as well as other subordinate classes. The respective positions of the bourgeoisie and the working class show that capitalism creates democratic pressures in spite of capitalists, not because of them. Democracy was the outcome of the contradictory nature of capitalist development, which, of necessity, created subordinate classes, particularly the working class, with the capacity for self-organization. Capitalism brings the subordinate class or classes together in factories and cities where members of those classes can associate and organize more easily; it improves the means of communication and transportation facilitating nationwide organization; in these and other ways it strengthens civil society and facilitates subordinate class organization. Though the working class has not proved to be the gravedigger of capitalism, it has very frequently been capable of successfully demanding its own political incorporation and an accommodation of at least some of its substantive interests. No other subordinate class in history has been able to do so on anywhere near the same scale. As Przeworski (1985, 1988) has frequently argued, democratic capitalism rests on a class compromise between labor and capital in which the interests of both sides are to varying extents accommodated.

Capitalist development and democracy are related primarily through these changes in the balance of class power. Yet our analyses also demonstrated that the level of democratic development can not be simply read off from the level of capitalist development. In part, this was due to the variability of the structure of class relations at a given level of capitalist development. We have just mentioned the structure of agrarian class relations as one such source of variability. The interrelations between dominant classes and the state are another. The timing of development and the type of integration into the world economy also greatly affected the structure of the economy and the class structure. This was most dramatically illustrated by the contrast between the advanced capitalist countries and the dependent countries of the Third World, but it was also a key source of early variation among the Latin American cases, as the nature of the export economy significantly affected their subsequent political development. In the West Indies, the extremely polarized nature of the Guyanese class structure, which was linked to the demands of sugar production in a geographic setting where irrigation was a necessity, was one root of the authoritarian direction of that country.

The comparative studies showed that the key source of variability across countries at a given level of development was the posture of the middle classes. Indeed, it can be said that, since the working class nowhere was strong enough to push through democracy alone, the middle classes assumed a pivotal role in the development of democracy. However, their role was ambiguous; it varied due to different relations to the dominant classes as well as due to variations in the middle classes' own interests. Moreover, owing to their intermediate position in the class structure and their internal heterogeneity, the interests of the middle classes were subject to a greater variety of social interpretation and construction. For this reason, even the urban middle classes were much more likely to come under the influence of dominant classes, sometimes supporting political movements which opposed their objective interests, by almost any interpretation of what those interests were.

The influence of the dominant classes on the politics of rural middle classes, poor peasants, and the agricultural proletariat was, in general, even greater than in the case of the urban middle classes. Where an alliance between the dominant classes, the state and an established church was formed, this church became an effective conduit for dominant class hegemony particularly over the rural middle and lower classes. Though peasants and rural workers shared an interest in democracy with the urban proletariat, they acted much less frequently in support of it, in part, because they followed the lead of large landlords and in part because they had much greater difficulty organizing themselves. However, to assert that the rural lower and middle classes were always backward, always on the receiving end of history, or always manipulated by other actors is a distortion of history. Our comparative studies demonstrated that in predominantly small-holding countries (e.g. the small European countries, the North and West of the United States, Canada, and New Zealand), family farmers, and in some cases poor peasants, acted as an independent, usually self-organized force and largely in favor of democracy. In the Caribbean, Central America, and some countries in Latin America (e. g. Peru), the plantation proletariat did organize also and usually weighed in as a democratic force.

This returns us once again to a point argued insistently in chapter 2: class interests are socially constructed. Though the variations in the class structure mentioned above go further in explaining cross-national differences than is admitted by culturalist and purely historicist interpretations, the differences can hardly be reduced to them. At any given historical conjuncture, a range of ideologies and political postures are objectively compatible with the interests of a class, given various time horizons, levels of risk aversion, and the need to choose between different, not fully compatible goals (consumption, power, leisure, participation, etc.) of various members of the class. Furthermore, nothing guarantees that many members of a given class will not choose a posture incompatible with most outside observers' interpretation of their objective interest. Indeed, our case studies were replete with examples of social groups who must have been very disappointed in the political movements they supported, the most recent example being the support of the middle classes in the southern Cone for the installation of bureaucratic authoritarian regimes in that region.[1] This suggests that a huge range of ideological and political orientations might be found in a given class in a given country; yet, empirically this is not the case. Ideologies inherited from past political and social organization of classes are a prime source of narrowing this range of variation. This persistence of political and ideological positions once they are embodied in organizational structures appeared repeatedly in our analyses: it was impossible to understand the posture of the German middle classes in the interwar period without reference to the political struggles and alliances of Imperial Germany; the legacy of Peronism was essential for the understanding of the political posture of the Argentine working-class and the agony of democracy in that country.

Discussing the posture of class forces one at a time, as we have done so far in this review, tends to obscure a point that was anticipated in our theoretical framework and that emerged as as dominant feature in all our comparative studies: the posture of one class can never be understood in isolation from that of all other classes, states and international actors in the historical situation. A few of the most clear-cut cases can be cited to underline this point: in Latin America, the posture of the middle classes toward full democracy was heavily conditioned by whether they could ally with segments of the upper-classes to effect their own inclusion. If they could not, and if a significant working class was present, they turned to an alliance with the working class and thus supported greater extension of suffrage. In Europe, the difference in the position of the German bourgeoisie and its Swedish counterpart was not a matter of subjective preference, but rather a matter of the different alliance options available to German and Swedish capitalists. In the 1930s in the Caribbean and Central America, planters everywhere favored harsh reactions to the labor uprising, but they had different alliance options with the state and in the international system, which led to different outcomes in the two areas.

Our studies also vindicated our interpretation of the effect of the growth of civil society on democracy as outlined in chapter 3 (see pp. 49–50). We agreed with modernization theory and pluralism on the positive effect of social mobilization and the development of formally autonomous social organizations and groups on democracy. They counterbalance the power concentrated in the modern state. However, we argued that the political effect of the growth of civil society can only be understood in connection with its articulation with the structure of class power. This proved to be a fruitful perspective that was theoretically detailed in the comparative historical studies in a number of ways. Several reminders should suffice here.

First, the growth of autonomous organizations in the subordinate classes, even when they are not initially political, can lead, and often does lead, to the development of a counter-hegemonic culture and more explicitly political organization, which begin to change the balance of class power in society. This can be most clearly seen in the pattern of relatively gradual transition to democracy through shifting class power, with the Scandinavian countries, the West Indies, and Costa Rica being ideal typical in this regard.

Second, under certain social conditions – generally where powerful and cohesive upper classes exist and form a strong alliance with the state – the organizations of civil society, or at least parts of it, may serve as conduits of authoritarian ideologies of the upper classes, thus weakening democracy. The most striking cases of this reactionary hegemony over the middle classes were Germany and Austria, which succumbed to authoritarian rule at high levels of socioeconomic development; but the generally conservative posture of the Brazilian middle classes and their support for the installation of the bureaucratic authoritarian regime make for another illustrative case. It is here where our analysis clearly proved superior to the pluralist analysis of secondary groups which ignores the class content of these organizations.

Finally, a strong hegemony of conservative (rather than reactionary) upper-classes can actually strengthen formal democracy as it can serve to defend the interests of the upper classes within the system and to keep the substantive demands of the lower classes off the immediate political agenda.[2] This is one of the primary reasons for the positive contribution of the existence of a strong party of the right for the survival of democracy, which proved important in a number of our Latin American cases, but also can be seen as one factor in the gradual and stable nature of suffrage extension in Britain.

To readers familiar with the social science literature on the social preconditions for democratic government, our treatment of culture may be striking as it denies the prominent role culture is given in the analyses of modernization theory.[3] Culture enters our analysis primarily as ideologies (in the broadest sense, that is, worldviews and value systems) of specific classes, including legacies of past alignments.[4] Our theoretical formulation of the social construction of class interests and application of this concept to the historical material covers much of what might appear as culture in structural functional analysis. Thus, culture is considered in its articulation with class interests in the same way that civil society was. Democratic cultures are largely a product of present and past structures of power in society which favor(ed) democracy. Thus, it was relevant for our analysis whether the culture, or ideological balance as we would designate it, in society favored democracy. In our analysis of Germany and Austria, we made this point very explicit; it was implicit in many other cases.

Aside from relating cultural phenomena systematically to class relations, we focused our attention more generally on those ideas, values, and symbols that are *organizationally and institutionally embedded*. This strategy proved fruitful in regard to religion. Our analysis indicates that it is the social organization of religion and its relation to classes and the state rather than its doctrinal content that was pivotal, though there is some relation between the two. Building on Lipset and Rokkan's (1967) work, we contended that sectarian Protestantism (but not Lutheranism) encouraged democracy because it strengthened civil society and tended to insulate its members from ruling-class hegemony. Dissenting religions in all countries in which they were strong were breeding grounds for popular democratic movements. By contrast, state churches, Catholic or Lutheran (and the parties supported by them), were conduits for ruling-class ideologies. However, in Latin America the post-Medellín "popular (Catholic) church" performed the same function of strengthening civil society through the organization of Christian base communities. In Europe churches that stood in opposition to ruling state–class alliances generally produced parties that were democratic forces. Again, our comparative analysis yielded a different interpretation of the statistical results found in cross-national quantitative analyses than those provided by the authors of those studies. By extending the Lipset–Rokkan analysis, we argued that the historic choices of state builders vis-à-vis religious institutions had a significant impact on the pattern of democratization, a clearly "Tocquevillian" effect of state–church alliances.

The state itself did play the essential role in shaping the chances for installation and consolidation of democracy that our initial framework attributed to it. In contrast to the relative consistency of class behavior, there is more systematic variation across regions in the role of the state. The same is true for the impact of transnational structures of power. Moreover, it is the interaction between these two factors and classes which helps explain the systematic differences in class alliances that can be observed across regions. Therefore, a discussion of the role of the state and transnational structures of power involves a review of variation across regions.

Consolidation of state power in the sense of the establishment of a monopoly on organized force was a fundamental prerequisite for the establishment of institutionalized contestation among elites or among elites and wider groups. We observed variation both across our regions and within regions in the timing of consolidation of state power and in the importance of the state as an anti-democratic force. We picked up the story of advanced capitalist societies at a point where states were consolidated already in virtually all cases. Significantly, it was in two of the breakdown cases, Germany and Italy, where consolidation of state power was problematic. Though there was a well consolidated core of state power in these cases, the question of the area over which this power was to be exercised remained contested until the second half of the nineteenth century. This meant that significant pressures for democratization emerged before the problem of national unity was resolved. It is this coincidence of problems that distinguishes the two Fascist from the two Catholic corporativist breakdown cases. In Latin America we observed sharper differences between countries, with Chile on one end of the spectrum, where state consolidation and contestation among elites were achieved early, and Venezuela on the other end, where armed struggles persisted until the turn of the century and there was no institutionalized contestation before 1945. On the whole, the process of state consolidation in Latin America was temporally closer to the emergence of pressures for mass incorporation. For the Caribbean states, the achievement of independence came late, but de facto consolidation of (colonial) state power had occurred much earlier. This made mass incorporation possible under colonial auspices. In Central America consolidation of state power has been most difficult. These states were weakened through foreign intervention through the early twentieth century and more recently have come under armed challenge from internal forces. Accordingly, it is not surprising that even institutionalization of contestation has been so difficult.

Establishing a monopoly on organized force required a strengthening of the coercive apparatus of the state, which in turn entailed its own perils for democracy. The coercive apparatus could be and frequently was used by the dominant classes to repress demands from subordinate classes for political inclusion or for material concessions. In the European breakdown cases the state was permeated by authoritarian forces allied with the dominant classes and contributed to the erosion of democracy. This penetration of the state was a direct outcome of the pattern of state-building. In Latin America the state played an overwhelmingly anti-democratic role in so far as its coercive arm was involved in politics both as an independent force and as an instrument used by the dominant classes to keep subordinate classes excluded. The prominent role of the coercive arm of the state in Latin American politics was partly a legacy of the independence and border wars of the nineteenth century, partly a result of the weakness and divisions of the dominant classes, and partly a result of external support.

Anti-democratic state involvement in Latin America took several forms, most prominently restrictions on contestation through repeated direct intervention and rule by the military, and/or systematic stifling of the organizational potential of the subordinate classes, particularly the urban working class, and/or exclusion by force of already organized subordinate classes. In Argentina, Brazil, Peru, and Ecuador, military intervention impaired contestation during the periods of restricted democracy. Civilian as well as military incumbents at times attempted to use the state apparatus to prevent the emergence of labor unions or to undercut any independent political articulation of the urban working class by incorporating it into state-sponsored organizations. The most successful example of such incorporation is the Mexican one under Cárdenas, but similar attempts, with varying success, were made by Vargas in Brazil, Perón in Argentina, Velasco in Peru, and Ibáñez in Chile. The bureaucratic–authoritarian states which emerged in the 1960s and 1970s in Argentina, Brazil, Chile, and Uruguay combined direct military rule with forceful exclusion of previously organized subordinate classes. Given the strength of civil society and its political articulation reached by that point, such exclusion implied the use of large-scale severe repression.

In the Caribbean, the colonial state was clearly non-democratic, but it slowly divested itself of some of its authoritarian powers and allowed for pressures for democratization from below to emerge and push that divestment further. After independence the Caribbean states were comparatively small and weak. Only in Guyana, where Burnham greatly expanded and strengthened the state, did the state come to play an anti-democratic role by bolstering the authoritarian rule of the PNC. In Central America, in contrast, the state has played a heavily anti-democratic role. Traditionally, it served as an instrument of dominant classes, at times in alliance with foreign interests, to repress lower-class challenges. In the post-World War II period the military came to dominate the state and to assume an increasingly autonomous role, supported by external material assistance and training for the coercive forces. Prevention of organization or repression of unions, professional associations, and allied political parties by military-dominated states became the modal pattern. Costa Rica is the exception from the pattern prevailing in Central America that proves the rule: this persistent democracy does not have a strong army.

To reiterate a central point of cross-regional variation in the role of the state, we found in our studies of the historical development of democracy that the degree of state autonomy at the point of the emergence of significant mass pressures for democratization was greatest in the Caribbean and Central America, least in Europe, with South America somewhat closer to the Caribbean and Central America than Europe. Though ultimately the source of this greater autonomy in the Third World countries was economic and political dependence, it developed in quite different ways in the two regions. In the case of the South American bureaucratic-authoritarian regimes, state autonomy resulted from a combination of state expansion due to dependent development, high domestic political conflict between dominant and subordinate classes, and foreign support for the coercive apparatus of the state. Even leaving aside the special case of British colonialism it is clear that direct foreign intervention played a much greater role in the genesis of state autonomy in Central America and the Caribbean.

Transnational power relations – war, the structural effects of economic dependence, and economically and geo-politically conditioned interventions of foreign powers – profoundly affected chances for democratization. The effect of these transnational structures of power on political development varied across the three regions and, to a lesser extent, within the regions. The broad contours of these variations and their causes were consistent with the expectations derived from our theoretical framework and the more subtle differences, though not anticipated, were explainable within the framework. At the most general level, it can be said that the strength of the effect of transnational structure varied with the length of independence of the nation and with the de facto degree of foreign domination, which was primarily a function of colonial history, size and proximity to world powers. Thus, transnational structures of power had the greatest influence on Central America and the Caribbean, the least on Europe, with Latin America and the former British colonies falling in between.

The key factor underpinning these differences was dependence in the world system, which had, in the cases we examined, generally unfavorable effects on the chances for democratic consolidation. As anticipated, the effects of geo-political dependence were more unambiguously negative than the effects of economic dependence. Actions on the part of dominant countries motivated by geo-political or a mixture of geo-political and economic interests, in particular the provision of massive economic and military aid to regimes challenged by leftist forces, or support for the military combined with pressures on incumbent leftist regimes, strengthened the state apparatus and allowed it to assume a high degree of autonomy from dominant as well as subordinate classes. The results were attempts to suppress organization of subordinate classes and imposition of harsh authoritarian rule; examples abound in Central and South America, from the early twentieth century to the Cold War. As expected, the strength of this effect was much greater in Central America than in South America.

The effects of economic dependence on the class structure were unfavorable for democracy in so far as delayed industrialization, based on imported technology, created a smaller urban working class than had emerged at comparable stages of development in the advanced capitalist countries. Also, where the export economy was based mainly on labor intensive agriculture, export-led growth strengthened anti-democratic large landowners. In contrast, export-led growth based on foreign-owned mineral production weakened the economic and political position of these landowners. Moreover, ISI – with or without strong participation of foreign capital – enlarged and strengthened urban groups and relegated large landowners to secondary importance. Foreign capital as a local actor weighed in on the anti-democratic side through opposition to reformist democratic regimes which attempted to mobilize resources for redistributive purposes (e. g. Arbenz in Guatemala, Goulart in Brazil, Allende in Chile). In the longer run, however, a strong presence of foreign capital in urban industrial growth could also strengthen pro-democratic tendencies not only by creating conditions for the organization of the urban working-class, but also by stimulating opposition to bureaucratic–authoritarian governments among the domestic bourgeoisie which in turn helped bring about the political openings that subordinate classes could take advantage of to pressure for democratization. Brazil in the 1970s and 1980s is a case in point.

To say that the non-European cases were more subject to the influences of transnational power is not to imply that European countries escaped the effects of the world political economy. Economic competition and interdependence (rather than dependence)[5] also had a great impact on the patterns of democratization there, even though it cannot be said that interdependence always aided or impeded democratization. The economic growth of the late eighteenth and early nineteenth century was an interdependent process. This is most clear in the case of the Scandinavian periphery, where the initial stimulus to industrialization was foreign demand, above all for wood and wood products. This led to the industrial spurt which created the industrial working class which in turn stimulated labor organization and thus democratization.

On the other hand, international competition is a necessary byproduct of interdependence, and the combination of these two factors meant that internationally transmitted recessions and depressions stimulated protective responses within countries. As we saw in chapter 4, the series of recessions between 1873 and 1896 stimulated political disputes about the level of tariffs and the politics of tariffs which were critically implicated in the coalition formation which subsequently influenced the politics of democratization. Whether the impact of tariff politics was positive or negative varied according to the internal constellation of power in the countries. The Great Depression of the 1930s also had an important impact on the breakdown or survival of democracy, but again its effect dependend on pre-existing domestic alignments.

In contrast to the other aspects of transnational power, war had a greater impact on democracy in Europe than in the other regions studied. Again, however, it did not have uniform effects on the countries. War could usher in democratic rule, but it could also strengthen anti-democratic tendencies. Defeat in war weakened dominant coalitions; where these coalitions were authoritarian, this implied an opening for democracy. Furthermore, mass mobilization for warfare empowered subordinate classes, at least temporarily, and thus strengthened democratic impulses. The impact of World War I on the breakthrough to full democracy in Europe was decisive in Germany, Austria, and Italy, and it accelerated the process in Sweden, Britain, and the Netherlands. On the other hand, involvement in wars could strengthen militaristic sentiment in society and increase the influence of the military in politics, as we saw in Germany, Spain, and Italy.

Still, elsewhere, war did also contribute to the development and demise of democracy. In the United States, soldiers' demands for suffrage rights at the time of the wars against Britain accelerated the broadening of suffrage. Over one hundred years later, the presence of black soldiers in the armed forces during World War II and afterward contributed to the movement which eventually resulted in the extension of suffrage to southern blacks. In Canada, the mass mobilization for World War I was critically implicated in the institution of universal suffrage there. In nineteenth century Latin America, on the other hand, repeated involvement in wars led to a build-up of the military and increased the political weight of the military.

The outcomes of other forms of direct military intervention short of war, and of diplomatic pressures by foreign powers, are also predicated on internal conditions. External imposition of any kind of regime is difficult, and particularly so of democratic rule. Short-term external intervention can tip the balance in favor of democratization only if the internal balance of class power and the state–society constellation are favorable. Long-term consistent pressures and incentives can be more effective in strengthening either authoritarian or democratic tendencies. We saw how US military aid and counterinsurgency doctrine strengthened authoritarian forces in Latin America; an example for the strengthening of democratic forces in cases not covered in our study would be the effects of the European Community's insistence on democratization as a prerequisite for membership of Spain, Greece, and Portugal. We encountered one of the rare situations where short-term external pressure for democracy did make a difference in the Dominican Republic in 1978, when pressures from the Carter administration in the United States induced the military to abstain from halting the vote count.

Colonialism was one historic form of domination by transnational structures of power and it constituted the epitome of non-democratic rule, imposed through a state which was largely autonomous from the civil society it ruled. It is surprising, then, that many authors (see e.g. Diamond 1989a, 1989b; Weiner 1987) have argued that British colonialism made a positive contribution to the development of democracy in its colonies through the transfer of British governmental and representative institutions to those countries and the tutoring of the colonial people in the ways of British goverment. In our case studies, we did find positive effects of British colonialism on the development of democracy but these were very different in the British settler colonies and the Caribbean plantation economies because of the way in which the colonies were integrated into the exploitative arrangements of the British economic empire. One can even see differences among the settler colonies on this dimension. The American colonies, settled during the mercantilist period, were a part of that closed trading system, and, thus, it suited British aims to grant them limited representative government but not self-government. With the industrialization of Britain, there was a growing perception that the greatest benefit for Britain could be derived from free trade, thus, Britain acquiesced to the demands of Canada, Australia, and New Zealand for self-government. In all four cases, the argument that the transfer of British institutions contributed to the democratic outcome does hold: early representative institutions generally specified suffrage rights similar to those prevailing in Britain. However, as we emphasized these resulted in vastly broader suffrage in these countries than they did in Britain owing to the wider distribution of property. Thus, the social structure of these countries determined that they would be much more democratic than Britain was at the same date.

In the Caribbean, by contrast, the British were involved in setting up a slave plantation system. Since direct exploitation of labor in a labor repressive system was an essential feature of the system, broad representative government was impossible. Only the white upper class was included, and "tutored," in British representative institutions. The American South, part of the circum-Caribbean slave plantation system (Beckford 1972), is an interesting combination of the two British colonial states. It combined relatively broad suffrage for whites with labor repression and political exclusion for blacks. It is perhaps not an accident that democracy came to both the British Caribbean and the American south in the 1960s, a time which also follows closely on the end of the profitability of the traditional plantation systems in the two regions. One cannot, of course, underemphasize the role of racism in legitimating the singling out of blacks for exploitation in these systems, and this racist ideology continued to justify treating the colonial subjects in the Caribbean differently from those in the British settler colonies even in the period after slavery. In the perception of the Colonial Office, the black masses were not fit for full citizenship and the colonial educational system, in assuming so, reinforced this perception.

None the less, we did find that the legacy of British colonialism helped explain why the British Caribbean developed in a democratic direction in sharp contrast to Central America. Our explanations differ from those of these other authors in so far as we see the contribution of British colonialism not in the form of "tutelage," that is, respect for the rule of law and experience with representative institutions, but rather in the form of room for the emergence of civil society. In the British Caribbean, colonialism prevented the landed upper class from using the state to repress protests and organizational attempts of subordinate classes, in contrast to the repression exercised by the large landlords in Central America. Colonialism was not able to bequeath democratic institutions where internal conditions were not favorable, though. In the Caribbean, parties and unions were firmly rooted in society at the point of independence, but in Africa they were not, mainly owing to the lower level of development of African countries. Accordingly, democratic regimes could be consolidated in the Caribbean whereas they gave way to the emergence of predatory states in Africa.

A final important note on transnational structures of power relates to the supra-national Catholic church. Here it is useful to contrast the Catholic church to the purely national state churches like the Lutheran church in northern Europe and the Anglican church in England. The latter were exposed to a much greater extent to the imprint of national power relations; indeed, they were largely instruments of the dominant state–class coalitions. Whereas the Catholic church historically was hardly distinguishable from these state churches in its closeness to and instrumentality for local elites, its transnational structure still meant that it had a larger relevant public which at times might lead it to function in a more autonomous way. Before World War I the Catholic church was an uncompromising opponent of liberalism and democracy. After World War II the most important parts of its constituency were citizens of democratic countries and the church adapted to these new conditions by developing close relations to Christian Democratic parties. Still, its dominant tendency remained conservative in the sense of discouraging challenges to class inequality. A significant change in the political orientation and social practice of the church occurred after the Second Vatican Council, and through its promotion of human rights and grass-roots organization in Latin America it made important contributions to democratization.

Revisions of theory, problems of generalization, open questions

The comparative historical studies built on a framework of conceptualizations, assumptions, and fundamental propositions; and they developed and elaborated the conceptions laid out in this framework. But they also led us to modify certain ideas in our original framework, and they introduced new themes. The middle classes turned out to be more central to the political developments in South America than they were in the advanced capitalist societies; working-class strength and ideology showed more complex effects on democracy than originally conceptualized; and the concept of labor repressive agriculture required modification. Yet the theoretically most far-reaching finding concerned political parties. Their role, particularly in moderating the threat perceived by elites to their interests by democratization, emerged as a crucial determinant of democratic consolidation. Finally, our studies also raised a number of questions which we were unable to fully investigate but on which we will offer some speculation.

In South America the working class was too weak to play the leading role in pushing for democratic rule. In effect, this role fell to the middle classes. The main reasons for this were the expansion of urbanization and the state as a result of the growth of the export economy, prior to significant industrialization. Thus, middle-class employees and the urban petty bourgeoisie and professionals could organize themselves into interest groups and political parties to promote their political inclusion, whereas the organizational potential and political weight of the urban working class remained restricted. Though ISI subsequently did enlarge the ranks of the urban industrial working-class and strengthened the labor movement, the transnational flows of technology kept the numerical strength of the working class below the levels reached by its counterparts in the advanced industrial societies. The main results of the greater numerical and organizational weakness of the working class vis-à-vis the middle classes in South America compared to the advanced capitalist societies were more restricted forms of democracy and more instability of democratic regimes. Middle-class commitment to democracy tended to be instrumental and contingent, aimed at their own inclusion and subject to abandonment in the face of militant lower-class pressures for radical reforms which affected the material conditions of middle-class life. As noted earlier, the different role of the working class in South America seems to, but does not really, contradict our basic argument about the effect of class relations on the chances of democracy: the weaker role of the working class in South America corresponds to a weaker and less stable development of democracy.

Working-class strength and ideology also emerged in a somewhat more complex relationship to democracy than we had originally conceptualized. Significant working-class strength was a necessary condition for the installation and consolidation of full democracy, but it was not a sufficient condition. Two factors could pervert the pro-democratic thrust of the presence of a strong working-class, namely the ideology and political practice of the actors originally mobilizing the working class and the weakness of working-class allies. First, where the bulk of the working class was mobilized by leaders like Perón in Argentina or by a dominant party linked to the state like the PRI in Mexico, loyalty to the leader and to the political arrangements which provided concrete benefits in the process of mobilization clearly outweighed pro-democratic commitments among the working-class organizations. The strong opposition of the leadership of the PRI-linked unions to the process of political liberalization in Mexico should serve as a stark reminder of the strength and durability of such loyalties. Second, high organizational strength of the working-class combined with a radical ideology heightened the threat posed by the enfranchisement of the working-class to the dominant classes. Where strong and radical working-class movements found strong allies in their push for democracy among the urban and rural middle classes, they generally managed to overcome the resistance of the dominant classes and effect the installation of democracy. In the advanced capitalist countries successful democratization by such alliances typically softened the radical character of working-class demands, which contributed to the stabilization of democracy. This was the case, for instance, in Sweden and Belgium. In contrast, where a powerful coalition of dominant classes exercised hegemony over large parts of the middle classes and radical working-class movements found only weak allies in their struggle for democracy, the extension of democratic rights to the lower classes tended to be delayed and subject to reversals, as in the European breakdown cases. In South America, where even the strongest working-class/middle-class alliances, those formed in the mineral export economies, were weaker than those in the advanced capitalist countries, they were capable of installing democratic regimes but provoked repressive reactions on the part of the dominant classes, with resulting high initial political instability.

One source of discontinuity between the experience of the advanced capitalist countries and later developers is the international learning process: social actors viewed one another and the institution of democracy differently because of the past experience of advanced capitalist countries. One important example of this is that labor became recognized as a potential power base by opportunistic political leaders: Argentina's Perón, Jamaica's Bustamante, and Grenada's Gairy would be unimaginable without the knowledge that elsewhere organized labor had propelled men into positions of political influence. Or to state it conversely, an opportunistic young politician in late nineteenth-century Europe would have been much less likely to see the nascent labor movement as a vehicle for his political ambitions. This same process of international learning also led the upper classes in late developers to perceive that labor was not necessarily a revolutionary threat, it could be integrated into the system.[6]

The findings of our comparative historical analyses allowed us to accept the more robust of the results of the cross-national statistical studies and provide alternative theoretical interpretations for these results. Our attempts to understand the mechanisms mediating the general relationship between economic development and democracy, as well as the complexities of specific cases, confirmed the importance of adopting a historical perspective. The sequencing of events was important for the installation and consolidation of democracy, as were particular conjunctures. For instance, it mattered whether strong competing parties emerged prior to the growth of the urban working class and thus could integrate these new forces into the political system without the spread of a threat which would have induced economic elites to seek allies in the military to keep the lower classes excluded. The early emergence of strong competing parties made the integration of new forces less problematic in Uruguay and Chile than, say, in Peru or Argentina. Late development of socialist and labor parties in France, Britain, and Switzerland was certainly responsible for the relatively positive posture of the bourgeoisie toward suffrage extension in these countries. We also saw that certain variables had different effects in different stages. For instance, factors which were favorable for the installation of democratic rule, such as the presence of radical mass parties capable of mobilizing working-class/middle-class alliances, were not necessarily favorable for its consolidation.

This striking feature of comparisons across the three regions studied here was anticipated and therefore not surprising. Factors such as dependent development, late and state-led development, international political constellations and events, and international learning, all conspired to create conditions in which the combinations of causes and thus the paths to democracy (and dictatorship) were different in different historical contexts and in different regions. This finding leads us to reject the assumption of cross-national statistical research that there is a homogeneous pattern of causation throughout history. Thus, the similarity of the correlation between development and democracy in different contexts is fortuitous. The pattern is not homogeneous and were one to attempt to statistically model the relationship between capitalist development and democracy, including the intervening variables (which would be essential to distinguish our theoretical explanation from that of modernization theory), one would have to develop regionally and historically specific models to test competing theories, which would be an absurdity given the number of cases. In our view, the only underlying homogeneity is the overall balance of power between classes and between civil society and the state. While this is enough to produce the correlation between development and democracy observed in the statistical studies, the same balance of power between pro- and anti- democratic actors can be produced in a large number of ways.

Does this mean, then, that we should actually have different theoretical frameworks to study the different regions? Certainly, the proponents of the corporatist approach would argue that this is the case (e. g. Wiarda 1980; 1982). Latin America, they argue, has to be understood on its own terms, as shaped by the Iberian legacy, and therefore models derived from the non-Iberian European experience are profoundly inappropriate for an analysis of Latin American political development. We disagree emphatically. Our theoretical framework has performed very well in accounting for developments within Latin America as well as for the differences between Latin America and the other regions in our study. The same key variables shaped the processes of democratization in all our cases, though these variables assumed quite different values and interacted in different ways across the cases and particularly across the regions. Cross-regional variations were systematic. They were shaped by the location of the regions in the world economy and system of states; they were influenced by the different timing of capitalist development and state-building; they expressed themselves in different constellations of class and state power; and thus they could be explained within our theoretical framework.

Class behavior was governed by the same factors, on the one hand the interest of subordinate classes in gaining a share of power, their capacity for organization, and the agent shaping their emerging political articulation, and on the other hand the interest of dominant classes in protecting their privileged position and the institutional channels to do so in a democratic context. What varied significantly across regions was the class structure and therefore the alliance possibilities both of subordinate and dominant classes. Further important sources of variation were the relationship of classes and class alliances to the state and the social construction of class interests.

Variations in the social construction of class interests were most manifest in the case of the working class. By the eve of World War I, social democracy was hegemonic in the working-class of the European core. By contrast, in Latin America and the Caribbean some individual political leaders made successful attempts to harness working-class organization for their own ambitions. In Latin America, there were also cases of successful state incorporation of the working-class into corporativistic schemes. We would suggest that this was at least in part a result of political learning and thus related to the phasing of domestic developments in relation to world historic development.

The balance of power between the state and civil society developed in the most favorable way for democracy in Europe, and least so in Central America, with South America closer to Central America than to Europe. In Central and South America the military emerged in an important political role from the difficult processes of achieving independence and consolidating state power. At later stages, economic dependency and foreign political domination or interventions increased the potential for state autonomy from civil society and for the development of the coercive apparatus into a domineering authoritarian albatross. Political domination in the case of British colonialism in the Caribbean, however, had a very different effect on the balance of power between state and civil society, in so far as the colonial state allowed for the growth of civil society and left a weak state apparatus after independence.

The impact of transnational structures of power also showed systematic variation across our regions, as we expected. As just discussed, economic and political dependency profoundly shaped both class structures and the character of the state apparatus, and thus class and class–state relations. The combination of these effects of transnational structures of power were most systematically and uniformly inimical to the development of an appropriate balance of class power and balance of power between state and civil society in Central America. In Europe, by contrast, the extent to which the effects of external influences were mediated by internal conditions and therefore varied in their impact was much greater.

One final point about the generalizability of our theoretical explanations needs to be addressed. One might argue that we only looked at cases of European extraction, that is, cases in Europe and areas where Europeans set up colonies and wiped out or marginalized the indigenous population. Of course, we have not presented any evidence for other regions, but we are prepared to argue that our framework would perform well in explaining the pressures for and obstacles to democratization in other regions. We have already demonstrated the usefulness of our theoretical framework for the analysis of regions which other authors, both culturalists and some dependency theorists, have considered to be very different from each other. We can also sketch an example of the usefulness of our framework for explaining cases from other regions, such as East Asia. In South Korea, for instance, the tremendous economic growth of the last three decades has created a stronger civil society, particularly a labor movement of some significance, and thus opened the possibility for the formation of an alliance between the working class and sections of the middle classes, led by students. This alliance has severely challenged the authoritarian state which had acquired a high degree of autonomy owing to the massive economic and military aid provided by the United States during and after the Korean War. This means that the balance of class power and the balance of power between the state and civil society has become less unfavorable for democratization, though the coercive apparatus remains excessively large in relation to the size of the country, which does not permit much optimism for the realization of full democracy in the near future.

It is possible that ethnicity would play a stronger role in other regions than it has in our cases. Much of the literature on democracy argues that deep ethnic divisions in a society make the installation of democracy more difficult, and cross-national statistical evidence confirms this (Bollen and Jackman 1985a; Hannan and Carroll 1981). Among the countries studied here, ethnic divisions were an important barrier to the development of democracy and assumed a central role in our analysis only in Guyana and the United States, even though a significant number of other countries might be characterized as "deeply divided" ethnically (Belgium, Switzerland, Spain, the Andean countries, Guatemala, and Trinidad and Tobago).[7] The selection of regions analyzed in this book probably leads to an underestimation of the importance of ethnic divisions for the fate of democracy in the modern world as a whole. The histories of state consolidation and nation-building of these countries distinguish them from most of the non-communist countries in the rest of the world. In western Europe, most states were either consolidated on the basis of relatively ethnically homogeneous groups, or the conquered populations were homogenized in centuries of domination. In Latin America, centuries of domination by the Spanish or Portuguese conquerors and then the Spanish- or Portuguese-speaking elites, led to homogenization in varying degrees in all countries except the Andean countries and Guatemala. By contrast, in Africa and Asia, colonialism was of more recent origin and it was imposed on peoples with strong ethnic and cultural identities and territorial attachments. The administrative units imposed by the imperial powers, and subsequently retained after independence, often did not correspond to the traditional ethnic divisions and thus more frequently resulted in deep ethnic divisions in the polity. Thus, it is not surprising that in the studies of the development of democracy contained in the Diamond, Linz and Lipset (1989a, 1989b) volumes on Asia and Africa, ethnicity appeared as a more important barrier to the successful installation of democracy than it did in our comparative historical studies.[8]

Given the relatively small number of ethnically divided societies analyzed here, then, it is fair to ask whether our generalizations would hold if a larger number of such national experiences were examined. Clearly, ethnic divisions in countries are subject to tremendous variation due to differences in the number of ethnic groups, their relative sizes, their relationship to class divisions, etc. ; thus, the specifics of one case will not apply to another. While we do believe that our political economy approach to the analysis of ethnic divisions, focusing on the chances of organizing subordinate interests in the struggle for power and control, is more fruitful than functional/pluralist emphasis on social integration and consensus, we remain open to the possiblity that our framework has to give more room to a direct impact of ethnic fragmentation on the chances of democracy.

Central to democratic consolidation in our original framework are the notions of balance of class power and of threat perception on the part of the dominant classes. We conceptualized the balance of class power as the relationship between the economic power of dominant classes and the organizational power of subordinate classes rooted in the structure of civil society and thus indirectly in the underlying class structure and the structure of the economy. We also recognized that perceptions of threat on the part of dominant classes are not simply reflections of objective conditions but rather symbolic constructs arising out of particular historical conjunctures. We did not specify any institutional mechanisms, though, which could mediate such threat perception. In our comparative analysis *political parties emerged as a crucial mediating mechanism.* The dominant classes accommodated to democracy only as long as the party system effectively protected their interests. Strong clientelistic, non-ideological multi-class parties as well as strong conservative parties could perform this function. In South America we saw that where such parties were lacking or lost their capacity to protect the economic interests of the dominant classes, the latter appealed to the military for intervention to prevent or to end democratic rule.

Variations in the strength of parties of the right can be seen as one source of the variable strength of dominant classes, independent of the strength of their opponents. Other sources of variability in dominant class strength which appeared in our studies are the degree of homogeneity of the economic base of elites and its international competitiveness, the strength of employers' organizations, which is facilitated by a high degree of concentration in the economy, and the penetration of the state apparatus – at present and building on earlier constellations – by the dominant classes.

Originally, we considered parties to be simply elements among others of the organizational structure of civil society. However, their crucial role in making democracy viable or not under very similar economic and social structural conditions forces us to question the adequacy of such a conceptualization. One solution to this problem is to introduce the distinction between civil and political society, as many authors on Latin American politics do, political society being comprised of political parties as the organizational manifestation of the political articulation of civil society. Another solution is to treat the political articulation of civil society as a distinct analytical dimension of civil society which is strongly affected by but cannot be reduced to the economic and class structure and the remainder of the organizational structure of civil society. Without an explicit conceptual discussion, we have opted for the latter solution in carrying out our comparative–historical analyses. Clearly parties should not be considered part of the state, though the state also heavily conditions the operation and structure of parties (see Lipset 1963: 327–65). Finally, whereas we can link the character and functions of political parties to some extent to economic, class, and state structures, they have to be understood in part also as a result of particular historical circumstances and as independent factors shaping the political trajectory of different countries. We have not made an attempt here to explain the origins of party systems beyond pointing to the work of Lipset and Rokkan (1967) on Europe and the difference between the types of parties emerging in mineral and agricultural export economies in South America.

Another modification of our theoretical framework concerns the concept of labor repressive agriculture. At the outset of the analysis we largely accepted Moore's emphasis on the importance of repressive (or political) vs. market mechanisms of labor control in explaining the variations in the posture of landlords toward democratization. This dichotomy proved to be too rigid. Landlord reliance on political mechanisms, ranging from slavery through indentured servitude to debt peonage, to limit labor mobility and insure an adequate supply of labor clearly is incompatible not only with democracy but also with the full introduction of liberal capitalist principles. However, landlord reliance on market control does not imply that democracy posed no threat to landlords' supply of cheap labor in cases where that was a requirement of profitable operation. There is a wide spectrum of political and organizational rights compatible with 'market' control of labor, if one uses the existence of full and free labor mobility as the dividing line between political and market control. Full democracy involves the right to organize as well as universal and equal suffrage, and this in turn may make it possible for rural labor and its political allies to use political power and union organization to drive up agricultural wages in a manner that leads landlords to perceive democracy to be incompatible with their definitions of adequate profits from their landholdings. As a result of these considerations, pressed upon us by the comparative historical studies, we have come to reconceptualize Moore's "labor repressive" landlords as "landlords dependent on a large supply of cheap labor."

This reconceptualization has broader implications than is immediately apparent. What differentiates landlords from capitalists, who, after all, might also be threatened by democratic reform in the same way? In much of the historical literature and in the sociological literature in the modernization tradition, landlords are seen as more conservative owing to their traditional values which are grounded in the prevalent social structures of agrarian societies – in particular the valuation of land as a status asset and a vehicle for domination over other humans rather than a purely economic asset. Without dismissing this line of argument entirely, we would suggest that the main reason for the reactionary posture of landlords is that their operations are simply more labor intensive, thus anything that raises the cost of labor is more expensive than it is to the average capitalist. This interpretation also serves to differentiate landlords dependent on large supplies of cheap labor from landlords, such as those involved in stock raising, not so dependent on labor.

This raises some questions on which we can only speculate. The same distinction, labor intensive vs. capital intensive, has been made among capitalists. It has been argued that those involved in labor intensive operations are more conservative owing to their greater dependence on cheap labor (see e.g. Ferguson 1983a, 1983b). This leads to the hypothesis that rising average capital intensity of production which accompanies economic development might lead the average capitalist to a more liberal posture and thus contribute to the explanation of why capitalist development is related to democracy. This assumes all other relevant factors are held the same. Taken by itself, this hypothesis would predict that Latin American capitalists should be more liberal than their European counterparts were at comparable stages of development, which we doubt. Yet if the other relevant factors were taken into account, the hypothesis may well be shown to be valid.[9]

Our analysis gives no clear-cut answer to the hypotheses that late development and state intervention in the economy inhibit democracy. Gerschenkron (1962) observed that late development within the European context was related to higher levels of state intervention and this in turn appeared to be associated with authoritarianism. As we discussed in chapter 2, de Schweinitz (1964) extends this argument to all late developers and expands it considerably. The empirical evidence here, though mixed, does not support a very strong relationship between authoritarianism and late development per se. In a cross-national statistical study, Bollen (1979) found no such relationship. Our analysis does indicate disadvantages for late developers through complex causal chains which link late development to dependent development and that, in turn, to class structure configurations, developmental bottlenecks, and geo-political dependence which did have a definite negative impact on democracy. However, this negative impact was nowhere near the insuperable barrier suggested by de Schweinitz.

Statistical studies have also indicated a negative relationship between the role of the state in the economy (as indicated by public expenditures as percent of GDP) and democracy (Bollen 1979; see also Cutright and Wiley 1969). This relationship is not very strong and it is not clear how it must be interpreted. Furthermore, one preliminary investigation on more recent data for developing capitalist countries indicates a positive relationship between public expenditures and democracy, though it is more plausible to explain this relationship by reversing the causality: democracy leads to more pressure for government spending (Kim 1988b). The difficulty here is probably a discrepancy between the concepts presented in the historical studies and theoretical arguments and the operationalizations in the statistical studies. When de Schweinitz and Gerschenkron refer to strong state intervention they have in mind, on the one hand, entrepreneurial activities, such as mobilizing capital and initiating new undertakings, activities that were performed by capitalists in early developers, and, on the other hand, state repression of labor. The measures used in statistical studies tap some of this, but they mainly capture variations among countries as indicated by social expenditure. To take concrete examples for the inadequacy of such an operationalization, Korea and Taiwan are very strong states in de Schweinitz's and Gerschenkron's sense, much more so than, say, Jamaica and Sri Lanka, but they are far outspent by the latter. In Jamaica the democratic socialist thrust of the PNP government of the 1970s and in Sri Lanka democracy combined with mass organization led to the expansion of social expenditure far beyond the levels prevailing in Korea and Taiwan (for Jamaica see Stephens and Stephens 1986; for Sri Lanka Herring 1987).

Nevertheless, our case materials do present some examples that might support Cutright and Wiley's (1969) much more carefully worded finding that social spending by authoritarian (and democratic) regimes does serve to stabilize those regimes. The most often cited historical example, Imperial Germany, is actually not the best case because we know in retrospect that Bismarck's welfare reforms (which even by the standards of the modern Third World were quite stingy) did not succeed in preventing the growth of a powerful labor movement pressing for democratic reforms. One possible reason is that these social expenditures were accompanied by rather repressive policies vis-à-vis the organizational attempts of subordinate classes. Mexico is a far better example and the amazing stability of the PRI regime must be attributed to successful co-optation caused in part by government social spending, accompanied by other redistributive and including measures vis-à-vis subordinate classes. Brazil under Vargas (1930–45) is another example, though clearly less successful than the PRI. And finally, we will suggest below that social welfare spending is one reason for the relative stability of another type of industrial authoritarian regime, Soviet and, to a lesser extent, East European communism.

A comparison of the experience of the advanced capitalist countries covered in chapter 4 with the later developers studied in the two following chapters raises a question that is perplexing in the context of our theoretical framework. Why were there more attempts to install democracy relative to the class balance of power in Latin America and the Caribbean? What we have in mind here primarily is that the working-class was significantly weaker in these two regions than in the large landholding cases among the advanced capitalist countries (the appropriate countries for comparison, given the landholding patterns in Latin America and the Caribbean). Let us be clear; we do not mean more cases of the successful installation of full democracy for that is not true, but rather more attempts to install democracy, full or restricted.

A number of explanations may account for this finding. First, if one includes the urban marginals or lumpenproletariat, there is a much larger urban (and therefore more easily organizable) subordinate class than if the working-class alone is considered. Second, in contrast to Europe and with the exception of Brazil, Latin American upper classes and the institutions they created lacked continuity with feudal and monarchical institutions and the traditional legitimation they enjoyed. Third, in part as a result of the weakness of traditional legitimation, the ideas of the European and American enlightenment proved to be stronger competitors to conservative (primarily Catholic) models of social order than in the large landholding countries of Europe. Fourth, the educated classes were oriented more towards Europe than towards Latin America and thus absorbed ideas and political models more appropriate to European than Latin American social reality. Given the prominent political role of the educated sectors of the middle classes in Latin America, these ideas came to influence political practice in the countries of the region. However, since most countries in the region lacked the underlying power relations to sustain institutions based on such ideas, frequently attempts at installation of democracy ultimately failed.

One might argue that the rhetorical triumph of democracy on a world scale since World War II has been a powerful force propelling Latin American and Caribbean countries toward the installation of democracy. This rhetorical triumph is not matched, of course, by actual triumph of even formal democracy, but it is not without its positive effects because external and internal legitimacy does affect regime stability. However, as the current situation in Central America demonstrates, the international pressures may be only for the appearance of the institutions of democracy without even its formal substance, and this may be a cover for the exclusion of certain groups from the political process. If the international legitimacy of democracy is the primary reason for its installation in a country and it is not underpinned by an appropriate balance of power, it is likely that "democracy" in the country will be a sham or that it will be subject to termination should economically and politically powerful groups feel threatened. This is one source of the frequence of sham democracy and rollbacks of democracy in the Third World in the post-World War II period.

An issue of significant practical interest and with important theoretical implications was raised by the cases of Venezuela and Colombia, namely the options for political engineering. In both of these cases, the leaders of the major parties and representatives of the dominant classes forged agreements on the establishment of democratic institutions which subsequently could be consolidated. From these cases one might draw the conclusions that political learning and deliberate institution-building could compensate for unfavorable structural conditions in making democracy possible. However, at least two caveats are in order. First of all, both Venezuela and Colombia had a crucial precondition for democratic consolidation, namely pre-existing parties which could be rebuilt and strengthened. Second, both contestation and inclusion were initially significantly limited in both cases, as the pacts provided for the protection of the vital interests of the dominant classes. Colombia remained a highly restricted democracy and accordingly never managed to channel protests through democratic institutions and to bring political violence under control. Venezuela did turn into a full democracy, but the resources from the oil economy played an important role in this achievement, as they allowed for social expenditures without threatening economic interests of the dominant classes. This, of course, severely limits the generalizability of the Venezuelan example.

Reflections

Turning toward the future

Does our analysis allow us to say anything about the prospects of democracy? Both the theoretical framework and the comparative studies focused on structural factors favoring or undercutting democratization and the stability of democratic politics. Our results can help us in developing reasonable anticipations of the longer-range future; they tell us less about short-run processes.

Prediction is always hazardous, of course, not only because of the limits of our theoretical understanding but even more so because of our limited ability to anticipate structural developments at the national and international levels on which predictions about the chances of democracy have to rely. We did develop explanatory accounts of a large number of cases and we did take care both to make these accounts theoretically coherent and to avoid ad hoc explanations fitting only one or a few cases. Though the resultant body of theoretical propositions is neither complete nor sufficiently specific to yield precise statements in individual cases, it does allow us to make some general assessments of the future chances of democracy in the areas covered in our study and to venture some expectations for other areas of the world.

Prediction is made easier in those cases where we can count on a good deal of historical continuity of structural conditions, institutions, and organizations, where in other words prediction from theoretical propositions can reasonably be combined with extrapolation. In turn prediction becomes much more hazardous if we try to anticipate the developments after a radical break in the institutional and organizational structure – as for example we are witnessing now in eastern Europe.

We may begin with a point about the future of authoritarian regimes. We touched on this at the end of chapter 3 when we discussed Moore's authoritarian capitalist path. Can this path actually lead to a modern, stable authoritarian regime? Our analysis leads us to think that in advanced capitalist countries authoritarian rule is unstable, because of the inevitable growth of a dense civil society and the development of a balance of class power which makes the smooth operation of an authoritarian regime problematic. Moreover, no modern capitalist authoritarian regime in the post-World War II era has developed an alternative legitimacy formula to democracy.

One of the most repressive of the bureaucratic authoritarian regimes of Latin America – Chile – is a good case in point. Despite massive repression and significant deindustrialization (and thus a weakening of the working class), the Chilean military government was unable completely to repress the labor movement (Valenzuela and Valenzuela 1986). Near total repression of civil society may have been possible at the level of development of Central America in the 1930s, but it is not possible at the level of development of the South American Southern Cone in the 1980s. Unlike the interwar Fascist regimes, the Chilean dictatorship also did not attempt to legitimate dictatorship as a permanent arrangement but, from the beginning, promised an eventual return to democracy, albeit a "protected democracy," free from the Marxist threat.

However, a caveat is necessary here. We do contend that modern capitalist dictatorship is unstable and that further economic development will result in greater pressures for democratization. Nothing says, however, that countries in the more developed parts of the Third World cannot, at current levels of development, vacillate for long periods of time between unstable dictatorship and unstable democracy. Given the current situation in Latin America and the Caribbean, nothing guarantees that these countries will experience the sustained growth in the next few decades necessary to induce the kind of structural change that would make democracy more stable.

There are a number of other factors that make us skeptical about the prospects of stable democratic regimes in Latin America. Several of these are by now well understood. The comparatively weak development of the working class and its organization was discussed extensively. We also touched on the greater autonomy of the state apparatus from civil society and the strong role of the military, which has been reinforced by foreign material and organizational assistance. In contrast to the military, the remainder of the state apparatus has been significantly weakened and its autonomy from external forces and from the export-oriented segments of the dominant classes reduced by the adjustment policies imposed to deal with the burden of the foreign debt in the 1980s. What this means is that the nature of the state has become less favorable for democracy and that these set-backs would make consolidation of democracy more difficult even if a solution to the debt crisis itself were found.[10] Moreover, in several Latin American countries party systems with two or more strong political parties have never developed. On the side of the subordinate. classes, the absence of strong parties with close links to other organizations in civil society keeps their capacity to exert sustained pressures for political inclusion limited; on the side of the dominant classes, the absence of strong right-wing or clientelistic parties enhances the uncertainty inherent in democratic procedures and the resulting perception of a potential threat to their interests. Consolidation of parties, in turn, is made particularly difficult in a situation where the political support of incumbent parties is more or less regularly decimated because of their inability to improve the economic situation and satisfy the material aspirations of the large mass of the electorate.

A last consideration deserves a little more discussion, partly because it leads us beyond Latin America. Given the difficulty of stabilizing newly installed full democracies in the context of moderate to high levels of popular mobilization and severe resource constraints, several Latin American governments have sought to conclude not only political but also socioeconomic pacts, that is, agreements among the main political actors on major social and economic policies. Even if socio-economic pacts can be reached, however, their actual enforcement and the achievement of the agreed-on policy targets depends on the existence of strong peak associations representing capital and labor which on their part are strong enough at all levels to deliver compliance of their constituencies, strong political parties, and an effective bureaucratic apparatus to monitor compliance with the pact. These are structural requirements which are fulfilled in relatively few countries – especially a handful of small democracies in Europe, most prominently Sweden, Norway, and Austria – and are particularly wanting in dependent capitalist countries. Moreover, as Przeworski's (1988) rational choice analysis demonstrates, the character of dependent capitalist economies is unfavorable for a compromise stipulated by a social pact under which labor forgoes current wage increases in exchange for capital's commitment to high reinvestment rates because the risk facing both capitalists and workers in relation to productivity of investment is higher than it is in advanced capitalist countries. These considerations leave one with a rather skeptical view of the chances for forging successful pacts for democratic consolidation in dependent capitalist countries.

What are the chances of democracy in the newly industrializing countries of East Asia, especially South Korea and Taiwan? So far it is quite clear that the dramatic success in economic development has not been matched by a corresponding "political development" of democratization that one might expect from functionalist equilibrium theory. Both countries share one condition favorable for democratization: in both a class of large landlords was destroyed nearly two generations ago. However, in both countries, too – and this is not unrelated – the state apparatus enjoys a substantial autonomy from civil society, and the military plays a central and powerful role within the state. Powerful business conglomerates, the *chaebols*, have begun to limit this autonomy in Korea, but the more important development for the chances of democracy is a strengthening of the working class and its organizations. The higher degree of industrial concentration in Korea than in Taiwan has led to the emergence of a stronger labor movement, but it has also created a stronger dominant class. Thus, the working class confronts not only a powerful non-democratic state but also a powerful capitalist class. Nevertheless, the working-class movement has put democracy more forcefully on the agenda in South Korea than in Taiwan, and it can be expected to keep up the pressure. In both countries, the easing of East–West tensions is removing the geo-political bases of support for the authoritarian regimes, namely the presumed threat from North Korea and mainland China.

As this chapter is being written, the collapse of bureaucratic state socialism in eastern Europe raises fascinating questions about the chances of democracy in these countries. While these questions technically fall outside the domain of an inquiry concerned with *capitalist* development and democracy, we should perhaps be prepared to rise to the challenge and seek to determine what our analysis would suggest.

A first point is simple. Without the transnational imposition of state socialism on the countries of Eastern Europe, a number of them would have experienced a thorough transformation of the balance of class power and a growth of organizational density in society sufficient to sustain democracy. As the periodic rebellions have shown, the authoritarian state socialist regimes in Poland, Czechoslovakia, East Germany, and Hungary were actually unstable and survived only with Soviet support.

State socialism was not, however, merely a foreign imposition. It also rested on the destruction of power based on the ownership of land and capital, on the radical denial of autonomous organizations, on an ideology-supported organizational penetration of society that had real effects even if much of its mobilization efforts existed to a large extent only on paper, and a provision of the necessities of life at nominal prices that constituted for the weakest segments of society a welfare system that was generous indeed. After decades of remarkable stability, this system failed both morally and – most important – economically. Once it became clear that the Soviet Union would not intervene with force as it had done earlier, the demise of the system came with a speed nobody had predicted.

A class analytic approach to the chances of democracy in the new Eastern Europe encounters a peculiar scene. One might begin by pointing to the absence of a large landowning class. This is indeed a striking contrast to what would be one of the central elements of a counterfactual scenario of developments in Eastern Europe without World War II. Above all, however, there is no capital-owning bourgeoisie to speak of.

Yet at the end of state socialism there still exists a class that bears some remarkable similarities to the powerful landlord classes of Western European and Latin American history: the *nomenklatura* or the elite of party, state, and enterprise managers.[11] As the classic aristocracy, the nomenklatura combines control of the means of production with political control. Labor control was achieved largely, though not exclusively, with political means.

What separates the state socialist nomenklatura from the landed aristocracy is above all the mode of cultural/ideological hegemony – based on long-established relations in a non-mobile society and partially grounded in religious traditions in one case, grounded in the promise of an affluent but just society and relying on a thorough organizational and ideological penetration of society in the other. The hegemony of large landowners is bound to decline everywhere, however haltingly in some cases. The hegemony of the communist party–state elites of Eastern Europe has collapsed and is unlikely to be revived.

Assuming that the nomenklatura in its past form will disappear, there is likely to emerge – to a large extent out of this nomenklatura – a new bourgeoisie that is weak economically and politically despite more or less strong infusions of direct foreign investment. It is a bourgeoisie without a history – without a heritage of organization, of alliances, but also of antagonisms. Thus one of the major factors determining choice in the social construction of class interest is missing. That also makes prediction of this construction of class interest more difficult. However, a fairly large and still autonomous state apparatus is bound to remain very important in economic affairs since even an aggressive privatization and free market policy will be partially blocked by the scarcity of private capital. It seems problematic to anticipate the new bourgeoisie to be a strong counterbalancing force to this state apparatus. Given its economic weakness as well as the background of its likely members, it is quite likely to be dependent on support by the state and to be able to form strong alliances with officials in central positions in the administrative apparatus.

Civil society was virtually denied any autonomous expression under state socialism. True, the Catholic church in Poland and to a lesser extent the Protestant church in East Germany were important exceptions to this rule, and there were minor others. But while these exceptions made a noticeable difference in the recent transitions, they do not change the overall assessment of the weakness of autonomous organizations in civil society in these countries. Assuming the persistence of a powerful state apparatus, this weakness seems to us the major problem overlooked in current optimism about the future of democracy in eastern Europe. There exists, of course, quite an array of party-linked organizations in civil society, but the question is whether these organizations can develop a life of their own or whether they collapse once their relationship to the party–state is severed.

Building strong organizations takes time, especially for the large subordinate classes. This is not primarily because it takes time to set up thousands of local and regional organizational units or to "build up" leading personalities in the media. A strong organizational representation of broad-based interests cannot be created overnight because it involves complex choices in the social construction of class interests as well as the development of trust in organization and leaders. To what extent existing organizations – unions, for instance, and even parties – can be reformed to become autonomous and trusted channels for people's interests and aspirations is an open and fascinating question.

A significant part in future developments will be played, of course, by the coercive apparatus of the state. Whether the security forces become the repository of authoritarian tendencies and intervene in politics on their own or in alliance with other forces in the state apparatus or in civil society, or whether they can be effectively subordinated to civilian authority, will to a large extent shape the room for maneuver open to pro-democratic forces. There are likely to be important contrasts among the different countries and regions of Eastern Europe in this respect.

A final consideration, analogous to the concluding comment on Latin America, adds to our skepticism: state socialist rule left the economies of Eastern Europe in shambles. Even with the best assumptions about economic recovery and growth, there is a fundamental discrepancy between the time horizons of politics – ranging from "solutions now" to two to four years – and the much slower pace of economic development. Rising dissatisfaction with economic conditions can be articulated spontaneously, even in the absence of powerful popular organizations. Policies of long-term promise and short-term sacrifice require strong organizations that have the trust of their constituencies. Unrest due to persistent economic deprivation – precisely if it remains unchanneled by deeply rooted unions, associations and parties – would increase the chances of authoritarian state action, unbalanced by strong forces in civil society.

Qualitative advance or decline in existing democracies?

What are the prospects that really existing democracies come closer to the ideal of political equality? Our analysis has focused entirely on formal democracy. While insisting that formal democracy itself was something of value, we set aside its relationship to true political equality. Further, what are the prospects that these formally democratic systems will deliver substantive social justice to their citizens?

Some of our findings give these questions a particular urgency, since they indicate that the establishment or stabilization of formal democracy was facilitated by keeping such issues off the agenda entirely or, where they were on the agenda, keeping them from becoming policy. To cite the two most important findings pointing in this direction, protection of elite interests through the existence of strong right-wing parties or other mechanisms and the absence of radical demands from movements representing the lower classes were found to be favorable to democracy.

Let us state at the outset that we do not believe that the ideal of democracy in the sense of complete political equality will ever be realized. However, in this closing section of the book, we will argue that significant progress towards greater political equality and substantive social justice is possible. These two goals are tied together: in order to reduce political inequality, it is necessary that the distribution of wealth, status and socioeconomic power become more equitable.

The actually existing democracies of today – defined by regular free and fair elections, responsibility of the state apparatus to elected representatives, and protection of civil liberties – vary a great deal in the degree to which they really give the many a voice in the determination of collective decisions. On the one hand, even if we exclude sham democracies, in some formal democracies the economically powerful are able to exert sufficient control over the political process that political decisions rarely challenge their interests. The masses respond by failing to show up at the polls to make electoral choices that appear to them to make little difference in the policy output of the government. On the other hand, other formal democracies are characterized by vibrant participation not only in elections but also in various organizations whose aim is to determine public policy and which arguably have proved to have some influence on policy. These differences appear not only if one examines the policy-making process but also the outcomes of that process. At one extreme, there are cases where formally democratic processes barely modify the distribution of power and economic resources. At the other end of the spectrum, the actual political power of the many has over time made a real difference in the distribution of scarce social and economic resources – of income and wealth, of power and influence, of honor and respect – and thus also in turn improved the bases of political equality. Changes away from a merely formal democracy toward the latter pole of the continuum represent both qualitative advances of democracy and of substantive social justice.

A first and theoretically simple implication of our analysis is clear: the same factors that advance the chances of democracy in the formal sense of the term – of what Robert Dahl has called polyarchy – also make democracy more real. The more the balance of class power favors subordinate class interests and the more a dense civil society aids in giving organizational expression to these interests and at the same time constitutes a countervailing force against unrestrained and autonomous state power, the greater the chances not only of installing democratic institutions and making them stable but also of increasing the real weight of democratic decision-making. The greater weight of the subordinate classes in the political process should in turn express itself in state policies which redistribute resources from the privileged to the underprivileged. This is what, in fact, has happened (Esping-Andersen 1990; Korpi 1982; Stephens 1979).

It is important to point out that reductions in class inequality do not follow automatically from the existence of democratic institutions; otherwise the quantitative analyses of the relation between democracy and economic inequality would have come to much more clear-cut results.[12] Rather, they depend on existing power relations and continued struggles; and these struggles, as we have seen, can raise complex problems.

Our comparative analyses suggested that given certain power constellations democratic institutions were particularly in danger if dominant class interests were not politically protected by a strong party. That this proposition suggested itself especially in the Latin American analyses is hardly an accident, since these cases tend to combine a smaller and weaker working-class presence with particularly great social and economic inequality. Where the working-class is large, well organized, and united, the chances are much better for substantial reductions of structured inequality and for democratic institutions to survive the very real conflicts involved. Cases such as Spain in the 1930s or Chile in the 1970s, in which democracy was terminated in part because radical demands from the working-class parties appeared as a threat to economic elites do not demonstrate that democratic institutions cannot be used to advance the substantive interests of the lower classes or even that there is some limit to the degree that those interests can be advanced in the context of formal democracy. Rather, they are cases in which the working-class parties pressed demands which were impossible to realize given the power balance in civil society.

In his most recent discussion of democracy, Robert Dahl acknowledges that class inequality poses problems for democracy but decides to "simply ... assume that an advanced democratic country would place high on its agenda the problem of how best to achieve an economic order that would strengthen the democratic process." (Dahl 1989: 333). He takes this position because he considers other problems even more formidable: "the long-run prospects for democracy are more seriously endangered by inequalities ... that are derived not from wealth or economic position but from special knowledge" (Dahl 1989: 333). The growing role of expert knowledge concentrated within state agencies and in the surrounding institutions of policy knowledge represents in his view a fundamentally new challenge to democracy, matched in importance only by the transition from the early "assembly democracies" to political systems that delegate most problems of implementation to the administrative state apparatus.

If we take the more conventional view that sees class inequality as more important for the fate of democracy, it is not altogether for conventional reasons. We are convinced that the challenge of knowledge expertise is answered fundamentally in the same way as the political power of bureaucratic administration. Both are indeed formidable problems; both point to an irreducible core of problems that make radical democracy impossible; but both can be contained and balanced by the forceful organization of socially and economically subordinate interests.

Policy knowledge can be produced and interpreted in quite pluralistic ways. In fact, in the late twentieth century the policy knowledge "communities" of the advanced capitalist countries are typically grounded institutionally in heterogeneous organizations that are affiliated with a range of political and class interests. The range is wider and takes subordinate interests more into account where working-class organization is strong. And it is only with strong organization of subordinate interests that the threat to democracy that is constituted by the ever growing need for expertise can be contained.

On its face, the claim that growing state activities – induced by democratically articulated demands – are a threat to democracy appears even stronger than the expertise vs. democracy thesis. If true, it would negate our proposition that reducing class inequalities is the central issue in making democracy more real; for such reductions most likely have to be brought about by politics and state action. We are convinced that this version of the classic claim of a fundamental contradiction between equality and freedom is mistaken. It is not the magnitude of state activities as such that interferes with democracy. It is the build-up of coercive power insufficiently controlled politically; and it is the growth of state strength not counterbalanced by a countervailing organizational strength of civil society, and especially of those interests that cannot rely on other sources of power than organization.

If countervailing organization of the many is so central to our argument, is it not possible that both theses – the thesis of the threat of expertise and the thesis of overwhelming state power – are mistaken as stated, but valid in a roundabout way: both strengthen the hand of organizational oligarchies vis-à-vis their constituencies, and both encourage deals among the leaders of peak organizations that are quite remote from the preferences of the members of the various organizations. We have spoken in chapter 2 of the "inherent ambiguity of collective action" and insisted that the tendencies toward oligarchy and collaboration at the apex of the organizational structure are variable and contingent outcomes of different conditions.

A major remedy for tendencies toward oligarchic autonomy within organizations would be increased participation at lower organizational levels. Participation in the governance of formally democratic organizations has complex determinants. Chief among them are skills and competence as well as a perception of being able to make a difference. This leads us into the question of democratizing decision making in spheres of life other than the specifically political arena. Though one may be skeptical of the thesis that stable and successful political democracy requires analogous patterns of modified and constrained authority in all spheres of life, it is quite plausible to argue that people's experience in settings that are not specifically political has a considerable effect on their skills, aspirations, confidence, and sense of efficacy.

If democracy has its ultimate rationale in the argument that human beings should have an autonomous say in all decisions that affect their lives and life chances, it is clearly an anomaly that the vast majority of adults in capitalist societies are subjected to an authority with few restraints in the arena of work – the sphere of life that next to family and other intimate personal relations matters most for most people. Economic democracy raises complicated questions that we cannot treat here.[13] However, extending democratic participation of workers into the decision-making of modern corporations has – aside from the intrinsic value of greater personal autonomy in a major sphere of life – quite important consequences for the chances of the democratic process in the more narrowly political sphere. It would diminish one-sided class power and thus increase the chances of making political democracy more "real." And it would very likely increase political participation and competence.

In fact, industrial democracy has always been on the agenda of working-class organizations and parties. Even the earliest trade unions fought for and sometimes won a small measure of shopfloor control. In Europe in the 1970s, workers' participation or, more broadly, economic democracy became the centerpiece of the program of many labor movements and social democratic parties. In almost all European countries, some modest legislative advance in this area was made, but the most ambitious agendas of, for instance, the Swedish trade unions and the French left, which would have made major steps toward democracy in industry, were never realized and the issue faded from the agenda in the face of the economic problems of the 1980s. Whatever the likelihood that industrial democracy returns to the top of the agenda of working-class movements, we are convinced that the control of private economic power and the reduction of social and economic inequality constitute the most promising path of advancing substantive democracy. Economic democracy would add to and complement other measures of reducing inequalities in society that affect political equality.

Our comments here fly in the face of the belief, all the more popular in the wake of the collapse of state socialism in Eastern Europe, that capitalism is a necessary precondition for democracy. Even an analyst otherwise sympathetic to our central argument, that it was the contradictions of capitalism and not capitalists that created democracy, might contend that these contradictions – and thus rather unencumbered capitalist economic conditions – are necessary for the survival of democracy. In particular, the Eastern European experience demonstrates in the view of many observers that private ownership of the means of production is a prerequisite for democracy because it insures the institutional separation of the economy from the polity.

This line of argument involves in the first place a misreading of the historical experience of Eastern Europe. Those regimes were set up with state ownership of production, command economies, and authoritarian polities; they were not democracies that became authoritarian due to an internal and democratic decision to nationalize industry. Much more relevant here are the examples of Norway and Austria. In those two countries, precisely such internal and democratic dynamics led to the wholesale nationalization of some industries and large-scale purchase of shares in other industries. Combining state-owned industry with state ownership of shares in industry, total public ownership of industry reaches 50 percent in Norway and far exceeds that in Austria (Esping-Andersen 1985: 225; Katzenstein 1984: 50). Not only are these countries formal democracies, but they, particularly Norway, have also achieved high levels of political participation and a high degree of economic equality when compared to other advanced industrial democracies.

We have insisted from the outset (see chapter 3) that democracy is impossible without some structural differentiation of the polity from the wider structures of inequality – and especially of power – in society. This involves in particular an institutional separation of polity and economy because fusing both creates overwhelming power concentrations.[14] However, we do not agree that private ownership of the means of production is necessary to achieve and maintain such a separation of powers. We are prepared to argue that a variety of forms of market socialism – with co-operative ownership, worker ownership, municipal and other forms of decentralized public ownership, "mutual fund socialism" along the lines envisaged by the Swedish Confederation of Trade Unions (Meidner 1978), or a combination of these forms – would not only be compatible with formal democracy, they would also help increase political equality and deepen substantive social justice as they would retain the institutional separation of the polity and the economy and at the same time would give those at the bottom more resources.

In this book, we have left the whole issue of inclusion of women in the electorate aside, as dynamics of this struggle follow quite different principles from that of inclusion of subordinate classes or ethnic groups and would require a whole separate analysis.[15] Also, before the 1970s women's issues were less politicized, and women did not form separate political blocs of major significance.[16] Nevertheless, any discussion of deepening democracy and extending political equality would be incomplete without some reflections on the prospects for greater equality in power relations between the sexes. It is similar to the issue of economic democracy as it involves extending equality of power into other spheres than the political sphere in the narrow sense, and it is likely to be similar in its consequences. However, we are convinced that the prospects for gender inequality and its impact on democratic politics are much more straightforward. In fact, the prospects for gender inequality may well be one of the last instances where we can speak of anticipating progress.[17]

The struggle for gender equality is bound to succeed in the long run; for the underlying factors shaping gender roles have changed irreversibly. Among these changes are not only declines in both mortality and fertility, freeing the major part of women's lives for other activities than reproduction; there are also changes in the structure of family and kinship, in the skills and strengths required at different kinds of work, in the legitimacy of ascriptive status distinctions, and last but not least in the chances of collective organization, even if women's interests lend themselves less easily to such organization than interests that are structurally less closely bound up with their opposites.

At the same time, the equalizing changes are likely to come slowly, because the elimination of male domination and privilege runs into very powerful obstacles, given the deep rooted nature of gender roles and relations. Finally, changes in gender relations, while they have an impact on all spheres of life and perhaps most on family relations, will for a large part and for a prolonged time be achieved by political means. Taken together, the long-term prospect of advances toward women's emancipation, the obstinate difficulties of change in gender relations, and the large role played by public policy in these matters mean that the struggles for gender equality will increase women's political participation over the long run and make it more intense. Aside from this broad effect on political participation produced by the arduous process of women's emancipation, approaching gender equality would in itself constitute a tremendous advance toward the broadest ideal of democracy.

In the end our conclusion is simple. It was neither capitalists nor capitalism as such but rather the contradictions of capitalism that advanced the cause of political equality. Capitalism contributed to democracy primarily because it changed the balance of class power in favor of the subordinate interests. This shift is in any country less than complete, and in addition the institutional stability of democracy is contingent on other factors as well. The democratic polity that capitalist development helped bring about offers the opportunity to advance democracy qualitatively, even though such advances are by no means assured.

Capitalism presupposes class inequality and has restructured it. It built on patriarchy and restructured it. Democracy has been a means of transforming capitalism. Where effective, it has contributed to a decline of both class and gender inequality. Further advances in the quality of democracy require further transformations of capitalism, because they require changes in the structure of power in society. Giving social and economic substance to political democracy is the essence of democratic socialism. Gender equality is one historical fulfillment of the democratic promise; democratic socialism is the other.

APPENDIX

Classification of Regimes

As explained in chapter 2, our conceptualization of democratic regimes is based on the dimensions of inclusion and contestation, and we distinguish between restricted and fully democratic regimes. Inclusion refers to the extent of suffrage and the non-proscription of political parties, contestation to institutionalization of opposition, freedom of association and expression, responsible government, and free and fair elections.

The minimum requirements to qualify as a democracy at all, as opposed to falling in the category of constitutional oligarchic or authoritarian systems are the following:

1 Low property or tax qualifications for the franchise, granting the right to vote to at least 60 percent of the adult male population; or literate adult male suffrage.
2 Direct popular elections of executive and/or legislature.
3 Responsible government: cabinet responsibility to the elected legislature and or to the elected executive.
4 Percent of population voting more than 5 percent (this is an indicator of formal and informal restrictions put on participation).
5 Compliance with election results.
6 Freedom of association and speech; protection from arbitrary arrest.

The criteria for differentiating a full from a restricted democracy are the following:

1 Universal male suffrage.[1]
2 No proscription of political parties.
3 No military intervention in politics.
4 No pacts or agreements imposing restrictions on the significance of election outcomes for access to political office and the distribution of political power.

[1] Our choice of male suffrage only as a criterion is explained in chapter 2. We are indebted to Karen Remmer for comments on this and other points of our classifications which forced us to rethink and/or sharpen our arguments.

5　Enforcement of free and fair elections; e. g. truly secret ballot and no intervention in the electoral process by local notables.

For our analysis of Europe, the main focus was on the transition from restricted to full democracy and the date of that change is stated in the text of that chapter. However, most of the countries were constitutional oligarchies at the beginning of the period under analysis (1870) owing to restrictions on suffrage, the absence of responsible government, or both. Though the transition to restricted democracy is not clearly dated, the analysis of the dynamics includes that transition also. For the British settler colonies, the suffrage was wide enough in every case for the country to qualify as a restricted democracy during the colonial period; the question was the granting or winning of responsible government. This poses no problem for the United States. In the other cases, we have treated them as restricted democracies when the legislative bodies of the country in question gained control over the making of all policies other than defense and foreign policy. For the British Caribbean, a similar criterion was used, but, in this case, this entailed the transition to full democracy because universal suffrage had already been achieved. The classification of regimes in Central America posed little problem since, with the exception of Costa Rica, few of them fell outside the authoritarian category in the time period under consideration.

By contrast, the analysis of South America covered a much longer time period than the other analyses and most of the countries moved back and forth among different regime forms. This motivated us to construct the more elaborate typology found in several tables in that chapter. Some comments on the classifications in these tables are in order here.

For a period to be classified as democratic, at least two separate popular free and fair elections had to be held. These elections could be of the same or of different types, such as one presidential and one congressional election, or one to a constituent assembly and one congressional or presidential election. Fixing the exact dates for such periods is somewhat arbitrary. One can date the democratic period from the introduction of the political reforms which protect it, or from the first national elections held under the new system, or from the inauguration of the new government. Where the introduction of the political reforms came as a clearly identifiable package (e. g. in Argentina in 1912), or where a dramatic regime change or announcement of elections ushered in the new period (e. g. Venezuela in 1945, or Bolivia in 1952), these dates were chosen, otherwise the date of the first election. Similarly, to date the end of the democratic period is easy in the case of coups, but more difficult in the case of slow erosion through growing harrassment of the opposition (e. g. Argentina 1949–51, or Uruguay 1968–73); in the latter case, a significant event, such as manipulated elections or the suspension of congress has been selected to indicate the date.

The distinction between full and restricted democracies, called exclusionary democracies by Remmer (1985–6), is crucial for Latin America, because among other things it draws attention to the fact that continued exclusion of the rural popular sector was often crucial for the installation and consolidation of "urban–democratic" regimes. Restricted democracies can further be distinguished according to the existence of restrictions on contestation or inclusion only, or on both. These categories include regimes with restrictions on inclusion based on suffrage qualifications and/or on provisions proscribing one or more parties; and/or with restrictions on contestation in the form of provisions whereby election outcomes are rendered irrelevant, such as by previously concluded political pacts on power sharing, with varying interference in the electoral process at the local level, and with high military involvement in politics of the "moderator" type (see Stepan 1971), i.e. interventions to block certain policies, or to prevent elections from having unacceptable outcomes, or to effect changes in the executive if elections did.

Periods with unqualified democratic rule according to these criteria have been rare indeed before the 1980s. Argentina 1912–30, 1946–51, and 1973–6, Uruguay 1919–33 and 1942–73, Chile 1970–3, Bolivia 1952–64, and Venezuela 1945–8 and 1968 to the present qualify. Objections to the classification of Argentina and Uruguay as fully democratic during their first periods of democracy could be raised on the grounds of the high proportion of immigrants among the lower classes. Whereas we argue that the disenfranchisement of a large part of the working class because of immigrant status reduced the threat posed to elites by democratization and thus facilitated the installation of democratic regimes in the two cases, we do maintain that the regimes can be classified as fully democratic. Disenfranchisement of non-citizens for national level elections is a universal feature of full democracies. Despite this de facto limitation, there was a clear difference between these two political systems, where more than half of the urban and rural lower classes could vote, and, say, the restricted democracy in Chile in the 1930s, where suffrage qualifications and de facto lack of a secret ballot kept virtually the entire rural lower class excluded. Moreover, by the 1940s the bulk of the working class was locally born, and thus these periods unambiguously qualify as fully democratic.

Restricted democracy with relatively mild restrictions, namely literacy qualifications only, existed in Chile 1958–70. The significance of these restrictions was further reduced by the comparatively low rate of illiteracy. In fact, one can argue that the electoral reforms of 1958 and the process of rural unionization during the 1960s gradually transformed the system into a full democracy, so that the enfranchisement of the illiterates in 1970 as such did not make a qualitative difference in the political process any more. Colombia 1936–49 is a borderline case, because suffrage was universal and contestation highly institutionalized, but control of local notables over the electoral process and thus fraud, as well as partly violent intimidation of the opposition, were widespread. Oquist (1980: 104) states that the entire period 1930–46 was characterized by widespread electoral fraud and coercion, which were accepted as a fact of political life. Moreover, in some municipalities the parties concluded pacts and fixed elections accordingly. Also, the local police was often highly partisan (Oquist 1980: 106). The 1942 elections were reportedly fraudulent (Oquist 1980: 109).

In Chile before 1958 the lack of enforcement of the secrecy of the ballot and interference in the electoral process by local notables, in addition to the literacy requirement, restricted democracy more significantly, particularly in rural areas. Inclusion was further limited in the period 1947–58 because the Communist Party was illegal, a party that had received over 10 percent of the vote in the two previous elections. Nevertheless, in the period 1932–58 the urban middle classes and large sectors of the urban working-class were included; the constitution of 1925 had established a permanent electoral register (which amounted to a de facto widening of the franchise) and the direct election of the president (Gil 1966: 58–9). Thus, one can regard this as a severely restricted democracy. Before 1920, Chile has to be classified as a competitive oligarchic system. Because Chile introduced literate male suffrage in 1874, it has frequently been referred to as a democracy with a long history. However, control of local notables over the process of registration and partly even the casting of ballots assured oligarchic domination to such an extent that it would be misleading to even classify Chile before 1920 as a democracy with severe restrictions, rather than a competitive oligarchic system. For instance, since the oligarchy felt that effective control threatened to slip out of their hands, and since the administration of suffrage was in the hands of municipal Committees of the Largest Taxpayers, they decided to greatly reduce participation through the process of registration. The number of registered voters dropped from 598, 000 in 1912 to 185, 000 in 1915. Before the 1923 elections the Presidents of the Chamber of Deputies and of the Senate agreed again to keep registration of voters much below 30 percent of those eligible (Valenzuela 1977: 213–15). The period 1920–4 was clearly a transition period between an oligarchic and a severely restricted democratic regime. Voter registration had greatly increased after the reforms of 1915 and participation rose above 5 percent in 1918, fell to 4. 5 percent in 1920, but rose again above 5 percent in 1921 (Drake 1978: 51). Participation had actually reached 8. 7 percent in 1912, but after that the oligarchy deliberately restricted registration (for the figures, see Remmer 1984: 84). Alessandri won with middle- and some working-class support; however, oligarchic groups still dominated Congress and managed to block any reform promoted by Alessandri.

The same label of severely restricted democracy can also be applied to the situations in Uruguay from 1903 to 1919, Colombia from 1958 to the present and Venezuela from 1958 to 1968. In Uruguay before the legal changes in 1915 and the constitution enacted in 1919 (also referred to as the constitution of 1917), there were literacy qualifications on the franchise (Nahum 1977: 75–6), voting was public by signed ballot (Vanger 1980: 100), and the election of the president was indirect. In the cases of Colombia and Venezuela, despite de jure full inclusion through universal suffrage, different factors have severely limited contestation and inclusion, and thus the effective representation of lower-class interests. In Colombia, the National Front agreement, which was in force from 1958 to 1974, not only provided for alternation in the presidency and a division of all important political positions, elected or appointed, between Liberals and Conservatives, but it explicitly prohibited third parties from participating in elections. After 1974, the practice of dividing executive positions and protecting the hegemony of the Conservative and Liberal Parties was continued. A constitutional reform in 1968 effected only a partial change in the Front arrangements. Competitive elections at the national level were held in 1974, but parity in the judicial branch was to be maintained, and in the executive branch it was to be maintained until 1978. However, even thereafter the party receiving the second highest number of votes was entitled to "adequate and equitable" representation, i. e. to participation in a coalition government (Hartlyn 1989). In 1971, ANAPO was recognized as a political party and thus made legal for electoral purposes. However, the dominance of the two traditional parties was further cemented, for instance, by the electoral reform law of 1979 which stipulates that the Electoral Court have four representatives each from the two major parties, and one from the third largest party. Even more serious in its implications for restrictions on democratic practice is the repeated recourse to declarations of the state of siege since the late 1940s.

In Venezuela, the Pact of Punto Fijo of 1958 committed the three main parties to a coalition government regardless of the outcome of the 1958 elections, to a common program which buried sensitive issues, and to a common defense of democracy. It deliberately excluded the Communist Party from participation in government. Coalition government and moderation in political programs, along with ostracism of the radical left, continued until the 1968 elections. Leftists were expelled from Acción Democrática and purged from leadership positions in unions. In the 1968 elections, the Communist Party, which by that time had come to reject insurrection, was allowed to participate through a front organization, and its legalization in 1969 signified the transition to full democracy. The fact that significant sectors of the thus alienated left took up arms and failed in their revolutionary goals critically weakened the entire left by not only physically liquidating many militants but delegitimizing radical leftist positions. Thus, the inclusion of the Communist Party was a risk of minor proportions for the established political forces. See Levine (1978: 97–101) and Karl (1986: 206–15) for discussions of the Pact and the subsequent marginalization of the left.

Periods of severely restricted democracy, with high military propensity to intervene directly through coups or indirectly through pressures on civilian political elites, occurred in Argentina 1958–66, Brazil 1945–64, Peru 1939–48 and 1956–68, and Ecuador 1948–61. In Ecuador, military involvement in this period was not as strong as in the other cases. Three elected presidents were able to serve their full terms, and no party or candidate was vetoed by the military. However, in matters of interest to the military itself, strong pressures were put on the incumbents, and a conflict between the president and a military officer in his cabinet almost led to the overthrow of the governement in 1953. Moreover, there were unsuccessful military revolts in 1950 and 1956. Thus, the military remained active behind the scenes and ready to intervene if the occasion were to arise. The main reason why none of the three presidents was overthrown was that no major social groups appealed for military intervention in this period. See Fitch (1977: 40–6) for the role of the military in this period.

In addition to strong military involvement, the proscription of the Peronist party greatly restricted the democratic quality of Argentine politics in this period. In Brazil, Peru, and Ecuador, literacy qualifications served to exclude the majority of the rural population in these periods. The illegal status of the Peruvian Aprista Party from 1939 to 1945, and of the Communist Party in

Peru and Brazil in the post-World War II period added a further exclusionary feature.

A final note on the classification of the current regimes in Brazil, Paraguay, Uruguay, Peru, and Chile: in Brazil the 1985 election of the president was indirect. Since then, most of the other criteria for democracy have been met; illiterates were enfranchised in 1985, direct elections for Congress and Governors were held in 1986 and for the presidency in 1989. However, as Stepan (1988: 103–12) demonstrates, the military retained a strong hold on important positions in the political system, such as on Cabinet seats and the National Security Council, and it exercised great political influence on the crucial issues which emerged during the first two years of the civilian government. The new constitution failed to significantly reduce the military's prerogatives in the political system and consequently Brazil remains closer to a restricted than a full democracy.

The ouster of Stroessner in Paraguay in February 1989 raised the question of a possible transition to democracy. However, not only were the elections following his ouster held under questionable rules and partly marred by fraud, but the fusion between the state (including the military) and the dominant party effected by Stroessner is still intact and obstructs genuine democratization.

Prior to the 1984 elections in Uruguay, the military engaged in some political manipulation, and a leading Blanco politician, Wilson Ferreira, was barred from participating; thus, the regime at that point should be classified as a restricted democracy. However, these restrictions did not seem to dramatically influence the election outcome (Gillespie 1986: 192), and de facto Uruguay started to function as a full democracy. The 1989 elections resulted in a transfer of power to the opposition.

Peru as of 1980 appeared to have made the transition to full democracy, with free and fair elections at all levels and universal suffrage including illiterates. The assumption of the presidency by Apra's Alan García in 1985, fulfilling the decades-long aspirations of Peru's only mass party, seemed to confirm the democratic quality of the system. However, the insurgency of Sendero and the government's countermeasures have created a situation where the rule of law is de facto suspended for large areas of the country. Thus, full democracy at the center coexists with essentially military rule in other areas of the country. Since the center has continued to operate according to democratic rules, Peru is classified as a full democracy.

Chile returned to democratic rule in 1990 with the inauguration of the Aylwin government, the president and congress having been elected in direct elections with universal suffrage. However, before handing over power, the Pinochet government had altered the legal and institutional frameworks such as to restrict greatly the new government's room for action in important areas of policy-making. Consequently, the new system has to be regarded as a restricted democracy.

Notes

1 Introduction: the Problem of Capitalist Development and Democracy

1 While these were city states with developed crafts and trade, they relied strongly on agriculture. However, though the Athenian system of self-rule acquired paradigmatic significance for the Western tradition of thought about democracy, it was actually a severely limited form of democracy. For it excluded the great majority of adults from participation – slaves, women as well as free men whose forebears did not belong to the established citizenry of Athens.

   The Swiss cantons after 1848 as well as such cases as Norway and the United States in the nineteenth century are better candidates for possible exceptions to the rule that democracy finds extremely inhospitable conditions in an agrarian society. These cases, which are discussed in chapter 4, may guide us in identifying the factors that actually account for the fact that democracy is rare under agrarian conditions. It is most likely not the domination of agricultural production per se but the concentration of property so often associated with it that works against democracy.

2 Throughout this book, we use the term "bourgeoisie" as equivalent to "capitalist class" or "big business." We exclude small businessmen (or petty bourgeoisie) as well as other "bürgerliche Stände," i.e. professionals, white collar employees, etc.

2 Capitalist Development and Democracy: The Controversy

1 The index of political development, to illustrate, is the sum of points given a country for each of the 21 years from 1940 to 1960 according to the following rules: two points for a *parliament* with more than one party, in which one minority party had at least 30 percent of the seats; one point for a multi-party parliament that violated the 30 percent rule; no points for parliaments without the above characteristics (including non-party parlia-

ments), for parliaments that do not exercise self-rule (for instance in colonies), and for systems without a parliament; one point for a *chief executive* elected directly or indirectly under conditions satisfying the 30 percent rule, half a point for a chief executive selected by other methods, including colonial appointment; no point for hereditary rulers and chief executives who abolished a multi-party parliament.

2 Cutright's index of political development was primarily determined by the length of time a country had an elected parliament and an elected head of the executive. Cutright and Wiley (1969) did not change this emphasis on longevity. This was criticized by Deane Neubauer (1967). Others have made the more general point that both Lipset and Cutright – by focusing on *stable* democracies – confounded the democratic character of a political order and its stability, so that their results could very well tell us as much about the stability of any regime as about the conditions of democratic government (see e.g. Bollen 1979). For a discussion of different measures of democracy and their empirical interrelations see Bollen (1980) and Bollen and Grandjean (1981).

3 This controversy involves not only data and measurement problems but also unresolved theoretical issues. Thus, it is not clear that literacy – in contrast to the level of economic development and the age structure of the population – is independent of democratic experience. A hypothesis of interdependence actually seems more plausible than an assertion of independence.

Bollen and Jackman (1989) attack Muller on further methodological grounds. They charge that his analysis is inadequate because it uses a combined measure of stability and democracy and because it does not employ a continuous measure of democracy. It is not necessary to go here into the details of the argument. However, it is important to insist that these are purely operational questions that cannot be decided for all subsequent studies. Reasonable decisions about operational conceptualization depend on available data and above all on the particular theoretical issues at hand. In regard to the latter it seems quite justified to relate years of democratic experience to inequality, as Muller (1988, 1989) does. Bollen's case is much stronger for studies that treat stable democracies as somehow more democratic than unstable democracies, as Lipset did in his early, pioneering essay (1959/1980).

4 Economic dependence was measured by export partner concentration and investment dependence. These measures were associated with military and one-party regime forms for the period 1960–75. However, not all associations were statistically significant, and for the period 1950 – 1965 the evidence suggested "no effects of national economic dependence over and above the influence of economic development" (Thomas et al. 1979: 197).

5 This conclusion was reached only after the international position of a number of *inconsistent* cases was reclassified. Even if such a partial, ad hoc reclassification is judged acceptable, Bollen's results still do not confirm the thesis that economic dependency has a negative impact on the chances

of democracy because this finding was obtained only after political measures had been added to the definition of world system status.

6 For the preceding see Weber (1906: 347). Weber's position on the relation between democracy and capitalist development is rather misrepresented when Lipset (1959/1980: 28) writes, referring to the same essay on democracy in Russia: "Weber ... suggested that modern democracy in its clearest form can occur only under capitalist industrialization." At best, this characterization fits Weber's view of the consequences of early capitalism, which he saw – together with Europe's overseas expansion, the ascendance of scientific rationalism as the hegemonic world view, and cultural ideals derived from Protestantism – as fostering freedom and democracy (Weber 1906: 348).

7 It is no accident that we find a similar focus on historical persistencies in the work of Reinhard Bendix, another pioneer of the renaissance of historical sociology during the last two decades. Bendix (1964: 8–9) quotes the memorable metaphor of Joseph Schumpeter (1947: 12–13): "Social structures, types and attitudes are coins that do not readily melt. Once they are formed they persist, possibly for centuries, and since different structures and types display different degrees of ability to survive, we almost always find that actual group and national behavior more or less departs from what we should expect it to be if we tried to infer it from the dominant forms of the productive process." For a discussion of certain theoretical problems in the use of this "Schumpeter Principle" see Rueschemeyer (1984, esp. 154–6).

8 In fact, Moore alludes a number of times to both factors (see especially 413–14, 439–441, 444, and 494) but does not integrate them fully into his analyses and explanations. Moreover, he expresses doubt about the importance of a pre-existing repressive capacity of the state as an independent actor as he contends that the English upper-classes could have created an adequate apparatus for repression had it been in their interest to do so. His position on intersocietal influences is in some sense quite radical, as he justifies his focus on the very large countries with the contention that the "fact that the smaller countries depend economically and politically on big and powerful ones means that the decisive causes of their politics lie outside their own boundaries" (Moore 1966: xiii). Most would consider this proposition vastly overstated even for the extremely small and dependent countries, and at the same time it led Moore to neglect the impact of international developments on large ones.

9 It is, however, a case with a very different historical development than we find in Britain or the United States. Theda Skocpol (1973) has pointed out that Moore's three instances of democratization really represent three profoundly different paths rather than one common route toward democracy.

10 While this point is critical for our overall assessment of the merits and accomplishments of the two research traditions, it ought not to be understood as a rejection of O'Donnell's argument in principle. It is logically and theoretically quite possible that the mix of causal conditions

changes over time. The specific claim that democracy becomes less and less likely is indeed at odds with Bollen's findings; but it is quite possible that a different mix of causal conditions has similar outcomes in the twentieth as in the nineteenth century.

11 We are aware that we use this appealing metaphor somewhat more loosely than is done in physics.

12 A move away from macro-structural explanations towards political–institutional if not outright voluntaristic ones is also detectable in the work of another collective project on democracy (Diamond, Linz and Lipset 1987). Emphasizing voluntaristic and intermediate organizational factors may, of course, feed on other sources as well. To give an account that stresses these rather than macro-structural factors may for instance be especially tempting when one confronts developments that were not foreseen – and whose very possibility was dismissed – less than fifteen years ago, as was the case with democratization in South America.

13 As Ragin explains: "Not only is human agency obscured in studies of many cases, but the methods themselves tend to disaggregate cases into variables, distributions, and correlations. There is little room left for historical process – that is, for the active construction by humans of their history" (Ragin 1987: 70).

14 The term "analytic induction" goes back to Florian Znaniecki who together with W. I. Thomas used similar strategies of building and testing theories in smaller-scale, social psychological research (Znaniecki 1934). Their conception was narrower than is intended here, restricted to the method of agreement. The concept was revived in broader and more inclusive form in recent discussions of how macro-historical work relates to theory building (see for instance Evans, Rueschemeyer and Skocpol (1985: 348–50). Skocpol and Somers (1980) and Skocpol (1984) speak about the same strategy when they refer to comparative history as "macro-causal analysis" or to procedures "analyzing causal regularities in history".

15 This argument does not simply refer to earlier investigations of the same kind. Equally important is the use of studies on other problems that are theoretically related to the issues at hand. These often concern smaller units of which there are far more cases. In research on democracy these may concern smaller, and often far more frequent, social units than countries or nations – unions for example, and other voluntary organizations (see, for instance, the classic study by Lipset, Trow and Coleman 1956). And they may concern sub-themes that constitute only one link in the larger chain of argument. The validity of such transfers of insight and understanding from one context or level of analysis to another is, of course, not unproblematic; but it can always itself be made the object of investigation. Surely it is precisely one of the major raisons d'être of theory to establish such connections between different areas of inquiry – to build canals linking the different stores of our knowledge, as Lichtenberg once put it.

16 The fact that we devote a whole chapter to the development and discussion of our theoretical framework gives our strategy a somewhat

ambiguous status in the threefold typology of comparative historical research developed by Skocpol and Somers (1980). They distinguish between "comparative history as the contrast of contexts," "comparative history as the parallel demonstration of theory," and "comparative history as macro-causal analysis". We see our endeavor as closest to the latter, but the full elaboration of a theoretical framework creates a certain similarity with the second type, in which a deductively constructed theory is applied to case after case. As argued above, we consider a thoroughly reflected analytic framework as critical for any form of analytic induction, including the one Skocpol and Somers call "macro-causal analysis". (In fact, as we have noted, Skocpol's own analysis of revolutions is built on such a framework.) At the same time, we see the construction of our framework only as the first phase, to be followed by comparative analyses that are informed by the framework, but at the same time test and revise it.

In Tilly's (1984: 80–84) classification, our study engages primarily in universalizing and variation-finding comparisons, but also includes elements of encompassing comparisons. We are interested in identifying the common factors which favor emergence and consolidation of democracy (a universalizing comparison), while we at the same time seek to account for the differences in national political trajectories (variation-finding comparisons). To the extent that we identify transnational structures of power as essential influences on the chances for democratization, we also treat our cases as parts of a larger interdependent system (an encompassing comparison).

The issues of relativism created by metatheoretical premises briefly alluded to in the text are very complex when fully confronted as problems in the philosophy of knowledge. That cannot be done in this context.

17 Mill's method of agreement compares cases, dissimilar in many respects, in which both the outcomes to be explained and the theoretically expected causal conditions are similarly present. The indirect method of difference looks for comparisons of cases similar in many respects but different both in the outcome to be explained and in the theoretically expected causal conditions. See Skocpol (1984) and Ragin (1987) for further discussion of Mill's designs in relation to contemporary comparative historical research.

3 Capitalist Development and Democracy: A Theoretical Framework

1 See Held (1987) for a thorough discussion of the historical succession of models of democracy, which also considers current debates on future possibilities of further democratization.

2 In the previous chapter, we discussed briefly the cross-national statistical evidence on the relationship between democracy and income inequality, which is still inconclusive (Bollen and Jackman 1985, 1989; Muller 1985, 1989; Weede 1989). It must be noted that these quantitative studies are extremely limited in distinguishing between democratic forms and democratically effective institutions.

3   Przeworski (1980, 1985) argues that the political choices of labor movements were made under severe constraints inherent in capitalist society and unfavorable to the interests of the working class. Yet it is hard to maintain that these choices did not in any way advance – that in fact they betrayed – the true interests of the working class.

4   Truly universal suffrage did not exist in the nineteenth and early twentieth centuries. What is critical is that electoral participation transcends class lines. Therefore, it seems reasonable to consider universal male suffrage as the historically crucial benchmark. This decision to focus on male suffrage will be explained further when we discuss gender inequality.

5   Dahl (1971) distinguishes in his definition of "polyarchy" two dimensions – inclusiveness of participation and what he calls public contestation of policy. The latter encompasses free and fair elections, responsible government as well as the protection of civil rights. His conceptualization is quite compatible with ours.

6   See the appendix for the empirical operationalization of these concepts employed in our comparative historical studies.

7   In our own past work we have emphasized the particular role of the strength of the working class vis-à-vis other classes in accounting for cross-national and cross-temporal differences in the strength of democratic impulses. See J. Stephens (1979c: 112–15), E. Stephens (1983), Stephens and Stephens (1986: 13–24, 337–8); Rueschemeyer (1980) offers a theoretical model of democratization that focuses on class conflict and on the means of the dominant classes to maintain their control.

8   As Therborn (1977) points out, there is little or no correlation between the extension of suffrage across class and across gender lines. An analysis of female suffrage would require another comparative study.

9   We say "production-related" rather than "economic" as only relationships and activities strictly necessary to the production and distribution of goods and services are excluded from this concept of civil society; employers' associations and labor unions are part of civil society. (On the complexities – as well as ambiguities – of the concepts of civil society and hegemony in Gramsci, see Anderson 1977; Mouffe 1979; and Laclau and Mouffe 1985). The version of his view of civil society given in the text is the one which we will employ in this book. Whether it is the most accurate reading of his thought is not our concern here.

10 In fact, our discussion reverses Gramsci's emphasis. His first concern was to argue that a dense civil society facilitated ideological domination by the dominant classes and thus made minority rule and democracy compatible. Then, he went on to argue that in such a society the strategy of the left should be to develop a counter hegemony through the development of a dense organizational life formed by the socialist and labor movements which insulate their followers from the dominant ideology.

11 "The proportion of the labor force engaged in the secondary sector around 1850 was as follows: Great Britain, 48.1 percent; France, 26.9; United States, 17.6 (no estimate is available for Germany at this time). Inci-

dentally, the second highest level was found in Belgium (36.6 percent), reflecting that country's industrial lead on the Continent. ... Britain at mid-century was already very close to its historical maximum, 51.6 percent in 1911. ... The British level was attained in only two other cases, Belgium (45.5 percent in 1910, peaking at 48.3 in 1961) and Germany (40.9 percent in 1910, peaking at 48.3 in 1961). Neither in France nor in the United States did the secondary sector work force ever constitute anywhere as high as proportion of the total. In France, the percentage rose slowly from the 26.9 percent level noted for 1850 to 33.1 in 1910, most of the increment occurring after 1880; in the United States, it climbed during the same period from 17.6 to 31.6 percent" (Zolberg 1986: 438). The "proportion of the labor force engaged in the secondary sector" is hardly an adequate definition of the working class, but it does indicate differences that affect class size, too.

12 The class conception used here is close to but not identical with others drawing on the traditions of Marx and Weber. The recent contribution by Wright (1985) substantially narrows the difference between Weberian and Marxist conceptions. Like Elster, Wright now considers all resources including skill and managerial position as well as property ownership as a determinant of class.

13 Here we deal, of course, with the old "class in itself/class in and for itself" problem. In contrast to the traditional view, we see the subjective and organizational expressions of class interests contingent on complex and variable historical conditions and not as an invariant and near-automatic outgrowth of the objective class structure. For a theoretical and empirical analysis of sources of cross-national variation in class consciousness see Stephens (1979a). For theoretical arguments insisting on a certain autonomy of collective goals from structural class position see Rueschemeyer (1986: 75, 186–7). Katznelson (1986) offers a model of class analysis that is quite compatible with our ideas, though we use here three instead of his four levels of class analysis. We have collapsed the first two of Katznelson's dimensions. They correspond very roughly to the distinction we make, following Weber and Giddens, between economic and social class. Wright (1978) makes a similar distinction between classes as positions (or "empty places") in the structure of production and class formation.

14 "Since the worker is at the same time the subject and the object of the exchange of labor power, a vastly broader range of interests is involved in this case than in that of capitalists, who can satisfy a large part of their interests somewhat apart from their functioning as capitalists. In the case of workers, those interests ... include not only material rewards but also such things as job satisfaction, health, leisure time, and continuity of employment. ... [In addition,] there is no common denominator to which all these heterogeneous and often conflicting needs can be reduced so as to 'optimize' demands and tactics. ... In contrast, capitalist firms as well as business associations do not have to take into consideration a comparative

multitude of incommensurable needs. All the relevant questions can be reduced to the unequivocal standards of expected costs and returns" (Offe and Wiesenthal 1980: 75).

15 The obvious exception is Czechoslovakia in 1948; but the communist seizure of power there can hardly be seen as an autonomous development from below.

16 In no country did a socialist party ever achieve a majority before World War I. In 1912 the then most potent socialist party, the German Social Democratic Party, reached with 34. 6 percent of the vote its high point of electoral support before World War I; it mobilized virtually the whole working class (except for a fraction of Catholic workers historically and organizationally tied to the Center Party), but fell far short of a majority (Zolberg 1986: 399; see also Przeworski 1980). Later, the SPD's electoral support increased somewhat, and in a few countries, for instance Finland (Alapuro 1988: 117–18), working-class parties gained a higher percentage of the vote. But in most other countries, neither the degree of working-class mobilization nor the size of the working class were as favorable as in Germany. For figures on the size of the working class and the socialist vote see Przeworski and Sprague (1986: 29–40).

17 Our concept of the state goes back to Weber – a set of organizations vested with the authority to make and enforce decisions that are binding for the people in a particular territory and that are implemented using force if necessary.

18 We will not review this debate at all but formulate our position in nearly apodictic brevity, since by now there exists a rich secondary literature; see Gold et al. (1975), Jessop (1982), Carnoy (1984), Skocpol (1985), Alford and Friedland (1985).

19 It will be remembered that one plausible interpretation of the ambiguous finding of Cutright and Wiley (1969) that the number of social security programs correlated with regime stability was to see this indicator as representing a powerful state apparatus rather than a state responsive to social policy demands. Similarly, Bollen (1979) found that the proportion of economic resources controlled by the state correlated negatively with democracy.

20 So labeled because of the striking analyses of such structural effects by Alexis de Tocqueville in his *The Old Regime and the French Revolution* as well as in *Democracy in America* (see Skocpol 1985: 21, and Evans et al. 1985: 253–4).

21 This interpretation radically neglects all internal factors favoring or obstructing democratization. That German democracy after World War I was also widely viewed as imposed and that this view quite plausibly contributed to its instability puts this interpretation of German democracy after World War II as imposed yet stable further into doubt.

4 Advanced Capitalist Countries

1 Our formulation of this point also avoids some of the ambiguities of Moore's analysis, which Skocpol has criticized elsewhere (see chapter 2). See Stephens (1989) for more extensive discussion of the implications of the European experience for Moore's and Skocpol's view of the state.

2 Kurth's work can be seen as a variant of the late industrialization thesis of de Schweinitz (see chapter 2), though Kurth is apparently unaware of the latter's work.

3 It is clear that Moore argues that the bourgeoisie's dependence on the state and the agrarian elite causes the class to absorb the values of the landed class, but it is not clear that he means that the bourgeoisie thereby adopts a political posture that is not in its interest, as Blackbourn and Eley (1984) imply, grouping Moore with a number of theorists, such as Dahrendorf (1967) who does hold this position. Moore's work can just as easily be read as indicating that the bourgeoisie's interests change in such a situation due to state aid and so on. Nevertheless, Blackbourn and Eley are clearly correct in asserting that Moore assumes that, in the absence of a powerful landed class closely allied with the state, the bourgeoisie will "naturally" adopt democratic politics.

4 The classification of landed class strength in table 4.1 is based on the comparative and country studies consulted for the analysis of the cases. Dovring's (1965) data, by far the most comprehensive compilation of data on landholding at the turn of the century, strongly indicate that political position of large landlords in the society is largely a product of their economic position, which in turn can be read off from landholding patterns. His data are not conclusive, however, because they do not control for land quality (distorting, for example, a comparison of England and Spain) and because the data for some countries includes crown- or state-owned lands, greatly skewing the distributions. It should be emphasized here that the comparative and case studies consulted revealed virtually no dissent from the classification presented in the figure.

5 The Congress of Vienna and subsequent power balance politics were especially important for the preservation of Belgium and the Netherlands. It should be noted that the association of agrarian elite strength with country size/great power status is an historical generalization of the European experience, which would not necessarily hold elsewhere.

6 It should be noted that the following discussion of the transition to democracy is based not only on the final reform establishing democracy as we have defined it but also on previous steps which resulted in suffrage extension to the majority of the working class and/or the establishment of cabinet responsibility to parliament (e.g. the 1884 suffrage extension in Britain or the 1901 establishment of parliamentary government in Denmark).

7 Given the power of the cantons, there were restrictions on political rights after 1848 in some of them; for instance, a conservative government in

Bern dissolved the Grütlivereine in 1850. Thus, Therborn argues that one should date Swiss democracy from the 1870s, when these cantonal restrictions were eliminated. Nevertheless, these restrictions paled in comparison to the provisions of the 1848 constitution, and we have in all cases used developments at the national level as a criterion for classifying countries.

8 The other candidate for the introduction of democracy would be the secret ballot reform of 1913.

9 The effect of this change in power relations already made itself felt on the material welfare of the mass of non-combatant working people in Britain. Winter (1986) shows conclusively that life expectancy rose and infant mortality declined dramatically during the war and that that was a result of, primarily, the improved material situation of the working class in the war economy and, secondarily, of health and welfare policy innovations.

10 On the transition to democracy in Sweden, see Rustow (1955), Verney (1957), Hadenius et al. (1970), Castles (1973), and Tilton (1974). For a detailed study of the role of the upper bourgeoisie, see Söderpalm (1969). Tilton and Castles both explicitly apply the Moore thesis to the Swedish case. Both point to the weakness of the landed aristocracy and the strength and independence of the peasantry in accounting for the democratic outcome in Sweden.

11 In Norway, the situation was yet more extreme as there were only three estates in the parliament, with no noble estate, due to the complete absence of feudalism noted in the text.

12 Rokkan made this observation in a lecture at Yale University in 1974.

13 For unconvincing attempts to rebut Harrison, see Himmelfarb (1966) and Cowling (1967).

14 The reason for the late development of a significant working-class party in relation to the level of industrialization, a characteristic that England shares with France and Switzerland, may lie in the fact that all three were earlier industrializers. The nature of industrialization in these countries (see the discussion of Kurth above) which created small dispersed work units may be one reason for this. Another obvious candidate is ideological diffusion among the late industrializers. For instance, earlier labor agitators in the Scandinavian countries and the Netherlands were heavily influenced by German Social Democracy and later the Second International. Thus, the initial organizers of the working class were socialists, and vaguely Marxists, in contrast to the British case.

15 One might argue that the late development of the Labour Party itself is partly attributable to the willingness of the Liberals to co-operate with working-class leaders. However, the Scandinavian cases argue against this as the Liberals were willing to co-operate with, and attempted to co-opt, elements of the working-class, and none the less, socialist parties emerged earlier and rapidly managed to gain the loyalty of the working class.

16 Sources for figures in this paragraph are: Mitchell (1978) for labor force, Rokkan and Meyriat (1969) for electoral statistics, and Stephens (1979c) for union membership.

17 In the interwar period this generalization about the working class is harder to sustain, since the splits in the working-class induced by the war and the Russian Revolution created anti-democratic minorities, above all the communist parties, whose political posture clearly contributed to the breakdown of democracy. Moreover, as Linz (1978) points out, the radical posturing of maximalist socialists frightened the middle classes, which contributed to the strengthening of the authoritarian forces, and even the moderate social democrats contributed to the outcome by inflexible postures vis-à-vis parties of the center. This said, we think it is fair to say that all of the parties of the social democratic left, which remained by far the largest of the working class parties in every country, maintained a commitment to democracy. Their mistakes do not make them anti-democratic.

18 Seton-Watson (1967: 282) argues that it was with the Libyan war that nationalism became anti-democratic and imperialist and began to attract business support.

19 This dominant view is expressed most succinctly in the works of Hans-Ulrich Wehler (see esp. Wehler 1985). Earlier works singled out for criticism, all emphasizing the role of the Junkers, include Veblen (1966, originally published in 1915), Schumpeter (1968), Gerschenkron (1943), and Moore. For critical, but sympathetic, discussions of Blackbourn and Eley, see Evans (1985) and Garst (1987).

20 Also see Sheehan (1978: 264–70) on the position of various liberal parties and factions on the suffrage question in the last decade of the Wilhelmine period. Not even the left Liberals favored the full reform of local government and, while they officially supported the introduction of responsible cabinet government, they "continually backed away from supporting an unambiguous call for parliamentary sovereignty" (Sheehan 1978: 270).

21 The figures given in the text ignore the votes for the USPD (German Independent Social Democratic Party), whose leadership was clearly democratic. But the party split into two factions, one of which re-entered the SPD (German Social Democratic Party). The other faction joined the Communist Party (KPD), whose disastrous line clearly contributed to the rise of Hitler.

22 See Abraham (1986) and Turner (1985). The Turner critiques of Abraham focus on the documentation of the instrumentalist argument about big business support for the Nazis. This is in fact not the main argument of the book. Rather, Abraham takes a class coalitions approach to the conditions for stable democracy not unlike the one proposed here. Turner's study sticks very close to the traditional historical case study method which, as we pointed out in chapter 2, is biased toward instrumentalist arguments, that is, explanations focusing on agency and process rather than structure.

23 For the structural argument to hold, it is not necessary to inject the subjective attitudes of businessmen as an intervening variable, but to make the argument without this link requires a more complex comparative

analysis and/or counterfactual, which is fortunately not necessary in this case. It is worth pointing out here that a Keynesian reflationary policy, which would have gone against the subjective preferences of business, might well have improved the economy as it did under the Nazis (Gourevitch 1986) and thus worked to stabilize the democratic regime.

24   Northeim, the town studied in Allen's book, was overwhelmingly Protestant, thus there was no Catholic subculture to speak of.

25   Note that the ideological content of these three campaigns (the Kulturkampf, the Agrarian League, and the Naval League) varied and that they were pressed by different, and sometimes conflicting, segments of the economic and political elite; roughly the state and the Liberals, the Junkers and the conservatives, and the state and heavy industry, respectively. Some might question whether the Kulturkampf was in any sense antidemocratic. While it is true that it is not as obvious as in the other two campaigns, it did result in repressive interference of the state towards Catholics and legitimated state discrimination in hiring practices against the enemies of the regime, not only Catholics, but also Social Democrats and Jews (see Blackbourn 1984: 243, 282; Sheehan 1978: 135–7).

26   The state prosecutor's plea began with a statement that sounded more like a campaign speech for a national hero than an indictment of a criminal. See Bracher (1970: 119–20).

27   Alapuro (1988: 216–18) argues that in addtion to the "Scandinavian social structure" (i. e. the dominance of small holding), the Finish upper classes did not perceive of a need to eliminate democracy as there was no working-class threat to the bourgeoisie, since the working class had been defeated in the abortive revolution of 1918.

28   As stated in the previous paragraph, the landed nobilities of the subject nationalities did often lead the nationalist pressures for autonomy.

29   Thus, the sociological counterpart to the Christian Socials in Germany was the DNVP, BVP, and the Zentrum. In the remainder of the party systems, the counterparts are closer: the PSU bloc contains the parties representing the secular urban upper classes and the labor bloc containing the working-class parties. The support for the latter two blocs is very roughly the same in the two countries. The difference lies in the remaining groups which are split in Germany with part supporting nationalistic monarchical authoritarianism and part democratic Catholicism, whereas in Austria they are united supporting the authoritarian Catholic corporativism of the Christian Socials.

30   In comparing Scandinavian liberalism to British (or Austrian) liberalism, it should be pointed out that it had a different social base. Lipset and Rokkan classify the British party as a P–D (Dissenting Sects) –U party and the Scandinavian parties as PD. This misses the urban middle-class component of Scandinavian liberalism, but it accurately catches the key difference: the Scandinavian bourgeoisie supported the parties of the right, not the Liberals. This is probably the main source of the more active support for democracy of the Scandinavian liberal parties as compared to the British.

31 The following remarks on nineteenth-century Spain are based on Carr (1982). See especially, pages 158ff, 203ff, 284ff, 287, and 342 on the social bases of the parties.

32 For the events of the Republic, see Preston (1983) and Malefakis (1970).

33 The struggle over the role of the Catholic church in Spanish society was the other burning issue of the Republic. But it is important to see that it is linked, in part, to the land question. In a Catholic small-holding society like Belgium, the church and Catholic political forces are more moderate. In Spain, where large landholders and the church are allied, it is not difficult to see why the discontent of segments of the masses was often strongly anti-clerical.

34 Strict adherence to our definition of full democracy, which requires male suffrage and no restrictions on contestation, would disqualify even the North and West in some periods as some states had literacy or tax qualifications for voting in the post-Jacksonian period, many states excluded blacks up to the Civil War, and, in certain periods (e.g. immediately after World War I and in the early part of the Cold War), the left was subject to persecution.

35 In the colonial period, some of the states enfranchised only those practicing the locally established religion and many states excluded Catholics.

36 The notable and interesting exception is Rhode Island. There suffrage remained restricted until the state began to industrialize. Then the middle and upper classes were unwilling to extend suffrage to the largely immigrant and Catholic propertyless industrial working class. This set the scene for the Dorr war in 1842, an unsuccessful insurrection carried out to force the expansion of suffrage.

37 Note, however, that not an insignificant numbers of planters were Federalists and later Whigs.

38 As Burch (1981: 16) notes, as late as 1880 Carnegie Steel was capitalized at only $5 million while at least 41 railroads had capital values of $15 million or more.

39 Business interests in the western alliance were not limited to markets. A key issue was the placement of the transcontinental railroad. See Ferguson (1983b: 41–9) for a discussion of the alignment of capitalist factions in this period.

40 The relationship of business to the progressive movement was complex since one reform thrust of the movement was aimed at monopolists, yet many medium and some large businessmen supported some of the reform efforts (see Wiebe 1962). Pro-progressive businessmen's attitude to the progressive goal of making government more responsive to the voters was at best ambivalent: As Wiebe (1962: 212) points out, they "wanted to purify democracy, they opposed extending it." On the decline in participation, see Burnham (1970, 1981) on the effect of the "System of '96," and see Ferguson (1983b: 52) for a summary table on the increase in suffrage requirements in this period. The reader may wonder why we continue to classify the North and West of the United States as a "full democracy"

given these increases in suffrage limitations. In our classifications, we did not place a polity in the "restricted democracy" category if it had residence or citizenship qualifications for voting. In 1912, nine states had property qualifications for voting, 16 tax (largely poll tax) qualifications, and 16 literacy or education qualifications for voting. These were largely concentrated in the South; thus, the overwhelming majority of northern and western states had no such suffrage limitations. The main legal barriers to participation in the North and West introduced in this period were residency and citizenship requirements. As Burnham (1970: 71–90) shows, this did cause a reduction in participation, but only a small portion of the drastic decline after 1896 can be directly linked to these new requirements. Other progressive reforms, which were aimed at urban machines but which weakened political parties' mobilizing capacity in general, were more important.

41 We use this term to differentiate these colonies from those that later became the United States, though it was not until Confederation in 1867 that it was applied to all of the provinces. Likewise, we refer to Québec and Ontario by the modern terms rather than Upper and Lower Canada or Canada East and West.

42 See Garner (1969) for an extremely detailed history of the franchise and other legislation affecting voting for the pre-Confederation period. In the very first elections in some colonies more liberal qualifications were employed owing to lack of population or to large populations still without proper titles to their lands. With the exceptions of British Columbia and Prince Edward Island, these were soon changed to more restricted property suffrage.

43 An enclave of labor repressive agriculture in the cotton and sugar plantations of Queensland, manned first by Indian and then South Sea island indentured labor, survived until the late 1880s when the combination of the decline in the power of the merchant–planter–squatter coalition in the colony, the rise of independent family farming and labor, and agitation by abolitionists fuelled by outrage at the excesses associated with the recruitment of indentured labor, including kidnapping, resulted in the eventual termination of the practice (Irving 1974: 152; Buxton 1974: 201).

44 Edward Wakefield's principles of systematic colonization aimed at the development of concentrated settlements along the lines of the English corn counties. To achieve the proper balance between land, capital, and labor, the price of land was to be set sufficiently high that purchase would be restricted to those of substantial means. The proceeds would be used to bring laborers to the colony and thus the labor shortages and dispersion of settlement characteristic of new colonies, such as the United States and Canada, which Wakefield loathed, would be prevented (Sinclair 1961: 44–7; Gardner 1981: 59–60). In fact, due to the availability of land, no large class of rural laborers ever developed in South Australia or New Zealand and thus the modal rural holding in both colonies resembled a North American family farm much more than English gentry estate.

45 This discussion of differing ways in which the historic authoritarian coalitions influenced interwar events helps explain why the analysis here comes to conclusions diametrically opposite to those in the recent work of Luebbert (1987, forthcoming) covering similar cases and a similar time period. Using percentage of the labor force in agricultural labor as the indicator of rural social structure, Luebbert contends that there is no correlation between rural social structure and regime outcome. The agrarian elite strength measure used here, which is a product of the underlying distribution of landholdings, shows something quite different. Luebbert then correctly points out that, in the arguments of Gerschenkron and Moore, the reason why landholder power resulted in an authoritarian outcome in Germany in the interwar period is, in large part, that they still exercised political control over the rural masses in this period. This path was not replicated in the other cases, he contends. Therefore, he concludes, landlord strength cannot explain the breakdown in these other cases. Our objection to this was made clear in our introduction to the breakdown cases: the mechanism suggested by Moore and Gerschenkron does not exhaust the ways in which late nineteenth-century coalitions and landlord power expressed themselves in the events of the 1920s and 1930s.

46 The discussion of Italy in this paragraph refers primarily to the Po Valley, which was the focus of the rural class struggles that led to the rise of Fascism. On Italy, see Cardoza (1982) and Corner (1975). On Spain, see Malefakis (1970).

47 In the four British settler colonies, tariff politics drove agriculture (including pastoralism) and industry apart. They all adopted protective tariffs in this period, but agriculture, which was internationally competitive, generally opposed them.

48 In both Sweden and Denmark, the king drew heavily on army officers, nobility, and higher civil servants to form cabinets whatever the composition of parliament until late in the nineteenth century. On Sweden, see the references cited above, particularly Rustow (1955) and Verney (1957). On Denmark, see Lind (1988).

49 On Scandinavia, see our discussion above, Stråth (1988), Rokkan (1967), and Tomasson (1970). On the importance of dissent for the early development of the labor movement and other opposition movements in England, see Thompson (1963). For a comparison of Scandinavia and Britain, see Stephens (1979b).

50 In his first version of the democracy essay, Lipset (1959: 92–3) points in this direction, but deletes this discussion from the 1960 book. This line of thought is, of course, further developed in his work with Rokkan (Lipset and Rokkan 1967) and in Rokkan's work (Rokkan 1967, 1970, 1975).

51 In an earlier version of this chapter (J. Stephens 1989), Finland was included because it appeared to be "Western" from the contemporary vantage point. However, as Alapuro's (1988) fine analysis shows, Finnish political development is more properly analyzed in comparison with that of

other East European countries that arose from the ashes of the Austrian, German, and Russian empires after World War I.

52   On eastern Europe, see Seton-Watson (1962) and Alapuro (1988); on Portugal, see Marques (1972); on the Balkans, focusing on Greece, see Mouzelis (1986).

5   Latin America

1   In this chapter, we will analyze the ten major South American countries and Mexico only; Central America will be dealt with in the next chapter. To avoid the lengthy "South America and Mexico," we will use "Latin America" to denote this set of countries, except where the context would make such usage ambiguous and the statements in question clearly do not apply to Central America.

2   Chile 1970–3, of course, is an important exception.

3   Tables 5.1 and 5.2 show our classification of regimes in the various countries and periods; an explanation of our decisions about the classification of regimes is given in the Appendix.

4   Our argument obviously draws on a wealth of case studies and comparative and theoretical analyses, but in order to keep the basic outlines of the argument here brief, we give all the citations in the next section with the presentation of the historical materials.

5   There is only one case of leading non-agricultural exports under domestic control, mining in Bolivia before the 1920s; Bolivia since the 1920s is a complex case and will be discussed in more detail below. The dominant agricultural export sectors in South America, in contrast to Central America, were primarily domestically owned. Foreign ownership in the Peruvian sugar industry was strong, but agricultural exports as a whole were still mainly under domestic control, and they constituted the dominant export sector only temporarily. Thus, we will use the terminology agricultural vs. mineral export economy which also implies national vs. foreign ownership, and where relevant we will specifically note exceptions.

6   If we extend the analysis to Central America and the Caribbean, the nature of ownership of the dominant agricultural export sector becomes important. In order for this relationship to hold, ownership of the large, labor intensive estates producing for the crucial export sector has to be domestic.

7   Note that some logically possible configurations of variables historically did not occur. The problem here is one of six cases; Argentina, Uruguay, Brazil, Colombia, Ecuador, and Paraguay; and three variables (labor intensity of agriculture, strength of industrialization, agent shaping the political articulation of civil society). Only two cases, Argentina and Uruguay, had non-labor intensive agriculture, and in these two cases the early industrializing thrust was comparatively strong and clientelistic parties played a crucial role. Of the four cases with labor intensive agriculture, Ecuador and Paraguay experienced very late and limited industrialization and thus very weak pressures for democratization; Brazil

was a case of significant industrialization from the 1930s on but weak pressures due to early and strong state encapsulation of the labor movement, and Colombia a case of moderate pressures due to delayed industrialization and the important role of elite-dominated clientelistic parties. Thus, the outcomes appear overdetermined and it becomes impossible to extract the primary reason for the different outcomes from the configuration of variables alone. Rather, one has to look at the historical record of the actions of the different actors towards democratization to make this assessment.

8　This can be explained by the fact that labor in mining was too independent and radical to be encapsulated, and that radical mass parties competed with the state in the organization of labor. For instance, the state in Chile under Ibáñez made incorporation attempts, but their effects were rapidly eroded during the following period of competitive party politics.

9　This is another case of overdetermination. In the only two cases, Argentina and Uruguay, where the working class had a significant presence and the leading role in the initial democratization was played by clientelistic rather than radical mass parties (because these were countries with agrarian export economies), the working class was of heavily immigrant extraction and thus the installation of full democracy did not have the effect of total inclusion. Furthermore, these were countries with non-labor intensive dominant agricultural export sectors. Thus, the threat posed to elites by democratization was reduced in both of these ways.

10　An explanation of the emergence of such parties is clearly beyond the scope of this study. We simply take their presence or absence as a given and use it as a variable in our analysis. Their emergence seems to depend on the early history of institutionalization of contestation and the intensity of intra-elite conflicts leading to repeated civil wars.

11　Our argument here is compatible with Rustow's who stipulates national unity as single background condition for the emergence of democracy, that is, enduring borders, a continuous citizenry, and the absence of any doubt among the citizens as to which political community they belong to (1970: 350–1). Our argument, however, puts less emphasis on citizens' attitudes than on effective state control over the national territory.

12　For a discussion of the problem of consolidation of the state and the role of caudillos in post-independence Latin America, see e. g. Cardoso and Faletto (1979: 36–41), Burns (1986: 90–132), and Safford (1985: 347–89).

13　In the interest of clarity, we have to provide a coherent exposition of the historical case material at some point and not scatter it among different analytical sections. Therefore, this section contains material that is also relevant for some of the other analytic issues.

14　Economic growth could of course also complicate the consolidation of state power, where it increased regional diversity and differential linkages of various regions to the international economy, as e. g. in Argentina.

15　For a discussion of dynamics in nationally controlled and enclave economies in this period see Cardoso and Faletto (1979: 66–73).

16 In the first years of the Republic, the middle sectors gained a share of political power, but they were quickly replaced by the oligarchy; see Burns (1980: 278–320).

17 In Argentina wheat, corn, and linseed together rivaled ranching as major export activity after the turn of the century and even surpassed it after 1910 (Díaz Alejandro 1970: 18). However, wheat farming was mostly done through a combination of tenancy arrangements and seasonal wage labor, that is, arrangements which were based on formal contracts and did not bind the labor force to a specific estate. Typically, a contract lasted for some three years, and then the land reverted to being used for ranching. This meant that there was a high turnover among the mostly immigrant tenants who had to look for a new place to work every few years (Allub 1983: 83). Thus, loss of control over a cheap supply of labor in the wake of democratization was not a threat to landowners. We are indebted to Art Stinchcombe for alerting us to these tenancy arrangements.

18 The Chilean case is different from the other three in so far as the middle-class–working-class alliance was an alliance of three separate parties, rather than one organized within one party. The Radical Party, which was the dominant partner in the Popular Front (it fielded the candidate for president), was clearly much less radical and thus mitigated the threat to the Chilean elites.

19 Zeitlin (1984) argues that there were significant divisions between the landowning and mining segments of the dominant class in the nineteenth century, so much so that they sparked two civil wars, and that the two segments only coalesced into the cohesive dominant class identified by Zeitlin and Ratcliff (1988) after the defeat of Balmaceda in 1891. However, Zeitlin's own data (1984) show the considerable overlap between landowners and capitalists, many of them having multiple holdings in different sectors. Thus, the statement that Chile's dominant class was more cohesive than the dominant classes in Peru and Venezuela remains accurate.

20 See Zeitlin et al. (1976), and Zeitlin and Ratcliff (1988) for a discussion of the importance of landlords in Chilean politics well into the second half of the twentieth century.

21 Bolivian politics from the 1920s on fit the pattern of enclave economies, though the character of the three tin companies was not typical of foreign-owned minerals companies. During the 1920s, the Big Three (Patiño, Aramayo, and Hochschild) managed to gain control over some 80 percent of tin production. Two of these owners were clearly of national origin, and the third one a German Jewish immigrant (Malloy 1970: 35–6). Though the companies were incorporated abroad and held extensive financial interests outside the country, they were also deeply entrenched in the national economy. For instance, Patiño was also the largest banker in Bolivia, and he and the other two tin magnates had interests in railroads, land, and commercial ventures (Malloy 1970: 43). Given their national origins, Patiño and Aramayo were legitimate political actors; Aramayo

came from an old elite family, and he in fact attempted to sponsor his own political party in the period 1936–8 and did so for the 1951 elections (Klein 1971: 37 and 45).

22 Industrial output as percentage of GDP was 23 percent in Argentina in 1929, compared to 12 percent in Brazil and 8 percent in Chile; in 1957 it had grown to 23 percent in Brazil and 20 percent in Chile (Furtado 1976: 108–11).

23 See Smith (1978: 14) and Rock (1975: 95) for a discussion of the importance of landowners in the Radical Party.

24 These characteristics were also present in Italy and France, and they weakened the labor movements there.

25 Portes and Walton (1981: 67–106) develop this conceptualization of the informal sector, and Portes (1985) discusses the development of the informal sector in Latin America, showing that it remained larger than in the United States at comparable stages of development.

26 As discussed in the Appendix, the formal introduction of universal male literate suffrage did not really bring in full democracy in Chile at that point. As late as the 1950s, suffrage qualifications, complicated registration procedures, and lack of a truly secret ballot kept the bulk of the rural population excluded, except where the landlords decided to use their labor force as suppliers of votes.

27 For basic information on the development of labor organization in the various countries, see Alexander (1965) and Alba (1968); for comparative historical analyses, see Spalding (1977) and Bergquist (1986).

28 In May 1969 automobile workers and students in Córdoba staged a strike, factory occupations, and demonstrations which were joined by many other sectors of the urban population and escalated into large-scale riots and battles with the police (see e. g. Rock 1985: 349).

29 Artisans and craftsmen can also be classified as working-class if they are employed, rather then being self-employed or employers.

30 For instance, A. Valenzuela (1977) makes a convincing case for the importance of patronage at the local level for all parties in Chile, including the left. Apra in Peru was famous for its organized mass base and for the services provided to its members through the Casas del Pueblo (see e. g. Hilliker 1971: 74–113).

31 See Finch (1981: 53–62) for a concise overview of the development of the labor movement in Uruguay.

32 Rial (1984: 14–15) argues that organized elite interest groups mainly exerted pressures directly on government agencies, rather than working through political parties. However, he gives examples where elite interests were effectively defended in parliament by party factions (see his footnote 8). Furthermore, incumbents in crucial positions in state agencies were appointed by the party-based governments, which meant that important concessions to elite interests had to meet with the approval of party leaderships.

33 See Bergquist (1986) and Spalding (1977) for discussions of the develop-

ment of the labor movement in Argentina, Smith (1969) and Rock (1975) for the political context, and Kenworthy (1973) and Page (1983) for Perón and his legacy.

34   There is a debate in the literature about the relative autonomy of the Brazilian state before 1930 (see the review by Graham 1987; also see Topik 1987). Whether the state acted on behalf of the oligarchy in the attempt to co-opt and control the emerging labor movement, or whether incumbents in state roles developed their own initiatives cannot be decided here. At any rate, such an attempt was made, the nature of the state apparatus facilitated the success of the attempt, and it had lasting effects.

35   The period 1930–7 does not really qualify as a restricted democracy because the Constituent Assembly of 1933 was not in its entirety elected by direct popular elections, as it included syndicate members, and Vargas was elected President by this Assembly, not by direct popular election.

36   Bergquist (1986: 12; passim) makes a similar argument concerning the radicalizing impact of foreign-dominated, capital intensive enclaves on the working and middle classes, but he does not see the role of the landowners as an important link. The greater strength of landowners in Chile in comparison with the other three cases certainly contributed to the conspicuous absence of anti-oligarchic and anti-imperialist policies under the Popular Front, in addition to the context of World War II.

37   Collier and Collier (forthcoming) and Collier (1986) classify Chile, along with Brazil, as a case of state incorporation. The reasons for disagreement are explained in the text.

38   Two reasons account for the difference in the success of the incorporation attempts in Brazil and Chile; first, in Chile there was no tradition of state involvement in the affairs of civil society comparable to state involvement in Brazil, and second an autonomous and radical labor movement with links to socialist and communist parties had already developed in the mining enclaves and could not be co-opted through state sponsorship and paternalism. R. Collier (1986) offers a comparison of incorporation attempts in these two cases which comes to the same conclusion that Vargas went further and produced more lasting effects than Ibáñez, but emphasizes other reasons for the difference in success, namely the effects of the Depression on the fall of Ibáñez and the timing of his regime in relationship to the spread of European Fascism.

39   See Bergquist (1986) on the development of the labor movement in Venezuela, and Martz (1966) on Acción Democrática and its relationship with the labor movement.

40   A short and unsuccessful incorporation attempt was made in Bolivia between 1936 and 1939 (Malloy 1970: 105). In the early years of his long rule (1919–30), Leguía in Peru made some attempts to co-opt and control labor (Collier and Collier, forthcoming, ch. 3). As far as competing parties are concerned, the Communist Party did promote labor organization in Peru, but it lost control over the labor movement to Apra by 1945 (Sulmont 1984: 48–62) and it was never able to build a mass base coming

close to Apra's. Various marxist parties were involved in labor organization in Bolivia, but they did not manage to develop strong bases outside the labor movement.

41 In the course of the Trujillo uprising several military officers who had been taken hostage were killed. This provoked an immediate bloody retaliation by the military, as well as a deep lasting enmity between the military and Apra. This is an example of an historical event which had consequences lasting much beyond the underlying structural conditions that had originally provoked the event. Aside from Klarén (1973), Pike (1967), Bourricaud (1970), Villanueva (1975; 1977) and Cotler (1978: 183–4) discuss the relationship between Apra, the oligarchy, the military, and other political actors.

42 See e. g. Lowenthal (1975), Stepan (1978), Philip (1978), and E. Stephens (1980) for an analysis of the emergence and the character of this regime.

43 For developments leading up to and following the 1952 revolution, see Malloy (1970), the essays in Malloy and Thorn (1971), and Mitchell (1977).

44 Stepan (1971: 57–66) develops the "moderator model" to characterize a situation where the military is frequently called into politics to moderate political activity, but not to effect significant changes in the political system. The military's main actions are coups against the executive and a transfer of power to alternative civilian groups.

45 Similarly, if we only look at cases where military subordination under civilian rule was successful, we could propose the following plausible hypotheses for Uruguay and Colombia. In both countries, the intense rivalry and armed conflicts between the two party camps prevented the emergence of a strong, professionalized army in the nineteenth century, as the regular troops were frequently confronted by armed irregulars. Thus, in Colombia the military could not offer any significant resistance to the attempts of civilian leaders to keep its size and budget small; as of 1940 the military was still the smallest relative to population in the western hemisphere (Ruhl 1980: 182–3). In Uruguay, the officers of the regular army were mostly of Colorado extraction, and the army fought under Batlle to put down the Blanco rebellion of 1904 (Finch 1981: 6–10). In order to be prepared for potential future Blanco rebellions, the army was strengthened by Batlle and his successor Williman. Therefore, it had no reason to accede to insistent Blanco calls for military intervention in 1910 to prevent a second Batlle presidency (Vanger 1980: 92; 170; 184). The majority of officers remained Colorado supporters, and the renewed military threat from the Blanco caudillos in 1932–3 helped the Colorado president to consolidate his control over the military (Taylor 1952: 310). However, these hypotheses do not help to explain why the military finally did become involved in politics. A comparative perspective draws our attention to the role of parties in channeling political pressures and mediating political conflicts without appeals for military intervention, and the fact that it was precisely when the parties fractionalized in situations of

intensifying social struggle and/or economic stagnation that elites turned to the military or the military started acting autonomously from civilian authority.

46 Parallel to our argument here, Di Tella (1990: 148) argues that civilian appeals are crucial catalysts of military intervention, and he stresses the importance of a strong party of the right for the consolidation of democracy. J. S. Valenzuela (1985) also emphasizes the importance of strong conservative parties, representing elite interests, for the viability of democratic regimes. O'Donnell and Schmitter (1986: 62–3) stress the importance of a strong showing of right-wing parties in the founding elections in a process of redemocratization.

47 Nun points out the middle-class character of the officer corps and the similarity in the political interests and actions of the military and the middle classes. In fact, he goes as far as to claim that "the armed forces became one of the few important institutions controlled by the middle-class" (1967: 76). Whereas his view ignores important internal dynamics in the military institution and cannot account for the cases where the military intervened on the side of the elites against middle class attempts to force an opening of the oligarchic system, it does draw attention to the frequent affinity between the political roles of the middle classes and of the military.

48 These conditions are not necessary ones, though, as the examples of Argentina 1912–30 and Bolivia 1952–64 demonstrate, where there were no strong parties competing with the Radicals and the MNR, respectively.

49 The conditions under which this is possible have occurred exceedingly rarely in South America, only in Peru 1968–75 and in Bolivia 1952–64, both countries with mineral export economies where the landowners did not control the crucial export sector. In the Chilean case, the land reform failed to deprive the landowning class of economic and political power; under Pinochet, significant amounts of land were restituted to the former owners. The Chilean case makes clear that satisfaction of the three conditions has to be an accomplished fact before they can sustain a fully democratic system. In Chile, the attempt to disempower the landowners and the simultaneous rapid strengthening of civil society, which raised the threat level to the elites, contributed to the erosion of the democratic system.

50 For characterizations of Mexican authoritarianism, see e. g. Weinert (1977: xii-xiii), Reyna (1977: 160–1), Cornelius (1986: 117–20), and Levy (1989). The Mexican system has been classified as bureau-cratic–authoritarian (e.g. Kaufman 1977: 194–5), but such a classification obscures some of the most interesting characteristics of Mexican authoritarianism, namely its comparatively high degree of legitimacy and low degree of outright repression.

51 Sources consulted for developments in Mexico in this period are Meyer and Sherman (1983), Skidmore and Smith (1984: 225–32), and Bazant (1987).

52 See Hansen (1971) for a detailed analysis of the Mexican economy and its political underpinnings from about 1880 to the 1960s.

53 Coatsworth (1983: 208–9), in examining the Moore thesis for the Porfiriato, analyzes the emergence of this central role of the state; he also argues that the revolution subsequently created the conditions for the establishment of the modern corporatist authoritarian regime (1983: 216).

54 A more than cursory discussion of the origins and course of the Mexican revolution is clearly beyond the scope of this chapter. An analysis and theoretical interpretation which fits well with our theoretical framework in so far as it focuses on class relations, the state, and transnational structures of power, is offered by Goldfrank (1975, 1979). Excellent analyses of the social bases of the Mexican revolution are Womack (1968), Wolf (1969), and Tutino (1986).

55 Again, no analysis of the course and outcome of the revolution is possible here, just a short mentioning of those factors of interest to our analysis. A number of factors worked together to obstruct the consolidation of power by Villa's and Zapata's forces. For instance, Zapata's forces were typical guerrillas dependent on their local environment, their interests were not the same as those of Villa's forces, US support for Carranza was important in turning the military tide in favor of the Constitutionalist armies, and Villa and Zapata lacked the political leadership qualities to match their skills as military leaders. See e. g. Meyer and Sherman (1983: 483–623) and Tannenbaum (1964) for an analysis of the course and outcome of the revolution; Gilly (1971) offers a detailed and interesting, albeit partisan account.

56 See Hamilton (1982) for an analysis of both the extent and the limits of state autonomy and redistributive reforms under Cárdenas.

57 This discussion of relations between the (post)revolutionary political leadership and organized labor relies heavily on Spalding (1977).

58 Though the military sector was eliminated in a renewed party reorganization in 1940, the top military leadership has continued to be involved in party politics; officers run for office, participate in party decisions, and influence candidate selection (Reyna 1977: 167–8). In 1946 the party was given its present name Partido Revolucionario Institucional (PRI).

59 See Hansen (1971) for an analysis of the Mexican growth model, its social consequences, and its roots in the political economy of the post-revolutionary period. Smith (1977: 19) discusses the relationship between the economic and the political elites.

60 Kaufman (1977: 212–15) points out another important difference which made the incorporation of subordinate classes more durable in Mexico than in Argentina and Brazil. The revolution and Cárdenas's reforms had eliminated the old agrarian export elites, and thus the subsequent governments did not have to appeal to labor support to counterbalance the opposition from these groups to their pro-industrialization policies. Accordingly, labor gained less room for independent and militant action than in the other two countries.

61 See Hellman (1983) for an informative discussion of the effective combination of co-optation and repression which is at the root of the PRI's continued hegemony.

62   Dahl (1971: 34–9) argues that the path from competitive oligarchy to polyarchy, i. e. first institutionalization of contestation and then inclusion, which was typical among the older polyarchies, is more likely to result in a stable regime than a simultaneous institutionalization of contestation and widening of inclusion, or a path where institutionalization of contestation comes after inclusion.

63   The same argument is often applied to the legacy of authoritarian institutions; successor authoritarian regimes tend to revitalize previously established forms of political control.

64   A discussion of the different types of authoritarian regimes is given at the end of the section on *Transitions to Authoritarianism*.

65   The exceptional features of the Chilean situation were discussed above. Thus, the statement here is not to be interpreted as an argument in support of the view that Chilean democracy broke down because of "hypermobilization" (Landsberger and MacDaniel 1976). It is not clear that the inclusion of the rural sector through rural unionization and political mobilization in the 1960s, the increase in urban unionization, and the enfranchisement of illiterates for the 1971 municipal elections per se were responsible for the breakdown of Chilean democracy. They certainly contributed to a turn among the large landowners and the bourgeoisie against the democratic regime, but it is plausible to argue that democracy would have survived if the electoral system had not produced a minority president with very radical reform designs confronting a hostile congress. For a discussion of the political institutional factors contributing to the breakdown, such as the presidential system and the constitutional reforms of 1970 designed to strengthen the executive, see A. Valenzuela (1989).

66   Lombardi (1982: 241) makes the point that a legacy of strong authoritarian institutions is a problem for democracy, but that Venezuela demonstrates that this does not mean that democracy requires a long tradition of pre-democratic institutions, but rather that such institutions can be created rapidly under conditions of a political vacuum, i.e. the absence of entrenched authoritarian institutions.

67   Rock (1975) and Smith (1978) disagree on the importance of the Depression for the 1930 breakdown in Argentina. Rock emphasizes the effects of the Depression, whereas Smith stresses the question of access to political power and the consequent illegitimacy of the system in the eyes of the conservatives. We agree with Rock that the Depression was clearly crucial and would argue that it was the perception of an acute threat to their interests which made the marginalization from political power intolerable for the agro-exporting interests. Waisman (1989: 69) agrees that the concern over "the effectiveness of democratic rules to protect its economic interests" motivated the agrarian upper class to install an authoritarian regime. For a discussion of the economic context of the post–1951 turn to authoritarianism see Wynia (1978: 61–73), for 1966 O'Donnell (1978: 149–59), and for 1976 Wynia (1978: 221–7), Di Tella (1983: 115–36), and Landi (1978: 49–70). Finch (1981: 106) makes the argument for Uruguay that the coup of 1933 brought a government to

power "whose primary and explicit objective was to defend the interests of the landowning class," which were threatened by the effects of the Depression on exports. He also provides an analysis of the interaction between the post–1955 economic and political crises (1981: 220–45). For the economic problems in Chile in 1922–4 see Mamalakis (1976: 29, 35), in 1970–3 Nove (1976) and Bitar (1986: 118–72); for Bolivia pre–1964 see Thorn (1971), and for Ecuador pre–1961 Schodt (1987: 80–1). The dynamics leading up to the 1948 coup in Venezuela are discussed by Lombardi (1982: 223–5), Martz (1966: 83–7), and Levine (1978: 89–92). The economic and political context of the 1948 coup in Peru is discussed by Pike (1967: 282–90) and Thorp and Bertram (1978: 187–201), and of the 1968 coup by Cotler (1978), Jaquette (1971: 148–74) and Thorp and Bertram (1978: 286–94). For the dynamics behind the breakdown in Colombia in 1948 see Oquist (1980: 111–27) and Wilde (1978: 51–8).

68 The regime characterizations given here are for modal types. Several regimes had mixed characteristics of traditional and populist authoritarianism. For instance, Peru in 1968 does not fit the mold of the traditional or populist authoritarian systems nor of the bureaucratic–authoritarian one. The regime was initially exclusively based on the military institution, and it never managed to build a strong organized social support base. Its reformism alienated all elite sectors, and its incorporation attempts towards the lower classes generated significant mobilization and organization, but stifled efforts to turn these organizations into strong support bases (E. Stephens 1980). It emerged at an intermediate stage of ISI and in the context of intermediate levels of popular mobilization. Thus, the threat from popular forces was less important as a motivating factor for the military than the inability of the democratic system to generate effective nationalist–developmentalist policies (see e.g. Stepan 1978 and Lowenthal 1975).

Ecuador in 1961 and 1963 does not fit the patterns of class coalitions and regimes outlined here either. No stable class and party coalitions were formed; rather, the President from 1961 to 1963 was under fire from right and left, elites and labor, and in 1963 the military took power with reformist intentions, ruling at least initially quite autonomously from forces in civil society (Schodt 1987: 82–3).

Brazil under Vargas cannot be easily classified either. The class base of the regime shifted somewhat; in the regime's early period it resembled the class base of the traditional authoritarian regimes with middle-class support, and under the estado novo it came to resemble the class base of populist regimes (see Skidmore 1967).

69 The critiques of O'Donnell's argument in Collier (1979) focus on the connection between the implementation of policies for the deepening of industrialization and the installation of bureaucratic–authoritarian regimes; they largely accept the point that the situation of economic stagnation after a period of rapid industrialization generated sharp social conflicts over economic policy.

70 Of course, alliances between sectors of economic elites and foreign capital

have a long history in Latin America, with predominantly negative consequences for democracy. These alliances strengthened domestic elite sectors and gave foreign capital considerable influence on domestic politics, which increased the capacity of both sets of actors to resist pressures from subordinate classes for widening of political inclusion and/or socio economic reforms. What was new in the 1960s was the particular composition of these alliances, with a crucial role played by civilian and military technocrats.

71 McClintock (1986) also points to the lower level of development in Ecuador and Bolivia compared to Peru as a factor making democratic consolidation less likely. Among the other factors increasing the chances for consolidation in Peru she mentions the legacy of the reforms under the Velasco regime and the guerrilla threat which induces the elites to perceive the choice as one between elections and civil war or revolution.

72 The growth of the illegal drug trade is also a major obstacle to the consolidation of democracy in Colombia and Peru. Corruption linked to the drug trade has a corrosive effect on the state, and powerful drug gangs have come to challenge the authority of the state, including its monopoly on organized use of force. Sectors of the security forces involved directly or indirectly, via corruption, in the drug trade have a strong incentive to defy the constitutional authority of democratic governments. Such defiance undermines the capacity of democratic governments to perform basic functions like enforcement of law and order, and consequently their legitimacy.

73 Peru is confronting additional serious threats to democratic rule in the form of the Sendero Luminoso insurgency and the drug traffickers. Large areas of the country are under the State of Emergency and de facto military rule, and some other parts are out of the control of the government.

74 Brazil is handicapped in still a third way. The military's role in politics is more firmly institutionalized than in the other cases (Stepan 1988), which raises the potential for continued high military involvement under a democratic regime and thus lowers the likelihood that a full democracy can be consolidated.

75 See Handelman (1976) for an analysis of the restricted room for union autonomy and the unpredictability of government reactions to demands from independent unions.

76 See Stevens (1974) for an analysis of the protest movement and the regime's response.

77 See Middlebrook (1986), Cornelius (1986) and Levy (1989) for analyses of the process of political liberalization in Mexico.

78 See Gómez and Klesner (1988) for a discussion of the emergence of the FDN.

79 The defeat of 11 trade union leaders belonging to the CTM and 29 leaders of "popular organizations" who ran as PRI candidates indicates that blue and white collar workers voted heavily for Cárdenas and the FDN (*Latin American Weekly Report*, January 12, 1989).

80 On the one hand, in July 1989 the PRI for the first time recognized the victory of an opposition party in a gubernatorial election, namely the PAN in Baja California (Norte), but on the other hand simultaneous elections in Michoacán, Cárdenas's home base, were highly fraudulent. Furthermore, PRD activities have met with increasingly violent responses from the state apparatus (e.g. *Latin American Weekly Report*, March 15, 1990).

81 It is important here to distinguish between conjunctures and incremental developments, as well as between economic conjunctures resulting in economically conditioned changes and political conjunctures resulting in impulses for change coming from the political sphere proper. Conjunctures are temporally distinct constellations of critical conditions. The effects of economic conjunctures are primarily mediated through the balance of power in civil society; the effects of political conjunctures through changes in the state or in the behavior of political parties. An example of effects of an economic conjuncture is the weakening of the landowning export oligarchy by the Depression; an example of effects of a political conjuncture are the experience of the Brazilian military in World War II and the international discrediting of authoritarian forces, which resulted in the military's decision to replace Vargas. Therborn (1979: 87–9) does not make this distinction. He identifies a Latin American democratic conjuncture which culminated in the mid-1940s but started in the mid- 1930s in Colombia and ended in 1952 in Bolivia; alternatively, he suggests that a wider conceptualization would have the conjuncture end in 1964, with the overthrow of Goulart. He argues that the Depression, the following boom during World War II and the post-War period, and the challenge from and defeat of Fascism were all important ingredients of this conjuncture. To use the concept of conjuncture in such an undifferentiated manner is to broaden its meaning to the point of destroying its analytical precision and usefulness.

82 In his study of 17 countries which were "developing democracies" (i.e. developing countries under democratic regimes) in the early to mid-1960s, Muller finds a statistically significant and quite strong negative correlation between US military aid per soldier received in the period 1953–63 and subsequent democratic political stability during the Johnson and Nixon administrations (Muller 1985: 461). In contrast, he finds no such relationship between indicators of economic dependence and democratic survival. This suggests that high levels of military aid did add to the troubles of democracy in South America. In fact, one might have to make a stronger argument about the significant independent effect of military aid on democratic breakdowns, were it not for two problems with the statistical analysis. (1) The use of military aid per soldier rather than per capita is questionable. (2) One could argue that military institutions that were more involved in politics to begin with requested (and received) US assistance to a greater extent. At any rate, one can accept Muller's explanation that military aid afforded strong influence to US policy-makers whose Cold War views often predisposed them to support authoritarian regimes, and one can add to this that the aid also strengthened the general potential of

the military to act politically, be it in alliance with sectors of elites or autonomously from civilian social and political forces.

6   Central America and The Caribbean

1   The purpose of this chapter is to illuminate the contrast between the strong authoritarian tradition of Central America and the strong democratic tradition of the ex-British Caribbean countries, as well as the special characteristics of the deviant cases in both areas. Thus, we chose the major countries in both sets for primary comparison, namely El Salvador, Guatemala, Honduras, and Nicaragua as typical, and Costa Rica as the deviant case in Central America; and Jamaica, Barbados, and Trinidad and Tobago as typical, and Guyana and Grenada as deviant cases in the ex-British Caribbean. Reference will also be made to the Dominican Republic which turned from a typical to a deviant case in the late 1970s. We did not include the micro-states in the ex-British Caribbean, nor Belize with its recent history of independence. Puerto Rico was omitted because of its lack of sovereignty and Panama because of the all-important presence of the canal. Furthermore, Haiti was omitted because of its French colonial heritage and Cuba because of the profound changes brought about by the revolution. Explaining the origins of the Cuban revolution would take the analysis here too far afield. However, we are prepared to argue that an inclusion of Cuba and Haiti in the analysis would not significantly affect our theoretical conclusions. Both Haiti and pre-revolutionary Cuba exhibit the traits of weak civil societies dominated by a state apparatus whose external anchoring was crucial.

For reasons of convenience we adopt the short-hand terminology "Central America" to refer to the Spanish-speaking countries of Central America and the Dominican Republic, and "the Caribbean" or "the West Indies" to refer to the ex-British countries of the Caribbean and Guyana.

2   It is worth briefly tracing the argument, for these authors arrived at this conclusion by no means independently. Diamond (1989: 11) cites Huntington (1984) and Weiner (1987) to support his own view that British colonialism did make some positive contributions to democracy. Huntington in turn (1984: 206) cites Weiner (1987, cited as manuscript by Huntington) to support his point that "British rule seemingly had a significantly different impact from that of other colonial powers."

3   Seligson (1987b: 167–92), in contrast to Huntington, argues that economic and sociocultural conditions in the Central American countries had grown past the critical threshold by the 1980s and thus brought these countries into the "zone of transition." His analysis concurs with ours, however, in emphasizing the importance of high inequality as an obstacle to the consolidation of democracy.

4   This might appear as an inconsistency with the last chapter where we argued that the Depression weakened the labor movements in South America. However, both effects occurred. In situations where a labor

movement already existed, increasing unemployment and falling business earnings frequently weakened its bargaining capacity and reduced its membership. In contrast, in situations where no or only minimal labor organization had emerged prior to the Depression, the social ferment resulting from the economic dislocations provided the impetus for labor protests and beginning attempts at organization.

5   See Woodward (1985) for a history of the five Central American republics and Espinal (1987) for the Dominincan Republic; LaFeber (1984) offers a historical treatment with special emphasis on US policies and their impact on the region, and Bulmer-Thomas (1987) provides a comparative analysis of the political economy of the region since 1920. Paige (1987) makes an interesting attempt to explain the different strength of the coffee oligarchies in Guatemala, El Salvador, Nicaragua, and Costa Rica, and their different responses to challenges from below with differences in the organization of coffee production.

6   See Anderson (1971) for an account of the 1932 events; Baloyra (1982; 1983) discusses the oligarchic–military relations; CAMINO (1982) and Gettleman et al. (1981) provide a good background to and discussion of the current situation.

7   Schoultz (1983), Adams (1970), and Jonas (1974) provide analyses essential for an understanding of developments in Guatemala.

8   For Honduras see Volk (1983) and Anderson (1981); for the Dominican Republic Rodman (1964), Wiarda and Kryzanek (1982), and Espinal (1987); excellent sources on Nicaragua are Millett (1977), Walker (1981) and Booth (1982).

9   In Honduras, the level of repression was significantly lower than in El Salvador, Nicaragua, the Dominican Republic, and Guatemala after 1954. Under Villeda Morales, who was installed in the presidency by the military in 1957, urban labor received some protection. However, his attempts at land reform brought him into confrontation with United Fruit and Standard Fruit and the US government, and in 1963 a coup brought army commander Lopez to power who ruled the country for the following 12 years. Unions continued to exist but mainly concentrated on the banana plantations and thus to a certain extent isolated, and owing to the weakness of political parties they had no significant political allies.

10 See below for a discussion of the post-World War II conjuncture.

11 The former law firm of Secretary of State John Foster Dulles had represented UFCO for a long time; Allen Dulles, the head of the CIA, had served on the company's board of trustees. For an analysis of these links and of US intervention in 1954 see La Feber (1984: 118–26), Schlesinger and Kinzer (1981) and Immerman (1982).

12 In addition to Woodward (1985), Ameringer (1978) and Seligson (1980) are useful general sources, though Seligson makes a different argument from ours. Booth (1989) offers a good account of the historical development of democratic rule. There is some controversy over the question of land inequality in Costa Rica. If one looks at the GINI index, a frequently used measure for inequality in land distribution, Costa Rica in

1960 ranked as high as Nicaragua and the Dominican Republic, and higher than Honduras (see Table 4 presented by Midlarsky 1989: 558). However, what differentiates Costa Rica from the other cases is the comparatively small proportion of small farms and large proportion of medium-sized farms (Muller et al. 1989: 582, 594). This demonstrates that the rural middle class managed to survive the process of land concentration. Gudmundson (1986: 56–81) argues that in the mid-nineteenth century landownership per se was not the basis of power of the Costa Rican elite, but rather took second place to commerce. At the same time, a process of differentiation among the peasantry set in and the more successful small-holders became coffee or market farmers. This class of family farmers remained an important social force into the middle of the twentieth century.

13   Weeks (1985: 117–18) argues that the crucial difference between Costa Rica and other Latin American countries is the absence of coercive pre-capitalist labor relations. The process of land concentration left a residual independent peasantry because of the open frontier in the south-west, and a relatively prosperous rural working-class because the labor shortage forced the large landowners to pay comparatively high coffee wages. Thus, we can infer that democratization posed less of a threat to large landowners, as they did not enjoy politically backed control over cheap labor to begin with but rather had become used to attracting labor through competitive wages.

14   The Communist Party had changed its name to Bloque de Obreros y Campesinos.

15   Figueres had been exiled by the Calderón government and he became a leading member of the Caribbean Legion, a group of exiles dedicated to the overthrow of dictators in the region. With the help of President Arevalo of Guatemala he put together a fighting force which won the civil war after a brief period of fighting. US action, though, was crucial for the outcome of the civil war. The US administration, particularly high level State Department officials, were suspicious of Figueres because of his social-democratic leanings, but they were even more concerned about the role of communists in Costa Rica. Thus, they prevented Somoza from aiding the government against the rebels and they went as far as to put US troops in the Canal Zone on alert for the case that armed communists would gain the military upper hand (La Feber 1984: 101ff).

16   The best source for general background information is Lewis (1968).

17   Lewis (1968: 229) points out that "the stranglehold of the resident whites, not only in estate agriculture but also in commerce meant that it took years after 1940 for a colored outsider family like the Wilsons to break into the trading monopoly of the famous 'Big Six' in the Bridgetown shopping emporia."

18   For examples of such alarmist reactions from the Jamaican case, see e. g. Post (1978: 325) and Sherlock (1980: 91).

19   Though we recognize that the French Socialists when in power did not promote independence of the overseas territories, but on the contrary

supported military action in Indo-China and later in Algeria (Smith 1978: 80), they did support political reforms in French territories, such as the establishment of legislative assemblies, which facilitated the emergence of nationalist movements (Gann and Duignan 1967: 338–40).

20 The idea of a federation had been promoted by the British Colonial Office and various forces in some of the Caribbean territories for some time. The Federation of the West Indies came formally into being in 1958; its capital was Port of Spain and its Prime Minister Grantley Adams of Barbados. Jamaican membership became an issue for internal electoral maneuvering, as Bustamante reversed his previously favorable position and Manley called a referendum to decide the issue.

21 It is difficult to identify whether the radical demands per se were responsible for the British reaction or whether it was Jagan's communist ideology; see below for further discussion.

22 The British TUC pressured its Jamaican counterpart to withdraw from the World Federation of Trade Unions because of the growing communist ties of this federation. The majority of the leadership of the Jamaican TUC, who constituted the left wing of the PNP, resisted these pressures. This aggravated existing internal tensions in the party, culminating in the expulsion of the left under the accusation of communist leanings and activities detrimental to the party. Eaton (1975: 135–50) and Munroe (1972: 79–80) discuss the internal tensions and the expulsion; see also Harrod (1972: 252–74).

23 These generalizations also apply to the smaller British West Indian islands not analyzed here (see Lewis 1968: 118–43 and Henry and Stone 1983). In general, the middle-class component was better organized and played a more important role in the larger islands, especially Jamaica, than it did in the smaller ones.

24 Though the percentage of rural families without or with insufficient land was high in Honduras as well (Goodwin 1988), the percentage of agricultural workers in total employment was high (Bulmer-Thomas 1987: 162–3). This meant that landlessness had different implications for the welfare of rural families in Honduras than in the neighboring countries. The illegal migration of Salvadorans into Honduras in search of land and jobs further underlines that land scarcity was less of a problem in Honduras.

25 We are indebted to Jeff Goodwin for drawing our attention to the importance of this variable; see e.g. Goodwin (1988).

26 For analyses of the political developments in the region in general and in the various countries, see the collections of essays edited by Blachman et al. (1986), Di Palma and Whitehead (1986), Diskin (1983), Grabendorff et al. (1984), and Hamilton et al. (1988).

27 On the revolution see Walker (1982).

28 One might ask whether these developments in Nicaragua do not represent still another path to democracy, namely via personalistic dictatorship and revolution. However, democracy in Nicaragua is far from consolidated, and the different outcomes in Cuba and Haiti suggest that the Nicaraguan

outcome might be quite atypical, should it end up in stable democracy. To attempt to analyze the causes of the different outcomes is beyond the scope of this chapter.

29 On oligarchic–military relations, see Baloyra (1982; 1983).

30 Population density in El Salvador is by far the highest among the Central American countries with 701 people per square mile, compared to 201 people in Guatemala, 102 in Honduras, and 53 in Nicaragua (estimates for 1985; see Woodward 1985: 363).

31 The discussion here owes much to the insightful analysis of the development of the civil war and of the impasse offered by Diskin and Sharpe (1986).

32 For developments in Guatemala over the last three decades see Torres-Rivas (1984), Davis (1983), Schoultz (1983), and Trudeau and Schoultz (1986).

33 For developments leading up to the democratic transition of 1978, see Hartlyn (1986) and Espinal (1986); for a more extended treatment of authoritarianism and democracy in the Dominican Republic, see Espinal (1987).

34 See Seligson (1980: 122–52) for a discussion of the very slow and timid approaches to land reform. Up to the early 1970s, only token attempts at reform were undertaken, and thereafter the emphasis of the program was on formalizing titles to land, not on expropriating large landholdings.

35 For the crisis of the 1980s and the impact of the regional turmoil on Costa Rica, see Blachman and Hellman (1986).

36 For political developments in Barbados through the 1970s, see Hoyos (1978); for the 1980s, see Watson (1988).

37 Ryan (1972) covers the early period of independence; Hintzen (1989) and Ryan (1989) carry the analysis into the 1980s.

38 Jefferson (1972) and Girvan (1971) provide essential information on the economic developments which constituted the background to the PNP's return to democratic socialism. For analyses of elite attitudes towards politics and the economy after the first decade of independence see Bell (1977–8), Bell and Baldrich (1982), and Bell and Gibson (1978). The dynamics of the 1972–80 period are discussed in Stephens and Stephens (1986).

39 Using our distinction between full and restricted democracy, any important electoral corruption would disqualify a country from being designated a full democracy and certainly corruption which resulted in the government defeating the opposition would disqualify a country from the democratic category altogether.

40 We use Africans here to refer to both the black and brown (i.e. mixed, colored, or mulatto) populations of the two countries.

41 The population in Trinidad was 56 percent black and mixed and 40 percent East Indian in 1970 (Hintzen 1989: 3). The Guyanese population was 44 percent East Indian in 1946 and 51 percent in 1970. The corresponding figures for black and mixed were 48 percent and 41 percent respectively (Greene 1974: 174).

42 For discussions of the ethnic/class structures of the two countries, see Hintzen (1989) and Despres (1967). For analyses of the relation between race, class, and mass political behavior, see Greene (1974) and Bahadoor-singh (1968).

43 For somewhat contrasting accounts of the events of 1953, see Spinner (1984: 33–58) and Depres (1967: 177–220).

44 The account below of events from 1962 to the 1970s is drawn from Hintzen (1989: 57–73), Manley (1979), and Spinner (1984: 89–154).

45 Burnham laid out these plans to an American anthropologist studying Guyana, before they occurred (personal conversation, 1987). The anthropologist also relates that UF leaders actively courted US–CIA intervention.

46 The following account of Grenada is based on Brizan (1984: 226–253), Jacobs and Jacobs (1980), and Thorndike (1985: 25–56).

47 The political economy of Grenada differs sharply from Guyana, however. Owing to the breakup of some of the large estates after emancipation, the availability of land, and the partial replacement of sugar with cocoa, nutmeg, mace, and (after 1955) bananas, all of which can be efficiently cultivated on small plots, the peasantry was quite strong in Grenada, rivaling that in Jamaica and St Vincent (Thorndike 1984: 29). On the other hand, 103 estate owners (few absentee) owned 46 percent of all land in Grenada in 1946 (Jacobs and Jacobs 1980: 143); thus, the domestic planter class was still of considerable economic and social significance. Another possible contrast between the two countries is difficult to assess: the strength of the middle-class nationalist movement before World War II. In Grenada, T. A. Marryshow and his Grenada Workingman's Association filled this role, having some support in the urban middle and working classes. Marryshow was elected to the local legislature a number of times. Here one is faced with the problem of size: does one multiply his movement by twenty to arrive at its Jamaican equivalent or does one conclude it was simply a one-man show and not a movement?

48 On the motivations for and impact of US intervention and military assistance programs, see Etchison (1975), Newfarmer (1984), Blachman et al. (1986).

49 Given the important role of the United States in building up the military in this region, one might restate this by saying that it was better to have British colonialism than American neo-colonialism which was essential in consolidating the repressive regimes of local elites. On the other hand, it might be added with some irony that the countries in which US intervention and rule were most direct, Cuba, Nicaragua, and the Dominican Republic, developed patrimonial dictatorships which generated revolutions (Goodwin 1988).

50 One could add two more critiques of the "tutelary democracy" argument. In so far as it hinges on the internalization of democratic norms by local elites, one has to admit that such norms are subject to erosion under changing conditions. Furthermore, despite the introduction of local representative institutions, the legacy of colonialism also had highly

authoritarian traits. For instance, in the discussion of post-colonial democracy in Asia, Diamond (1989b: 13) points out that Pakistan and Bangladesh built on the British martial law tradition. The interesting question then becomes under what conditions which aspects of the colonial legacy became decisive, or under what conditions other norms replaced those internalized under colonial rule. Again, our analysis indicates that which legacies and norms are enduring is largely determined by power relations in society, between the state and society, and in the international system.

51   See Evans (1989) for a discussion of the emergence and developmental consequences of predatory state apparatuses.

7   Conclusions and Reflections

1   We do not mean to include here the case of movements pressing their self-defined interests beyond their capacity to effect such policies given the power balance in society, as in the cases of the socialist movements of Spain in the 1930s and Chile in the 1970s. In our view, these movements correctly assessed the interests of their class constituents; they were mistaken in their analysis of the relative social power of the supporters and opponents of socialist transformation.

2   This is the prototype of Gramsci's rule through consent.

3   For instance, see the recent discussions by Weiner (1987) and Diamond (1989a, 1989b).

4   This is not to deny that a national society theoretically could be characterized by a national system of values commonly held by members of all classes as hypothesized by structural-functionalism; but this theoretically polar case would be one of total ideological hegemony of the dominant class. It is unlikely that this degree of national consensus on the ideology of dominant classes ever exists in capitalist societies (Mann 1970; Abercrombie and Turner 1982). Societies vary not only in the extent to which upper-class ideologies (or cultures) are accepted and the extent to which the various classes throw up their own counter-ideologies, but also in the extent to which the ideologies are held by very distinctive "camps" (to use the Austrian terminology) based in the class structure. For instance, in Sweden, the growing strength of Social Democracy initially led to the development of highly class-segregated camps along Austrian lines, but in the decades of Social Democratic political domination in which class lines became more fluid, the high degree of class segregation in ideological orientation also declined. But, Social Democratic counter-hegemony did not decline, rather it broke out of its class boundaries (Stephens 1976). Swedish "political culture" today should be seen as the product of a class compromise between a very powerful social democratic labor movement and the capitalist class. Solidarity and equality (but not socialism) are now almost national cultural values, though pockets of upper- and upper-middle-class dissent certainly exist. These values

certainly were not dominant at the turn of the century. We argue that this sort of value transformation occurs on the value of democracy with the growth and victory of democratic movements and the installation and persistence of democratic rule.

5 On the distinction between interdependence and dependence see Caporaso (1978). A similar distinction is implicit in Senghaas's (1985) discussion of European industrialization.

6 However, as we noted above, if the country in question lacked a power constellation favorable to democracy, it is likely that it would be rolled back if the economic elites began to feel threatened by popular demands.

7 The phrase "central role" is important here. An in-depth analysis of a number of these cases would reveal that ethnic divisions did play a significant role in the political developments in the country (e.g. see our analysis of Trinidad) and in some cases (e.g. Spain) played a contributing role in the events that led to the breakdown of democracy. Our distinction here is that one might plausibly argue that "democracy broke down in Guyana because it was ethnically divided" but that a similar statement about Spain would not be plausible.

8 However, ethnic heterogeneity and democracy were not at loggerheads in all of these cases either. As Bardhan (1987) argues, in India democratic institutions offered an arena for elite bargaining among ethnically and economically fragmented interest groups.

9 Another factor that has been used to differentiate the political posture of capitalists in different sectors of the economy is orientation toward export or toward domestic markets. Curiously enough, this may be hypothesized to have exactly the opposite effect in Latin America from the effect it is supposed to have had in advanced capitalist countries. It might be argued that export oriented industry in Latin America has no interest in the domestic market but does have an interest in keeping wage costs low and thus favors repressive labor policies. The literature on advanced capitalist countries maintains that export orientation is associated with more liberal policies toward labor, but it is not very explicit on why this should be so (e.g. see Ferguson 1983a, Gourevitch 1986, Kurth 1979). In part, this would appear to be due to the fact that the export oriented industries were generally capital intensive and thus export orientation per se was irrelevant. From Kurth's work, it is apparent that one dimension that differentiated domestic industry in post-war Latin America from that in late nineteenth-century and inter-war Europe is that Latin American industry was involved in production of light consumer goods while its European counterpart was heavy industry and thus not involved in production for a consumer market and consequently had no interest in high wages. Kurth's explanation which connects the reactionary posture of domestically oriented (and often internationally uncompetitive) heavy industry to armament production and thus imperialism further suggests that the relation between domestic market/export orientation may well be contingent on a country's status in the interstate system. The Swedish case supports this as it follows the Latin American pattern of conservative

export industry and liberal domestic manufacturers (Söderpalm 1969, 1976).

10 In some countries, most notably Bolivia and Colombia, but also Peru, Mexico, and Panama, the state apparatus has been corroded to an even greater extent by the corrupting influence of the drug trade. Where the rule of law itself is severely endangered, democracy clearly cannot take hold.

11 This parallel was suggested by Chris Gowlland in a seminar of D. Rueschemeyer.

12 See chapter 2 for a review of this literature.

13 There is, of course, a rich body of theoretical and empirical literature on this topic, including a journal, *Economic and Industrial Democracy*, devoted entirely to it. For example, see Dahl (1985), Pateman (1970), Stephens (1980), Stephens and Stephens (1982), Sirianni (1987), Vanek (1970), Zwerdling (1980).

14 Bureaucratic state socialism in Eastern Europe did indeed fuse polity and economy. Ironically, this led to an increasing domination of politics by economic concerns; see Rueschemeyer (1990).

15 Pateman (1990) demonstrates how women have been excluded not only from democratic practice but also from democratic theory. She argues for the incorporation of women into the presumably universal status of citizenship and the concomitant rights on the basis of recognized gender differences.

16 This in itself points to a major difference to class and ethnic divisions. The struggles of subordinate classes and ethnic groups for social, economic, and political inclusion dominated the political agenda before these actors achieved political inclusion.

17 For the following see Rueschemeyer and Rueschemeyer (1990).

References

Abercrombie, Nicholas and Turner, Bryan S. 1982: The dominant ideology thesis. In Giddens, A. and Held, D. (eds), *Classes, Power, and Conflict: classical and contemporary debates*. Berkeley: University of California Press.

Abraham, David 1986: *The Collapse of the Weimar Republic: political economy and crisis*. New York: Holmes and Meier.

Adams, Richard N. 1970: *Crucifixion by Power: essays on the Guatemalan national social structure, 1944–1966*. Austin: University of Texas Press.

Alapuro, Risto 1980: Mass support for Fascism in Finland. In Larsen, S. U., Hagtvet, B. and Myklebust, J. P. (eds), *Who Were the Fascists: social roots of European Fascism*. Bergen: Universitetsforlaget.

——1988: *State and Revolution in Finland*. Berkeley: University of California Press.

Alapuro, Risto and Allardt, Erik 1978: The Lapua movement: the threat of rightist takeover in Finland. In Linz, J. and Stepan, A. (eds), *The Breakdown of Democratic Regimes: Europe*. Baltimore: Johns Hopkins University Press.

Alba, Victor 1968: *Politics and the Labor Movement in Latin America*. Stanford, CA: Stanford University Press.

Alejandro, Carlos F. Diaz 1970: *Essays on the Economic History of the Argentine Republic*. New Haven: Yale University Press.

Alexander, Robert J. 1965: *Organized Labor in Latin America*. New York: The Free Press.

Alford, Robert R. and Friedland, Roger 1985: *Powers of Theory: capitalism, the state, and democracy*. Cambridge and New York: Cambridge University Press.

Allen, William S. 1984: *The Nazi Seizure of Power: the experience of a single German town 1922–1945* (Revised Edition). New York: Franklin Watts.

Allub, Leopoldo 1983: *Origenes del autoritarismo en America Latina*. Mexico, D.F. : Editorial Katun.

Ameringer, Charles D. 1978: *Don Pepe: a political biography of Jose Figueres of Costa Rica*. Albuquerque: University of New Mexico Press.

Aminzade, Ronald. D 1981: *Class, Politics, and Early Industrial Capitalism: a study of mid-nineteenth-century Toulouse, France.* Albany: State University of New York Press.

——Forthcoming: *The Origins of Democratic Institutions: political parties and class formation in France.*

Anderson, Perry 1977: The antinomies of Antonio Gramsci. *New Left Review.* 100.

Anderson, Thomas P. 1971: *Matanza: El Salvador's communist revolt of 1932.* Lincoln: University of Nebraska Press.

——1981: *The War of the Dispossessed: Honduras and El Salvador, 1969.* Lincoln: University of Nebraska Press.

Andrey, Georges 1983: Auf der Suche nach dem neuen Staat (1798–1848). In *Geschichte der Schweiz und der Schweizer.* Basel: Helbing und Lichtenhahn.

Angell, Alan 1968: Party systems in Latin America. In Veliz, C. (ed.), *Latin America and the Caribbean: a handbook.* New York: Praeger.

——1972: *Politics and the Labour Movement in Chile.* London: Oxford University Press.

Apter, David A. 1965: *The Politics of Modernization.* Chicago: University of Chicago Press.

Baer, Werner 1965: *Industrialization and Economic Development in Brazil.* Homewood, IL: R. D. Irwin Inc.

Bahadoorsingh, Krishna 1968: *Trinidad Electoral Politics: the persistence of the race factor.* London: Institute of Race Relations.

Baloyra, Enrique 1982: *El Salvador in Transition.* Chapel Hill: University of North Carolina Press.

——1983: Reactionary despotism in El Salvador. In Diskin, M. (ed.), *Trouble in Our Backyard.* New York: Pantheon Books.

Bardhan, Pranab 1987: Dominant Proprietary Classes and India's Democracy. In Kohli, Atul (ed.), *India's Democracy.* Princeton: Princeton University Press.

Bazant, Jan 1987: Mexico. In Bethell, L. (ed.), *Spanish America After Independence, c. 1820 – c. 1870.* New York: Cambridge University Press.

Beckford, George 1972: *Persistant Poverty.* New York: Oxford University Press.

Bell, Wendell 1977–8: Independent Jamaica enters world politics: the start of foreign policy in a new state. *Political Science Quarterly,* 92.

Bell, Wendell and Baldrich, Juan 1982: Elites, economic ideology and democracy in Jamaica. In Czudnowski, M. M. (ed.), *International Yearbook for Studies of Leaders and Leadership.* DeKalb, IL: Northern Illinois University Press.

Bell, Wendell and Gibson, J. William 1978: Independent Jamaica faces the outside world. *International Studies Quarterly,* 22 (1).

Bendix, Reinhard 1964: *Nation-Building and Citizenship: studies in our changing social order.* New York: Wiley.

Berg, Ronald H. and Weaver, Frederick Stirton 1978: Toward a reinterpretation of political change in Peru during the first century of independence. *Journal of Interamerican Studies and World Affairs* (1) (February).

Bergquist, Charles W. 1978: *Coffee and Conflict in Colombia, 1886–1910.* Durham, NC: Duke University Press.

——1986: *Labor in Latin America: comparative essays on Chile, Argentina, Venezuela, and Colombia.* Stanford: Stanford University Press.

Best, Lloyd 1967: Independent thought and Caribbean freedom. *New World Quarterly*, 3 (4). Reprinted in Girvan, N. and Jefferson, O. (eds), *Readings in the Political Economy of the Caribbean.* Kingston, Jamaica: New World Group, 1971.

Bitar, Sergio 1986: *Chile: experiment in democracy.* Philadelphia, PA: Institute for the Study of Human Issues.

Blachman, Morris J. and Hellman, Ronald G. 1986: Costa Rica. In Blachman, M. J., Leogrande, W. M. and Sharpe, K. (eds) *Confronting Revolution: security through diplomacy in Central America.* New York: Pantheon Books.

Blachman, Morris J., Leogrande, William M. and Sharpe, Kenneth (eds) 1986: *Confronting Revolution: security through diplomacy in Central America.* New York: Pantheon Books.

Black, Cyril E. 1966: *The Dynamics of Modernization.* New York: Harper and Row.

Blackbourn, David 1984: The discreet charm of the Bourgeoisie: reappraising German history in the nineteenth century. In Blackbourn, D. and Eley, G. *The Peculiarities of German History: bourgeois society and politics in nineteenth-century Germany.* Oxford: Oxford University Press.

Blackbourn, David 1984: The discreet charm of the bourgeoisie: reappraising Eley, G. *The Peculiarities of German History: bourgeois society and politics in nineteenth-century Germany.* Oxford: Oxford University Press.

Blanksten, George I. 1951: *Ecuador: constitutions and caudillos.* Berkeley: University of California Press.

Blewett, Neal 1965: The franchise in the United Kingdom 1885–1918. *Past and Present*, 32.

Block, Fred 1977: The ruling-class does not rule: notes on the marxist theory of the state. *Socialist Revolution* 7.

Bloom, Jack M. 1981: *Class, Race, and the Civil Rights Movement.* Bloomington: Indiana University Press.

Bollen, Kenneth A. 1979: Political democracy and the timing of development. *American Sociological Review*, 44.

——1980: Issues in the comparative measurement of political democracy. *American Sociological Review*, 45.

——1983: World system position, dependency, and democracy: the cross-national evidence. *American Sociological Review*, 48.

Bollen, Kenneth A. and Grandjean, Burke 1981: The dimension(s) of democracy: further issues in the measurements and effects of political democracy. *American Sociological Review*, 46.

Bollen, Kenneth A. and Jackman, Robert 1983: World system position, dependency, and democracy: the cross-national evidence. *American Sociological Review*, 48.

——1985a: Economic and noneconomic determinants of political democracy in the 1960s. In Braungart, R. G. (ed.), *Research in Political Sociology.*

Greenwich, CT: Jai Press.
——1985b: Political democracy and the size distribution of income. *American Sociological Review*, 50.
——1989: Democracy, stability, and dichotomies. *American Sociological Review*, 54.
Booth, John A. 1982: *The End and the Beginning: the Nicaraguan revolution.* Boulder; Westview Press.
——1989: Costa Rican democracy. In Diamond, L., Linz, J. and Lipset, S. M. (eds), *Democracy in Developing Countries: Latin America.* Boulder: Lynne Rienner.
Bornschier, Volker and Chase-Dunn, Christopher 1985: *Transnational Corporations and Development.* New York: Praeger.
Bourricaud, François 1970: *Power and Society in Contemporary Peru.* New York: Praeger.
Bowles, Samuel and Gintis, Herbert 1986: *Democracy and Capitalism: property, community, and the contradictions of modern social thought.* New York: Basic Books.
Boyer, John 1981: *Political Radicalism in Late Imperial Vienna: origins of the Christian social movement 1848–1897.* Chicago: University of Chicago Press.
Bracher, Karl Dietrich 1970: *The German Dictatorship: the origins, structure, and effects of National Socialism.* New York: Praeger.
Brenner, Robert 1976: Agrarian class structure and economic development in pre-industrial Europe. *Past and Present*, 70.
——1977: The origins of capitalist development: a critique of neo-Smithian Marxism. *New Left Review*, 104 (July–August).
Bridges, Amy 1986: Becoming American: the working-classes in the United States before the Civil War. In Katznelson, I. and Zolberg, A. R. (eds), *Working-Class Formation.* Princeton: Princeton University Press.
Brizan, George 1984: *Grenada: island of conflict.* London: Zed.
Broadbent, John Edward 1966: *The Good Society of John Stuart Mill.* Unpubl. Ph. D. diss., University of Toronto.
Brown, Robert Craig and Cook, Ramsay 1974: *Canada, 1896–1921: a nation transformed.* Toronto: McClelland and Stewart.
Bruneau, Thomas 1982: *The church in Brazil: the politics of religion.* Austin: University of Texas Press.
Bulmer-Thomas, Victor 1987: *The Political Economy of Central America since 1920.* Cambridge: Cambridge University Press.
Burch, Philip H. 1981: *Elites in American History: the Civil War to the New Deal.* New York: Holmes and Meier.
Burnham, Walter Dean 1970: *Critical Elections and the Mainspring of American Politics.* New York: Norton.
——1981: The System of 1896: an analysis. In Kleppner, P. et al. (eds), *The Evolution of American Electoral Systems.* Westport, CT: Greenwood Press.
Burns, E. Bradford 1980: *A History of Brazil.* New York: Columbia University Press. Second Edition.
——1986: *Latin America: a concise interpretive history.* Englewood Cliffs, NJ: Prentice-Hall. Fourth Edition.

Buxton, G. L. 1974: 1870–90. In Crowley, F. K. (ed.), *A New History of Australia*. Melbourne: William Heinemann.

Calleo, David 1978: *The German Problem Reconsidered: Germany and the world order, 1870 to the present*. Cambridge: Cambridge University Press.

CAMINO, Central America Information Office 1982: *El Salvador: Background to the Crisis*. Cambridge: Central America Information Office.

Caporaso, James A. 1978: Dependence, dependency and power in the global system: a structural and behavioral analysis. *International Organization*, 32 (1).

Cardoso, Fernando Henrique and Faletto, Enzo 1979: *Dependency and Development in Latin America*. Berkeley: University of California Press.

Cardoza, Anthony L. 1982: *Agrarian Elites and Italian Fascism: the Province of Bologna, 1901–1926*. Princeton: Princeton University Press.

Carnoy, Martin 1984: *The State and Political Theory*. Princeton: Princeton University Press.

Carr, Raymond 1982: *Spain 1808–1975* (Second Edition). Oxford: Oxford University Press.

Carsten, F. L. 1973: *The Reichswehr and Politics 1918–1933*. Berkeley: University of California Press.

Castles, Francis G. 1973: Barrington Moore's thesis and Swedish political development. *Government and Opposition*, 8 (3).

Cavarozzi, Marcelo 1986: Political cycles in Argentina since 1955. In O'Donnell, G., Schmitter, P. C. and Whitehead, L. (eds), *Transitions from Authoritarian Rule: Latin America*. Baltimore: Johns Hopkins University Press.

Chambers, William Nisbet 1967: Party development and the American mainstream. In Chambers, W. N. and Burnham, W. D. (eds), *The American Party Systems: stages of political development*. New York: Oxford University Press.

Chase-Dunn, Christopher 1975: The effect of international dependence on development and inequality: a cross-national study. *American Sociological Review*, 40 (6).

Chilcote, Ronald H. and Edelstein, Joel C. (eds) 1974: *Latin America: The Struggle with Dependency and Beyond*. New York: Wiley.

Childers, Thomas 1983: *The Nazi Voter*. Chapel Hill: University of North Carolina Press.

Christiansen, Nils Finn 1988: The role of the Labour movement in the process of democratisation in Denmark 1848–1901. In Stråth, B. (ed.), *Democratisation in Scandinavia in Comparison*. Gothenburg: Department of History, University of Gothenburg.

Ciria, Alberto 1974: *Parties and Power in Modern Argentina (1930–1946)*. Albany: State University of New York Press. First published in 1964 as *Partidos y Poder en la Argentina Moderna (1930–1946)* by Editorial Universitaria de Buenos Aires.

Chirot, Daniel 1977: *Social Change in the Twentieth Century*. New York: Harcourt, Brace and Jovanovich.

Clark, C. M. H. (ed.) 1955: *Select Documents in Australian History 1851–1900*. Sydney: Angus and Robertson.

Coatsworth, John H. 1983: Orígenes del autoritarismo moderno en México. In

Allub, L. (ed.) *Orígenes del autoritarismo en America Latina.* Mexico, D.F.: Editorial Katún.

Collier, David 1979: The Bureaucratic–Authoritarian model: synthesis and priorities for future research. In Collier, D. (ed.), *The New Authoritarianism in Latin America.* Princeton: Princeton University Press.

Collier, Ruth Berins 1986: *Historical Founding Moments in State-Labor Relations: Brazil, Chile, Mexico, and Venezuela.* Paper delivered at the World Congress of the International Sociological Association, New Delhi, India, August.

Collier, Ruth Berins and Collier, David Forthcoming: *Shaping the Political Arena: critical junctures, trade unions, and the state in Latin America.*

Conaghan, Catherine M. 1987: Party politics and democratization in Ecuador. In Malloy, J. M. and Seligson, M. A. (eds), *Authoritarians and Democrats: regime transition in Latin America.* Pittsburgh: University of Pittsburgh Press.

Connolly, C. W. 1981: The middling-class victory in New South Wales, 1853–62: a critique of the bourgeois–pastoralist dichotomy. *Historical Studies,* 19.

Cornelius, Wayne A. 1986: Political liberalization and the 1985 elections in Mexico. In Drake, P. W. and Silva, E. (eds), *Elections and Democratization in Latin America, 1980–85.* San Diego: Center for Iberian and Latin American Studies, University of California, San Diego.

Corner, Paul 1975: *Fascism in Ferrara 1915–1925.* London: Oxford University Press.

Cotler, Julio 1978: A structural–historical approach to the breakdown of democratic institutions: Peru. In Linz, J. J. and Stepan, A. (eds), *The Breakdown of Democratic Regimes: Latin America.* Baltimore: Johns Hopkins University Press.

Cowling, M. 1967: *1867: Disraeli, Gladstone and Revolution.* Cambridge: Cambridge University Press.

Creighton, Donald 1971: *The Story of Canada.* London: Faber and Faber.

Cueva, Agustín 1982: *The Process of Political Domination in Ecuador.* New Brunswick, NJ: Transaction Books.

Cuneo, Dardo 1967: *Comportamiento y crisis de la clase empresaria.* Buenos Aires: Editorial Pleamar.

Cutright, Philips 1963: National political development: measurement and analysis. *American Sociological Review,* 28 (April).

Cutright, Phillips and Wiley, James A. 1969: Modernization and political representation: 1927–1966. *Studies in Comparative International Development.*

Daalder, Hans 1966: The Netherlands: opposition in a segmented society. In Dahl, R. (ed.), *Political Oppositions in Western Democracies.* New Haven: Yale University Press, 188–236.

Dahl, Robert A. 1956: *A Preface to Democratic Theory.* Chicago: University of Chicago Press.

——1971: *Polyarchy: participation and opposition.* New Haven: Yale University Press.

——1985: *A Preface to Economic Democracy.* Berkeley: University of California Press.

——1989: *Democracy and its Critics*. New Haven: Yale University Press.

Dahrendorf, Ralf 1967: *Society and Democracy in Germany*. Garden City, NY: Doubleday.

Dalziel, Raewyn 1981: The politics of settlement. In Oliver, W. H. and Williams, B. R. (eds), *The Oxford History of New Zealand*. Wellington: Oxford University Press.

Danns, George K. 1982: *Domination and Power in Guyana: a study of the police in a third world context*. New Brunswick, NJ: Transaction Books.

Davis, Shelton H. 1983: State violence and Agrarian crisis in Guatemala. In Diskin, M. (ed.) *Trouble in Our Backyard: Central America and the United States in the Eighties*. New York: Pantheon Books.

Dean, Warren 1966: The planter as entrepreneur: the case of Sao Paulo. *Hispanic American Historical Review*, XLVI (2) (May).

de Garis, B. K. 1974: 1890–1900. In F. K. Crowley (ed), *A New History of Australia*. Melbourne: William Heinemann, 216–259.

de Schweinitz, Karl 1964: *Industrialization and Democracy: economic necessities and political possibilities*. New York: Free Press.

Derry, T. K. 1973: *A History of Modern Norway 1814–1972*. Oxford: Clarendon Press.

Despres, Leo A. 1967: *Cultural Pluralism and Nationalist Politics in British Guyana*. Chicago: Rand McNally.

Deutsch, Karl W. 1961: Social mobilization and political development. *American Political Science Review*, 55.

Diamond, Larry 1989a: Introduction: persistence, erosion, breakdown, and renewal. In Diamond, L., Linz, J. J. and Lipset, S. M. (eds), *Democracy in Developing Countries: Asia*. Boulder: Lynne Rienner.

——1989b: Introduction: roots of failure, seeds of hope. In Diamond, L., Linz, J. J. and Lipset, S. M. (eds) *Democracy in Developing Countries: Africa*. Boulder: Lynne Rienner.

Diamond, Larry, and Linz, Juan J. 1989: Introduction: politics, society, and democracy in Latin America. In Diamond, L., Linz, J. J. and Lipset, S. M. (eds) *Democracy in Developing Countries: Latin America*. Boulder: Lynne Rienner.

Diamond, Larry, Linz, Juan J. and Lipset, Seymour Martin 1987: Democracy in developing countries: facilitating and obstructing factors. In Gastil, R. D. (ed.), *Freedom in the World: political and civil liberties, 1987–88*. New York: Freedom House.

——(eds) 1989a: *Democracy in Developing Countries: Africa*. Boulder: Lynne Rienner.

——(eds). 1989b: *Democracy in Developing Countries: Asia*. Boulderr: Lynne Rienner.

Díaz Alejandro, Carlos 1970: *Essays on the Economic History of the Argentine Republic*. New Haven: Yale University Press.

Dinkin, Robert J. 1977: *Voting in Provincial America: a study of elections in the thirteen colonies, 1689–1776*. Westport, CT: Greenwood Press.

——1982: *Voting in Revolutionary America: a study of elections in the original thirteen states, 1776–1789*. Westport, CT: Greenwood Press.

Di Palma, Giuseppe and Whitehead, Lawrence (eds) 1986: *The Central*

American Impasse. New York: St Martin's Press.

Diskin, Martin (ed) 1983: *Trouble in Our Backyard: Central America and the United States in the 1980s*. New York: Pantheon Books.

Diskin, Martin and Sharpe, Kenneth E. 1986: El Salvador. In Blachman, M. J., Leogrande, W. M. and Sharpe, K. (eds), *Confronting Revolution: security through diplomacy in Central America*. New York: Pantheon Books.

Di Tella, Guido 1983: *Argentina Under Perón, 1973–76*. New York: St Martin's Press.

Di Tella, Torcuato S. 1968: The working-class in politics. In Veliz, C. (ed.), *Latin America and the Caribbean: a handbook*. New York: Praeger.

———1990: *Latin American Politics: a theoretical framework*. Austin: University of Texas Press.

Dore, Ronald P. 1959: *Land Reform in Japan*. London: Oxford University Press.

———1973: The late development effect. In Evers, H. -D. (ed), *Modernization in South-East Asia*. London: Oxford University Press.

Dore, Ronald P. and Ouchi, Tsutomi 1972: Rural origins of Japanese Fascism. In Morley, J. (ed), *Dilemmas of Growth in Prewar Japan*. Princeton: Princeton University Press.

Dovring, Folke 1965: *Land and Labour in Europe in the Twentieth Century* (Third Revised Edition). The Hague: M. Nijhoff.

Drake, Paul W. 1978: *Socialism and Populism in Chile, 1932–52*. Urbana: University of Illinois Press.

Drake, Paul and Silva, Eduardo (eds) 1986: *Elections and Democratization in Latin America, 1980–1985*. San Diego, CA: Center for Iberian and Latin American Studies, University of California, San Diego.

Dybdahl, Vagn 1969: *Partier og Erhverv*. Aarhus: Universitetsforlaget.

Eaton, George E. 1975: *Alexander Bustamante and Modern Jamaica*. Kingston, Jamaica: Kingston Publishers.

Eley, Geoff 1983: What produces Fascism: preindustrial traditions of a crisis of a capitalist state. *Politics and Society*, 12 (1).

———1984: The British model and the German road: rethinking the course of German history before 1914. In Blackbourn, D. and Eley, G., *The Peculiarities of German History: bourgeois society and politics in nineteenth-century Germany*. Oxford: Oxford University Press.

Elster, Jon 1985: *Making Sense of Marx*. Cambridge: Cambridge University Press.

Elwitt, Sanford 1975: *The Making of the Third Republic: class and politics in France 1868–1884*. Baton Rouge: Louisiana State University Press.

Erickson, Charlotte 1957: *American Industry and the European Immigrant, 1860–1885*. Cambridge, Mass.: Harvard University Press.

Erickson, Kenneth Paul 1977: *The Brazilian Corporative State and Working Class Politics*. Berkeley: University of California Press.

Espinal, Rosario 1985: Democratization in the Dominican Republic: a challenge to the existing theories of Latin American political development. Paper delivered at the Meeting of the American Sociological Association, Washington, D. C. (August).

———1986: An interpretation of the democratic transition in the Dominican Republic. In Di Palma, G. and Whitehead, L. (eds), *The Central American*

Impasse. New York: St Martin's Press.

———1987: *Autoritarismo y Democracia en la Política Dominicana.* San José: CAPEL.

Esping-Andersen, Gøsta 1985: *Politics Against Markets: the social democratic road to power.* Princeton: Princeton University Press.

———1990: *The Three Worlds of Welfare Capitalism.* Cambridge: Polity Press.

Etchison, Don L. 1975: *The United States and Militarism in Central America.* New York: Praeger.

Evans, Peter 1989: Predatory, developmental and other apparatuses: A comparative analysis of the Third World state. In Portes, Alejandro and Kincaid, Douglas (eds), *Sociological Forum,* 4, (4).

Evans, Peter B. 1979: *Dependent Development: the alliance of multinational, state and local capital in Brazil.* Princeton: Princeton University Press.

Evans, Peter, Rueschemeyer, Dietrich and Skocpol, Theda (eds), 1985: *Bringing the State Back In.* New York: Cambridge University Press.

Evans, Peter and Stephens, John D. 1988: Development and the world economy. In Smelser, N. (ed), *Handbook of Sociology.* Newbury Park: Sage.

Evans, Richard J. 1985: The myth of Germany's missing revolution. *New Left Review,* 149.

Farneti, Paolo 1978: Social conflict, parliamentary fragmentation, institutional shift, and the rise of Fascism: Italy. In Linz, J. and Stepan, A. (eds), *The Breakdown of Democratic Regimes: Europe* Baltimore: Johns Hopkins University Press.

Ferguson, Thomas 1983a: From Normalcy to New Deal: industrial structure, party competition, and American public policy in the Great Depression. *International Organization,* 38.

———1983b: Party realignment and American industrial structure: the investment theory of political parties in historical perspective. In Zarembla, P. (ed), *Research in Political Economy,* vol. 6. Greenwich, CT: JAI Press.

Finch, M. H. J. 1981: *A Political Economy of Uruguay Since 1870.* New York: St Martin's Press.

Fitch, John Samuel 1977: *The Military Coup d'Etat as a Political Process: Ecuador, 1948–1966.* Baltimore: Johns Hopkins University Press.

Fitzmaurice, John 1983: *The Politics of Belgium: Crisis and Compromise in a Plural Society.* New York: St. Martin's Press.

Flora, Peter, Alber, Jens et al. 1983: *State, Economy and Society in Western Europe, 1815–1975,* vol. 1. Chicago: St James Press.

Furtado, Celso 1968: The industrialization of Brazil. In Veliz, C. (ed), *Latin America and the Caribbean: a handbook.* New York: Praeger.

———1976: *Economic Development of Latin America.* Cambridge: Cambridge University Press. Second Edition.

Gann, L. H. and Duignan, Peter 1967: *Burden of Empire: An Appraisal of Western Colonialism in Africa South of the Sahara.* Stanford: Hoover Institution Press.

Gardner, W. T. 1981: A colonial economy. In Oliver, W. H. and Williams, B. R. (eds), *The Oxford History of New Zealand.* Wellington: Oxford University Press.

Garner, John 1969: *The Franchise and Politics in British North America*

1755–1867. Toronto: University of Toronto Press.

Garretón, Manuel Antonio 1986: The political evolution of the Chilean military regime and problems in the transition to democracy. In O'Donnell, G., Schmitter, P. C. and Whitehead, L. (eds), *Transitions from Authoritarian Rule: Latin America*. Baltimore: Johns Hopkins University Press.

Garst, Daniel 1987: *Capitalism and Liberal Democratic Political Development: state structures in Britain and Germany prior to World War I*. Ph. D. Dissertation, University of Minnesota.

Geertz, Clifford 1963: The integrative revolution: primordial sentiments and civil politics in the new states. In Geertz, C. (ed), *Old Societies and New States*. Glencoe, IL: Free Press.

Gerschenkron, Alexander 1943: *Bread and Democracy in Germany*. Berkeley: University of California Press.

——1962: *Economic Backwardness in Historical Perspective*. Cambridge, Msss.: Harvard University Press.

Gettleman, Marvin E. et al. 1981: *El Salvador: Central America in the New Cold War*. New York: Grove Press.

Giddens, Anthony 1973: *The Class Structure of Advanced Societies*. London: Hutchinson, and New York: Harper and Row.

——1981: *A Contemporary Critique of Historical Materialism*. Berkeley: University of California Press.

Gil, Federico G. 1966: *The Political System of Chile*. Boston: Houghton Mifflin Company.

Gillespie, Charles G. 1986: Uruguay's transition from collegial military–technocratic rule. In O'Donnell, G., Schmitter, P. C. and Whitehead, L. (eds), *Transitions from Authoritarian Rule: Latin America*. Baltimore: Johns Hopkins University Press.

Gillespie, Charles and Gonzalez, Luis E. 1989: Uruguay: the survival of old and autonomous institutions. In Diamond, L., Linz, J. and Lipset, S. M. (eds), *Democracy in Developing Countries: Latin America*. Boulder: Lynne Rienner.

Gilly, Adolfo 1971: *La revolución interrumpida*. Mexico: D.F.: El Caballito.

Girvan, Norman 1971: *Foreign Capital and Economic Underdevelopment in Jamaica*. Mona, Jamaica: Institute of Social and Economic Research, University of the West Indies.

Gitermann, Valentin 1941: *Geschichte der Schweiz*. Thayngen: Augustin-Verlag.

Gold, David A., Lo, Clarence, Y. H. and Wright, Eric Olin 1975: Recent developments in Marxist theories of the state. *Monthly Review*, 27 (5).

Goldfrank, Walter 1975: World system, state structure, and the onset of the Mexican Revolution. *Politics and Society*, V (4).

——1979: Theories of revolution and revolution without theory: the case of Mexico. *Theory and Society*, 7 pp. 135–65.

Goldstone, Jack 1982: The comparative and historical study of revolutions. *Annual Review of Sociology*, 8.

Gómez, Leopoldo and Klesner, Joseph L. 1988: Mexico's 1988 elections: the beginning of a new era of Mexican politics?. *LASA Forum*, XIX, (3) (Fall).

Good, David F. 1984: *The Economic Rise of the Habsburg Empire 1750–1914*. Berkeley: University of California Press.

Goodman, Paul 1967: The first American party system. In Chambers, W. N. and Burnham, W. D. (eds), *The American Party Systems: stages of political development*. New York: Oxford University Press.

Goodwin, Jeff 1988: Revolutionary movements in Central America: a comparative analysis. CRPSO Working Paper No. 7, Harvard University.

Gourevitch, Peter 1986: *Politics in Hard Times: comparative responses to international economic crises*. Ithaca: Cornell University Press.

Grabendorff, Wolf, Krumwiede, Heinrich W. and Todt, Jörg (eds) 1984: *Political Change in Central America: internal and external dimensions*. Boulder: Westview Press.

Graham, Richard 1987: State and society in Brazil, 1822–1930. *Latin American Research Review*, 22 (3).

Greene, J. E. 1974: *Race vs. Politics in Guyana*. Mona, Jamaica: Institute of Social and Economic Research, University of the West Indies.

Gross, N. T. 1973: The Habsburg Monarchy 1750–1914. In Cipolla, C. M. (ed), *The Fontana Economic History of Europe: the emergence of industrial societies–1*. Glasgow: Fontana.

Gruner, Erich 1977: *Die Parteien in der Schweiz*. Bern: Francke Verlag.

Gudmundson, Lowell 1986: *Costa Rica Before Coffee*. Baton Rouge: Louisiana State University.

Gulick, Charles A. 1948: *Austria from Habsburg to Hitler*. Berkeley: University of California Press.

Hadenius, Stig, Wieslander, Hans and Molin, Björn 1970: *Sverige efter 1900*. Stockholm: Aldus.

Hagopian, Frances and Mainwaring, Scott 1987: *Democracy in Brazil: origins, problems, prospects*. Working Paper No. 100. Notre Dame, IN: The Helen Kellogg Institute for International Studies, University of Notre Dame.

Hamilton, Nora 1982: *The Limits of State Autonomy: Post-Revolutionary Mexico*. Princeton: Princeton University Press.

Hamilton, Nora A., Frieden, Jeffry, Fuller, Linda and Pastor, Jr., Manuel (eds) 1988: *Crisis in Central America: regional dynamics and US policy in the 1980s*. Boulder: Westview Press.

Hamilton, Richard F. 1980: *Who Voted for Hitler?*. Princeton: Princeton University Press.

Handelman, Howard 1976: The politics of labor protest in Mexico: two case studies. *Journal of Interamerican Studies and World Affairs*, 18 (3).

——1981: Ecuador: postscript. In Handelman, H. and Sanders, T. G. (eds), *Military Government and the Movement toward Democracy in South America*. Bloomington: Indiana University Press.

——1986: Prelude to elections: the military's legitimacy crisis and the 1980 constitutional plebiscite in Uruguay. In Drake, P. W. and Silva, E. (eds), *Elections and Democratization in Latin America, 1980–1985*. San Diego: Center for Iberian and Latin American Studies, University of California, San Diego.

Hannan, Michael T. and Carroll, Glenn R. 1981: Dynamics of formal political structure: an event–history analysis. *American Sociological Review*, 46.

Hansen, Roger D. 1971: *The Politics of Mexican Development*. Baltimore: Johns Hopkins University Press.

——1974: *The Politics of Mexican Development.* Baltimore: Johns Hopkins University Press.

Harrison, Royden 1965: *Before the Socialists.* London: Routledge.

Harrod, Jeffrey 1972: *Trade Union Foreign Policy: a study of British and American trade union activities in Jamaica.* Garden City, NY: Doubleday.

Hartlyn, Jonathan 1986: Democratization and "political learning": the case of the Dominican Republic. Paper delivered at the Meetings of the Latin American Studies Association, Boston (October).

——1989: Democracy in Colombia: the politics of violence and accommodation. In Diamond, L., Linz, J. and Lipset, S. M. (eds), *Democracy in Developing Countries: Latin America,* Boulder: Lynn Rienner.

——1990: The Dominican Republic. Paper presented to a conference organized by the World Peace Foundation. Kingston, Jamaica.

Hartwell, R. M. 1977: The pastoral ascendancy, 1820–50. In Greenwood, G. (ed), *Australia: a social and political history.* London: Angus and Robertson.

Held, David 1987: *Models of Democracy.* Cambridge: Polity Press, and Stanford: Stanford University Press.

Hellman, Judith Adler 1983: *Mexico in Crisis.* New York: Holmes and Meier. Second Edition.

Henry, Paget and Stone, Carl (eds) 1983: *The Newer Caribbean: decolonization, democracy, and development.* Philadelphia, PA: Institute for the Study of Human Issues.

Herring, Ronald J. 1987: Food policy in a dependent welfare state: internal and external determinants of entitlements in Sri Lanka. In Hollist, Ladd and Tullis, LaMond (eds), *Pursuing Food Security, International Political Economy Yearbook, volume III.* Boulder: Lynne Rienner.

Hewitt, Christopher 1977: The effect of democracy and social democracy on equality in industrial societies. *American Sociological Review,* 42.

Hibbs, Douglas A. 1973: *Mass Political Violence: a cross-national causal analysis.* New York: John Wiley.

Hicks, Alexander, and Swank, Duane. 1984: Governmental redistribution in rich capitalist democracies. *Policy Studies Journal* 13.

Hierro, Luis Antonio 1977: *Historia Uruguaya. Batlle: democracia y reforma del Estado.* Montevideo: Ediciones de la Banda Oriental.

Hilliker, Grant 1971: *The Politics of Reform in Peru: the aprista and other mass parties of Latin America.* Baltimore: Johns Hopkins University Press.

Himmelfarb, G. 1966: The politics of democracy: the English Reform Act of 1867. *Journal of British Studies,* 6 (1).

Hintze, Otto 1975: Military organization and the organization of the state. In Gilbert, F. (ed.), *The Historical Essays of Otto Hintze.* Oxford and New York: Oxford University Press; first published 1906.

Hintzen, Percy 1989: *The Costs of Regime Survival: racial mobilization, elite domination, and control of the state in Guyana and Trinidad.* Cambridge: Cambridge University Press.

Hirschman, Albert O. 1969: The political economy of import-substituting industrialization in Latin America. *Quarterly Journal of Economics,* February.

Hoyos, F. A. 1978: *Barbados: a history from the Amerindians to independence.* London: Macmillan.

Huntington, Samuel 1968: *Political Order in Changing Societies.* New Haven: Yale University Press.

——1984: Will more countries become democratic? *Political Science Quarterly,* 99 (2).

Hurtado, Osvaldo 1980: *Political Power in Ecuador.* Albuquerque: University of New Mexico Press. Originally published in 1977 as *El poder politico en el Ecuador* by Pontificia Universidad Catolica del Ecuador, Quito.

Imaz, José Luis de 1970: *Los que mandan (Those Who Rule).* Albany: State University of New York Press. Originally published in 1964 as *Los Que Mandan* by Editorial Universitaria de Buenos Aires.

Immerman, Richard H. 1982: *The CIA in Guatemala: the foreign policy of intervention.* Austin: University of Texas Press.

Ingham, Geoffrey K. 1974: *Strikes and Industrial Conflict.* London: Macmillan.

Irving, T. H. 1974: 1850–70. In Crowley, F. K. (ed.), *A New History of Australia.* Melbourne: William Heinemann.

Jackman, Robert W. 1973: On the relation of economic development to democratic performance. *American Journal of Political Science,* 17.

Jacobs, W. Richard and Jacobs, Ian 1980: *Grenada: the route to revolution.* Havana: Casa de las Americas.

Jagan, Cheddi 1972: *The West on Trial: the fight for Guyana's freedom.* East Berlin: Seven Seas.

James, David R. 1988: The transformation of the southern racial state: class and race determinants of local–state structures. *American Sociological Review,* 53.

Jaquette, Jane S. 1971: *The Politics of Development in Peru.* Ithaca: Cornell University, Latin American Studies Program, Dissertation Series, No. 33.

Jefferson, Owen 1972: *The Post-War Economic Development of Jamaica.* Mona, Jamaica: Institute of Social and Economic Research, University of the West Indies.

Jessop, Bob 1982: *The Capitalist State: marxist theories and methods.* New York: New York University Press.

Johnson, Richard 1976: Barrington Moore, Perry Anderson and English social development. Working Papers in *Cultural Studies,* 9.

Jonas, Susan 1974: Guatemala. In Chilcote, R. H. and Edelstein, J. C. (eds), *Latin America: the struggle with dependency and beyond.* New York: John Wiley.

Kahl, Joseph A. 1976: *Modernization, Exploitation and Dependency in Latin America.* New Brunswick, NJ: Transaction Books.

Karl, Terry Lynn 1986: Petroleum and political pacts: the transition to democracy in Venezuela. In O'Donnell, G., Schmitter, P. C. and White-head, L. (eds), *Transitions from Authoritarian Rule: Latin America.* Baltimore: Johns Hopkins University Press.

Katzenstein, Peter 1984: *Corporatism and Change: Austria, Switzerland and the politics of industry.* Ithaca: Cornell University Press.

——1985: *Small States in World Markets: industrial policy in Europe.* Ithaca:

Cornell University Press.

Katznelson, Ira 1986: Working-class formation: constructing cases and comparisons. In Katznelson, I. and Zolberg, A. R. (eds), *Working-Class Formation: nineteenth-century patterns in western Europe and the United States.* Princeton: Princeton University Press.

Katznelson, Ira and Zolberg, Aristide. R. (eds) 1986: *Working-Class Formation: nineteenth-century patterns in western Europe and the United States.* Princeton: Princeton University Press.

Kaufman, Robert R. 1977: Mexico and Latin American authoritarianism. In Reyna, J. L. and Weinert, R. S. (eds) *Authoritarianism in Mexico.* Philadelphia, PA: Institute for the Study of Human Issues.

——1989: Economic orthodoxy and political change in Mexico: the stabilization and adjustment policies of the de la Madrid Administration. In Stallings, B. and Kaufman, R. (eds) *Debt and Democracy in Latin America.* Boulder: Westview Press.

Kehr, Eckart 1973: *Battleship Building and Party Politics in Germany, 1894–1901.* Chicago: University of Chicago Press.

Kenworthy, Eldon 1973: The function of the little-known case in theory formation or what peronism wasn't. *Comparative Politics.* 6 (1) (October).

Kim, Heung Sik 1988a: Japanese Fascist development: a test of Moore's thesis on the social origins of Japanese Fascism. Unpublished paper. Northwestern University.

——1988b: The scope of the public economy in third world countries: a comparative analysis. Unpublished paper. Northwestern University.

Klarén, Peter F. 1973: *Modernization, Dislocation, and Aprismo: origins of the Peruvian aprista party, 1870–1932.* Austin: University of Texas Press, for the Institute of Latin American Studies.

Klein, Herbert S. 1971: Prelude to the revolution. In Malloy, J. M. and Thorn, R. S. (eds), *Beyond the Revolution: Bolivia since 1952.* Pittsburgh, PA: University of Pittsburgh Press.

Kocka, Jürgen 1985: Problems of working-class formation in Germany: the early years, 1800–1875. In Katznelson, I. and Zolberg, A. (eds), *Working-Class Formation.* Princeton: Princeton University Press.

Korpi, Walter 1978: *The Working Class in Welfare Capitalism.* London: Routledge.

——1982: *The Democratic Class Struggle.* London: Routledge.

Kryzanek, Michael J. 1979: The 1978 election in the Dominican Republic: opposition politics, intervention and the Carter administration. *Caribbean Studies,* 19 (1 and 2).

Kurth, James 1979: Industrial change and political change. In Collier, D. (ed.), *The New Authoritarianism in Latin America.* Princeton: Princeton University Press.

Laclau, Ernesto and Mouffe, Chantal 1985: *Hegemony and Socialist Strategy: towards a radical democratic politics.* London: Verso.

LaFeber, Walter 1984: *Inevitable Revolutions: the United States in Central America.* New York: Norton. Expanded Edition.

Laitin, David D. 1985: Hegemony and religious conflict: British imperial control and political cleavages in Yorubaland. In Evans, P. B., Rueschemeyer, D. and Skocpol, T. (eds), *Bringing the State Back In*. Cambridge and New York: Cambridge University Press.

Landi, Oscar 1978: *La tercera Presidencia de Perón: Gobierno de emergencia y crisis política*. Documento CEDES/G. E. CLACSO No. 10. Buenos Aires.

Landsberger, Henry A. and McDaniel, Tim 1976: Hypermobilization in Chile, 1970–1973. *World Politics*, 28 (4) (July).

LASA Forum 1985: *Report of the Latin American Studies Association Delegation To Observe the Nicaraguan General Election of November 4, 1984*. Pittsburgh: Latin American Studies Association.

Leff, Nathaniel H. 1967: Import constraints and development: causes of the recent decline of Brazilian economic growth. *Review of Economics and Statistics*, November.

Lepsius, M. Rainer 1978: From fragmented party democracy to government by emergency decree and national socialist takeover: Germany. In Linz, J. and Stepan, A. (eds), *The Breakdown of Democratic Regimes: Europe*. Baltimore: Johns Hopkins University Press.

Lerner, Daniel 1958: *The Passing of Traditional Society: modernizing the Middle East*. New York: Free Press.

Leuchtenburg, William E. 1986: The pertinence of political history: reflections on the significance of the state in America. *Journal of American History*, 73 (3)

Levine, Daniel H. 1978: Venezuela since 1958: the consolidation of democratic politics. In Linz, J. J. and Stepan, A. (eds), *The Breakdown of Democratic Regimes: Latin America*. Baltimore: Johns Hopkins University Press.

Levy, Daniel C. 1989: Mexico: sustained civilian rule without democracy. In Diamond, L., Linz, J. J. and Lipset, S. M. (eds), *Democracy in Developing Countries: Latin America*. Boulder: Lynne Rienner.

Lewis, Gordon 1968: *The Growth of the Modern West Indies*. New York: Modern Reader.

——1987: *Grenada: the jewel despoiled*. Baltimore: Johns Hopkins University Press.

Lewis, Paul H. 1982: *Socialism, Liberalism, and Dictatorship in Paraguay*. New York: Praeger.

Lind, Gunner 1988: Military state and bourgeois democracy. In Stråth, B. (ed), *Democratisation in Scandinavia in Comparison*. Gothenburg: Department of History, University of Gothenburg.

Linz, Juan J. 1967: The party system of Spain: past and future. In Lipset, S. M. and Rokkan, S. (eds), *Party Systems and Voter Alignments*. New York: Free Press, pp. 197–282.

——1970: An authoritarian regime: Spain. In Rokkan, S. (ed.), *Mass Politics*. New York: Free Press.

——1975: Totalitarian and authoritarian regimes. In Greenstein, F. and Polsby, N. (eds), *Handbook of Political Science*, vol 3. Reading: Addison-Wesley.

——1976: Some notes toward a comparative study of Fascism in sociological historical perspective. In Laqueur, W. (ed.), *Fascism: a reader's guide*.

Berkeley: University of California Press.

——1978: *Crisis, Breakdown and Reequilibration*. Baltimore: Johns Hopkins University Press.

Linz, Juan J. and Stepan, Alfred (eds) 1978: *The Breakdown of Democratic Regimes: Latin America*. Baltimore: Johns Hopkins University Press.

Lipset, Seymour Martin 1959/1980: Some social requisites of democracy: economic development and political legitimacy. *American Political Science Review*, 53; reprinted in Lipset, S. M., *Political Man*, exp. edn. Baltimore: Johns Hopkins University Press.

——1960: *Political Man*. Garden City: Anchor Books.

——1963: *The First New Nation: the United States in historical and comparative perspective*. Garden City, NY: Anchor Books.

——1980: *Political Man: the social bases of politics*, exp. edn. Baltimore: Johns Hopkins University Press.

Lipset, Seymour Martin and Rokkan, Stein 1967: Cleavage structures, party systems, and voter alignments: an introduction. In Lipset, S. M. and Rokkan, S. (eds), *Party Systems and Voter Alignments*. New York: Free Press.

Lipset, Seymour M., Trow Martin, and Coleman, James S. 1956: *Union Democracy: what makes democracy work in labor unions and other organizations?*. Glencoe, IL: Free Press.

Lombardi, John V. 1982: *Venezuela: the search for order, the dream of progress*. New York: Oxford University Press.

Lorwin, Val 1966: Belgium: religion, class, and language in national politics. In Dahl, R. (ed), *Political Oppositions in Western Democracies*. New Haven: Yale University Press.

Loveman, Brian 1979: *Chile: the legacy of Hispanic capitalism*. New York: Oxford University Press.

Lowenthal, Abraham F. 1971: *The Dominican Intervention*. Cambridge: Harvard University Press.

——(ed) 1975: *The Peruvian Experiment: continuity and change under military rule*. Princeton: Princeton University Press.

——1986: Armies and politics in Latin America: introduction to the first edition. In Lowenthal A. F. and Fitch, J. S. (eds), *Armies and Politics in Latin America*. New York: Holmes and Meier. Revised Edition.

Luebbert, Gregory M. 1987: Social foundations of political order in interwar Europe. *World Politics*, 39.

Lukes, Steven 1967: Alienation and anomie. In Laslett, P. and Runciman, W. G. (eds), *Philosophy, Politics and Society*, 3rd series. Oxford: Basil Blackwell.

——1974: *Power: a critical view*. London: Macmillan.

Lutchman, Harold Alexander 1974: *From Colonialism to Co-operative Republic: aspects of political development in Guyana*. Rio Piedras, Puerto Rico: Institute of Caribbean Studies, University of Puerto Rico.

Lyttelton, Adrian 1973: *The Seizure of Power: Fascism in Italy 1919–1929*. New York: Scribner's.

McAdams, Doug 1982: *Political Process and the Development of Black Insurgency, 1930–1970*. Chicago: University of Chicago Press.

McClintock, Cynthia 1986: The prospects for democratic consolidation in three "least likely" Andean nations. Paper delivered at the Meetings of the Latin American Studies Association, Boston, October.

McCormick, Richard P. 1967: Political development and the second party system. In Chambers, W. N. and Burnham, W. D. (eds), *The American Party Systems: stages of political development*. New York: Oxford University Press.

McMichael, Philip 1984: *Settlers and the Agrarian Question: foundations of capitalism in colonial Australia*. Cambridge: Cambridge University Press.

McNaught, Kenneth 1988: *The Penguin History of Canada*. London: Penguin Books.

McNaughtan, I. D. 1977: Colonial liberalism, 1851–92. In Greenwood, G. (ed), *Australia: a social and political history*. London: Angus and Robertson.

Macpherson, C. B. 1973: *Democratic Theory: essays in retrieval*. Oxford: Oxford University Press.

——1977: *The Life and Times of Liberal Democracy*. Oxford: Oxford University Press.

Magraw, Roger 1983: *France 1815–1914: the bourgeois century*. Oxford: Fontana.

Maier, Charles 1975: *Recasting Bourgeois Europe*. Princeton: Princeton University Press.

Main, Jackson Turner 1961: *The Anti-Federalists: critics of the constitution 1781–1788*. Chapel Hill: University of North Carolina Press.

Mainwaring, Scott 1986: *The Catholic church and Politics in Brazil, 1916–1985*. Stanford: Stanford University Press.

Malefakis, Edward 1970: *Agrarian Reform and Peasant Revolution in Spain*. New Haven: Yale University Press.

Malloy, James M. 1970: *Bolivia: the uncompleted revolution*. Pittsburgh: University of Pitttsburgh Press.

——1971: *Revolutionary Politics*. In Malloy, J. M. and Thorn, R. S. (eds), *Beyond the Revolution: Bolivia since 1952*. Pittsburgh: University of Pittsburgh Press.

——1987: The Politics of Transition in Latin America. In Malloy, J. M. and Seligson, M. A. (eds), *Authoritarians and Democrats: regime transition in Latin America*. Pittsburgh: University of Pittsburgh Press.

Malloy, James M. and Gamarra, Eduardo A. 1987: The transition to democracy in Bolivia. In Malloy, J. M. and Seligson, M. A. (eds), *Authoritarians and Democrats: regime transition in Latin America*. Pittsburgh: University of Pittsburgh Press.

——1988: *Revolution and Reaction: Bolivia, 1964–1985*. New Brunswick, NJ: Transaction Books.

Malloy, James and Seligson, Mitchell (eds) 1987: *Authoritarians and Democrats: Regime Transition in Latin America*. Pittsburgh: University of Pittsburgh Press.

Mamalakis, Markos J. 1976: *The Growth and Structure of the Chilean Economy: from independence to Allende*. New Haven: Yale University Press.

Mandle, Jay R. 1978: *The Roots of Black Poverty*. Durham, NC: Duke University Press.

Manley, Robert H. 1979: *Guyana Emergent: the post-independence struggle for nondependent development*. Boston: G. K. Hall.

Mann, Michael 1970: The social cohesion of liberal democracy. *American Sociological Review*, 35.

——1973: *Consciousness and Action amongst the Western Working Class*. London: Macmillan.

——1986: *The Sources of Social Power*,vol. I: a history of power in Agrarian societies. Cambridge: Cambridge University Press.

——Forthcoming: *The Sources of Social Power*, vol. II: a history of power in industrial societies. Cambridge: Cambridge University Press.

Marais, J. S. 1968: *The Colonisation of New Zealand*. London: Dawsons of Pall Mall.

Marques, Antonio Henrique de Oliveira 1972: *History of Portugal*. New York: Columbia University Press.

Marsh, Robert M. 1979: Does democracy hinder economic development in the latecomer developing nations? *Comparative Social Research*, 2.

Marshall, T. H. 1950: *Citizenship and Social Class*. Cambridge: Cambridge University Press.

Martz, John D. 1966: *Acción Democrática: evolution of a modern political party in Venezuela*. Princeton: Princeton University Press.

——1972: *Ecuador: conflicting political culture and the quest for progress*. Boston: Allyn and Bacon, Inc.

Marx, Karl 1852: The Chartists. In Bottomore, T. B. and Rubel, M. (eds), *Karl Marx: selected writings in Sociology and Social Philosophy*. New York: McGraw Hill, 1964.

Marx, Karl and Engels, Friedrich 1848: Manifesto of the communist party. In *Karl Marx and Friedrich Engels, Collected Works VI*. New York: International Publishers, 1976.

Matthew, H. C. G., McKibbon, R. I. and Key, J. A. 1976: The franchise factor in the rise of the Labour party. *The English Historical Review*, 91 (361).

Meidner, Rudolph 1978: *Employee Investment Funds*. London: Allen and Unwin.

Mendez Vives, Enrique 1977: *Historia Uruguaya, Tomo 5, 1876–1904: El Uruguay de la modernización*. Montevideo: Ediciones de la Banda Oriental. Tercera Edición.

Meyer, John 1980: The world polity and the authority of the nation–state. In Bergesen, A. (ed.), *Studies in the Modern World System*. New York: Academic Press.

Meyer, Michael C. and Sherman, William L. 1983: *The Course of Mexican History*. New York: Oxford University Press. Second Edition.

Michels, Robert 1908/1949: *Political Parties*. Glencoe, IL: Free Press; first German publication 1908.

Middlebrook, Kevin J. 1986: Political liberalization in an authoritarian regime: the case of Mexico. In Drake, P. W. and Silva, E. (eds), *Elections and Democratization in Latin America, 1980–85*. San Diego: Center for Iberian and Latin American Studies, University of California, San Diego.

Midlarsky, Manus I. 1989: Land inequality and political violence. *American Political Science Review*, 83 (2).

Miller, Kenneth E. 1968: *Government and Politics in Denmark*. Boston: Houghton Mifflin.

Millett, Richard 1977: *Guardians of the Dynasty: a history of the US-created Guardia Nacional de Nicaragua and the Somoza family*. Maryknoll: Orbis Books.

Mitchell, B. R. 1978: *European Historical Statistics 1750–1970*. New York: Columbia University Press.

Mitchell, Christopher 1977: *The Legacy of Populism in Bolivia: from the MNR to military rule*. New York: Praeger.

Montgomery, David 1979: *Workers' Control in America*. Cambridge: Cambridge University Press.

Montgomery, Tommie Sue 1982/1983: Cross and rifle: revolution and the church in El Salvador and Nicaragua. *Journal of International Affairs*, 36 (2).

Moore, Barrington 1966: *The Social Origins of Dictatorship and Democracy*. Boston: Beacon Press.

Morris, Aldon D. 1984: *The Origins of the Civil Rights Movement: black communities organizing for change*. New York: The Free Press.

Moskos, Charles C. 1967: *The Sociology of Political Independence*. Cambridge: Schenkman.

Mouffe, Chantal (ed) 1979: *Gramsci and Marxist Theory*. London and Boston: Routledge.

Mouzelis, Nicos P. 1986: *Politics in the Semi-Periphery: early parliamentarism and late industrialization in the Balkans and Latin America*. London: Macmillan.

Muller, Edward N. 1985: Dependent economic development, aid dependence on the United States, and democratic breakdown in the third world. *International Studies Quarterly*, 29.

——1988: Democracy, economic development, and income inequality. *American Sociological Review*, 53.

——1989: Democracy and inequality: reply to Weede. *American Sociological Review*, 54.

Muller, Edward N., Seligson, Mitchell A. and Fu, Hung-der 1989: Land inequality and political violence. *American Political Science Review*, 83 (2).

Munroe, Trevor 1972: *The Politics of Constitutional Decolonization: Jamaica 1944–1962*. Mona, Jamaica: Institute of Social and Economic Research, University of the West Indies.

Nahum, Benjamín 1977: *Historia Uruguaya, Tomo 6, 1905–1930: La época Batllista*. Montevideo: Ediciones de la Banda Oriental. Tercera Edición.

Neebe, Reinhard 1981: *Grossindustrie, Staat und NSDAP, 1930–1933*. Göttingen: Vandenhoeck aund Ruprecht.

——1987: Die Verantwortung der Grossindustrie für das Dritte Reich: Anmerkungen zu H. A. Turners Buch *Die Grossunternehmer und der Aufstieg Hitlers. Historische Zeitschrift*, 244.

Neira, Hugo 1973: Ecuador. In Bernard, J.-P. et al. *Guide to the Political Parties of South America*. Baltimore: Penguin Books.

Neubauer, Deane E. 1967: Some conditions of democracy. *American Political Science Review*, 61.

Newfarmer, Richard (ed) 1984: *From Gunboats to Diplomacy: New US policies for Latin America*. Baltimore: Johns Hopkins University Press.

Nordlinger, Eric A. 1977: *Soldiers in Politics: military coups and governments*. Englewood Cliffs, NJ: Prentice-Hall.

North, Liisa 1976: The military in Chilean politics. In Lowenthal, A. F. (ed.), *Armies and Politics in Latin America*. New York: Holmes and Meier.

Nove, Alec 1976: The political economy of the Allende regime. In O'Brien, P. (ed), *Allende's Chile*. New York: Praeger.

Nun, José 1967: The middle-class military coup. In Veliz, C. (ed), *The Politics of Conformity in Latin America*. London: Oxford University Press.

Nunn, Frederick M. 1970: *Chilean Politics 1920–1931: the honorable mission of the armed forces*. Albuquerque: University of New Mexico Press.

O'Donnell, Guillermo A. 1973: *Modernization and Bureaucratic Authoritarianism*. Berkeley: Institute of International Studies.

——1976: Modernization and military coups: theory, comparisons, and the Argentine case. In Lowenthal, A. F. (ed.), *Armies and Politics in Latin America*. New York: Holmes and Meier.

——1978: Reflections on the bureaucratic authoritarian state. *Latin American Research Review*, 13 (1).

——1979a: Tensions in the bureaucratic authoritarian state and the question of democracy. In Collier, D. (ed), *The New Authoritarianism in Latin America*. Princeton: Princeton University Press.

——1979b: *Modernization and Bureaucratic Authoritarianism: studies in South American politics*. Berkeley: Institute of International Studies, University of California, Berkeley; first published 1973.

O'Donnell, Guillermo and Schmitter, Philippe C. 1986: *Transitions from Authoritarian Rule: tentative conclusions about uncertain democracies*. Baltimore: Johns Hopkins University Press.

O'Donnell, Guillermo, Schmitter, Philippe C. and Whitehead, Laurence (eds), 1986: *Transitions from Authoritarian Rule: prospects for democracy*. Baltimore: Johns Hopkins University Press, 4 vols.

Offe, Claus and Wiesenthal, Helmut 1980: Two logics of collective action: theoretical notes on social class and organizational form. *Political Power and Social Theory*, 1.

Olson, Mancur, Jr. 1963: Rapid growth as a destabilizing force. *Journal of Economic History*, 23.

——1965: *The Logic of Collective Action: public goods and the theory of groups*. Cambridge, Mass.: Harvard University Press.

Oquist, Paul 1980: *Violence, Conflict, and Poltics in Colombia*. New York: Academic Press.

Orloff, Ann Shola and Theda Skocpol 1984: Why not equal protection? Explaining the politics of public social spending in Britain, 1900–1911 and the United States, 1890s–1920. *American Sociological Review*, 49 (6).

Page, Joseph 1983: *Perón: a biography*. New York: Random House.

Paige, Jeffery M. 1975: *Agrarian Revolution*. New York: Free Press.

——1987: Coffee and politics in Central America. In Tardanico, R. (ed.), *Crisis in the Caribbean Basin*. Beverly Hills: Sage Publications.

Parsons, Talcott 1960: Some reflections on the institutional framework of economic development. In Parsons, T., *Structure and Process in Modern Societies*. Glencoe, IL: Free Press.

Pateman, Carole 1970: *Participation and Democratic Theory*. Cambridge: Cambridge University Press.

——1990: Promise and paradox: women and democratic citizenship. Los Angeles: Center for Social Theory and Comparative History, University of California.

Philip, George 1978: *The Rise and Fall of the Peruvian Military Radicals 1968–76*. Athlone.

——1985: *The Military in South American Politics*. London: Croom Helm.

Pike, Fredrick B. 1967: *The Modern History of Peru*. New York: Praeger.

Piven, Francis Fox and Cloward, Richard A. 1971: *Regulating the Poor: the functions of public welfare*. New York: Vintage Books.

Portes, Alejandro 1985: Latin American class structures: their composition and change during the last decades. *Latin American Research Review*, 20 (3).

Portes, Alejandro and Walton, John 1981: *Labor, Class, and the International System*. New York: Academic Press.

Post, Ken 1978: *Arise Ye Starvelings: the Jamaican labour rebellion and its aftermath*. The Hague: M. Nijhoff.

——1981: *Strike the Iron: a colony at war: Jamaica 1939–1945*. Atlantic Highlands, NJ: Humanities Press.

Potash, Robert A. 1969: *The Army and Politics in Argentina 1928–1945, Yrigoyen to Perón*. Stanford: Stanford University Press.

——1980: *The Army and Politics in Argentina 1945–1962, Perón to Frondizi*. Stanford: Stanford University Press.

Preston, Paul 1983: *The Coming of the Spanish Civil War: reform, reaction, and revolution in the Second Republic*. New York: Methuen.

Price, Roger 1972: *The French Second Republic: a social history*. London: Batsford.

Przeworski, Adam 1980: Social democracy as a historical phenomenon. *New Left Review*, 122.

——1985: *Capitalism and Social Democracy*. Cambridge and New York: Cambridge University Press.

——1988: Capitalism, democracy, pacts: revisited. Paper delivered at the conference on the micro-foundations of democracy, University of Chicago, April 29 – May 1, 1988.

Przeworski, Adam, and Sprague, John 1986: *Paper Stones: a history of electoral socialism*. Chicago: University of Chicago Press.

Putnam, Robert 1967: Toward explaining military intervention in Latin American politics. *World Politics*, 20 (October).

Rabinbach, Anson 1983: *The Crisis of Austrian Socialism: from Red Vienna to Civil War 1927–1934*. Chicago: University of Chicago Press.

Ragin, Charles 1987: *The Comparative Method: moving beyond qualitative and quantitative strategies*. Berkeley: University of California Press.

Remmer, Karen L. 1984: *Party Competition and Public Policy: Argentina and Chile, 1890–1930*. Lincoln: University of Nebraska Press.

——1985–6: Exclusionary democracy. *Studies in Comparative International Development*, 20 (4). (Winter).

Reyna, José Luis 1977: Redefining the authoritarian regime. In Reyna, J. L. and Weinert, R. S. (eds) *Authoritarianism in Mexico*. Philadelphia, PA: Institute for the Study of Human Issues.

Rial, Juan 1984: *Partidos políticos, democracia y autoritarismo*. Montevideo: Centro de Informaciones y Estudios del Uruguay; Ediciones de la Banda Oriental.

Rock, David 1975: *Politics in Argentina 1890–1930: the rise and fall of radicalism*. Cambridge: Cambridge University Press.

——1985: *Argentina 1516–1982*. Berkeley: University of California Press.

Rodman, Selden 1964: *Quisqueya: a history of the Dominican Republic*. Seattle: University of Washington Press.

Rokkan, Stein 1966: Norway: numerical democracy and corporate pluralism. In Dahl, R. (ed), *Political Oppositions in Western Democracies*. New Haven: Yale University Press.

——1967: Geography, religion, and social class: crosscutting cleavages in Norwegian politics. In Lipset, S. M. and Rokkan, S. (eds), *Party Systems and Voter Alignments*. New York: Free Press.

——1970: *Citizens, Elections, Parties*. Oslo: Universitets Forlaget.

——1975: Dimensions of state formation and nation-building: a possible paradigm for research on variations within Europe. In Tilly, C. (ed), *The Formation of National States in Western Europe*. Princeton: Princeton University Press.

Rokkan, Stein and Meyriat, Jean 1969: *International Guide to Electoral Statistics*. The Hague: Mouton.

Rostow, Walt W. 1961: *The Stages of Economic Growth: a non-communist manifesto*. Cambridge: Cambridge University Press.

Rubinson, Richard 1976: The world economy and the distribution of income within states. *American Sociological Review*, 41.

Rueschemeyer, Dietrich 1969: Partielle Modernisierung. In Zapf, W. (ed), *Theorien des sozialen Wandels*. Cologne: Kiepenheuer und Witsch. Expanded English version: Partial modernization. In Loubser, J. J., Baum, R. C., Effrat, A. and Lidz, V. M. (eds), *Explorations in General Theory in the Social Sciences*. New York: Free Press 1976.

——1980: Über sozialökonomische Entwicklung und Demokratie. In Levy, R. (ed), *Weltgesellschaft und Sozialstruktur* (Festschrift für Peter Heintz). Diessenhofen, Switzerland: Ruegger.

——1984: Theoretical generalization and historical particularity in the comparative sociology of Reinhard Bendix. In Skocpol, T. (ed), *Vision and Method in Historical Sociology*. Cambridge and New York: Cambridge University Press.

——1986: *Power and the Division of Labour*. Cambridge: Polity Press, and Stanford: Stanford University Press.

——1990: Planning without markets: knowledge and state action in East German housing construction. *Eastern European Politics and Societies*, 4 (3).

Rueschemeyer, Dietrich and Evans, Peter B. 1985: The state and economic transformation: toward an analysis of the conditions underlying effective intervention. In Evans, P. B., Rueschemeyer, D. and Skocpol, T. (eds), *Bringing the State Back In*. Cambridge and New York: Cambridge University Press.

Rueschemeyer, Dietrich and Rueschemeyer, Marilyn 1990: Progress in the distribution of power: gender relations and women's movements as a source of change. In Alexander, J. and Sztompka, P. (eds), *After Progress*. London: Unwin Hyman.

Ruhl, J. Mark 1980: The military. In Berry, R. A., Hellman, R. G. and Solaún, M. (eds), *The Politics of Compromise: Coalition Government in Colombia*. New Brunswick, NJ: Transaction Books.

Rustow, Dankwart 1955: *The Politics of Compromise*. Princeton: Princeton University Press.

——1970: Transitions to democracy: toward a dynamic model. *Comparative Politics*. 2 (3).

Ryan, Selwyn 1972: *Race and Nationalism in Trinidad and Tobago: a study of decolonization in a multiracial society*. Toronto: University of Toronto Press.

——1989: *Revolution and Reaction: parties and politics in Trindad and Tobago 1970–1981*. St Augustine, Trinidad: Institute of Social and Economic Research; University of the West Indies.

Safford, Frank 1985: Politics, ideology and society in post-independence Spanish America. In Bethell, L. (ed), *The Cambridge History of Latin America*, vol. III. Cambridge: Cambridge University Press.

Sanders, Thomas G. 1964: *Protestant Concepts of Church and State: historical backgrounds and approaches for the future*. New York: Holt, Rinehart, and Winston.

Schlesinger, Stephen and Kinzer, Stephen 1981: *Bitter Fruit: the untold story of the American Coup in Guatemala*. Garden City, NY: Doubleday.

Schmelz, Frieder 1981: *Paraguay im 19. Jahrhundert*. Heidelberger Dritte Welt Studien. Heidelberg: esprint Verlag.

Schmitter, Philippe 1971: *Interest Conflict and Political Change in Brazil*. Stanford: Stanford University Press.

Schodt, David W. 1987: *Ecuador: an Andean enigma*. Boulder: Westview Press.

Schoultz, Lars 1983: Guatemala: social change and political conflict. In Diskin, M. (ed), *Trouble in Our Backyard*. New York: Pantheon Books.

Schumpeter, Joseph 1947: *Capitalism, Socialism and Democracy*. New York: Harper and Brothers.

——1968: *Imperialism and Social Classes*. Cleveland: World Publishing Co.

Schwartz, Michael 1976: *Radical Protest and Social Structure: the southern Farmers' Alliance and cotton tenancy, 1880–1980*. New York: Academic Press.

Seligson, Mitchell A. 1980: *Peasants of Costa Rica and the Development of Agrarian Capitalism*. Madison: University of Wisconsin Press.

——1987a: Democratization in Latin America: The current cycle. In Malloy, James and Seligson, Mitchell (eds) 1987: *Authoritarians and Democrats:*

Regime Transition in Latin America. Pittsburgh: University of Pittsburgh Press.

——1987b: Development, Democratization, and Decay: Central America at the Crossroads. In Malloy, James and Seligson, Mitchell (eds), *Authoritarians and Democrats: Regime Transition in Latin America.* Pittsburgh: University of Pittsburgh Press.

Senghaas, Dieter 1985: *The European Experience: a historical critique of development theory.* Dover, NH: Berg.

Seton-Watson, Christopher 1967: *Italy from Liberalism to Fascism.* London: Methuen.

Seton-Watson, Hugh 1962: *Eastern Europe between the Wars 1918–1945.* Hamden, CT: Archon Books.

Sewell, William H. Jr. 1986: Artisans, factory workers, and the formation of the French working-class, 1789–1848. In Katznelson, I. and Zolberg, A. R. (eds), *Working-Class Formation: nineteenth-century patterns in western Europe and the United States.* Princeton: Princeton University Press.

Sheehan, James J. 1978: *German Liberalism in the Nineteenth Century.* Chicago: University of Chicago Press.

Shefter, Martin 1986: Trade unions and political machines: the organization and disorganization of the American working-class in the late nineteenth century. In Katznelson, I. and Zolberg, A. R. (eds), *Working-Class Formation: nineteenth-century patterns in western Europe and the United States.* Princeton: Princeton University Press.

Shepherd, Philip L. 1986: Honduras. In Blachman, M. J., Leogrande, W. M. and Sharpe, K. (eds), *Confronting Revolution: security through diplomacy in Central America.* New York: Pantheon Books.

Sherlock, Philip 1980: *Norman Manley: A biography.* London: Macmillan.

Silva Michelena, Jose A. 1973: Diversities among dependent nations: an overview of Latin American development. In Eisenstadt, S. N. and Rokkan, S. (eds), *Building States and Nations: analyses by region*, vol. II. Beverly Hills: Sage Publications.

Simon, Walter 1978: Democracy in the shadow of imposed sovereignty: the first republic of Austria. In Linz, J. and Stepan, A. (eds), *The Breakdown of Democratic Regimes: Europe.* Baltimore: Johns Hopkins University Press.

Sinclair, Keith 1961: *A History of New Zealand.* London: Oxford University Press.

Sirianni, Carmen (ed) 1987: *Workers' Participation and the Politics of Reform.* Philadelphia, PA: Temple University Press.

Skidmore, Thomas E. 1967: *Politics in Brazil 1930–1964: an experiment in democracy.* New York: Oxford University Press.

Skidmore, Thomas E. and Smith, Peter H. 1984: *Modern Latin America.* New York: Oxford University Press.

Sklar, Richard L. 1979: The nature of class domination in Africa. *Journal of Modern African Studies*, 17 (4).

——1979: *States and Social Revolutions: a comparative analysis of France, Russia and China*. Cambridge and New York: Cambridge University Press.

——1984: Emerging agendas and recurrent strategies in historical sociology. In Skocpol, T. (ed.), *Vision and Method in Historical Sociology*. Cambridge and New York: Cambridge University Press.

——1985: Bringing the state back in: strategies of analysis in current research. In Evans, P. B., Rueschemeyer, D. and Skocpol, T. (eds), *Bringing the State Back In*. Cambridge and New York: Cambridge University Press.

Skocpol, Theda and Somers, Margaret 1980: The uses of comparative history in macrosocial inquiry. *Comparative Studies in Society and History*, 22 (2).

Smith, Brian H. and Rodríguez, José Luis 1974: Comparative working-class political behavior: Chile, France, and Italy. *The American Behavioral Scientist*, 18 (1) (September/October).

Smith, Peter H. 1969: *Politics and Beef in Argentina: patterns of conflict and change*. New York: Columbia University Press.

——1977: Does Mexico have a power elite? In Reyna, J. L. and Weinert, R. S. (eds), *Authoritarianism in Mexico*. Philadelphia, PA: Institute for the Study of Human Issues.

——1978: The breakdown of democracy in Argentina, 1916–30. In Linz, J. J. and Stepan, A. (eds), *The Breakdown of Democratic Regimes: Latin America*. Baltimore: Johns Hopkins University Press.

——1979: *Labyrinths of Power: political recruitment in twentieth-century Mexico*. Princeton: Princeton University Press.

Smith, Tony 1978: A comparative study of French and British decolonization. *Comparative Studies in Society and History*, 20.

Smith, Wayne S. 1983: The return of Peronism. In Turner, F. C. and Miguens, J. E. (eds), *Juan Perón and the Reshaping of Argentina*. Pittsburgh: University of Pittsburgh Press.

Söderpalm, Sven Anders 1969: *Storföretagarna and Det Demokratiska Genombrottet*. Lund: Gleerups.

——1976: *Direktörsklubben: storindustrin i svensk politik under 1930– och 40– talen*. Stockholm: Zenit/Rabén & Sjögren.

Spalding, Hobart A. 1977: *Organized Labor in Latin America: historical case studies of urban workers in dependent societies*. New York: Harper and Row; Harper Torchbooks.

Spinner, Thomas J. 1984: *Political and Social History of Guyana 1945–1983*. Boulder: Westview.

Statistical Abstract of Latin America: 1963. University of California, Los Angeles: Center of Latin American Studies.

Stepan, Alfred 1971: *The Military in Politics: changing patterns in Brazil*. Princeton: Princeton University Press.

——1978: *The State and Society: Peru in comparative perspective*. Princeton: Princeton University Press.

——1985: State power and the strength of civil society in the southern cone of Latin America. In Evans, P. B., Rueschemeyer, D. and Skocpol, T. (eds), *Bringing the State Back In*. Cambridge and New York: Cambridge University Press.

——1988: *Rethinking Military Politics: Brazil and the southern cone*. Princeton:

Princeton University Press.

——(ed) 1989: *Democratizing Brazil: problems of transition and consolidation*. New York: Oxford University Press.

Stephens, Evelyne Huber 1980: *The Politics of Workers' Participation: the Peruvian approach in comparative perspective*. New York: Academic Press.

——1983: The Peruvian military government, labor mobilization, and the political strength of the left. *Latin American Research Review*, 18(2).

——1988: Economic development, social change, and political contestation and inclusion in South America. Paper delivered at the meetings of the Latin American Studies Association, New Orleans, March.

Stephens, Evelyne Huber and Stephens, John D. 1982: The labor movement, political power, and workers' participation in western Europe. *Political Power and Social Theory*, 3.

——1986: *Democratic Socialism in Jamaica: the political movement and social transformation in dependent capitalism*. Princeton: Princeton University Press.

——1987: Democracy and authoritarianism in the Caribbean basin: domestic and international determinants. Paper delivered at the XII, International Congress of the Caribbean Studies Association in Belize City, Belize, May.

——1988: Evaluating human rights in Jamaica. In Donnelly, J. and Howard, R. (eds), *International Handbook of Human Rights*. New York: Greenwood Press.

——1990: Capitalists, socialism, and democracy: an analysis of business attitudes towards political democracy in Jamaica. *Comparative Social Research* 12.

Stephens, John D. 1976: The consequences of social structural change for the development of socialism in Sweden. Ph. D. dissertation, Yale University.

——1979a: Class formation and class consciousness: a theoretical and empirical analysis with reference to Britain and Sweden. *British Journal of Sociology*, 30 (4).

——1979b: Religion and politics in three northwest European democracies. *Comparative Social Research*, 2.

——1979c: *The Transition from Capitalism to Socialism*. Urbana: University of Illinois Press.

——1989: Democratic transition and breakdown in Europe, 1870–1939: a test of the Moore thesis. *American Journal of Sociology*, 94 (5) (March).

Stevens, Evelyn P. 1974: *Protest and Response in Mexico*. Cambridge, MA: M. I. T. Press.

Stinchcombe, Arthur 1968: *Constructing Social Theories*. New York: Harcourt, Brace, and World.

Stråth, Bo 1988: Continuity and discontinuity in passing front I and II: Swedish 19th century civil society: culture, social formations, and political change. In Stråth, B. (ed), *Democratisation in Scandinavia in Comparison*. Gothenburg: Department of History, University of Gothenburg.

Sulmont, Denis 1984: *El movimiento obrero peruano (1890–1980): reseña histórica*. Lima: Tarea. Cuarta edición.

Tannenbaum, Frank 1964: *Mexico: the struggle for peace and bread*. New York: Alfred A. Knopf.

Tasca, Angelo 1938: *The Rise of Italian Fascism 1918–1922*. New York: Howard Fertig.

Taylor, A. J. P. 1976: *The Habsburg Monarchy, 1809–1918: a history of the Austrian empire and Austria–Hungary*. Chicago: University of Chicago Press.

Taylor, Philip B. Jr. 1952: The Uruguayan Coup d'Etat of 1933. *Hispanic American Historical Review*, 32 (3) (August).

——1962: *Government and Politics of Uruguay*. Westport, CT: Greenwood Press, Publishers. (Reprinted 1984 by Greenwood Press. Copyright 1962 Tulane University.)

Therborn, Göran 1977: The rule of capital and the rise of democracy. *New Left Review*, 103.

——1979: The travail of Latin American democracy. *New Left Review*, 113–14.

Thomas, Clive Y. 1984: *The Rise of the Authoritarian State in Peripheral Societies*. New York: Monthly Review Press.

Thomas, George M., Ramirez, Francisco O., Meyer, John W., and Gobalet, Jeanne G. 1979: Maintaining national boundaries in the world system: the rise of centralist regimes. In Meyer, J. and Hannan, M. (eds), *National Development and the World System*. Chicago: University of Chicago Press.

Thompson, Dorothy 1984: *The Chartists*. London: Temple Smith, and New York: Pantheon Books.

Thompson, E. P. 1963: *The Making of the English Working Class*. New York: Vintage.

——1978: *The Poverty of Theory and Other Essays*. London: Merlin.

Thorn, Richard S. 1971: The economic transformation. In Malloy, J. M. and Thorn, R. S. (eds), *Beyond the Revolution: Bolivia since 1952*. Pittsburgh: University of Pittsburgh Press.

Thorndike, Tony 1985: *Grenada: politics, economics and society*. Boulder: Lynne Rienner.

Thorp, Rosemary and Bertram, Geoffrey 1978: *Peru 1890–1977: growth and policy in an open economy*. London: Macmillan.

Thorp, Rosemary and Whitehead, Laurence (eds) 1979: *Inflation and Stabilisation in Latin America*. New York: Holmes and Meier.

Tilly, Charles 1975: Reflections on the history of European state-making. In Tilly, C. (ed.), *The Formation of National States in Western Europe*. Princeton: Princeton University Press.

——1984: *Big Structures, Large Processes, Huge Comparisons*. New York: Russell Sage Foundation.

Tilton, Timothy 1974: The social origins of liberal democracy: the Swedish case. *American Political Science Review*, 68 (2).

Tomasson, Richard F. 1970: *Sweden: Prototype of Modern Society*. New York: Random House.

Topik, Steven 1987: *The Political Economy of the Brazilian State, 1889–1930*. Austin: University of Texas Press.

Torres-Rivas, Edelberto 1984: Problems of democracy and counterrevolution in Guatemala. In Grabendorff, W., Krumwiede, H.-W. and Todt, J. (eds), *Political Change in Central America: internal and external dimensions.* Boulder: Westview Press.

Trebilcock, Clive 1981: *The Industrialization of the Continental Powers 1780–1914.* London: Longman.

Trudeau, Robert and Schoultz, Lars 1986: *Guatemala.* In Blachman, R. J., Leogrande, W. M. and Sharpe, K. (eds), *Confronting Revolution: security through diplomacy in Central America.* New York: Pantheon Books.

Tumin, Jonathan 1978: Pathways to democracy: a critical revision of Barrington Moore's theory of democratic emergence and an application of the revised theory to the case of Netherlands. Ph. D. Dissertation, Harvard University.

Turner, Henry A. 1985: *German Big Business and the Rise of Hitler.* New York: Oxford University Press.

Tutino, John 1986: *From Insurrection to Revolution in Mexico: social bases of Agrarian violence 1750–1940.* Princeton: Princeton University Press.

Urrutia, Miguel 1969: *The Development of the Colombian Labor Movement.* New Haven: Yale University Press.

US Senate 1975: *Covert Action in Chile 1963–1973.* Staff Report of the Select Committee to Study Governmental Operations with Respect to Intelligence Activities. Washington, DC: Government Printing Office.

Valenzuela, Arturo 1977: *Political Brokers in Chile: local government in a centralized polity.* Durham, NC: Duke University Press.

——1989: Chile: origins, consolidation and breakdown of a democratic regime. In Diamond, L., Linz, J. and Lipset, S. M. (eds), *Democracy in Developing Countries: Latin America,* Boulder: Lynne Rienner.

Valenzuela, Arturo and Valenzuela, J. Samuel 1986: Party oppositions under the Chilean authoritarian regime. In Valenzuela, J. S. and Valenzuela, A. (eds), *Military Rule in Chile: dictatorship and oppositions.* Baltimore: Johns Hopkins University Press.

Valenzuela, Julio Samuel 1985: *Democratización Vía Reforma: La expansión del sufragio en Chile.* Buenos Aires: Ediciones del ides.

Vanek, Jaroslav 1970: *General Theory of Labor-Managed Market Economies.* Ithaca: Cornell University Press.

Vanger, Milton I. 1963: *José Batlle y Ordoñez of Uruguay: the creator of his times, 1902–1907.* Cambridge, MA: Harvard University Press.

——1980: *The Model Country: José Batlle y Ordoñez of Uruguay 1907–1915.* Hanover, NH: University Press of New England, for Brandeis University Press.

Veblen, Thorstein 1966: *Imperial Germany and the Industrial Revolution.* Ann Arbor: University of Michigan Press

Veliz, Claudio (ed.) 1968: *Latin America and the Caribbean: a handbook.* New York: Praeger.

Verney, Douglas 1957: *Parliamentary Reform in Sweden 1866–1921.* Oxford: Clarendon Press.

Villanueva, Victor 1962: *El militarismo en el Perú.* Lima: Empresa Grafica T. Scheuch.

——1975: *El Apra en busca del poder (1930–1940)*. Lima: Editorial Horizonte.
——1977: *El Apra y el ejército (1940–1950)*. Lima: Editorial Horizonte.
Viola, Eduardo and Mainwaring, Scott 1984: Transitions to democracy: Brazil and Argentina in the 1980s. Working Paper No. 21. Notre Dame, IN: The Helen Kellogg Institute for International Studies, University of Notre Dame.
Volk, Steven 1983: Honduras: on the border of war. In Diskin, M. (ed), *Trouble in Our Backyard*. New York: Pantheon Books.
Waisman, Carlos 1989: Argentina: Autarkic industrialization and illegitimacy. In Diamond, L., Linz J. J. and Lipset, S. M. (eds), *Democracy in Developing Countries*. Boulder: Lynne Rienner.
Waite, Peter B. 1971: *Canada, 1874–1896: arduous destiny*. Toronto: McClelland and Stewart.
Walker, Thomas W. 1981: *Nicaragua: the land of Sandino*. Boulder: Westview Press.
——(ed) 1982: *Nicaragua in Revolution*. New York: Praeger.
Wallerstein, Immanuel 1974: *The Modern World-System: capitalist agriculture and the origins of the European world-economy in the sixteenth century*. New York: Academic Press.
——1976: Semi-peripheral countries and the contemporary world crisis. *Theory and Society*, 3.
Waswo, Ann 1977: *Japanese Landlords: the decline of a rural elite*. Berkeley: University of California Press.
Watson, Hilbourne 1988: The 1986 general elections and political economy in Barbados after Barrow. *Caribbean Affairs*, 1 (4) (Oct.–Dec.).
Weber, Max 1906: Zur Lage der bürgerlichen Demokratie in Russland. *Archiv für Sozialwissenschaft und Sozialpolitik*, N.S. 22.
——1922/1968: *Economy and Society*, 2 vols. New York: Bedminster Press; second printing Berkeley: University of California Press, 1978; translation of *Wirtschaft und Gesellschaft*, 4th edn. Tübingen: J. C. B. Mohr (Paul Siebeck), 1956; first published 1922.
Weede, Erich 1989: Democracy and income inequality reconsidered: comment on Muller. *American Sociological Review*, 54.
Weeks, John 1985: *The Economics of Central America*. New York: Holmes and Meier.
Wehler, Hans Ulrich 1985: *The German Empire 1871–1918*. Dover, N H: Berg Publishers.
Weiner, Myron 1987: Empirical democratic theory. In Weiner, M. and Özbudun, E. (eds), *Competitive Elections in Developing Countries*. Washington: American Enterprise Institute, pp. 3–34.
Weiner, Myron and Özbudun, Ergun (eds) 1987: *Comparative Elections in Developing Countries*. Washington, DC: American Enterprise Institute.
Weinert, Richard S. 1977: Introduction. In Reyna, J. L. and Weinert, R. S. (eds), *Authoritarianism in Mexico*. Philadelphia, PA: Institute for the Study of Human Issues.
Weinstein, James 1967: *The Decline of Socialism in America 1912–1925*. New York: Monthly Review Press.

Whitehead, Laurence 1986a: Bolivia's failed democratization, 1977–1980. In O'Donnell, G., Schmitter, P. C. and Whitehead, L. (eds), *Transitions from Authoritarian Rule: Latin America.* Baltimore: Johns Hopkins University Press.
——1986b: International aspects of democratization. In O'Donnell, G., Schmitter, P. C. and Whitehead, L. (eds), *Transitions from Authoritarian Rule: comparative perspectives.* Baltimore: Johns Hopkins University Press.
Wiarda, Howard J. 1980: Is Latin America democratic and does it want to be? The crisis and quest of democracy in the hemisphere. In Wiarda, Howard J. (ed), *The Continuing Struggle for Democracy in Latin America.* Boulder: Westview Press.
——(ed) 1982: *Politics and Social Change in Latin America: the distinct tradition.* Amherst, MA: University of Massachusetts Press.
Wiarda, Howard and Kryzanek, Michael J. 1982: *The Dominican Republic: a Caribbean crucible.* Boulder: Westview Press.
Wiebe, Robert H. 1962: *Businessmen and Reform: a study of the Progressive movement.* Cambridge: Harvard University Press.
Wiener, Jonathan M. 1976: Review of reviews: the social origins of dictatorship and democracy. *History and Theory,* 15 (2).
——1978: *Social Origins of the New South: Alabama, 1860–1885.* Baton Rouge: Louisiana State University Press.
Wilde, Alexander W. 1978: Conversations among gentlemen: oligarchical democracy in Colombia. In Linz, J. J. and Stepan, A. (eds), *The Breakdown of Democratic Regimes: Latin America.* Baltimore: Johns Hopkins University Press.
Williamson, Chilton 1960: *American Suffrage: from property to democracy 1760–1860.* Princeton: Princeton University Press.
Winter, J. M. 1986: *The Great War and the British People.* Cambridge, MA: Harvard University Press.
Wolf, Eric R. 1969: *Peasant Wars in the Twentieth Century.* New York: Harper.
Womack, John Jr. 1968: *Zapata and the Mexican Revolution.* New York: Alfred A. Knopf.
Woodward, C. Vann 1974: *The Strange Career of Jim Crow.* New York: Oxford University Press. Third Revised Edition.
Woodward, Ralph Lee, Jr. 1985: *Central America: a nation divided.* New York: Oxford University Press. Second Edition.
World Bank 1986: *World Development Report 1986.* Oxford University Press.
Wright, D. G. 1970: *Democracy and Reform: 1815–1885.* London: Longman.
Wright, Erik Olin 1978: *Class, Crisis, and the State.* London: New Left Books.
——1985: *Classes.* London: New Left Books.
Wynia, Gary W. 1978: *Argentina in the Postwar Era: politics and economic policy making in a divided society.* Albuquerque, NM: University of New Mexico Press.
Zeitlin, Maurice 1984: *The Civil Wars in Chile (or the bourgeois revolutions that never were).* Princeton: Princeton University Press.
Zeitlin, Maurice, Neuman, W. Lawrence and Ratcliff, Richard Earl 1976: Class segments: Agrarian property and political leadership in the capitalist

class of Chile. *American Sociological Review*, vol. 41 (December).

Zeitlin, Maurice and Ratcliff, Richard Earl 1975: Research methods for the analysis of the internal structure of dominant classes: the case of landlords and capitalists in Chile. *Latin American Research Review*, 10 (3) (Fall).

——1988: *Landlords and Capitalists: the dominant class of Chile*. Princeton: Princeton University Press.

Znaniecki, Florian 1934: *The Method of Sociology*. New York: Farrar & Rinehart.

Zolberg, Aristide R. 1986: How many exceptionalisms? In Katznelson, I. and Zolberg, A. R. (eds), *Working Class Formation: nineteenth-century patterns in western Europe and the United States*. Princeton: Princeton University Press.

Zwerdling, Daniel 1980: *Workplace Democracy*. New York: Harper and Row.

Index